SOCIAL WORK WITH CHILDREN AND THEIR FAMILIES

SOCIAL WORK WITH CHILDREN AND THEIR FAMILIES

PRAGMATIC FOUNDATIONS

SECOND EDITION

Christopher G. Petr

OXFORD
UNIVERSITY PRESS
2003

OXFORD
UNIVERSITY PRESS

Oxford   New York
Auckland   Bangkok   Buenos Aires   Cape Town   Chennai
Dar es Salaam   Delhi   Hong Kong   Istanbul   Karachi   Kolkata
Kuala Lumpur   Madrid   Melbourne   Mexico City   Mumbai   Nairobi
São Paulo   Shanghai   Taipei   Tokyo   Toronto

Copyright © 2003 by Oxford University Press, Inc.

Published by Oxford University Press, Inc.
198 Madison Avenue, New York, New York 10016

www.oup.com

Oxford is a registered trademark of Oxford University Press

Library of Congress Cataloging-in-Publication Data
Petr, Christopher G.
Social work with children and their families: Pragmatic foundations
/ Christopher G. Petr. — 2nd ed.
p.   cm.
Includes bibliographical references and index.
ISBN 978-0-19-515755-0
1. Social work with children—United States.   2. Family
social work—United States.   I. Title.
HV741.P47   2003
362.7'0973—dc21   2002015612

Printed in the United States of America
on acid-free paper

PREFACE

Pragmatism: 1. character or conduct that emphasizes practicality. *Random House Unabridged Dictionary* (2nd ed.), 1993

Goals and Purposes

This book aims to provide the graduate-level or senior-level undergraduate student with the essential foundation of knowledge necessary for beginning social work with children and families. In the spirit of pragmatism, this textbook emphasizes practical knowledge that is relevant and useful to students, rather than abstract theories and ideas that are difficult to connect and translate to the real world of the social worker. This knowledge is practical in the pragmatic sense of synthesizing and integrating sometimes very divergent ideas and viewpoints. Through the pragmatic process of mediating divergent perspectives, social workers can learn to formulate purposeful actions that make a difference for clients.

Unquestionably, multiple and often divergent viewpoints populate the world of social work with children and families. Social workers tend to work with those children and families that other professionals see as the most difficult, multiproblem cases. These children are often involved with numerous professionals who work in separate and often segregated systems of care such as child welfare, mental health, and education. The viewpoints and perspectives of all these professionals are often widely disparate: they can disagree on innumerable issues including the target of concern (e.g., individual or family), the definition of the problem, the cause of the problem, the goals of the case plan, and the best means to achieve the goals. When the parent and child's opinions are added to this mix, even more complexity results. Divergent viewpoints are not limited to the level of individual opinion. The professional literature is replete with hundreds of different practice modalities and interventions, scores of theories about human behavior, contradictory and incomplete research, and conflicting social policies. How, then, do we best prepare social workers for beginning-level practice?

Organization of the Text

Social work education programs typically organize courses into four sequences: policy, practice, human behavior, and research. Although attempts are made to make connections between and among these sequences, students can experience them as fairly distinct and divergent. This book is broad in scope, covering material in all four arenas. But unlike the distinct sequences, this textbook seeks to synthesize and integrate the knowledge from all four domains that is most relevant and useful to beginning practitioners in child and family service agencies, with particular emphasis on linking practice and policy. Eight pragmatic perspectives, numerous case vignettes, and four in-depth examples help to integrate the material, linking policy and practice in a pragmatic way.

This text's general approach is to integrate policy and practice issues in child and family settings in a way that is relevant to students in their field internships and future employment. The major mechanisms for this integration are eight pragmatic perspectives, which are first introduced in chapter 1: later, an entire chapter is devoted to each perspective. Each of the eight pragmatic perspectives presents an important point of view on children and families that has implications for both direct practice and policy. These eight pragmatic perspectives are:

1. Combating adultcentrism (chapter 4)
2. Family-centered practice (chapter 5)
3. Strengths perspective (chapter 6)
4. Respect for diversity and difference (chapter 7)
5. The least restrictive alternative (chapter 8)
6. Ecological perspective (chapter 9)
7. Organization and financing (chapter 10)
8. Achieving outcomes (chapter 11)

This is a time of dramatic change in the systems of care for children and families in this country, be it child welfare, children's mental health, or public education. Change in the system is proceeding with some fairly clear directions and in accordance with these eight perspectives. Students need to understand these directions and how they create a context that has direct applications for their direct client work. The traditional system of care for children and families has *not* been organized or driven by these eight pragmatic perspectives. In fact, the system has been largely characterized by opposing perspectives: the system has been adultcentric, professional- and child-centered rather than family-centered, pathology-oriented rather than strengths-focused, insensitive to diversity, dominated by highly restrictive alternatives, individually rather than ecologically focused, organized in a fragmented and inefficient fashion, and focused on process rather than outcome. Thus, this text presents a frame of reference that helps students act in accordance with the most progressive initiatives in the field. Because these perspectives are so highly associated with change and reform, students may find that their efforts to act in accordance with the perspectives are sometimes met with hostility and resistance by some social workers and other professionals. Many long-time practitioners in the field have been operating under a different system, and not all agree with the direction of the reforms.

In these times of rapidly changing policies, it is important not to neglect the role and importance of direct, face-to-face practice. Certain generic engagement and interviewing skills are essential to beginning-level social work practice, regardless of specific setting. Children and families present unique interviewing challenges that this book addresses through practice principles and techniques that apply across settings and agencies (chapters 4 and 5). Students will learn a value-based framework for practice that enables them to establish the rapport and interpersonal connection essential to successful working relationships. This focus on engagement and interviewing is supported by research results on the characteristics of successful helpers. This extensive body of research concludes that it is not the professional's theoretical approach that is the most important factor in achieving successful outcomes; instead, it is the client's experience of the professional as a warm, involved, and skilled communicator that is most essential (Coady, 1993). Because this research indicates that many different theoretical approaches can be successful—but only if they are employed from a firm interpersonal foundation—this text will focus on the basic engagement skills and attitudes that are the prerequisites for success. Onto this foundation, the student can build more advanced theoretical knowledge from the multitude of approaches available.

A clear underlying assumption of the book is that social work practice with children is a very difficult and complex undertaking. Social work in any one specific setting requires knowledge about the other major settings, or service systems, because children and families cross many systems, often in a fragmented manner. Often social workers are called upon to help children and families negotiate the complex maze of programs and services. Essential knowledge includes the history and purpose, guiding policies, available services, and most effective intervention strategies for each specific setting. Social workers need to be familiar with the language and jargon of each system, and with the roles that various professionals fulfill in each system.

Two major settings for social work practice with children and families are presented in this text: child welfare (chapter 2) and children's mental health, including special education for children with emotional and behavioral disorders (chapter 3). These two fields of practice are centrally important to the social work field and to social work employment. Since social workers also work in other service systems that serve children and families, including education, juvenile justice, health care, and developmental disabilities, some information about these systems will be presented throughout the text to illustrate the breadth and complexity of the child and family arena.

In summarizing the organization of this text, the reader is first introduced in unit 1 to the general issues, laws, policies, practices, and vocabulary of the *child welfare* and *children's mental health* service systems (chapters 1–3). Next, each of the eight pragmatic perspectives is presented in depth in unit 2, and specific connections about how each perspective applies in child welfare and children's mental health are made (chapters 4–11). At the end of unit 2, a list of suggested learning activities is presented for the reader's consideration—the list may be particularly useful to instructors in devising assignments. Finally, unit 3 presents in-depth case examples from child welfare (chapter 12) and children's mental health (chapter 13) that demonstrate the utility of the eight pragmatic perspectives in actual practice.

All case vignettes and case examples in this text are either entirely fictitious or fictitious composites of the author's professional experiences. *Case vignettes* are short accounts of client interactions that highlight and illustrate specific principles. These occur throughout the text. *Case examples* are in-depth, lengthy narratives with commentary and analysis using the eight pragmatic perspectives. These occur in chapters 12 and 13.

The in-depth case examples demonstrate how the eight pragmatic perspectives apply to everyday social work, showing the reader how the eight perspectives are interrelated—how they sometimes overlap and even contradict each other. At any one point, with any one particular client, in any one particular program and setting, the day-to-day decisions of the social worker may be guided more by one perspective than by another. Sometimes, social workers must choose between two or more competing perspectives. This is one reason that social work in child and family settings is so difficult and complex: there is no single perspective, no single theory or approach that can guide practice in all situations. With knowledge of the eight perspectives, students can better decide what is most purposeful and appropriate in a given situation.

Both the case vignettes and case examples are intended to reflect and mirror the real and imperfect world of social work in child and family settings. Thus, the reader should not be surprised if mistakes are made, conflicts are unresolved, and goals are only partially achieved. The author believes that these realistic portrayals of social work prepare the student for practice better than canned, stilted case examples in which everything works out perfectly. Because the latter are not realistic, they falsely delude students into expecting that social work practice is easier and "cleaner" than it actually is.

The content and organization of this text have been developed by the author over several years of teaching and scholarship at the University of Kansas School of Social Welfare, outpatient work with children and families at the Bert Nash Mental Health Center in Lawrence, Kansas, and policy/program involvement at the local, state, and national levels. The text has been developed and piloted in SW 830: Social Work in Child and Family Settings, which is a graduate-level "integrative" course designed to help students learn the foundation material for clinical and administrative social work in the child and family arena. This text assumes that the student has taken introductory courses covering content on generic social work practice and interviewing skills, child and family development, cultural diversity, policy, and research.

Changes in the Revised Edition

There are three important changes in the second edition. First, as described above, the sequencing of the chapters has been changed, placing content on the two service systems earlier, so that readers have an orientation to the service systems from the beginning. This change was made based on experience of the author and other colleagues in using the text to teach classes. In the second edition, each pragmatic perspective now has its own full chapter, with an overview section followed by sections that make specific connections to child welfare and children's mental health.

The second change reflects the addition of new subject content. General topics include updated statistics on the well-being of children and families in the United States, gender issues for boys, family-centered interagency collaboration, and the strengths perspective in group work. In child welfare, new topics include resiliency, the role of police in child welfare investigations, accreditation of child welfare agencies, updated statistics on the extent of abuse and neglect, gay and lesbian youth in foster care, updates on privatization initiatives, and the Adoption and Safe Families Act of 1997. In children's mental health, new topics include reactive attachment disorder, medications with preschoolers, mental health services in the juvenile justice system, bias in mental health assessments, 1997 amendments to the Individuals with Disabilities Education Act relating to positive behavioral supports and transition to adulthood, and empowering the voice of youth.

The content of the second edition has been strengthened through the incorporation of more than 60 new references. The majority of these references pertain to evidence-based studies that shed light on many key issues. This increased focus on evidence-based practice was recommended by respected colleagues, and is further emphasized through the addition of research capsules that appear in various chapters of the text. Research capsules highlight evidence-based best practices programs that have been shown to be effective interventions in helping children and families achieve outcomes. These include well-designed studies that show the effectiveness of (1) family foster care compared to group homes, (2) community-based treatment compared to hospitalization, (3) community involvement through the Big Brothers/Big Sisters program, and (4) prevention and early intervention programs.

Acknowledgments

Many individuals provided support for this undertaking. Pat Litzelfelner provided detailed feedback on the early manuscript, and her insights, particularly in relation to the strengths perspective, improved the text significantly. I am grateful to Elena Sifferlin and Carol Porter, who located and summarized source materials for the first edition in expeditious fashion. Uta Walter and Jocelyn Martin have been long-time research assistants for state children's mental health projects, and have been the sharpest and hardest working research assistants that anyone could hope for. Their work has contributed significantly to this product. More recently, Sharon Barfield, Kirsten Oelklaus, Shara Davis, and Tara Swaim have continued this tradition. Cheri L'Ecuyer provided important consultation on formatting, charts, and word processing.

I am indebted to scores of clients and students who have taught me much about how to practice as well as how to teach. Conversations I have had with numerous colleagues over the years have shaped my thinking about effective work with children and families. These include Jim Kreider, whose clinical skills with children and families are unsurpassed; Annette Kahn, my earliest clinical supervisor and teacher; Rud and Ann Turnbull, who have served as inspirations for what family-centered practice means; Barbara Huff of the Federation of Families for Children's Mental Health, whose untiring advocacy efforts and unsurpassed dedication to cultural competency have reaped huge benefits for families across the United States; John Poertner and Ira Cutler, who were instrumental in initiating ideas about how to change the system of care in Kansas; Tom McDonald, whose focus on outcomes and research has broadened my appreciation for this aspect of the system of care; Candace Moten, who offered me the opportunity to learn about family preservation; Judge Jean Shepherd, for her inspirational commitment to the welfare of children and families; and Reva Allen, who embraced the idea of family-centered practice with a passion. I am grateful also for the support of this project offered by my dean, Ann Weick. She, together with other current and former colleagues at the School of Social Welfare, including Dennis Saleebey, Charlie Rapp, Wally Kisthardt, and Pat Sullivan, introduced me to the importance and relevance of the strengths perspective in social work practice.

Finally, I cannot publish a book about children and families without recognizing my own children and family: my wife, Julie; grown twin sons Jonathan and Kyle; and young son David. They have immeasurably enriched my life.

CONTENTS

U N I T

I

Overview of the Systems of Care for Children and Their Families

The purposes of unit I are twofold. First, in chapter 1, the reader is introduced to the field of social work in child and family settings. The current status of the health and well-being of children and families is presented using data from three recent national reports. This is followed by a brief look at what social workers do to try to meet some of the needs of children and families. The chapter ends with a brief introduction to the eight pragmatic perspectives that are at the core of effective social work practice with children and their families. These eight pragmatic perspectives are:

1. Combating adultcentrism
2. Family-centered practice
3. Strengths perspective
4. Respect for diversity and difference
5. Least restrictive alternative
6. Ecological perspective
7. Organization and financing
8. Achieving outcomes

Unit I is completed by two chapters that help the reader understand the terminology, laws, policies, and practice issues in the two major service systems: child welfare and children's mental health. The child welfare chapter, chapter 2, presents information about child abuse and neglect, foster care, and adoptions. The chapter is organized according to the three main purposes of the child welfare system: protection of children, preservation of families, and permanency planning. Chapter 3 focuses on the children's mental health system. It is organized into three sections: the first presents an overview of the purpose, history, and policy initiatives in this arena; the second section discusses assessment and treatment issues; the final section provides an overview of special education services for children with serious emotional and behavioral disorders.

CHAPTER 1

Introduction to Social Work in Child and Family Settings

Overview

This chapter introduces the reader to the general problems, issues, and needs facing children and families in the United States. After outlining the disappointing statistics about the health and well-being of children and families, the chapter introduces the role of the social worker in responding to the needs of children and families from within the three major settings of child welfare, mental health, and education.

General Status of Children and Families in the United States

Despite unprecedented advances in the nation's overall standard of living, the well-being of children and families in the United States is discouragingly low. Numerous studies and reports have confirmed the need for a better societal response to the needs of children and families. Three of the most influential of these reports will be discussed and cited in this section.

The first of these reports is the final report of the National Commission on Children, published in 1991, titled *Beyond Rhetoric: A New Agenda for Children and Families*. Chaired by Senator John D. Rockefeller IV, the National Commission on Children was created by Congress and the president in late December 1987 by Public Law 100-203 "to serve as a forum on behalf of the children of the Nation." Its members were sworn in and began their work in February 1989, charged with assessing the status of children and families in the United States. After two and a half years of intense investigation and deliberation, the bipartisan commission documented the status of America's children and families and issued a call for a broad-based societal commitment to children and their families. Although this report is somewhat dated, it is included because of its comprehensiveness and its impact on raising awareness and stimulating action.

The second report is a statistical yearbook produced annually by the Children's Defense Fund. Since 1973, advocacy for an improved societal response to the needs of children and families has been spearheaded by the Children's Defense Fund based in Washington, D.C., and headed by Marian Wright Edelman. The Children's Defense Fund tracks the status of children and families in the United States and advocates for change. Typical of the Children's Defense Fund's efforts is *The State of America's Children Yearbook: 2001*, which outlines the status of children and families in six different areas of health and well-being. These six areas are family income, health, child care, education, children and families in crisis, and juvenile justice/youth development.

A third important source for documentation of

the status of children and families in the United States is the Annie E. Casey Foundation's *Kid's Count Data Book,* published annually since 1985. The *Kid's Count Project* is a national and state-by-state effort that provides policy makers and citizens with annual benchmarks of child and family well-being. Data for each state are provided in 10 critical dimensions of children's lives, allowing states to see how they have advanced or regressed from one year to the next. These 10 dimensions are percent of low-birthweight babies; infant mortality rate; child death rate; rate of teen deaths by accident, homicide, and suicide; teen birth rate; percent of teens who are high school dropouts; percent of teens not attending school and not working; percent of children living with parents who do not have full-time, year-round employment; percent of children in poverty; and percent of children in single-parent families. In 48 states, the Casey Foundation funds efforts to break the statistics down even further, to the county and city level, so that local citizens and officials can track the status of children at the community level.

Although many of the statistics reported in these sources improved during the 1990s, many areas of concern remain. The following statistics from the above reports (National Commission report=NC; Children's Defense Fund, *The State of America's Children 2001*=CDF; Annie E. Casey Foundation, *Kid's Count Data Book, 2001*=KC) help the reader grasp the significance and magnitude of the problems facing children and families today.

Family Income

- Despite some modest improvements in recent years, one in six American children remain in poverty. (CDF)
- The child poverty rate in the United States is the highest among the top 17 developed nations. (KC)
- More than 40% of children in female-headed households were poor in 1999. (KC)
- Thirty-three percent of African American children were living in poverty in 1999. (CDF)

Health

- The infant mortality rate for African Americans is 13.8 per thousand, more than twice as high as for white Americans. (CDF)

- The child death rate has fallen steadily the last few years, but the United States still ranks 23rd among developed countries in number of child deaths due to injury. (KC)
- The percent of overweight children has more than doubled since the 1960s. (CDF)
- The percentage of infants born at low birth-weight has continued to climb from a low of 6.7% in 1984 to 7.6% in 1998. (CDF)
- Despite recent programs, nearly 15% of children in America remain without health insurance. (CDF)

Housing and Homelessness

- From 1991 to 1997, rents rose at twice the rate of general inflation. (CDF)
- In 1999, more than 3.6 million children lived in families either paying at least half their income on rent, or living in severely substandard housing. (CDF)
- The U.S. Conference of Mayors reported that the average demand for emergency shelter rose between 1999 and 2000 in the 25 cities surveyed. (CDF)

Children and Families in Crisis

- Almost 1 million cases of child abuse or neglect were confirmed in 1998. (CDF)
- Approximately 568,000 children were estimated to be in out-of-home placements in September 1999, an increase of 48% over the past decade. (CDF)
- In the fall of 1999, 60% of children in care were children of color. (CDF)
- Between 3.3 and 10 million children witness domestic violence in their homes each year. (CDF)
- The percentage of children in single-parent families increased 13% between 1990 and 1998, and from 5.8 million in 1960 to 19.8 million in 1999 (KC); over 50% of black children in 1989 were living in single-parent households. (NC)

Mental Health

- An estimated 1 in 10 children in the United States suffers from serious emotional and behavioral disorders. (CDF)
- Only 20–25% of those in need of drug and/or alcohol treatment receive it. (CDF)

- Suicide is the second leading cause of death among teenagers. (NC)
- It is estimated that as many as 70% of children and adolescents in need of treatment are not receiving mental health services. (NC)

Education and Child Care

- Nearly 40% of fourth graders scored below basic reading level in 1998. (KC)
- Nearly 7 million children between ages 5 to 14 care for themselves on a regular basis without any adult supervision. (CDF)
- Dropouts are 3.5 times more likely to be arrested than high school graduates, and 6 times more likely to be unmarried parents. (NC)

As bleak as the above indicators are for children and families overall, the health and welfare of poor and minority-race children and families are dramatically worse. The infant mortality rate for black children is more than twice that of whites (CDF). African American and Hispanic youth are twice as likely as whites to be neither in school nor working (KC). Thirty-three percent of African American children are living in poverty (CDF). A disproportionate percentage of children of color are removed from their homes and placed into foster care (CDF).

These statistics document that the health and well-being of many American families is at high risk. Some of that risk can be attributed to the unprecedented stresses and pressures that face children and families today: "[T]he family is imperiled by extraordinary social, demographic, and economic change and instability" (NC, p. xi). The family as a social institution is changing rapidly. Families are smaller, and children are a declining proportion of the total U.S. population. In 1960, children accounted for 36% of the population, in 1990 they were 26% (NC, p. 17). More children live with only one parent, usually their mothers, and many have little contact and involvement with their fathers. The percentage of children in single-parent families increased 13% between 1990 and 1998, and from 5.8 million in 1960 to 19.8 million in 1999 (KC). About half of all marriages in the United States are expected to end in divorce, and each year, more than 1 million children are affected by marital separation or divorce (NC,

pp. 18–19). More mothers are employed, so that children and parents spend less time together. Between 1970 and 1990, the proportion of mothers with children under age six who were employed or looking for employment rose from 32% to 58% (NC, p. 21).

Despite the smaller size of families and the greater number of women in the work force, children are the poorest group in the United States. One in six children are poor. Poverty is a pernicious influence that can have a devastating influence on overall child and family well-being (Sherman, 1994). Poor children eat fewer nutritious meals. Poor children often live in shelter that is not safe. Poor children have fewer opportunities to learn, because parents cannot buy stimulating toys, books, preschool classes, extra school supplies, eyeglasses, and other accoutrements, that enhance learning. Poor children and their families experience more stress, which results in more conflict, including violence. Poor children live in neighborhoods that are unsafe and crime-ridden. Poor children and their families are less able to buy health care and health supplies. Poor children and their families are less able to afford transportation, which limits their access to jobs, health care, and other services.

Thus, it is not surprising that the health and well-being statistics for poor children are worse than for the non-poor. The human and economic costs of poverty are far reaching (Sherman, 1994). Poor children are less healthy, less successful in school, more likely to be victims of child abuse and neglect, and more likely to become delinquent or violent. Poverty kills: low-income children are two times more likely to die from birth defects, three times more likely to die from all causes combined, four times more likely to die in fires, and five times more likely to die from infectious diseases and parasites. Economically, poverty costs society billions of dollars in reduced future worker productivity and employment, and billions more in education, special education, medical care, and corrections costs. Poverty stacks the odds against children from before their birth. As Marian Wright Edelman proclaims, "Poverty forces children to fight a many-front war simultaneously, often without the armors of stable families, adequate health care and schooling, or safe and nurturing communities" (Sherman, p. xvii).

Many of today's families are under siege as they attempt to adapt to all these pressures (Weick & Saleebey, 1995). Yet political and social structures have been slow to move beyond rhetoric in addressing the concerns. The values of rugged individualism and economic self-sufficiency are paramount in the American image; hence, other values and philosophies that would be more conducive to supporting the family unit are seldom realized. The American family is perceived as an isolated unit that succeeds or fails by its own hand. Instead of *universal* programs such as children's allowances, health care, and maternal leave, the United States institutes *residual* programs, which people can access only as a last resort, when in severe need, and only after the resources of the family, kinship network, and other sources have been exhausted. When help is needed, the residual approach presumes it will be minimal, time limited, and highly selective according to specific predetermined categories of need (Wilensky & Lebeaux, 1958). The great majority of families are expected to fend for themselves. While there is something to be said for targeting scarce resources on those most in need, a residual system is highly bureaucratized, is often difficult for families to access, and is stigmatizing to recipients. Rather than preventing problems before they occur, a residual system focuses on responding to crises, and on treatment of problems after they occur.

Clearly, there is much for society to do. There is widespread agreement that the United States is failing large segments of its children, youth, and families. Although most children continue to grow up to be healthy and productive citizens, large segments of children are at high risk for failure. Social institutions can and should do more to adequately support the growth and development of our country's most valuable future resource: children.

Social work is one of the primary professions charged by society to help children and families meet their needs. Two major arenas or settings for social work practice with children and families are *child welfare* and *mental health*. Specific knowledge about these settings is important for all social workers, because children and families have multiple needs that cross over from one setting to another. This specific knowledge will be presented

later in the text. First, however, the remainder of chapter 1 provides an overview of the history and evolving role of social workers in child and family settings (next section), and of the eight pragmatic perspectives that influence and guide practice and policy (chapters 4–11).

Brief History of Social Work with Children and Families

(The material in this section is adapted from Petr & Spano, 1990.)

From its beginnings as a profession in the early part of this century, social work has a strong history of involvement with children and families. Early professional efforts were built on a foundation of religious and philanthropic initiatives on behalf of children dating back to least the mid-1800s. These early efforts were characterized by dynamic philosophical tensions that have continued, largely unresolved, to the present day. The discussion that follows highlights two of these tensions: first, the appropriateness of out-of-home, institutional, and other segregated responses to the needs of children; second, interrelated to the first, is the nature of the relationship of the social work professional to a child and to that child's family.

During the nineteenth century, societal efforts on behalf of children and families focused on the plight of dependent, neglected, and dependent children (Petr & Spano, 1990). Whereas colonial America had relied on non-institutional responses to social problems, Jacksonian America developed a flurry of institutional responses. During the nineteenth century, America built orphan asylums, houses of refuge, and reformatories. These institutions varied in program and in the specific populations they served. However, they shared a common ideological perspective on the needs of children: society was facing an imminent breakdown because of a crumbling social structure, especially family structures. Social stability could be reestablished through rehabilitation based on discipline and structure provided away from the negative influences of the person's family and larger environment. Thus, by the mid-1800s, America's response to dependent and needy children was to target efforts directly at the children, providing them with rehabilitation in institutions that isolated them from the families and environments that were considered the sources of their problems.

This approach led to the establishment and the proliferation of large institutions whose purposes were to discipline, control, and reform America's troubled youth. Many of these youth were the children of parents confined to almshouses, institutions for the poor and destitute. Investigations into the conditions of these almshouses resulted in recommendations that children be removed from almshouses and placed in separate institutions (Meckel, 1985). Between 1861 and 1890, the number of child-caring institutions, called orphan asylums, grew from 75 to 600 (Trattner, 1974). Other institutions, variously called training schools, reformatories, and houses of refuge, were established for delinquent children. Thus, by the end of the nineteenth century, institutional child advocacy efforts had resulted in the creation of hundreds of large institutions for the care of troubled children, and these were seen as improvements over the previous conditions in almshouses. These institutions attempted to segregate children from adults, including their families. They also attempted to segregate dependent children from delinquent children.

Meanwhile, in opposition to the movement toward institutional solutions, Charles Loring Brace, who in 1853 became director of the New York Children's Aid Society, was championing the cause of "placing out." This was a controversial program that sought to place troubled urban children with rural farm families in midwestern states. Between 1853 and 1878, the program placed about 50,000 children, but the program was not without controversy (Trattner, 1974). Catholic critics charged that the program sought to convert Catholic children to Protestantism, and many midwestern state officials claimed that the majority of children placed were troublemakers.

By the end of the nineteenth century, placing out was the solution officially sanctioned by most child advocates, as evidenced by the endorsement of the National Conference on Charities and Corrections Committee on Children in 1899. Even though placing out was fraught with problems, so too were child-caring institutions, which were plagued by overcrowding, poor staffing, rigid discipline, and monotonous routine. Even though child-caring institutions were probably an improvement over almshouses, they were not considered to be the solution to the children's needs. Thus, "the nineteenth century, which began with attempts to get needy children into institutions, ended with attempts to get them out of those institutions" (Trattner, 1974, p. 107).

But institutions did not disappear from the scene, and tensions between institutional and noninstitutional responses remained. Between 1900 and 1925, many policies and programs that emphasized deinstitutionalization were initiated. One of these was "mother's aid," or "mother's pensions," which provided subsidies to children in their own homes. These programs were founded on the belief that poverty alone should not cause children to be removed from their homes. Another policy response to troubled children was the establishment of juvenile courts, which sought to rehabilitate children on probation whenever possible, rather than place them in a reformatory.

One would expect that with the official endorsements of child advocates and the initiation of these deinstitutionalization efforts, use of institutions would have declined. But that was not the case. The number of child care institutions in the United States increased from 698 in 1890 to 1,151 in 1910 (Warner, 1922). In 1923, the number of children supported in institutions (138,760) surpassed the number supported in homes (121,000) (Bureau of the Census, 1927). Community- and family-based options apparently came to supplement, rather than supplant, the predominant institutional system of care.

Several different factors contributed to the resilience of the institutional response. One factor was the financial incentives provided by states to institutions. A second factor was the difficulty of changing established patterns and beliefs. A third factor was that many parents preferred the institution because they knew where the child was, could visit the child, and were not in competition with other parent caregivers for the child's affections. A fourth factor was that benefactors preferred the institution because it was so visible and its work was so manifest (Warner, 1922).

A fifth important source of resilience of institutional responses was the social work profession's own ambivalence about the proper role of institutions in the care of dependent, neglected, and troubled children. On the one hand, the fledgling profession supported non-institutional responses in many ways. For example, a survey of child-placing institutions in the early 1920s found that agencies placed priority on saving families rather than children (Staff, 1923). There were also published successes in the use of social workers at intake to reduce unnecessary admissions to children's homes (Staff, 1928).

On the other hand, the budding profession was highly influenced by the emergence of the social sciences paradigm in the Progressive Era. The progressive, social science perspective enticed the social work profession with promises of definitive answers to social ills and a more central place in society for social workers, who were seeking professional status. Social work in the Progressive Era was fueled by a religiously based moral mission to combat the corrupting influences of industrialized city life. Progressive reformers believed that moral education was the key to success, and they couched the importance of moral education in a scientific rationale.

This religious-scientific combination made it quite reasonable for the professional to ignore the family. Because parents were considered to build their children's characters, it followed that the parents of children with character flaws were unworthy parents who did not have a moral right to rear their children. Instead, the best interests of the child could be assured only by professional experts whose scientific training in emerging personality theories and child development qualified them to choose and monitor the type and quality of care. This system fostered a hierarchy of credibility, at whose top sat the professional expert, whose expertise about the proper care of children superseded the child, the parent, and the public at large (Hanson, 1987).

Thus, by the 1920s, social work with children and families had certain key characteristics. First, it rested on a strong moral foundation that criticized and blamed parents for the maladies of their children. Second, it infused a scientific rationale for this stance by using emerging explanations of personality that supported its stance. Third, it opted for the social casework method, which emphasized an individual focus that further separated the interests of children from their families.

During the 1920s and 1930s, the establishment of child guidance clinics fostered attention to the behavioral and emotional issues of children. As an outgrowth of the mental hygiene movement, these clinics sought to prevent the development of serious, adult mental illness through early detection and treatment. Although that treatment was oriented toward outpatient care, child guidance clinics also were involved with assessing the need for institutionalization.

Because of the growing awareness of children's mental health issues, many child-caring institutions began to change their focus from custodial care of dependent children to treatment of children with emotional disorders. By the late 1930s, these institutions hailed their new role in the continuum of care for mentally ill children. For example, Verry (1939) asserted the advantages of institutionalization for this population and Whitman (1939) noted that "many old endowed institutions have transformed their work and now render up-to-date service in the analysis and diagnosis of problem children" (p. 1). Thus, an additional factor in the resiliency of institutions has been their ability to change with the times.

From the 1940s to the present, societal and professional ambivalence about the role of institutional, segregated, out-of-home care in the care of children continued. Despite philosophies such as "Least Restrictive Alternative" and the lack of research data to support their effectiveness, institutional and segregated responses to children remain strong. This holds for child welfare, mental health, and education, as will be discussed more fully in subsequent chapters.

Additionally, despite a growing body of professional literature that espouses a more family-centered, strengths-oriented approach, many professionals and professional training programs continue to hold to the Progressive Era attitudes that are rooted so strongly in our history and our consciousness. Many professionals see themselves as the experts who best know what is in the best interests of the child. Many professionals refuse to consider strengths and competencies in parents, preferring instead to hold them solely accountable and to blame for their children's maladies.

The result is a system of care for children and families that is ambivalent about the role of segregated, institutional solutions. The result is also a system of care that is conflicted about the proper relationship between professionals, children, and parents. These two central themes are reflected in many of the eight pragmatic perspectives that serve as the unifying framework for this text. In future chapters, the reader will enter the complex and confusing world of social work in child and family settings and hopefully finish those chapters with a clearer understanding of how to think and act in that complex, ambivalent world in ways that best promote the well-being of children and families.

Social Work in Child and Family Settings Today

Today, social work in child and family settings is intensely challenging—physically, mentally, and emotionally—yet it can be extraordinarily rewarding. Social workers help children and families with a vast range of difficulties and issues. The historical tensions described above are often evident in the everyday work of frontline social workers. For example, in *child welfare*, one of the primary service systems in which social workers are employed, the predominant issues are the investigation of child abuse and neglect, the care of children in foster care, and adoption. The following vignette illustrates the roles and tensions involved in the everyday work of a social worker in child welfare.

CASE VIGNETTE: Susan

Susan is a 23-year-old recent graduate of an accredited Bachelor's in Social Work (BSW) program. Her first social work job is with the county child welfare department's Child Protection Unit (CPU), conducting assessments and providing services to children and families who have been reported for child abuse and neglect. In the course of a routine day, Susan will encounter children who have been severely physically or sexually abused by family members, or children who have not eaten, bathed, or seen their parents for days. Susan will also follow up on reports of children whose situations are not so dramatic, where suspicions of physical or sexual abuse are difficult to confirm. She also will interview parents whose parenting abilities are considerably curtailed by poverty, unemployment, racism, discrimination, violence, drug or alcohol addiction, physical or mental illness, or homelessness. These same parents may possess significant strengths and talents that are underrecognized and underutilized. Susan's primary social work task is to ensure the safety and well-being of the children while trying to maintain and preserve the families of the children as principal resources. Often, Susan faces the dilemma of whether it is best to remove the children into state custody and foster care, or leave the children within the family and arrange for the types of services and supports that can assure the safety and long-term well-being of the child and family.

Susan is just one of a multitude of social workers within the department, most of whom work in units other than child protection. Some work in the income maintenance unit, some in family preservation, others in foster care, still others in adoptions. These units are organized by purpose and function, but Susan knows of social welfare departments in rural areas of the state and in other states who organize units differently, so that individual workers do child protection, family preservation, foster care, and adoptions, with no particular special area of emphasis. She also knows of fellow social workers who perform many of these same functions, but who are employed by private, nonprofit social agencies rather than by the state or local government.

Susan's social work activities are not limited to provision of direct services. She also serves on the board of directors of a local battered women's shelter and on the statewide Child Abuse Prevention Coalition. She recently has been active on the local Human Resource Commission's Committee to combat racial discrimination in employment.

Social work is the primary profession in child welfare, but it is secondary in many other service systems and agencies. A second major service system for social work with children and families is *children's mental health*. Social workers in mental health settings, along with psychologists, psychiatrists, nurses, and other professionals, target children with serious emotional and behavioral problems and their families. Settings include public and private nonprofit community mental health centers, private practice groups, psychiatric units of hospitals, and state institutions for the mentally ill. Jon's job is an example of one typical role for social work in mental health settings.

CASE VIGNETTE: Jon

Jon, 36, has been a clinical social worker at the Community Mental Health Center for several years, having received his Master's in Social Work (MSW) degree 10 years ago. Jon provides assessments and counseling to children and families on an outpatient basis, including play therapy, group therapy, and family therapy. The children have a wide range of mental health diagnoses, including Attention Deficit Hyperactivity Disorder (ADHD), depression, and conduct disorder. Jon coordinates his work with other members of the mental health center staff, including social work case managers, who help clients link up with needed resources in the community. He also collaborates with community professionals in other agencies such as school, child welfare, and public health.

One of the more difficult situations for Jon is deciding when hospitalization is appropriate and necessary for clients. Such a decision is considered when children are in need of increased structure and medical supervision, such as during suicidal episodes. The primary resource for inpatient hospitalization is the psychiatric unit of the nearby community hospital, which provides short-term care. Occasionally, when children must be hospitalized for weeks or months, the regional state psychiatric hospital is utilized. Another difficult decision is determining which members of a troubled family to meet with, and how often. It is frustrating that there seems never to be enough time or money for him to be as thorough as he would like to be in his approach.

Like Susan, Jon also is involved in community activities aimed at improving social conditions. He is a member of the local Homelessness Task Force and the Interagency Coordinating Council. At the state level, he participates on the Children's Mental Health Committee of the state chapter of the National Association of Social Workers (NASW).

Child welfare and children's mental health are the two major systems of care that will be the focus of this book, but social workers serve children and their families in other arenas as well. These other systems of care include *education, juvenile justice, health care,* and *developmental disabili-*

ties. In *education*, school social workers provide a variety of direct services to children and families, as well as consultation to teachers and administrators. Commonly, social workers act as the liaisons between the school and the community, helping children and families access the resources they need to succeed in school. Many school social workers target children with special needs or disabilities in *special education*, the federal program that ensures a free and appropriate education to all children, regardless of disability. In this text, information about special education will be presented in chapter 3 on children's mental health, with emphasis on how the special education and mental health systems interact for children with emotional and behavioral disorders.

CASE VIGNETTE: Carmelita

Carmelita, 54, has been a school social worker for 23 years, ever since receiving her MSW from a program that included specialization in school social work. She splits her time between a middle school and two elementary schools. She works with a school psychologist on an evaluation team that identifies and assesses children for special education services. In addition to evaluations, she provides direct social work services to children and families, as well as consultation to special education teachers. Her direct work with children and families focuses on removing barriers to the child's educational success at school. This includes providing a social-skills group for children with behavioral disorders, parent support groups for parents of children with mental retardation, and a peer counseling group for young teenagers with alcohol and drug problems. Her consultation to teachers includes behavior management strategies for children with emotional and behavioral disorders, inservice training on ADHD, and support for engaging and communicating with parents.

A critical function of Carmelita's work is to help the team determine the appropriate level and type of special education services. Some children can be maintained in regular classrooms, which is the official goal of recent inclusion initiatives. Other children may need the help of separate resource rooms, learning centers, or even self-contained classrooms. A few children may even be best served outside of the regular school system, in special schools for the blind, hearing impaired, or emotionally and behaviorally disordered. In her 23 years of school social work, Carmelita has seen the emphasis shift away from special schools and self-contained classrooms toward inclusion in regular classrooms, a shift that is difficult for many teachers, other professionals, and even some parents, to accept.

Carmelita also serves as liaison between the school and other community agencies. In this capacity, she sometimes alerts child welfare authorities of possible child abuse or neglect, coordinates services with mental health professionals regarding children with emotional and behavioral disorders, and helps obtain appropriate resources for children with hearing impairments. These indirect services on behalf of clients are complemented by community activities that enhance educational opportunities for all children. Carmelita organized the Committee for Multicultural Education and participates on a Head Start Policy Board.

In the field of *juvenile justice*, social workers help children and youth who have been accused of committing crimes. Sometimes, when helping efforts with the child and family fail to prevent repeated and serious criminal behavior, the child can be placed into state custody for the purposes of punishment and/or rehabilitation. In the *health care* system, social workers work with children and their families both in public health settings and in general and specialty hospitals. In these settings,

children and their families need help from social
workers to prevent minor health problems from becoming more serious, to cope emotionally with the
stresses and pressures of serious illness, and to find
resources in the community. In the field of *developmental disabilities*, social workers help children
and their families to understand the nature of the
disability and to face the challenges that ensue as
the child grows older. These challenges include
finding qualified professional service providers,
accessing financial supports, and advocating for
appropriate educational services. Although it is beyond the scope of this text to cover these systems
in great depth, the reader is cautioned not to think
of child welfare and children's mental health as
the only arenas for social work practice with children and their families. The above vignettes offer
a glimpse of what social workers do in settings that
serve children and their families. The reader will
be reacquainted with Susan, Jon, and Carmelita
periodically throughout the text, by way of various case vignettes and case examples. The work is
not easy or simple. Social work with children and
their families can be quite difficult and complex.
Some of the factors that contribute to the difficulty
and complexity are introduced below.

Human beings, including clients and other professionals with whom the social worker interacts,
are themselves very complex, difficult to understand, and sometimes stuck in their traditional
ways of doing things. As advanced social work
students know from their human behavior and
psychology courses, there are literally hundreds
of different theories of human behavior, none of
which has generated any consensus among professionals or the public. Yet it is these same complicated people—clients and other professionals—
with whom social workers must interact and influence everyday.

A complicating and often frustrating aspect of
social work with children and families is that many
clients receive services from more than one system at the same time (see figure 1.1). Figure 1.1
depicts only three systems of care, but some children are involved in four, five, or even six service
systems. Consider that a child who has been physically or sexually abused often has emotional and
behavioral problems that necessitate services from
special education and mental health. If that child
develops a serious illness, or commits a crime, then

FIGURE 1.1
Children and Families Across Service Systems

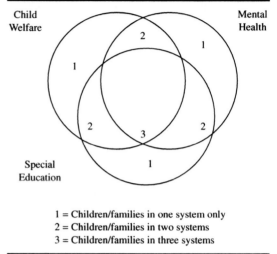

1 = Children/families in one system only
2 = Children/families in two systems
3 = Children/families in three systems

the health care and juvenile justice systems are
engaged as well. It may be unusual for a single
child to be involved in so many systems, but it is
not unusual for families who have many children
to be so involved.

So, Susan, Jon, and Carmelita sometimes find
that they are working with the same children and
families at the same time. While there may be a
need for many service systems to become involved
with a given family, effective service requires
close coordination and clarity about professional
roles and functions. There is a real danger that parents can feel confused and overburdened by the
number of professionals involved. Yet professionals can interpret these feelings as lack of motivation. This perceived lack of motivation can then
reinforce the all-too-common professional point of
view that many, if not most, families in the service
system are "dysfunctional families" who are to
blame for their children's difficulties. But from the
point of view of the parents of these same families,
the issue is one of "dysfunctional service systems
and professionals," not "dysfunctional families."

Figure 1.1 may appear to be a chaotic maze to
the reader. From the family point of view, the service system can appear to be just that. Today, the
provision of services to meet the needs of children
and families is an enormous undertaking. All levels of government—federal, state, and local—are
involved, as are a multitude of private nonprofit

and private for-profit organizations. There is little organization or direction to the overall system. The residual approach demands that families complete lengthy paperwork and stigmatizing interviews to establish eligibility. Services are funded by categories, but a given child and family's needs may not fit into any specific category. Different services are located in different parts of a community, and access to them can be difficult and time consuming. The services may not be affordable for the family, or may be offered at times and locations that do not match well with the family schedule. Thus, families can often become frustrated in attempting to navigate the maze of programs and professionals. The system can, indeed, appear to be very dysfunctional to the families in need.

An array of services can be helpful to families, but more services also means more professionals involved in the lives of a given family. Social workers often work with families who are struggling to overcome numerous difficulties and challenges, families who often are involved with many services and many professionals. The viewpoints and perspectives of these professionals can be widely disparate, and many can hold onto outdated and inappropriate attitudes regarding the role of professionals in the lives of families. Professionals often disagree on what should be done for and with the child and family. Some focus on the child as the unit of attention, others on the parents or entire family. Disagreements can arise over the definition of the problem, the cause of the difficulties, or the most appropriate solution. The downside of accessing services, from the family point of view, is the threat of outside intrusion from opinionated professionals, and subsequent loss of control.

Eight Pragmatic Perspectives

Despite these daunting complexities, social work in child and family settings can be very rewarding. Social workers can, and do, help children and families overcome obstacles and meet their goals. The following chapters provide the beginning student with the essential foundational knowledge to help children and families succeed. This knowledge includes current trends and reforms in the provision of services, trends that are embodied in catch phrases such as "community-based," "family-centered," "integrated," "least restrictive alternative," "culturally competent," "prevention," "decentralization," "privatization," and "outcome-driven." These trends and reforms are incorporated into the eight pragmatic perspectives that form the unifying framework for this text. The reader will learn how the eight pragmatic perspectives influence policy and their own direct practice.

To be effective, the social worker must understand policy trends, sensitively interview adults and children, help families negotiate the complex maze of service delivery, and juggle many roles and responsibilities. With the practitioner working in concert with progressive social policy, it is possible to create a system of care that can reverse the alarming statistics that were presented at the beginning of this chapter. Understanding and implementing the eight pragmatic perspectives discussed in subsequent chapters can improve the well-being of children and families at the individual and collective levels. These pragmatic perspectives are introduced below, then are discussed in more detail in subsequent chapters, including specific applications of each perspective to the systems of child welfare and children's mental health.

Pragmatic Perspective 1: Combating Adultcentrism. When social workers and other professionals interact with children, they need to be aware of potential bias in their understanding and responses to the children. This potential bias stems from the difference in age between the adult professional and the child. The younger the child, the greater are the differences that must be bridged—differences such as language, communication, and worldview.

This potential bias is called "adultcentrism." Adultcentrism is akin to two other, more familiar, forms of bias—egocentrism and ethnocentrism. An egocentric person demonstrates an excessive preoccupation with oneself and has an exaggerated view of their importance. An egocentric person thus has difficulty seeing another person's point of view and perspective. A parallel phenomenon occurs with ethnocentrism, when a person believes that their own cultural, racial, or ethic group is superior to all others. An ethnocentric person has difficulty understanding or appreciating other cultures, and may judge people from other cultures as not being as competent or as "good" as people from his or her own culture.

In adultcentrism, adults can display a similar bias in relation to children. Children are different from adults in many ways, and adults can have a biased view of these differences. Since children are on their way to becoming adults, adults can view adulthood as being superior to childhood. Adults know more and are more competent at all human tasks and skills, aren't they? Children are seen as growing up to become adults—that is their goal and purpose in life, to become well-adjusted and law-abiding adult citizens. So children are viewed as less competent and generally inferior. But this view is a biased one, and can lead to poor communication, devaluing of competencies, and overly rigid limits on decision making. Adultcentrism can be combated the same way that egocentrism and ethnocentrism can be—through learning about children as children, by suspending one's own beliefs, and by learning how to communicate in children's own language.

Pragmatic Perspective 2: Family-Centered Practice. Effective social work practice with children emphasizes the crucial importance of families in children's lives. Traditionally, professional services have too often been overly focused on the individual child to the detriment of the child's relationship with his or her family. Historically, professional expertise and authority supplanted parental expertise and authority, as professionals have tended to blame parents, especially mothers, for their children's difficulties. Parents have been reluctant to seek professional help for fear they will be criticized and misunderstood, a result of being held to unrealistic, idealistic professional parenting standards. The result (perhaps unintended) has been the undermining of parental authority and responsibility, and the erosion of the family as a social institution by well-intentioned professionals who have superseded parents as the "real" experts on children. This lack of professional support for the family mirrors the way that the culture as a whole undermines parenthood and the family (Mack, 1997).

Family-centered practice seeks to reverse the traditional stance in which the professional views him/herself as a consultant to the parent. To this end, there are three essential elements of family-centered practice. First, the professional sees the family, not just the individual child, as the unit of focus and attention. The professional truly believes that the child cannot be viewed as independent from his or her family, and that the family is the child's most important and enduring resource. Second, the professional guards against unwarranted breaches of parental authority and responsibility by honoring the parents' right and obligation to make informed decisions about their child's care. Professionals may have information, knowledge, and expertise that the parent can use in making the decisions, but the professional should not presume that their expertise usurps the right and responsibility of parents to make the decisions. Third, family-centered professionals employ a strengths approach. Rather than blaming and criticizing parents, family-centered practitioners focus and build on family strengths and capacities.

Pragmatic Perspective 3: Strengths Perspective. This perspective was introduced as a key element of family-centered practice. It also applies to the social worker's approach to individual children and to the relationships with other professionals that work with the child and family. A strengths perspective is an antidote to the negative, pathology orientation that has characterized much of traditional professional education and practice. Strengths assessments are characterized by such factors as discovering what the client wants, discovering the uniqueness of clients, mutuality in deciding goals and strategies, and avoiding blame (Cowger, 1994). No matter how desperate a situation may appear, a strengths-oriented practitioner believes that every person and family has strengths and resources to bring to the situation.

Pragmatic Perspective 4: Respect for Diversity and Difference. Children and families come in many different shapes, sizes, and colors, so that today's social workers need to be skilled at working with diverse populations. Diversity can involve age (as in the case of adultcentrism), race, culture, gender, sexual orientation, and/or disability. Whenever differences exist between the practitioner and the client, there is a potential for miscommunication, inaccurate judgments, and ultimately, ineffective practice because client outcomes are negatively affected. If a social worker strongly believes that homosexuality is wrong, how can that worker help a teenager who is struggling with his or her own sexual identity? How can that social worker effectively help a gay couple raise a young child with behavioral problems? Overt and covert forms of prejudice and discrimination have resulted in a system of care that does not treat all children and families equally, in which the health and well-being of poor and minority race children fall short.

There are many ways for social workers to improve their competence in this area. One way is to understand and appreciate the dynamics of powerlessness and how people respond to the lack of power in their lives. Another is to strive for cultural competence in social work organizations. Practitioners can also learn to appreciate the experience of immigration by employing such tools as cultural mapping.

Pragmatic Perspective 5: Least Restrictive Alternative. The "least restrictive alternative" influences the delivery of services at both a policy and direct-service level. Simply put, the concept of the least restrictive alternative holds that, whenever possible, children should be served in the environment that is least restrictive to their personal liberty. In practice, this often means the environment that is most comfortable and normal for the child. For example, rather than placing children who have serious mental illness in state hospitals or residential treatment centers, out of their homes and away from their families, services should be geared to treating the child and helping the family while the child remains in his or her home and community.

Least restrictive environment is closely associated with another term, *continuum of care.* In each of the systems of care, there is a continuum of service options for children that range from low to high in restrictiveness. For example, children in education can be served from placement in a regular classroom full-time (at the low end of the continuum), to placement full-time in a self-contained special education classroom within the same school (middle of the continuum) to placement outside the school and community in a spe-

cial facility such as a school for the hearing impaired (high end of the continuum). Although the least restrictive alternative is a guiding principle of services, it is not without controversy. Parents and professionals often disagree among themselves about what is the most appropriate level on the continuum of care, and these disagreements can be very contentious, sometimes resulting in scarred relationships and seemingly irresolvable tensions.

Pragmatic Perspective 6: Ecological Perspective. The social work profession has, since its inception, embraced a person-in-environment perspective unique among all the helping professions. The ecological perspective is the latest manifestation of this approach. The ecological perspective seeks to understand the origins of and solutions to problems and struggles of individuals by looking to the interface of the person and the person's larger social environment including family, friends, coworkers, and professional service providers. The needs of clients can be blocked by gaps in available resources, poor access to services, and lack of knowledge about available supports.

One tool that social workers employ for ecological assessment is the "ecomap" (Hartman, 1978). This assessment form helps workers assess the relationship of parents and children to environmental supports such as work, school, friends, extended family, religion, health care, and recreation. Operating from an ecological perspective, the social worker often acts as a case manager, works for increased community involvement and ownership of children and families, and advocates for the client and for systems change.

Pragmatic Perspective 7: Organization and Financing. The systems of care for children and families need to be accessible, affordable, and efficient in order to have the maximum impact and benefit. Unfortunately, these characteristics are not always present. Service agencies often receive funding from many different sources, including fee for service, government grants, private foundations, and insurance companies. These funding sources often determine the categories of services that clients are eligible to receive and the way the agency organizes to deliver those services.

Current issues in the organization and funding of services include decentralization, privatization, managed care, and service integration. Decentralization is characterized by the diffusion of responsibility, planning, and implementation of services from higher to lower levels of the organizational hierarchy. Privatization is a growing trend in the delivery of services to children and families. It is characterized by the belief that the private sector can be more efficient and effective in providing services than can the governmental, public sector. Managed care, a way to finance services that originated in the health care system, has been spreading to the child welfare and mental health systems in recent years. Managed care systems intend to control the cost of service delivery without sacrificing quality, but critics contend that managed care systems inevitably must compromise quality in order to gain cost control. Service integration efforts aim to reduce the fragmentation of service delivery systems to improve efficiency and coordination. These efforts can take the form of restructuring and "decategorizing" services, or instigating interagency and community planning councils, local government authorities, and neighborhood revitalization efforts.

Pragmatic Perspective 8: Achieving Outcomes. Traditionally, governmental and private agencies that provide services to children and their families have not been required to document that their services have resulted in improved outcomes for their consumers. More recently, taxpayers, lawmakers, government officials, and private funders have pushed for better accountability. When significant dollars are invested, investors want to know that children and families are being helped, and that society's goals for children and families are being achieved.

Sometimes termed *results-based accountability*, this new outcome emphasis may seem simple and straightforward, but there are in fact many complex barriers to its successful implementation. These barriers include resistance among providers, distinguishing process outcomes from final outcomes, conflicts between individual and systems goals, disagreement about which outcomes to measure, the difficulty and cost in accurately measuring and interpreting outcomes, determining whether the outcomes achieved justify the costs, and weighing prevention versus treatment.

It is very important that the reader understand that, together, these eight pragmatic perspectives represent a clear and dramatic departure from traditional professional practice in many other disciplines. That is, services for children and their families have historically been adult-centric, child- and professionally centered rather than family-centered, focused on pathology rather than strengths, insensitive to diversity, supportive of treatment in highly restrictive environments, uninterested in the broader context, poorly organized and chaotically funded, and unable to document successful outcomes. Thus, practicing social work according to these perspectives can be a courageous and often frustrating endeavor. Even though these perspectives represent the most progressive ideas about current "best practices" in the field, all can be considered controversial as well. Not every professional in every discipline agrees that these perspectives represent the best direction.

CHAPTER 1 SUMMARY

This chapter has provided an introduction to the field of social work with children and families. Disappointing and disheartening statistics about the overall health and well-being of children and families in the United States indicate that there is a need for much stronger and more effective efforts. Social workers work with children and their families in two major settings, or systems of care: child welfare and children's mental health. At the same time, those children and families can also be receiving services from several other systems of care, including education, special education, juvenile justice, health care, and developmental disabilities. These settings each have their own history, policies, laws, and functions. Although they are sometimes described and analyzed as distinct systems of care, children and families cross systems with regularity.

Eight pragmatic perspectives were introduced briefly. These are intended to help students see and understand the commonalities across settings and give them a frame of reference for understanding and acting in very complex and difficult situations. Each pragmatic perspective is a lens through which the social worker can view the client's situation, and each perspective helps the social worker see the situation in a different light. Together, the perspectives inform and direct the actions of the worker so that those actions are consistent with the most important principles in the field.

The next two chapters provide the student with basic and fundamental knowledge about the two major systems of care that employ social workers: child welfare and children's mental health. These chapters explain the laws, policies, terminology, and practice issues in the two fields. With this foundation in place, later chapters then present more in-depth coverage of the eight pragmatic perspectives, including specific ways in which they apply in the two major settings. Finally, the book ends with two chapters that present detailed case examples of successful practice and the ways in which the eight pragmatic perspectives were incorporated into each case.

CHAPTER **2**

Social Work in Child Welfare Settings

Overview

This chapter introduces the reader to the world of social work in child welfare settings. The reader is exposed to the continuum of services from intake and investigation through adoption. This continuum of services is presented in the context of the three main goals or functions of the child welfare system: protection of children, preservation of families, and permanency planning.

Introduction to the Field

Of the two major settings for social work practice this text presents, child welfare is the first to be closely examined, because of the vital and crucial role that social workers perform in the child welfare system. Unlike mental health and education, where social work plays "second fiddle" to other professional disciplines—psychiatrists, psychologists, and educators—social work in child welfare is the dominant profession and force. As Ann Hartman (1990), a leading social work author and educator, put it, "Social work has a very special role in the child welfare system. Our profession was born in that system. The social institution known as child welfare has been primarily a social work domain since the early 1900s" (p. 484). Because children and families in the child welfare system are often known to other systems such as mental health and education, social workers employed in these other settings are obliged to have a good working understanding of the issues, policies, and practices in child welfare. School social workers and mental health professionals spend a good portion of every working week interacting with social workers and

other professionals in the child welfare system—making reports of suspected abuse and neglect, providing information about progress, coordinating care plans, attending case conferences and review hearings, even testifying in court.

It is the social workers employed in these other settings who have the responsibility for explaining, interpreting, and sometimes defending the child welfare system to colleagues. The higher education and training programs for schoolteachers, principals, psychologists, psychiatrists, and other professionals rarely include information about the child welfare system. These professionals are unlikely to be aware of the laws, values, and policies that structure child welfare practice. It is easy, and common, for these professionals to engage in "child welfare/social worker bashing" because they do not understand or appreciate the nature of child welfare work. Thus, it is incumbent on social workers in mental health, education, and other settings to educate other professionals about how and why the child welfare systems functions as it does.

The child welfare system is a huge enterprise, consisting of efforts by public, governmental agencies at the local, state, and federal levels as well

18

as private efforts by countless nongovernmental agencies. Even when child welfare is narrowly defined as concerning the abuse and neglect of children, people new to the field are often astounded to learn that child welfare activities consume billions of dollars of the federal budget, and millions more from the budgets of each of the states. For example, in FY 1992, the federal appropriation for foster care services alone was over $2 billion (Pecora, Whittaker, & Maluccio, 1992). In addition to the amount of money expended, thousands of people are employed in the child welfare field.

This vast undertaking works toward three primary purposes: the protection of children, the preservation of families, and permanency planning for children in care. Encompassed under these three purposes is the child welfare continuum of services for children and families: intake and investigation, prevention of placement, reunification, foster parenting, residential group care, adoption, and independent living.

Protection of Children

Overview

Brief History. Individuals have expended efforts to protect and care for abused and neglected children at all times in history. However, concerted and organized efforts by either the public or private sector are a relatively recent phenomenon. In the United States, most states passed legislation in the late 1800s to allow courts to remove children from parents for their protection and placement in almshouses, orphanages, or families, but these laws did not specify responsibility for the investigation and enforcement of the laws. Curiously, this responsibility came to be assumed by private organizations for the prevention of cruelty to children, which sprang from existing organizations for the prevention, and cruelty of animals. In the mid- and late 1800s, the protection of animals was a much more highly organized and effective movement than was the protection of children. Beginning with the founding of the New York Society for the Prevention of Cruelty to Children in 1875, other similar societies were founded throughout the United States. These societies, modeling the purposes and strategies of the animal protection

societies, were formed to investigate cases of alleged child maltreatment, present cases to the court for resolution, and advocate for the passage of laws that enhanced children's welfare (Downs, Costin, & McFadden, 1996).

Concerted efforts by the medical profession, legislatures, and the public sector to protect children from the abuse and neglect of their parents are a relatively recent phenomenon in the United States (Lindsey, 1994). Prior to 1962, there were very few references to child abuse in the medical literature. Although social welfare efforts on behalf of children had existed for more than 100 years, the abuse and neglect of children did not fully capture the public's attention until the publication of a medical survey on "the battered child syndrome" by C. Henry Kempe and associates in 1962 (Kempe, Silverman, Steele, Droegmueller, & Silver, 1962). In this article, the authors documented the brutality that could be afflicted on children by their parents, and the public was moved to action. Child advocates called on states to pass laws for the reporting of child abuse and the protection of children. This "rediscovery" of child abuse prompted states to act, so that by the mid-1960s every state had passed new legislation regulating child abuse. Since the passage of these laws, the number of reports of child abuse has risen each year, from 9,563 in 1967 to 2,936,000 in 1992 (McCurdy & Daro, 1993, as cited in Lindsey, 1994, p. 93).

In 1974, the United States Congress initiated federal involvement through passage of the Child Abuse Prevention and Treatment Act of 1974 (P.L. 93-247). This law established the National Center on Child Abuse and Neglect, provided financial assistance for demonstration projects for the prevention, identification, and treatment of child abuse and neglect, and mandated that states provide for the reporting and investigation of child abuse (Pecora, et al., 1992). Of course, not all child maltreatment is reported, despite these state laws that mandate that professionals and others report suspicion of child abuse. Of those reported, not all are substantiated on investigation. Nationwide, in 1996, there were over 3 million children reported to be abused and neglected in the United States (compared to 2 million in 1986), of which about one-third of the reports were substantiated by child welfare authorities, ranging from 92% confirmed in Alaska to 3.7% in North Dakota (Petit, Curtis, Woodruff, Arnold, Feagans, & Ang, 1999). The wide variances in the percentage of reports that are substantiated are the result of different definitions, procedures, training, and data collection in each state.

Recent findings suggest that the incidence of child maltreatment is increasing dramatically. A national survey commissioned by the federal government found that the number of abused and neglected children grew from 1.4 million in 1983 to 2.8 million in 1993. During the same period, the number of children that were seriously injured quadrupled, climbing from 143,000 to 570,000 (U.S. Department of Health and Human Services, 1996).

Poverty, Substance Abuse, and Child Maltreatment. The relationship between poverty and all forms of child maltreatment is very strong. Studies by the federal government have found that child maltreatment is almost 7 times more likely to occur in families with incomes under $15,000 than families over $15,000 (U.S. Department of Health and Human Services, National Center on Child Abuse and Neglect, 1988, as cited in Downs, et al., 1996), and 22 times more likely than in families with incomes over $30,000 (U.S. Department of Health and Human Services, 1996). Children of single parents were 80% more at risk of suffering serious injury from abuse or neglect (U.S. Department of Health and Human Services, 1996). Even though child maltreatment crosses all income categories, and can be concealed more easily in families of higher social status, most authorities agree that poverty is a major source of stress and frustration that can lead parents to take out these frustrations on their children.

Substance abuse is believed to be a contributing factor in a high percentage of abuse and neglect cases. Most authorities have viewed the drug epidemic of the 1980s, particularly the abuse of crack cocaine, as a primary reason for the collapse of many families and for the large increases in the number of children being removed from their homes and placed into foster care. The link between substance abuse and neglect appears to be especially strong (Nelson, Saunders, & Landsman, 1990). When a parent is addicted, the drug

or alcohol becomes all-consuming, and the needs of the children are not attended to.

Types of Maltreatment. Physical abuse, sexual abuse, psychological or emotional abuse, and neglect are the four broad types of maltreatment for which children in need are reported to state authorities. In 1996, of all substantiated cases of abuse and neglect, physical abuse constituted 21%, sexual abuse 11%, emotional abuse 5%, and neglect 45% (Petit, et al., 1999). Each of these terms is imprecisely defined, so that the lack of consensus about what constitutes a certain type of abuse presents a multitude of challenges for the children, their parents, the professionals who investigate and intervene, and researchers who study incidence, prevalence, and treatment.

Psychological abuse is perhaps the most difficult to define and specify, because it accompanies most other forms of abuse and can less frequently be confirmed as a specific, separate phenomenon. Psychological or emotional abuse involves the active or passive failure of the adult to provide for the positive development of the child's sense of self and social competence (Pearl, 1994). Specific forms of emotional abuse include verbal assaults on the child, corrupting the child, isolating the child from family and community so as to deny the child human contact, and rejecting the child's needs and requests.

The following sections briefly define physical abuse, sexual abuse, and neglect and discuss the prevalence, causes, effects, and treatments for each.

Physical Abuse

Definition, Incidence, Causes, and Treatment. Physical abuse involves the intentional physical injury of children. The injury can be major (such as broken bones, fractured skulls, or serious burns) or minor (such as small bruises and minor burns). Physical abuse can be an acute, single event or it can be chronic over time. Physical abuse can be familial, when perpetrated by a parent or sibling, or extrafamilial, when perpetrated by someone outside the family such as a teacher or baby-sitter. Violence against children can also take the form of corporal punishment, which many would view as a form of physical abuse because it inflicts physical injury.

In 1996, approximately 230,000 children were confirmed as having been physically abused in the United States. This represents an incidence rate of 3.5 per 1,000 children in the population. There were also 930 maltreatment-related fatalities nationwide in 1996, a slight decline from 1,127 in 1990 (Petit, et al., 1999). Physical abuse is about four times as likely in families struggling with poverty (U.S. Department of Health and Human Services, 1988).

While it is probably impossible to isolate the specific causes of any one occurrence of physical abuse, four theoretical perspectives offer different possible explanations (Pecora, et al., 1992). None of these perspectives has been sufficiently developed or tested to qualify as the definitive model for understanding abuse and neglect. The psychological model holds that there is something psychologically deficient in the parent or caretaker that triggers the abuse. Perhaps the parent has a personality disorder or some type of mental illness that stands in the way of effective parenting. Abusive parents may lack empathy for others, especially children, and thus have less tolerance and too-high expectations. These emotionally needy parents might be susceptible to subtle or blatant forms of role reversal, in which the child is expected to take care of the parent, rather than vice versa. Parents may lack education in proper discipline and childhood development, or they may have been damaged emotionally and cognitively by abuse they themselves suffered as children. Substance abuse may render a parent incapable of caring for a child, so that treatment of the parent, perhaps in an inpatient facility, would be needed to correct this deficit. Although many parents who abuse have themselves been abused as children, the vast majority of children who are abused do not grow up to be abusive parents.

The sociological perspective focuses on the social context of the abuse, rather than on the personality of the parents. Cumulative environmental stresses from poverty, unemployment, living conditions, social isolation, and other factors can precipitate abuse, as individuals' normal coping patterns are eroded by the stress. Societal tolerance of violence also fits into the sociological perspective. A third perspective is the socio-situational model of abuse, in which the interactions between the child and abuser are seen as determining the abuse. In this model, specific attributes of the child, such as disability, temperament, or behavior, are seen as stressors on the parents that block the development of positive bonding.

In the final perspective, the interactive model, all of the above perspectives are seen as interlinked; each may be present, to some extent, in incidents of physical abuse. This perspective calls for an individualized approach that utilizes multiple perspectives to devise a treatment plan that fits the particular situation. A thorough history, environmental mapping, family interactional assessment, and psychological assessment are necessary to provide a broad and holistic perspective on the problem.

Effects of Physical Abuse on Children. Children who have been physically abused over a period of time can adapt to the experience in a variety of ways. Some become quite compliant, trying to behave so well that there could be no reason for parents to become angry. Others become aggressive with peers and/or adults, exhibiting behavior problems of defiance and opposition that require heavy investments of adult time and energy. This aggression can be understood from a variety of perspectives. Perhaps it is due to identification with the powerful adult aggressor. Perhaps a defiant and defensive posture serves to protect the child from others' aggression, in the spirit of "the best defense is a good offense." Perhaps the aggression is partly the result of social learning, because adults have modeled an aggressive and violent means of coping with the world. Another common response is for the child to blame himor herself for the abuse, to cope with the abuse by rationalizing that it was a necessary response of the adult to a "bad" child. Thus, many abused children have a poor self-concept and lack confidence in their capabilities. Still other children can respond to the abuse as a traumatic event, which may result in symptoms of Post-Traumatic Stress Disorder (PTSD), including dissociation, intrusive thoughts and nightmares, and a numbing of emotional involvement with others.

The long-term effects of physical abuse on adult functioning are not clear. While it makes intuitive sense that such trauma *must* have some negative effect on short and long-term development and functioning, research studies have shown a surprising level of resilience and coping ability among adults who were abused as children. Although some studies report a greater likelihood that abused children will experience problems such as depression, substance abuse, criminal behavior, and abusive behavior toward their own children as adults, there is no certainty that an individual abused child will have any one of these problems (Crouch, 1994). If there is some form of irreparable and certain harm that occurs, it has not been detected by current measurement tools.

Treatment for the Abused and the Abuser. Treatment for children who have been abused can range from individual play therapy to out-of-home placement in a safe environment. For trauma victims, the key therapeutic goals involve developing feelings of safety, trust in the world, and a sense of control over circumstances. These goals can be achieved through a variety of methods, including court orders of no contact with the perpetrator, individual play therapy, family counseling, and corrective emotional experiences with adult caregivers and therapists. It is often therapeutic for the abusive parent to apologize and take responsibility for the event, to relieve the child of feelings of guilt and self-blame.

For the abusive parent, treatment can include a number of options, depending on which causal explanations and theoretical perspectives appear to have the most relevance to the particular family. As mentioned above, a thorough approach to the problem involves a holistic perspective and assessment of the psychological, environmental, and interactional dynamics of the situation. Many treatment programs that target the needs of the perpetrator emphasize parent education classes, developing social support networks, anger management training, and relaxation or stress-reduction skills. Sometimes, abusive parents who were themselves abused as children need to confront and integrate their own abuse before real change can occur. A holistic approach generally entails some environmental intervention to reduce the effects of stressors and some interactional or family work to repair the damage of the abuse and build a more positive relationship.

Sexual Abuse

Definition, Incidence, Causes, and Treatment. Sexual abuse of children involves sexual contact or interaction for sexual stimulation and gratification of a parent, adult caretaker, or older child. Sexual abuse can be classified as sexual assault, incest (also called intrafamilial abuse), and exploitation. Sexual assault involves force and violence that usually results in some form of injury. Sexual assault is usually a one-time event and is usually perpetrated by someone outside the immediate family. Incest is sexual abuse of children by someone within the child's family, so closely related that they are forbidden to marry. Incest usually occurs over a long period of time and does not necessarily involve violence or physical assault resulting in injury. Exploitation is a form of sexual abuse that involves prostitution and pornography. Often, both parents are sexually involved with the children and use the children for financial gain. Some sexually abused children also report that they were subjected to sadistic and ritualistic abuse associated with satanic worship (Monteleone, Glaze, & Bly, 1994).

National statistics indicate that 119,357 reports of sexual abuse were confirmed nationwide in 1996, representing an incidence rate of 1.8 per 1,000 children in the general population (Petit, et al., 1999). The actual prevalence of sexual abuse may be much higher, because of the secrecy, taboos, and fear of reporting associated with victimization. More girls than boys are reported as victims, but sexual abuse of boys may be vastly underreported. A rigorous study of San Francisco women found that 28% reported unwanted sexual experiences before age 14, and that 16% experienced incest before age 18 (Russell, 1983, as cited in Pecora, et al., 1992, p. 167). Finkelhor (1979) found that 9% of the men and 19% of the women in a survey of 796 college students had experienced sexual abuse, including noncontact sexual abuse, during childhood (Finkelhor, 1979). Sexual abuse is more than four times as likely to occur in poor families (U.S. Department of Health and Human Services, 1988).

The four broad theoretical perspectives on child maltreatment, described in the above section on physical abuse, can also be applied to sexual abuse, but most of the literature focuses on psychological factors and family dynamics. Unlike physical abuse, in which it seems logical that environmental stressors can lead to impulsive, angry responses that target children, it is more difficult to conceptualize how environmental stressors such as poverty and unemployment can lead to sexual abuse. The societal taboo regarding sexual abuse is stronger than physical abuse, so it is thought that perpetration of the act must result from some strong personality deviance.

About 85% of perpetrators are males, and psychological profiles indicate a range of personality characteristics that are associated with sexual abuse. *Situational child molesters* are those who do not have a strong sexual preference for children per se, but engage in sexual acts with children because of low self-esteem, availability, feelings of power and dominance, experimentation, or insecurity. *Pedophiles* have a strong sexual preference for children. They are usually blocked in their social and heterosexual relationships. Not all child molesters are pedophiles, and not all pedophiles are child molesters, because some pedophiles do not act out their fantasies (Monteleone, et al., 1994).

On the family systems level, sexual abuse, particularly incest, can be viewed as representing dysfunction in the family, not in the individual. According to this thinking, the sexually abusive behavior might actually be a symptom of some other problem within the family, such as marital conflicts or lack of emotional boundaries. This systems thinking has been criticized, however, because it allows the perpetrator to avoid responsibility by blaming something in the family system (Conte, 1986, as cited by Pecora, et al., 1992, p. 170).

Although not prevalent in the literature, community and societal factors may play a role in sexual abuse. Just as society is tolerant of violence, so is it tolerant of the sexualization of children, as evidenced by advertisements and commercials for clothes and cosmetics. When a child reports sexual abuse, he or she is not always believed, so that a potential perpetrator could feel relatively safe and not fearful of being caught. When families are forced to live in small, inadequate housing, a climate for poor emotional, physical, and sexual boundaries can develop as people are forced to sleep in the same bed and personal privacy is difficult to achieve.

Effect of Sexual Abuse on Children. Children who have been sexually abused often display greater knowledge about sexual matters and display more sexual behaviors than other children of the same age. However, while most sexually abused children will display sexualized knowledge and behavior beyond their years, many show no such behavioral indicators, and not all children who do demonstrate sexual behavior have been sexually abused. Intense and chronic sexual abuse can result in dissociative reactions and multiple personality. Sexual abuse is highly correlated with the problems of attempted suicide, running away, and adolescent drug abuse and prostitution (Monteleone, et al., 1994). Like other forms of abuse, sexual abuse often engenders feelings of guilt and low self esteem in victims. They may feel betrayed with a corresponding loss of security and trust in adults, powerless as a result of the fear and helplessness of not being able to end the abusive situation, and stigmatized by the shame and guilt of having been involved in a socially unacceptable situation (Finkelhor & Browne, 1986).

Treatment for the Sexually Abused and Sexual Abuser. Because children experience sexual abuse differently, careful attention must be paid to the age, developmental level, and circumstances of each individual case. Often, these children need play therapy, group therapy, and family therapy to resolve their guilt, learn to express anger, develop skills of self-protection, and reestablish trust in adults. To ensure the child's safety while avoiding the potential trauma of placement, many programs urge that the alleged perpetrator leave the household and have only supervised contact with the child. If the child, rather than the perpetrator, must leave the home, the child can feel punished, as if he or she were the one to blame for the abuse.

Treatment for sexual offenders is complex and difficult, requiring highly specialized training and skills. Because denial is usually a strong component of the offender's defenses, some legal leverage is often employed to pressure the offender to admit that he has a problem and needs treatment. Since many cases involve the child's word against the adult offender's, many offenders cling to the defense of denying the problem, in hopes that no one will believe the child. If legal authorities take a hard line by arresting the alleged perpetrator and threatening to prosecute, offenders may agree to treatment in lieu of court hearings or jail sentences. Once in treatment, offenders hopefully learn to take responsibility for their actions, apologize to the victim, and gain control of their sexual behavior through a variety of treatment approaches (Giaretto, 1981).

Orten and Rich (1988) developed a useful tool (figure 2.1) for the social worker to use to assess the family situation in cases of incest or intrafamilial abuse. Successful work with the family requires attention to the historical, behavioral, and attitudinal characteristics of each of the three primary participants: the abused child; the offender, who is usually a male caretaker in a father role; and the mother. According the authors' review of the literature, the key assessment and treatment issues for the offender are whether or not he admits to the behavior, takes responsibility for it, and shows some empathy for the child. Prognosis is also affected by the severity of the abuse, the past relationship with the child, history of alcohol or drug abuse, antisocial behavior, and history of prior sexual abuse offenses. For the mother, the key variables are whether or not she believes the child, has a good past relationship with the child, bonds with therapists, takes action to protect the child, demonstrates ability to be independent, has an active social support system, absolves the child of all guilt and blame, has a history of alcohol or drug abuse, and has a physical or mental handicap that limits her ability to protect the child. For the child, the key characteristics are age, level of cognitive, emotional, and physical development, confidence in the mother's ability to protect, ability to identify adult resources outside the family, and ability to develop rapport with a therapist.

To assist in the assessment of these factors, each characteristic is rated on a measurement scale from 1 to 5. Low numbers indicate positive ratings on the attribute, while high numbers indicate the need for improvement and attention in that area. By calculating a total score, the worker can gain a sense of the overall prognosis and compare the score at various points in time to monitor overall progress. Use of the scale can help the worker and family focus on the key issues that families need to address to overcome the problem and remain intact.

Child Neglect

Definition, Incidence, Causes, and Treatment. Child neglect is a broad category of child maltreatment that describes the failure of adult caretakers to provide for the basic needs of their children. Neglect can be mild or severe, acute or chronic. Neglect is generally thought of as an act of omission, rather than commission. In investigating and confirming serious neglect it is important to establish not only that the parent's inattention to the child's needs resulted in harm to the child, but also that the caretaker had been informed of the child's need by a competent professional if that need would not have been apparent to most adults, and that the caretaker was physically and financially able to provide the care (Munkel, 1994). Several types of neglect can be identified, corresponding to the various needs of children, such as health, shelter, education, nutrition, emotional care and nurturing, and proper supervision. Physical neglect is a broad term that encompasses health, shelter, nutrition, supervision, and other forms of physical health and well-being.

The number of confirmed reports of all types of child neglect was 499,871 in 1996, which is about double that of physical abuse and more than four times that of sexual abuse. This represented an incidence rate of 7.5 per 1,000 children in the population (Petit, et al., 1999). Physical neglect is the most frequently reported type of neglect, followed by educational neglect and emotional neglect (Pecora, et al., 1992). Neglect was nine times as likely to occur in poor families than in the population as a whole (U.S. Department of Health and Human Services, 1988).

Because the range and scope of neglect is so broad, and because family situations in which neglect occurs are very complex, no one theory explains why neglect occurs. The psychological model of parent inadequacy appears to apply to many parents who are confirmed for neglect. Many neglectful parents are drug abusers or suffer from serious mental disorders, such as depression (Nelson, et al., 1990). The sociological model also applies to neglect because poverty and social isolation are so highly associated with neglectful behavior. Money is necessary to meet children's needs, and social support is helpful in relieving the stress of living in poverty. In many cases, the

FIGURE 2.1. FAMILY ASSESSMENT: FATHER–DAUGHTER INCEST

Father or father-figure					Score
1	2	3	4	5	___
Admits incestuous behavior		Cautious or vague in acknowledging incestuous behavior		Categorically denies abuse	
1	2	3	4	5	___
Accepts responsibility for incest		Projects blame onto wife, alcohol, etc.		Blames victim	
1	2	3	4	5	___
Seems to understand impact on child and shows remorse		Minimizes seriousness of incident and impact on child		Main concern is about consequences for self	
1	2	3	4	5	___
Abuse limited to touching, fondling, exposure; no use of force		Abuse included manual or oral-genital contact or intercourse, use of threats		Rape through threat or force, injured or terrorized child, involved child in pornography	
1	2	3	4	5	___
Past relationship with child showed general empathy		Role reversal, lack of empathy for child		History of physical abuse or extreme discipline	
1	2	3	4	5	___
No history of alcohol or drug abuse		Sporadic alcohol or drug abuse		Alcoholism or drug addiction	
1	2	3	4	5	___
No history of antisocial behavior or criminal acts		Few and less serious law infractions		Extensive antisocial behavior, criminal record	
1	2	3	4	5	___
No previous history of sexual abuse		History of sexual abuse of current victim and/or other children in family		Past or current sexual abuse of children outside family	

Total ___

FIGURE 2.1. (*continued*)

Mother					Score
1	2	3	4	5	
Believes child		Vague about incident, doubts child's reports		Does not believe child, denies abuse	____
1	2	3	4	5	
Historically adequate relationship with child		Ambivalent bond to child, role reversal		History of abuse, neglect, inadequate parenting	____
1	2	3	4	5	
Quickly forms bonds with therapist		Forms bond with therapist after resistance		Distrustful, resists help	____
1	2	3	4	5	
Takes action to protect child, i.e., reports incident		Minimizes need to protect or takes ineffectual action		Primary concern is protection of partner and self	____
1	2	3	4	5	
Demonstrates ability to be independent		Dependent on partner but can act independently with support		Strong dependency on partner	____
1	2	3	4	5	
Active social support system		Limited social support system		Socially isolated	____
1	2	3	4	5	
Holds adults responsible for limits of sexuality and for protection of children		Partially blames daughter or blames alcohol, etc.		Blames daughter for incestuous behavior	____
1	2	3	4	5	
No history of alcohol or drug abuse		Sporadic alcohol or drug abuse		Alcoholism or drug addiction	____
1	2	3	4	5	
No physical or mental handicap that limits ability to protect		Intellectual, physical, or psychiatric condition that compromises ability to protect child		Serious physical, intellectual, or psychiatric handicapping condition	
				Total	____

FIGURE 2.1. (*continued*)

Child					Score
1	2	3	4	5	
Adolescent, age 13 years or older		Latency, age 6 through 12 years		Preschool age, age 5 years or younger	
1	2	3	4	5	
Normal intellectual, emotional, and physical functioning		Borderline intelligence, mild physical or emotional handicaps		Vulnerable child—serious mental, physical, or emotional handicap	
1	2	3	4	5	
Expresses confidence in mother's ability to protect		Protective of mother or sees mother as being unable to protect		Fearful of mother or sees her as potential abuser	
1	2	3	4	5	
Can identify available adult resource person outside family		Can identify possible adult resource persons		Socially isolated, distrustful of adults	
1	2	3	4	5	
Easily develops rapport with therapist		Able to develop bond with therapist after being cautious initially		Distrustful, resists therapist and other helpers	
				Total	

psychological and sociological exist together and can be highly interrelated in terms of cause and effect. That is, the substance abuse and personality problems may be caused, or at least be exacerbated, by poverty in some cases, while in other cases they may be the reasons for the poverty.

The interactional model of understanding neglect is also pertinent, especially in situations in which the parent and child do not form a strong bond or attachment, such as nonorganic failure to thrive. Nonorganic failure to thrive is an interactional disorder in which infants fail to grow and develop properly. The children are often thin and emaciated, with potbellies and mottled skin. They are usually emotionally and verbally unresponsive (Munkel, 1994). Families in which failure to thrive

occurs have been characterized as highly disengaged. Communication and interaction between family members is minimal. This disengaged style results in a lack of nurturing and bonding with the infant, who in turn responds by withdrawing and not communicating his or her needs to the parents, because past attempts to communicate those needs have not been acknowledged or responded to by the parents (Alderette & deGraffenreid, 1986).

Effects of Neglect on Children. Children who have been neglected can suffer severe psychological, physical, and developmental harm, and even death. Even though child neglect receives much less media attention than physical abuse or sexual abuse, it is more prevalent than these other forms of child maltreatment and its consequences can be just as serious (Downs, et al., 1996). As in the case of physical and sexual abuse, the effects of neglect are not irreversible. Not all children who were neglected grow up to be neglectful parents, nor do all of them struggle as adults with major psychological problems or criminal behaviors. Still, it is likely that adults who were seriously neglected as children are more likely to be unable to trust others, have low self esteem, have problems with anger, and be socially inept and isolated (Munkel, 1994).

Treatment for Neglected Children and Their Families. Treatment for neglected children means ensuring that their needs are provided for, particularly the needs that have been neglected. They may need food, medical attention, shelter, or supervision. They may also need attention to their psychological and emotional needs, so that they receive love, attention, and stimulation. They usually need to develop a trust that adults will take care of them (Polansky, Chalmers, Buttenweiser, & Williams, 1981). Individual or group psychotherapy and placement in foster care may be necessary to meet those needs, because the family may not be able to change fast enough to ensure the child's well-being.

Treatment for the families of seriously neglected children is considered a long-term proposition that requires casework for longer than six months. Families need a combination of family supports in the form of concrete services and clinical interventions to change long-standing family and personal dynamics (Pecora, et al., 1992). Concrete services include help with housecleaning, housing, employment, transportation, education, finances, and other needs. Clinical services involve the establishment of trust and a stable relationship between a caseworker and the family. Clinical services may also involve the therapeutic services of drug abuse, alcohol, and mental health counselors. In time, families need to learn to overcome their social isolation and loneliness by establishing positive social support networks.

Investigation of Abuse and Neglect

Complex Decision Making. Social workers are called upon to investigate the reports of intrafamilial abuse and neglect that come to the attention of child welfare agencies. Because abuse and neglect of children, if confirmed, can also be a criminal action for which the perpetrators are arrested and tried in criminal court, these investigations are often conducted in cooperation with police officers. Although they may overlap, the roles of the police officer and child welfare worker are not the same and should not be confused. The social worker's job is to determine whether or not to confirm the report, to ensure the safety of the child, and to provide or arrange for ameliorative services to the family. The police officer's job is to participate in ensuring for the safety of the child while preparing evidence for a possible criminal investigation. The social worker must decide whether or not to confirm or substantiate the report, decide what level and intensity of services and what degree of supervised contact with the alleged offender are needed to safely maintain the child in the home, and decide whether to petition the juvenile court (or family court) for custody if the child's safety can be assured only through out-of-home placement in state custody.

There are few clear guidelines or objective standards for making any of these decisions. Even when there is direct evidence of physical harm, there can be different explanations for how the child was harmed. Without witnesses, the determination of abuse may rest with the child's word against the parents'. Social workers may be influenced by parent cooperation or defensiveness, past history, the role of substance abuse, child vulnerability, and other factors. The level and intensity of needed services is based on an assessment of the factors that contributed to the abuse and how to ameliorate them, both of which are subject to opinion and interpretation. The most severe and/or chronic cases of abuse are the category for which foster care placements are necessary, sometimes on an immediate basis because the child is in imminent danger. But professionals can disagree about whether the level of abuse in a case is moderate or severe, and about whether or not the parents are amenable to treatment and services.

If the report is substantiated, the child welfare worker must somehow determine the level of risk to the child of repeated abuse or neglect. This involves balancing risk to the child with the importance of family ties and relationships, and with the risk of harm to the child if placed out-of-home. If the child welfare system wanted to protect children at all costs, it would take no risks with abusive parents—all abused and neglected children would be removed and placed in safe families or group homes. Such a conservative, cautious approach would thus lead to the placement of many children in state custody. Essentially, this was the situation that developed in the 1950s, 1960s, and 1970s in this country, and federal legislation was passed in 1980 to ameliorate some of the problems that this approach created. In effect, the legislation expanded the mandate and mission of the child welfare system, from an almost exclusive focus on the safety of children to inclusion of the goals of preservation of the family and permanent relationships. (More on this legislation will be presented in later sections.)

When investigating reports of abuse and neglect, the worker is faced with the realization that the safety of children can *never* be guaranteed, whether they are placed at home, with a foster family, or in residential care. It is naive to assume that a child will be safe in state custody. Abuse and neglect occurs in foster homes and group homes at alarming rates: the chance of a child being abused or mistreated in residential care may be as high as one in five (Rindeleisch & Rabb, 1984). In one midwestern state, soon after being honored as the statewide foster parent of the year, a foster parent was arrested, convicted, and jailed for sexually molesting foster children in his care. In addition to the safety risk inherent in placement, there is a risk of temporary or permanent damage to the already fragile parent-child relationship. There is the added risk of the child moving from placement to placement while in foster care, and languishing in foster care while reunification and/or adoption efforts bump along. In 1990, in 22 states, 57% of the children leaving foster care had been in placement for between 1 and 5 years, and only 18% had been in care for fewer than 6 months (Curtis, Boyd, Liepold, & Petit, 1995).

Risk Assessment. Because these decisions about placement and risk are so complicated, many have sought some type of systematic, objective means to assess risk that would not rely so heavily on the personal judgment, experience, and subjectivity of the individual worker. Intended as an aid, not as substitute, for worker judgment, various risk

assessment tools have been developed. These instruments are intended to help determine whether a child is likely to be maltreated at some future time, not to determine whether abuse exists in the present or has existed in the past. Systematic risk assessment can standardize data collection in an agency, help make decisions more consistent across different personnel, prioritize cases for investigation and services, and help determine the level and intensity of services needed. "High risk" families would receive priority for more immediate and intense intervention, compared to "low risk" families (Downs, Costen, & McFadden, 1996).

Typically, risk assessment instruments contain items that have been shown from research and practice to predict later maltreatment of a child. In a thorough review of eight of the most common of these instruments, McDonald and Marks (1991) identified 88 separate variables that are measured, of which any one single instrument measures no more than 44, and as few as 13. Less than half of these 88 variables had been empirically tested. Two variables were common to three rigorous, empirical studies of the recurrence of abuse: access of the perpetrator to the child and the number of children in the home. Other high-risk factors associated with abuse include the child's characteristics of age, physical or behavioral disabilities, and perception of difference by the caretaker. The abusing caretaker's mental health status, level of stress, unemployment, and lack of social support have been found to be related to abuse.

Ideally, social workers would use these risk assessment instruments and their own clinical judgment to make decisions about which children need out-of-home placement, and which can safely remain with their families. Lindsey (1994) has presented a strong critique of decision making in child welfare intake and assessment. According to his analysis of data, the best predictor of out-of-home placement is the economic security of parents. Children whose parents are self-supporting or who received government assistance were more likely to remain in the home and receive supportive services than were those whose parents were without reliable income. Guidelines for the removal of children may well be vague and inconsistent, but "findings suggest that an underlying guideline does exist, although it may not be stated explicitly in many agencies: adequacy of income" (p. 154).

Police Investigations of Abuse. Abuse and neglect of children is also a matter for the criminal justice system, because the perpetrators can be prosecuted as criminals. Whereas the social work investigation focuses on protection of children as the goal, police investigations focus on criminal investigation and potential arrest and prosecution of the perpetrator. Although criminal investigations do not generally proceed except in the most egregious cases, there is often a need for both types of investigations. In order to avoid duplication and confusion, many communities conduct joint investigations of situations such as sexual abuse that are likely to involve criminal investigation, often with established teams designated for this purpose.

Some experts have called for a greater role for the police in the investigation of child abuse and neglect (Pelton, 1998). In this expanded role, the responsibility for the investigation and for the protection of the child would rest with law enforcement. Child welfare would be freed of its coercive, authoritative function and thus be free to focus on providing help and assistance to needy families. With the roles clearly delineated, there would be little overlap of function between the law enforcement and child welfare, and families would see the child welfare agency with less fear and trepidation.

Of the 26 states that have moved in this direction of assigning more responsibility to law enforcement, Florida has initiated some of the most dramatic changes (Kresnak, 2001). In four Florida counties, the sheriff's offices have completely taken over all child abuse and neglect investigations, and they employ some social workers as well as police officers. Critics fear that housing investigations within law enforcement will result in more removals of children into foster care, because they are not trained in the nuances of abuse and neglect and may have little empathy or patience with parents. Out-of-home placements have risen, but it is not clear whether this would have happened under child welfare as well, because new laws have mandated removal under certain conditions. An early legislative evaluation report noted that the four sheriff's offices were outperforming child welfare agencies on only two indicators: the percentage of alleged victims seen within 24 hours

of a report and the percentage of cases closed within 30 days. But the sheriff's offices are better funded as well, spending almost 40% more per investigation than child welfare.

Preservation of Families

Public Law 96-272: The Adoption Assistance and Child Welfare Act of 1980

Overview. As mentioned in the previous section, the preservation of families became a major goal of the child welfare system with the passage of federal legislation: the Adoption Assistance and Child Welfare Act of 1980 (P.L. 96-272). The intents and purposes of this act have been widely discussed, and it is considered to be the most important piece of federal legislation to impact child welfare practice. Overall, the legislation was designed to promote permanently stable situations for children who come to the attention of child welfare authorities. It was enacted to combat the documented impermanence of foster children who had been shown by extensive research to languish and "drift" in foster care. The philosophy, professional attitudes, and financial incentives of state child welfare systems of the 1960s and 1970s had focused on "child saving" rather than "family saving," to the detriment of thousands of foster children who grew up in foster care with few permanent ties to family. Instead of supporting permanent relationships in biological or adoptive families, the system kept too many children too long in long-term foster care, in a kind of limbo status that left them without the kinds of permanent bonds and supports generally considered essential to healthy development. There was also a serious concern that many children were unnecessarily placed, because services to maintain them in their families were inadequate or nonexistent.

Reasonable Efforts. P.L. 96-272 makes it clear that the most desirable permanent placement for children is with their own family. Thus, the preservation of families is an explicit goal of this legislation. To encourage this end, the law requires that, in order to receive certain federal dollars that help pay for child welfare services, states must comply with the provisions of P.L. 96-272. States must make judicial determination that reasonable efforts were made to prevent the unnecessary placement of children in out-of-home care (42 USC 672 [a] [1]). If placement is necessary, the state must make reasonable efforts for the child to return to his or her family (42 USC 672 [a] [15]).

Unfortunately, P.L. 96-272 did not define what constituted "reasonable efforts." Although this determination must and should be made on an individual, case by case basis, general guidelines for have been developed which describe a range of services and supports which should be available to families, as depicted below.

Reasonable Efforts: Range of Services
(adapted from *Making Reasonable Efforts: Steps for Keeping Families Together,* n.d.)

- Intensive, home-based family services and counseling
- Crisis intervention
- Cash payments for emergency needs, and ongoing financial support
- Food and clothing
- Housing
- Emergency shelter
- Respite care
- Child day care
- Treatment for substance abuse
- Treatment for physical, sexual, emotional abusers and their victims
- Parenting skills training
- Life skills training
- Household management and homemaker services
- Transportation

Reasonable efforts to prevent placement or reunify children are to be provided for as long as necessary to prevent removal or facilitate reunification, without time limits. Workers should be available for emergencies 24 hours a day, including weekends. The parents, child, and worker should mutually arrive at goals and contracts. The intensity of services should increase during crisis times, when removal is imminent, and immediately after removal *(Making Reasonable Efforts,* n.d.).

The parent perspective on reasonable efforts is similar to the above. Parents of children with disabilities, who comprise about 20% of the children in foster care, have stressed the need for a wide range of services and supports including respite care, special education, counseling, financial support, and information/referral (Petr & Barney, 1993). When parents of children with disabilities experienced a crisis that threatened out-of-home placement, they most often characterized the crisis as precipitated by the child's behavior, a problem in the system's ability or willingness to support the child and family, general stress, or the parent's inability to provide care. Parents stressed the importance of family-centered attitudes and values from programs and professionals. They expressed a need for professionals to stop blaming parents and to develop greater levels of sensitivity to the stresses that parents face in raising a child with a disability.

The remainder of this section will highlight the two areas for reasonable efforts specified in the P.L. 96-272: programs designed to prevent unnecessary removal of children from their homes, often called family preservation or intensive home-based services; and reunification services.

Prevention of Placement

One of the most essential and most widespread strategies to prevent the unnecessary removal of children from their homes is intensive, home-based family services, also called intense family preservation services (IFPS). This section will describe the general characteristics and theoretical base for IFPS programs, describe one program (Homebuilders) in some detail, review the evaluation research on IFPS effectiveness, and briefly discuss family preservation models that are alternatives to the IFPS model.

General Characteristics and Theoretical Base of IFPS. Intensive family preservation services are time-limited, problem-focused services delivered in a family's home for up to several hours each week. The primary goals of IFPS are to protect children, to maintain and strengthen family bonds, to stabilize crisis situations, to increase the skills and competencies of family members, and to facilitate the family's use of a variety of formal and informal services and supports (Whittaker & Tracy, 1990). Ultimately, attainment of these goals will increase the safety of the child and prevent the unnecessary removal of children from the family into state custody.

Goals of Intensive Family Preservation Services (IFPS) (adapted from Whittaker & Tracy, 1990)

- Protect children
- Maintain and strengthen family bonds
- Stabilize crisis situations
- Increase skills and competencies of families
- Facilitate the family's use of formal and informal services and supports

---

Although IFPS programs can differ by type of staffing patterns, public or private auspices, specific target population, frequency and intensity of service, and program components, they generally share some common characteristics. Families are referred and accepted based on at least one child being at imminent risk of placement. Service is time-limited, typically lasting between 1 and 5 months. Each worker carries a small caseload, as few as two families at any one time. The low caseloads allow the workers to make frequent visits to the family home, up to several hours in one week. Workers maintain flexible hours, 7 days a week, so that they are available for emergencies and crises and can schedule visits at times that are most convenient for the family. The service approach combines teaching skills to family members, helping the family access resources, and family counseling to help family members understand and improve the way they function as a unit (Whittaker & Tracy, 1990).

According to Barth (1990), IFPS programs are built on four major theoretical frameworks, one or more of which might be emphasized by any one particular program. *Crisis intervention theory* holds that people are most motivated and amenable to change when they are in a crisis state, or a state of disequilibrium. Crisis theory postulates that people tend to reach a new state of equilibrium within four to six weeks. The time-limited, crisis response characteristics of IFPS are consistent with these crisis intervention ideas. Yet crisis theory was developed in relation to everyday people who were confronted with untenable and unexpected circumstances and events, which may not characterize the IFPS population.

The second theoretical base for IFPS is *family systems theory*. Although there are a multitude of different types of family systems theories, they share in common a focus on the family, rather than the individual child. Depending on the specific school of thought, the focus can be on intergenerational patterns and dynamics, communication and interactions among family members, subsystem boundaries, power relationships, or other aspects of family functioning.

The third theoretical base is *social learning theory*. Social learning theory was originally applied mainly to individual, young children, and it was not a theory widely applied to work with families until the 1970s. Social learning theory focuses on the family interactions that punish or reward competent behaviors. Workers employing this theory might focus on parent training in which parents are taught effective discipline and communication skills, or on teaching negotiation skills to parents and teenagers. Workers focus on how behaviors are learned and reinforced in a family and tend to assume an educational or teaching role in helping the family learn new behaviors.

The fourth theoretical base for IFPS is *ecological theory*. The ecological perspective is presented in detail in chapter 9. In IFPS, the ecological model applies when workers help the family gain access to resources needed for a safe and healthy environment. Workers do not simply talk with the family about communication patterns, like many office-based family therapists might do. Instead, they "get their hands dirty," helping the family advocate for and obtain concrete services to meet basic needs.

Homebuilders Model of IFPS. The Homebuilders model is one of the earliest and most widely used models of IFPS. Begun in Tacoma, Washington, in 1974, the program has conducted trainings in all 50 states. The model attempts to serve families within four weeks, and workers' caseloads are limited to two families at any one time. Homebuilders has emphasized program evaluation from its beginnings, and data about program effectiveness are widely available (see next section for a discussion of research on IFPS) (Kinney, Haapala, Booth, & Leavitt, 1990).

The program philosophy of Homebuilders reflects many family-centered principles. The program emphasizes instilling hope in families, treating clients as colleagues, and believing that most clients are doing the best they can. Homebuilders has been categorized as fundamentally a social learning—based program that uses interventions based on the other three above theories to a more limited extent.

The following case example, previously published as an example of the Homebuilders model in action (Kinney, et al., 1990, pp. 60–63), demonstrates the mix and range of theories and interventions Homebuilders uses. This case example is instructive because it illustrates the wide range of interventions that must be employed to successfully work with a family in which abuse has occurred. The reader is invited to identify specific interventions that are employed and note the theoretical base for each.

The Clark Family: Child Abuse

[Reprinted with permission from *Reaching High-Risk Families: Intensive family preservation in human services,* ed. J. K. Whittaker, J. Kinney, E. M. Tracy, & C. Booth, pp. 60–63. Copyright © 1990 by Aldine de Gruyter.]

The Clark family was referred to Homebuilders by a public health nurse. [Currently all referrals are routed through the Department of Social and Health Services.*CGP*] The nurse requested that the Homebuilders intervention coincide with the release of the Clarks' infant daughter from the hospital. The baby had been born prematurely and had spent the first 3 months of her life in the hospital.

The nurse requested intensive services because she was concerned about the family situation. The Clarks' 3-year-old son recently had been diagnosed as hyperactive and as having some brain damage. Children's Protective Services and the nurse were also questioning three concussions that the boy had had over the last year. The nurse and CPS were certain that unless Homebuilders was available to see the family, both children would have to be placed in foster care.

The nurse discussed her concerns with the parents, and they consented to allow a Homebuilders therapist to come to their house. The family had no phone, so the therapist dropped by unannounced for a visit. Mrs. Clark was home at the time, so the therapist asked if she could stay awhile and talk.

After sitting down, the first thing the therapist noticed was the smell of gas leaking from the furnace. Mrs. Clark said she thought she had smelled gas, but hadn't felt up to walking to the public phone to call her landlord. The family's pediatrician had ordered her to get a telephone installed because of the uncertain condition of the baby, but since her husband was not working regularly, they couldn't afford to pay the installation fee.

The therapist suggested that Mrs. Clark dress herself and the children warmly, open the window and turn the furnace down. While she did that, the therapist went to a public phone and called the landlord to send out a repairman.

When the therapist returned, Mrs. Clark talked about her situation. She said she had been very depressed since the baby's birth, and that she often felt that the child did not belong to her. She was also extremely upset about her son's "wild" behavior. She wondered if the boy had a "bad seed" in him like his uncle who was in prison. She had begun to think that she might kill him rather than watch him grow up to be a murderer like his uncle.

Mrs. Clark was very thin, pale and weak. She had a chronic cold, and had lost her front teeth due to poor health. Now twenty-two, she had had three children and four miscarriages in 5 years of marriage. She also said she was very lonely. Her husband usually was away from the home from midmorning to late at night. He worked as an insurance salesman, but he had not sold a policy in five months. The woman told the therapist that every other counselor they had seen had told her that her husband was "rotten" and that she should leave him. She said she loved him and that he didn't beat her. The family had moved to Washington from Idaho several months previously so that they could remain married, yet still be eligible for state aid. Currently they were receiving funds from the WIN program.

The next day the therapist approached a local charitable organization and secured the $25 needed to have a telephone installed. She also got two old bedsheets that could be nailed up as curtains, since Mrs. Clark had expressed fears about sitting alone at night with no curtains for privacy. She had told the therapist that one night recently a strange man had been peering in her window. She had been raped once before and was scared it might happen again.

During the next home visit, they focused a lot on the three-year-old son. Mrs. Clark said that she did not love him, and described a variety of what she labeled as self-destructive and wild behaviors that he engaged in. She reported incidents such as him throwing himself backward off furniture, touching the hot stove and laughing, turning on the kitchen burners, banging his head against the wall until he passed out, biting, scratching, and hitting other people. Although he was three, he still had not started talking. She was concerned that Children's Protective Services would think she was abusing him because he hurt himself so much, and because they locked him in his room at night. The Clarks did this because the boy slept only two or three hours at a stretch, and if he were not locked in his room, he would go into the kitchen and eat until he vomited. She said CPS thought she should put him in an institution because she couldn't handle him. He would not kiss or show any affection to people. She said he had been removed from the home by Children's Protective Services in Idaho the previous year when she had "a nervous breakdown" and was hospitalized. Since moving to Tacoma, the parents had already voluntarily placed the boy once for 72 hours because the mother felt she "couldn't cope" with him any longer. She was also afraid she might harm him because he made her so angry sometimes.

Before leaving that day, Mrs. Clark and the therapist made a list of what she could do if she felt her son's behavior was so bad that she would want to place him again. The Homebuilder let her know she thought it was a good idea to lock him in his room sometimes and explained the concept of Time Out. The list also included calling the Homebuilder (the family's phone was to be installed the next day). Then they made an appointment to take the son to Mary Bridge Children's Hospital Learning Center to see about enrolling him in a special school program. Finally, the therapist talked with the mother about making some free time for herself, and volunteered to baby-sit for several hours later that week. Mrs. Clark accepted the offer.

Later that week, the Homebuilder was alone with the children for five hours while she was babysitting. She learned a lot about the young boy. She observed him engage in some of the behaviors Mrs. Clark had reported. By the end of the day, however, she determined that he responded to a positive reinforcement and Time Out. During the afternoon she taught him to play a kissing game. The information gathered that day was invaluable. It was proof for both the therapist and the mother that the little boy could change, and that he did care about people. His mother cried the first time they played the kissing game.

During the second week of the intervention, Mrs. Clark began to talk more freely about her discontent with her marriage. She said that she knew her husband wasn't really working all the times he was gone. She expressed resentment over the fact that he dressed nicely when she had only one outfit, that he was free to play all day and night while she sat confined in their apartment, that he would not let her get a driver's license but also would not drive her places. Feeling she had reached a teachable moment, the Homebuilder began to talk about territoriality and assertiveness training. The Homebuilder also called the woman's DSHS caseworker and received authorization to get her front teeth replaced.

Mr. Clark was beginning to get curious about what was happening. One day he stayed home to meet the therapist. While his wife was at the dentist, he and the Homebuilder spent several hours talking. He shared his own frustrations about having to be on welfare. The Homebuilder told him that she wanted him to be a part of the counseling process and he agreed to attend the next session. After their discussion he seemed more willing to participate.

During the last weeks of the intervention, the therapist focused primarily on teaching the parents some behavioral child-management skills. The son had begun attending the Mary Bridge school program, and Mrs. Clark rode the bus with him every day. The Homebuilder was pleased to see this, as it gave the mother a chance to watch the teachers, and to make friends with the staff there. Mrs. Clark reported having some positive feelings about her son, and no longer felt she should send him away. She also began to feel much better about herself. She had temporary caps on her teeth, and began to smile more. She was also beginning to gain a little weight.

As the end of the intervention approached, the therapist and Mrs. Clark explored ways she could continue receiving counseling. She decided that she wanted to go back to a counselor at the mental health center. She had seen the counselor a couple of times right after the baby was born last summer, and thought she could trust her. She made an appointment.

During her last week with the family, the therapist helped the Clarks move to a better apartment in the neighborhood, where they felt safer. It wasn't until after the move that the family found out the Mary Bridge bus would no longer be able to transport the boy to school. Mrs. Clark became very upset, but quickly calmed down and began to problem-solve. She talked with the counselors at Mary Bridge and followed their suggestion to see if the boy could be transferred to Child Study and Treatment Center's day care program. There were no openings at the center, but he was put on the waiting list.

A follow-up call from this family several months later revealed that although there had been a number of upsetting events that had happened after the Homebuilder left, they were still together as a family. Mrs. Clark had been seeing her counselor and had continued to work on being more assertive. She and her husband were also going for marital counseling. Mr. Clark had quit selling insurance and was enrolled in a job training program. The son was attending the new school, and the mother was participating in a parent education program required by the school. The Clarks reported that their son was starting to talk and did not seem as "wild." The infant daughter was doing fine as well.

Homebuilder costs for the Clark family intervention totaled $2,937. If the mother had been placed in a psychiatric hospital, the cost of hospitalization would have been $5,926. If the two children had been removed by Children's Protective Services, the cost of their placement would have been $15,000 or $7,500 each. Total costs would have been $20,926.

Commentary. Although the original authors did not analyze this case, interventions and their theoretical base will be discussed here as an educational tool for the reader to more fully understand and grasp the nature of intensive family-based services.

Many of the therapist's interventions were ecologically based, including the first intervention. The therapist took direct action to notify the landlord about a needed concrete service: repair of the gas furnace, which was potentially life-threatening. Soon after that, the therapist arranged for a phone to be installed and obtained makeshift curtains to address the mother's concern about privacy. During the second visit, the therapist offered to provide a concrete service herself when she offered to baby-sit later in the week to provide free time for the mother to do something for herself. Other ecological-based interventions included enrolling the son in a special learning center, getting authorization to have the mother's front teeth fixed, and helping the family move to a better, safer apartment.

Crisis intervention theory could be used to conceptualize the disequilibrium in the family brought on by the premature birth of a new baby and the baby's entry into the family after a three-month hospitalization. A crisis situation also existed relative to the potential placement of the three-year-old son. Crisis intervention principles were also demonstrated by how quickly the worker responded to the referral, the quick and direct action that the worker and family took to fix the gas furnace, and the list the worker and mother made to help her through the next time she felt in a crisis over her son's behavior to the extent that she wanted to place him out of the home.

Family systems theory was evident in the therapist's focus on interactional and communication patterns in the family. The therapist listened to both parents' frustrations about the marriage and apparently helped the mother be more assertive about her issues and needs. However, most of the family systems interventions were based on social learning theory: "During the last weeks of the intervention, the therapist focused primarily on teaching the parents some behavioral child-management skills," which consisted of positive reinforcement and Time Out. The strategy of teaching the child to play a kissing game, which reportedly helped spur a dramatic turnaround in the mother-child relationship, could also be seen as stemming from social learning theory, in that the child and parent were taught new skills that positively reinforced the relationship.

Overall, this case example depicted the potential of the Homebuilders model to effect positive change. At the beginning, the worker faced a family clearly struggling with major problems and difficulties: poverty, illness, serious marital conflict, severe child behavioral difficulties, and poor parenting skills. The purpose of the program—prevention of unnecessary placement—was achieved and all five goals of IFPS programs listed above were addressed. Safety of the children was assured while family bonds were strengthened, resources were acquired, and parenting skills were learned.

It is also important to note that not all of the family's problems were solved at the time of closure. Individual counseling for mother and marital therapy continued, and "a number of upsetting events" transpired after termination. Rather than attempting to completely alleviate all of the family's issues, Homebuilders' efforts aimed at stabilizing the family situation and getting them headed in the right direction. This focus on achieving limited objectives is essential to a brief intervention program. Armed with renewed hope, parenting skills, and resources, the family was able to stay together without the intensive level of help afforded by the Homebuilders therapist.

Evaluation of IFPS. Unlike many human service programs, IFPS has been committed to evaluation of effectiveness since its beginnings. The Homebuilders model has been especially diligent and exemplary in this regard. Early evaluations of the Homebuilders model were quite positive and encouraging. By 1987, after seeing almost 3,500 cases, Homebuilders reported that 97% had avoided placement in state funded care, three months after termination. Twelve months post-termination, placement had been averted in 88% of the cases. The program also has attempted to assess the cost-effectiveness of the program, by translating the prevention of placement into cost savings for the state. Assuming that all cases would have been placed without Homebuilders (all referrals were judged to be at "imminent risk" of placement) and using average costs of out-of-home placement and average length of stay in care in Washington, Homebuilders calculated that the cost of the program was more than $31 million less than the cost of placement (Kinney, et al., 1990).

But these early evaluations were based on the tenuous assumption that all of the cases referred to IFPS were truly at imminent risk of placement. Later evaluations tested this assumption by designing a comparison group drawn from the same target population pool. In this way, the outcomes for families receiving the IFPS interventions could be measured against the outcomes for similar families, also judged to be at imminent risk for placement, who received the normal level of service from the child welfare agency. These controlled studies of IFPS have not shown nearly the same dramatic results.

One of the surprising findings of these studies was the low rate of out-of-home placement in both the control and comparison groups. For example, in a California study, 82% of the treatment group avoided placement, while the figure was 83% for the comparison group. In a Nebraska study, the figures were 96% for the treatment group, 89% for the comparison. In New Jersey, the percentages were 94% for the treatment group and 83.5% for the comparison group (as cited in Pecora, et al., 1992, p. 292). Apparently, most of the cases identified as at imminent risk for placement were not, in fact, imminently at risk. Clearly, in conducting cost-effectiveness studies, programs cannot assume that all of their cases would have been removed to state custody in lieu of treatment.

Although these more recent controlled studies failed to verify the early dramatic claims of placement prevention and cost savings, neither do the results of these studies prove that IFPS is ineffective. Flaws in the designs of the studies can explain the apparent lack of success, so that a number of factors must be considered in interpreting the results. In many cases, the families in the comparison group received substantial assistance, so the level of assistance and intervention between the two groups may not have been dramatically different. Intensity of service in the IFPS groups varied dramatically across different programs. The comparison group and treatment group may not have been identical, or matched, on key characteristics such as household size, income,

severity of abuse and neglect, or level of parent substance abuse. Also, placement rates and cost-effectiveness may have been overemphasized as outcomes. Other important outcomes to track are improvements in child functioning at home and school; changes in parental functioning in such areas as employment, substance abuse, or anger management; and improvement in family functioning, such as less conflict and better communication (Pecora, et al., 1992). It is also important to track the safety of the child as a program outcome, to determine whether children are abused and neglected less when served in IFPS programs.

Although design flaws may account for the disappointing results, it is also important to scrutinize the characteristics of the IFPS model itself. The results of the comparison-group studies do not prove that the IFPS model is ineffective, but they do raise the question of whether the intervention itself may not be powerful enough or long-term enough to effect long-lasting change in families whose children are at risk for placement. IFPS programs have been less effective with the issue of child neglect, and it has been recommended that more emphasis should be placed on linking these families with neighborhood services that can continue on a long-term basis (Berry, 1992). More rigorous studies of various models must be undertaken before we know which interventions work best to achieve which outcomes with which kinds of families.

Alternatives to the IFPS Model of Family Preservation. One alternative to the short-term IFPS model is a long-term model of family counseling and support designed for work with families "in perpetual crisis" (Kagan & Schlosberg, 1989). Developed at the Parsons Child and Family Center in Albany, New York, in work with over 1,000 families, this model recognizes that many families whose children are at high risk for placement have long histories of severe problems and seem to operate in a state of chronic crisis. Use of the model prevented placement in 88% of families served, with high ratings of client satisfaction. The model emphasizes the building of a long-term relationship with a single worker who helps the family overcome past traumas, losses, and lack of trust that developed over generations. Emphasizing a family systems approach over ecological or social learning theories, this model views perpetual crises in families as a lifestyle pattern that enables families to avoid more long-standing issues and dilemmas.

Short-term IFPS programs are probably not adequate for families in which severe substance abuse is present (Downs, et al., 1996). Family preservation programs for this population involve longer term case management and close coordination among providers of substance abuse treatment, mental health, health, child care, and other services. Often, families need transitional housing for parents in exiting inpatient treatment programs, extensive child care options, and family planning services. Programs for recovering addicts need to recognize that relapse is common, so that the parent and staff develop means to anticipate relapse so that children can be protected prior to a crisis.

Reunification

(This section is adapted from Petr & Entriken, 1995.)

Overview and Definitions. The second arena for which "reasonable efforts" must be made under P.L. 96-272 is the reunification of foster children with their families. Although P.L. 96-272 emphasizes both the prevention of placement and reunification, subsequent child welfare programming and research have emphasized prevention-of-placement programs, as described above. Because of this lack of emphasis, the knowledge base for reasonable efforts to achieve reunification is not as developed as for family preservation programs focused on prevention.

Outcome-based research on reunification is limited and has yielded mixed results. Lahti (1982) reported findings from a comparison group study of programmatic efforts to secure permanent placements for 259 children in foster care, either by reuniting them with their families of origin or by placing them with adoptive families. Project efforts resulted in significantly more children being placed in adoption than was true in the comparison group, but there were no significant differences between groups in the numbers of children returning to parents. This result was confounded, however, by differences between the project and comparison group selection procedures. The project group was

selected from a pool in which caseworkers considered family reunification to be unlikely, while the comparison group did not have this restriction. In a study reported by Fein and Staff (1993), 68 mostly preschool-aged abused and neglected children received reunification services for at least six months. Of these, 26 (38%) were reunified, but seven of these returned to foster care. Thus, 28% of the families remained reunified by the end of the second year of the program. In a control-group study of reunification, E. Walton, Fraser, Lewis, Pecora, and W. K. Walton (1993) reported that, after a 90-day service period, 93% of the treatment group were reunited, compared to 28% in the control group. Twelve months after treatment, 75% of the treatment children were in their homes, compared to 49% of the control children.

The relative inattention to reunification may be due, in part, to the greater complexity and difficulty inherent in attempting to reunite children with their families, as compared to prevention of placement (Allen, 1992). During placement, a multitude of new people and systems typically become involved with the child, including the court, attorneys, out-of-home care providers, foster care workers, new school personnel, and therapists. The child and family may feel relief at the placement and may be ambivalent about reintegration (Hess & Folaron, 1991). Greater challenges may exist regarding teaching and learning parenting skills when the child is not in the home, and families may have to overcome a sense of failure and incompetence (Kreiger, Maluccio, & Pine, 1991). In addition, successful reunification is more difficult to achieve the longer the child is in placement (George, 1990).

Definitional problems complicate the process of reunification even further. Petr and Entriken (1995) draw an important distinction between reunification and reintegration. *Reintegration* refers to the physical reintegration of children with their families. *Reunification* is a more encompassing term that includes physical reintegration as one component. In addition to physical reintegration, reunification involves optimal emotional reconnection with the family and reconnection to the community of origin. Emotional reconnection includes such activities as family counseling to heal wounds and maintaining contact through letters, visits, and phone calls. For those foster children placed outside their community and neighborhood, reconnection with the community underlines the community's role in sharing with the family the responsibility for the growth and nurturance of its young members. Stable and long-lasting relationships with teachers, neighbors, and friends can be almost as important to the child as relationships with family members. Thus, this definition views reunification on a continuum, not dichotomously. Return to the community and emotional reconnection to the family are important reunification goals, even when physical reintegration is not desirable or feasible.

Barriers to Reunification. Like all social programs, reunification efforts are constrained by agency, policy, and program contexts. Social workers attempting reunification should be aware of five major systems barriers that have been found to impede reunification efforts (Petr & Entriken, 1995).

Five System Barriers to Reunification
(adapted from Petr & Entriken, 1995)

- Lack of attention to reunification goals and principles
- Geographic distance
- Policies of residential and youth correctional facilities
- Lack of community-based programs and coordination
- Barriers to family involvement

First, the foster care system may focus on care and treatment of the child, with few resources devoted to reunification. Despite the mandate of P.L. 96-272, reunification may not be the driving force of service delivery in foster care. High caseloads and financial disincentives for reunification may inhibit workers and caretakers from focusing concerted efforts on reunification. When reunification is actively addressed, the focus may be exclusively on physical reintegration, with little regard to emotional reconnection or community reintegration.

Second, geographic distance can be a formidable barrier to reunification efforts. When children are placed outside of their neighborhoods and communities, it is difficult for the local foster care worker to keep in contact with the child and to arrange visits with family. Workers have to commit valuable time to travel, when it may seem more efficient to stay home and work on several other cases. Distance inhibits family visitation and involvement, especially for working families struggling to find the time or means to visit the child. Roles and responsibilities between the local foster care worker and placement staff can become blurred, so the responsibility for organizing and coordinating reunification efforts is not clearly assigned. Finally, geographic distance can impede the formation of community-based supports and services, because it is difficult for community professionals to plan for the coordination of services for a child they do not know and whom they feel little obligation to serve without the child first establishing physical residency in the community.

Third, policies of residential facilities may be antithetical to reunification efforts. Visits and phone calls may be treated as earned privileges, rather than as rights. Parents may be seen as unwelcome intrusions that divert the child's attention from focusing on the facility's intervention program. There may be no staff members whose duties are to facilitate discharge and reintegration into the community.

Fourth, there may be a lack of effective and coordinated community-based programs for these children and their families. Specialized treatment programs for seriously emotionally disordered children and their families, and intensive sexual abuse treatment programs, may not exist. Linkages between child welfare, mental health, and education may be inadequate or nonexistent.

Fifth, there may be strong and entrenched negative attitudes about the parents of foster children, who may be stereotyped as dysfunctional, unmotivated, and uncaring. From the parents' point of view, professionals may expect an unreasonable level, or standard, of family functioning before considering reintegration. The standard of functioning, for both the child and family, may be much higher for reintegration than it was for removal. That is, the level of functioning required to keep a child in a home prior to removal may be lower than the standard required for the child to return to a family after removal.

Permanency Planning

Public Law 96–272 and Permanency Planning

Purpose of P.L. 96-272. Permanency planning is "the systematic process of carrying out, within a brief time-limited period, a set of goal-directed activities designed to help children live in families that offer continuity of relationships with nurturing parents or caretakers and the opportunity to establish life-time relationships" (Maluccio, Fein, & Olmstead, 1986, p. 5).

As mentioned above, the intent of the Adoption Assistance and Child Welfare Act of 1980 (P.L. 96-272) was to ensure a higher level of permanence for children. Before passage of P.L. 96-272, several problems existed in the foster care system (Pecora, et al., 1992). First, despite the temporary purpose of foster care, research had shown that foster care placement had become a permanent status for many children entering the system. Second, many foster children moved from one placement to another with little sense of permanency or continuity, a situation termed *foster care drift*. Third, children were inappropriately and unnecessarily placed out of their homes, with little efforts to preserve the family. Fourth, disproportionate numbers of minority and poor children were in foster care. Fifth, separation of children from their parents was, for some children, a serious traumatic event that could have lifetime adverse consequences.

Specific provisions of P.L. 96-272 supported change in the child welfare system to address these problems. In order to continue to receive certain federal dollars, states had to rewrite their laws governing child welfare to meet the requirements of P.L. 96-272. One of the central requirements was for reasonable efforts to prevent unnecessary placement of children and to reunify foster children with their families, in those cases where placement was necessary. These efforts to prevent placement and reunify foster children were described above.

Once a child is placed into state custody, reasonable efforts to reunify the child with the family are only one of a range of requirements concerning the care of the child. Through provisions for case plans and periodic case reviews, the law institutes a planning process that is intended to result in permanency for the child. These provisions include the following:

Case Plans and Case Reviews. P.L. 96-272 includes provisions for case plans for each child in care. Specifically, the law requires that "each child has a case plan designed to achieve placement in the least restrictive (most family-like) setting available and in close proximity to the parents' home, consistent with the best interests and special needs of the child" (42 USC 675 [5] [a]). These case plans are to be written documents that include discussion of the appropriateness of the placement, documentation of reasonable efforts, a plan for the proper care of the child, assurances that services are provided "to improve the conditions of the parents' home, facilitate return of the child to his own home or the child's permanent placement of the child" (42 USC 675 [1]).

At 6-month intervals or more often, the court or an administrative panel must review the status of each foster child case. This review is to determine the "continuing necessity for and appropriateness of the placement, the extent of compliance with the case plan, the extent of progress which has been made toward alleviating or mitigating the causes necessitating placement in foster care, and to project a likely date by which the child may be returned to the home or placed for adoption or legal guardianship" (42 USC 675 [5] [b]). In addition to these six-month reviews, P.L. 96-272 attempts to promote permanency by requiring a dispositional hearing no later than 18 months after the original placement. The purpose of this dispositional hearing is to reach some final and permanent decision regarding the future living status of the child. The options to be considered are (a) return to the parent; (b) continuation in foster care for a specified period; (c) placement for adoption; or (d) continuation in foster care on a permanent or long-term basis (Sec. 475 [5] [c]).

Thus, the language and provisions of P.L. 96-272 are fairly clear about the goals and mission of the state with respect to foster children or potential foster children, and about how important permanency planning is to the achievement of those goals. States have clear guidelines for their child welfare systems. First, make reasonable efforts to maintain children safely in their own homes. Second, make reasonable efforts to reunify children who must be placed out-of-home with their families. Third, if progress toward reunification is slow, continue foster care for a specified time. Fourth, if reunification efforts fail, then place the child for permanent adoption. Long-term foster care, which had been the norm for many children in foster care, was officially relegated by the law to be the last and least preferred option. The law encourages states to make a permanent decision about the child's living situation within 18 months of placement.

The next sections continue the discussion of the continuum of care in child welfare by reviewing foster care, independent living, and adoptions.

Foster Care

For our purposes, foster care is a general term for the care of children in state-sponsored out-of-home placement. Relative placement, often called kinship care, is the type of placement for about 25% of all children in out-of-home care (Petit, et al., 1999) This form of care will be discussed in the subsequent chapters under the pragmatic perspectives related to family-centered practice and respecting diversity and difference. In addition to kinship care, children in foster care may be living in family foster homes (foster parenting), residential group facilities, or independent living.

Data on Children in Foster Care. The number of children in out-of-home care in the United States increased 65% in the 10 years from 1984 to 1993, from 270,000 in 1984 to 445,000 in 1993. Between 1990 and 1993, the overall increase was 10%, encompassing increases in 38 states. In the same years, in five of the largest states, 24% of the children entering foster care were less than 1 year old. In 1990, only 18% of the children entering foster care exited foster care within 6 months, and only 33% exited within one year; 57% stayed from 1 to 5 years, and 10% were in care over 5 years. The average length of time spent in out-of-home care dropped from 2.4 years in 1977 to 1.7 years in 1990. In 1990, 60% of those exiting foster care returned home, 32% moved to independent living or extended families, and 8% were adopted (Curtis, et al., 1995).

These data reflect a mixed result for permanency planning as set out in P.L. 96-272, and as described in the previous section. The number of children in foster care has increased rather than declined. But perhaps these are necessary placements due to increased abuse and neglect, and the figures would be even higher were it not for reasonable efforts to prevent placement. The average length of time spent in foster care has been reduced, but for most children, it is still well over one year. In 1996, most (56%) of the children who left foster care in the states reporting returned to their families, indicating some continued focus on reunification (Petit, et al., 1999).

Family Foster Care. (Material in this subsection is adapted from Petr, 1995.) Family foster care is provided by foster parents. Foster parenting is the temporary provision of parenting services, in a family home, to children whose birth parents cannot or will not provide adequate care for them. Government child welfare agencies in each state license foster parents, who may work directly for the state or for a private child welfare agency that contracts with the state. Foster parents are paid a monthly maintenance rate to support the child, based on the age and special needs of the child. Effective foster parents are believed to possess the following characteristics: the ability and willingness to learn and accept help from outside agencies, warmth and the ability to understand and accept children, a high frustration tolerance, good communication skills, good physical and emotional health, and a sense of humor (Jordan & Rodway, 1984).

The number of foster families has been declining in the United States in recent years. Current estimates place the number at 100,000 in 1991, down from 142,000 in 1978 (Evans, 1993). Numerous factors may account for this decline. Foster parenting is recognized as a difficult and challenging undertaking. Foster children often exhibit behavioral and emotional problems, due to a combination of factors including the abuse and neglect they may have experienced, drug and alcohol problems, and/or difficulty adjusting to a new family after the trauma of separation. Birth parents may intrude and undermine the foster parents' efforts, while the financial and service support from the state agency may be minimal. Foster parents must work 24 hours a day, often with inadequate training and support. The lifestyle of the American family has changed so that more women, who have traditionally been the primary foster caretakers, now are employed full-time outside the home.

Another important factor in the decline of foster parenting is the role confusion engendered in the move toward permanency planning. Permanency planning's emphasis on reunification and adoption further complicates the role of the foster parent. On the one hand, foster parents can serve a useful function in helping children reunite with their birth parents, by encouraging visitation and serving as role models for birth parents. On the other hand, studies have also shown that foster parents are one of the best adoption resources for foster children (Barth, Berry, Yoshikami, Goodfield, & Carson, 1988). This dual function places foster parents in a dilemma, because it is hard to be both an adoption resource and a promoter of reunification at the same time. If they view themselves as an adoption resource, can they in good conscience promote and participate actively in reunification? But if social workers ask that foster parents focus on reunification, and not consider themselves as adoption resources, will this not hurt the child's chances for adoption if reunification fails? If foster parenting is defined in a more neutral and distant fashion, as only providing temporary care to the child, isn't this wasting a potent reunification or adoption resource?

To address these issues, many foster parents and professionals advocate the professionalization of foster parents (Pecora, Whittaker, Maluccio, & Barth, 2000). Professionalization would involve enhancing the status and compensation of foster parents, so that they are viewed as essential members of the professional team. Foster parents would receive ongoing, intensive training, supervision, and support, including respite care and quick access to social workers. There is some empirical evidence for the notion that foster parent training and support can make a difference. In a study of 650 families in New York, A. Sanchirico and K. Jablonka (2000) found a significant relationship between foster parent training and support and the reunification-promoting activities of foster parents. However, on a discouraging note, 48% of the sample received neither training nor support, and only 18.9% of the sample received both training

and support. Professionalization could result in a degree of specialization, so that foster parents and their training could be matched to specific types of children, such as children with HIV. It could also result in a career ladder, with recognition of highly qualified and effective foster parents as "master" foster parents.

To date, professional foster parenting has not been widely implemented. Implementation has been hampered by inadequate fiscal resources to pay for the expense of adequate compensation, lower worker caseloads, training, and other support services (Pecora, et al., 2000). But if resources are not offered to enhance the attractiveness of foster parenting, then the availability of foster homes can be expected only to decline. This decline would mean that increasingly higher numbers of foster children who have no kinship placement options would be living in residential group facilities, undermining the principle of least restrictive alternative that is the hallmark of permanency planning.

Residential Group Facilities. Residential group facilities can be emergency shelters, group homes, or residential treatment facilities. Unlike family foster homes, residential group facilities are staffed by professional houseparents and other paid staff, who may or may not have professional degrees in the helping professions. Emergency shelters are used when a child needs an immediate placement to ensure his or her safety. After a few days or weeks, the child then returns home or is moved to a foster home, group home, or residential treatment facility. Group homes are staffed by paid houseparents, child care workers, and other support staff. Length of stay for children in group homes can be months or years. Group homes generally house a small group of children, sometimes according to age and gender. Residential treatment facilities are larger facilities that accept the most troubled and behaviorally disordered children for treatment. They tend to be the most highly structured and restrictive.

Residential group facilities can be large or small: in California, the average number of children per facility is about 10; in Texas, the number is almost 50. The number of residential group facilities per state varies from 1 in Vermont, to 1,424 in California. Across the United States residential group facilities have the capacity to house over 117,000 children, which is about one-fourth of the number of children in foster care (Curtis, et al., 1995).

Although they vary in size, scope, and programming, residential group facilities have in common provision of 24-hour care to groups of children by paid professional staff. This form of care is generally regarded as a more restrictive form of care than family foster care, and thus is targeted for children who require more structure and supervision than can be provided by foster parents. Typically, children's daily activities are highly structured by rules and daily routines. Children may receive intensive, individualized education and therapy, especially in residential treatment centers.

An article in the literary magazine *Atlantic Monthly* profiled some of the better-known residential group facilities (Weisman, 1994). According to the author, children in these facilities are placed there because they are too damaged to handle the intensity of real family life. Many are still loyal to their parents and need the greater level of emotional distance that relationships with paid staff provide. A highly structured and controlled environment helps the child feel safe, develop trust in adults, and lower their psychological defenses.

The Villages, with 19 group homes located in Kansas and Indiana, was founded by Karl Menninger, one of the founders of the Menninger Clinic, in 1964. Menninger envisioned placement at the Villages to be a permanent one for children who had no family resource. The average length of stay is 2.5 years. Married couples are the houseparents in all but one of the homes. The Villages believes that the therapeutic value of family life helps many children who might otherwise be housed in more restrictive residential treatment facilities. The structure at the Villages is old-fashioned and family-like. Children are typically expected to attend church, perform daily chores, clean their rooms, dress neatly, and obey houseparents. Some children receive individual therapy and medications for emotional and behavioral problems.

Boys Town, in Omaha, Nebraska, is a large residential treatment center caring for 556 boys and girls who live in smaller, group home—like houses with teaching parents and other children.

Boys Town is a small village unto itself, with 75 houses on 400 acres of landscaped property, complete with schools, churches, town hall, and swimming pools. The treatment program at Boys Town is designed to develop practical and replicable techniques for changing the behavior of children with emotional disorders. Houseparents are "family teachers" who receive intensive training on the nine component parts of a "teaching interaction." An elaborate point system is in place in which children can earn or lose points at home and school depending on their behavior. Points can then be cashed in for extra privileges and purchases.

Woodland Hills, in Duluth, Minnesota, houses 48 boys and girls, aged 13 to 17, most of whom have been substance abusers and gang members. The treatment program at Woodland Hills is based on developing a positive peer culture, the essence of which is helping others. Residents are placed in preexisting groups of 10, and the peer-group therapy that takes place is the essence of treatment. The teenagers learn to care about each other, and eventually themselves. Rather than serving as teaching parents who correct and reinforce behaviors on an intensive basis, staff members at Woodland Hills are experts in group process and helping the residents communicate to each other and care about each other. Unlike Boys Town and other behavioral programs, staff workers intervene directly as little as possible.

Research on the effectiveness of residential group care is inconclusive and controversial. What is the definition of success? For how long after discharge should a residential treatment facility be held accountable for the child's adjustment, behavior, and accomplishments? Are comparison groups required, and if so, can they be designed? A review of the research findings on the effectiveness of residential group care is beyond the scope of this text; however, the major problem that has been identified is maintenance of the gains made by the child after discharge. In other words, residential group facilities can effect change in residents while they participate in the programs, but it is less clear whether that change lasts very long after discharge. In a review of several studies, Pecora and colleagues (1992, p. 421) concluded that two significant factors have been shown to impact a child's postdischarge adjustment: community supports and family involvement. The quality of community supports and the level of contact and involvement with the family are better predictors of postdischarge adjustment than severity of the child's presenting problem, specific treatment technique, or progress made at the residential placement. If confirmed by future studies, this conclusion is powerful support for the ecological and family-centered perspectives espoused in this text. Group-care institutions, rather than focusing exclusively on the child, will be well served to involve families in their programs and target their interventions with children more toward their interactions with family and community, and less with in-house staff. Curiously, none of the above three "exemplary" programs highlighted in the *Atlantic Monthly* article emphasizes either ecological or family-centered approaches.

Independent Living. Independent living programs are intended to help older adolescents, living in foster care, make a successful exit from foster care into adult self-sufficiency. Enactment of independent living programs was stimulated by the Independent Living Initiative of 1986 (P.L. 99-272). For many older teenagers in foster care, neither adoption nor reunification is a practical permanency outcome. When these children reach the age of majority, it is important for the child welfare system to have prepared them for successful living, because many will not have the support of family as they enter adulthood. Rather than the term *independent living,* a more appropriate term for the challenge that these teenagers face is *interdependent living.* This latter term more appropriately emphasizes the need for these teenagers, like all other people, to form networks of support and mutual dependence in personal community relationships. Some of the tasks and skills that interdependent living programs emphasize are money management and daily living skills, nurturing of their own children, responsible decision making regarding sexuality, developing supportive relationships, and participating in the community (Maluccio, Krieger, & Pine, 1990).

A study of the exit outcomes for over 2,500 foster children in California, who were at least 17 and had spent at least 18 months in foster care, yields some clear insights into the older foster care population and offers implications for the design and implementation of independent living programs (Courtney, et al., 1996). Half of these children had entered care at age 13 or older, and one quarter at age 15 or older. The average length of time from first placement to discharge was 5 years, and 10% had spent more than 10 years in placement. In this study population, 60% of the children exited the system through emancipation or independent living; 17% returned home, to a relative, or were adopted; and 23% exited in some undesirable fashion such as running away from placement. The authors conclude that the high percentage of children returning to their biological parents, together with the high percentage of those emancipated and those who ran away and likely returned to their families, suggests that independent living programs should pay more attention to the maintenance of family and kinship ties as a central component of the support-building process. If foster children are strongly drawn back to their families, then independent living programs should not only acknowledge this fact but also work to help ensure that these relationships are as supportive as possible.

Adoption

Definition. Adoption creates a legal relationship of parent and child between individuals who are not each other's biological parent and child. Adoptions can be of two types: agency adoption or independent adoption. Adoption agencies can be private or public. In an agency adoption, birthparents relinquish their rights to the agency, and the agency finds the adoptive parents and gives its consent to an adoption by the adoptive parents. In independent adoptions, birthparents and adoptive parents find each other, and consent to adopt is given directly to the adoptive parents. Only six states do not authorize independent adoptions, and even in those states, the only required stipulation to independent adoptions is that an agency arrange for the parental rights to be terminated (McDermott, 1993).

Material in this section will focus on adoptions of children in the foster care system, as one of the efforts to secure permanency for children who have been abused or neglected.

Data on Adoptions. Overall, there were about 125,000 adoptions in the United States in 1992, of which about 40% were public agency adoptions. This number means that about 2 of every 100 children in the population are adopted. About 68% of all public adoptions are children with special needs, and about 4% are transracial adoptions. Of those states reporting rates of public adoption disruptions in 1993, disruption rates ranged from 3% to 15% (Curtis, et al., 1995).

P.L. 96-272 and Special Needs Adoptions. As previously discussed, the Adoption Assistance and Child Welfare Act of 1980 (P.L. 96-272) set out to change the child welfare system through permanency planning that would either prevent children from coming into foster care unnecessarily, reunify children with their families if placement did become necessary, or place children for adoption when reunification was not feasible or in the best interests of the child. To facilitate the adoption process, P.L. 96-272 encourages states to develop adoption subsidy programs for special needs children and will reimburse the states for 50% of the costs of these subsidies (Barth, 1992).

Adoption subsidies are somewhat controversial among the public as well as the social work profession. The rationale for the subsidies is that they can help hard-to-adopt children find permanent adoptive homes. However, P.L. 96-272 also states that subsidies can be used only when a nonsubsidized placement cannot be found. This requirement can adversely affect continuity of care for the child because it gives preference to strangers who might agree to a nonsubsidized adoption over foster parents who have been receiving support for the child in foster care, but would lose that support if they agreed to a nonsubsidized adoption. Another disincentive to adoption by foster parents is that adoption subsidies are almost always less than the foster care rate (Barth, 1992).

Although the definition of "special needs," and thus eligibility for adoption assistance, varies somewhat from state to state, the following characteristics are generally included: age of over 4 years at adoption, emotional or behavioral problems, adoption as part of a sibling group, presence of a developmental disability or medical condition, and being a member of a minority race (Rosenthal, 1993).

Characteristics of "Special Needs" Children in Adoptions (adapted from Rosenthal, 1993)

- Older than 4 years at adoption
- Emotional or behavioral problems
- Adopted as part of a sibling group
- Developmental disability or medical condition
- Member of minority race

From Foster Care to Adoption. Despite P.L. 96-272 and the increased efforts to help children in foster care find permanent homes, adoption of these children remains a complex, lengthy, and arduous process. In a government study of 20 states in 1991, foster children who were eventually adopted spent an average of 3.5 to 5.5 years in foster care prior to the adoption (as cited in McKenzie, 1993). This length of time is often required for the child to move through three phases of the adoption process, each of which can take months or years (McKenzie, 1993).

The first phase is reunification, in which reasonable efforts must be made to reunify the child with the family. In many states, adoption cannot even be considered until after a legal finding and dispositional hearing have certified the failure of reunification efforts. Although P.L. 96-272 encourages states to decide between reunification and adoption within 18 months of placement, the decision to cease reunification efforts is seldom an easy or clean one. Often, parents make some progress, but not enough to ensure the safety and well-being of the child, in the professionals' opinion. Sometimes children are reunited, only to be removed again, and reunification efforts start all over. Severance of parental rights is a serious legal matter that many courts and individuals view as an extreme intrusion of the state that should be granted only as a very last resort.

The second phase is preparation for adoption planning, including severance of parental rights. Severance of parental rights is a complicated legal matter that requires the focused and concerted efforts of attorneys to complete the necessary technical work to bring the case to court and secure the legal termination. During this stage the child and social worker are dependent on the legal profession and the legal system. While this legal process drags out, the child is left waiting, and the parent may continue to demand reunification services and regular visitation. The social worker must attend to the needs and confusions of the child, deal with the parents' demands, and work with the legal staff for speedy resolution of the case in court.

The third phase of the foster-care-to-adoption process is active adoption planning. Once reunification attempts have failed, and once the child is legally free to be adopted, much hard work is yet to be done. If family members and foster parents are not adoption resources, then a new family must be recruited, assessed, trained, and otherwise prepared. The child, too, must be supported through the long waiting period and then prepared for the adoption (more on preparation of children for adoption will be presented in the next chapter under the pragmatic perspective of combating adultcentrism). Once a tentative match has been found and processed, a period of preparation and visitation can begin. Even after the child moves in, the adoption is not final, and many states require that the child live with the adoptive family for several months before the adoption can be legally finalized.

There is a growing awareness and recognition of the need for services and supports to the child and family after adoption has occurred. These services help the child and family adjust to each other and prevent the disruption or breakdown of the placement. These supports can include financial subsidies, individual and family counseling, parent support groups, respite care, parenting skills classes, coordination of services, reading lists and materials, retreats, and intensive family preservation services for adoptive families in crisis (Barth, 1992; Rosenthal, 1993).

Outcomes of Adoptions. If one considers the population of all people who were adopted as children, the research on long-term adjustment is fairly positive. Most adoptees become well-adjusted adults, although there is some indication that, as a group, they are somewhat more likely to have emotional, behavioral, or academic difficulties than nonadopted peers growing up in intact

homes with biological parents. Some differences emerge at 5 to 7 years of age, when children begin to understand the meaning and implications of adoption. Evidence of differences in the teenage years, adulthood, and between genders is not strong or conclusive. Research has demonstrated that "special needs" children who have experienced abuse and neglect, or multiple changes in their caretaking environments, are more likely to experience adjustment difficulties and adoption disruption (Brodzinsky, 1993).

An adoption disruption is defined as a termination of the adoption prior to legal finalization, during the period of time that the child is living with the adoptive parents on a trial basis. In a review of the literature on adoption disruptions, Rosenthal (1993) concluded that the overall disruption rate for older children with special needs is between 10% and 15%. He concluded that this low percentage represented a high success rate, considering that adoption would probably not have been an option for any of these children 20 years ago. Key predictors of increased risk of adoption disruption are listed below. Contrary to the expectations of some, adoption risk is not greater for families with low income or education, minority groups, or single-parent families, and is only slightly greater for children with developmental disabilities.

Factors That Increase the Risk of Adoption Disruption (adapted from Rosenthal, 1993)

- Older-aged children
- Inadequate background information
- Unrealistic parental expectations
- Low levels of support from relatives and friends
- Child history of physical, and particularly sexual, abuse
- Child history of prior psychiatric hospitalization
- Children with behavioral problems
- Adoptive placement with "new" adoptive parents rather than foster parents

These research results offer guidelines to social workers in the adoption field regarding "best practices" to enhance the chances of adoption success. Specifically, prior to adoption, social workers should move swiftly to adopt the child at the youngest age possible, fully inform the prospective adoptive parents of all the background information, educate the parents about what expectations are reasonable, help adoptive parents build support systems among relatives and friends, and place children with their foster parents when feasible and appropriate.

Family Preservation and Support Services, Omnibus Budget Reconciliation Act of 1993

One of the more significant pieces of federal legislation in the child welfare arena to be enacted since the Adoption Assistance and Child Welfare Act of 1980 is the Family Preservation and Support Services Program, contained in the Omnibus Reconciliation Act of 1993 (Allen, Kakavas, & Zalenski, 1994). In times of fiscal austerity, the Clinton administration was able to pass new federal legislation that could serve as a catalyst for states to develop innovative programs for the support and preservation of families. Almost $1 billion was made available to states over a five-year period. In the first year, states were required to prepare a comprehensive plan for statewide service delivery in the ensuing 4 years. States were encouraged to involve a wide range of constituent groups in the planning process and to support integration and coordination between systems of care that serve children and families.

The program makes a clear distinction between family preservation services and family support services, requiring that states specify plans for each. Neither program can consume more than 25% of funds unless ample justification is given. The definitions of the two separate programs follow.

Definition of Family Preservation and Family Support Services under Omnibus Reconciliation Act of 1993 (adapted from Allen, et al., 1994)

- Family Preservation Services: *Services for children and families designed to help families (including adoptive and extended families) at risk or in crisis.* Such services can include helping promote planned permanent living arrangements including reunification and adoption, preplacement preventive services such as intensive family preservation services, respite care to provide temporary relief to families, and parenting skills training.

- Family Support Services: *Community-based services to promote the well-being of children and families—designed to increase the strength and stability of families (including adoptive, foster, and extended families), to increase parents' confidence and competence in their parenting abilities, to afford children a stable and supportive family environment, and otherwise enhance child development.* Such services can include in-home visits, parent support groups, programs to improve parenting skills, respite care, structured activities to strengthen parent-child relationships, drop-in centers, information and referral services, and early developmental screenings.

Implementation of this federal legislation is in the early stages, so evaluation of impact is premature. However, indications from the year's planning process point to an emphasis on family support services over family preservation (James Bell Associates, 1996). That is, the trend is for states to target more of their dollars toward programs that are preventive and more universal in nature, rather than at help for families in crisis. A number of factors were influential in this development. First, many states had initiated family preservation programs prior to this federal law, so that the need did not seem to be as great in that area, whereas the needs in prevention were underdeveloped. Second, dollars for prevention are so difficult to access that many states saw this as a rare opportunity to fund prevention efforts. Third, the broad diversity and local nature of the planning process encouraged states to view the needs of children and families broadly in order to reach some consensus among the planning participants (John Zalinsky, personal communication, May 6, 1996).

In 1997, the Family Preservation and Support Services Program was reauthorized, expanded, and renamed the Promoting Safe and Stable Families Program as part of the enactment of the Adoption and Safe Families Act (ASFA), a major change in law that is discussed in greater detail below. The new provisions expand the scope of services to include reunification and adoption services, and they require assurances that the safety of children served will be the paramount concern. Funding was authorized for $305 million for FY 2001 (Pecora, et al., 2000).

Public Law 105-89: The Adoption and Safe Families Act of 1997 (ASFA)

The Adoption and Safe Families Act was passed in 1997 to change and to clarify many of the policies enacted by the Adoption Assistance and Child Welfare Act of 1980. In essence, ASFA builds on the foundation principles established in the 1980 Act, such as permanency planning and reasonable efforts, and provides new definitions, timelines, and incentives to clarify what is expected of states. Overall, the new law places more emphasis on the safety of children and on adoption as a permanency outcome. Discussion of the specific provisions of this law will be organized by the three purposes of child welfare services: protection of children, preservation of families, and permanency planning.

ASFA and the Protection of Children

Because of concerns that the 1980 law was being implemented in a way that emphasized family preservation and reunification at the expense of child safety, ASFA asserts that in providing these services, the health and safety of the child is to be the paramount concern. States are now required to conduct criminal-records checks for all prospective foster and adoptive parents and to deny applications if serious offenses related to children are uncovered. The law also requires the Secretary of the Department of Health and Human Services (HHS) to develop a set of outcome measures to assess state performance with respect to various outcomes, including child safety. Also, ASFA establishes a "fast track" to adoption, in that it stipulates that the reasonable-efforts requirements to preserve and reunify families are not applicable in cases where severe parental misconduct has been found by the court. These circumstances are listed below.

Provisions of ASFA: Circumstances in Which Reasonable Efforts to Preserve and Reunify Families Are Not Required

- The parent has subjected the child to "aggravated circumstances, including but not limited to abandonment, torture, chronic abuse, and sexual abuse."
- The parent has committed murder or voluntary manslaughter of another child of the parent, or aided in such a crime.
- The parent has committed a felony assault that resulted in serious bodily injury to one of his or her children.
- The parental rights of the parent to a sibling have been involuntarily terminated.

ASFA and the Preservation of Families

The ASFA legislation reauthorizes the Family Preservation and Support Services Act, as described above, and it continues to require reasonable efforts to preserve families, within the new parameters and exceptions described above. Thus, the changes now do not require family preservation services in exceptionally egregious circumstances and do require that safety be the paramount concern if family preservation services are initiated. In addition, ASFA establishes clearer and shorter timelines in which reunification services are expected to show results. In other words, re-unification services are expected to succeed within a shorter timeframe, or termination of parental rights is to proceed. These new features may have been motivated by widespread frustration with re-unification outcomes, especially for children who have been in foster care for several months. The specifics of these new ASFA requirements are discussed in the next section.

ASFA and Permanency Planning

ASFA is the first federal law to set out the guide-lines and timelines for the termination of parental rights. Unless certain exceptions apply, the state must file a petition to terminate the parental rights of children who have been in foster care for 15 of the past 22 months (often called the "15 of 22" provision). Exceptions can be made if the child is being cared for by a relative, if the state has not provided the necessary services to return the child to the home, or if the state documents to the court a compelling reason why filing for termi-nation would not be in the child's best interests. For children newly entering the foster care system, ASFA requires a permanency hearing to decide on the permanency plan (return home, adoption and termination of parental rights, legal guardianship, independent living) within 12 months of entering care, reducing the timeline from the 18 months in previous federal legislation.

Although the exceptions for the filing of termi-nation of parental rights are broad, the effect of these changes is to emphasize adoption as a per-manency option. The guidelines reduce the time in which reunification services are expected to pro-duce results, and they set out an expectation that termination will result if efforts to reunify are not successful in that time. Other incentives toward adoption are included in other provisions of the law. ASFA extends the reasonable efforts man-date to include reasonable efforts toward adop-tion, and it allows for these reasonable efforts to occur concurrent with reasonable efforts to re-unify the child with the family. ASFA requires that states do more to provide health care cover-age to adopted children with special needs, autho-rizes new funding for technical assistance to pro-mote adoptions, and addresses cross-state barriers to adoption.

Another, more subtle incentive toward adoption is implicit in one of the exceptions to reasonable efforts to reunify families listed in the box above. Since reunification efforts are not required for par-ents whose rights have been *involuntarily* termi-nated on a child, a parent for whom reunification efforts are failing may be more inclined to *volun-tarily* relinquish rights to one child in order to pre-serve the possibility of reunification services for other children. They might think that they should not fight the termination proceeding on one child, because if they were to lose, then it would be eas-ier for the state to terminate their rights on other children.

In addition to all of these provisions, ASFA au-thorizes adoption incentive payments to the states. That is, states receive a bonus payment for the number of children adopted in 1999–2003 that exceeds the average number adopted in previous baseline years. The amount of payment is $4,000 for a foster child and $6,000 for a special needs fos-ter child. These incentives were intended to help meet a goal, set by President Clinton in 1996, to at least double the number of adoptions by 2002.

Prior to ASFA, states reported outcomes and other data on a strictly voluntary basis, but ASFA now requires all states to report information on the functioning of their child welfare systems to the federal government. The General Accounting Office issued its first report on outcomes under ASFA in 2002, and a summary of its findings is discussed in chapter 11.

CHAPTER 2 SUMMARY

This chapter was organized according to the three principal goals of the child welfare system: protection of children, preservation of families, and permanency planning. Under the topic of protection of children, the areas of physical abuse, sexual abuse, and child neglect were discussed with respect to their definitions, prevalence, causes, effects on children, and treatment. The investigation of abuse and neglect was considered, emphasizing the complex decision making involved and the use of risk assessment matrices.

Regarding the goal of preservation of families, an overview of P.L. 96-272, the Adoption Assistance and Child Welfare Act of 1980 was presented, focusing on the importance of making "reasonable efforts" to prevent unnecessary out-of-home placements of children and to facilitate the reunification of foster children with their families and communities. With regards to prevention of placement, the chapter described the general characteristics and theoretical base of Intensive Family Preservation Services (IFPS), particularly the Homebuilders model of IFPS. Evaluation research on the effectiveness of IFPS was discussed, with consideration of the possible reasons for the mixed results. Alternatives to IFPS were considered, especially for those families requiring either longer-term support or help with substance abuse. Reasonable efforts with respect to reunification were next addressed. The concept of reunification was differentiated from reintegration: the latter refers to the physical reintegration of foster children with their families, while the former encompasses a continuum that includes reintegration plus community reunification and emotional reconnection with families. Five systems barriers to reunification were identified and discussed.

Several important topics were highlighted under the goal of permanency planning. These included the relevant provisions of P.L. 96-272, such as case plans and case reviews, different types of foster care for children, independent living programs for older adolescents, transitioning from foster care to adoption, data and outcomes of adoptions, and special needs adoptions. Finally, the chapter concluded with information about the Family Preservation and Support Services Program established in 1993, which provides ongoing funding to states to enhance their prevention efforts for families.

The chapter concluded with a discussion of important federal legislation passed in 1997: the Adoption and Safe Families Act, commonly referred to as ASFA. The provisions of AFSA have resulted in a greater emphasis on protection of children and on adoption as a preferred permanency option, with a corresponding reduction of emphasis on prevention of placement and reunification as a permanency option.

CHAPTER 3

Social Work with Children and Families in Children's Mental Health Settings

Overview

This chapter, organized into three sections, introduces the reader to the world of social work with children and families in mental health settings. The first section covers the background and context of social work and children's mental health, including the purpose and scope, historical background, and important federal legislation and initiatives. The second section presents an overview of assessment and treatment in children's mental health. This section includes information on common diagnostic categories, psychological testing, common medications, and a survey of a range of interventions, including play therapy, cognitive-behavioral therapy, family therapy, and case management. The third section focuses on special education services for children with emotional and behavioral disorders. Although technically a part of the educational system, not the mental health system, special education plays a vital role in the lives of these children, and there is often a high level of coordination between the education and mental health systems in providing services for these children.

Background and Context of Services

Two recent reports from the Surgeon General of the United States have focused attention on children's mental health. These two reports are *Mental Health: A Report of the Surgeon General*, issued in 1999, which contains a chapter on children's mental health; and *Report of the Surgeon General's Conference on Children's Mental Health: A National Action Agenda*. The latter report expressed a vision of mental health services that reflected a commitment to the following four principles: (1) Promoting recognition of mental health as an essential part of child health; (2) integrating family, child, and youth-centered mental health services into all systems of care that serve children and youth; (3) engaging families and incorporating perspectives of children and youth into the development of all mental healthcare planning; (4) developing and enhancing a public-private health infrastructure to support these efforts.

Just as in child welfare, social workers in mental health settings operate within a context of laws, policies, and practices that influence the nature of their interactions with clients. This section will discuss the purpose and scope of social work in this arena, the historical context, and federal legislation and initiatives that have shaped policy and practice in the field.

Purpose and Scope

The purpose of professional efforts in children's mental health is to improve the emotional and behavioral functioning of children who suffer from emotional and behavioral disorders. There is a wide range of different types of these disorders, which include depression, conduct disorder, and attention-deficit/hyperactivity disorder. The common diagnostic categories will be reviewed in a later section of this chapter. Because these disorders have traditionally been thought of as forms of mental illness, the medical model is dominant in this field, and mental health agencies are often organized and structured in conjunction with the health and medical care system in a community.

Social workers in mental health settings can perform various functions and roles, based on their level of education, specialized training, and the particular type of setting in which they are employed. Social workers with master's degrees (MSWs) and state certification or licensure (if required) can engage in counseling or psychotherapy with children and families (often termed clinical or psychiatric social work) and can perform supervisory and administrative functions. Bachelor's level social workers (BSWs) typically serve as case managers, group leaders, activity therapists, and team coordinators. Specialized training can be obtained in play therapy, family therapy, and any number of specialized theoretical models and/or specific types of behavioral and emotional disorders. Social workers can be employed to work with these children and families in a wide variety of settings: long-term residential treatment facilities, short-term inpatient units of psychiatric or general hospitals, day treatment or partial hospital programs, community mental health centers, independent private practice, and in special education programs in school systems.

Unlike child welfare, in mental health care, social workers are not usually the dominant group of professionals. Often, social workers function in multidisciplinary teams that include psychiatrists, psychologists, psychiatric nurses, special education teachers, and others. Similar to social workers, some of these professionals may also conduct individual, group, or family therapy and perform supervisory or administrative functions. In addition, each has specialized training and expertise. Psychiatrists are medical doctors who have completed basic medical training plus specialized training in general psychiatry or child psychiatry. Psychiatrists are the only members of the team who can legally prescribe medications for children, although psychiatric nurses can also assess and monitor medications under supervision from a psychiatrist. (Psychiatrists are not the only type of doctors who prescribe medication for children with emotional and behavioral disorders—pediatricians and other medical doctors may do so also). Psychologists in mental health settings have a master's degree or doctorate in psychology and are usually licensed or certified in their respective states. Psychologists are trained to administer and interpret various psychological and intelligence tests, as will be described below. Psychiatric nurses are nurses who have received additional training and education in mental disorders and, together with psychiatrists, possess expertise regarding medications. Special education teachers typically have master's degrees in special education with an emphasis in emotional and behavioral disorders. Other specialized professionals include activity therapists, art therapists, and music therapists.

The remainder of this section discusses the history of children's mental health in the United States and presents some of the important federal legislation that has shaped policy and programming for children with emotional and behavioral disorders.

Historical Background

(Material in this section is adapted from Petr and Spano, 1990.)

Before the 1920s, needy children were generally thought of as dependent or delinquent, not as mentally ill or emotionally disordered. This began to change with the establishment of child guidance clinics, an outgrowth of the mental hygiene movement that sought to prevent the development of serious mental illness through early detection and outpatient treatment. By 1931, 232 child guidance clinics had been established, usually in connection with some other community agency such as juvenile courts, hospitals, or schools (Bremner, 1971).

Many of these child guidance clinics developed close working relationships with child-placing agencies and children's residential institutions, because one of their functions was to assess the need for removal from the home and placement in foster care or an institution. As this relationship solidified, and the view of children continued to incorporate a mental health orientation, many children's institutions began to change their focus from custodial care of dependent and neglected children to treatment of children with emotional disorders. In many institutions, this development first took the form of the "study home," in which the institution reserved a certain number of its beds for the short-term observation and assessment of children with personality or behavioral problems. By the late 1930s, this change in focus was being noted and hailed in the literature: "Many old endowed institutions have transformed their work and now render up-to-date service in the analysis and diagnosis of problem children" (Whitman, 1939, p. 1). During the 1930s and 1940s, hospitals joined these children's institutions by establishing short- and long-term treatment units.

One of the results of the increasing role of institutions in the care of children with mental disorders was that the continuum of care came to be dominated by institutional, rather than community-based and outpatient, responses. In addition to the private residential treatment centers described above, state hospitals for the mentally ill typically have units reserved for children and adolescents, and private hospitals admit children for short-term treatment. Between 1950 and 1970, a phenomenon characterized as *transinstitutionalization* occurred for institutionalized children in the United States. Under transinstitutionalization, the total number of institutionalized children remained nearly constant at just over 140,000, but the number of children in mental hospitals and residential treatment centers tripled, and the number of children in homes for the dependent and neglected was reduced by one-half (Petr & Spano, 1990). The tensions between institutional and community-based outpatient care have continued into the 1990s, as will be discussed in more depth in the next chapter under the pragmatic perspective of least restrictive alternative.

The poor state of children's mental health in the 1970s was eloquently documented in an influential study published by the Children's Defense Fund in 1982 (Knitzer, 1982). This oft-cited study asserted that only one-third of the 3 million children with serious emotional disorders were receiving mental health services, many of which were inappropriate. The report targeted the lack of state and federal initiatives as a major cause of the chaotic and ineffective system.

Important Federal Legislation and Initiatives

Community Mental Health Centers. The most significant federal initiative in the mental health arena has been the passage of legislation in 1963 that enabled the development of community mental health centers (CMHCs), which are nonprofit agencies sometimes linked to state or local governments. After years of study, debate, and advocacy by key individuals, Congress passed legislation that was designed to prevent the development of serious mental illness and reverse society's overreliance on state mental hospitals for the care and treatment of mentally ill individuals. This development was spurred by the introduction of psychotropic drugs, patient's rights, and a growing belief in the power of early intervention and prevention. By 1975, 600 CMHCs had been established nationwide (Foley & Sharfstein, 1983).

Despite the professed emphasis on prevention and early intervention, the implementation of CMHCs was characterized by a form of adult-centrism, which relegated services to children to a lower status and priority than services to adults. It was not until 1975 that CMHCs were required to provide specialized children's services (Foley & Sharfstein, 1983), and according to a 1980 study by the National Institute of Mental Health (NIMH), the proportion of CMHC budgets directed at children had decreased over time to 17% (Knitzer, 1982). In 1981, federal funding for CMHCs shifted from direct categorical financing to block grants awarded to the states. Under this legislation, CMHCs no longer were required to provide specialized services for children, so that funding and programming suffered accordingly (Jerrell & Larsen, 1986). In response to this decline, Congress amended the block grant legislation to require that states set aside 10% of their mental health grant funding for children and other underserved populations and areas (Dougherty, 1988). In addition, block grant funding is conditional upon the state submitting a state plan for the development of a system of care for children's mental health (Lourie, Katz-Leavy, DeCarolis, & Quinlan, 1996).

Federal Initiatives in the 1980s and 1990s.
In 1984, in response to concerns about the lack of state programming for community-based children's mental health systems, the National Institute of Mental Health initiated the Child and Adolescent Service System Program (CASSP). Begun in 10 pilot states, CASSP eventually was implemented in all 50 states. The overall purpose of CASSP was to develop a state-level focus and capacity for planning and developing local systems of care for children with serious emotional and behavioral disorders and their families. An evaluation of the initial 10 states concluded that these states had been generally successful in achieving the goals of the program. Specifically, states were judged to have improved their leadership capacities, local coordination of services, family participation, cultural responsiveness, technical assistance, and evaluation capacities (Schlenger, Etheridge, Hansen, Fairbank, & Onken, 1992).

In 1992, Congress increased its support for children's mental health in its Reorganization Act of 1992 (P.L. 102-321) (Staff, 1994). Under this reorganization, a new Substance Abuse and Mental Health Services Administration (SAMHSA) was established within the Department of Health and Human Services. Within SAMHSA, the Center for Mental Health Services (CMHS) assumed responsibility for the CMHC block grants. Ten percent of the CMHC block grants are to be used for supporting an integrated system of community mental health services for children and adolescents. Within CMHS, a new Child, Adolescent, and Family Branch was created, under which CASSP was reorganized into two distinct programs: one to support the continued development of community infrastructures to develop systems of care, and the second to continue to give parent organizations assistance in developing parent support networks. (See figure 3.1.) In addition to this reorganization, Congress funded the Comprehensive Children's Mental Health Services Program. Under this program, 22 grants were awarded to communities to develop local interagency systems of care that provide a comprehensive array of services through collaborative efforts between agencies. The range of services includes day treatment, case management, respite care, home-based child and family services, family-based crisis and

FIGURE 3.1
Organizational Diagram for Federal Children's Mental Health Services

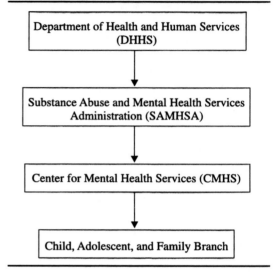

other emergency services, therapeutic foster care and group homes, and transition programs.

There have also been significant federal initiatives regarding children's mental health in the areas of research, training and advocacy. Since 1984, CMHS and the Department of Education's National Institute on Disability and Rehabilitation Research (NIDRR) have jointly funded two national research and training centers focused on children's mental health. One is the Research and Training Center on Family Support and Children's Mental Health based at Portland State University in Portland, Oregon. The focus of this center is on improving services to families of children with emotional and behavioral disorders. Center activities and topics of interest to families and professionals in the mental health field are published in the center's bulletin, *Focal Point.* The second research and training center is the Research and Training Center for Children's Mental Health at the Florida Mental Health Institute, University of South Florida, in Tampa. This center's focus is on improving the systems of care for children with emotional and behavioral disorders and their families. It, too, publishes a bulletin, entitled *Update,* about its activities and issues concerning systems of care. The federal government finances advocacy for children and adults with mental illnesses through the Protection and Advocacy for Mentally

Ill Individuals Act of 1986 (P.L. 99-319). As will be discussed more thoroughly in the next chapter, this law authorizes protection and advocacy agencies in all states and territories to pursue all remedies to assure the rights of mentally ill people who reside in public and private facilities or who have been recently discharged from such facilities.

Assessment and Treatment in Mental Health Settings

Overview

Along with other professionals on the mental health team, social workers are called upon to provide assessments and treatment for children with emotional and behavioral disorders and their families. This section presents basic information about the terms and techniques used in the classification and treatment of these children and their families. While not endorsing the pathological or deviance model, it is important for social workers in mental health settings to understand the language and terminology that are used, to facilitate communication with others on the team. As previously stated, the mental health system is part of the health system, so the medical model of disease, diagnosis, and treatment prevails.

"Theories of mental disorder are essentially theories of dysfunction" (Wakefield, 1992a, p. 385). To avoid a deficit and pathology orientation in assessment, the social worker must identify strengths in the child and frame an understanding of the problem in the most normalized terms possible. A section in chapter 6 on the strengths perspective includes guidelines on how to conduct assessments in a way that honors client strengths and that frames answers to the above question in the least pathological and most normalized terms.

The point of an assessment is *not* to reach a diagnosis. As will be clear in the following summary of diagnostic categories, a diagnosis is only a description and categorization of the symptoms and behaviors. A diagnosis, in itself, does not help anyone understand why the behaviors are occurring nor what to do about them. The point and purpose of an assessment is to both understand the presenting problems and to formulate a plan for improving the situation, based on that understanding. The assessment question is "Why, at this particular time, is this particular child engaging in these particular behaviors?" (Lucco, 1991). In answering this question, the social worker looks at the child in his or her situational context and considers biological, psychosocial, and developmental domains. A diagnosis is a component of an assessment in mental health, and sometimes can facilitate communication and treatment, but formulating a diagnosis is not the same as completing an assessment.

Since social workers must understand the basics of how mental disorders are classified and treated if they are to function effectively in or with the mental health system, this section presents basic information on common diagnostic categories, types of psychological tests and rating scales, major medications prescribed by physicians, and common types of interventions such as play therapy, cognitive-behavioral therapy, family therapy, and case management.

Definition and Prevalence

What is the definition of an emotional and behavioral disorder? Who is the target population for children's mental health services? Currently, there is no universally accepted definition. For federal funding and planning purposes, the Center for Mental Health Services adopted a definition of "children with serious emotional disturbance" in 1993. The major characteristics of this definition are as follows (see box on p. 56).

With respect to prevalence of serious emotional disturbances, a recent review of prevalence research concluded that prevalence rate was between 9% and 19% (Friedman, Kutash, & Duchnowski, 1996). This is the percentage of children with both a diagnosable condition *and* substantial functional impairment. The number of youth with diagnosable mental disorders is far greater than the number with serious emotional disorders.

Common Diagnostic Categories for Children

DSM-IV. The above definition is a broad one that encompasses a number of specific mental disorders. The authoritative source for the classification, or diagnosis, of mental disorders is the fourth

Definition of Children with Serious Emotional Disturbance (Center for Mental Health Services) (Source: Brazelton Center for Mental Health Law as cited in Friedman, Kutash, & Duchnowski, 1996, p. 72)

- *Age:* birth to age 18.
- *Diagnosis:* must have a diagnosable emotional, behavioral, or mental disorder under *DSM-IV* (with the exception of "V" codes, substance abuse, and developmental disorders, unless they co-occur with other diagnoses)
- *Functional impairment:* the disorder must have resulted in functional impairment that substantially interferes with the child's role or functioning in the family, school, or community activities.

edition of the *Diagnostic and Statistical Manual of Mental Disorders,* commonly referred to as the *DSM-IV* (American Psychiatric Association, 1994). Although the *DSM* has been criticized on many fronts, particularly regarding the conceptual validity of the diagnostic categories, each revision of the *DSM* has been generally recognized as an improvement over past efforts (Wakefield, 1992a; Wakefield, 1992b; Vaillant, 1984). Debate is especially strong regarding the construct validity of the disruptive behavior disorders: attention-deficit/hyperactivity disorder, conduct disorder, and oppositional-defiant disorder (H. C. Johnson, 1989; Waldman, Lilienfeld, & Lahey, 1995).

As mentioned above, in using the *DSM-IV,* professionals must keep in mind that the categories of mental disorder are descriptions of behavior that do not usually elucidate the source of the disorder. For example, with respect to conduct disorder, which is perhaps the most commonly diagnosed mental disorder in children, a child must exhibit 3 or more of 15 listed behaviors in the last 12 months. But these criteria do not help the professional to distinguish whether the behavior is the result of poor moral development, biochemical imbalance, impulse control, social pressure, adaptation to environmental conditions, or some other cause: "An adolescent who behaves in such ways may be rebellious, foolish, coerced, or desperate rather than disordered" (Wakefield, 1992b, p. 242).

Attention-Deficit/Hyperactivity Disorder (ADHD). This category of childhood disorder is

diagnosed with increasing frequency. More than 6,000 scientific papers, 50 textbooks, and numerous articles in newspapers and popular journals have increased the public's awareness of this disorder and its treatment (Barkley, 1995). ADHD is estimated to affect 3–5% of school-aged children, with males affected at a rate at least four times that for females. ADHD is characterized by difficulty in sustaining attention, lack of impulse control, and excessive activity (sometimes termed hyperactivity). The inability to sustain attention is evident in such behaviors as failing to listen to others, losing things, making careless mistakes, and being easily distracted from tasks. Impulse control problems include such behaviors as blurting out answers to questions before they have been finished, interrupting others, and poor money management. Hyperactivity includes talking excessively, repeatedly leaving the seat in class, and excessive fidgeting or squirming. To receive an ADHD diagnosis, symptoms must have persisted for at least 6 months to a maladaptive degree, some of the symptoms must have been present before age 7, some impairment must be present in two or more settings, and there must be clear evidence of impairment in social, occupational, or academic functioning. Subtypes of the disorder are predominantly inattentive type and predominantly hyperactive-impulsive type (American Psychiatric Association, 1994).

The characteristics of ADHD may be deficits in some situations and strengths in others (Barkley, 1995). ADHD children do not perform well in structured situations that require one to be cool, calm, objective and rational. But many activities in life call for great personal conviction and emotional expression. People with ADHD may excel in the performing arts, in sales, and in occupations that emphasize socializing over solitary work.

Conduct Disorder. Conduct disorder is one of the most frequently diagnosed conditions, and its prevalence is estimated to be between 6 to 16% of males and 2 to 9% of females. Conduct disorder involves the violation of the basic rights of others or violation of major societal norms and rules. These behaviors are categorized as aggression to people and animals, destruction of property, deceitfulness or theft, and serious violations of rules. To receive the diagnosis of conduct disorder, behaviors in three of these four categories must have been present in the last 12 months, and in at least one of the categories in the last 6 months. The *DSM-IV* cautions that the diagnosis of conduct disorder should be applied "only when the behavior in question is symptomatic of an underlying dysfunction within the individual and not simply a reaction to the immediate social context" (American Psychiatric Association, 1994, p. 88).

Oppositional-Defiant Disorder. This disorder usually becomes evident between age 8 and early adolescence, and affects from 2 to 16% of the population. Oppositional-defiant disorder involves recurrent negative, defiant, and disobedient behavior. Four of the following behaviors must have occurred frequently in the last 6 months: losing temper, arguing with adults, defying or refusing to comply with adult requests, deliberately annoying others, blaming others for mistakes or misbehavior, being touchy or easily annoyed, being angry or resentful, or being spiteful or vindictive. This disorder can co-occur with and be diagnosed along with ADHD, but oppositional-defiant disorder is not diagnosed if the criteria are met for conduct disorder (American Psychiatric Association, 1994).

Generalized Anxiety Disorder. This category includes the formerly separate diagnosis of overanxious disorder of childhood. The prevalence rate for generalized anxiety disorder in the total population is 3 to 5%, and the diagnosis is somewhat more frequent for females. This disorder involves difficulty in controlling anxieties and worries about a number of events or activities. The anxiety is generalized in that it is not focused on a single worry or fear such as speaking in public. In children, these worries may focus on performance in academics or sports, on punctuality, or on apprehensions about catastrophic events such as earthquakes. These children may be perfectionistic and unsure of themselves and may require excessive reassurance about their performance or other worries. In addition, in children, at least one of the following six symptoms must be present: restlessness, fatigue, difficulty concentrating, irritability, muscle tension, or sleep disturbance (American Psychiatric Association, 1994).

Depression. It is important to distinguish between three subtypes of depression, which range from mild to severe. *Adjustment disorder with depressed mood* is the development of depressed mood, tearfulness, or feelings of hopelessness in response to an identifiable psychosocial stressor(s) that has occurred within the last 3 months. The level of distress must be more than what would be expected given the nature of the stressor(s), or result in significant impairment of social or occupational functioning. *Dysthymic disorder* has more severe depressive symptoms that have lasted for 2 years (1 year in children and adolescents). In children, the mood can be irritable rather than depressed. Two of the following six symptoms must accompany the depressed or irritable mood: poor appetite or overeating, sleep difficulties, low energy or fatigue, low self-esteem, poor concentration or difficulty making decisions, and feelings of hopelessness. In *major depressive episode,* the person experiences a depressed mood or the loss of interest in nearly all activities for a period of at least 3 weeks. In addition, four of the following seven symptoms must be present: changes in weight or appetite, sleep disturbance on a daily basis, daily psychomotor agitation or retardation, daily fatigue, feelings of worthlessness or guilt on a daily basis, daily difficulty thinking, concentrating or making decisions, and recurrent thoughts of death or suicide (American Psychiatric Association, 1994).

The recognition of depression as a condition that occurs in childhood is a recent development

(Gustavsson, 1995). Although the *DSM-IV* describes essentially the same features and symptoms for adults and children, many children's mental health professionals believe that other types of symptoms and behaviors may indicate that a child is depressed. Rather than display the classic symptoms, children may defend against their feelings of despair by becoming aggressive or displaying somatic symptoms such as headaches or abdominal pain. Severe depression can lead to suicide, a growing problem discussed more fully below.

Eating Disorders. The two major types of eating disorders are anorexia nervosa and bulimia nervosa. In *anorexia nervosa,* the person refuses to maintain a minimally normal body weight, is intensely afraid of gaining weight or becoming fat, and has distorted perceptions of body size or shape. In *bulimia nervosa,* the person's weight is usually within a normal range, but the person shares the anorexic's fear of gaining weight and poor body image. The distinguishing characteristics of bulimia are binge eating and inappropriate compensatory behavior to prevent weight gain, such as self-induced vomiting, misuse of laxatives, or fasting. These behaviors must occur, on average, at least twice a week for 3 months. If binge eating occurs during anorexia, then the diagnosis is anorexia nervosa, binge-eating/purging type, and a separate diagnosis of bulimia is not made. More than 90% of anorexia nervosa and bulimia nervosa cases occur in females. The onset of both disorders most frequently occurs in late adolescence. Serious medical conditions requiring hospitalization can result from either of these disorders (American Psychiatric Association, 1994).

Post-Traumatic Stress Disorder (PTSD). This condition develops in response to the experience of a traumatic event in which the person responded with fear, helplessness, horror, or in the case of children, disorganized or agitated behavior. Traumatic events that children may experience include war, violent personal assault such as physical or sexual abuse, kidnapping, severe automobile accidents, natural or manmade disasters, and diagnosis of a life-threatening illness. Symptoms of PTSD involve reexperiencing of the traumatic event, persistent avoidance of stimuli associated with the

event and numbing of general responsiveness, and persistent symptoms of increased arousal, such as sleep difficulties, irritability, and hypervigilance. Children may reexperience the traumatic event through repetitive play expressing themes or aspects of the event, frightening dreams, and reenactment of the event. Symptoms usually occur within 3 months of the event, and duration of the symptoms must be for more than 1 month. The disorder is specified as *acute* if the duration of symptoms is less than 3 months, *chronic* if the duration is 3 months or longer, and *with delayed onset* if at least 6 months have passed between the traumatic event and the onset of symptoms (American Psychiatric Association, 1994).

Reactive Attachment Disorder of Infancy or Early Childhood (RAD). Reactive Attachment Disorder describes a condition that is caused by grossly pathological care and results in marked disturbance in the ability to form and maintain social relations that begins before age 5. There are two subtypes of RAD: the inhibited type, in which the child fails to appropriately initiate or respond to social interactions; and the disinhibited type, in which there is a pattern of indiscriminate sociability or a lack of selectivity in social attachments. By definition, either of these subtypes is presumed to be the result of pathological caregiving.

Although this diagnosis is derived from a strong theoretical base about the importance of attachment and bonding in a child's developmental growth, the RAD diagnosis is quite controversial in the mental health field. The controversy is based on issues of both diagnosis and treatment (Hanson & Spratt, 2000). With respect to clarity and accuracy of diagnosis, there are problems with obtaining an accurate and detailed social history, with the level of severity that must be evident, and with the somewhat arbitrary determination of age 5 as the cutoff. Most importantly, there is concern about the presumption that this disorder is caused by pathogenic care. According to Hanson and Spratt (2000), studies have shown that many children who are known to have suffered from extremely poor caretaking do not develop attachment disordered behaviors, while many other children who do have these behaviors did not suffer from pathogenic care. Because of the lack of conceptual clarity, children may be misdiagnosed and over-diagnosed with the RAD label, especially children in foster care who have been known to experience severe abuse and neglect at a young age.

Beyond diagnosis, some of the treatment techniques for RAD are also highly controversial. Chief among these are coercive techniques such as holding, and rage-reduction therapy (James, 1994). These techniques involve prolonged restraint (holding) and aversive stimulation (tickling, poking, yelling). The idea is to provoke the child into an angry rage that is then controlled, accepted, and treated by the adults. Through this process, the child is believed to learn to trust and attach to adults, as the adult provides nurturance and caring as well as confrontation. These techniques are criticized because they have not been empirically validated and because they may traumatize or retraumatize the child.

Adjustment Disorders. Adjustment disorders describe situations in which people develop emotional or behavioral symptoms in response to an identifiable psychosocial stressor(s). Adjustment disorders are classified according to the type of symptom: adjustment disorder with depressed mood, with anxiety, with mixed anxiety and depressed mood, with disturbance of conduct, or with mixed disturbance of emotions and conduct. The symptoms must develop within 3 months after the onset of the stressor(s), and resolve within 6 months of the termination of the stressor or its consequences, unless the symptoms are a response to a chronic stressor or one that has enduring consequences. Stressors may be single or multiple, recurrent or continuous, and associated with developmental events (American Psychiatric Association, 1994).

Divorce is a common stressor for children that often results in a diagnosable adjustment disorder. Research on children's adjustment to divorce has shown that children of divorce, as a whole, use more mental health services, have more conduct problems, succeed less in school, and are more likely to become divorced as adults. Factors associated with the quality of a child's adjustment are the passage of time, the quality of the child's relationship with the residential parents, the custodial parent's own adjustment and

emotional well-being, the economic status of the child's residential family, and the level of conflict between the divorced parents. High-level parental conflict involves ongoing legal disputes, disagreements about parenting practices, hostility, and verbal or physical violence. Studies of divorce indicate that from one-fourth to one-third of divorced parents remain hostile and in conflict 3 to 5 years after their separation. Many communities have initiated court-mandated parent education programs, divorce adjustment workshops, support groups, divorce mediation, and educational/therapeutic groups for children to ameliorate or minimize the negative effects of divorce on children (Emery, 1988; Johnston, 1994).

Common Psychological Tests and Assessment Tools

Although social workers are not usually trained to administer or interpret psychological tests, it is important for them to have a basic understanding of the range and scope of these tests so that they can understand and use the results of the tests in their work with children. This section describes some of the assessment procedures most commonly used by psychologists. These are divided into two types: *projective* and *objective*. Regardless of specific type, no one test alone should ever be used to diagnose or plan treatment. The results of the tests must be considered in relation to other data obtained from the child, parents, teachers, and direct observations.

Projective tests are the more controversial because they rely on the judgment and experience of the tester and rest on an assumption that is not universally endorsed. The assumption is that people will respond to an ambiguous stimulus or situation in a way that reveals important information about their unique needs, attitudes, and ways of perceiving the world. Whether an inkblot, a picture, or an incomplete sentence, the person will "project" their way of viewing the world and their own issues and perspectives into the situation. In contrast, the so-called objective measures of personality attempt to minimize the subjective interpretations of the psychologist by standardizing the administration and interpretation of the data. Objective tests are typically paper-and-pencil questionnaires completed by the child, parents, or teachers. The person completing the questionnaire responds to items by responding "true" or "false" or by indicating some level of agreement with a statement. Responses are then grouped and categorized so that the presence of personality traits or behavioral patterns can be discerned. Although these tests contain a highly subjective element because the responses represent the subjective view of the responder, they are called objective tests because they are quantifiable and produce numerical, norm-referenced scores that are reliable regardless of the individual professional administering the test. Below, three types of projective tests are presented: Rorschach Inkblot Test, Thematic Apperception Test (TAT), and the sentence completion method. This is followed by four common objective measures: the Minnesota Multiphasic Personality Inventory (MMPI), the Wechsler IQ test, the Child Behavior Checklist (CBCL), and the Child and Adolescent Functional Assessment Scale (CAFAS).

Rorschach Inkblot Test. The Rorschach is a projective personality test frequently used with children, particularly adolescents and preadolescents (Wodrich, 1997; Ames, Metraux, & Walker, 1995). The Rorschach, the oldest of the projective techniques, was developed by a Swiss psychiatrist, Hermann Rorschach, beginning in 1911. The Rorschach is administered by presenting 10 standard inkblots to the child, one at a time, and asking the child what the child sees in the inkblot. The child's answers are recorded verbatim in this first phase of the administration. Next, the "inquiry" phase of the administration, the examiner asks the child to identify the aspects of the inkblot that determined the child's response to each card. These aspects include the color, shading, texture, form, and detail of the inkblot. In the final phase of the test, the examiner scores and interprets the responses using one of several scoring systems that have been developed. Criteria used in this scoring include the location of the percept (whether it was the entire blot, a large detail, or a small detail), the primary determinant of the percept (such as color, shading, or form), the content of the percept (such as animal, human, or anatomical), the originality or conventionality of the percept, and the

"form level" of the percept (to what degree the percept makes sense based on what others typically see). Based on the overall responses, interpretations about the child's orientation to the world can be made. For example, if a child consistently sees things in the inkblots that few others see (poor form level), some question about their reality contact might be made. In severe cases, this might indicate a tendency toward psychosis and schizophrenia, while in milder cases it might reflect simply an unconventional and creative way of seeing the world. For another example, a child who responds primarily to small details in the blots, and not to the overall whole, may be the type of person who is so concerned with the small details in life that he or she has difficulty getting the big picture (Wodrich, 1997).

Sound and accurate interpretation of the Rorschach depends on knowing the typical or normal responses for children who are not emotionally or behaviorally disordered. Studies have shown that, in children, responses vary significantly by age and gender (Ames, et al., 1995). Gender differences are not readily apparent in children under 10 years of age, but from 10 to 16, differences are marked and consistent. Boys' responses tend to be more global, fewer in number, and less precise in form, while girls' responses tend to be fuller, more detailed, more reflective of movement, color, shading, and human forms.

Thematic Apperception Test (TAT). A second popular projective test is the TAT, which was developed at Harvard University by Henry Murray and Christina Morgan and introduced in 1935 (Wodrich, 1997). The TAT consists of a number of picture cards, most of which depict scenes of human interaction in vague situations. The examiner shows a card to the child and asks the child to tell a story about the picture on the card. Although there are 30 cards altogether, the examiner selects a subset for each child, and either tape-records or writes the child's responses, including responses to the examiner's queries for clarification or explanation.

The interpretation of the responses is quite impressionistic, as there is no scoring system or research-based normative data, as there is with the Rorschach. Thus, the TAT is most useful not for establishing a clear diagnosis, but for revealing the way that children view their social reality. Psychologists attempt to identify the theme of each story and to look for patterns in the themes across many stories. The central character or "hero" of the story may be representative of the child and his or her experience in some important ways. The hero may have worries, anxieties, or needs that parallel the child's. The stories may reveal attitudes about school, what makes the child feel sad or unhappy, the child's reactions to parental conflict, or parent-child relationships. Interpretations must be made with caution, especially since it is tempting for the psychologist to choose certain cards that can tend to prove a hypothesis. For example, certain cards tend to produce stories with more aggressive themes, and it would be inaccurate to label a child as having aggressive tendencies solely because he or she responded to the cards with stories reflecting aggression. The TAT may be most valuable as a source of new hypotheses about how to understand a child, or to collaborate existing hypotheses (Wodrich, 1997).

Sentence Completion. Sentence completion tests consist of stems, or beginning parts of sentences, that the child simply completes in his or her own words. Older children and teenagers can write their responses, while younger children can respond orally. Sample incomplete sentences include:

> I am ashamed . . .
> In school I . . .
> People think that I need . . .
> Sometimes I think about . . . (Wodrich, 1997)

Like the TAT, the child's unique responses can reveal the child's perceptions, concerns, and needs. The examiner looks for themes and patterns in the responses, rather than focusing on any one single response. Also like the TAT, the interpretation of responses tends to be highly impressionistic, as no universally accepted scoring guidelines have been developed.

Minnesota Multiphasic Personality Inventory (MMPI). The MMPI is an objective personality inventory that was developed at the University of Minnesota beginning in the 1930s (Wodrich, 1997). Although it was developed for use with adults, the MMPI is the most widely used psychological instrument in the field, and it is commonly used with adolescents. The MMPI consists of 556 items to which the respondent answers either "true" or "false." Research with clinical and nonclinical populations has resulted in a scoring system that utilizes several scales, each of which deals with a type of mental disorder or personality type. For example, the items on the 556-item questionnaire that have been empirically shown to distinguish between depressed and nondepressed populations are included in the "depression" scale. The MMPI also has three validity scales that give the examiner a clear indication of whether or not the respondent provided honest and candid answers.

The higher a person scores on a certain scale, the more likely the person is to have that mental disorder or personality type. Because the MMPI has been used so extensively on so many people, personality profiles can be constructed from the combination of the scale scores, and these profiles can be used to predict the person's success rate in psychotherapy or their tendency to abuse alcohol or drugs. The MMPI is popular among psychologists with adolescents because it is time efficient and objective. However, it does require a sixth-grade reading level and it is important that responses be evaluated relative to adolescent, not adult, norms.

Weschler IQ Test. The Weschler IQ test is a measure of the child's essential intellectual functions (Siegel, 1987). Three separate IQ scores are computed: Verbal, Performance, and Full (both Verbal and Performance). Half of the population falls in the average range, between scores of 90 and 109. Most states identify students with IQs above 130 as gifted and those with IQs below 70 as having mental retardation (Turnbull, Turnbull, Shank, & Leal, 1995). Several subtests administered in both the verbal and performance sections of the test allow for the specification of intellectual strengths and weaknesses in several different areas of intellectual functioning.

While the primary purpose of the Weschler is to assess and quantify intellectual functioning, a lesser-known capability is its use in screening for emotional maladjustments. Emotional problems are one possible cause of *scatter* scores, which reflect inconsistencies in the child's test performance. For example, when the Verbal and Performance scores differ by 15 to 20 points, there may be some emotional conflict that is involved. Likewise, scatter scores within a single subtest may reflect a pattern of successes and failures that have been produced by emotional conflict.

In addition to the quantitative dimension represented in scatter scores, valuable insights into the child's psychological make-up can be inferred from the answers given and the approach the child takes to the tasks. The Weschler is not merely a paper-and-pencil test—the examiner asks many open-ended questions that allow for responses with rich intellectual and emotional content. A competent examiner makes note of these emotional dynamics and does not merely report the IQ scores. For example, a child's scores may be negatively influenced by anxiety or an oppositional orientation toward adults. Specific worries and poor self-concept can be projected into the responses as themes and patterns. For example, Siegal (1987) describes how a 12-year-old boy, entering puberty at a much slower rate than his peers and thus worried about his own small size, projected these worries into several responses. In describing how beer and wine were similar, the child commented how both would stop the growth of a little kid who drank them. A yard and a pound were similar in that a small person could measure height and weight by them. The child's obsession with his body image intruded into his thinking and restricted his ability to fully use his intellectual abilities.

Many people believe that the Weschler and other IQ tests (such as the Stanford-Binet and Leiter) are biased against minorities. Objections center on the assertion that IQ tests measure achievement, not innate ability, and that they have been validated on white students. The federal courts, however, have upheld their use in special education classification. In *Pace v. Hannon,* a federal judge ruled that only 9 of 488 questions on three separate IQ tests were racially biased or suspect. In addition, the judge noted that the judgment of the examiner is crucial to interpreting responses. Examiners can, and should, be trained to know the

child's social, cultural, and economic background and to interpret answers in a culturally sensitive way (Turnbull, et al., 1995).

The Child Behavior Checklist (CBCL). The CBCL is a 118-item scale that parents complete for children aged 4–16 years, developed by Thomas Achenbach and colleagues (Wodrich, 1997). The CBCL was developed using both clinical and nonclinical samples, and it has been shown to reliably discriminate between the two. Although its intent is not to yield a diagnosis, the 118 items are clustered into narrow diagnostic groupings such as depression, hyperactivity, and social withdrawal. Two broad groupings are also used: internalizing behaviors and externalizing behaviors. Three additional scales can be administered to assess the child's broader functioning: the Activities Scale, the Social Scale, and the School Scale. By using one or more of the four supplemental forms (Teacher's Report Form, the Youth Self-Report Form for children older than 11, and the Direct Observation Form), the evaluator can get a more complete picture of the child from various perspectives, although these ratings frequently do not correspond to each other. The CBCL is a thoroughly validated instrument that can be useful in assessment and in empirical research.

The Child and Adolescent Functional Assessment Scale (CAFAS). The CAFAS is both a clinical and research tool developed by Kay Hodges and colleagues that has been used as an outcome measure is several large research studies (Hodges, Wong, & Latessa, 1998). Rather than identifying specific problematic behaviors and feelings, the CAFAS asks the clinical staff to assess the level of the child's or adolescent's functioning in several domains: role performance, behavior toward self and others, moods/emotions, thinking, and substance use. Two other domains related to adequacy of caregiver resources are also included. In each domain, the staff person assigns one of four levels of functioning: none or minimal level of dysfunction, mild impairment, moderate impairment, or marked impairment. Several examples for each level and each domain are given to assist the staff person in making this assessment. For example, "expelled or equivalent from school" is an indication of severe impairment in the role performance domain. Each level of functioning has a corresponding score, with higher values assigned to higher levels of impairment, so that by summing the scores in each domain, one can generate a total score. By administering the CAFAS at intake and at 6-month intervals, clinicians and researchers can evaluate the effectiveness of clinical and systemic interventions on the functioning of clients.

Use of Medications to Treat Emotional and Behavioral Disorders

Overview and Cautions. Recently, pediatric psychopharmacology (or the use of psychotropic medications to treat the emotional and behavioral disorders of children and adolescents) has been characterized by both growth and controversy (Jensen, Vitiello, Leonard, & Laughren, 1994). Use of medications to treat children has become increasingly common as more psychiatric disorders have been recognized in younger ages and the biological origins of these disorders have been investigated. Two recent articles in the *Journal of the American Medical Association* discussed the increased use of psychotropic medications in young children under six (Zito, et al., 2000; Coyle, 2000). The former article reported results of a study of two Medicaid programs and a managed-care organization in which prescriptions for methylphenidate (Ritalin) for 2- to 4-year-olds nearly tripled in the early 1990s, to the point that 1–1.5% of all children in this age range were prescribed this medication. These articles also report that prescriptions for young children appear to be increasing in Canada and France. In one city in France, 12% of children beginning school were receiving psychotropic medications.

However, for all diagnostic categories except ADHD, "there is an extremely limited and in some cases non-existent research base" (Jensen, et al., 1994, p. 4) to support the use of psychotropic medications. Even with ADHD, the most commonly prescribed drug, methylphenidate, carries a warning against its use in children under age 6 (Coyle, 2000). Jensen and colleagues (1999) reviewed the empirical research on both the safety and efficacy of various classes of psychotropic medications for children, and concluded that most medications were being prescribed based on clinical opinion, case reports, or uncontrolled studies. Only a few classes of medications, including stimulants for ADHD, were based on at least two randomized controlled trials.

Despite this lack of research and the resulting official recommendation that most of the psychotropic medications are not recommended for children below age 12, physicians often exercise their own clinical judgment and use the results of research on adults to prescribe medications to children for these other diagnostic categories. This, despite the fact that children's responses to medications are not necessarily the same as adults, and there is concern about the effects of medications on the developing brain of young children. Thus, "it appears that behaviorally disturbed children are now increasingly subjected to quick and inexpensive pharmacological fixes as opposed to informed, multimodal therapy associated with optimal outcomes" (Coyle, 2000, p. 1060).

According to the National Institute of Mental Health's Web site (at www.nimh.org), the following medications have been approved by the Food and Drug Administration for use with children, with dosages depending on body weight and age (table 3.1).

The use of medications to treat emotional and behavioral disorders is fraught with ethical and moral considerations (Barkley, et al., 1991). Children do not generally seek psychiatric treatment, so issues of informed consent, coercion, and social control emerge. Long-term effects on brain growth and overall development have not been thoroughly studied. Because of its inexpensiveness and convenience, treatment by medication can be overemphasized, with the result that the importance of the social and ecological context in the etiology and maintenance of behavioral disorders can be minimized and obscured. Reliance on drugs may create a double standard in which the distinction between the prohibition on illicit drug use and the encouragement of prescription drugs may be confusing to children. With these considerations in mind, professionals must pay attention to numerous pragmatic issues inherent in medication trials with children.

Pragmatic Considerations in Use of Psychotropic Medications with Children (adapted from Barkley, et al., 1991)

- Is the medication designed to benefit the child or the child's caregivers?
- Are the behavioral targets of the medication clearly identified and communicated to all concerned?
- How will the effects of the medication be monitored?
- Is the physician prescribing the medication knowledgeable about the medication and its side effects and available to the family and other caregivers?
- Have alternative therapies been offered and attempted?
- Have contraindications and potential interactions with other medications been assessed?
- Have risks and benefits of this and alternative therapies been fully explained to the parents and child, and informed consent of the guardian and assent of the child been obtained?
- Within the family, who will be responsible for compliance with the recommended dose and schedule? Can the family afford the medication?
- When will the medication be discontinued, if it is successful? When will it be discontinued if there is no sign of improvement?

TABLE 3.1
Psychotropic Medications Approved by FDA for Use with Children

Brand Name	Generic Name	Approved Age
Stimulant Medications		
Adderall	amphetamine	3 and older
Concerta	methylphenidate	6 and older
Cylert*	pemoline	6 and older
Dexedrine	dextroamphetamine	3 and older
Dextrostat	dextroamphetamine	3 and older
Ritalin	methylphenidate	6 and older
Antidepressant and Antianxiety Medications		
Anafranil	clomipramine	10 and older (for OCD)
Luvox	fluvoxamine	8 and older (for OCD)
Sinequan	doxepin	12 and older
Tofranil	imipramine	6 and older (for bed-wetting)
Zoloft	sertraline	6 and older (for OCD)
Antipsychotic Medications		
Haldol	haloperidol	3 and older
(generic only)	thioridazine	2 and older
Orap	pimozide	12 and older (for Tourette's syndrome)
Mood Stabilizing Medications		
Cibalith-S	lithium citrate	12 and older
Depakote	divalproex sodium	2 and older (for seizures)
Eskalith	lithium carbonate	12 and older
Lithobid	lithium carbonate	12 and older
Tegretol	carbamazepine	any age (for seizures)

*Due to its potential for serious side effects affecting the liver, Cylert should not ordinarily be considered as first line drug therapy for ADHD.
Source: National Institute of Mental Health Website: www.nimh.nih.gov/publicat/childqa.cfm

ADHD and Medication. Because medication has been so thoroughly researched (for children older than 6) and so widely used in the treatment of ADHD, and yet remains controversial, some detailed discussion of ADHD and medication is warranted here.

According to medical experts, Ritalin and other medications are safe and effective, yet these medications have gained a negative reputation with the general public because of several factors. First, many children are misdiagnosed and perfunctorily placed on Ritalin without a comprehensive evaluation. Second, the medication may not be monitored properly, so that side effects are not recognized. Third, parents are not always informed and empowered as consumers. As a result, either side effects can be missed altogether or parents can be inappropriately alarmed at the appearance of a side effect (Wodrich, 1994).

The most common and most thoroughly researched forms of medication for ADHD are stimulants. The three types of stimulants most commonly prescribed are methylphenidate (Ritalin), *d*-amphetamine (Dexedrine), and pemoline (Cylert). Stimulants work by increasing the action of chemicals in the brain, resulting in increased ability to focus attention. At one time, it was thought that Ritalin had a paradoxical effect on ADHD children, calming them while stimulating other children and adults. This was a myth, because stimulants have been shown to increase alertness and on-task behavior, while decreasing distractibility, in most adults and children (Wodrich, 1994). Ritalin and Dexedrine are quick acting, short lasting, and are eliminated from the body within 24 hours. Some changes in behavior can be noticed within 30–60 minutes of taking the medication, with effects lasting 3 to 6 hours and peaking within 1–3 hours. Sustained-release versions of Ritalin and Dexedrine have been developed, but they may not have as powerful an effect. Cylert has a longer-lasting effect, from 7 to 9 hours, but may take longer to exert a full effect and may build up in the body (Barkley, 1995).

Hundreds of studies have documented that 70–90% of children treated with one of these stimulants will improve. The more severe the symptoms of inattentiveness and impulsivity, the more likely a child is to respond. With Ritalin, children are usually begun on a low dose (5 mg) taken in the morning and at noon. Increases of 5 mg per week are common until a good response is found, to a maximum of about 20 mg per dose, two or three times daily. The dosage for Dexedrine is generally half that for Ritalin, because of its greater potency. Dosages for Cylert, which is longer lasting, are given once a day in the morning, and range from 37.5 to 112.5 mg, depending on the age, weight, and response for each child (Barkley, 1995).

The side effects of stimulants range from mild to severe, and from 1 to 3% of children with ADHD cannot tolerate any level of stimulant medication. Approximately half of children medicated with stimulants will experience decreased appetite, insomnia, anxiousness, irritability, or proneness to crying, usually at a mild level. About a third will report stomachaches and headaches.

Up to 15% of children taking stimulants may develop tics and nervous mannerisms, which usually disappear after withdrawal of the medication, and very rarely develop into full Tourette's syndrome (Barkley, 1995). Overdosage can cause an acute paranoid reaction in children, and about 2% of children treated long-term with therapeutic doses develop paranoid reactions (Wodrich, 1994).

Other types of medications for ADHD children are antidepressants and clonodine. Antidepressants include Norpramin or Pertofrane (desipramine), Tofranil (Imipramine), Elavil (amitriptyline), and Prozac (fluoxetine). These have been shown to be potentially useful in treating ADHD when the child has not responded well to stimulants, experienced strong side effects to stimulants, or has depression or anxiety in addition to ADHD. Effects of these drugs may not be seen for days or weeks, and they do not move out of the body quickly, as do stimulants. Thus, it may take several weeks to withdraw the child gradually from the medication. Side effects include problems with heartbeat and heart rhythm, increased risk of seizures, dry mouth, constipation, blurred vision, near-sightedness, and difficulty urinating. Rare but serious side effects include mental confusion, psychotic reactions, rashes, sensitivity to sunlight, and nervous tics. Prozac is a different type of antidepressant that has slightly different side effects but does not seem to cause the slowing of heart activity characteristic of the other antidepressants (Barkley, 1995).

Clonadine, a drug used to treat high blood pressure in adults, has also been used with ADHD children who have not responded favorably to the stimulants. It may be most useful in the treatment of ADHD children who are oppositional and defiant. Like stimulants, clonadine is quick acting and short lasting, but unlike the stimulants, it builds up in the body and should never be discontinued abruptly. The most common side effect is fatigue or sleepiness, which may persist for 2 to 4 weeks in many children, and longer in as many as 15% of the children experiencing this side effect. Other somewhat common side effects include decrease in heart rate, drop in blood pressure, headaches, dizziness, nausea, constipation, and dryness of mouth. More rarely, children may experience depression, erratic changes in heartbeat, nightmares, increased appetite, weight change, increased anxiety, coldness in the fingers or toes, or water retention (Barkley, 1995). Recently, concern has been heightened about the safety of clonadine for children, especially when it is used in combination with other medications for the treatment of ADHD and its co-occurring disorders (Zito, et al., 2000).

Common Types of Therapy Utilized in Mental Health Settings

The following information is intended to give the reader a broad introduction to the types of therapy commonly employed in mental health settings. Social workers must assess their own level of skill and expertise and receive appropriate training and supervision before practicing these or any other specific therapies with clients.

Play Therapy. Play therapy is a nonadultcentric way of working with young children because it respects the basic medium by which children communicate. Webb (1991) describes it as "a psychotherapeutic method, based on psychodynamic and developmental principles, intended to help relieve the emotional distress of young children through a variety of imaginative and expressive play materials such as puppets, dolls, clay, board games, art materials, and miniature objects" (p. 27). Because of the emphasis on relieving emotional distress, play therapy is most often used with children who have been emotionally damaged by some event or events, such as violence, physical

or sexual abuse, death of a loved one, physical illness, divorce, or natural disaster (Webb, 1991; Gil, 1991). Although play therapy is traditionally viewed as a long-term approach, it can be effective in many short-term situations as well (Kaduson & Schaefer, 2000).

The play therapist attempts to create a warm, accepting climate in which the child can communicate, in their play and actions, their fears, worries, and feelings. To encourage the child to express him/herself, the therapist can use a variety of nondirective and directive techniques, based on the needs of the child and phase of the therapeutic process. Nondirective techniques are especially appropriate in the beginning stages, so that the child does not feel intruded upon and experiences safety in the ability to control the session. Nondirective techniques include being an active observer, following the child's lead, and demonstrating unconditional warmth and acceptance. Directive techniques include structuring the type of play and choosing the play materials, asking the child questions, suggesting motivations and feelings, and directing the play toward certain themes or solutions.

Whether directive or nondirective, the play therapist utilizes a wide range of materials and methods to facilitate maximum expression and communication from the child. Each child may have a preferred medium of expression, so a range of choices helps ensure an appropriate match. Art supplies such as colored markers, watercolors, finger paints, and modeling clay facilitate drawing and other symbolic forms of expression. Dolls and puppets allow children to recreate scenes from home, school, and playground without directly talking about themselves. When children project their own feelings and behaviors onto the puppets or dolls, as well as those of parents and others in their environment, the therapist can gain a keener understanding of how the child experiences a situation. Doll play allows the child and therapist to talk about the actions, feelings, and thoughts that belong to the puppets and dolls, providing emotional distance for the child who then does not have to acknowledge them as his or her own. Board games, although less useful in encouraging expression of emotional content, can be helpful in developing social skills, self discipline, cooperation, frustration tolerance, and a sense of competence and mastery. Play telephones and tape recorders encourage verbal communication in a way that is fun and that affords some emotional distance.

Play therapy is often complicated by complex emotional dynamics that occur between the child and therapist, especially when the child has experienced a trauma involving interactions with an adult, such as abuse and neglect (Gil, 1991). These children have learned that the world is unsafe and that adults are not necessarily to be trusted. Thus, the relationship with the therapist is emotionally charged with the anxiety, uncertainty, and tremendous neediness that the child brings from past relationships. Many children defend against these feelings by being hostile and aggressive, others by being extremely compliant and passive. In many cases, the goal of the therapy is to provide a corrective experience with an adult that can repair much of the emotional damage that has been caused. Through the process, children learn that emotional intimacy with an adult does not necessarily lead to harm. Rather than experience emotional closeness as a threat that leads to anxiety, children can experience it as safe and rewarding. The hope is that the child will learn that adults can be trusted. With this in mind, the therapist needs to move quite slowly and cautiously in building a relationship. Limits must be clearly set and calmly, consistently enforced, so that the child learns the boundaries of the relationship and feels safe within those boundaries. Because play therapy can be emotionally draining, the therapist must guard against burnout through regular supervision and other means of support and renewal.

Cognitive-Behavioral Therapy. Cognitive-behavioral therapy with children and adolescents has become increasingly popular since the 1980s, as evidenced by the publication of well over 500 journal articles in the late 1980s and early 1990s. Cognitive-behavioral therapy is a training, or teaching model, that helps children change their cognitions, behaviors, mood, or motivation through gaining new knowledge and skills. This type of therapy assumes that children's behavior is highly influenced by their thoughts, or cognitions. Problems are clearly defined and specified in terms of behaviors, values or belief systems, personal interactions, or environments (Butterfield & Cobb, 1994).

The problems are then solved through one of two slightly different, yet congruent means: analysis and correction of cognitive errors that underlie the problem, or through remediation of cognitive deficits by teaching children how to cope with the world successfully. The first method emphasizes the role of irrational thoughts in influencing behavior, as in many cases of childhood phobias, depression, and social withdrawal. The second perspective explains problematic behaviors in terms of cognitive deficits. Children lack cognitive knowledge and skill regarding how to solve problems, manage their emotions and behaviors, and get along with others.

Assessment techniques reflect the emphasis on both the cognitive and the behavioral aspects of a problem. A variety of assessment tools are used to establish the level of cognitive functioning. Various checklists, questionnaires, surveys, and scales can be used to specify and measure the problem behaviorally. When the child, parents, and teachers each complete these scales, different results and perspectives are often obtained. Once identified, problems are prioritized and treatment interventions are designed. Although it is tempting for the therapist to be directive and authoritative in prioritizing problems and designing interventions, progressive behavioral therapists recommend that therapists outline options for clients but ensure that the child and family make their own choices (Butterfield & Cobb, 1994).

Cognitive-behavioral methods can take a variety of forms, depending on the nature of the problem and the level of cognitive development in the child. Strictly behavioral methods are employed with most children under age 8, because most that age have not developed the verbal skills and rational thinking necessary for cognitive techniques. For younger children, these methods include modeling and environmental manipulations that emphasize reinforcement, punishment, and alteration of stimulus conditions. For older children, these techniques can be supplemented with self-instructional techniques in which children learn to talk to themselves to gain control of their behavior, or visual imagery in which mental images are used to influence behavior or emotions. For adolescents, who have mastered more complex language and cognitive skills, methods such as compromise, verbal persuasion, reciprocity, and concern for the continuity of relationships can be employed.

Family Therapy. After years of focus on individuals and individual pathology, family therapy burst on the mental health scene in the 1970s and has become perhaps the most widely utilized method of intervention with children. The profession of social work played a major role in the development of this method. Social work has been concerned with families and family functioning since its inception. Many social workers were pioneers in the family therapy field, and social workers continue to be important contributors to the literature. The broad and complex field of family therapy has been thoroughly covered elsewhere, most notably by Nichols and Schwartz (1995). This section presents a brief introduction to the various schools, or theoretical approaches, of family therapy, some of the commonalities and differences that are shared by the various schools, and a brief critique of family therapy.

There are many different schools, or theoretical models, of family therapy. In other words, there is no one right way to conduct family therapy. Families are very complex and intricate entities that cannot really be understood in their entirety. This may be one reason why professionals historically shied away from meeting with families as a whole: individuals are perplexing enough! Therapists need somehow to simplify the knotty and complicated interactions in families so that they can get a firm handle on the issues and see some course of action more clearly. Thus, each school of family therapy is a sort of map of the family territory, a perspective on the family, which leads the therapist and family members toward a focus on certain dynamics and issues, and away from others.

Despite their differences, schools of family therapy share some commonalities. All see the family (albeit an ill-defined family) as the unit of attention, and view problems of individuals within a family context. All schools deal with change in families and individuals, and with resistance to change. This change in some way focuses on how members in the family interact with each other and recognizes the triadic nature of human relationships.

Some of the major theoretical models of family therapy to emerge in the 1960s and 1970s are

psychoanalytic, experiential/humanist, Bowenian, structural, communication/strategic, and *behavioral* (Goldenberg & Goldenberg, 1991). A comparison of these schools relative to the following eight factors is presented in table 3.2 below: the major time frame of interest, the role of unconscious processes, insight versus action orientation, role of the therapist, unit of study, major theoretical underpinnings, goals of treatment, and major theorists.

As Nichols and Schwartz (1995) insightfully point out, each of the numerous schools of family therapy are based on different assumptions about people and families—about the nature of people and the way that change happens. None is more true or right than others—all are *theoretical* models and none has proven more empirically valid than others.

> Those who view people as mechanistic black boxes will try anything to alter the communications among those boxes, and do so from a position of distance, like the expert repairman. Those who understand people from a lens of power and see symptoms as control operations . . . also work from a strategic distance and develop strategies to diffuse the power of the symptom or the power arrangements in the family that made it necessary. Those who see people as chameleon-like in the degree to which they change when family relationships change . . . use their own relationship with the family to change its structure and, consequently, work from a position of proximity. Those who believe people basically want intimacy and love . . . will get close to family members in order to help them feel and share tender feelings. Those who see people as dominated by irrational emotionality will create a reflective atmosphere in which clients learn to stay rational in the face of family upset. (pp. 105–106)

The failure of theorists and adherents of the various schools of family therapy to articulate their basic assumptions is one of the many criticisms that have been laid against family therapy in recent years. One assumption endorsed by many schools was that the family would change in response to the power and expertise of the therapist. Many of these traditional schools viewed the therapist as the distant expert who had the knowledge, power, and responsibility to effect change in families through using powerful interventions and directives. This

TABLE 3.2
A Comparison of Six Theoretical Viewpoints in Family Therapy

Dimension	Psychodynamic	Experiential/ Humanistic	Bowenian	Structural	Communication/ Strategic	Behavioral
1. Major time frame	Past: history of early experiences needs to be uncovered	Present; here-and-now data from immediate experience observed	Primarily the present, although attention also paid to one's family of origin	Present and past; family's current structure carried over from earlier transactional patterns	Present; current problems or symptoms maintained by on-going, repetitive sequences between people	Present; focus on interpersonal environments that maintain and perpetuate current behavior patterns
2. Role of unconscious processes	Unresolved conflicts from the past, largely out of the person's awareness, continue to attach themselves to current objects and situations	Free choice and conscious self-determination more important than unconscious motivation	Earlier concepts suggested unconscious conflicts, although now recast in interactive terms	Unconscious motivation less important than repetition of learned habits and role assignments by which the family carries out its tasks	Family rules, homeostatic balance, and feedback loops determine behavior, not unconscious processes	Problematic behavior is learned and maintained by its consequences; unconscious processes rejected as too inferential and unquantifiable
3. Insight vs. action	Insight leads to understanding, conflict reduction, and ultimately intrapsychic and interpersonal change	Self-awareness of one's immediate existence leads to choice, responsibility, and change	Rational processes used to gain self-awareness into current relationships as well as intergenerational experiences	Action precedes understanding; change in transactional patterns more important than insight in producing new behaviors	Action-oriented; behavior change and symptom reduction brought about through directives rather than interpretations	Actions prescribed to modify specific behavior patterns
4. Role of therapist	Neutral; makes interpretations of individual and family behavior patterns	Active facilitator of potential for growth; provides family with new experiences	Direct but non-confrontational; de-triangulated from family fusion	Stage director: manipulates family structure to change dysfunctional sets	Active; manipulative; problem-focused; prescriptive, paradoxical	Directive: teacher, trainer, or model of desired behavior; contract negotiator
5. Unit of study	Focus on individual: emphasis on how family members feel about one anther and deal with each other	Dyad: problems arise from interaction between two members (for example, husband and wife)	Entire family over several generations; may work with one dyad (or one partner) for a period of time	Triads; coalitions, sub-systems, boundaries, power	Dyads and triads; problems and symptoms viewed as interpersonal communications between two or more family members	Dyads; effect of one person's behavior on another; linear view of causality
6. Major theoretical underpinnings	Psychoanalysis	Existentialism; humanistic psychology; phenomenology	Family systems theory	Structural family theory; systems	Communication theory; systems; behaviorism	Behaviorism; social learning theory
7. Goals of treatment	Insight, psycho-sexual maturity, strengthening of ego functioning; reduction in interlocking pathologies; more satisfying object relations	Growth, more fulfilling interaction patterns; clearer communication; expanded awareness; authenticity	Maximization of self-differentiation for each family member	Change in relationship context in order to restructure family organization and change dysfunctional transactional patterns	Change dysfunctional, redundant behavior sequences ("games") between family members in order to eliminate presenting problem or system	Change in behavioral consequences between people in order to eliminate mal-adaptive or problematic behavior
8. Major theorists and/or practitioners	Ackerman, Framo, Boszormenyi-Nagy, Stierlin, Skynner, Bell	Whitaker, Kempler, Satir	Bowen	Minuchin	Jackson, Erickson, Haley, Madanes, Selvini-Palazzoli, Watzlawick	Patterson, Stuart, Liberman, Jacobson, Margolin

From H. Goldenberg & I. Goldenberg, Family Therapy: An Overview, 3d ed. Copyright © 1991. Reprinted with permission of Wadsworth, a division of Thomson Learning.

orientation obscured the importance of a therapeutic alliance, maintained a deficit and pathology orientation, and led to blaming the "resistance" in a family for their failure to change. In seeking to change the family system from outside of and "above" the family system, these therapists acted contrary to general systems theory notions about the essential and primarily autonomous nature of living systems (Petr, 1988). According to general systems theory, systems change results from the reaction of a system not to external stimuli (in this case, the therapist's interventions and directives), but to a complex set of factors that includes but is not limited to the external stimuli. Thus, family systems retain a great deal of autonomy and may or may not respond to external stimuli presented by the therapist.

Harriet Johnson (1986), in her critique of family therapy, agreed with the above discrepancy between family therapy and systems theory, describing the issue as one in which family therapists tend to view families as closed rather than open systems. Just as importantly, most family systems theories limit the "system" to the interpersonal interactions among a nuclear family. This construction excludes the influence of individual biology on human functioning (as in the established biological basis for schizophrenia) and ignores the influence of the larger human system of extended family, community, and social institutions. She also criticized the "guruism" that had developed in the field, in which charismatic proponents of various schools of thought made extravagant claims about the universal applicability of their theories without any empirical substantiation.

In addition to all of these criticisms, family therapy has been taken to task for its lack of sensitivity to issues of gender, race, culture, and sexual orientation. Case examples in the literature were typically white, middle-class, two-parent families from which the theories were presumed to universally generalize to all populations. At the heart of the matter is what the therapist presumes to be normal and what is considered pathological. Any deviation from the norm can be seen as the cause of any particular problem and the target of change.

The traditional male/female role division has been viewed as the norm in the family therapy literature, and the combination of a dominant, overinvolved mother and distant, ineffectual father has been the most commonly cited example of a "dysfunctional" family system. Not only was family therapy guilty of sex stereotyping, it was also guilty of minimizing the power differentials between men and women in families. Feminists strongly criticized the traditional systemic view that male violence against women was the result of the interacting influence of all members in the family, which implied that blame and responsibility should not be focused on the male (Nichols & Schwartz, 1995). This sex-role stereotyping and ignoring of power differentials with regard to gender are similar to racial and cultural stereotyping that can occur when therapists do not understand a race or culture and project their own ethnocentric views onto the family. Ho (1987), among others, helped practitioners understand that differences in cultures were not necessarily pathological, and that family therapy concepts were not universally applicable to all races and cultures.

In recent years, then, family therapy has been "deconstructed" from a variety of fronts. New perspectives have emerged to address some of the criticisms and concerns. These include feminist approaches, solution-focused therapy, collaborative/conversational approaches, medical and psychoeducational approaches, the work of Michael White, and the internal family systems model. (For a discussion of these new perspectives, see Nichols & Schwartz, 1995, pp. 444–474.)

Group Work. Group work with children and families is somewhat of a neglected topic in the professional literature. Recent books on practice with children and families pay scant attention to group work, focusing instead on individual and family modalities (see, for example, Webb, 1996; Herbert, 1989; Allen-Meares, 1995; Gil, 1991; Wachtel, 1994). In addition, some books devoted to the topic of group work pay scant attention to group work with children, in rather adultcentric fashion (Zastrow, 1993; Stempler & Glass, 1996).

Despite its potential advantages in terms of cost and development of peer social support, group work is thought to be underutilized with many children, including those in foster care who have mental health issues (Mellor & Storer, 1995). This underutilization may be due to concerns about children overidentifying with the victim role in groups or with lack of professional training and experience (Gil, 1991).

Social skills training and divorce adjustment are two problem areas in which research has demonstrated the effectiveness of group work (LeCroy, 1994; Kalter & Schreier, 1994). A brief summary of the recommended guidelines for each of these types of groups will be presented to acquaint the reader with the potential of group work to improve children's functioning.

As outlined by LeCroy (1994), group work is an effective means of teaching social skills to children because of the interactions, feedback, and variety of practice opportunities that are afforded in the group context. Additionally, the group interactions are more motivating for young people than are individual sessions. In LeCroy's model, 11 social skills are taught in 11 separate group sessions. These 11 skills are (1) creating positive interactions; (2) getting to know others: starting conversations; (3) making requests: getting more of what you want; (4) expressing your feelings directly; (5) getting out: how to say "no"; (6) asserting your rights: tell it like it is; (7) identifying how others feel: the art of empathy; (8) dealing with those in authority; (9) responsible decision making; (10) learning to negotiate: conflict resolution; (11) when you're in need: asking for help. Each session follows a similar format and organization. First, the skill for the session is introduced, its importance discussed, and examples are given. Second, the adult leader in a role-play models the skill and the leader reviews how it was used. Next, each group member practices the skill in role-play situations outlined by the leader. Finally, group members are asked to generate more situations in which the skill can be used and may be asked to practice between sessions.

The developmental facilitation model of divorce adjustment (Kalter & Schreier, 1994) has been used in over 35 states in 1,500 sites, and its positive effects have been documented by evaluations that have tracked children up to 4 years postintervention. A group format was chosen because of its efficiency, peer support, and greater comfort level for children. The groups have five major purposes: (1) to normalize the experience of parental divorce; (2) to clarify concerns and questions about divorce; (3) to provide a safe place for children to address emotionally painful aspects of the divorce; (4) to help children develop coping skills relative to their own feelings and family interactions; and (5) to communicate the child's concerns, conflicts, and questions to the parents.

This model was first developed for children in grades 4–6, and then adapted for younger children grades 1–3. The groups are time limited (lasting 8 to 10 sessions) and are organized around key adjustment issues and themes. These themes include (1) predivorce fighting and arguing; (2) learning from parents about the separation and divorce; (3) changes brought on by the transition away from a two-parent family; (4) visitation and custody issues; (5) continuing hostility between parents; (6) parent dating; and (7) remarriage and "blended" family life.

The group structure allows for and encourages indirect expression of thoughts and feelings. Dolls, puppets, and talking about imaginary children and families allow children to safely express their own fears and worries, one step removed from their own painful reality. For example, in the first session, the group constructs an imaginary story about a family that is headed for divorce. Each participant in turn contributes something to the story line, and later, the leaders pick out themes and employ universalizing statements that normalize children's concerns. In later sessions, children role play "Divorce Court," complete with legal pads and cross examination of parents; create a skit involving children waiting for the noncustodial parent to pick them up for a visit; and develop a Divorce Newspaper that includes interviews with group members and reports on results of a group poll on the "five worst (best) things about divorce" or "what parents need to know about how kids feel about divorce."

Case Management. With the onset of CASSP and the ensuing focus on systems of care and their coordination, case management for children and adolescents with emotional and behavioral disorders and their families has developed rapidly. Like case management with other populations, several common concerns drive the development of case management with this population. These include concerns about service fragmentation, a focus on the needs of the whole person and family, the desire for continuity of care, and the need for individualized treatment (Early & Poertner, 1993).

General case management purposes and functions are described more fully in the next chapter. In children's mental health, several approaches to case management have been employed (Early & Poertner, 1993). The outpatient therapy approach views case management as an adjunct to the outpatient therapy process, which is itself driven by the medical model's orientation toward diagnosis and treatment of mental illness. The brokerage approach places the case manager in the role of making arrangements for clients to receive services. The case manager is the expert on resources in the community: what services exist, how to access them, and how to advocate for and with families to get them. The interagency team approach brings the major service providers together to assess the need for services and coordinate their delivery. Finally, the strengths approach focuses less on problems and more on goals. The case plan is built on what the child and family do well, and the child and family direct the case planning process, not the professionals. The "wraparound" approach to service delivery combines elements of all of these approaches and will be discussed more thoroughly in the next chapter on the ecological perspective.

Unlike family preservation, multisystemic therapy, and other short-term models, case management services can be provided for months or even years, and thus case management is employed as a long-term support to children and families. Although case management is widely employed by mental health agencies nationwide, there is no clear consensus about its components, so that model specification and fidelity are problematic. Also, case management has a very limited empirical base of support.

Although case management is discussed in this text under the heading of "common types of therapy," it is usually referred to as an intervention or service rather than as a therapy, because the intent is not to change the individual or family directly, but to indirectly help them obtain the needed resources and supports. Because of this distinction, some tension can arise in mental health agencies between therapists and case managers over the relative value and effectiveness of the respective services. Case management is not only the new kid on the block with a different focus, but case managers are often professionals with BSWs or other bachelor's degrees, while therapists typically have master's degrees or PhDs. If the effects of these competitive tensions are not minimized, client outcomes can be adversely affected.

Adolescent Suicide

The topic of adolescent suicide warrants special attention because of its serious nature and its increasing incidence in the population. When depression or other mental disorder results in self-inflicted death of a young person, the importance of effective mental health prevention and treatment programs becomes dramatically obvious to all concerned.

Between 1967 and 1987, the suicide rate among 15- to 19-year-olds almost tripled, from 3.6 to 10.3 per 100,000 (Berman and Jobes, 1991, as cited in Kirk, 1993, p. 8). This count is probably conservative because many youth suicides may not be officially labeled as such because of ambiguity about the cause of death and the stigma for the family. Legally, suicide must be proven (Hicks, 1990). Clearly, there are many more suicide attempts than suicide completions, with conservative estimates targeting 50–100 attempts for every completed suicide (Kirk, 1993).

Identifying the causes of youth suicide is extremely complicated because of the myriad number of individual and contextual factors. Despite this complexity, Kirk (1993) has identified three sets of interrelated factors that appear to apply generally to a large group of potentially suicidal teenagers: adolescent stress, family issues, and clinical depression. According to Kirk, teenagers at high risk for suicide are those with a history of previous attempts, who have thoughts about killing themselves and have a specific plan and means for completing the act, and have symptoms of agitation or depression. While these factors can serve as broad guidelines for assessment of risk, readers are cautioned that many individuals do not fit group profiles: talk of suicide should always be taken seriously and an experienced professional should always evaluate the individual's situation for risk.

The following guidelines are practical techniques to guide suicide intervention.

Pragmatic Guidelines for Suicide Intervention (adapted from Kirk, 1993)

- Be available and accessible.
- Make therapeutic contact and establish rapport, communicating the three *C*s of caring, confidence, and competence.
- Assess for imminence—evaluate for suicide intent, plan, and method.
- Interrupt the suicide process by using empathy to defuse negative emotions, opposing suicide intent, and offering a plan for professional help and social support that includes some choice for the adolescent.
- Obtain a commitment to the plan of help, including an antisuicide agreement, if necessary.
- Make referrals
- Follow up with adolescent and referral sources
- Document the intervention and report the problem to relevant adults

---

Mental Health Needs and Services in the Juvenile Justice System

The mental health needs of children in the juvenile justice system have long been ignored. Unlike the child welfare system, in which abused and neglected children are often viewed as having been victimized and traumatized, and thus deserving of mental health treatment, children who commit crimes are seen as needing supervision and punishment for their crimes. Just like children in the child welfare system, children in the juvenile justice system can be placed into state custody—into foster homes, group homes, detention centers, youth correctional facilities, and even residential treatment facilities. Most commonly, however, juvenile offenders are assigned to probation within the community.

A recent study documented the level of severity of mental health needs in the juvenile justice population, even among those on probation (Lyons, Baerger, Quigley, Erlich, & Griffin, 2001). Using stratified, random sampling techniques, the authors used the Children's Severity of Psychiatric Illness (CSPI) scale to evaluate the mental health needs of 473 youth on probation in the community, 120 youth incarcerated in correctional facilities, and 50 youth offenders adjudicated to residential treatment in a mental health facility. The CSPI revealed SED diagnosis for 45.9% of the community probation subsample, 67.5% of the correctional facility sample, and 88% of the residential treatment sample. Analysis of the two institutional subsamples revealed significant differences, including findings that those in the correctional sample had a higher suicidal risk, were a greater danger to others, were more sexually aggressive, and had greater substance abuse problems. The residential treatment group had greater emotional disturbance, more impulsivity, and more severe past abuse. The authors emphasized that this level of need justified increased mental health assessment and intervention in all aspects of the juvenile justice system.

Multisystemic Therapy (MST) is a home- and community-based intervention developed by Scott Henggeler and colleagues to respond to the mental health needs of the juvenile offender population (Henggeler, et al., 1998). The research base for MST is much better than for most new therapeutic interventions: at least eight randomized trials of MST have been conducted with demonstrated effectiveness. Studies have shown that MST has reduced the long-term rates of re-arrest among violent and chronic juvenile offenders by 25% to 70% over control groups. Out-of-home placements were reduced 47% to 64% compared to comparison groups. MST has also demonstrated effectiveness in preventing hospitalizations for children with serious emotional problems, as discussed further in chapter 8.

MST shares many of the characteristics of family preservation programs discussed in the previous chapter, but it is also unique in at least three aspects: (1) MST has a solid research base and commitment to ongoing research; (2) MST has a specific training manual and training program that, together with close supervision and monitoring of what clinicians actually do, ensures higher levels of fidelity to the model; and (3) MST actively targets peer interventions to facilitate development of friendships with prosocial peers. Multisystemic therapy has nine core principles that guide interventions:

Nine Core Principles of Multisystemic Therapy

1. The therapy works on finding the fit between the identified problems and their broader systemic context.

2. The therapy is positive and strengths-focused.

3. The therapy works on increasing responsible behavior among family members.

4. Interventions are present focused and action-oriented, targeting specific and well-defined problems.

5. Interventions target sequences of behaviors within or between multiple systems that maintain the identified problems.

6. Interventions are developmentally appropriate.

7. Interventions require continuous effort by family members.

8. Interventions are evaluated continuously from multiple perspectives, with providers assuming accountability for overcoming barriers.

9. Interventions empower caregivers to maintain their ability to address family members' needs across multiple systemic contexts.

Special Education for Children with Emotional and Behavioral Disorders

History of Social Work in Schools

The first school system to establish social work in schools was Rochester, New York, in 1913, through the employment of visiting teachers (Radin, 1989). The major function of these visiting teachers was to help the school and parents better understand each other by serving as a school-home liaison. The need for such a liaison was stimulated by compulsory school attendance laws passed in all states in 1918. The visiting teacher's job involved educating and supporting parents to ensure that their children attended school every day. In a complimentary fashion, the visiting teachers also worked to sensitize the school to the realities of children's lives away from school, and to advocate on behalf of children to help the school meet the children's needs.

During the 1930s, school social workers shifted their approach to coincide with the burgeoning mental hygiene movement that began in the 1920s (Freeman, 1995). The role of the social worker began to change from home-school liaison to clinical caseworker who sought to understand and treat children with behavioral problems. The role also involved general casework regarding the physical and social needs of children adversely affected by the Depression.

By the 1960s, many school social workers began to focus on changing the school as a social system (Radin, 1989; Freeman, 1995). In the social action and social change climate of the times, schools came to be targeted as one of the social institutions that perpetuated poverty, racism, and other social ills. Many school social workers began to target school policies and procedures that contributed to these social ills, rather than just doing casework with individual children. For the most part, however, practitioners failed to attain the leadership positions needed to reform the system, and casework for family and parents remained the primary approach.

The passage of the Education for All Handicapped Children Act of 1975 (P.L. 94-142) had a dramatic and profound impact on social work (Allen-Meares, Washington, & Welsh, 1996). This Act mandated that states must provide a free and appropriate education to all children, regardless of ability or disability. With the implementation of this law, special education became an integral program in all school districts nationwide. The impact on social work stemmed from the law's specific naming of social work as one of the required "related services" that must be provided to help children benefit from special education. As specified in the law, social workers are to provide the following services:

Social Work Services in Special Education Mandated by P.L. 94-142
(adapted from Meares, et al., 1996, p. 154)

- Preparing the social or developmental history for children with handicaps
- Providing group and individual counseling services to the child and family
- Attempting to solve those problems in a child's living situation (home, school, community) that affect the child's adjustment in school
- Mobilizing school and community resources to enable the child to receive maximum benefits from his or her educational program

---

Although the school-home liaison role and systems change role could be a part of the above services, the law clearly views the social worker role as primarily caseworker for the child and family. The inclusion of social work as a required related service solidified social work's role in the interdisciplinary school team. Although social work as profession is not the dominant profession in school systems, and probably never should be, neither can it any longer be viewed as unimportant or marginal to the school's principal functions. The law enabled the employment of many more social workers in school districts and enhanced their image and role.

Federal Legislation: Individuals with Disabilities Education Act (IDEA)

Children with serious emotional and behavioral disorders in schools were targeted for special education services, along with other children with other types of disabilities, in the Education for All Handicapped Children Act of 1975 (P.L. 94-142). In 1990, this Act was amended and replaced by the Individuals with Disabilities Education Act (P.L. 101-476), commonly referred to as IDEA, which

was reaffirmed and amended in 1997 (P.L. 105-17). Prior to this federal legislation, many children with disabilities were excluded from local schools altogether. Now, all students are guaranteed a free and appropriate public education through federal law.

IDEA provides state and local school districts with federal money to help provide special education services to children with disabilities. Special education is specially designed instruction to meet the unique needs of a student with a disability. IDEA defines the types of disabilities that are eligible for special education, lists specific "related services" (including social work services in schools) that must be available, and establishes six principles to govern the provision of special education. These six principles are zero reject, nondiscriminatory evaluation, appropriate education, least restrictive environment, procedural due process, and parent participation (Turnbull & Turnbull, 2000). In the following paragraphs, these six principles will be discussed as they apply to students with emotional and behavioral disorders between the ages of 3 and 21.

Zero Reject. This principle asserts that every child, regardless of disability, is entitled to a free and appropriate public education. Thus, children with emotional and behavioral problems cannot be denied access to public education, regardless of their behavior. Since the behaviors of some of these children can be quite disruptive, suspension and expulsion from school are frequently considered options. But whereas "troublemakers" who are not identified as special education students can be expelled, recent court rulings have established guidelines and limits for the long-term suspension and expulsion of special education students. Short term suspensions, for up to 10 days, can be imposed on all students, whether disabled or not. Exclusion for more than 10 days, however, constitutes a change in the placement of the special education student and can be accomplished only through proscribed due process procedures. These procedures must include an evaluation of the relationship of the misbehavior to the disability, because special education students cannot be expelled for behaviors that are a result of their disability (Sorensen, 1995). Rather than expulsion, educators may change the placement of the child to homebound, special school, or residential placement, so that appropriate educational services are continued.

Nondiscriminatory Evaluation. Schools must screen and evaluate students to determine if they have a disability as defined by federal and state law, and if they need special education services. IDEA refers to children with emotional and behavioral disorders as "seriously emotionally disturbed" and defines them as follows:

Definition of "Seriously Emotionally Disturbed" under IDEA (Turnbull, et al., 1995, p. 190)

The term means a condition exhibiting one or more of the following characteristics, displayed over a long time and to a marked degree that adversely affects a student's educational performance:

A. An inability to learn that cannot be explained by intellectual, sensory, or other health factors

B. An inability to build or maintain satisfactory interpersonal relationships with peers and teachers

C. Inappropriate types of behavior and feelings under normal circumstances

D. A general pervasive mood of unhappiness or depression

E. A tendency to develop physical symptoms or fears associated with personal or school problems

The term includes children who are schizophrenic but not children who are socially maladjusted, unless they are seriously emotionally disturbed.

States and local school districts do not have to use this exact language in their own definitions, so that some variation in definition exists from one state and locality to another. Also, ambiguous terms in the above definition are subject to interpretation and make identification complicated and imprecise. How long is "over a long time"? What exactly is a "marked degree"? How does one distinguish between social maladjustment and serious emotional disturbance, especially when social maladjustment is a characteristic of the definition (part B)?

Despite the vagaries in the definition, the job of the special education evaluation team is to determine whether children referred by teachers meet the above definition. This evaluation team typically consists of special education teachers, counselors, school psychologists, and school social workers. Team members can use behavioral rating scales, behavior checklists, interviews, ecological and family assessments, self-concept measures, and direct observations to complete the evaluation. Direct observations typically make use of structured recording sheets to collect data about the frequency, duration, and intensity of target behaviors (Turnbull, et al., 1995).

In 1990–1991, according to the U.S. Department of Education, the number of students between the ages of 6 and 21 being served under this disability category was 356,050, or 8.5% of the special education population (Turnbull, et al., 1995). However, while major studies indicate that at least 3–5% of all children have serious emotional and behavioral disorders, only about 1% of all school-aged children is receiving special education services for this disability. Possible reasons for this underidentification include reluctance to identify children with conduct disorders who are seen as willful troublemakers rather than as children with disabilities, the costs associated with education and treatment, the stigma associated with the label, the ambiguousness and subjectivity involved in identification, and insensitivity to the "internalizing" type of disorders such as depression, anxiety, and social withdrawal (Turnbull, et al., 1995).

For all types of disability categories, racial minorities have historically been overrepresented in special education compared to their proportion of the general school population. This has been especially true for African American children, who are overrepresented in all disability categories, including emotional and behavioral disorders. In this context, the importance and necessity of a "nondiscriminatory" evaluation becomes clear. Although the overrepresentation could be due to low socioeconomic status that correlates with disability because of the poorer health care and nutrition that poor children receive, the overrepresentation could also be due to biased referral and assessment procedures (Artiles & Trent, 1994). With the end of widespread school segregation based on race, it is possible that special education has unwittingly become the vehicle for continued racial segregation: instead of being excluded altogether, minorities can be segregated to special education programs.

Appropriate Education. Once a child is identified as having a disability, the child is then entitled to special education services that provide the child with an appropriate education, based on the child's strengths and needs. The special education program is individualized by mandate, and the vehicle for that individualization is the Individual Education Plan (IEP). The IEP is a document that describes the plan to meet the child's educational needs. It includes evaluation information, annual goals, short-term objectives to meet the annual goals, procedures for determining attainment of the objectives and goals, the listing of all related services that will be provided, and the type of placement that will be provided, including specification of the amount of time the student will participate in the general education program.

After the evaluation is complete and the disability is established, school personnel must conduct an IEP conference that includes the child's teacher; a school professional, other than the child's teacher, who is responsible for providing or supervising the special education program; the person conducting the evaluation; the parent or parents, if they desire to attend; and the child, if appropriate. Other people, such as friends, advocates, or community professionals may attend at the discretion of the parent or school. For adolescents who are 16, the IEP must include an Individual Transition Plan (ITP), which describes the services the student needs for transition from school to adulthood. The purpose of the ITP is to promote and secure successful outcomes for special education students, such as

postsecondary education, vocational training, employment, or independent living (Turnbull, et al., 1995).

Special education programming for children with emotional and behavioral disorders varies widely by individual, school, and state. The authors of a national study of exemplary programs and practices concluded that there was overemphasis on behavior management to the detriment of learning (Knitzer, Steinberg, & Fleisch, 1990). It appears that it is easy for programs to lose sight of the primary educational purpose in the attempt to control and manage children's behavior. Also, the study found that children lacked access to mental health services and that parent involvement tended to be superficial and perfunctory.

Least Restrictive Environment. In school systems, the least restrictive environment calls for children with disabilities to be educated, to the maximum extent appropriate, with students who do not have disabilities. Statistically speaking, this principle has been the most difficult to implement for children with emotional and behavioral disorders. According to a 1993 U.S. Department of Education report, children with emotional and behavioral disorders are being educated in highly segregated environments (cited in Turnbull, et al., 1995, p. 215). More than 50% of those identified are educated in either separate schools (13.9%) or separate, self-contained classrooms (37.1%). By comparison, for all students in special education, only about 30% are educated in either a separate school (4.6%) or separate, self-contained classrooms (24.9%).

Several different terms have been associated with the least restrictive environment as it applies in special education. Sometimes these terms are used interchangeably, but there are subtle differences in the precise meaning of each term that are important to differentiate. These terms are *mainstreaming, inclusion,* and *regular education initiative* (REI). In the early years of special education, professionals used the term *mainstreaming* in association with least restrictive environment. Usually, mainstreaming presumed that special education students would be based in a separate school or classroom, as the responsibility of special education teachers, and would be mainstreamed in regular schools or classes for part of the day. Inclusion, on the other hand, asserts that all students belong in regular classrooms and that responsibility for the child's education rests with the regular education teacher. In collaborative inclusion models, the special education and regular teacher collaborate on the educational plan, but the instruction and support are delivered in the regular classroom, not in resource rooms of separate self-contained classrooms. The REI was a precursor to the inclusion movement. Initiated in the mid-1980s by Madeline Will, then assistant secretary of the Office of Special Education and Rehabilitative Services of the U.S. Department of Education, the REI position criticized the separation of general and special education and sought to make general education more accommodating and accepting of students with disabilities (Turnbull, et al., 1995).

Thus, *inclusion* is the current term most often used to refer to the way in which educators and advocates are implementing the least restrictive alternative principle. Inclusion remains a controversial topic because it eliminates the choices on the continuum of care that are most restrictive and segregated. These options are also the most individualized, according to some opponents of inclusion, and best meet the needs of some children with disabilities, particularly those with learning disabilities who need a less distracting environment than is offered in regular classrooms (Vaughn & Schumm, 1995). Also, some children with disabilities, particularly those with serious behavioral problems, may be too disruptive to other students in general classrooms.

Inclusion requires close cooperation and team teaching between special education and general education teachers, so that the special education teachers, as well as the students, are integrated into regular classrooms. Ideally, inclusion results in positive effects for both the disabled and nondisabled students. Students with disabilities gain in the areas of social interaction, language development, appropriate behavior, and self-esteem. Students without disabilities learn to accept their classmates and become more compassionate, helpful, and friendly to them. Teachers involved in collaborative inclusion listed the following advantages and disadvantages:

Teacher Views of Collaborative Inclusion (adapted from Marston & Heistad, 1994)

Advantages:
- meets the needs of more students who are *not* identified as special education
- students are exposed to more than one teaching style
- decrease in behavior-related problems
- better able to serve at risk students

Challenges:
- inadequate space—classrooms too small
- lack of time for cooperative planning
- less time devoted to the needs of special education students
- scheduling conflicts
- different teaching philosophies

Procedural Due Process. IDEA includes due process procedures to ensure accountability in the special education process. If a parent and the educational agency disagree about the type of placement, the goals and strategies of the IEP, or anything else concerning the child's education, then IDEA affords either party the opportunity to have a hearing before a neutral party, called a due process hearing officer. In a due process hearing, the parents and schools may have lawyers and present evidence. Appeals of the due process hearing officer's decision can be made to the state education agency, and the loser in that decision can sue in court. In addition to this procedural safeguard, parents are entitled to access to the student's records; to a free nondiscriminatory independent evaluation, paid for by the education agency, if a court determines that the agency's evaluation was not appropriate; and to written notice in their native language of any plans to change the child's classification, IEP, or placement (Turnbull, et al., 1995).

For children with emotional and behavioral problems, procedural due process is especially relevant with respect to the issue of suspension and expulsion from school. As discussed above, children with disabilities cannot be excluded from school for more than 10 days without an official change in placement as reflected in a new IEP. Long-term suspension and expulsion can occur only when an evaluation team has determined that the misbehavior was not related to or caused by the child's disability (Sorenson, 1995).

Parent-Student Participation. IDEA encourages parent and student participation in the evaluation process, in the development of the IEP, and in procedural due process. Although the intent is to develop a climate of collaboration, parents and children are often passive participants, at best. Even in regular education, schools have traditionally been child and professional centered, not family centered. The parent involvement provisions of special education legislation have not resulted in increased involvement of parents in their child's education (Yanok & Derubertis, 1989).

Most school-based efforts to involve families have focused on family therapy or wraparound approaches which attempt to change or support the family in dealing with the child with emotional or behavioral problems at home (Knitzer, et al., 1990). Few have focused on increasing the parents' involvement in the special education process itself. A notable exception is the Parents Involved Network (PIN program) in Pennsylvania (Fine & Bordon, 1989). PIN is a parent-run, self-help organization begun in 1984 to support and advocate for parents of children with serious emotional disorders. All staff members are themselves parents, and the focus of the organization is on parent involvement in the educational process of their children. Staff members accompany other parents to IEP meetings, provide information, run parent support groups, and teach parents advocacy skills to use in schools and legislatures.

Birth to Age 3. The above discussion of special education applies to children aged 3 to 21. IDEA also proscribed special education provisions for children from birth to 3, under part H of the legislation. Provisions for this age group differ somewhat from those for older children. For infants and toddlers, the state may assign responsibility to an agency other than education, such as maternal and child health. States do not have to serve all children of this age with disabilities, but may target and focus their efforts. Instead of an IEP, professionals develop an Individualized Family Service Plan (IFSP). As reflected in its title, the IFSP is more focused on the family than is the IEP. It is designed to enhance the family's capacities to meet the child's special needs, thus ensuring the child's optimal development and perhaps minimizing the need for special education services when the child reaches school age (Turnbull, et al., 1995).

1997 Amendments to IDEA

In 1997, Congress reauthorized and amended IDEA. Two new provisions that have particular relevance to children with emotional disorders and their families will be highlighted in this section: positive behavioral interventions and supports; and transition to adulthood.

Positive Behavioral Interventions and Supports (PBIS). The 1997 amendments to IDEA included language that specifically addressed concerns that local schools were using negative and aversive techniques to attempt to control he behavior of students with disabilities. Although the amendments do not prohibit such practices, they do require that IEP teams consider appropriate strategies, including positive behavioral interventions and supports (PBIS) to address behavior that impedes a student's own, or others, learning (Turnbull & Turnbull, 2000). This language is particularly pertinent to children with emotional and behavioral disabilities, because it requires that schools at least think about, and seriously consider, whether positive interventions and supports could be helpful.

According to Turnbull and Turnbull (2000), PBIS is an approach that broadens the range of potential interventions to include four interrelated components. Of particular note is a social work philosophy that emphasizes the role that the larger system plays in influencing children's behavior. Rather than simply adopting a traditional behavioral management approach that targets the individual student and his or her behavior, PBIS looks also to the systems and environments surrounding the child. First is the level of systems change.

Here, the school looks at the philosophies, practices, personnel, and organization of the school for needed changes and supports. For example, the system level may not fully support the philosophy of inclusion, or teachers may need more training and support in a specific area. Second is the area of environmental alterations, in which physical or instructional accommodations may need to be made to address environmental factors that negatively influence student behavior. Third is recognition that a student's behaviors can become more appropriate if the student receives proper instruction on how to build the behavioral skills, and if parents, teachers, and others also receive guidance on how to interact with the student. Finally, the fourth component of PBIS focuses on behavioral consequences for the student that are based on a functional behavioral assessment that seeks to understand the factors that contribute to the occurrence, maintenance, and resolution of the problem behaviors.

Transition to Adulthood. Amendments in 1997 lowered the age at which transition services for children with disabilities must be provided from age 16 to 14. Much attention has been focused recently on the transition needs for children with serious emotional disorders. According to studies cited by Deschenes and Clark (2001), these youth have poor transition outcomes: they have the highest dropout rate among all special education students; only 7–26% of those who do graduate go on to enter postsecondary education; they are more likely than any other group their age to have employment problems; and they are more likely to demonstrate substance abuse, unplanned teenage pregnancies, involvement with the criminal justice system, and poor work, marital, and occupational adjustment.

Synthesizing the results of studies of best practices for these children in their struggles to successfully transition to adulthood, Clark, Deschenes, and Jones (2000) have established six guidelines for best practices in this area. These six guidelines are quite consistent with the eight pragmatic perspectives presented in this text.

First, the transition process must be characterized by person-centered planning based on the young person's interests, strengths, and cultural and familial values. The emphasis on self-determination and social supports results in more interest and involvement from the young person. The second guideline emphasizes individual services and supports that encompass all of the four transition domains. These four domains are employment, educational opportunities, living situation, and community-life adjustment with natural supports. Third, exemplary transition services are characterized by extensive coordination of services and supports to provide continuity. Fourth, the transition team provides a safety net of support, demonstrating unconditional commitment and sense of hope and affirmation for the youth's inherent dignity and worth as a human being. The team realizes that progress can proceed in fits and starts, and they stick with the young person during the tough times as well as the successful times. Fifth, the team focuses on enhancement of the young person's competencies in skills related to work, independent living, and self-advocacy. Finally, transition programs must be driven by outcomes at the individual and system levels, including process measures for assessing system improvement.

Transition to Adulthood: Four Domains
(Clark, Deschenes, & Jones, 2000)

1. Employment
2. Educational opportunities
3. Living situation
4. Community-life adjustment (skills and activities related to functioning across all of the domains)

CHAPTER 3 SUMMARY

Social work in mental health settings requires knowledge and understanding of the policy context stemming from federal and state initiatives, and of practice-level assessment and intervention strategies. This chapter began with an overview of the purpose and scope of social work in mental health settings, and it traced historical developments in children's mental health that highlighted the tension between institutional and community-based approaches to service delivery. Recent federal initiatives that have attempted to build a stronger set of policies and organizing principles for the delivery of mental health services were discussed. In the realm of assessment and treatment, the second section sought to familiarize the reader with the terms and procedures used by mental health professionals. Various diagnostic categories, types of psychological tests, medications, and forms of interventions were presented. The final section covered the important area of special education for children with emotional and behavioral disorders. The federal Individuals with Disabilities Education Act of 1990 (IDEA) sets out policies, procedures, and safeguards that govern services to these children in public school systems.

II

Eight Pragmatic Perspectives in Social Work with Children and Their Families

Unit II, consisting of chapters 4–11, presents the eight pragmatic perspectives that serve to focus and integrate the material in this text. These perspectives represent breaks from traditional professional practice and policy; as such, they guide the beginning professional toward policies and practices that are critical to reform and improvement of the service delivery system. It is important that macro-level policy and micro-level practice be in sync with each other. Each of the eight pragmatic perspectives serves as a lens through which social work practice situations can be viewed. They serve as conceptual frameworks for organizing and integrating practice and policy in ways that break from old traditions and offer hope for better child and family outcomes. They help the beginning social work practitioner understand and act in purposeful ways in complex and difficult situations. In acting in accordance with these perspectives, the social worker's actions will be compatible with larger policy trends and values that are rapidly reforming the human service system.

CHAPTER 4

Pragmatic Perspective 1: Combating Adultcentrism

Overview

Adultcentrism is the tendency of adults to view children and their problems from a biased perspective, thus creating barriers to effective practice with children. The first section of this chapter (1) examines the roots of social work's adultcentrism in history and developmental theory, (2) discusses how adultcentrism influences practice, and (3) considers ways for practitioners to combat adultcentrism in their practice. The second and third sections offer specific and concrete practice guidelines and techniques for engaging young children and adolescents that help the practitioner combat adultcentrism, regardless of service system setting. The final sections discuss specific ways to combat adultcentrism in the child welfare and children's mental health arenas.

Adultcentrism in Social Work Practice with Children

(This section is adapted from Petr, 1992.)

Introduction and Background

The social work profession has a long-standing commitment to child welfare and the improvement of the quality of life for children. Yet social work with children is a complex and demanding undertaking. One of the factors that complicates work with children is the simple fact that they are very different from the adult practitioners who work with them. Children are not adults—they have a different worldview, different ways of communicating, different status and power, and different rights. Sensitive practitioners have long recognized these differences and sought creative ways to bridge the gaps. Their task is akin to that of bridging cultural, racial, or gender differences.

Effective practice with different ethnic cultures requires vigilant monitoring of potential ethnocentric bias and prejudice, and similarly, the potential for sexist bias must be confronted in situations of gender difference.

The purpose of this chapter is to elucidate analogous potential bias in our work with children. The premise is that the effectiveness of our work with children can be undermined by adultcentrism, a complex set of attitudes, values, and behaviors that can skew our relationship with children and thus negatively affect our work. Simply defined, adultcentrism is the tendency of adults to view children and their problems from a biased, adult perspective (Goode, 1986). This bias does not typically stem from some blatant, pernicious, or even conscious intent. Adultcentrism is more subtle, and although the analogy is not a perfect one, adultcentrism can be understood as being similar to ethnocentrism, a concept long familiar to social workers, and originally defined as "a view of things in which one's own group is the center of everything, and all others are scaled and rated to it" (Sumner, 1906). With respect to children and adults, adultcentric bias is evident when we measure children by adult standards, when we fail to suspend our assumptions about them, when we decline to see the world from their point of view. The negative consequences of adultcentrism can be the same as those of ethnocentrism: miscommunication (with children), inaccurate judgments (about children's intents and motivations), misuse of power (to limit children's self-determination), and undermining strengths and competencies (setting expectations too high or too low).

It may be difficult for the reader to readily endorse the idea that our relationships with children are subject to adultcentric bias, because most adults have children's best interests at heart and genuinely think of themselves and society as being child-centered. Contemporary manifestations of adultcentrism are in fact often nebulous and elusive, especially when compared to the drastic adultcentrism that has characterized adult-child relationships in Western European tradition. Long ago, children were regarded as little more than chattel whose purpose was to aid their parents and adult society. Economic and emotional dependency on adults could not be prolonged beyond the early years. A short life expectancy and harsh economic conditions mandated that children grow up fast and become absorbed into the life of adults as soon as possible, even at 6 or 7 years of age (Aries, 1962; Kadushin, 1980). Beginning in the seventeenth century, notions about childhood began to change. This shift was due not to changes in demographic conditions or a reduction in child mortality, but to the growing influence of Christianity on attitudes and customs (Aries, 1962). As Christianity itself began to emphasize the moral aspect of religion above the sacred aspects, attention was turned to the importance of children's education. Thus, gradually, "it was recognized that the child was not ready for life, and that he had to be subjected to a special treatment, a sort of quarantine, before he was allowed to join the adults" (Aries, 1962, p. 412).

Eventually, by the nineteenth century, education and social welfare programs began to consider the unique developmental aspects of childhood. Child welfare policies and programs to protect and care for needy and delinquent youth flourished, including child labor laws, juvenile courts, and child guidance clinics (Trattner, 1974). Interest in the study of childhood began in earnest in the late 1800s, and the first center in the world devoted to the study of normal child development, the Child Welfare Research Station, was established at the University of Iowa in 1917 (Crissey, 1992). More child research centers were established around the United States in the 1920s and 1930s, so that by the middle of the twentieth century, many sophisticated theories about child development had evolved. In more recent times, the legal and human rights of children have been recognized by the United Nations and a "children's rights" movement is in place, as exemplified in the work of the Children's Defense Fund and the *Children's Rights Report,* a monthly newsletter of the American Civil Liberties Union.

Clearly, progress has been made and our society is generally less adultcentric, more attuned to children than ever before in history. Yet, while the United States is in many ways a child-focused society, critics point out many contradictions and areas for continued improvement. For example, the United States is one of a handful of countries that has refused to ratify the United Nation's Convention on the Rights of the Child ("Child Rights," 1990). Only 33% of the families responding to a recent national survey state that society places a great deal of value on children (Gallup, 1988). Our infant mortality rate ranks twenty-second in the world (Children's Defense Fund, 1995), and reports of child abuse have recently increased dramatically (Children's Defense Fund, 1990). The United States has become the first society in history in which the poorest group in the population is children (Phillips, 1990). The fact that an organization such as the Children's Defense Fund exists is, paradoxically, a sign of progress and at the same time an indictment of our society's disregard of children, for if we truly valued children, there would be no need for such an organization. Many would argue that the commentary on American adult/child relationships made more than 50 years ago by noted anthropologist Ruth Benedict (1934) still applies, to some degree, today: "Our children are not individuals whose rights and tastes are casually respected from infancy, as they are in some primitive societies, but special responsibilities, like our possessions, to which we succumb or in which we glory, as the case may be. They are fundamentally extensions of our own egos and give special opportunity for the display of authority" (p. 245).

Social work is not immune from these societal contradictions and ambivalences. While social work has been vigilant in detecting and combating ethnocentrism, it has been less aware of the need to address adultcentric attitudes and tendencies in students and the larger society. For example, current Council on Social Work (CSWE) Accreditation standards specifically mandate that the curriculum provide content on ethnic minorities and women, but make no mention of children. Generic practice texts include little if any significant material on practice with children (see, for example, Compton & Galaway, 1989; Hepworth & Larsen, 1993; L. C. Johnson, 1989; McMahon, 1996; Sands, 1991). This situation is particularly vexing and perplexing in light of the fact that a significant proportion of graduates are employed in child-related settings.

Analysis and confrontation of potential adultcentric bias can help practitioners remain vigilant in their determination to bridge the gaps between themselves and the children they work with. The remainder of this section will (1) explore adultcentric bias in child development theory, (2) discuss examples of adultcentrism in assessments and interventions, and (3) consider ways to combat adultcentrism in practice.

Adultcentrism in Child Development Theory

Most social work practitioners are knowledgeable about the general tenets of child development. Major stage theories of child development are studied in educational programs in standard human behavior texts. On the one hand, these stage theories have helped adults, students, and the general public become more sensitive to the unique needs and capabilities of children. This enhanced sensitivity has influenced countless child welfare and educational programs, as developmental notions have been incorporated to enhance the quality of life for children.

Yet stage theories of child development are sometimes accorded such reverence that the voices of critics are not often heard or appreciated. These critics maintain that our society's subtle, yet powerful, adultcentric biases are revealed in the way that we study and learn about children. They assert that embedded in stage theories of child development are two subtle, yet central adultcentric biases: first, that children are incomplete; second, that children are essentially incompetent.

First, the stage theories reflect the adult bias that children are unfinished, incomplete, and in process. Child development theory rests on the fundamental premise that children grow, develop, and mature in stages toward the end goal of adulthood (Kagan, 1984). But this concept of developmental stages subtly, but inherently, implies that those who have not achieved the end stage of adulthood are necessarily, and by definition, undeveloped. Children in development are incomplete: less knowledgeable, less serious, ultimately less important than adults (Waksler, 1986). If children are not fully adult, by implication they are not fully human (Goode, 1986). The following chart (adapted from Grotberg, 1976) depicts the incomplete bias:

Children Are	Adults Are
dependent	independent
amoral	moral
egocentric	sociocentric
illiterate	literate
irrational	rational
emotionally unstable	emotionally stable
unproductive	productive
present oriented	future oriented

So, although our society no longer views children as miniature adults, stage theory encourages us to view them as small, incomplete beings on their way to becoming adults. If all goes well, children will progress through the stages toward the valued end of well-adjusted, socially productive adulthood. Thus, one can see how closely stage theories of development become intertwined with the process of socialization or "acculturation" to the dominant, adult culture. The legitimate but perhaps overemphasized demands of the socialization process can lead adults to define children as vehicles for the transmission of social values

(Denzin, 1977). This emphasis on the socialization aspects of adult-child relationships can lead to theoretical formulations about children that mirror the adult view that children are as yet incomplete beings (Mackay, 1973). As a result, stage theories of child development subtly support a notion of adult-child relationships that overemphasizes the socialization function and promotes the view of children as incomplete beings.

The second adultcentric bias in stage developmental theory is closely related to the first. Beyond viewing children as incomplete, we view them as essentially incompetent and incapable, because we measure their competence against our own. No matter what skill is mastered, what new knowledge is acquired, what developmental stage and milestone are reached, that competency is only briefly celebrated before our attention turns to the next competency on the ladder toward adult proficiency. We quickly return to the process of scaling children according to how well they are mastering adult competencies.

All of this is not to say that we should abandon our stage development theories or cease helping children grow and mature. But this second bias regarding competence is problematic in two ways. First, our child development theorists have consistently underestimated the competencies of children at any given age. That is, the clear trend in developmental research is to "discover" competencies in children that developmental experts previously had not thought possible. This is particularly true in the area of infant development research, which has experienced rapid growth in the last two decades. Infants, being the most distant from adults on a stage scale, were traditionally assumed to be the most incompetent and incapable. Margaret Mahler and colleagues (Mahler, Pine, & Berman, 1975) went so far as to describe newborns up to 3 months old as "autistic," believing that infants basically did not interact with their environments. Research has shown that nothing could be farther from the truth. One of the early works that challenged the myths of the infant stage was *The Competent Infant* (Stone, Smith, & Murphy, 1973). The editors collected scores of research articles documenting infant capabilities, including neonate motor, sensory, perceptual, and learning abilities. In a more recent text, Snow (1989) writes: "[E]ven at birth infants possess remarkable abilities. We used to believe that babies were blind at birth. We now know that the newborn can not only see, but is capable of other sophisticated functions" (p. 8).

This tendency to underestimate children's competencies is documented in recent qualitative research and so-called resiliency studies. Regarding the former, a recent assessment of qualitative research with children (Fine & Sandstrom, 1988) concluded that these studies revealed that children are more mature and capable than expected: "Some studies find that children are much more sophisticated than we have given them credit for being. They are more verbally effective, emotionally considerate, or socially knowledgeable. They are more 'mature' than we as 'grownups' believe. We know of no study that has found that children are more 'childish' than we have given them credit for" (p. 72). The resiliency studies challenge child development's long-held assumption that early experience has a permanent impact on a child's later development of competence. In a thorough review of longitudinal studies (Clapp, 1988) that addressed this issue, the author concluded that although early experience can have serious negative effects, this is in no way universal, as many studies have demonstrated that many children make impressive recoveries. While the past is important, the present is itself a potent force that pressures each person to adapt and come to terms with it (Clapp, 1988). These impressive recoveries reinforce the notion that children have more strengths and competencies that we typically attribute to them.

The competence bias is also problematic when we and our theories are so focused on the socialization and growing up processes that we fail to view children as children, with their own knowledge, skills, and even culture. We *know about* children, but do we *know* children? Just as the dominant white culture now strives to view the values and knowledge of minority cultures as being simply different, not worse than or inferior to white culture, so too adults need to view children as having a culture that is merely different, not "less than" our own. Yet we seldom seem interested in children as children. We seldom study children in their natural environments and from their own perspective of what is important. When that has been done, the results have been surprising. For example, Glassner

(1976) studied grade school children during unsupervised recess at a public school in St. Louis. Although the main purpose of the study was to determine the extent of integration within the student population (which he found to be quite high), an unexpected finding was the degree to which a separate "kid society" existed, complete with its own norms, hierarchy, and subgroups. This society focused almost totally on itself, with little or no interaction with adults. In fact, Glassner claimed that he never heard a child talk about teachers, classroom activities, parents, or home life.

In summary, stage theories of child development and research have made considerable contributions to our understanding of children. But a close, critical analysis reveals that child development's stage theories have some implicit adultcentric biases that can negatively affect our view of, and thus our work with, children. The next section identifies how adultcentrism affects social work assessments and interventions.

Adultcentrism in Social Work Assessments and Interventions

Stage theories of child development constitute one of the major knowledge foundations of social work practice with children. The adultcentric aspects of this knowledge can be intensified in social work assessments because of the ongoing tension the profession feels between being "helpers" while at the same time being representatives of the larger society's interests in social control and socialization (Pincus & Minahan, 1973; Specht, 1988). Social workers engage children in a variety of settings, including residential institutions, mental health centers, schools, court probation offices, child protection, and foster care and adoption. In many of these settings, the role of the social worker is something of the "socialization expert." The professional is asked by the parent, teacher, or court system to diagnose the child, then "shape up" and "correct" the child: in effect, to socialize the child to the adult society's standards. This socialization agenda can magnify the effects of adultcentrism, so that social workers must be constantly vigilant in combating the subtle adultcentric agendas of their agency contexts.

For example, in child mental health assessments, there is a danger of judging normal childhood behaviors as abnormal and pathological. In the child and adolescent section of the *Diagnostic and Statistical Manual of Mental Disorders*, 4th ed. (1994), published by the American Psychiatric Association, one finds many diagnostic indicators that could apply to almost any child. For example, the criteria for oppositional disorder can be seen as describing much of normal adolescence. A child must exhibit at least four of eight behaviors for at least 6 months, including "often argues with adults" and "is often touchy or easily annoyed by others" (p. 94). What normal adolescent isn't touchy and doesn't argue? Although the manual does state that the behavior must be exhibited "more frequently than is typically observed in individuals of comparable age and developmental level" (p. 94), no guidelines are provided about what is typical. Thus, a child can be diagnosed with any number of mental disorders for exhibiting *normal* behaviors *more frequently* than one professional thinks is average for the child's mental age. Might not some professionals be diagnosing childhood itself?

In a humorous yet scathingly perceptive parody of child assessment, Smoller's "The Etiology and Treatment of Childhood" (1986) exposes this tendency. Although written as satire, one can see how stage development theory's adultcentric themes of incompleteness and incompetence intertwine with a socialization agenda to produce an adultcentric case plan. Writing tongue-in-cheek, Smoller says the "clinical features of childhood" include congenital onset, dwarfism, emotional liability and immaturity, knowledge deficits, and legume anorexia. The causes of childhood include the psychological-based theory of "learned childishness," which postulates that individuals who are treated like children eventually give up and become children. Despite intensive treatment, many victims of childhood remain children. The following case was presented as "typical."

> Billy J., age 8, was brought to treatment by his parents. Billy's affliction was painfully obvious. He stood only 4'3" high and weighed a scant 70 pounds, despite the fact that he ate voraciously. Billy presented a variety of troubling symptoms. His voice was noticeably high for a man. He displayed legume anorexia and, according to his parents, often refused to bathe. His intellectual

functioning was also below normal—he had little general knowledge and could barely write a structured sentence. Social skills were also deficient. He often spoke inappropriately and exhibited "whining behavior." His sexual experience was non-existent. Indeed, Billy considered women "icky."

His parents reported that the condition had been present from birth, improving gradually after he was placed in a school at age 5. The diagnosis was "primary childhood." After years of painstaking treatment, Billy improved gradually. At age 11, his height and weight have increased, his social skills are broader, and he is now functional enough to hold down a "paper route." (p. 9)

Turning to the arena of interventions with children, social workers must pay particular attention to issues of defining the client, self-determination, and social control. Is the client the child, or the parent, or the teacher? What are the ethical and practical limits to self-determination with children? How much social control of children is warranted? While these issues are extant across all practice methodologies, behavior modification and family therapy illustrate them particularly well.

Behavior therapy, which focuses on changing children's behaviors through the use of reinforcers and consequences, is a powerful and often effective methodology taught in many schools of social work (Association for the Advancement of Behavior Therapy, 1981). Yet it remains controversial with respect to issues of control and the impact on children's self-directed behavior. Its supporters emphasize its commitment to empiricism and measurable outcomes (Thyer, 1989), while critics question its emphasis on social control (Schrag, 1978) and other ethical issues (Stolz, 1978). While a comprehensive review of this controversy is beyond the scope of this chapter, social work's commitment to self-determination and client-centeredness require awareness of the adult-centric potential of the theory and/or its application. For example, in a recent national study of supposedly exemplary school programs for children with behavioral and emotional disorders, the authors identified a "troubling pattern" they called "the curriculum of control" (Knitzer, Steinberg, & Fleisch, 1990): "The curriculum emphasis is often on behavioral management first, learning, if at all, second. Central to many of the classrooms we

visited was a great concern with behavioral point systems. Yet often, these seemed largely designed to help maintain silence in the classroom, not to teach children how better to manage their anger, sadness or impulses" (p. xii).

In a review of outcome research on behavior therapy with children, Graziano and Bythell (1983) questioned whether the modality is client-centered or more focused on adult agendas of socialization and social control. Even when changes took place, they questioned whether those changes were of personal and/or clinical significance for the youth involved. By way of example, they cited programs for quiet children, who adults decide are socially withdrawn and in need of behavioral intervention, without consideration of whether their quietness was problematic for the child, in the child's own opinion.

Family therapy models, although widely diverse in orientation, generally share a systems orientation that can lead to devaluation of children's perceptions. As Johnson (1986) points out in her critique of family therapy, "A fairly obvious dilemma is that some interventions may foster the best interests of one family member, at the same time . . . countervailing those of another member" (p. 303). When agendas clash, family workers understandably can become confused about who is the client. Since children are less verbal and less powerful than parents in the family hierarchy, the problem definition and treatment plan can be overly influenced by the adults, unless the therapist moves strongly to incorporate and empower the children. Although this issue has recently begun to be addressed (see, for example, the entire issue of the *Family Therapy Networker,* vol. 15, no. 4, July/August 1991), family systems theories have not typically identified this issue nor encouraged the therapist to seek out, validate, or legitimize the child's perspective (Hoffman, 1981). This certainly does not mean that the social worker should side with the child against the parents. As will be elaborated upon in the next chapter on family-centered practice, it is crucial that all members of a family feel respected and supported. It does mean, however, the social worker should maximize the input of the child within the limits of the family and agency context.

In summary, the danger in practice with children is to overidentify with the goals and point of view of the adults. This danger is intensified by the agency context that often emphasizes social control and by practice methodologies that implicitly or explicitly legitimize the adult point of view. Children have relatively little power in the world, since adults are the authority figures and exercise their power over children, in families and in agencies. Thus, practitioners working with children, themselves adults, must be vigilant in combating these adultcentric forces. The social worker must do this while maintaining positive relationships with the adults in the child's life, which is not always an easy task.

Recommendations for Combating Adultcentrism

This section offers suggestions on ways social workers can maintain this vigilance. Although some of these suggestions may not be new to experienced practitioners, they serve as reminders and as validation for their approach, while orienting beginning practitioners to some guiding principles for effective practice with children.

Principles for Combating Adultcentrism

1. Take time to learn about and value children as children.
2. Routinely conduct individual interviews with children.
3. Involve the child as fully as possible in decisions that affect the child's life.
4. Support changes in social work research and education.

First, practitioners can take time to learn about and value children, as children. A powerful way to combat any bias is to enter, as much as is possible, the world of the other. For our work with children, this means suspending our usual adult-child interactions long enough to just observe children as they are, in their natural settings such as playgrounds, backyards, video parlors, and malls. What are children like when they are not responding to adults? What is important to them in their

own world? By routinely taking the time to get outside and beyond our usual modes of interacting, we gain insight not only into their worlds, but also into our own subtle biases. Through the process, we may even rediscover the playful, childlike parts of ourselves that our adultness has suppressed.

A second way for the social worker to empower children and combat the tendency to identify with the adults in the system is to routinely conduct individual interviews with children, even when the presenting problem and theoretical orientation of the therapist and agency favor a family systems approach. In this way, the child's perspective is included in our assessments and interventions, assuming that we know how to communicate with and "interview" them. A more thorough discussion of how to engage and interview children and adolescents will be presented in the next sections of this chapter, but it should be noted here that one does not interview young children in the traditional, verbal way that one employs with adults. Our adult verbal communication style does not match a child's preference for communicating through play, metaphor, drawing, and physical activity. So, if we insist that a young child sit quietly and talk with us about a problem, even if we do so individually, we may not obtain much valuable information.

Although it may come as a surprise to some readers, intrafamilial sexual abuse is one of the few family problem areas in which this routine individual interview process is recommended in the literature. It is widely recognized that children will not generally reveal incidents of incest in a family context—the prohibitions are just too strong (Sgroi, 1982). But might not this be the case for many other problems as well? Why do we so often assume that children will tell us their perspective and opinions about school problems, alcohol and drug abuse, their parents' behaviors, and other issues in family meetings, even when we think to ask them? Not only will new information be obtained, but also the child's investment in goals and problem definition will enhance participation and motivation. (Specific guidelines for interviewing and engaging children and adolescents are offered in following sections.)

Third, social workers can employ the cardinal social work value of self-determination by involving a child more fully in the decisions made by social workers and other adults that directly affect a child's life (Bush & Gordon, 1982). This does not mean that we blindly allow children to be totally self-determined. Just as with adults, there are limits to self-determination related to capacity and respect for others' rights. But we can more diligently and routinely include children's perspective and wishes in our decision making.

There are at least four valid reasons to do so. First, it is reasonable to postulate that, in many circumstances, children have interests that are appreciably different from their adult caretakers (Melton, 1982). Examples of these conflict-of-interest situations include parents or guardians admitting their children to mental hospitals, placement decisions in child welfare, and divorce custody. Second, ethical considerations stemming from the value of respecting children and equalizing power differentials compel us to pay attention to their views in the interest of equality and fairness. By doing so, we communicate confidence in their abilities and strengths to problem solve. Third, solicitation of children's views can enhance their satisfaction with the ultimate decision. For example, foster children who had a voice in their placement reported significantly greater satisfaction with their placements than those who had not been afforded input (Bush & Gordon, 1982). Finally, children's views and preferences can inform public policy. For example, while adults have long been ambivalent about the role of institutions in the care of children (Petr & Spano, 1990), children themselves unequivocally prefer non-institutional placements (Bush, 1980). In the field of adoption, children's views challenge the predominant adult, professional view that most foster children want to be, and should be, adopted (Bush & Gordon, 1982).

The final recommendation is that practitioners support changes in social work research and education, areas that indirectly, yet strongly, affect social work practice. In the research arena, studies on the effectiveness of programs too often fail to include the perspective of the children who are directly affected. Recent studies of adoption, which focused on data obtained from social workers, parents, and records, are a case in point (Barth, 1988; Kagan & Reid, 1986; Reid, Kagan, Kaminsky, & Helmer, 1987). While these studies yielded important information about adoption practices, the results would have been enriched, and perhaps even changed, if the researchers had included the opinions and perspectives of children themselves. In their review of permanency planning research, Barth and Berry (1987) acknowledge this current shortcoming and argue that data about children's satisfaction should be incorporated into permanency planning research as one of four indicators of the suitability of placements. Practitioners should support utilization of both quantitative and qualitative methodologies (Cook & Reichardt, 1979) into research designs. Although many ethical and logistical barriers must be overcome before engaging in qualitative methods such as participant observation with children (Fine & Sandstrom, 1988), these approaches can be powerful weapons against adultcentrism because of the emphasis placed on immersing oneself in the world of the subject to better know and understand that world.

Practitioners can support changes in educational curriculum that incorporate these research issues into research classes. In other areas of the curriculum, content on child development theory must include a critique of the adultcentric bias of stage theories, along the lines articulated here. The works of Stern (1985) and Gergen (1983) offer frameworks for exposing social workers to nontraditional development theories, which emphasize the power of the individual as an autonomous, active agent. This emphasis is also found in much of the general systems literature, and has strong implications for the worker-client relationship (Petr, 1988). Social work practice classes and texts need to address the specific issues in working with children as a special population, just as most now do in relation to working with ethnic minorities. The content of this material should include: (1) specific ways to communicate with and understand the language of children; (2) a clear acknowledgment and confrontation of the socialization and social control aspects of social work with children, as they manifest themselves in various practice settings and methodologies, and the implications of these aspects for cherished social work values such as self-determination and empowerment; and (3) specific exercises and activities which thrust students into the world of children (playgrounds, video parlors, day care centers) so that they can better know, not just know about, children.

Pragmatic Connections: How to Combat Adultcentrism When Engaging and Interviewing Young Children

As introduced above, professionals can combat adultcentrism by regularly conducting individual interviews with children. Effective communication with young children requires social workers to modify the comfortable verbal style that they employ to interview adults. Young children communicate nonverbally and indirectly; their preferred modes of communication are play, metaphor, drawing, and physical activity.

The remainder of this section will present specific guidelines and techniques for combating adultcentrism when engaging and interviewing young children. Specific ideas will be presented on how to create a climate for engagement, how to understand the indirect, metaphoric style of communication in children, especially as this is expressed in their drawings, and how to communicate in words with older and more verbally oriented children. These ideas and techniques are generic in that they apply to children regardless of specific agency setting. In the later units on child welfare and mental health, engagement issues specific to those settings will be addressed: in child welfare, interviewing victims of abuse; in mental health, play therapy as an intervention modality.

Creating a Climate for Engagement

When interviewing adults, a social worker might help establish a conducive climate for engagement by offering the client coffee or a soft drink, by having comfortable chairs and furniture, and by beginning the interview with relaxed conversation about the weather or the adult's work and hobbies. After a brief period, the client is ready to talk about the issues and problems that are the reason for the interview.

Similarly, with young children, the social worker wants to put the child at ease and establish a comfortable climate for rapport. Offering a child a drink of water, possibly a soft drink, and a small snack of crackers, fruit, or cookies is a great way to break the ice. It is important that the food and drink *not* be contingent on the child's behavior, at this initial stage, any more than the offer of food and drink to an adult would be contingent

on the adult's behavior. The issue at hand is not control and socialization, but engagement. The noncontingent offer of a snack or a drink to a child communicates that the relationship between the child and social worker is not going to be based solely on socialization and control, that some unconditional positive regard will be a part of the relationship mix.

Young children are very oriented toward food and drink, even more so than adults. To young children, food and drink are symbolic of nurturance and caretaking. Young children know that they are dependent on adults to provide them with the basic sustenance of life. The initial, unconditional offer of food and drink is a type of metaphoric communication to the child, for it says, indirectly, to the child: "This is a caring and nurturing place where people will try to understand you and meet your needs."

There are other ways that the social worker can help the child feel at ease. While adults like to sit in comfortable chairs and sofas, children often prefer to sit on the floor. It is important for the social worker to "start where the client is at" in literal, physical ways with children, not just in verbal ways as they would with adults. This means getting out of the chair and sitting on the floor, even if the child has not yet done so. It is especially important to do so if the child is already on the floor, because it communicates a willingness to adapt to the child and the child's view of the world, rather than force the child to "come up" to the adult's world. On the floor, the adult and child are in the child's world, and the child is not being "looked down on" by the adult.

Sometimes, especially with older and more verbal children, engagement may be facilitated by initial chitchat with the child. Whereas with adults this chitchat would probably be about the weather or the adult client's work, family, or interests, with children the focus is different. Chitchat commonly centers on areas that are relevant to the lives of young children, such as toys, games, TV programs, and events in the very immediate past or present. Young children are neither past nor future oriented; in contrast to most adults, young children are intensely present. Adult comments or questions about anything not immediate are likely to be met with silent, perhaps puzzled, responses. Because many children resist answering questions, it is often helpful for the worker to share something about the worker's own activities of experiences that day, to help the child feel comfortable doing the same.

Engaging and Clarifying

With adults, after the client is feeling relaxed and comfortable, it is important to discuss the purposes of the interview and the presenting problems or issues. This general principle is important with children, too, because it sets the boundaries for the relationship and alleviates any anxiety they may have about the strange setting and the new adult in their life. While important, this communication can be strained and difficult, because young children cannot cognitively conceive of themselves as having any "problems," and verbal communication must be aimed at their level of vocabulary.

One way to transition from the "settling in" to the "work" phase is to ask the child, in simple terms, if they know the reason for the meeting. Children seldom ask for help with problems; more often, it is someone else who wants the child to see a social worker. Still, some acknowledgement of the reason for the meeting is important so that the child is informed and at some level gives his or her consent. Otherwise, the child may be anxious about the intentions of the worker or may imagine that the purpose is something other than what the worker thinks it is.

> *Social worker:* "So, Johnny, did your mother (teacher, etc.) talk with you about how come we are meeting today?" or "Johnny, I talked with your mother (teacher, etc.) about how come she wanted us to meet today, and I wonder, did she talk with you about that too?"

The social worker should not be dismayed or discouraged if the child shrugs his or her shoulders or answers "I don't know." These are very common responses, because young children have a very difficult time conceptualizing and talking about problems. Even if they are able to conceptualize and verbalize well, children still may not be sure if they have the "correct" answer, or may be reluctant to self-disclose to a relative stranger. Still, it is recommended that the worker start with this question because it communicates a respect for the child's perspective and agenda, rather than reacting to the adult's understanding of the agenda. It is very unproductive for the social worker to push the child for an answer, even when the social worker knows that the reasons for meeting have been told the child by the parent or teacher just minutes before the interview, because confrontation at this point can only lead to a pointless power struggle. It is not important for the child to " 'fess up" or to "admit to the problem" at this point. The child's quiet, equivocal answer is not necessarily a sign of denial or resistance or uncooperativeness, and should not be treated that way. What is important is that the child and social worker begin to communicate with each other, which means avoiding power struggles, if at all possible.

The appropriate and productive response by the social worker is to accept the child's response matter-of-factly, and then proceed to share the social worker's own understanding about the purpose of the meeting. This clarifies the boundaries of the relationship and sets a tone of communication that is genuine and straightforward. If the social worker fails to clarify his or her own understanding of the situation, in language the child can understand, then the child could be left with understandable fears and anxieties about the adult's agenda. An appropriate response to the child's "I don't know" would be:

> *Social worker:* "OK, well, let me take a minute to tell you what I think we're meeting for. My job is not a teacher or a doctor or a nurse. I don't have a classroom of kids to teach like a teacher does, and I don't give shots like a doctor or nurse does. I meet with kids to help them and their families and their teachers and everybody with everybody's worries and the things that are bothering everybody. I try to help everybody feel better or get along better or whatever."

At this point, the child may have questions or volunteer more about the worries and bothers that are the presenting problems. This would indicate that the child potentially will be able and willing to talk directly about some of the issues, in the fashion of an adult or older child. But since verbalization is not the preferred mode of communication for most young children, the social worker should not expect questions or elaboration, and should be prepared to move on in whatever direction the child leads. First, however, the practitioner should state briefly his or her understanding of the specific ways others hope he or she can help.

> *Social worker:* "I don't know you or your situation very well, so I don't really know how I can help everybody in your situation. I did talk a little bit with your mother [teacher, etc.], and she said you are a really great kid who is smart in math and takes good care of his pet cat. She hoped I could help you and her and everybody with all the worries she has about your getting in trouble so much at school [or whatever the concerns of the adults are]."

Again, a brief pause here can prompt the child to offer information or ask questions, but it is perfectly OK if the child does not. Note also how the language of the social worker includes comments about the child's strengths and does not single out the child as the problem or the target for change. Instead, the language emphasizes a systems perspective that emphasizes "everybody," not just the child.

At this point, if the child does not verbalize questions or offer more information, the social worker could be tempted to ask the child directly if they have anything to add or to say about the situation. This is not necessarily the wrong thing to do, but it does continue the communication in a verbal mode, which may inhibit the child communicating in other ways. The child could begin to think that the worker is not accepting of his or her quietness, or the child could become wary that the worker is going to insist on the adult way of communicating. A safer and more cautious approach is to invite the child to communicate in other, more comfortable, ways.

Listening, with Caution, to the Language of Metaphor

Rather than continue to attempt verbal communication with a young, reticent child, the social worker can change the focus to nonverbal interactions and communication. This shift from the language of words to the language of play and metaphor can open up possibilities for communication and understanding, if the social worker is attuned to the indirect and subtle ways that young children communicate, and if the social worker

does not overinterpret or misinterpret the meaning of the communication (Garbarino, Stott, & Faculty of the Erikson Institute, 1989).

The need for caution in interpretation cannot be overemphasized. Accurate interpretation of a child's indirect communications requires patience, knowledge of child development, an extended base of experience, feedback from the child about the accuracy of the interpretation, repetition of the same message or theme in various contexts, consultation with colleagues, and corroboration from other sources of information.

For example, a teacher may notice that a child in a preschool group is spanking her doll and calling it bad. Knowing that children often use play to reenact their own situations, the teacher may interpret this play as an indication that the child is being inappropriately disciplined at home. But this conclusion would be quite premature and inappropriate. While this child's behavior *may* reflect her home life, it is just as possible that it could reflect her own inner concerns about being "bad" as she develops her conscience. The play may reflect a fantasy or a wish to be punished or controlled, not a reality. Numerous other interpretations are possible as well. Because children are so present oriented, their play can often reflect something about what has happened in the very recent past. In the above situation, for example, the girl may be repeating or copying the play that she just recently observed an older girl exhibiting.

Therefore, it is important to emphasize that the information presented in this section is offered as a brief glimpse into the ways that children may communicate. Readers are cautioned not to jump to conclusions from any single source of information. While children's indirect and nonverbal communications can offer clues and hypotheses for understanding behavior, they should never be considered alone and in isolation as conclusive of anything. In fact, this holds for their verbal communication as well. The young child's world is so focused on the present, and so full of imagination and fantasy, that accurate communication can be very difficult, complex, and time consuming.

Bearing this caution in mind, a few examples of the potential power of the language of children are offered. This information is not intended as training on how to communicate and conduct interviews. Rather, the information acquaints the reader with some of the techniques that various professionals use to try to combat adultcentrism, in the hope that this may stimulate the reader to seek additional training and experience.

Three common techniques, used by many school psychologists and mental health professionals, are the Draw-a-Person (DiLeo, 1983; Klepsch & Logie, 1982), the Kinetic Family Drawing (Burns, 1982), and unstructured play. These techniques are founded on the supposition that children will often project information about themselves and their families into drawings and play activities. That is, rather than talk directly about themselves and their families, children will communicate important information about the way they see themselves and their families indirectly, through their drawings and play.

Draw-a-Person. In the Draw-a-Person, the child is presumed to be drawing a self-portrait that has important clues about his or her self-image. However, it is important that the adult ask the child to draw a person, and leave it at that, with no further explanation. If the adult asks the child to "draw a picture of yourself," the projection process is disrupted, and the child may get overly focused on technical aspects and accuracy of the physical portrait, thus losing the emotional and psychological projections. After giving the instruction, the adult should avoid further communication until the child completes the drawing.

The completed drawing, and the ensuing discussion about it, can be important modes of communication. Although much has been made about the possible symbolism of a multitude of physical details in the drawing itself, the reader is reminded that no professional should make conclusions about children or their situations from drawings alone. There is a Peanuts cartoon in which Charlie Brown inspects a drawing made by Linus. "This is a very nice drawing of a man, Linus. I notice, however, that you've drawn him with his hands behind his back. You did that because you yourself have feelings of insecurity." Linus replies angrily, "I did that because I myself can't draw hands!" The lesson is that drawings can be useful, if they are cautiously interpreted in the context of the child's comments about them.

The most global, general level of interpretation is the safest (DiLeo, 1983). What is the general im-

pression of the figure drawn? Does it appear happy, sad, mad? Does it appear to be well grounded on a firm foundation or weakly supported? Next, notice any physical features that stand out, or are absent. Special attention to specific parts of the body may mean special anxiety or concern about that body part or what it symbolizes. Children who feel clumsy, for instance, may draw large feet or big shoes. Children with physical disabilities or illnesses often exaggerate the area of concern in their drawings. Children with asthma may draw large noses and mouths, or children with hearing problems may accentuate the ears.

It has been widely noted that many children who have been sexually abused will draw attention in their drawings to genital areas and "private parts." Unfortunately, too often this one piece of information can be misinterpreted as "proof" that the child is being sexually abused. There can in fact be other explanations for why a specific child's drawing is more sexualized than other children of the same age. The child may have been recently exposed to nude pictures in a magazine or movie while visiting at a friend's house. The child may live in a family where nudity is not discouraged in the privacy of the home. An overly sexualized drawing may indicate only that the child may have sexual knowledge and awareness beyond their years. That knowledge may have been obtained through sexual abuse experiences but it may have been obtained much more innocently and harmlessly. (More discussion of this subject will be presented later in this chapter).

The most revealing part of the Draw-a-Person exercise is usually not the drawing itself, but the discussion of the drawing with the child. Assuming that the drawing is a reflection of the child in some way, the adult can use discussion about the drawing to facilitate communication with the child, about the child, but indirectly. Talking about the drawing, not about him- or herself, provides important distance for the child. It is important for the adult to focus on the person in the drawing at first, and not to connect the aspects of the person directly to the child and his or her life until the end of the interview, if at all.

Thus, the Draw-a-Person exercise is a tool to open communication and engage the child. As is true in other interview situations, the discussion about the drawing should proceed from the general to the specific, from open-ended questions to more specific questions. This allows the child the greatest freedom of expression and minimizes responses that react to the adult's agenda. Thus, the adult could first say, "Tell me about what you drew." Depending on the child's response, the adult might pursue other questions such as "What is the person thinking [or feeling, or doing]?" Perhaps a story of the person begins to evolve, and the adult can ask, "What is going to happen next?" Later, the adult might point to specific parts of the drawing and ask for clarification and/or elaboration, such as, "Tell me about this part" or "I notice that the person in the drawing doesn't have any arms." Some children will not want to discuss their drawing at all; others will discuss the drawing but will resist direct connections to themselves. At the end of the interview, it is often productive for the adult to attempt this direct connection by noting something about the person in the drawing that is like the child. For example, the adult might say, "You said that this person in your drawing is thinking about the trouble they got into at school. Do you ever get into trouble at school?"

Two examples from *Silent Screams and Hidden Cries* by Agnes Wohl and Bobbie Kaufman (1985) illustrate how children communicate something about themselves in their drawings.

FIGURE 4.1
"Harriet"

Source Reprinted with permission from Agnes Wohl & Bobbie Kaufman, *Silent Screams and Hidden Cries*, p. 31. Reproduced by permission of Routledge/Taylor & Francis Books, Inc.

The first impression of the figure drawn by Harriet, age 8, is of a cute, somewhat frail, gentle, and shy child. The viewer may find him- or herself drawn to cuddle, hug, or protect the child. This sense of vulnerability is linked to the tiny eyes, short arms, and sense that the child is off balance and falling. According to the authors and the child's therapist, the drawing is an accurate self-portrait of how Harriet appears to the adults in her world. She is described as quiet and non-intrusive, one who watches but does not speak out. The authors note that her style of interacting serves her well in coping with her family life. Harriet's parents are separated, and the father has terrorized the family by breaking into their home at night and threatening to kill the mother. Like viewers responding to the drawing, adults find Harriet engaging and easy to love. She has been successful in getting adults outside the family to protect and nurture her.

Brian is a 10-year-old who witnessed much violence on the part of his father toward his mother. The mother finally decided to leave with Brian and his 4-year-old brother James when she overheard the two of them plotting to kill their father. According to the authors, Brian's picture is an accurate reflection of how Brian feels about himself and how he presents himself to the world. The first overall, global impression is of a figure that is upright, smiling, and apparently at attention. But the figure also appears stiff, rigid, and controlled, ready to defend and ward off any threats. Brian first began to draw a person in the lower half of the page, tried to erase and correct it, then began again. The erasures may indicate general anxiety about himself and the need to alter and perfect. The authors note the omissions of hair and ears in the drawing. Since hair has been interpreted as the traditional symbol of masculinity and strength (the biblical story of Samson comes to mind in this regard), Brian may be denying these qualities in himself and rejecting the role model presented by his father. The absence of ears may be symbolic of one of Brian's coping mechanisms. Can he protect himself by not having to hear the verbal abuse that his father spews at his mother?

Kinetic Family Drawing. The Kinetic Family Drawing is similar to the Draw-a-Person in that it is based on the assumption that the drawing will

FIGURE 4.2
"Brian"

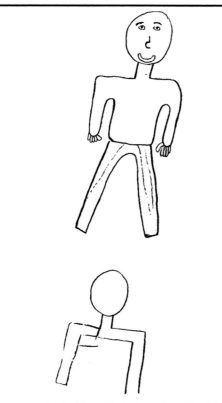

Source   Reprinted with permission from Agnes Wohl & Bobbie Kaufman, *Silent Screams and Hidden Cries*, p. 33. Reproduced by permission of Routledge/Taylor & Francis Books, Inc.

in some way be a projection or reflection of the child's perceptions, but this time the projection is of the child's own view of their family situation, rather than of him- or herself. Here, the instructions are "Draw a picture of your family doing something." The kinetic aspect of the drawing is embodied in the "doing something" phrase. This kinetic component adds richness to the projection, because it involves the interactions of family members with each other. As with the Draw-a-Person, the most global, most general level of interpretation is the most cautious. What seems to be the child's place and role in the family (where and how does he or she belong?) and what appears to be the child's view of the place and role of other family members? Thus, the specific content or plot of the family drawing is not as important as the themes and perspectives that they reflect.

The drawing in and of itself can be revealing,

but the most important aspect of the exercise is the discussion with the child. Of particular note in the drawing itself are the size and placement of the child relative to other family members, the distance between family members, and the inclusion or exclusion of certain members. These can give clues as to who the child might feel closest to and most distant from in the family, whether the child perceives the parent relationship to be close or distant, and who in the nuclear and extended family are included in the child's conception of family.

As with the Draw-a-Person, the adult should initially refrain from any communication, including clarification of the instructions, so as not to inhibit the range of the child's expression. After the drawing is completed, the discussion proceeds from general and open-ended comments about the drawing, then to specific questions about the drawing, and finally to comments and questions relative to connections between the drawing and the child's life. Initial comments from the interviewer might be "Tell me about your picture"; "What is happening in the picture"; "What are [specific people] thinking [feeling, doing, etc.]"; "What is going to happen—how is it going to end up?" Intermediate questions could be "I notice that, in this picture, your stepbrother is not here"; or "Are your grandparents anywhere around in this picture?" At the end of this discussion, the adult can pursue themes or issues in more detail, and with less reference to the drawing. "So, that argument that your parents had in your drawing there, does that happen a lot?"; or, "In the drawing, you and your brother were fighting a lot. Does that happen a lot in real life?"

In 8-year-old Marilyn's drawing of her family, the initial impression is inviting and almost festive. The sun is out, the family is rosy-cheeked and smiling, and Marilyn appears to be carrying a balloon. This may be Marilyn's expression of how the family attempts to present itself to the world. Behind this facade are indications of conflict and turmoil, as Marilyn describes when she tells about her picture. The father is calling Marilyn to feed her, but the mother tells him to shut up, because Marilyn is ill. Dad begins screaming because Marilyn is not next to him and isn't coming to be close. The position of the mother may reflect her use of herself as a buffer between the conflicts of Marilyn and her father, but Marilyn may experience her

Figure 4.3
"Marilyn's Family"

Source Reprinted with permission from Agnes Wohl & Bobbie Kaufman, *Silent Screams and Hidden Cries*, p. 77. Reproduced with permission of Routledge/Taylor & Francis Books. Inc.

mother as determined to keep her and father apart. The drawing may reflect Marilyn's identification with her mother, as indicated by the similar stance, triangular dresses, and the repetition of hearts in the mother's dress and Marilyn's balloon.

In summary, the reader should keep the following guidelines in mind when using the Draw-a-Person or Kinetic Family Drawing:

Unstructured Play. A third, less structured way to obtain information is to allow the child to play freely, and to note the themes and issues that emerge in the play. (This technique is important in nondirective play therapy, which was discussed

Guidelines for Use of Children's Drawings in Assessments

1. Don't jump to quick conclusions or interpretations. Consider the drawings as one piece of the puzzle that must be viewed in the context of other data from family, school, and environment.

2. Listen and watch for metaphoric, indirect communication.

3. Discuss the drawing with the child, beginning with general, open-ended comments and moving toward detail and specifics.

4. Check out interpretation (the link between the drawing and the child's own life) with the child and others before making conclusions.

in chapter 3. After creating the climate for engagement and briefly clarifying the purpose of the meeting as described above, the adult can allow the child a period of free time. "OK, now we're going to have some play time, where you can play with whatever you like." It is important to establish basic limits to the play, but not rigid ones that suppress freedom of expression. For instance: "There are only three rules: don't hurt yourself, don't hurt anybody else (like me), and don't break anything."

Many children will use this playtime to communicate something about themselves and their situation. For example, a young girl may begin spanking a doll and calling her bad, as discussed above. Different children choose to do different things, and their choices are in some way statements about who they are and how they view their worlds. One child may play quietly by herself, revealing little about herself and interacting little with the adult. The interviewer might wonder, "How might this behavior be reflective, or not reflective, of how this child is in the world? Is she usually shy and withdrawn? If not, what about this situation could explain the contradic-

tion?" Another child may choose to read books out loud to impress the adult with their reading ability. This, too, may be an important indicator of how the child sees him- or herself. Still other children may engage in puppet play that reflects key family themes, interactions, or concerns.

The appeal of this unstructured play approach is that individual children can have the opportunity to express and communicate what they choose to communicate on their own terms, in their own unique way. The potential drawback of such an unstructured approach is that it produces so much indirect and complex communications that the risk of misinterpretation is at its highest. At the risk of belaboring the point, the reader is reminded that all of the interviewer's thoughts and questions should be tentative and incomplete—no conclusions should be drawn from any one piece of data or interaction. With this caveat again in the reader's mind, the following brief illustration is offered to give the reader a feel for how such an unstructured interview might proceed, the difficulties and complexities involved, and the tentative meaning that can be drawn.

CASE VIGNETTE: Bill

Bill is a very verbal and imaginative 5-year-old boy who has been recently getting in lots of fights at kindergarten. He is aggressive verbally with his teacher—talking back and calling her names—and he has gotten into fistfights with classmates during recess about three times a week for the last week. The kindergarten teacher has referred Bill to the school social worker, Carmelita, who conducts a brief interview with Bill to attempt to get his point of view on the situation. After offering Bill a drink of water and briefly introducing herself, her role, and the reason to meet, the following exchange occurred:

BILL: How come there are toys here and I'm not playing with them?

CARMELITA: (Leaving chair and sitting on floor.) Well, I was just going to say, we can have some talk time and some play time—which do you want to do first?

B: Play time.

C: OK. The only rules are not to break things and not to hurt anybody.

B: (Nodding, goes over to the puppets and briefly touches and examines them and some toys around them. Picks up one puppet). This is coyote. "Grrr, grrr. I just woke up from a nap."

C: Hi, coyote, did you just wake up from a nap?

B: Yes, I'm cranky when I get up from a nap.

C: Oh, I see.

B: Grrr . . .

C: What do you do, coyote, when you are cranky after a nap?

B: Grrr . . . (Abruptly takes hand out of puppet.) My hand is getting really hot and sweaty. (Bill begins to look open and glance at books.) This cat is mean.

C: The cat in the book is doing mean things?

B: Yeah. See? (Shows pictures in book to C)

C: What mean things is the cat doing?

B: See? (Points to pictures. The cat is doing things like spilling the milk, knocking over plants, tracking mud into the house.)

C: Yes, I see. What do you think is going to happen to the cat?

B: (Long pause . . . continues to page through the book . . . long pause . . . looks up at C) Is it about time for the talk time now?

Commentary. This is not a particularly exemplary interview. The interviewer attempted to lead too much, rather than staying with Bill by reflecting and understanding what Bill might be trying to say. For example, Bill abruptly terminated the play with the coyote when Carmelita asked what the coyote does when he's cranky after a nap. The mistake here is that Bill is showing what coyote does—he growls—but the interviewer's question doesn't acknowledge this. Instead, the interviewer misses the communication of the child and resorts to the more adult mode of verbalization. The question about what will happen next ignores the behavior and asks Bill to describe more verbally what the coyote does, and Bill isn't ready or willing to do this. A better comment would have been "You growl and go 'Grrr' when you are cranky after a nap."

Later, the interviewer again rushes too fast to her own agenda by asking what is going to happen to the cat. But Bill has given no indication that he is interested in what happens to the cat. So far, Bill just wants Carmelita to notice what the cat is doing. A more facilitative comment from Carmelita would have been "I see that the cat is spilling the milk here. Here it is knocking over the plant. And here it is tracking mud into the house!" These responses would have better demonstrated the abilities to listen and to follow the child's lead.

Despite the interviewer's mistakes, some valuable information about Bill's view of himself in the situation was obtained. Consider that, of all the things that Bill could have chosen to do or say, the topics and themes he chose to focus on paralleled his own situation. Is this merely a coincidence? Like the coyote and the cat, Bill is reported to be cranky and mean, is he not? Although the teacher did not use those words, Bill himself may be struggling with how to characterize and understand his own behavior. Is he cranky when he wakes from a nap and at other times, and is this why he is getting into fights? Or is he mean like the cat in the book? The interviewer could tentatively hypothesize that Bill is himself struggling to grasp the meaning of his behavior, and that he may want some help in understanding and changing that behavior. His unstructured time was not spent in superfluous play or avoidance of the issues; in fact, Bill seemed ready to get right down to business!

Open-Ended Questions

In addition to the above techniques and strategies, communication with children can be facilitated by open-ended questions that can reveal concerns and issues, either directly or indirectly. A series of open-ended questions can be introduced as "something fun, something to help me get to know you better." The answers to the questions can reveal what the child thinks is most important, what the child's worries and concerns are, and something about the child's strengths. Many different open-ended questions are possible. The following interview and commentary exemplify the potential of this technique.

CASE VIGNETTE: Kerry

Kerry is a 10-year-old female whose single mother has just been released from prison after serving 9 months for writing bad checks. Mom is concerned about Kerry's defiance at home and has sought help from the local mental health center to get control of the situation before it gets worse. Kerry has two younger siblings. The social worker, Jon, met individually with Kerry, and the interview included the following exchange:

JON: If you had three wishes, and all three wishes could come true, what would you wish for?

KERRY: I'd wish for a car that runs. And second for us all going to Florida and spend summer vacation there. And third for my Mom getting a job.

J: OK. What would you do with a million dollars?

K: Well, I'd put some away for college. I'd get us a new house. I don't know what else.

J: Let me ask you this. If you could stay at home or go to school, which would you do, if you had the choice?

K: Go to school, probably. My friends are there, and if I want to go to college I have to get good grades. And if I don't go to school my Mom could get in big trouble.

J: What is the best thing that ever happened to you in your whole life?

K: Probably Mom and I getting back together.

J: What is the worst thing that ever happened to you?

K: Mom getting taken away by the police. I know that for sure, that's the worst thing.

J: What do you want to be when you grow up?

K: I want to go into the Air Force. I have to be a navigator, because I can't be a pilot with my eyesight.

J: Tell me about the things that scare or frighten you.

K: When I see a policeman driving by our house or something. I think they're coming to get my mom like before. The police came to arrest her and in court they were standing by her and I didn't like it.

J: Tell me about things that get you mad.

K: Well, not much really. I got a little mad today when Mom said I couldn't ride my bike down here.

J: Tell me about what makes you sad.

K: I get sad when somebody gets hurt and it's my fault.

J: Tell me about when you are the happiest.

K: When I get good grades. Two years ago I got Cs and Ds and this year I'm getting Cs and Bs and As.

Commentary. In just a short amount of time, Jon has learned quite a bit about Kerry. Unlike many kids whose three wishes are for material possessions, Kerry is more focused on immediate needs for the family. Rather than spending money on her immediate wants, Kerry said she'd spend a million dollars on her future education and on immediate family needs. She is clearly concerned for the welfare of her mother and the family, as many of her answers indicate. She appears to be goal oriented and other-directed, in that she is concerned about her mother and sensitive to the feelings of others. The power struggles with her mother are reflected in her response to what makes her mad—she gets angry when her mother tells her she can't do something. Finally, Kerry may have been traumatized by the arrest and incarceration of her mother—she has strong feelings and memories of the event that may need further assessment and intervention.

It is important to note that Jon did not pause to respond to each answer to each question. For example, it may have been tempting to ask Kerry what was wrong with her eyesight, when she mentioned this as a reason she could not be a pilot. But Jon asked a question, noted the response, and then went on to the next question. This interview procedure has advantages and disadvantages. Its principal advantage is that the answers are not unduly influenced by Jon's reactions. If Jon were to react and follow up to one or more questions, then later answers could easily be influenced by the direction that the previous elaborations took. Kerry might begin to sense what Jon thinks is a "good" or "right" or "interesting" answer, and modify her answers accordingly. By not reacting, Jon communicates neutrality and acceptance, allowing Kerry to give her own answers, not those she thinks Jon will like best. The principal disadvantage of this style of interviewing is that the lack of responsiveness can be interpreted by Kerry as indifference or disinterest, rather than as acceptance. This difficulty can be mitigated by stating early on that the interviewer will come back to some of the questions to talk more about them after they have finished asking and answering all of them first. In Kerry's situation, Jon followed up by asking more about all of the questions, so that Kerry could elaborate and clarify in more depth. Both breadth and depth of answers are important, and the interviewer must try to structure the interview to obtain both.

The responses to open-ended questions can be as revealing for what they leave out as for what they include. In Kerry's situation, for example, Jon noted that Kerry never mentioned her absent father, her siblings, or the grandparent whom she had stayed with the last few months. Unlike many other kids of her age, she also did not focus much on friends and fun activities. When this happens, it is appropriate for the interviewer to ask specific questions about the omissions at the end of the

interview. In Kerry's case, Jon learned that Kerry expressed a modest desire to visit more frequently with her father, and that she felt isolated and friendless at school. Although these issues were not foremost in Kerry's mind, or her mother's, they were included as lower priority concerns on the case plan.

Pragmatic Connections: How to Combat Adultcentrism When Engaging and Interviewing Adolescents

What Is Important to Adolescents?

Combating adultcentrism in relationships with adolescents begins with developing an empathy and sensitivity to the adolescent's world. Adolescence has long been recognized as a time of turmoil, confusion, and change. The overriding developmental issue is forming an identity. Teenagers struggle with the question "Who am I?" In answering that question, teenagers can try on various roles and identities. They can make strong statements about who they are *not* by rebelling against parents and established convention. They can be very sensitive to being treated like children, yet they are not yet responsible enough to be treated as adults.

How Do Teenagers Form an Identity?

- Separating and individuating from family
- Avoiding feelings of dependence
- Seeking privacy
- Finding places to belong outside of family
- Developing competence and self-management through decision making
- Coping with developing sexuality

The struggle to form an identity is manifested in many ways. To a teenager, finding a strong sense of self often means separating and individuating from family. Teenagers would much rather spend time with their friends than their parents or siblings. It is children, "little kids," who spend time with their families; teenagers are often embarrassed to be seen with their parents. Children are also dependent on their families. Teenagers often feel that it is important for them not to be dependent on anyone, especially not parents. This strong need not to be a dependent little kid can lead to counterdependence, in which the teenager is organized around resisting any sort of direction or authority. Similar to the 2-year-old whose favorite word is "no," a teenager can satisfy the need to feel separate by opposing and resisting, by defining self in opposition to others. Agreement can feel like sameness, and disagreement can heighten a sense of difference and separateness.

Related to the formation of identity are the need for privacy, the need to belong, the need to demonstrate competence, manage one's own affairs, and make decisions, and the need to cope with body maturation and developing sexuality. Privacy accentuates separateness and allows the time and place for independent thinking. Rejecting family as the sole source of identification, the teenager needs to develop a sense of belonging somewhere outside the family. This leads not only to more time with friends, but also to seeking out adult role models to identify with. Since a sense of competence is so highly associated with self-concept, teenagers need to accomplish tasks and develop a sense of responsibility. For teenagers who do not display particular aptitude for traditional school subjects, sports, or other school-related activities, a part-time job is often the key to meeting this need. Development of a sense of competence is achieved in part through successful decision making. Teenagers need to make choices and decisions for which they take responsibility. By learning from their mistakes and relishing in their successes, teenagers prepare for the difficult decisions of adulthood. Finally, adults tend to forget that adolescence is a time of "raging hormones." The teenager's sense of self is constantly challenged by rapid changes in physical features and emotional mood swings. Many teenagers face anxiety about sexual orientation—about whether they are homosexual or heterosexual. The intense interpersonal relationships that can characterize adolescence can at times be all consuming.

Adolescents, then, are a different breed. Not yet adults, they are no longer children. An example of how adolescents just don't seem to fit can be found in the health care system. Teenagers are too old for pediatricians, yet are not welcomed by physicians who treat adults. According to a survey reported by the *Los Angeles Times*, only 31% of pediatricians and 34% of internal medicine doctors said they liked working with adolescents (Roan, 2000). Few people are aware that physicians can obtain board certification in adolescent medicine—only a few hundred have done so.

Adults who lose sight of these developmental realities are susceptible to adultcentrism. It is easy to treat teenagers as either older or younger than they actually are—it is difficult to know what expectations are reasonable. Because they can be so oppositional, it is tempting to take a social control posture that unduly restricts choice and decision making.

Pragmatic Principles for Engaging and Interviewing Adolescents

In forging relationships with adolescents, it is important to keep the above developmental issues in the forefront of one's thinking. Ideally, relationships built on solid respect for developmental realities will be longer lasting and more rewarding to both parties. The following generic relationship principles are intended to help workers establish the kind of foundation that can lead to success.

Principles for Engaging and Interviewing Teenagers

1. Offer choices or negotiate
2. Address confidentiality
3. Be consistent and genuine
4. Focus on strengths and interests

Offer Choices or Negotiate. Regardless of the setting or the purpose of the social work involvement, adults can seek to maximize the choices of adolescents as much as possible. This gives the adolescent some sense of control and influence, communicates respect by maximizing self-determination, and helps the adolescent feel less like a little child.

This principle can and should be applied to even to such "mundane" decisions as where and when to meet. Many teenagers are uncomfortable with the face-to-face formality of office visits. They prefer meeting in a more informal atmosphere such as parks, playgrounds, or coffee shops. Office visits are also passive in tone, whereas teenagers prefer activity and movement. Talking while taking a walk, or while driving around in a car, are more comfortable contexts for many teenagers. Not only are these choices less passive, they also allow for some distance from the direct intensity of face-to-face eye contact. Scheduling times for meeting should respect the teenager's schedule so that they do not have to cancel or postpone important activities such as part-time jobs or extracurricular school events.

Whereas the key dynamics of the relationship between adults and young children are control and nurturance, the key dynamic to the adult-teenager relationship is negotiation. While the adult-young child relationship is replete with "Yes" and "No," the adult-teenager world is full of "Yes," "No," and "Maybe." The adult needs to carefully determine whether a "Yes," "No," or "Maybe" is called for in a given situation. Many adults need to learn this because their style with children is so cut and dried, "Yes" and "No." With teenagers, whenever possible, the adult should strive to be very clear about a "No," in which no negotiation is possible, and a "Maybe," in which there is room for discussion and negotiation. Meanwhile, the teenager needs to respect "No," but also needs to learn how to make a "Maybe" into a "Yes," through positive behavior and/or verbal persuasion.

It is vital that the worker practice this principle in direct interactions with the teenager. Too often, social workers err in thinking that their focus with clients is to talk about issues and problems "out there" in the world, thus missing the opportunity to make purposeful use of self in the immediate relationship. The following interaction illustrates how the negotiation principle can be operationalized in immediate fashion in an initial interview between a teenager and a social worker.

CASE VIGNETTE: Bob

BOB: I don't know why I'm here. I'd really rather be out with my friends. What is this all about anyway?

JON: I'm not totally clear what this is about myself, although I did talk to your parents briefly on the phone yesterday. I can certainly understand that you would rather be spending time with your friends. Is someone making you come today, or did you have some choice about it?

BOB: I don't know. They just said to come see you, so here I am. Can I smoke in here?

JON: No, I'm afraid you can't smoke here—that's a hard and fast rule that I don't make exceptions for. It would be OK to take a break later to go smoke outside, if you really want to. Or we can take a walk or go for a drive or something—we don't have to sit here in the office. As far as coming to see me, my understanding is that your mother and teacher are worried about you and think that talking to me would help. But I don't know if you agree with them or if you have any choice about coming.

BOB: Well, I don't know what they are so worried about and I don't want to come here. Do I have to?

JON: I don't know if you have to or not. Should we call your mom and teacher and find out what they say about it?

Commentary. In the above interchange, the social worker, from the beginning, establishes a clear "No" regarding smoking, and communicates a clear "Maybe" about the issue of having a choice about attendance. It would be a mistake to elicit the client's view of his problems, or focus the conversation on the adults' concerns, because these would only heighten the client's opposition and communicate a disrespect for the client's agenda. Instead, the worker focused on the issue that is paramount to the client, and offered to get it resolved first. This communicates respect for the client's view of the situation and doesn't force somebody else's agenda on the interview prematurely. The teenager is learning that the worker will be firm in areas that are non-negotiable, but will also listen to the teenager and show respect for the issues that the teenager brings.

In the above example, the social worker employed the recommended principles in the direct, immediate relationship with the teenager. In addition, the social worker can promote the choice and negotiation themes in the other contexts that envelop teenagers. On the home front, the social worker can educate the parents about the importance of negotiation to a teenager's development, and help them to make clear distinctions about the "No"s and "Maybe"s in their own home, considering their own values and lifestyle. At schools, in group homes, and in mental health facilities, social workers can promote policies and attitudes that respect the developmental realities and needs of teenagers, while at the same time respecting the adult needs to properly socialize teenagers and maintain a minimum of structure and control. Within a school classroom, group home, or mental health facility, how far can choice and negotiation be expanded without risking chaos?

Address Confidentiality. The need for privacy and individuality renders teenagers particularly sensitive to the issue of confidentiality. When the social worker respects the teenager's need for confidentiality, within limits, this is communicating respect while at the same time expecting the teenager to accept some reasonable limitations. The limits of confidentiality vary according to type of agency setting, worker comfort, and parent wishes. The important practice principle is to negotiate and clarify the limits of confidentiality

early in the helping process. If this early clarification and contracting is not accomplished, there is a strong possibility of major disruptions to the helping process at a later stage.

Some limits to confidentiality are applicable across settings, and these should be conveyed to the teenager. Social workers must report suspicion of abuse or neglect to the proper authorities. Some client information must be shared with supervisors and colleagues, or in case records. Social workers must notify parents and other authorities if the teenager is dangerous to self or to others. In addition, depending on the setting and worker comfort, social workers may feel compelled to break confidentiality if the teenager reports using alcohol and drugs, or reveals illegal activity, or brags about breaking important school or parent rules.

In the author's opinion, these potential limits to confidentiality should be discussed with the parents and teenager at the first encounter, if at all possible. Parents may assume that the social worker will tell them certain information, and if the social worker learns that information but does not inform the parent, then the parent can feel betrayed. Similarly, the teenager can feel betrayed if the social worker had not forewarned them that the worker could not keep certain information confidential. School social workers, who often informally counsel children without much formal parent contact, can find these recommendations particularly difficult to implement with parents. It may not be possible for them to formally contract with all parents about confidentiality—or about any other issue, for that matter. Some mental health and child welfare professionals may also find these recommendations difficult to implement, because they fear that if they inform the teenager ahead of time about the limits of confidentiality, then the teenager will never talk about the most important issues such as physical abuse or drug abuse that are the very same issues that prompted professional involvement.

However, in addition to the practical benefits of avoiding major confrontations later, it is recommended that workers address confidentiality early in the helping process because it is a way to metaphorically address the individuation issue. By addressing confidentiality, the worker is indirectly saying that the teenager's privacy is important and is to be respected. Addressing confidentiality early also sets the foundation for a negotiation tenor to the interactions. But because of limits to confidentiality, the teenager, worker, and parents usually must negotiate and reach agreement on what the ground rules will be. This sends a message that negotiation is central to the process.

This contracting process can be arduous and contentious. For example, suppose that the parent of a teenager with alcohol and drug problems initially wants the social worker to reveal incidents of drug and alcohol use. The social worker is willing to respect this parental wish, but the social worker is not willing to do so without informing the teenager of the agreement. The social worker explains to the parent how a secret agreement for the social worker to surreptitiously inform on the teenager would break confidentiality and thus be unethical. It would also severely damage the teenager's trust in adults if the teenager were ever to find out about the agreement. "But," the parents respond, "our teenage son will never tell you about drug use if he knows you are going to tell us!" The social worker empathizes with the dilemma, and offers a compromise. "Suppose that you as parents, your teenager, and I all agree that I will inform you and your teenager when I have information that leads me to believe that the drug and alcohol use is becoming abuse, that it is a problem that is negatively affecting the teenager's functioning. This would allow your son to discuss his drug use in confidence, and he would know directly from me when I thought his drug use was to the point where I needed to inform his parents so that we could all try to help him." Both the parents and the teenager might respond by asking, "What is the difference between use and abuse?" This question could lead to a very productive discussion of each party's point of view on that issue. The parents may believe that any use is abuse, while the teenager may believe that use never could lead to abuse. Through the issue of confidentiality, important substantive work on the presenting problem has begun.

In the end, it is likely that neither the parent nor the teenager will be completely happy with the suggested compromise. The parent might continue to insist that the social worker secretly inform on the teenager, and the teenager might want assurances of total confidentiality. Neither of these positions is tenable to the social worker, so negotiation of disagreement must ensue. This negotiation process is valuable on the process level in that the process itself models and parallels the type of adult-teenager interactions that the social worker hopes to establish between this particular teenager and the adults in the teenager's world. It also enhances the trust building process between parties, because conflicts and disagreements are being discussed openly and respectfully. The negotiation process is also valuable at the content level, because it introduces the distinction between drug use and drug abuse, and it "forces" both the teenager and the parents to struggle with their own definitions of each.

Be Consistent and Genuine. Teenagers need adults who are stable and consistent, to counteract the teenager's own emotional instability and unpredictable nature. Teenagers gain a sense of security when they see that their own volatility will not shake or overpower the solidity of the world around them. This is, of course, easier said than done. It often helps adults to remember and constantly remind themselves not to take the teenager's acting out personally. Usually, the teenager's hostility and anger is not, fundamentally, based on dislike for the adult, although it can appear to be that. More often, the hostility and anger is an expression of the teenager's own struggles relative to individuation and the need for emotional distance. If the adult can view the behavior in those terms, it is easier to remain calm, patient, and steady, because the adult can minimize and control the emotional reactions that stem from personalizing the behavior.

This is not to say that the adult should forego setting limits or never get angry. Genuineness is a trait highly valued by teenagers, who are keenly attuned to phoniness and hypocrisy. Adults need to show genuine interest in teenagers, listen to them, and offer choices, but they also need to be clear and strong about the limits they believe in. When angry or upset, adults should not pretend to be calm and unaffected. When pushed by the teenager, the adult should genuinely and appropriately express anger and model effective conflict resolution. In addition, teenagers value adults that they can depend on. Practitioners must be careful not to promise something that they cannot or do not deliver. Follow-through is a must—if you say you are going to do something, be sure to do it.

The importance of genuineness was noted years ago by Seymour Halleck (1963) when he discussed the negative consequences of professional dishonesty with teenagers. Denial, rationalization, and displacement of anger are some of the categories of "lies" that professionals have commonly exhibited. Halleck asserted that adolescents, especially troubled ones, cannot be expected to cooperate with adults who are unwilling to admit that they sometimes find teenagers intolerable. Halleck also exposed the lie of adult morality, in which adults portray themselves as being well in control of their aggressive and sexual impulses. In confronting teenagers about their own chaotic sexuality and poorly controlled aggression, adults imply to teenagers that these impulses can be readily controlled, if only the teenagers would be more mature and adult. While it may be unrealistic and inappropriate for workers to reveal all of their own deficiencies and past transgressions, it is also inappropriate and unrealistic for professionals to portray themselves and other adults as superior moral beings.

The following case vignette illustrates how Jon, the social worker in a mental health setting, operationalized the above principles with Moe, a 15-year-old.

CASE VIGNETTE: Moe

Moe is 15, an above average student, and interested in science fiction. He is also severely overweight and mildly depressed. He has little energy for anything, is quiet, and has never had many friends. He also gets in trouble for sneaking around, lying, and ignoring adults.

Moe has lived in foster care for 3 years. He was removed from home due to serious neglect (his parents had serious drug problems and didn't provide for his basic needs) and some physical abuse (slapping and spanking that left bruises). He has lived at a local group home for boys for the last 6 months, since his previous foster parents moved out of state. The whereabouts of Joe's parents are unknown.

Jon has been seeing Moe weekly for counseling for the past 2 months. Moe has great difficulty talking about problems or counseling goals. The group home parents, who referred Moe for counseling, really like Moe and want him to be happier. They also want him to stop lying so much. They think it would help if Moe talked with Jon about his parents and how they mistreated him.

Just 10 minutes before Jon's appointment with Moe, the group home parent calls to inform Jon that Moe was caught engaging in oral sex with one of the other boys in the group home. He and the boy were observed having oral sex in the back of a van when the kids were being transported to an outing. The group home parents grounded Moe for the behavior, restricted other privileges, and warned him that another episode would result in his expulsion from the home. He won't talk about the incident with the group home parents or staff, instead offering feeble denials that he did anything. The houseparents hope Moe will talk with Jon about the incident and that Jon will fill them in.

Before meeting with Moe, Jon considers how he should approach this situation. How can Jon make most purposeful use of himself in the situation? At the beginning of the interview, should Jon tell Moe what the houseparents have told him (which would be consistent with the genuineness or honesty practice principle)? Or should Jon wait for Moe to bring it up (which is consistent with the practice principle about choice and decision making)? If Jon does talk with Moe about the incident, what would Jon ask or say? What issues might this situation provide a window of opportunity to discuss? Will the houseparents consider Jon a failure if Moe refuses to talk with Jon? Should Jon relay what Moe says to him, if he does open up, back to the houseparents?

With little time to think these issues through, Jon calls Moe into the office and begins the interview:

JON: Hey, Moe, how's everything for you today?

MOE: OK, I guess. Nothing special.

JON: (Deciding that he is uncomfortable keeping a "secret" from Moe, yet wanting to afford Joe some choice in the matter.) Listen, Moe, before we get started today, I wanted to let you know that your houseparents called me just a few minutes ago to give me some information about how you've been doing lately, like they do every so often. I don't know what all you have on your list of things to talk about today, but that's one of the things we can talk about, if you want.

MOE: I don't really have anything I want to talk about today. What did the houseparents say about me?

JON: Well, like I said, we don't have to talk about this if you don't want to. But what they told me was that you were caught having sex with another boy in the van a couple of days ago, and they thought it might help if you and I talked about it. (Jon is trying to be brief, nonjudgmental, and respectful of self-determination in Moe's choice of whether or not to discuss the situation. He wants to ask questions that are as open-ended as possible, to allow Moe to point the direction of the interview.)

MOE: Oh, yeah, that. Well, I'm not gay or anything, you don't have to worry about that.

Commentary. In the last response, Moe indicates that the most important aspect of this incident to him may relate to the identity formation issue. Another child might have focused on the punishment, or on the worry that he would be expelled. It was very important that Jon had not directed Moe toward any particular response. Jon may have hoped or expected that this situation would have provided a window of opportunity to focus on Joe's feelings about the rules and consequences in the home, or his feelings of abandonment. He may wonder whether Moe's parents sexually abused him in the past, or whether Moe was the aggressor in this incident. If Jon had hoped and wondered these things, he might have said something like, "The houseparents said they grounded you for having sex in the van with another boy. Is it clear to you that you could be expelled? Are you worried about that?" Or, "Tell me more about what actually happened between you and the other boy. Was it your idea or his?"

Because Jon was open to allowing the interview to be guided by Moe's agenda, he was able to talk with Joe about some very important developmental and identity issues. Following Joe's lead, they talked about what "gay" means to Moe,

and how Jon would accept Moe for who he was, whether he was gay or not. Moe was eventually able to talk about the incident in terms of his feelings of closeness to the other boy. On two occasions in the interview, Moe was reluctant to reveal information for fear that Jon would report back to the houseparents. Because the information did not concern immediate safety issues, Jon was able to assure Moe of confidentiality, and later, in Moe's presence, to inform the houseparents of the nature of the interview in the most general terms.

So the interview that day and later interviews were able to focus on the identity theme and Moe's growing awareness of his emotional needs and how to meet them. In the process, as Moe himself alluded to other important issues, such as Moe's history of sexual abuse, the details of the particular incident, and Moe's reactions to the punishment, then Moe and Jon were able to discuss them. By affording Moe self-determination regarding whether or not he discussed the incident, choice about what aspect of the incident was most important to him, and respect for confidentiality, Jon was able to engage Moe in a therapeutically productive discussion of a potentially explosive issue.

Combating Adultcentrism in Child Welfare

How is adultcentrism typically manifested in child welfare, and what can social workers do to combat it? A real danger in child welfare is for social workers and other adults to superimpose their own agendas and biases about children who have been abused and neglected on those same children, at all stages of the child welfare process.

Combating Adultcentrism in Intake and Investigation

During the intake and investigation of alleged abuse and neglect, adultcentrism can rear its head when the social worker meets with the parents and conducts an individual interview with the child. A neutral, objective stance is essential. If the social worker interviews the parents first, there is danger that the adult social worker could overly empathize and identify with the parent's point of view about the child and the incident, perhaps minimizing the incident and its impact. So, the social worker must guard against this potential adultcentrism by interviewing the child individually and keeping open to hearing the child's point of view. Otherwise, the social worker might not see the need to interview the child, or might approach the child with an already biased point of view.

In a different way, adult bias can also creep into the interview with the child when the adult social worker has a mindset that the alleged abuse did occur and that the child needs help in talking about it. Then, in conducting individual interviews with children, the adult social worker may put words in the child's mouth, or lead the child to say something which the child believes is the "right" answer, the one that the social worker wants to hear. In this situation, it is not the parents' point of view but the social worker's own values and bias that generate the adultcentrism.

Competent interviewing of children is perhaps nowhere more crucial than in the investigation of child abuse. This is especially true for young children, who do not communicate well in words. Faculty at the Erickson Institute for the Advanced Study of Child Development have written an excellent resource to guide child welfare workers and other adults in their efforts to obtain information from and communicate with children (Garbarino, et al., 1989). The book presents over 100 practice principles for interviewing children, principles that consider the impact of child development, cultural diversity, adult bias, and other factors on communication with children. A thorough coverage of these principles is beyond the scope of this book, but a selected few are presented to illustrate the complexity of the task of interviewing children.

Practice Principles for Conducting Investigative Interviews with Children in Child Welfare (adapted from Garbarino, et al., 1989)

- There are few fixed and specific formulas for communicating effectively with children; it is essential that the adult adapt to the characteristics of each child and each situation.

- In general, the more confident and mature the child, the more positively familiar the setting, and the more conversational the inquiry, the more effective the process of communication and the more valid the information will be.

- The more sources of information an adult has about a child, the more likely the adult is to receive the child's messages properly.

- Children rarely invent or fantasize allegations of sexual abuse on their own initiative; adults are a more likely source of false allegations.

- In using play and storytelling, it is important to note the repetition of a theme, for it indicates that the theme has some special meaning for the child.

- Interviewers are responsible for adjusting their interviewing methods to the communicative competencies of the child.

- Children are most likely to offer information that is reliable when talking about events that are part of or related to their own interests or part of their everyday experience.
- School-age children may feel that adult interviewers already know the answers to the questions they are asking and thus may either severely curtail their responses or not respond at all.
- There may be powerful incentives for adults to suppress, ignore, or minimize information from children about the quality of care they receive; this adult disbelief can be a powerful inhibitor to children.
- Those who operate within the legal system must be—or at least must be advised by—informed and sensitive child development experts who can interpret the system for children and interpret children to the system.

Interviewing children who are the alleged victims of sexual abuse presents unique and specific challenges. A widespread interviewing method entails the use of sexually anatomically correct dolls, which are used to facilitate communication with young and reticent children. Because of the dolls' sexual detail, children can demonstrate the abuse they have experienced. But, despite widespread use by a variety of professionals, the dolls remain controversial because it is not clear whether or not the dolls themselves might stimulate demonstrations of sexual activity and abuse by nonabused children. In other words, do the dolls stimulate the type of play and explicit sexual activity among nonabused children that are demonstrated by abused children?

The research on this question is not conclusive. Garbarino and colleagues (1989) concluded that at least three studies (White, Strom, & Santilli, 1986; Sivan, Schor, Koeppl, & Noble, 1988; Goodman & Aman, 1987) have reported that the dolls are not suggestive to children who are not suspected of being abused. However, at least one study (Boat & Everson, 1988) noted extensive demonstrations of sexual activity between dolls by a few children in a sample of nonreferred children, so that the authors of the study concluded that demonstration of sexual abuse cannot be considered a clear indication that abuse has occurred. These findings encourage social workers to be cautious in their interpretation of doll play by children, and to use multiple tools and sources in assessment. While explicit and graphic enactments of sexual and violent behavior with sexually detailed dolls are prob-

ably not normal responses to the dolls, and thus warrant further inquiry, the enactments should not be viewed as proof positive that sexual abuse has occurred.

Combating Adultcentrism in Foster Care

At the stage in the continuum of services when the child may have to come into temporary state custody and out-of-home placement, adultcentrism can manifest itself in not completely informing the child about procedures, and not maximizing choice and decision making regarding the details of the placement process. To combat adultcentrism in the placement process, the worker can provide the child with information about potential placements, seek the child's ideas about potential relatives or friends who could serve as placement resources, and allow the child to visit the chosen placement before a final decision is made. Involving children in the decisions can ultimately make for better child adjustment to the placement (Bush & Gordon, 1982).

Once a child is placed out-of-home, there is a danger that adultcentrism can manifest itself through an emphasis on social control rather than supportive treatment. Many abused and neglected children will exhibit behavioral problems that stem directly from their abusive experiences. If controlling and improving these behaviors through behavior modification and social control are the exclusive or predominant focus of the adult caretakers, then the reasons for the placement can become blurred to the child and adults alike. Although abuse and neglect on the part of the parents was the reason for removal, the child could come to believe that it was the child's own behavior that was responsible for the breakup of the family. The system can perpetuate and solidify this thinking by requiring that the child's behavior must improve before the child can return home. To combat this tendency, social workers and other adults must be vigilant in seeking to help the child and other adults understand the connections between the abuse and the child's behavior, and balance behavioral interventions with cognitive and emotional treatment of the abuse and neglect that are at the roots of the misbehavior. They also must keep clear about the reasons for the removal from home and base reunification on ability of the parents to address and remediate those concerns.

Bibliotherapy can be an effective, nonadultcentric way to help children adjust to foster care and adoption. Children must deal with separation from their biological parents and siblings and adapt to a new living situation, including a new school in many situations. Children's books are an effective way to communicate with children in their own language. When children read about others who were facing similar problems but were able to overcome them, then they can gain new insights about their own situations. They can see that they are not alone, that others have successfully coped and adjusted to foster care and adoption. Depending on the child's age, reading level, and special needs, the social worker and foster parent can select books that can be read and discussed with an adult (Pardeck & Pardeck, 1987). Usually, it is not necessary for the child to make direct, overt connections from the book to the child's own life. The child can be encouraged to discuss the events, themes, and feelings of the characters in the book itself. This indirect approach allows sufficient emotional distance for the child to gain awareness and insights while avoiding direct focus on the self.

Combating Adultcentrism in Adoption

Adults should not assume that all children want to be adopted (Bush & Gordon, 1982). Some, fearing permanent loss of contact with their biological parents or their foster parents, prefer to remain in long-term foster care. To avoid adult projection of bias, each child should be involved in the decision to the extent they are interested and capable to do so. Although researchers have, for the most part, ignored the child's impact on adoption outcome, it is logical to hypothesize that the level of the child's motivation and involvement in the adoption process is predictive of long-term adjustment.

Social workers can help prepare children for adoption by helping them (1) understand and cope with their feelings about the past, (2) understand the difference between biological, foster, and adoptive family roles, (3) deal with separation, and (4) anticipate future success (Fahlberg, 1991).

Compiling a Life Story Book with the child can be one of the most effective mediums for achieving these goals. The Life Story Book is a tool that has been used to help children adjust to placement and foster care since the 1960s (Aust, 1981). The Life Story Book is a scrapbook or photo album that starts with the child's birth and contains photos, drawings, mementos, and memories of the child's life experiences. Together with a foster parent, social worker, or therapist, children create the Life Story Book, and in the process, talk about themselves, their parents, their past experiences, and their expectation for the future. Typically, original birth certificates, photos of family, foster parents, and other important adult figures, and written positive comments from previous caseworkers, relatives, and teachers are included. Adults should use this technique cautiously and introduce it gradually, as many children resist remembering past experiences that were painful or provoke anxiety. After initial excitement, children may resist the Life Story Book and become more confused, aggressive, or self-destructive. The Life Story Book belongs to the child and can be updated as changes occur. Thus, the Life Story Book can remain a source of information, support, and personal history after the adoption and into adult life.

In summary, adultcentrism can be combated in child welfare by the following:

Recommendations to Combat Adultcentrism in Child Welfare

- Conduct individual interviews of children during investigations.

(cont.)

- Involve children in foster placement and adoption decisions.
- Help the foster child and adult caretakers understand the links between the child's behaviors and the abuse or neglect.
- Consider bibliotherapy and Life Story Books to help children adjust to foster care and adoption.

Combating Adultcentrism in Mental Health

Adultcentrism in Assessment and Treatment

As introduced in chapter 2, the assessment process of diagnosing and labeling children can be inherently adultcentric in that the strengths and competencies of the child are not routinely identified or appreciated. Strong adult socialization agendas on the part of teachers and parents can skew our tolerance for individual uniqueness and diversity. The result can be that any behaviors that deviate from those preferred by adults can be viewed as symptoms of mental illness. In the extreme, this process can result in the pathologizing of normal childhood. Where, for example, does a normal level of activity in children stop and ADHD begin? Where do normal teenage mood swings stop and depression or bipolar disorder begin? Despite so-called objective criteria, the assignment of mental disorder is ultimately a subjective judgment of the adults and professionals involved. For example, experts in ADHD have noted that the diagnosis of ADHD occurs when a significant number of adults in the child's environment lose their tolerance for the child's behavior. People with ADHD may not adapt well to situations that require calm, solitary, unemotional responses, yet they may do well in environments that call for a person to be passionate and socially exuberant (Barkley, 1995). Given this reality, does a child with ADHD behaviors have a mental disorder or is there simply a mismatch between the child's strengths and the environment?

Adultcentrism in the assessment phase can be followed by adultcentrism in treatment. Behavior modification is a powerful technology that not only focuses on deficits rather than strengths, but also takes an adult perspective in the definition and treatment process, so that it can be used by adults for inappropriate social control purposes. How often do children identify their own behavior as the problem, compared to how often they see adults and others as the problem? Play therapy, when conducted in a nondirective fashion, is a less adultcentric treatment because it recognizes the need for the adult to communicate with children in children's preferred communication modes of play and activity. Yet play therapy focuses on emotional healing and may not be the modality of choice for children with conduct disorder, ADHD, and other disorders that are primarily behavioral or neurobiological in nature.

Another intervention that combats adultcentrism is the various types of youth mediation or conflict resolution programs that have blossomed in recent years in schools, juvenile justice, neighborhoods, and mental health agencies (Umbreit, 1991). In many of these programs, especially those based in elementary and secondary school settings, youth themselves are trained to be conflict-resolution mediators of peer conflicts. When conflicts erupt in the halls or on playgrounds, student mediators are called in to help the combatants resolve the conflict. These peer mediator programs have been shown to reduce playground conflict and to lower suspension rates for fighting. Even when the mediators are adults, as they are in most juvenile justice and parent-child mediation programs, the message is that youth have the capacity to communicate, negotiate, and compromise— they do not necessarily need, nor do they necessarily benefit from, adult-imposed solutions.

Family therapy can be adultcentric when the therapist does not recognize the power imbalances in families and does not seek out the opinions and perspectives of children. Although the therapist must respect and honor the hierarchy in the family, the therapist does not have to do this to the total exclusion of the child's point of view. Although some authors have encouraged the inclusion of children in family sessions, it has been common practice for many family therapists to work exclusively or primarily with the parents alone or the parents and older, more verbal children (Wachtel, 1994). As discussed in previous chapters, it is important for the professional to conduct separate, individual interviews with children and to honor and validate children's opinions. This does not mean, however, that the practitioner should overrule the decision-making prerogative of parents in families. As discussed previously, the tension between combating adultcentrism and honoring family decision making as a part of family-centered practice is ongoing, just as it is in parenting when parents struggle with how much control and input to afford children based on their age, maturity, and other factors.

Informed Consent from Children

Across the assessment and treatment process, the extent to which the child should be included in the decision making is a controversial subject. Perhaps the subject is nowhere more controversial than in the area of medication. What constitutes informed consent for medications for mental disorders in children? Does the concept of informed consent even apply in this situation, where the parent perhaps should have the total power of decision making? Do professionals practice informed coercion in the guise of informed consent?

Krener and Mancina (1994) have addressed these issues in a thoughtful article that recognizes the complexity of the issue, addresses the ethical dilemmas involved, and offers guidelines for informed consent with minors to guide practitioners in this area. The following material is condensed from their article. Although the model is specific to informed consent for medications, the principles involved can be generalized to other forms of work with children as well.

Legally, informed consent from a minor is not required for medical procedures except those involving consent for participation in research protocols. Rather, consent for a child must be obtained by proxy, from the authorized adult. Children are considered by law to lack the competence to make medical decisions. Yet professionals are well aware that the cognitive competence of children varies by age and developmental level, and that many children have a definite will and opinion about their own care. So, although there is no legal requirement to obtain the child's consent directly, clinical and ethical concerns may point to a more complete consent process than is required by law.

The ideal consent process involves the parent(s), the child, and others such as mental health or school staff. Ideally, agreement is obtained from all parties before the child takes medication. Coercion of the child can lead to mistrust and conflict that can spill over into other areas of the adult-child relationship. If children are informed about the reasons for taking the medicine and its potential benefits, cooperation can more readily be obtained than by telling the child that he or she has to take the medicine. If the child is reluctant, a trial period can be proposed as a compromise, so that the child does not think they have to take the medication forever.

One way to negotiate this potential minefield is to distinguish between informed *consent* and informed *assent*. For legal and ethical reasons, the child cannot officially give his or her consent, but that does not mean that the adult should not explain matters to the child and attempt to gain his or her assent to the helping process. This idea of assent has relevance in the mental health arena beyond formal helping procedures, such as the taking of medications. In all of the forms of therapy described in chapter 3, the practitioner can inform the child of the process, answer questions, and otherwise explain things on the child's level. The child's reactions and questions may lead to modifications that enhance the child's participation, motivation, and feelings of ownership. Even if the child does not agree with the total plan, the child has a clear idea of what is being done and why.

Empowering the Voice of Youth

Youth with serious emotional and behavioral disorders are rarely consulted about their own opinions about the services they receive, nor have these been helped to form their own self-help and advocacy organizations (Choi, 2000). At least two avenues are available for empowering the voice of these youth as a group: consumer satisfaction surveys and consumer-run organizations. When adults have taken the time to systematically survey the opinions and satisfaction of youth, important and sometimes surprising information can be gleaned. A discussion of the results of a statewide consumer satisfaction survey is presented in chapter 11.

Petr, Holtquist, and Martin (2000) advocate for youth-run consumer organizations that can meet the developmental, transitional, and associational needs of these youth. The idea of consumer-run organizations for youth stems from the success of similar organizations for adult consumers and the families of children with mental disorders. As successful as these organizations are, they are not designed to meet the needs of youth. Adolescents with emotional and behavioral disorders do not seek role models from among adults with severe mental illness, and their developmental need for individuation from their parents makes participation in family-run organizations problematic. A consumer-run organization for youth could provide opportunities for peer activities and support, information on educational and employment opportunities, and opportunities to become politically active. Barriers to the formation of such organizations identified by the authors included sponsorship, funding, and leadership. Ideally, sponsorship of the group would come from an existing mainstream organization for youth such as the YMCA or a community recreation cen-ter, with support and training from parents and mental health professionals. Funding could come from private organizations or from the state mental health department as a regular line in their budget. Young consumers are not likely to have the knowledge, skills, or confidence to provide the initial leadership to get such an organization established, so the leaders to spearhead such an organization would probably have to drawn from parents and mental health professionals, who would gradually hand over leadership functions to the youth themselves.

An example of one such youth organization is the Health in Action program in King County, Washington (Stevenson, 2000). Young people aged 13–20 have established their own mission and goals aimed at making changes in the system of care. By sharing their experiences with the system, the group hopes to recruit more youth interested in making changes in the system, to develop mentoring for youth in the system, to support youth leadership training and participation, and to sustain a community of active youth who are ongoing participants and leaders in the system.

CHAPTER 4 SUMMARY

This chapter has presented and discussed the concept of adultcentrism, the tendency of adults to view children from a biased, adult perspective. Adults tend to view children as incomplete and incompetent compared to adults. This tendency can lead to miscommunication, inappropriately high or low expectations, an overemphasis on socialization and social control, and undermining strengths and competencies.

The chapter elaborated on several strategies for social workers to employ to combat adultcentrism. These strategies included entering the world of children, gaining knowledge of how children are when they are free of adult influence and interaction, through direct observation of children in natural settings. Policymakers and direct practitioners should seek out the opinions of children and maximize self-determination. It is important for social workers to communicate with children in their own language: the nonverbal and indirect language of activity, play, and metaphor.

Considerable attention was paid to combating adultcentrism in the engagement and interviewing process. For young children, the use of drawings, unstructured play, and open-ended questions are congruent with their own preferred modes of communication. Vigilant caution must be maintained in the interpretation of meaning from these communications. When communicating with teenagers, it is vital that the social worker understand the central issues and tasks related to the core developmental theme of identity formation. Teenagers need to separate and individuate from their families, and they want to spend inordinate amounts of time with their friends; they strive to avoid feelings of dependence; they want and need privacy; they search for a place to belong outside the family; they need to develop a sense of competence and self-management through decision making; and they struggle to cope with developing sexuality and emotional mood swings. In relationships with adolescents, the chapter recommended that social workers offer choices and promote negotiation; address confidentiality early in the helping process, with both teenagers and their parents; and be as consistent and genuine as possible.

Specific suggestions were offered on how to combat adultcentrism in child welfare, from intake and investigation to foster care and adoption. In the children's mental health field, combating adultcentrism involves vigilance in the assessment and treatment process, attention to informed consent issues, and youth empowerment.

CHAPTER 5

Pragmatic Perspective 2: Family-Centered Practice

Overview

One of the contemporary trends in service delivery to children and families is termed *family-centered practice*. This chapter is divided into three sections. In the first section, family-centered practice is defined and its three major components are thoroughly explicated. Specific pragmatic connections of abstract concepts are provided in the form of a case vignette and specific guidelines for how to engage and interview families. The first section concludes with pragmatic connections to the fields of policy and research. The second and third sections discuss ways in which family-centered practice applies in child welfare and children's mental health.

What Is Family-Centered Practice?

(This section is adapted from Allen & Petr, 1996.)

Since its inception as a profession at the turn of the century, social work has been concerned with both children and families. The specific term *family-centered* has been used to describe a preferred form of service delivery in social work since at least the 1950s (Birt, 1956). The term *family-centered* has also been used in other disciplines, across service systems, and in federal legislation. Family-centered services are often deemed to be essential to the process of achieving better child and family well-being outcomes. If the family as a social institution is to be supported and strengthened, then professionals must place the entire family in the center of the process, not the individual child. Despite its broad use, the term *family-centered* can still cause confusion because it can mean different things to different people.

Definition. Family-centered service delivery, across disciplines and settings, recognizes the centrality of the family in the lives of individuals. It is guided by fully informed choices made by the family and focuses upon the strengths and capabilities of these families (Allen & Petr, 1996).

The above definition of the term was the result of an extensive cross-disciplinary literature review of 120 professional articles that included 28 separate definitions.

The definition emphasizes three core elements of family-centered practice: the family as the unit of attention, informed choice, and a strengths perspective.

Family as the Unit of Attention

Of the 28 definitions reviewed, all (100%) made some reference to the family as the central unit of concern and attention. Family-centered practice recognizes that children cannot be served appropriately without diligent consideration of the family with whom they live. The entire family becomes the focus of assessment, planning, and intervention. For the direct-service social work professional, focusing on the core element of the family means always considering the child to be, first and foremost, a member of a family. Whenever a family-centered professional seeks to help an individual child, that professional believes that the child's family is the most important source of support and influence in the child's life, and the best way for the professional to help the child is to support the child's family in providing for the child's needs.

Historically, service providers across disciplines have tended to focus exclusively on the child, resulting in what has been termed *child-centered* service delivery. Professionals have historically been trained to diagnose and work with individual children. If the family was considered at all, it was viewed as the source of the problems, as an obstacle to the child's growth, or as irrelevant to the intervention process. Families have disputed and resented this approach and have pushed for changes in service delivery systems. Parents, not professionals, have been the primary impetus for change toward a family-centered approach in which the family is the central unit of attention (Collins & Collins, 1990; Turnbull & Turnbull, 1990).

Today's professionals remain ambivalent about whether to focus on the children in need of services or on their families. As introduced in chapter 1, this ambivalence is rooted in a mentality first exhibited during the Progressive Era of the early twentieth century. Children's problems were viewed as the result of poor parenting by people who had character flaws that caused the children's difficulties. Under this paradigm, the professional's superiority was assumed, and the choice about the nature of the care was removed from the child, the family, and public scrutiny. So although service delivery was child-centered, it was also adultcentric and professional-centered, because the professional was the expert who dominated decision making.

The White House Conference on Families in 1979 laid the foundation for political initiatives that began to focus on the needs and capacities of

families, not individual children (Langley, 1991). This conference reflected the growing influence of the *family support* movement, which argues that sufficient community support is essential to enable families to take care of their own members (Singer, Powers, & Olson, 1996). Family support programs are designed to strengthen individual and family functioning in ways that empower people to act on their own behalf (Dunst, Trivette, Starnes, Hamby, & Gordon, 1993).

The family as a social institution is under considerable strain and is in danger of crumbling. Parents today face unprecedented cultural obstacles in raising their children, to the extent that parents feel they must protect their children from the ravages of a hostile environment (Mack, 1997). If the family as a social institution is to survive, then society must do more to support the abilities of families to care for their children. Focusing on individual children as the unit of attention in service delivery has tended to undermine the integrity of families, as professionals substituted their own knowledge and expertise for that of parents. Rather than being a support to parents, professionals have tended to criticize, blame, and supplant them.

Informed Family Choice

Belief in the family's competence to make informed decisions is the second core element of family-centered practice. The family is viewed as the consumer and director of the service delivery process, as the party that has ultimate decision-making authority. Thus a family-centered approach would maximize family choice in each of the following areas: the definition of the family; who will make decisions for the family; the unit of attention of the service delivery process; the nature of the family-professional relationship; the sharing of information; and the identification of needs, goals, and interventions.

Choice Regarding the Definition of the Family. Merriam-Webster's Collegiate Dictionary defines *family* as "a group of individuals living under one roof and usually under one head." This definition is an adequate starting point for an understanding of family-centered practice and certainly improves upon the dyadic (parent-child or mother-child) view of the family often encountered in practice. However, family-centered service delivery allows—in fact, requires—the family itself to define its boundaries, to decide who is a part of it and who is not. The definition of family proposed by the Commission on Families of the National Association of Social Workers better suits family-centered practice: a family is "two or more people who consider themselves family and who assume obligations, functions, and responsibilities generally essential to healthy family life" (Barker, 1991, p. 80).

Ho (1987) and others remind us that ethnicity and culture, among other things, affect our thinking about family membership and structure. Extended family ties tend to be strong among ethnic minority families and may play a vital part in the functioning of the family. Even nonrelatives, such as pastors and close friends, may be considered and function as members of the family. The family-centered practitioner respects the choice of the family as to who is a part of it and incorporates their definition into the design of service delivery.

Choice Regarding Who Makes Decisions. Although the ultimate incarnation of family-centered practice might involve all family members in reaching consensus decisions about service delivery, such consensus is not always possible or desirable. Consistent with family systems theory, caregivers of families—usually the parents—are recognized as the heads of the household and, therefore, the primary decision makers for the unit. Family-centered practitioners encourage each family member to be as involved as possible in the service-delivery process and acknowledge the normality of conflict that may result (Friesen & Koroloff, 1990), but this does not alter the position that the parents/caregivers ultimately must be responsible for making choices regarding care.

Recognizing parents as the primary decision makers in families does not negate the perspective that family members and professionals need to maximize the self-determination options for those children, especially as they grow into adolescence and adulthood. Thus, a family-centered approach needs to guard against adultcentrism. Just as it is not suggested that professionals preempt the roles and choices of parents, it is not suggested that parents assume responsibilities that could be accepted by or make decisions that could be made by their children. The growth and empowerment of the child do not have to be ignored as the family unit is supported.

Choice Regarding the Unit of Attention. The family-centered professional respects the family's right to choose who among them will be involved in the service delivery process. The practitioner must initiate contact with the family unit in some form, and the dyad of the child and primary caregiver is a reasonable starting point. However, over time, the professional must respond to the wishes of the family regarding the expansion or reduction of this unit of attention.

Choice Regarding the Nature of the Family-Professional Relationship. In family-centered service delivery, the family also makes choices regarding the nature of the family-professional relationship (Leviton, Mueller, & Kauffman, 1992). At the logistical level, the family should be afforded choices about the times and places for meetings, so that services are accessible to them at times and places that are convenient.

In professional-directed approaches to care, the professional is in charge of care and the family as a unit may be either avoided entirely or else involved in service delivery in ways that are determined by the professional and serve that person's goals. The dominant family-professional style advocated by current family-centered practitioners emphasizes collaboration, in which professionals and families are equal partners and work together as a team toward mutually defined goals (Friesen & Koroloff, 1990). A recent emphasis of family-centered models goes beyond the concept of collaboration by placing the family firmly in control of the service delivery process, with the professional serving as the agent of the family (Dunst, Trivette, Davis, & Cornwell, 1988; Tower, 1994). As professionals at the Kennedy Institute's Department for Family Support Services found in their work with parents of children with special needs, parents value professionals' knowledge and clinical expertise in relation to their child; however, they state that only they have the necessary expertise to determine whether the recommendations of professionals can be successfully incorporated into their own families' lifestyles (Leviton,

TABLE 5.1
Family-Centered Continuum

Range of Parent-Professional Relationship	View of Parents
Professional-Centered	Adversary (parents are the problem)
	Student or patient (dependent on expertise of professional)
	Partner (but family is the agent of the professional, who determines roles and responsibilities
	Colleague (parents are consumers who have expertise and knowledge)
Family-Centered	Employer (professionals are the agents of families)

Adapted from Dunst, Johanson, Trivette, & Hamby (1991).

et al., 1992). The Institute's model of service delivery conceptualizes the professional role as one of "consultant." This relationship is somewhat analogous to the employer-employee relationship, in which the professional works *for* the family, not just *with* the family, as is emphasized in collaboration models.

The nature of the parent-professional relationship can be conceptualized as a continuum, with professional-centered approaches at one end and family-centered at the other end (see table 5.1). As one moves along the continuum, parents are viewed less as adversaries and more as partners and colleagues. At the farthest end of the continuum, professionals view themselves as the employees of the family.

This model of family-professional relationship does not mean that professionals never give their opinion, or never disagree with the family. Just as employees will occasionally disagree with their employer, professionals are obligated to offer their point of view to the family in a respectful and timely way. For example, the professional may think that certain information would be helpful to obtain from the parents to understand a situation better, or the professional may think that a certain course of action would be more productive than another. Certainly, these professional opinions should be shared. But if the professional and the family disagree, the professional defers to the wisdom of the family, unless there is some overriding legal or ethical issue.

Choice Regarding the Sharing of Information.
In family-centered practice, information flows in both directions, and the family is in control of the information it discloses as well as the information

it receives (Dunst, 1991; Leviton, et al., 1992). Only relevant information is requested, and the family is given choices about the medium in which the material is provided, for example during face-to-face interviews instead of filling out a form. As members of the intervention team, family members have access to the same information (files, reports, case notes, etc.) as other team members and control over how information from various sources is shared (Collins & Collins, 1990). Families differ regarding the amount of information they want from professionals, and the family-centered practitioner offers them choices about how much information they are given regarding their child's and their situation, the activities of the professionals involved, and community resources. This approach to care attempts to maximize the family's choices as to the form in which the information is provided—for example, whether the information is shared verbally or in written or videotaped formats. Regardless of format, communication between family members and professionals should be as free of jargon and of patronizing and blame-laden language as possible (Collins & Collins, 1990; Leviton, et al., 1992).

Choice Regarding the Identification of Needs, Goals, and Intervention. Family-centered practice begins by identifying child and family needs, strengths, resources, and goals as the family sees them (Dunst, et al., 1988; Friesen & Koroloff, 1990; Turnbull & Turnbull, 1990). The professional may present additional potential areas of concern to the family for their consideration, acknowledging their right to accept or refuse these ideas. The child's and parents' situations are viewed holistically within the context of the broader family, so that the consideration of needs and goals is as comprehensive as the family wishes it to be, regardless of the presenting concern.

Just as the family makes choices regarding the identification of needs and goals, so also does it provide suggestions and make choices regarding the interventions that are used to reach these goals (Jones, Garlow, Turnbull, & Barber, 1996). Professionals and family members together compile as extensive an array as possible of intervention options and of formal and informal resources needed to meet the goals of the family. Family members are given a full explanation of the potential costs and benefits of each option and whatever other assistance is needed to help them develop a plan from among their options. In the process, the family and professional negotiate their respective responsibilities for implementing the plan.

The family also maintains the right to choose the level and nature of its involvement in the service delivery process. As Turnbull and Summers (1987) note, some families want to be decision makers and some do not; some place a priority on implementing home intervention programs and others do not; some like support groups, some benefit from written self-help materials, some wish to be designated as team leaders or as case managers—and others do not. Families may choose to avail themselves of some service options and not others; and in fact, some families may choose not be involve themselves with the formal service delivery system at all. Family-centered professionals must maintain a flexible perspective on how family members may be involved in the helping process and expect the nature of this involvement to differ from family to family and, within any one family, to change over time.

Limits to Choice. As discussed above, the principle of maximizing family choice and decision making does not preclude professionals from voicing their professional opinion, offering their expertise, or disagreeing with the family. Thus, the process is not one in which the family dictates to the professionals, but one in which families make informed decisions based on collaboration and consultation with professionals. Even then, the idea of families making as many decisions as possible is a complex, sensitive, and controversial issue that requires attention to the limits of that

decision making—to times and circumstances in which family decision making is restricted.

Although family choice is central to the concept of family-centeredness, there are limits to any person's self-determination, in any sphere of activity. First, the person must have the capacity to make the choice. Some family members may be too young or have too severe a mental disability to make fully informed choices. However, family-centered practice takes a broad view of capacity, believing in the strengths and capabilities of families to make reasonable, informed decisions and in their right to make decisions that may differ from those of professionals (Finkelstein, 1980). When in a genuine crisis state, family members may need the professional to make decisions because they are temporarily overwhelmed and cannot decide what to do. In effect, during these situations, the family members can decide that they want the professionals to decide what to do.

Second, the parent or family must be ready and willing to assume responsibility for decisions. In terms of family members of infants in neonatal intensive care units, research has indicated that families want to be introduced to their role of decision-maker gradually and to be taught the skills they need to be effective in this role (Summers, Behr, & Turnbull, 1989). Professionals must attempt to determine the readiness of family members to participate in the service delivery process and to offer opportunities for involvement based upon these levels of readiness.

Third, self-determination cannot infringe upon the rights of others or violate laws. Choices must be made within a legal framework that respects the rights of all parties. For example, professionals do not sanction parents' choices to physically, emotionally, or sexually abuse their children.

Fourth, a person cannot "self-determine" how another should behave. Even though the family-centered practitioner is the "employee" of the family, employees cannot and should not always do what the employer asks. Professionals are obligated to inform families when they disagree about means or ends, when they are being asked to do something of which they are not capable, when what the family wishes conflicts with limits of the professional's expertise or licensure or with limits placed by the organization that employs them, or when they cannot perform or condone certain behaviors because they are illegal or unethical.

Fifth, logistical considerations also can limit the choices of families. Often, needed resources may not be available to fulfill all the wishes of a family. The cost of services can be prohibitive, and difficult decisions sometimes must be made regarding the allocation of scarce resources to underserved populations (Jones, et al., 1996).

Strengths Perspective

The third core element of family-centered practice is a commitment to family strengths and capabilities. (The strengths perspective will be discussed in more detail as pragmatic perspective 3 in the next chapter.) One cannot engage in family-centered practice without having a strong belief in the importance of the family and a strong respect for the inherent strength and capability of family members. Too often, across disciplines, professionals have focused almost exclusively upon the deficiencies of children and families, to the extent that families feel under attack rather than supported by the very people who have been trained to be helpful. Family-centered service delivery is an antidote to this blaming of families and represents a significant shift in the way in which professionals and families consider each other.

In this approach to service delivery, an awareness of and respect for families' positive attributes, abilities, talents, resources, and aspirations guides the help-giving process (Saleebey, 1992). The professional sometimes may need to encourage family members themselves to adopt this perspective by helping them to identify as strengths relevant aspects of their life of which they lack conscious awareness, which they take for granted, or which they have viewed only as problems but which have functional, productive qualities.

Family-centered professionals are committed to finding the strengths and capabilities of children and families, to using those strengths to overcome deficiencies, and to support rather than criticize. Strengths come in a variety of forms, and practitioners must be creative and open-minded in their perspectives of what makes a certain characteristic or behavior a positive contribution to a family's life. This attitude can be challenged when professionals interact with families who are different from themselves in race, culture, sexual orientation, or socioeconomic status. The family-centered professional must guard against judging competency through an ethnocentric lens that distorts or clouds the strengths and competencies of other, different cultures and lifestyles.

The functional aspects of a particular family's life must be identified, sanctioned, and expanded to those areas that do not work as well. Professionals may not learn about a family's capabilities because social systems fail to create opportunities for them to be displayed (Dunst, et al., 1988). One of the functions of the professional, then, is to create such opportunities, thereby enabling the family to apply the full repertoire of skills they possess.

There is evidence that many members of families with children with special needs feel that their lives have been enhanced and strengthened by the presence of those children. They report, among other things, that the experience has made them and their families stronger, that they have become more patient and compassionate, that they have a greater appreciation for the simple things in life, that their religious faith has been strengthened, that their social networks and career opportunities have expanded, that they feel a greater sense of love and joy in their lives, and that they have a greater appreciation of the value of different kinds of people (Summers, et al., 1989). Clearly, family members bring to the help-giving process attributes that are to be valued and respected and that can drive the service delivery process in positive, affirming directions.

Pragmatic Connection: Case Illustration of Family-Centered Practice

One of the pragmatic implications of family-centered principles for the direct-service practitioner is that family-centeredness can help the worker to define the client, and thus to focus the work, in situations in which defining the client is difficult and complex. Because the first element of family-centered practice is to define the family as the unit of attention, it follows that family-centered social workers should endeavor to define families as their clients. In social work practice classes and texts, much attention is placed on being "client-centered." Client-centeredness is also emphasized for social work practice at the indirect, or administrative, levels of social work practice (Rapp & Poertner, 1992). In client-centered work, social workers focus intently on listening to what the client's wants and needs are, helping the client to formulate goals and interventions that are client generated and thus highly relevant to the client's life space. Being client-centered helps enhance client motivation and maximizes the social work value of self-determination.

Despite the attention paid to being client-centered, little attention is paid to defining who the client actually is. The presumptive mind-set is that social workers work with individual adults, that the individual adult is asking for some help and is thus defined as the client. While this situation may hold for many social workers, and while it may be expedient and strategic to simplify situations for beginning-level students, defining the client in the child and family arena is seldom such a simple task. Beginning practitioners who oversimplify this important process run the risk of encountering serious difficulty.

Consider the following situation, one that exemplifies the difficulty that social workers often have in determining exactly who they are working for; in other words, exactly who is the client.

CASE VIGNETTE: Johnson Family

Jon, the social worker at the mental health center, gets a referral for services from a teacher, Mrs. Jones, at the local school. According to Mrs. Jones, Randall Johnson, a 9-year-old boy, is acting up in class. He often shouts angrily at her, fights with other children, and refuses to do his homework. Mrs. Jones feels that he needs evaluation and treatment for his apparent conduct disorder. She has talked with Randall's mother, Brenda, about the situation and she has agreed to bring Randall to the mental health center for evaluation.

When Jon meets with Randall's mother, he learns that she has a different view of the situation. Brenda believes that the teacher, who is white, is overreacting and perhaps prejudiced against Randall, who is biracial. Brenda reports that she and her husband have no problem with Randall's behavior at home, and that the school personnel need to be less critical and more supportive of Randall so that he can experience school as a more positive and nurturing place. She feels excluded by the school and has been frustrated in her attempts to communicate and work together with Mrs. Jones.

When Jon meets with Randall, he learns that Randall has yet a third perspective on the situation. Randall agrees that he has been acting up in school, but he likes Mrs. Jones and is confident that he can get his behavior under control by himself, because it isn't as bad or serious as Mrs. Jones thinks it is. Randall's main concern is his parents. Randall has been wanting to spend more time with his friends, but his parents don't like them and don't allow him to play with them much. Also, Randall and his parents have argued loudly about the issue and he has gotten spanked for seeing the friends without permission.

Commentary. The teacher, Mrs. Jones, sees Randall as the problem and wants Jon to work with Randall to improve his behavior. Randall's mother, Brenda, believes that the school and Mrs. Jones are the problem, not Randall. She wants Jon to change how the school personnel and Mrs. Jones view Randall. Randall himself believes that his behavior at school is only a minor problem that he can correct by himself. He sees his parents as the problem and wants Jon's help to get them to let him see his friends more often. The teacher essentially says, "Shape up the child!" The parent says, "Shape up the school!" The child says, "Shape up my parents!"

So who is Jon's client? Who is he working for? The principal actors in this scenario have very different expectations and goals—whose expectations and goals are to take precedence? Different professionals might well answer the question differently, depending on their own training, experiences, values, and sensitivity to organizational and financial pressures.

For example, suppose that Jon had just recently received a memo from the director of the mental health center where he works that apprised the staff of the center's financial difficulties. In the memo, the director noted that the center had recently suffered financial setbacks due to drastically fewer numbers of clients referred to the center by community agencies, most particularly the school system. The director warned that layoffs were possible if the situation did not improve, and advised staff to be particularly sensitive to communications with referral sources, particularly the local schools. In this circumstance, would Jon not be likely to view the teacher as his primary client, as the person whom he was essentially working for and most accountable to? Would he not be likely to focus on the child as the problem?

Or suppose that Jon had received professional training that emphasized a child-centered approach to practice. The training curriculum was heavy on child development, individual and group play therapy, and children's rights. Children's misbehavior was seen as a response to family dysfunction, and the behavior could be improved by a combination of sensitive, corrective emotional experiences provided by the professional in individual sessions with the child, and family meetings in which the professional educated the parents about the child's needs and the ways they should meet them. The curriculum emphasized that the professional was the expert whose role was to help the family better understand and deal with the child, while helping the child adjust and cope with the emotional impact of the negative environment in individual sessions. In this circumstance, would Jon not be likely to view the child as the client, as the person whom he was trying most to help? Would he not tend to focus on the parents as needing to change?

Finally, consider the professional in Jon's position who is himself a parent of a special-needs bi-racial child. Suppose that his own experience with the school system has not been a positive one, and he fully understands how the school system can fail children and blame parents. His experience with the school in some ways mirrors Brenda's. Additionally, his professional training emphasized the importance of the social environment on children's behavior, and warned against "blaming the victim." Instructors and coursework encouraged professionals to take a strong advocacy position to change the social context, rather than targeting individuals for change. In this circumstance, would Jon not be likely to view the parent, Brenda, as his client and join with her in attempting to change Mrs. Jones and the school?

Experienced professionals might respond to the question "Who is the client?" by answering "All of the above." When a professional chooses just one player in the complicated world of children and families as his or her client, the work may be simplified and more focused, to some extent, but the risk of failure is high if all of the principal players do not see some benefit to them from participating in the process. Any one party can sabotage progress, and the key is finding common issues and goals that everyone can invest in. Ideally, then, all three of the key actors in this scenario (teacher, child, mother) should be viewed as clients, and all of their concerns and perspectives should receive equal weight. Yet, this ideal situation is much easier said than done. People do not always want to work together, and even when the desire and motivation to work together is there, they may not be able to find common ground. In addition, the validation of the point of view of certain actors may be more important to the overall achievement of outcomes than the validation of other perspectives.

Because of these complex and difficult realities, it is important to have a guiding philosophy and value frame that can help guide the social worker's approach to situations such as the above. The worker's orientation has implications not only for the specific case, but also for long-range policy and program impact. That is, if all professionals were consistently child-centered, what would the world of child and family services look like? What if everyone was consistently professional-centered? We have seen the poor overall results of the traditional child-centered and professional-centered approaches. Is it time to give family-centered approaches a chance to work?

Returning to Jon and his dilemma, how can the philosophy of family-centeredness help him identify the client and, thus, guide his practice? If Jon were a family-centered social worker, how would he initially address the situation?

First of all, on the phone with the teacher, Jon would acknowledge and validate Mrs. Jones's concerns, agree that the situation seemed to warrant further evaluation (perhaps eventually to include direct observation by Jon at the school), and let her know that his first step would be to meet with Randall and his mother to find out their respective points of view. With this approach, Jon would acknowledge and validate the teacher's concerns while clearly noting the importance of establishing rapport and trust with the family. Jon would also mention that the referral is an appropriate one because his agency is concerned for the welfare of children and families in the community, and tries to help kids and their families be successful. These statements begin to operationalize and communicate the first aspect of family-centered practice: the family is the unit of attention. The client, or unit of attention, is not the child alone, nor the school in which the problems are occurring. The unit of attention is first and foremost the child within his family; the child and family's interactions with the school are important, but the school is not itself the unit of attention.

Next, Jon would symbolically reinforce that the family is the unit of attention by meeting first with Randall and Brenda together, not separately, unless Brenda objected. Jon would communicate to them, as he did to Mrs. Jones on the phone, that his role and focus was to help Randall and his family be successful (to get what they want and need) in the community. He would communicate this orientation early to Brenda, so that she would be clear that the concerns of herself, her child, and the rest of the family are Jon's principal focus. In order to fully include Randall as part of the family process, and to combat Jon's own potential for adultcentrism, Jon would request that Brenda permit him to meet individually with Randall. He would explain that, in this way, Jon and Brenda could obtain information about how Randall views the situation, and thus be as clear as possible.

Jon would stress that this information could be important to Brenda's decision-making process about how to understand the situation and planning what to do about it.

These actions begin to incorporate the second element of family-centered practice: informed choice. Jon makes it clear that Brenda is in charge of the decision-making process, but he also indicates that his orientation is toward the family, not just the parent. In other words, neither the parent alone, nor the child alone, is the client. The unit of attention (client) for Jon is the family. Later in the first interview, Jon would ask for information and opinions from both about several other issues, but Jon would support Brenda making the ultimate decisions about each of these issues. These other issues would include when to meet, where to meet, who in the nuclear and extended family is to be involved in the meetings, and when and how to involve Mrs. Jones and the school.

The control of the decision-making process is key to defining who is the client. The social worker must ask, "Who should be in charge here, who is it that is best to make decisions about this child?" A family-centered practitioner believes in supporting families first and foremost, so strives to have families make as many decisions as possible. This is the essence of family-centered practice, because families who are in control of decision making are truly at the center of the process.

In many families, the idea that families are to make decisions may translate to one or both of the parents making the decisions, with little or no input from the children, in rather adultcentric fashion. In Jon's situation, for example, Brenda might not want Jon to interview Randall separately, and might not be terribly interested in Randall's point of view. Unless this results in abuse or neglect of the children, the family-centered practitioner will accept this situation, though not necessarily approve of it. One of the choices afforded to families is the choice about what decision-making processes and hierarchy is best for them. Although the social worker may point out the pros and cons of various options, and may even tell the family that he or she disagrees with the way decisions are made, in the end, the family-centered practitioner accepts how a given family does things in their family, unless serious legal or ethical issues such as abuse and neglect are involved. Although it is not always easy to draw this legal and ethical line, the social worker cannot force parents and other family members to be less adultcentric, and in the end must accept a wide range of diversity and difference in family styles, some of which derives from racial and cultural differences.

What the social worker can do is focus on self, combating adultcentric attitudes and behaviors within himself or herself. The social worker can also present information about the potential benefits of a less adultcentric approach to decision making, without ever asserting that the social worker knows best what should be done. The social worker may even express the opinion that a certain course of action is preferable, offering this "dissenting" opinion in the spirit of providing the parents with additional information that might be useful to them. Whenever the professional indicates that he or she knows what is best and dictates any course of action, then the professional undermines the family by not believing in their competence.

One cornerstone of the strengths perspective is this same belief that families can and should decide what is best for their family. Family-centered practitioners respect family choice because they believe in the competence and decision-making capability of families. The strengths perspective informs family-centered practice in other ways as well. In the above case example, Jon could begin to operationalize this strengths perspective by alerting the family that part of his job is to help people to see and build on their strengths, to counter the tendency to get overly negative and critical. An initial "strengths assessment" of the child, parents, teacher, and school would be a part of this process. Jon would constantly be alert for opportunities to compliment the child and parents. Jon might strive to begin and end each meeting with family members acknowledging something positive about other family members. (More on the strengths perspective is included in chapter 6 on pragmatic perspective 3.)

Summary of Essential Elements of Family-Centered Practice

This section has presented the critical elements of family-centered practice: the family as the unit of

attention, informed choice, and a strengths perspective. Family-centered practice can help guide the social worker in critical stages of the helping process—initially, by defining the client as the family; later, by structuring the interactions with the family toward maximizing family decision making and utilizing a strengths perspective. Defining the family as the unit of attention is only the first step in family-centered practice, for it is the way that the family is treated by the professional that distinguishes family-centered practice from other forms of professional practice. A case scenario was presented in which the pragmatic usefulness of the concept was demonstrated and discussed.

This scenario underscored that a critical tension in operationalizing a family-centered approach is the potential danger that family-centeredness can lead to acceptance of adultcentric decision making within families. Parents vary greatly on how much input and involvement they allow their children to have in family decisions. In more authoritarian families, if family-centered practice means respecting the hierarchy and decision-making processes within a family, how can the social worker do this and maximize the self-determination of the children (combat adultcentrism) at the same time? Although this tension can never be fully resolved, social workers are encouraged to respect and ultimately accept family decisions as long as they do not result in outright abuse and neglect of children or violate laws and policies. Social workers can focus their efforts to combat adultcentrism on the social worker's own actions and attitudes toward children, and on informing the parents about the potential benefits of a less adultcentric decision-making style. The role of the professional is to make suggestions and offer options for the family to consider.

Pragmatic Connection: How to Engage and Interview Families

Social workers across all agencies that serve children and families must know how to engage families in the helping process. The key to successful engagement is sensitive, family-centered interviewing that respects the integrity of the family, affords choices, and focuses on strengths. The following *Do*s and *Don't*s of family interviewing offer clear and specific guidelines for interviewing families that operationalize family-centered principles.

Family Interviewing *Do*s and *Don't*s

Do:

- Make connections with each individual.
- Respect family hierarchy.
- Explore each person's view of the problem(s).
- Use compliments.
- Respect the sanctity of the variability of family rules and customs.
- Offer some hope of change for the better.

Don't:

- Criticize parents in front of their children.
- Enforce rules or correct children's behavior directly—work through the parents.
- Offer advice prematurely.

Do

Do Make Connections with Each Individual. In initial interviews, family members can be understandably tense and apprehensive. Take a few minutes to visit with each person in the family. Offer coffee or something else to drink and encourage people to feel at ease by providing comfortable chairs and relaxed furnishings. Ask people about their jobs, the weather, what they did in school today, or some other topic to "break the ice." It is important that this process not continue for too long; if it does, family members might begin to doubt whether the social worker is ever going to "get down to business" and take the work seriously. Be sure to speak individually with each person. This lets all members know that you are interested in each of them and that you will not be inclined to ignore anyone later.

Do Respect Family Hierarchy. Because the parents are the leaders of the family, it is important to respect this role, not only so that the parents will feel appropriately respected, but also so that the children observe the respect and deference that is paid to their parents. This respect can be demonstrated by speaking first to the parents, by asking their permission to complete each stage of the assessment process, and by soliciting their opinions about what has been helpful in the past and/or would be helpful in the present or future. Within the parental subunit of a given family, the mother, father, or grandparent may be at the top of the hierarchy. The family-centered social worker brings no preconceived notions about what sort of hierarchy and decision-making process is best. Instead, the social worker initially accepts and respects the way that individual families organize themselves. The social worker intervenes in the family's organization only when that organization is clearly blocking achievement of goals, and then only with the family's sanction. Additionally, the social worker can respect family hierarchy by respecting the role of older children. In most families, older children are afforded more status and more responsibility in the household, so it would be consistent to engage the older children next after the parents.

Do Explore Each Person's View of the Problem. Beyond the initial contact with each family member, the interviewer should also later be sure to engage each family member in a more lengthy discussion of the presenting problems and issues of concern. This is important to combat adultcentrism (as discussed more fully in chapter 4) and to maximize the amount of information introduced into the decision-making process. The interviewer should use active listening techniques that clarify and expand on information, leading to better understanding. The goal is to understand the needs of the family member as that person sees them, not as someone else sees them. It is important to remember that understanding does not mean agreement. The interviewer should avoid indicating agreement with any one individual's perspective, at least initially, because this inhibits discussion of alternate perspectives and leaves the impression of "taking sides." It is often helpful for the interviewer to elicit the perspective of family members who are not in attendance. This can be done by asking those present to convey the absent person's perspective and/or by calling the person on the phone either during or after the interview. This process communicates to the family that all individuals are important and valid to the process, and that the social worker will be thorough and fair in his or her approach to the helping process.

Do Use Compliments. Many children and families have experienced long histories of being criticized by professionals, neighbors, and relatives. Even if they have not, families typically fear that the professional will criticize them. This stems from the traditional deficiency-oriented approaches in which it has been the job of professionals to find out what the problem is and what is causing the problem. So, whether or not the family has had extensive experience with the system, it can be a real breath of fresh air to hear something positive about themselves. When possible, compliments in the initial interview should be aimed at the parents, at each child, and at the family as a whole. The compliments do not have to be monumental or earthshaking, but they do have to be genuine. To parents, it is often appropriate to compliment them for their interest and concern, for rearranging their busy schedules to come to the meeting on time, and/or for their determination to get help for their child. It is also often helpful to tell the parents something that the professional likes about the children. This is an indirect compliment, in that children are often seen as extensions of parents, but it is no less important than direct compliments, because parents yearn to feel proud of their children. Especially for the child targeted for help, compliments can begin to reverse the negativity that often surrounds the child. Even small compliments, such as "Johnny has a really cute smile," if offered in a timely and genuine fashion, can go far toward establishing a positive therapeutic alliance. For compliments targeted to each child, the interviewer's compliments could range from noticing a hat, scarf, or other garment, to commenting about how smart and insightful a particular comment was, to praising a child on his cooperation or his showing respect to his parents by not interrupting. With respect to the family as a whole, it can be useful for the social worker to point out norms or roles in the family that appear positive. For example, the interviewer could compliment the family

on their ability to communicate to each other, or on how neat it is that the older children help out with the younger children, or on how hardworking everyone is. In addition, the worker can begin to combat and reverse negativity and criticism in the family itself by asking family members to share something positive about another family member at the beginning and end of every meeting.

Do Respect the Sanctity of the Variability in Family Rules and Customs. All families are unique in the ways in which they are organized, in the ways that they support and challenge individuals, even within a given race or ethnic group. It is highly disrespectful for a social worker to communicate that there is one best way to parent, that there is one way to deal with a child or a situation. The worker is guilty of stereotyping if he or she assumes that because the family belongs to a category of race or ethnicity, that family will behave in a certain way. The role of the social worker is to help the family be successful in a way that is consistent with the unique ways they do things in their family, as long as those ways do not constitute child abuse or neglect. The successful social worker conveys a nonjudgmental attitude; he or she genuinely believes and respects that there are many different roads to success. In specific terms, the social worker can begin to operationalize this attitude by asking questions about how things are done, listening to the answers, and never commenting on the ways things are done except to ask if the family is itself satisfied with things. When it comes time to problem solve, the social worker remembers and validates the family norms, and makes it clear that solutions must fit how the family operates.

Do Offer Some Hope for Change for the Better. No matter what the presenting problem is, family members want to leave an initial meeting feeling like their time has been well spent, that there is some hope for improvement in the situation. This hope does not have to take the form of a concrete action plan with specific goals and objectives. It is more important that each family member leaves with a willingness to return to talk and work some more. For voluntary clients, the measure of a successful first interview is whether or not the client returns again. This will depend on whether the client feels that they were truly heard by the social worker, and whether the social worker conveyed some sense of optimism that things can and will improve. This optimism can be conveyed in part by using genuine compliments throughout the interview. It is also helpful to make a statement at the end of the meeting that conveys optimism and hope, based on a restatement of the strengths and positives observed. Normalizing statements, which frame the issues as ones which many families struggle successfully with, can help reduce feelings of stigma and connote that even though it will be a struggle, the family, like most families, can succeed.

Don't

Don't Criticize Parents in Front of Their Children. This maxim could read, "Don't even come close to criticizing parents in front of their children." This prohibition follows from the principle of "Do Respect the Family Hierarchy." Criticism, even the so-called constructive variety, is difficult to hear and incorporate under any conditions. Criticism damages the therapeutic alliance and inhibits motivation. Any criticism of parents in front of their children undermines the parents' authority, further damaging the working relationship. Social workers should be vigilant about this maxim because it is not criticism per se that is the issue, but the client's perception of criticism. Thus, the worker should refrain from any statement (including giving advice as discussed below) that could even remotely be interpreted as criticism. If a worker feels that it is imperative to say something that could be interpreted as criticism, he or she should ask that the children exit the interview temporarily so that they are not present during the discussion. (Of course, one exception to this general rule occurs when the social worker observes outright physical abuse.) When and if a worker senses that a family member has felt criticized, the social worker should immediately address the possibility with the client, process any miscommunication, and apologize to the family member, adding that it is not the intent or purpose of the worker to criticize but to support, and that the worker appreciates the willingness of the family member to share his or her experience and allow the worker to correct the mistake.

Don't Enforce Rules or Correct Children's Behavior Directly—Work through the Parents. Almost every parent has experienced a situation at a relative's or neighbor's in which their child misbehaves and the relative or neighbor quickly jumps in to directly correct the child. While this correction may be well intentioned, and may stem from a desire to enforce the rules that exist in the relative or neighbor's own household, it is nevertheless disrespectful of the parent's role and authority. If there is any correcting to be done, the parent is the one who is to do it, unless, of course, they are not present. When others jump in, it is rarely perceived by the parent as helpful; rather, it feels like an intrusion into the parent's domain that implies that the parent cannot or will not discipline their own child. The appropriate and respectful approach is to work through the parent. The worker should first allow time for the parent to correct the behavior in his or her own way and time. If the parent does not notice or take action, the worker should politely state the issue with the behavior (e.g., "If Johnny keeps playing with the toy that way, I'm afraid someone is going to get hurt"). It is then up to the parent to correct the behavior or to ask the worker to deal with the child directly. In either case, the child experiences that the worker has deferred to the parent as the one who is chiefly in charge.

Don't Offer Advice Prematurely. Beginning social work professionals are often eager to jump in and use their newfound professional knowledge and expertise to give advice to people on how to solve their problems, because they are trained to be problem solvers. It usually takes little time for them to realize that much of their wonderful professional advice is falling on deaf ears. The helping process can be conceived as having three phases: exploring, understanding, and doing. Giving advice is appropriate only in the doing, or action, stage of the process, and even in that phase giving advice can be inappropriate or ill-timed. A general guideline for practitioners is to never offer advice unless (1) advice has been directly asked for by the client, or (2) the worker has checked out with the family whether direct advice and suggestions would be helpful. Students should be aware that the latter situation is clearly the less preferred option, because the client may answer affirmatively only to please the worker, with no real interest in incorporating the advice. Here, the worker must be keenly attuned to nonverbal cues that either support or contradict the affirmative verbal message.

Family-Centeredness in Policy and Research

Family-Centeredness at the Community and State Levels

As mentioned earlier in this chapter, broad-based family support efforts that bolster the ability of families to care for themselves are family-centered. The family support movement endorses the motto of an African saying: "It takes a whole village to raise a child." The Family Resource Coalition, a national group founded in 1981, facilitates the development of family support programs across the country (Weissbourd, 1987).

Although these family support programs vary in shape, size, and target population, one common element is the family resource center (Chamberlin, 1996). A family resource center is a place where parents of children living in an area can come with their children to socialize with other parents, learn parenting and other skills, get temporary relief from child care, obtain help with problems, and develop cooperative arrangements for sharing goods and services. For many families, these resource centers can provide the support that is missing from absent extended family networks. Sometimes, these family resource centers are affiliated with school systems, as will be discussed more fully in chapter 10. Other times, family resource centers are established independent of school systems, through cooperation of agencies and governments.

Two examples of successful family resource centers illustrate how they work. The Addison County Parent/Child Center serves a rural Vermont county of 32,000 people (Chamberlin, 1996). Activities include a drop-in center where parents can come during the day to participate in various support groups, use the washer or dryer, or play with their child. Parents can have somebody else watch their child while they have a cup of coffee or participate in other activities. Area service agencies use the center to coordinate services, and vans are available to transport families to and from the center. Center personnel provide educational programs to the county's three high schools on such topics as child development, parenting, and pregnancy prevention. Home visitors are available to meet with new mothers who have special concerns.

In Seattle, under the leadership of the mayor and city council, a network of neighborhood family support centers are being established (Miller, 1993). Centers are based on the principles of being open to all families, building on family strengths, developing self-sufficiency, and cultivating respect for diversity. The centers seek to decrease feelings of isolation, promote positive parent-child relationships, and support positive child development.

In some states, family support programs also involve direct cash subsidies to families of children with disabilities (Bergman & Singer, 1996). These programs are based on the proposition that families should control the kinds of supports they receive, not the service system. One way to ensure that the family is the locus of control is to give resources directly to them in the form of money or vouchers, rather than giving the resources to service agencies. In Michigan, for example, families of children with the most severe disabilities can receive $242 a month to spend as they see fit. Once a year, families are asked to report how they spent the money. The three most common uses of the funds have been for clothing, educational aids and toys, and general household expenses. Other uses included purchase of respite care, transportation, and home renovations. More than 50% of participants reported that the subsidy "very greatly" or "greatly" improved the overall lifestyle of the family, improved the ability of the family to care for the child with the disability, helped the family do more things together, and eased the family's financial worries (Bergman & Singer, 1996).

A crucial defining principle of family support programs is *empowerment* (Jones, Garlow, Turnbull, & Barber, 1996). In other words, family support programs aspire to help families increase a sense of mastery and control over their lives so that they can obtain the resources necessary to meet their needs. Hence, an empowering organization seeks to maximize the family's control within the program itself, to facilitate access to resources, to maximize choice, and to facilitate participation.

Families control what services they receive and who provides them, they define their needs, and they decide the extent of their program involvement.

Family-Centeredness at the Organizational Level

Enactment of family-centeredness at the organizational level may require a radical shift in the way that administrators have traditionally operated. At the organizational level, adoption of a family-centered approach involves four tasks: assessment of the organization's policies and procedures relative to family-centeredness and cultural competence, creating support for family participation, providing staff and family training, and expanding programmatic and fiscal flexibility (Allen, Petr, & Brown, 1995).

How Organizations Can Improve Family-Centeredness

1. Assess policies and procedures
2. Create support for family participation
3. Provide staff and family training
4. Expand programmatic and fiscal flexibility

Assess Policies and Procedures. In beginning to address family-centeredness, it is important for organizations to review the organization's mission statements, policies and procedures with respect to the core elements of family-centeredness. This review should include an examination of the group's name, goals, hiring practices, and outreach and advocacy efforts. What values, attitudes, and intentions toward families and diverse populations are conveyed by these aspects of the organization, and are they consistent with the three core elements of family-centered practice? The review process itself should involve parents and children as consumer representatives whose perspectives are valued.

The assessment should pay particular attention to the use of language and physical space within the organization. Language, both written and spoken, should be respectful of family strengths and diversity. Organizations should use "people-first" language, such as "children with mental retardation" rather than "mentally retarded children." The phrase "dysfunctional family" should be outlawed. Instead of "patient" or "case," organizations should use "consumer," "client," "user," or "participant." In terms of ethnicity, families should be described in terms that the family prefers, whenever possible. For example, if a family prefers "African American" to "black," then use "African American." Because so many people are biracial, intake forms should allow for more than one choice in the identification of racial heritage. If the organization serves consumers whose primary language is not English, translation of written documents and interpreters are appropriate.

The organization should strive to have family-centered principles reflected in the organization and use of physical space. Are spaces welcoming and furnished for children? Do the spaces contain toys that are gender balanced and culturally varied? Are the reading materials in waiting rooms representative of and interesting to people served? How accessible is the service space to a full range of consumers, including the disabled and those who rely on public transportation? Are offices open at convenient times?

Create Support for Family Participation. Families should be afforded the option of participating in organizational decision making, as well as decisions specific to their own service plan. Organizations can also support family participation beyond the borders of the organization, by educating families about how systems operate, and how to advocate for their family's and children's needs in other forums. Organizations can help families develop articulate voices by encouraging support groups, by including children and parents as trainers of staff, and by including family members on decision making and planning groups in more than a token fashion. Families encounter many barriers to such participation, so organizations must be prepared to "go the extra mile" to support meaningful involvement. This support includes provision of concrete aid in the form of child care, transportation, and reimbursement for expenses such as meals or time taken from work.

Provide Staff and Family Training. Because family-centered professional practice entails a radical shift from traditional professional-centered approaches, organizations need to provide staff with training and support to accomplish change. Parents and children are excellent sources of training for staff, in that they can share their personal experiences of what they find helpful in interactions with professionals. This collaboration in training can lead to other collaborative efforts between families and staff to identify and meet gaps in service delivery. Parents themselves may desire training from staff or outside facilitators on issues. These might include how to understand the nature of various disabilities and diagnoses, how to influence legislation, or how to discipline children more effectively. It is important to find out from families themselves what training they desire. Staff members are often discouraged with the attendance when they offer an educational program, typically parent education, without first finding out if parents want that kind of training.

Expand Programmatic and Fiscal Flexibility. Family-centered service delivery intends to meet the needs of the individual family, regardless of the nature and extent of those needs. Rather than fitting the family into a service category, family-centeredness requires fitting services to the individual needs of the family. Each organization in a community cannot provide a full range of services to families, but each organization can designate at least one staff person to help families access other resources, and each organization can be involved in community development activities to ensure the existence of comprehensive and coordinated service delivery systems in the community. Within an organization or community, flexibility of programming may depend on flexibility of funding. Mechanisms to achieve this flexibility include freeing existing funds by reducing the degree to which they are tied or committed to specific programs, tapping new funding sources, and contributing organizational funds to an interagency funding pool that can be used to address needs not addressed by categorical funding. (More on the organization and financing of services is presented under pragmatic perspective 7 in chapter 10; more on family-centeredness at the interorganizational level is presented under pragmatic perspective 6 in chapter 9.)

Family-Centeredness in Research

In the research arena, family-centered principles apply to the process of conducting research as well as to the outcomes that are studied. That is, the research process itself can and should incorporate the elements of family-centeredness in the design and methodology. In addition, the level or extent of family-centeredness can and should be studied as an outcome of service delivery.

Incorporating Family-Centered Principles in the Research Process. In conducting research, researchers can model family-centeredness by including families at all stages of the process, from design to dissemination. This inclusion process has been referred to as Constituency-Oriented Research and Dissemination (CORD) (Fenton, Batavia, & Roody, 1993). In a CORD process, researchers seek input from families about what families think are the most important issues to research. Researchers work with families to design research that meets family needs and respects families as subjects. Data collection and interventions are sensitive to family issues and maximize the informed choice and strengths components of family-centeredness. Dissemination of results is targeted not just to professionals, but also to families so that the information can be used by families in ways that improve the life of the family or help the family advocate for change.

Family-Centeredness as an Outcome for Study. In studying the extent of family-centeredness in service delivery, researchers can view family-centeredness as an end outcome in itself. Or it can be considered a means to achieving better child and family well-being outcomes. It may be most helpful to view it as both. Even if child and family well-being outcomes were unimproved, family-centeredness on the part of professionals and programs would be valuable in and of itself because most families prefer it. Thus, endorsement of family-centered principles should not be dependent on whether or not the implementation of those principles results in better statistical outcomes. Still, many families, policy makers, and program funders are interested in not just in whether programs are family-centered, but also in whether or not family-centeredness correlates with or affects other outcomes. For example, would a family-centered approach in child welfare affect the incidence of repeat child abuse and neglect? Would a family-centered process in special education result in fewer absences, higher academic achievement, and more time spent in regular classrooms? Would a family-centered approach in mental health result in improved child behavior or fewer hospitalizations?

In order to ascertain the level of family-centeredness of professionals and programs, or to ascertain whether family-centeredness makes a difference in outcome, the concept must be measurable. Examples of two measurement scales designed to measure family-centeredness are discussed next. Both were developed at the Beach Center on Families and Disability at the University of Kansas.

The Family-Centered Program Rating Scale (FAMPRS) was designed to assess the level of family-centeredness in early intervention programs for young children with special needs and their families (Murphy & Lee, 1991). It consists of 59 statements about program features. Respondents, who can be either parents or professionals, rate each feature's importance and the program's performance on each feature. English or Spanish versions are available. Scores for 11 categories, or subscales, of features are produced. These 11 subscales are flexibility and innovation in programming, providing and coordinating responsive services, individualizing services and ways of handling complaints, providing appropriate and practical information, communication timing and style, developing and maintaining comfortable relationships, building family-staff collaboration, respecting the family as decision-maker, respecting the family's expertise and strengths, recognizing the family's need for autonomy, and building positive expectations. The reliability of the subscales was moderate to high, with internal consistency coefficients (Cronbach's alpha) ranging from .71 to .87 for parent raters, and .63 to .87 for professional staff. Evidence for construct validity was adduced from principal components analysis that established that each subscale measures a statistically independent construct.

The FAMPRS can be used by early intervention programs for program evaluations, program planning, and staff development. By administering the

scale periodically, evaluators can track direction and change over time. The scale can be useful in staff development, targeting areas of strength as well as areas for improvement and training. Because the scale includes ratings of both performance and importance, the agency can target areas for improvement based on the discrepancy between the scores. The highest priority would be areas that were rated as high in importance but low in performance. The lowest priority would be areas rated low in importance but high in performance. In addition, because there is a version for parents and staff, the agency can compare the views of staff with those of parents, on both the importance and performance ratings. The agency might find a high or low level of consistency between the groups, which could stimulate discussion. For example, what if staff rated their performance as higher than parents? Or, what if there was a big discrepancy between what the two groups thought was important?

The second example of a scale to measure family-centeredness is the Family-Centered Behavior Scale (FCBS) (Allen, et al., 1995). The FCBS was designed to assess the level of family-centeredness exhibited by professionals in their interactions with families. It was designed to be relevant within any service system that works with families who have children with a special need, whether this need be physical, developmental, emotional, or social. The FCBS consists of 26 items describing family-centered behaviors that might be performed by agency staff members. Family members rate the performance of professionals on each item. The 26 items exemplified the three essential constructs of family-centeredness discussed above: family as the unit of attention, informed family choice, and a strengths perspective. A companion scale (FCBS-I) on which parents measure importance of each scale item can be used in conjunction with the FCBS. Both scales are available in English and Spanish.

Construction of the FCBS and FCBS-I involved participation from parents and professionals through a CORD committee. Before the scale was mailed to a national validation sample, it was discussed and modified by several professional and parent groups and field tested by parents. Strategies were explored to increase the ethnic, gender, and socioeconomic diversity of the national mail sample, as well as to include a full range of special needs. Half of the national sample was asked to rate the "best" staff member with whom they had recently worked, and half were asked to rate the "worst" staff member. A 32-item scale was mailed to over 1,700 households nationwide.

Evidence of scale validity was documented in three analyses. First, the scale was able to differentiate between "best," "worst," and "only" staff members. Difference of means of these groups were significant at the .0014 level or higher for all scale items. Second, respondents rated all of the 26 behaviors as important to them: the item means ranged from 3.2 to 4.7 (3=important, 5=extremely important). Third, items correlated positively with respondent overall satisfaction with the staff member. Zero-order correlations between scale items and satisfaction ranged from .31 to .81, and all but four of the correlations were above .52.

Reliability of the FCBS was assessed using Cronbach's alpha to test for internal consistency. The standardized alpha for the 32-item scale was .9712. Temporal reliability was also assessed through test-retest procedures, with the test-retest correlation being .9601. On the basis of the validation study results, six of the original 32 items were eliminated from the scale, two because they performed poorly in several analyses and four because they elicited a relatively large number of "I don't know" or missing responses.

Like the FAMPRS, the FCBS can be used in program evaluation and staff development. When both the performance and importance versions of the scales are used, a "difference" score, which indicates the discrepancy between ratings of importance and ratings of performance, can be computed. The difference score on each item is computed by subtracting the Importance rating from the Frequency rating. Difference scores close to zero indicate a fairly good match between how important consumers think a behavior is and how frequently it is performed. Difference scores above zero signify that the performance of the behavior is higher than its importance, while difference scores less than zero indicate behaviors of special concern, because they are performed to a lesser degree than their importance. Ideally, there would be a strong match between the level of importance and the level of performance, as indicated

---

Family-Centered Behavior Scale (FCBS)—Sample Items

The staff member:

1. Accepts our family as important members of the team that helps our child.

2. Helps us get all the information we want and/or need.

3. Helps us get the help we want from our family, friends, and community.

5. Points out what my child and family do well.

7. Respects our family's beliefs, customs, and ways that we do things in our family.

9. Makes it clear that we as a family, not the professional, are responsible for deciding what is done for our child and family.

10. Plans meetings at times and places that are good for our family.

12. Treats us with respect.

16. Helps my family meet our needs as we see them.

18. Understands that I know my child better than anyone else does.

22. Makes sure we understand our family's rights.

23. Accepts our feelings and reactions as normal for our situation.

24. Wants to hear what we think about this program.

---

by difference scores close to zero. The goal for the parent and the conscientious professional is for those behaviors that are highly important to be frequently practiced.

An interesting finding of the validation study of the FCBS was that behaviors measured by the scale are performed much less frequently than their importance. The national sample of 443 respondents reported difference scores close to or greater than zero on only 4 behaviors out of 26. Apparently, professionals are doing well on these four behaviors: The staff member . . . "makes negative judgments about us because of ways that we are different from the staff member (such as race, income level, job, or religion)" (item 13); "talks in everyday language that we can understand" (item 20); "blames me for my child's problems" (item 4); and "criticizes what we do with our child" (item 11).

All of the rest of the items on the scale were rated by parents as higher on importance than on performance, indicated by difference of means that were at least 0.41. Of these 22 items, the 5 with the worst difference scores were: The staff member . . . "helps my family get services from other agencies and programs as easily as possible" (item 19); "makes it clear that we as a family, not the professional, are responsible for deciding what is done for our child and family" (item 9); "helps us get the help we want from family, friends, and community" (item 3); "helps us get all the information we want and/or need" (item 2); and "points out what my child and family do well" (item 5). These items represent the areas of professional behaviors are in most need of improvement, according to the parents in this study.

These research findings indicate professional strengths in the areas of respecting and communicating with parents. Although professionals do not openly blame and criticize parents, neither do they point out the strengths in the child and family, what the child and family do well. Considering the importance to parents in the sample, professionals are also falling short in the areas of linking families to formal and informal services, responding to parents' needs for information, and respecting the parents' decision-making prerogatives.

Family-Centered Practice in Child Welfare

Family-Centeredness in Family Preservation

Many, if not most, parents view the child welfare system with suspicion and distrust. A sensitive, family-centered approach to parents who have been accused of abuse and neglect requires some understanding of how parents generally perceive the child welfare system and their caseworkers. In a small, qualitative study of parental perceptions, Diorio (1992) found that parents felt quite vulnerable and powerless in relation to the child welfare system. Parents were found to have little knowledge about their due process rights, instead believing that the child welfare agency had limitless power to intervene in their family at any time. Social workers can counter these perceptions by carefully and respectfully informing parents of their rights and choices in the investigation and assessment process, thus introducing the informed choice component of family-centered practice.

In child welfare, family preservation programs are usually characterized as family-centered, because these programs are based on the premise that the family should be the unit of attention for services (the first core element of family-centered services), and that all reasonable efforts should be made to maintain a child within this most important unit. This represents a dramatic reversal of the historic tendency of child welfare to be child-focused and oriented to child-saving rather than family-saving. Family preservation program staff members must maintain flexibility, from family to family, in allowing each family to define the boundaries of the family unit that is to be involved, so that extended family, broader kinship networks, friends, neighbors, clergymen, and others can be included if the family so desires.

This flexibility is particularly important in divorced families in which single mothers are struggling to raise several children who have limited contact and support from the father(s). Initially, these fathers may be reported to be "deadbeat dads" who have little interest or involvement in the children. But family preservation workers should attempt to contact and assess the father's willingness to be involved, because they often can be an untapped resource for the children. In some cases, lack of involvement, from the perspective of the father, is due to being pushed away by the mother and/or children, and the father will welcome the opportunity to be involved. In other divorce situations, a high level of involvement and conflict between the divorced parents presents a different set of challenges in defining the boundaries of the unit of attention, as the workers must decide whether to work with the children in the two separate family units, only one of the two, or to somehow view the two separate units as one.

Most family preservation programs attend to the second core element of family-centeredness, informed family choice. Of course, the limits to family choice are clear in this population as well, because parents do not have the choice to continue to abuse or neglect their kids. Some degree of choice can be afforded with respect to participation in the program, when to meet, for how long, and how often. Most family preservation programs are "home-based," meaning that the worker and family meet in the family home. Although most families prefer the convenience, informality, and flexibility that home-based services afford, some families may view professional presence in the home as intrusive. These families may prefer to meet in an office, in the park, or in some other location. Family preservation programs should not view the "home-based" component as a mandatory requirement.

Because child welfare workers are under the dual and sometimes conflicting mandates to protect children and to preserve families, some conflict can arise in defining the client. Some programs attempt to handle this conflict by assigning each mandate to a separate worker—the family preservation worker's focus is preserving the family, and the child protection worker focuses on child safety. This situation is typical of family preservation programs that are privatized—the private sector worker focuses on supporting the family while the public sector social worker retains responsibility for monitoring the safety of the child. The role of the family preservation worker can be characterized as family-centered, while the role of the protective service worker can been viewed as a check on the potential adultcentrism of the family preservation efforts.

Family-Centeredness in Foster Care

In the foster care arena, family-centered principles can (and should) guide many of the decisions and actions of the workers. Placement is sought first with relatives, then in a foster family, so that the child lives in some type of family unit if at all possible. The preferred permanency planning goal, under P.L. 96-272, is reunification with the biological family unit. Family-centered foster care workers seek to place the child in close proximity to the family, so that visits can be easily arranged to maintain the family ties. Family-centered workers view visits between foster children and their parents and siblings as a right, not an earned privilege. Even if there is a need for supervised visits, these should be frequent and not contingent on the child or parent's behavior.

An innovative family-centered development in foster care is "shared family care," in which both the natural parents and the host caregivers simultaneously care for the child and work toward reunification and independent care by the parents (Barth, 1994). In effect, the entire family enters into foster care or residential group care, so that the children and parents are not separated. Shared family care may be most applicable to situations in which a parent needs extended residential treatment for severe drug or alcohol abuse. Instead of the children having to enter foster care during the parent's treatment, the treatment facility accepts the parent and the children into care. In this way, the parent-child bond is maintained, the children can participate in the parent's treatment, and the staff can work with the parent on improving parenting skills that had been eroded by drug or alcohol use. In foster families, the role of the foster parent is moving toward the attitude of shared care with the biological parent. Although it is unusual for the whole family to reside with the foster family, the foster parents assume the role of mentor and teacher to the parents, while consulting with the parents on all major decisions from discipline in the foster home to special education and other educational decisions at school.

A prime example of family-centeredness in child welfare, one that often avoids formal foster care and its attendant reunification efforts, is the process of Family Group Conferences (Allan, 1991; Firman, 1993; Connolly & McKenzie, 1999), originated in New Zealand and now operational, in modified form, in many states in the United States. Family Group Conferences were established in New Zealand as part of the Young Persons and their Families Act of 1989. This law mandates that when the state becomes involved with a child who has been abused or neglected and is at risk for out-of-home placement, the power of decision making regarding the protection of the child must be given to the family. The social worker convenes a Family Group Conference, inviting all members of the child's nuclear and extended family (including tribal members); if necessary, the state subsidizes the cost of travel to the meeting. During the first portion of the conference, the professionals and family members share information about the issues regarding the child's safety and well-being. During the second portion, professionals generally leave the family alone to develop a plan for the care and protection of the child, usually within the family system itself. The role of the state, except under extraordinary circumstances, is to sanction the plan and negotiate resources that will be required to implement it.

In these Family Group Conferences, all three core elements of family-centeredness are in strong force: the family is made the unit of attention through the efforts to avoid state custody and involve extended kinship networks; informed choice is maximized in placing the decision about the child clearly in the hands of the family; the strengths perspective manifests in the belief that the family is competent to decide what is best, and that strengths and resources exist in all families. Many child welfare workers, accustomed to assuming responsibility for making placement decisions, would be hesitant to adopt such an approach: "How do we know that the family decision is a good one, that the child will be safe?" Proponents, noting the extent of abuse and neglect in foster care and group homes, ask the same question about traditional placement methods, and maintain that families will protect the children at least as well as the state system can. After 4 years of implementation in New Zealand, outcomes suggest that the law has stimulated improvements. Among these outcomes are a 90% reduction in the use of state foster care in some areas of New Zealand, more accurate family assessments, and the generation of a greater variety of care alternatives (Firman, 1993). Still, not all family group conferences are successful, and the degree of success may depend on the commitment of professionals to family decision making and the participation of a wide range of family members who work toward finding solutions rather than denying the severity of the problems (Connolly & McKenzie, 1997).

Family-Centeredness in Adoptions

When children are placed for adoption, the informed-choice element of family-centeredness is vitally important in preparing the adoptive family for the adoption. The adopted family must have full access to all information and history about the child, regardless of the potential impact. In other words, they must know what they are getting into; otherwise, the adoption can fail when the adoptive parents experience behaviors or needs for which they were not prepared. Adoption workers may hesitate to provide all of the information for fear that the information will frighten away prospective parents. Limited research findings suggest that adoptive parents do not always feel that they have been fully informed, and adoptive parents have successfully sued child welfare agencies for withholding important information (Barth, 1992). The social workers in many of these types of cases claim that they have provided full information, so whether the social workers failed to inform or the parents failed to fully hear and appreciate the information is open to debate. To ensure adequacy of communication, social workers can document, in writing, the information that was discussed with the adoptive parents and have the adoptive parents sign to indicate that they received and understood the information.

Family-centeredness also applies to the adoption arena with respect to the continuation of the relationship of the adopted child to his or her biological parents and siblings. Proponents who favor the practice promote "open" adoptions; those who oppose it call for "closed" adoptions. In cases of private adoptions of newborns, when the biological parents know, or even select, the adoptive parents, the issue of open or closed can be negotiated between the parties. In public adoptions of infants, current law in most states is that the birth records be sealed (Cohen, 1992). In cases of older children who have had a long-standing relationship with their biological parent, when parental rights are severed the issue of ongoing contact is left up to the court and the adoptive parents (Barth, 1992). Proponents of open adoptions for older children argue that ongoing contact helps the child maintain a sense of belonging, continuity, and support over a lifetime. Opponents, on the other hand, fear that ongoing contact will keep the adopted child from making the necessary emotional connection and commitment to the adoptive parents. While neither the child nor the biological parent should be forced to maintain contact if they choose otherwise, a family-centered approach would support the option for continued contact if the child, the biological parents, and the siblings so choose.

Family-Centered Practice in Children's Mental Health

Perpetuation of Blaming

In mental health settings, the family is now usually the unit of attention for professionals who work with troubled children. Although the advent of the family therapy modality and family systems thinking in the 1970s succeeded in shifting the unit of attention in the mental health field from the individual child to the child's family, several criticisms have been leveled at the family therapy field. First, family therapy has been criticized for unduly ignoring or minimizing the needs of the individual child and excluding the child from the process. Second, the second and third components of family-centeredness (maximizing family decision making and strengths perspective) have not been characteristics of most family therapy models, at either the theoretical or operational levels.

In their extensive literature review of the empirical research on families with children with emotional disorders, Early and Poertner (1993) found that parents, and mothers in particular, are frequently blamed for their child's condition. The authors found that many of these studies confused correlation with cause and effect. That is, the studies documented a correlation between parent dysfunction and childhood behavioral and emotional problems, but then proceeded to attribute the former as the cause of the latter, without documenting the temporal order of the two variables. In other words, a child's behavioral and emotional problems could be the cause of the parents' "dysfunction," rather than vice versa.

Barkley (1995), in his work with ADHD children and their families, is one of the few researchers to have recognized the importance of distinguishing between correlation and cause, exposing the myth that poor parenting is the cause of ADHD. While he found a correlation between negative parenting behaviors and negative behaviors in children, further evaluation using Ritalin and placebos indicated clearly that the parenting behavior was in response to the children's behavior,

not the cause of it. In addition, correlations have been found between ADHD in children and the general psychological functioning of their parents, but biology and genetics are the most likely link: "It is not the psychiatric problems of these family members and the resulting 'bad' family environment that cause ADHD in the child but the genes that the parents and child have in common" (p. 72).

In light of the tendency to confuse correlation with cause, it is not surprising that the parents of children with emotional problems report that they experience encounters with many mental health professionals as blaming and exclusionary (Collins & Collins, 1990). In their validation study of the Family-Centered Behavioral Scale, Petr and Allen (1997) documented that the system of care for children with emotional and behavioral disorders (EBD) is much less family-centered than systems of care for children with other types of disabilities (non-EBD), as judged by parent perceptions of professional behaviors. All of the parents surveyed (EBD and non-EBD subsamples) were in general agreement about which behaviors were most important, but the samples differed on how often the behaviors were performed. The three most important behaviors for both the EBD and non-EBD samples were: The staff member . . . listens to us; treats us with respect, and accepts us as important members of the team that helps our child.

While there was general agreement about which professional behaviors are most important, those behaviors were reportedly performed much less frequently by professionals serving the EBD population. The EBD subsample rated each and every behavior on the FCBS as being performed significantly less frequently than the non-EBD sample reported. These results indicate that professionals who work with the EBD population may be less attuned to family-centered behaviors than are other professionals who work with children with other types of special needs; thus, parents of children with EBD may view professionals in the system more guardedly and with more caution and distrust than other parents.

Genograms

A popular clinical tool in family therapy is the genogram, which is a map of the current and historical context of a family: "A genogram is a format for drawing a family tree that records information about family members and their relationships over at least three generations" (McGoldrick & Gerson, 1985, p. 1). The genogram helps families see how a particular presenting problem may be connected to the past and present family context.

Creating a genogram involves drawing a map of the family structure, recording family information on the map, and delineating family relationships. When completed, the genogram is a graphic depiction of the family that (1) highlights important events such as births, deaths, and divorces, (2) identifies birth order and sibling position of family members, (3) records information such as occupation and health status, (4) focuses on life-cycle transitions and adaptations, and (5) explores patterns in relationships such as closeness, distance, and conflict, over the generations. The genogram is insight-based—change in families and improvement in the presenting problem are predicated on the family understanding itself and the presenting problem in some fresh and new way that triggers behavioral change.

Genograms are not inherently family-centered, nor are they inherently family-blaming. Multigenerational genograms can be complex and time-consuming, with the attendant risk that the family can feel that its presenting problems are not being fully attended to. The family-centered practitioner must guard against using the genogram to identify patterns of pathology or to attribute blame. At its best, the genogram can be useful in helping clients explore relationships within the "family as the unit of attention." A genogram offers a way for the family to expand the boundaries of its image of itself from nuclear to extended. Advocates of the genogram believe that it is a practical way of engaging the whole family in a therapeutic process, because it conveys an interest in the family's history and experience, not just its present problems. Advocates also believe that genograms can be used to reframe and normalize an issue the family would otherwise view as a toxic and rigid. For example, a father, who is himself an oldest child, has been accused by his wife and children as being overcontrolling. The family might be told that it is not surprising that the father is so responsible in his parenting since oldest children commonly are (McGoldrick & Gerson, 1985).

Family-Centeredness in Policy and Programs

In mental health administration, much can be done to enhance the family-centeredness of service delivery (Friesen & Koroloff, 1990). A family-centered system of care in the mental health field would include the three components of family-centered practice in the policies, procedures, and organization of the mental health system. Some of the specific strategies for administrators are listed below.

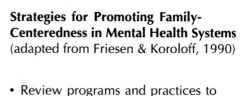

Strategies for Promoting Family-Centeredness in Mental Health Systems
(adapted from Friesen & Koroloff, 1990)

- Review programs and practices to be sure that they do not explicitly or implicitly blame families.
- Institute programmatic and fiscal flexibility to ensure that the full range of family needs are addressed by someone in the community.
- Support full participation of family members at every clinical and organizational decision point, including participation in task forces, committees, and boards of directors. Full participation will require information, training, and provision of child care, transportation, and reimbursement for expenses.
- Institute a training and consultation program for staff in family-centered practices.
- Encourage the development and maintenance of parent support and advocacy groups.
- Develop mechanisms in the personnel evaluation and program monitoring systems to assess the level of family-centeredness within the organization. These could include direct systematic feedback from families and review of case records and agency documents.

A prime example of family-centeredness in children's mental health is the family-designed system of care in Essex County, New York (Tannen, 1996). In this project, called Families First, a group of parents and concerned citizens has set out to develop a system of services and supports that are designed and implemented by parents of children with emotional and behavioral disorders. Reversing the professional tendency to blame parents for their children's emotional problems, this project was based on the idea that most parents are doing the best they can and that serious emotional disorders are the result of multiple causes, including biochemistry, genetic predisposition, and severe environmental stressors. When parents were asked what they wanted and needed in a mental health system, their priorities were for nontraditional support services rather than formal professional services. They wanted informal services such as respite, information and referral, someone to advocate for their needs, concrete assistance, and a family center. In hiring staff, including social workers and case managers, preference is given to parents of children with special needs. Families First initiated interagency networking, organized parent support groups, recruited citizen volunteers, and used the wraparound approach (see chapter 10 for a full discussion of this approach) with individual families to secure needed resources. In response to the need for respite, several inns and hotels in the county agreed to provide free rooms to parents during off-peak times. In effect, the project focused on creating a parallel system of care that both provided different services and sought to change the existing system through better utilization and coordination of existing services.

In Georgia, the decision-making component of family-centeredness has been implemented in a dramatic way. In that state, the Georgia Parent Support Network, a parent advocacy organization affiliated with the Federation of Families for Children's Mental Health (see description under pragmatic perspective 6 below), was highly involved in changing the state's system for delivering mental health services. A new Georgia law created 19 regional boards to plan, purchase, and evaluate mental health services, and 51% of the board seats are reserved for consumers and their family members. In January 1996, the Georgia Parent Support Network successfully bid on the regional contract to implement, monitor, and evaluate services for children with serious emotional disabilities in Fulton County, City of Atlanta. So in Atlanta, the entire children's mental health system, including the professionals and programs, is being directed by a family advocacy organization, which has the power to hold the system accountable. The notion of professionals being the agents of families, of working *for* families, has taken on new meaning in Georgia (Smith, 1996).

Family-Centeredness in Special Education

In special education settings for school-aged youngsters, a child-centered approach continues to dominate service delivery. As discussed in chapter 4, the principal tool for evaluation and service planning is the Individual Education Plan (IEP), which focuses specifically on the child's needs, not the family's. It is not even required that parents attend IEP meetings. When they do, they often find themselves overwhelmed by the number of professionals, the amount of information, and the lack of time to discuss issues. In contrast, the tool for evaluation and service planning for young children (0–3) is the Individual Family Service Plan (IFSP). With this age group, the family is clearly central to the process, and the needs of the child are placed within the family context. Perhaps, as young children and their families enter the regular school system, they will be disappointed with the change in focus from family to child, and will advocate for a more family-centered approach by the special education staff.

The PIN program in Pennsylvania, discussed in chapter 4, is one rare example of a family-centered initiative in special education. Another innovative program in special education that seeks to have the family as the unit of attention and to empower families in the service system is the WRAP project in LaFrange, Illinois (Eber, 1993). This school-based project (discussed more fully in chapter 9 under pragmatic perspective 6) also combines interagency collaboration, reallocation of funding, interagency planning, and wraparound services to pursue the goal of inclusion for children with severe emotional and behavioral problems.

CHAPTER 5 SUMMARY

An important trend in the delivery of services to children and families is the trend toward *family-centered* practice: "Family-centered service delivery recognizes the centrality of the family in the lives of individuals. It is guided by fully informed choices made by the family and focuses upon the strengths and capabilities of these families" (Allen & Petr, 1996).

Family-centered practice involves three core elements: the family as the unit of attention, an emphasis on informed family choice, and a strengths perspective. These elements contrast with traditional child-centered and professional-centered approaches that target the child as the unit of attention, provide little family choice, and are deficit oriented. In family-centered practice, the professional is the agent of the family. The professional works *for* the family to help the family meet its needs. Family-centered professionals need to guard against adultcentrism by ensuring that the views of the children are taken into consideration, so that the unit of attention is the family, including all its members, not just the parents.

At the direct practice level, family-centered practice has important pragmatic implications for conducting face-to-face interviews with families. Family-centered social workers make connections with each individual, respect family hierarchy, explore each person's view of the problem, use compliments, respect the sanctity of the variability of rules and customs, and offer some hope of change for the better. They strive not to criticize parents in front of their children, not to enforce rules or correct children's behavior directly when parents are present, and not to offer advice to parents prematurely.

At the policy level, family-centeredness appears in family support programs and policies that seek to build community supports for ensuring the success of families. Two family support strategies are family resource centers and cash subsidies. At the organizational level, administrators can improve the level of family-centeredness by assessing policies and procedures, creating support for family participation, providing staff and family training, and expanding programmatic and fiscal flexibility.

In the research arena, the measurement of family-centeredness is important to enable evaluation of programs and professionals, as well as to study the links between family-centeredness and client outcomes. Family-centeredness is an end in itself, but it is also a means to the achievement of better child and family well-being outcomes. Two measurement scales, the Family-Centered Program Ratings Scale (FAMPRS) and the Family-centered Behavior Scale (FCBS) have been developed to stimulate evaluation and research of family-centered practice.

In child welfare, the chapter discussed family-centered issues in family preservation, foster care, and adoptions. In relation to children's mental health, family-centered practice issues were discussed with respect to the perpetuation of blaming, genograms, the administration of policies and programs, and special education.

Pragmatic Perspective 3: Strengths Perspective

Overview

The strengths perspective is an approach to social work practice that has been introduced in previous chapters as an essential component of the social worker's efforts to combat adultcentrism and to engage in family-centered practice. In the first section of this chapter, the strengths perspective is further explained, beginning with an introductory case vignette that depicts the differences between a strengths and deficiency orientation. This is followed by discussions of the strengths perspective in direct practice, the solutions-focused model of practice, and the strengths perspective in policy development. The second and third sections discuss applications of the strengths perspective in child welfare and children's mental health settings.

Strengths Perspective: Introduction

A strengths perspective is an antidote to the pervasive deficiency approach that has traditionally characterized professional practice with children and adolescents. As introduced in chapters 2 and 3, the strengths perspective is integral to combating adultcentrism and practicing from a family-centered orientation. With respect to individual children, the strengths perspective counters the tendency of adult professionals to view children as incomplete and incompetent. A strengths-oriented practitioner is quick to point out areas of competence in children, works to reinforce positive attitudes and behaviors, and maximizes opportunities for children to be involved in decision making that affects their lives. With families, a strengths-oriented professional practices the behaviors on the Family-Centered Behavior Scale. These in-

clude not criticizing or blaming parents, and respecting the beliefs, customs, and unique ways that each family operates.

Students in field internships are often amazed at how negative other professionals are in their comments about children and their families. Whether it is in the teacher's lounge at public schools, in a team meeting at the psychiatric unit of the hospital, or a staffing conference or court hearing in child welfare, many professionals express negative and cynical attitudes toward clients. This focus on deficiencies, or pathology, skews perceptions and inhibits holistic understanding of situations. It furthers poor client self-esteem and sets the stage for fulfillment of negative prophesies. Interventions based on this inadequate and pessimistic foundation have much less chance to succeed.

The following case scenario depicts a negative, deficiency orientation to a situation.

CASE VIGNETTE: Lyle

At a staff meeting at the child welfare office, Susan listened to a colleague present the following information about a child and family:

WORKER 1: This case is concerning Lyle, age 5, who is reported to be neglected by his parents. The report came in from his kindergarten teacher, who says he is very hungry and sleepy when he gets to school, his clothes are always dirty, and sometimes he smells from urine and feces on his clothes. I interviewed his mother, who appears to be a real loser. She was asleep at noon when I made the home visit. The house was a disaster area. She has two older school-age children, both of whom were home from school, supposedly sick. We have had previous reports of neglect on the older kids. The mother has a history of failed marriages and living with men for short periods of time. The last guy she lived with beat her up regularly. She is an alcoholic who has been in inpatient treatment three different times in the last 7 years. She gets food stamps, but she probably cashes those in for money to spend on booze. She had a pretty defensive and uncooperative attitude, mostly quiet.

WORKER 2: This appears to be another of those cases where the mother is a drunk, living off the taxpayers, who can't get it together to take care of her kids.

WORKER 1: Right. We can try to get her to take better care of the kids, and with pressure from us she probably will for a short while so we don't take her kids, but then it will be back to the same old story.

Commentary on Case Vignette. There are no factual errors in Worker 1's account of the situation—the child did come to school as described, she was asleep at noon, the house was a mess, the mother was quiet and reluctant to discuss the situation, and the mother did have a history of the problems mentioned. But Worker 1 provided the team with no factual information about strengths of the child and family—information that could lead the professionals to a dramatically different point of view and action plan. When only the negative, deficiency-oriented facts are seen, the perspective is skewed. Observe how your own attitudes about this child and family change when information on strengths is added to the above.

CASE VIGNETTE

SUPERVISOR: We haven't heard anything about this woman's and family's strengths. Were you able to identify any?

WORKER 1: No, not really. I only saw the woman one time, and it was real brief because I had to go see another family. It's a stretch to find strengths in families like this.

WORKER 3: Well, I know a little about this family. I had them for an intake about a year ago, and worked with them for about 3 months. The mother actually has a bachelor's degree in English literature, but isn't able to use it for much. She has bouts of clinical depression, which medication can help with, but she isn't always able to afford the medication. She does have a history of alcohol abuse, but when I worked with her she had been on the wagon for over a year and was regularly attending Alcoholics Anonymous. She also has had poor success in relationships with men, and it's a positive if she's not living with any man right now. When I terminated the case, she was working night shift at a local factory and having a sister come watch the kids at night. She's a pretty hard worker. She puts a real high value on education and gets the kids to do their homework every night—they were getting A's and B's when I knew them.

Supervisor: Well, that paints a little different picture. Maybe she's still working the night shift and having problems getting her sister to stay with the kids at night. Or maybe she hasn't been able to afford her medication and is depressed.

The addition of strengths and positives provides a balance to the deficiency perspective. Suddenly, the reader may have found some hope in the situation, some way to imagine a resolution of the problems, as did the supervisor and professionals.

The above scenario and dialogue place the reader in the professional position or role. To illustrate even more fully the power of a strengths perspective, the reader is now asked to enter the worldview of the client. As a client, would you find it helpful to have all the negatives about yourself and the situation emphasized? Or would you find it to be a real breath of fresh air for some professional to put your problems and issues in a wider, more holistic context that first emphasized your strengths, capabilities, and resilience? Would it be most helpful for you to leave a meeting with a professional feeling criticized or feeling supported?

Continuing the example introduced above, a traditional deficiency-oriented professional, who bases his or her opinions on the first information, might approach the family with the following feedback and plan. Remember to put yourself in the position of the parent and imagine that the professional is talking directly to you.

CASE VIGNETTE

Worker 1: (To Lyle's mother) You are going to have to dry out and shape up if you want to keep your kids. The house has got to get cleaned up and you have got to stop drinking. We can help you get alcohol treatment. But with your history, I have to warn you that the kids are at very high risk for placement. Lyle has got to go to school clean and well fed. I will be monitoring the situation to see that Lyle is taken care of.

How do you feel as the client hearing this? Are you motivated to work hard with this professional on the issues? Do you feel comfortable in expressing your opinions, disagreement, and discomfort, or are you inclined to keep quiet for fear of being further labeled as "resistant" or a "troublemaker"?

Contrast that experience with the following, more strengths-based approach.

CASE VIGNETTE

Worker 1: (To Lyle's mother) I want you to know that I think we need to do something about Lyle's situation—it's not good—but I have a lot of confidence that things can get better. I'm here to help support you in this, not to criticize and blame. I know you have struggled with lots of problems in the past, including alcohol and depression, but I also know that you care a lot about your kids, you work hard, you want your kids to succeed at school, and you have been able to conquer the depression and alcohol in the past. I want to help you get things back on track.

Now what are you feeling as the client? Do you feel more encouraged and motivated to work? Do you feel more comfortable about raising questions and concerns? Which approach is more likely to succeed with you?

Strengths Perspective in Direct Practice

Overview and Guidelines for Strengths Practice

The above scenario points out the contrast between the strengths and deficiency approaches. One of the first articles to articulate a strengths perspective for social work practice was published in *Social Work* in 1989 (Weick, Rapp, Sullivan, & Kisthardt, 1989). An extensive body of literature has since evolved that further explicates the strengths perspective. Despite criticisms that the approach is "Pollyannaish," is merely simplistic positive thinking, and ignores or downplays real problems, supporters believe that it offers professionals a new way of thinking and acting (Saleebey, 1996). Much of this literature is directly relevant to social work with children and families.

Goldstein (1990) explored and contrasted the concepts of "strength" and "pathology," concluding that the strength orientation is more responsive to the humanistic, ethical, and political conditions that characterize the helping process. According to Goldstein, a pathology approach is inadequate because it tends to reduce the complexities of the human state to narrow compartments of diagnostic schemes. This oversimplified approach cannot succeed as well as a strengths approach that, rather than being concerned with control, classification, and precision, emphasizes instead the vital and dynamic search for structure and security.

Saleebey (1996) further emphasized the differences between a strengths approach and conventional pathology-based approaches. These differences are summarized in the following table.

TABLE 6.1
Comparison of Pathology and Strengths

Pathology	Strengths
Person is defined as a "case"; symptoms add up to a diagnosis.	Person is defined as unique; traits, talents, resources add up to strengths.
Therapy is problem focused.	Therapy is possibility focused.
Personal accounts aid in the evocation of a diagnosis through reinterpretation by an expert.	Personal accounts are the essential route to knowing and appreciating the person.
Practitioner is skeptical of personal stories, rationalizations.	Practitioner knows the person from the inside out.
Childhood trauma is the precursor or predictor of adult pathology.	Childhood trauma is not predictive; it may weaken or strengthen the individual.
Centerpiece of therapeutic work is the treatment plan devised by practitioner.	Centerpiece of work is the aspirations of family, individual, or community.
Practitioner is the expert on clients' lives.	Individuals, family, or community are the experts.
Possibilities for choice, control, commitment, and personal development are limited by pathology.	Possibilities for choice, control, commitment, and personal development are open.
Resources for work are the knowledge and skills of the professional.	Resources for work are the strengths, capacities, and adaptive skills of the individual, family, or community.
Help is centered on reducing the effects of symptoms and the negative personal and social consequences of actions, emotions, thoughts, or relationships.	Help is centered on getting on with one's life, affirming and developing values and commitments, and making and finding membership in or as a community.

Source: D. Saleebey (1996), p. 298. Copyright © 1996 by National Association of Social Workers, Inc.

Cowger (1994) asserted that a strengths approach is congruent with client empowerment, in contrast to a deficiency approach that reinforces social structures that victimize and disempower clients. If assessment focuses on deficits, then it is likely that client deficits will continue to remain the focus. This deficit focus can lead to self-fulfilling prophesies, to an inability to discern the client's potential for growth, to reinforcement of clients' poor self image, and to client dependence. Cowger proposed the following 12 guidelines for strengths assessments.

Twelve Guidelines for Strengths Assessments (adapted from Cowger, 1994)

1. Give preeminence to the client's understanding of the facts.
2. Believe the client.
3. Discover what the client wants.
4. Move the assessment toward personal and environmental strengths.
5. Make assessment of strengths multidimensional.
6. Use the assessment to discover uniqueness.
7. Use language the client can understand.
8. Make assessment a joint activity between worker and client.
9. Reach a mutual agreement on the assessment.
10. Avoid blame and blaming.
11. Avoid cause-and-effect thinking.
12. Assess, do not diagnose.

Give Preeminence to the Client's Understanding of the Facts. The focus should be on the client's view of the situation, as stated in the client's own words. Social and behavioral scales and other paper and pencil assessment tools that categorize the client and the client's problems should not be overused or imposed on the client. These are appropriate only insofar as they identify strengths that can be applied in the situation or pinpoint obstacles to achieving client objectives.

Believe the Client. While it is true that some clients, like all other people, may prove to be untrustworthy in certain areas over time, it is a mistake to prejudge clients as untrustworthy. To do so would be contrary to social work values such as respect for client self-worth and dignity.

Discover What the Client Wants. What are the client's goals, and how does the client believe they can be attained? Although goals and interventions are ultimately subject to negotiation, starting with the client's own goals can enhance and support the client's own motivation.

Move the Assessment toward Personal and Environmental Strengths. While some attention must be paid to obstacles, solutions to difficult situations lie in strengths, so that dwelling on obstacles may have little success.

Make Assessments of Strengths Multidimensional. These multidimensions include the client's own interpersonal skills, motivation, and emotional and cognitive strengths. They also include strengths external to the client that are present in the family, significant others, community groups, and public institutions.

Use the Assessment to Discover Uniqueness. The strengths assessment helps the practitioner appreciate the individuality of the client, thus allowing both the practitioner and the client to appreciate what sets the client apart from other people.

Use Language That the Client Can Understand. Professional jargon is a barrier to effective practice. Both the written and spoken word should be in simple language that is easily understood by those who are not trained in the professional discipline.

Make Assessment a Joint Activity between Worker and Client. By stressing the importance of the client's understanding of the situation and the client's goals, the social worker can minimize the power imbalance between worker and client. If motivation is to be sustained, the client must feel some ownership of the process.

Reach Mutual Agreement on the Assessment. Social workers must openly share their own opinions and agendas, so that the final assessment document is openly negotiated. Hidden, privately held assessments make the client vulnerable to manipulation.

Avoid Blame and Blaming. Typically, neither the client nor any one aspect of the environment is to blame for situations. Rather, client situations are usually the result of a multitude of complex interactions and events. If clients are blamed, they can feel discouraged, unsupported, and lower in self-esteem. If blame is assigned to others, this may encourage learned helplessness or lower motivation.

Avoid Cause-and-Effect Thinking. Causal thinking can be overly simplistic and lead to blaming. Assessment should focus on here-and-now strengths and solutions, not antecedents in the past that focus narrowly on individual inadequacy. Too much attention to past causal factors distracts energy from the resolution of the problem.

Assess; Do Not Diagnose. Diagnosis is associated with a medical model of labeling. Unpopular or unacceptable behavior is seen as the symptom of some underlying pathological condition. Assessment is a much broader process than diagnosis, and it focuses on understanding the child's behavior in his or her ecological context (Lucco, 1991).

Solution-Focused Model

Of the above recommendations and guidelines, students often find that the most difficult to implement is the admonishment to avoid cause-and-effect thinking. It has been assumed that solutions to problems rest on an understanding of their cause. That is, a problem cannot be solved unless its causes are fully understood, so that interventions can be properly targeted. The problem-solving process, then, has always been predicated on the following steps.

> **Steps in Traditional Problem-Solving Process**
>
> **Step 1:** Identify or define the problem.
> **Step 2:** Understand the causes of the problem.
> **Step 3:** Find solutions to the problem, which eradicate or counteract the causes.

The above process is ingrained in our thinking. We learn this basic, logical way of thinking in grade school. This way of problem solving is essential to our hard sciences, where hypotheses about the cause of problems are tested by the scientific method. This way of problem solving is clearly evident in medicine, and people are exposed to it every time they see a doctor. It is evident when our automobile is not performing and we take it to the car mechanic and say, "Find the cause of the problem, then fix it!" In many arenas, this problem-solving process has served us well. But in the complex and multifaceted world of human problems, simple cause-and-effect thinking provides only simplistic, incomplete solutions.

A recently proposed alternative problem-solving model is a radical departure from the traditional problem-solving process described above (de Shazer, 1985; Walter & Peller, 1992). Called "solutions-focused," this form of problem solving asserts that it is not necessary to understand the cause of a client problem in order to solve it. Solutions to problems are to be found not in their causes, but in the strengths and coping capacities that people have developed in dealing with the problem. Rather than search for causes of problems, solution-focused practitioners look for exceptions to the problems, for times when the problem has not been an issue. It is these times of relative success that hold the key to the solution. What was different about that period of time? What strengths and resources did the client draw on, personally and environmentally? What positive coping mechanisms did the client employ? What was the client doing right?

Steps in Solution-Focused Problem-Solving Process

Step 1: Identify or define the problem.

Step 2: Understand the exceptions to the problem.

Step 3: Find solutions based on the exceptions to the problem.

The first step of the problem-solving process is the same for both the traditional and the solution-focused models: identify or define the problem. Both models require that clients and workers be able to bring the problem out of the realm of the vague and abstract, to define the problem in concrete terms. But the models radically depart on the second step of the problem-solving process. Rather than analyze the cause of the problem to find solutions, the solutions-focused model analyzes the exception to the problem: the times when the problem is not, or has not been, an issue.

This directs the client to strengths and coping capacities that the client may not have recognized (De Jong & Miller, 1995). The worker and client talk about the exception times, when the client has demonstrated competence in relation to their goals, not about the problem times and the client's deficiencies relative to the problem. Because it avoids cause-and-effect thinking and directs the client to discussions about competencies, the solutions-focused model is more compatible with a strengths perspective than is the traditional problem-solving model.

A brief example of the solutions-focused approach will illustrate the contrast between the two problem-solving methods.

CASE VIGNETTE: LaShonna

Carmelita, our school social worker, began work with a 7-year-old girl, LaShonna, and her teachers. The presenting problem was that LaShonna got into lots of fights at recess at school. These were usually with other girls, but sometimes also with boys, and they had resulted in bruises and minor injuries to children. The parents had been notified, were concerned, and were willing to do whatever was needed to help LaShonna.

Carmelita knew that there were many different ways to approach the situation. From a traditional cause-and-effect model, several different explanations were possible. It could be that LaShonna is angry or stressed about something at home or at school, and this is causing her to act out on the playground. In this case, individual and/or family counseling could get to the root of the problem. Or it could be that she has not learned to control her emotions and behavior and needs a behavior modification program that can reshape her behavior using various consequences. It could be that Carmelita lacks basic social skills and could benefit from a social-skills education group. Or it could be that Carmelita's aggression is caused by some form of physical, biochemical imbalance that medication could regulate. It could be that LaShonna is responding to some stimulus on the playground, so that a close observation of what occurs before the fights could help everyone understand what is causing it. Although these approaches differ on their specific focus, they all derive from the traditional problem-solving model discussed above because they seek to understand what is causing the problem and then to intervene to correct or ameliorate the cause.

Instead of these approaches, Carmelita chose to implement a solutions-focused method. Carmelita asked the teachers and LaShonna to observe and note what was different about those occasions when the fighting did not happen on the playground. She asked them to focus on the exception to the problem, rather than on the problem itself and its cause. This was not easy for the teachers or for LaShonna to do. They had hardly ever noticed those occasions when the fighting didn't happen, and they continued to report to Carmelita on the fights themselves. Soon, though, with Carmelita's persistence, LaShonna and her teachers began to closely note and observe those times when LaShonna was successful at recess. They noticed that, at those successful times, LaShonna played with three specific girls, avoiding contact with almost everyone else. They also noticed that, on successful occasions, when a situation arose with the potential for conflict, LaShonna yelled at the other student, then walked away.

Carmelita pointed out that LaShonna had been solving her problem all along, on some days. Though not aware of it, what she had been doing to solve the problem was to play with three specific girls, and to yell and walk away from potential trouble. Rather than focus on what LaShonna had been doing wrong, Carmelita helped her to see what she had been doing right. LaShonna discovered, and Carmelita reinforced, the strengths that LaShonna was displaying during times of success. Rather than feeling inadequate and criticized, LaShonna felt bolstered, smart, and competent. With her new awareness and resolve, LaShonna and her teachers were able to implement the solutions to the problem: play with the three girls, and yell and walk away from trouble. As a result, none of the above interventions—individual and family therapy, behavior modification, social skills group, medication—was necessary in this particular case.

Strengths Perspective in Group Work

The principles of the strengths perspective are useful in group work with children and adolescents. According to Malekoff (2001), the early social group work traditions were laden with a strengths and empowerment perspective, but those traditions have been transformed into current group work practices that are the antithesis of the strengths perspective: "Much of what passes as group work today is nothing more than curriculum-driven pseudo group work with little interaction amongst group members, no mutual aid, cookbook agendas, and canned exercises. The emphasis is on controlling kids, shoving education down their throats, and stamping out spontaneity and creativity" (p. 247).

The author discusses the following seven principles for a strengths-based approach to group work with youth.

Strengths Perspective and Resilience in Children

The common presumption in a deficit approach is that children who face stressful, high-risk situations will invariably have little success as adults. This notion has been challenged by adherents

---

Seven Principles for Strengths-Based Group Work (adapted from Malekoff, 2001)

1. Form a group based on addressing shared needs, not on the basis of diagnosis or label.
2. Structure the group to include the whole person, not just the hurt and troubled parts.
3. Value verbal and nonverbal activities that don't define success as kids talking politely and insightfully.
4. Turn control over to the group members to encourage mutual aid and what each member has to offer.
5. Keep a dual focus on the individual needs and the need to change not only oneself, but also one's surroundings.
6. Treat parents as allies and not as enemies.
7. Value the developmental life of a group and understand that each group has a unique personality.

of the strengths perspective who argue that it is possible for many children to overcome these challenges without a great deal of professional help. There is a growing body of research that studies *resilience* in children, or the capacity to achieve positive outcomes in the face of high-risk situations (Kirby & Fraser, 1997). Many of these studies are longitudinal studies that have tracked large groups of children from an early age into adulthood, identifying both risk and protective factors that appear to influence outcome. Overall, it appears that about one-third of those children who experience high-risk, stressful childhoods grow up to be well-adjusted, successful adults.

Although this research has not been able to identify the specific ways in which risk and protective factors interact, a general model of resilience has emerged. Kirby and Fraser (1997) have discussed this model that identifies risk and protective factors at three systems levels. At the broad environmental level, risk factors can negatively influence the overall development of the child. Chief among these risk factors are poverty, racial discrimination, and few opportunities for education and employment. The protective factors at this broad environmental level are opportunity and family support. At the family, school, and neighborhood level, risk factors involve child maltreatment, parental conflict, parental psychopathology, and generally poor parenting. Protective factors at this level are social supports in the neighborhood and community, the presence of a caring and supportive adult, and effective parenting with a positive parent-child relationship. At the individual level of biological and psychosocial characteristics, the risk factors are gender and biomedical problems. Boys appear to have more difficulty coping with stressors such as divorce, while girls have relatively more difficulties in school. Protective factors at the individual level include an easy temperament, competence in normative roles, self-esteem, and higher levels of intelligence.

The resiliency literature provides a foundation for the strengths perspective in practice. Rather than focusing on the negatives in a child's situation, this literature encourages practitioners to look for the strengths and protective factors that can be bolstered to mitigate against the high-risk factors. In addition, the literature encourages that prevention activities be aimed at multiple systems, to reduce or eliminate the high-risk conditions that spawn poor adult outcomes.

Strengths Perspective in Policy Development

Consistent with Cowger's view that a strengths approach can lead to client empowerment, Weick and Saleebey (1995) discuss and analyze how policy and practice must support family strengths as we move into the twenty-first century. Families have been criticized, categorized, and therapized from narrow, deficiency-oriented perspectives for too long. Reversing this trend toward a strengths approach requires attention to the political, economic, racial, and social context of families' lives. The goal of social work with families is to help families gain access to knowledge, resources, and tools that assist them to solve their problems and achieve their aspirations. Social workers can accomplish this goal by becoming agents of the family, helping them develop strategic and tactical plans and maneuvers that can help them solve their problems and achieve their aspirations.

A strengths perspective is also important at the social policy level, where it can be useful in reformulating the problem-focused, pathology-centered approaches that dominate policy development (Chapin, 1995). Traditionally, policy analysis has focused on finding the causes of the social problem, and too often has located those causes within the individual deficiencies of those people who are affected by the problem. Even when the root of the problem is located in environmental and institutional barriers, traditional problem analysis has taken a blaming approach, rather than identifying the strengths and resources in the individual and community.

A strengths approach to policy development would differ from the traditional approach in several ways (Chapin, 1995). First, the voice of the client would strongly dominate the process. From identification of needs, to identification of barriers, to identification of successful intervention strategies, to identification of desired client outcomes, the experiences of those affected would drive the process. Since clients are viewed as people with strengths rather than as deficient or pathological, the strengths-oriented policy specialist views their inclusion as a necessity. Second, the strengths perspective recasts the foundation of the policy-making process from a social problems foundation to a human needs foundation. This emphasis on human needs rather than social problems mitigates the blaming and labeling process, focusing the analysis on the various legitimate ways that people get help in meeting those needs without being negatively labeled. Rather than focusing on problem definition and analysis, the strengths approach focuses on common human needs and the barriers to meeting those needs. Third, the strengths approach alters the relationship between the policymakers and those who are to be helped. In the traditional approach, the policymaker was the expert who analyzed a social problem, developed policy goals and solutions, and informed the public. In contrast, utilizing the strengths perspective, the policymaker gives voice to client perspectives, helps negotiate definitions and goals that include those perspectives, and includes the client as collaborator in the entire process, including evaluation. When policymakers view the people experiencing the problem as cocreators of social policy, then new possibilities emerge. Action can be guided by client stories of survival and strength, rather than misconceptions about client deficiencies. Often, this can lead to identification of informal community resources that policymakers can bolster.

Strengths Perspective in Child Welfare

Strengths Perspective with Parents of Abused and Neglected Children

The strengths perspective may encounter its most difficult challenge in its application to the parents that populate child welfare. Social workers can be revolted at the harm that parents can perpetrate on children. "How could anybody do this to a child?" and "They should lock those parents up and throw away the key" are common, gut-level responses to child abuse and neglect. With these feelings, it is hard to avoid the deficiency perspective, to focus instead on the strengths and capabilities of the parents.

The key to successful implementation of a strengths perspective with this population is to believe that abusive and neglectful parents are like all other people in that they have the ability and motivation to grow and achieve competence (Pecora, et al., 1992). It is important to believe that most people are doing the best they can, given their circumstances. Workers view the parents as capable of learning new skills and are sensitive to the pressures and stresses imposed by societal conditions that limit the power of parents and interfere with their coping efforts. Thus, the parents are seen as needing not treatment for their pathology, but help and support in learning skills and developing a sense of mastery and control. Situations and problems are reframed as stemming from lack of knowledge, inadequate coping and support, or disempowering social conditions. The social worker's task is to help secure the necessary services and supports needed to sustain the growth and empowerment of the parents. These efforts may involve parent education, self-help groups such as Parents Anonymous, communication-skills training, anger-management classes, job training, and other supports.

By taking a positive approach in the assessment and intervention phases, the worker can build the parent's self esteem and reverse critical, negative patterns in the family. Solution-focused questions that focus not on the abuse and neglect but on exception times when the parents and family have been able to avoid or prevent abusive situations can help the family discover solutions to the problem.

Strengths Perspective with Children Who Have Been Abused and Neglected

The concept of resiliency in children is both helpful and potentially dangerous in working with children who have been abused and neglected. One has only to "walk a mile in the shoes" of an abused or neglected child to appreciate the tremendous strength and resiliency that most possess. Even though many may appear to struggle in school or with behavior, if a person imagines how he or she would be functioning if the same abuse had happened to oneself, then usually the person is amazed at how much worse the child's functioning could be, and how relatively well the child is doing. Like most people, most children are doing the best they can, given their circumstances.

But there is a potential danger in the resiliency and strengths perspectives with abused children of minimizing the impact of the abuse and down-playing the needs of the abused child. An inappropriate, cavalier extension of the strengths perspective is to say, "He'll be OK. Kids are tough and they can cope with anything. They are very resilient. He's a survivor." In order to avoid this inappropriate application of the strengths perspective, social workers need to know that the resiliency of children is highly variable from one child to another. First, some children are born with constitutional make-ups that are stronger and more adaptable than others. Second, for all children, resiliency is associated with environmental supports and opportunities. So, the correct conclusion to be drawn about resiliency in abused children is that, although many do better than expected, many others struggle in their development, and most do not do as well as kids who have not been abused. The development of resiliency in all abused and neglected can be enhanced through the provision of environmental supports.

Strengths Perspective in Children's Mental Health

There are several ways in which the social worker can maintain a strengths perspective in working with children with serious emotional disorders and their families. Three will be discussed in this section: the disability model, systematic assessment of strengths, and avoiding blame.

The Disability Model

Poertner and Ronnau (1992) advocate that practitioners adopt a disability model of childhood emotional disorders. This frame of reference is deemed less stigmatizing because the general public views a disability as something that can be compensated for and coped with. A disability is a condition that an individual can adapt to, functioning successfully with support—not an illness that can be cured. Under this model, the emotional disability is only one of the child's characteristics. Other strengths, abilities, interests, and characteristics account for other aspects and portions of their lives. They have the capacity to learn, grow, and offer informed opinions about their disability and their care. Adopting a disability model places the

child within the purview of the disability rights movement, with its attendant focus on inclusion in the mainstream of society and the importance of society making reasonable accommodations for the youth.

Systematic Assessment of Strengths

Teresa Early (2001) has identified and discussed several measurement instruments that can be used to measure child and family strengths. A prime example is a structured measurement scale to assess the emotional and behavioral strengths of children (Epstein, 1999). The Behavioral and Emotional Rating Scale (BERS) was developed to supplement the deficit-oriented assessment scales prevalent in the mental health field. The 52-item scale is completed by teachers or other direct-service providers and identifies strengths on five dimensions: interpersonal strengths, family involvement, intrapersonal strengths, school functioning, and affective strengths. Examples of items include: for interpersonal strengths, "accepts no for an answer" and "admits mistakes"; for family involvement, "interacts positively with siblings" and "participates in family activities"; for intrapersonal strengths, "smiles often" and "demonstrates a sense of humor"; for school functioning, "attends school regularly" and "exhibits interest in school activities"; for affective strengths, "accepts a hug" and "asks for help." The BERS has been normed on a national sample of 2,176 children without disabilities and 861 children with emotional and behavioral disorders.

Avoiding Blame

As initially discussed in the previous chapter, the assessment and diagnosis process is a fertile ground for the tension between a deficiency and strengths approach. Diagnostic labels carry stigma and encourage attention to pathology. In answering the assessment question, "Why, at this particular time, is this particular child exhibiting these particular behaviors," the social worker must normalize and contextualize the behavior as much as possible, without minimizing or discounting the seriousness of it. In other words, child behaviors can emanate from a variety of sources and be viewed from a number of perspectives. Serious misbehavior to one person might be within a normal range to another. Even when it is agreed that a misbehavior is serious, opinions about the causes of that behavior can vary widely. Thus, it is essential that the professionals do not label behavior as pathological if it can legitimately be seen as falling within a normal range. When behavior is seen as seriously problematic, it is essential that professionals not assume that the source of the behavior is rooted in individual psychopathology, willful misbehavior, or dysfunctional family dynamics.

This is not a call for underdiagnosis. It is, however, a caution against overdiagnosis. A strengths approach does not ignore legitimate problems in a Pollyannaish fashion. When children are struggling, it is important to give them the help and the resources they need to succeed. Too often, professionals have minimized the legitimate issues of children, with homilies such as "she'll grow out of it" or "he's just an excitable boy." But a strengths approach is cautious about overreacting to children's behavior and making things more serious and complicated than they need to be. The following guidelines are offered to help social workers remember to begin answering the above assessment question with consideration for the potential relevance of the most normal, least pathological point of view on the presenting problem behaviors. Before jumping to conclusions about severe pathology, the social worker is first obliged to rule out other, more normalized, ways of viewing the behavior.

Guidelines for Avoiding Blame in Mental Health Assessments

Steps in answering the question: "Why at this particular time is this particular child engaging in this particular behavior?"

- **Step 1:** Is the behavior within a "normal" range?
- **Step 2:** Was the child "born that way"?
- **Step 3:** Is the behavior some type of adjustment reaction?
- **Step 4:** Is the behavior a result of severe trauma?
- **Step 5:** Is this a learned behavior?

Step 1: Is the behavior within a "normal" range? In chapter 2, the idea was introduced that normal childhood behavior can be labeled as deviant or pathological. Professionals are trained to diagnose and identify pathology, so they tend to find pathology wherever they look. In this assessment step, the social worker considers the possibility that compared to other children, this child's behavior is normal, but adults are viewing it as abnormal or pathological. When this is the case, the focus of intervention for the social worker becomes the adults who have, for some reason, singled the child out. Adults might do this out of lack of knowledge of developmental norms, racial or other type of bias, a tendency to exaggerate and overreact, or for some other reason. Often in a mental health setting, parents are unsure about whether or not certain behaviors are serious or within the normal range, and they are seeking some objective input from a professional. Parents may in fact be reluctant to seek such input from professionals because of fear that the problems will be blown out of proportion.

Step 2: Was the child "born that way"? In this step, the social worker considers that the behavior can be attributed, in large part, to the child's constitutional make-up and temperament. In this level of understanding, the child's behavior is seen as "abnormal" compared to most children, but relatively "normal" for this particular child. As more biomedical research is conducted, more and more adult and childhood mental disorders are discovered to have a biochemical etiology. In adults, examples of this are schizophrenia, depression, and bipolar disorder. Although these conditions can be exacerbated by environmental conditions, and a small proportion of sufferers do not have a biochemical basis for their disorder, the predominant professional view now is that environmental and interpersonal dynamics are not the primary cause for these disorders in most people.

In children, autism and ADHD are two conditions that have a strong biological or neurological basis. But our focus should not be confined to diagnostic categories. For all children, it is important to understand their basic temperament and whether the current behavior is an extension of that temperament or a departure from it. For example, was the aggressive, loud, and oppositional 9-year-old boy an active, assertive, and vocal baby, or was he quiet and passive?

When a child's constitution is found to be a major factor, then biomedical responses such as medication become a more crucial element of the treatment. Adults can view the child as having a medical condition or a disability, so that the goal for the child, family, and adults becomes one of coping with the condition rather than curing the behavior. With such a mindset, some adults may become more realistic in their expectations and more patient in their responses.

Step 3: Is the behavior some type of adjustment reaction? In this step, the social worker considers the stresses and pressures emanating from the child's environment. The child's presenting problem is not viewed as essentially normal, nor is there a strong constitutional component to the behavior. The child's behavior may be a reaction to (a) a troublesome event or situation, or (b) a developmental stage. Troublesome events or situations include divorce, death, change of residence or school, loss of family income, discrimination, and so forth. When children become stressed or worried, they often do not know how to cope with their anxieties, so that they "act out" their anxieties behaviorally. In addition to stressful events, these anxieties may be triggered by a stage of development or a developmental task that is challenging or frightening to the child. In these cases, the environmental pressures stem from internal and external demands for the child to "grow up."

With this view and understanding of the problem, the adults can see the behavior as a sort of symptom of an underlying adjustment issue at the symptom's core. Interventions can then be targeted more at ways in which the environment can help the child cope with the situation, and not exclusively on the behavior itself. This level of understanding is often well received by adults, because the behavior can be understood as an almost normal, albeit not very successful, way of coping with the situation. This way of framing the problem does not blame anyone and points a relatively clear direction for how the child and family can resolve the problems.

Step 4: Is the behavior a result of severe trauma? This step could be seen as an extension of the previous one, in that the child's behavior is a reaction to some event or circumstance. The difference is in the degree of severity of the event, and the extraordinary difficulty that most people have in coping with the event. Traumas such as sexual abuse, physical abuse, neglect, exposure to violence, and natural disasters fall into this category. When any of these exist in a client history, regardless of how long ago, it is important to consider that there may be a link between the traumatic event and the behavior.

Play therapy and other forms of expressive therapy may be indicated to help these children cognitively and emotionally integrate their past experiences. Family therapy and cognitive-behavioral therapy may also be used, as long as they recognize the link between the child's behavior and the trauma. Mental health centers and psychiatric hospitals are full of adults who were traumatized as children and did not receive expert help as children in coping with the trauma.

Step 5: Is this a learned behavior? In this fifth step, the social worker considers that the behavior is in some way learned and reinforced. From parents, peers, or other sources, the child has learned that the behavior is acceptable and it has some positive consequences. This perspective is categorized as more pathology-oriented than previous ones because blame is often attributed. The child may be viewed as engaging in "willful misbehavior," having intentional control over the behavior and an unwillingness to change. The parents may be blamed for having modeled the behavior or for not having implemented effective measures to correct or resolve the problems. From a family systems or family therapy perspective, the child's behaviors may be seen as a way for the parents to deflect attention away from their marital problems, thus serving to keep the family together.

In this context, interventions can focus on the behavior itself using behavior modification, or on teaching the parents how to help the child unlearn the behavior, or on addressing the more subtle family dynamics that reinforce the behavior. If extreme caution is maintained to avoid blaming, this way of framing the problem can lead to educational interventions which are less stigmatizing to parents. The message communicated to the parents is not that they are bad or crazy or incompetent, but that they are uninformed. This approach presumes that they are competent and willing to change once they have the information.

Note that the above steps are not mutually exclusive. Often more than one perspective is useful in fully understanding a child's behavior. There may be trauma, adjustment issues, constitutional factors, and learning dynamics that all must be recognized and addressed for a thorough and complete understanding and resolution of the problems to occur.

CHAPTER 6 SUMMARY

The strengths perspective is vital to social work with both children and families. For too long, professionals have operated from a deficiency perspective that focuses unnecessarily on the negative aspects of behavior. The strengths perspective is integral to combating adultcentrism, engaging in family-centered practice, and respecting diversity and difference. Specific guidelines for conducting strengths assessments in direct practice were presented and discussed. The solutions-focused approach to problem solving was introduced, with particular attention placed on the contrast between this approach and traditional problem solving with respect to the issue of cause-and-effect thinking. Next, a discussion of the utility of the strengths approach in policy development was presented. Finally, direct applications of the strengths perspective in child welfare and children's mental health were discussed, with particular emphasis on the concept of resiliency in the child welfare arena and guidelines for avoiding blame in the children's mental health arena.

CHAPTER 7

Pragmatic Perspective 4: Respect for Diversity and Difference

Overview

The fourth pragmatic perspective, respect for diversity and difference, explores this important process as it specifically applies to child and family settings. This chapter presents an overview of the problem of prejudice and discrimination, followed by discussions of the dynamics of powerlessness, cultural competence, cultural mapping, understanding gay and lesbian adolescents, and gender bias. The chapter concludes with specific applications in the child welfare and children's mental health service systems.

Overview of the Problem of Prejudice and Discrimination

Because the United States is home to an increasingly diverse and heterogeneous population, today's social work practitioners must be comfortable with diverse populations (Pinderhughes, 1995). Interactions among people from different cultural and social backgrounds are becoming more and more common, and will be even more commonplace in the future. Between 1991 and 2025, the population of ethnic minorities and people of color in the United States will double (U.S. Bureau of the Census, 1991). Children from racial minorities constitute the most rapidly growing group in the population: by the year 2010, one in every four children will be a child of color (Chan, 1990). As society has become more tolerant, more and more Americans are publicly acknowledging their gay and lesbian sexual orientation. Many of these people are also the primary parents or caregivers of children, so that the definition of family is taking on new meaning. Children with disabil-

ities are becoming more visible in schools and communities as advocacy efforts continue to have an impact at the federal, state, and local levels. Preparing social workers for practice with diverse populations has never been more important. Although there has been much progress in the United States in reducing prejudice and discrimination, the experiences of many of those who are in some way different from the middle-class, white, male majority indicate that much improvement is still required.

The need for improvement is also evident in the grim comparisons of the health and welfare of minority and poor children as compared to the rest of the population. As mentioned in chapter 1, the infant mortality rate for black children is more than twice that for whites; fewer black children and poor children receive childhood immunizations; the reading levels of black, Native American, and Latino children are well below that for whites; black children stay in foster care longer than whites; and young Latinos and blacks are twice as likely to be unemployed as whites.

The struggle to combat potential bias is a constant in social work practice with children and families. The chapter on combating adultcentrism (chapter 4) analyzed how adult bias can negatively affect practice with children; how adults, because of their difference in age, see the world very differently than do children; and how this different worldview can be imposed on children to their detriment. In addition to this age difference, many other differences between the social workers and their clients can be sources for miscommunication, inaccurate judgments, and ineffective practice. These include differences of race, ethnicity, income, gender, disability, and sexual orientation. Whenever a difference exists, there is a danger that the difference will be viewed or judged as better or worse (usually worse), rather than as simply different. The goal is to value and respect differences as they are, rather than view them as something deviant that needs to be changed. Adults don't need to push so hard for children to like adults; heterosexuals do not need to try to change homosexuals; whites do not need to change African American values and lifestyles.

For beginning social work direct practice clinicians, this pragmatic perspective is important because any bias in the interactions that social workers have with clients can negatively affect the outcome. It is important that social workers be aware of their potential weaknesses in this area and combat those weaknesses with diligence. Awareness of one's own propensity to place value judgments on differences can be heightened by being aware of the various ways that prejudice can manifest itself.

The most obvious form of prejudice is conscious and overt discrimination. In this situation, a person consciously believes that the observed difference makes the other person inferior and defective. While few social workers would consciously judge racial differences in this way, many may be aware of conscious prejudices in the realm of gender or sexual orientation. For example, based on family or cultural mores, some men may view women as inferior. Or, based on religious upbringing, some heterosexuals may believe that homosexuality is a moral deficiency.

Beyond conscious bias and discrimination, there are three more subtle unintentional forms of prejudice social workers also need to examine. One form occurs when different standards are applied to different people, without conscious awareness. For example, without being aware of it, a teacher can single out the behavior of an African American child for disciplinary action when the same behavior conducted by a white child is ignored. Or similar differential treatment may occur with respect to males and females. In child welfare, the physicians, nurses, and social workers in the emergency room of a hospital may unconsciously respond to the injuries of poor children, or people of color, in a different way than they do the white upper class. The bruises on a poor, minority-race child may be seen as reason to report for child abuse and neglect, whereas the same bruises on an upper-middle-class white child may be quickly accepted as the result of an accident. Thus, without intention, the same behavior or circumstance is responded to differently, using a different standard, because of the difference in the person exhibiting the behavior or circumstance.

A second form of subtle prejudice occurs when a person or group uses a standard for judgment that appears to be objective, but is in fact biased. Whereas the above form of prejudice involved imposing different standards for the same behavior, this second form of unintentional prejudice involves using just one standard, but without realizing that the standard is itself biased. The thinking is, "I'm not prejudiced, because I use the same standards for judging people, regardless of who they are." But what if the standard is itself biased and ethnocentric? Standardized tests to measure intelligence are an example of this subtle form of discrimination. These tests have been widely criticized as being unfair to racial minorities, and to a lesser extent, females. The same standard is applied to all groups, but the standard favors one group over another. Another example occurs in child welfare, when a standard for child-raising or parenting that is culturally specific is applied to all groups as if it were a universal standard. In a white, rural community, the standard for proper child care may not be the same standard as in the urban, African American inner city. Parenting norms vary across race and culture regarding the use of corporal punishment, the age and length of time that children can be left alone unattended, and the age at which older siblings can be expected to care for younger ones. Attempting to apply one universal standard for child care and parenting to all races, cultures, and socioeconomic classes may not respect the diversity of norms that exist in the population.

A third form of subtle, and largely unconscious, prejudice occurs when a well-intentioned person minimizes the significance or meaning that an event or situation might have to the person who is different. The difference between the two people is responsible for a different perspective on a situation, but this different perspective is not appreciated or respected fully. For example, in schools, heterosexual school social workers may not fully appreciate the pain and suffering that young gay and lesbian teenagers feel. In the field of adoptions, whites have a difficult time understanding why most African Americans insist that African American children be adopted by African Americans. The well-intentioned social workers want

the children raised in permanent homes, and they cannot understand why a child can't be adopted by a white family, if no African American adoptive homes are available.

In this form of prejudice, the social worker can conduct a "check" on their own potential for prejudice by reversing the situation, and assessing whether the social worker's feelings would be the same when the situation is reversed. Suppose that there were many white children available for adoption, and many African American families to adopt them. Would the white social worker be so quick to want the child adopted? In this reversed situation, wouldn't there be more time, energy, and money spent to recruit white adoptive families than is being spent now to recruit African American adoptive parents?

The following case vignette underscores how this third form of prejudice can negatively affect outcome.

CASE VIGNETTE: Kevin

Kevin is a 12-year-old African American male who has been living in the same group home with the same houseparents for 5 years. He has special needs in the areas of mental retardation and behavioral/emotional functioning. Susan has been his foster care worker for the last 2 years. Kevin was removed from his mother's care when he was 7 due to serious, repeated neglect and abuse that stemmed from his mother's severe alcoholism. Over the 5 years, his mother has made only sporadic attempts to get Kevin back, and has had only brief periods of sobriety. The official goal of the case plan is reintegration with the mother (Kevin's father is deceased), but Susan and the rest of the professionals working with Kevin believe that long-term foster care in the group home is more realistic. Kevin has done well at the group home, the houseparents like him and are committed to him, and he has a sense of permanence in the group home. Adoption, in the professionals' opinion, would disrupt his attachment to the group home parents, disrupt his contacts and attachment to his biological mother, and be difficult to accomplish because of Kevin's race, age, and special needs.

The only problem is that Kevin wants to live in an African American family. Kevin has awareness and interest in his racial heritage, and although he likes his white houseparents and gets along with the mostly white kids at the group home, Kevin yearns to be raised in an African American family. Over the 5 years he has been at the group home, Kevin has stated this preference numerous times, but the well-intentioned professionals minimized his concerns, as the situation was stable and Kevin seemed to be doing well. As his perspective was repeatedly ignored, Kevin began to escalate his behavior. He "ran away" from the group home (going just a few blocks) and said that he wanted to kill himself. When asked to explain his behavior, Kevin at first was silent, and then cited his anger at not getting certain privileges at the home. With further discussion, Kevin repeated that he wanted to live in a black family if he couldn't go home to his mother. At first, the professional staff did not take Kevin seriously, viewing his behavior as "manipulative," trying to get extra privileges.

But when he repeated the behavior twice more, Susan began to listen. She realized that her past opinion about Kevin's best interests were both adultcentric and racially biased. Why had she so quickly dismissed Kevin's perspective? She reversed the situation, and considered how her opinion would change if Kevin had been a white child, placed with African American parents and mostly African American residents. Susan had to admit that, in such a reversed situation, she might have given more weight to Kevin's perspective. She could more easily identify with how hard it would be for a white child growing up in an African American household. Based on her new appreciation of the situation, Susan moved the system toward severance of parental rights and adoption. As it turned out, Kevin was adopted by a relative, and he maintained contact with both his biological mother and his former houseparents.

The following sections present several topics to help the reader in the ongoing struggle to respect diversity and difference. These include the dynamics of powerlessness, cultural competence, culturagrams for cultural mapping, understanding gay and lesbian adolescents, and combating gender bias.

Dynamics of Powerlessness

Minority groups in the United States share in the experience of powerlessness. It is important for social workers to understand the experience of powerlessness in their clients' lives and to be sensitive to the power dynamics that can operate between themselves and their clients. The ideas of Pinderhughes (1995) have illuminated the importance of the dynamics of powerlessness to the practice of social work and are the basis for this section.

Power is "the capacity to influence for one's own benefit the forces that affect one's life space" and/or "the capacity to produce desired effects on others" (Pinderhughes, 1995, p. 133). Because the dominant society has long viewed people of color, women, and gays as inferior, society has used stereotyping, discrimination, and stratification to assign lesser value to these groups. These processes have created policies and structures that limit access to opportunities and resources and lessen the quality of life. In this context, people in these disaffected groups can feel powerlessness at several interrelated levels. At the society level, the group is assigned lower status; at the institutional level, the group has little authority; at the interactional level, members of the group are dominated; and at the individual level, members feel less mastery, competence, and control.

It is important for social workers to empathize with how people respond, or adapt, to this lack of power in their lives. In order to combat a view of themselves as powerless victims, people respond to a lack of power in a variety of ways. Some disempowered people struggle to prove their worth to the larger society by trying to counteract the stereotypes perpetuated about them that suggest they are incompetent, dumb, dangerous, immoral, and dependent. Others become guarded, aggressive, dependent, or stubbornly autonomous. Another way of coping with powerlessness is to transform impotence into an active force by transforming the negative stereotypes into active positive forces. For example, African Americans have changed the use of the word *bad* to mean "good," and use the hated word *nigger* as a term of affection and warmth (Pinderhughes, 1995).

Regardless of the specific type of behavior, social workers must consider that the problematic behavior of a member of a disempowered group may be related to a sense of powerlessness, and not necessarily to individual or family pathology. If behaviors are viewed as the adaptive, coping responses to powerlessness, then they are less likely to be seen as deficient or pathological. This different view of the behavior can lead to much different types of intervention strategies, strategies that focus on empowerment of the individual or group. These strategies are designed to help clients view problems and needs in a larger social context, to see the connections between their behaviors, their sense of powerlessness, and powerless societal roles. Clients can be helped to see how powerless social roles can undermine individual and family functioning, how behaviors that begin as adaptive responses to a harsh and powerless situation can become exaggerated to the point that they become maladaptive. For example, a rigid, controlling, and physically abusive father could learn that his behavior might reflect a misdirected and exaggerated desire to protect his family and gain a sense of personal control in a chaotic and racist environment. In the same manner, a cautious lifestyle developed in response to powerlessness can become immobilization, persistence can turn to stubbornness, and protectiveness can become smothering.

Social workers, particularly those of the dominant group, must also understand how people respond to having power. Generally, they feel gratified, competent, and in control, and they behave in ways that exert influence and control. Everyone needs to feel a sense of power, but practitioners must guard against getting this need met through interactions with clients, because this can lead to exploitation. As one who has experienced power in the world, it is critical that the dominant-group social worker not misuse that sense of power with clients. If the professional is white, male, and/or middle class, and the client is a person of color, female, or poor, the situation is ripe for misuse of power. This can occur if the professional is not aware of his or her own power needs and the ways in which he or she exercises influence and control in the world. Professionals can misuse power by focusing on the pathology of others, by holding themselves out as superior experts who possess privileged knowledge, and by reinforcing client perceptions of themselves as incompetent and unworthy.

Cultural Competence

Effective practice with diverse populations requires culturally competent individual practitioners and organizations. To become culturally competent practitioners, social workers must develop a set of abilities and capacities that facilitate their work with diverse populations. Social workers must be able to see the world through the eyes of their clients, by learning about the values, beliefs, and customs of the group(s) to which the client belongs. They must be able to assess their own values, beliefs, and culture to ferret out and change false assumptions and stereotypes. Social workers must be able to think and behave flexibly and without judging, respecting and valuing diversity as a positive, enriching characteristic of human life. In learning about the cultural values and norms of a diverse group, the social worker must be able to assess how the general knowledge about the group does or does not apply to a specific child or family.

At the organizational level, cultural competence manifests itself in the policies and programs of the organization. In order to help organizations assess their own organizational development toward cultural competence, Cross (1988) presented the idea of a cultural competence continuum. There are six points along the continuum: cultural destructiveness, cultural incapacity, cultural blindness, cultural pre-competence, cultural competence, and cultural proficiency.

Cultural Competence Continuum for Organizations (adapted from Cross, 1988)	
Best	Cultural Proficiency
	Cultural Competence
	Cultural Pre-competence
	Cultural Blindness
	Cultural Incapacity
Worst	Cultural Destructiveness

Cultural Destructiveness. In this most negative point on the cultural competence continuum, the dominant group assumes superiority and consciously sets out to eradicate the lesser cultures and groups. Overt bigotry and significant power differentials allow the dominant group to disenfranchise, control, and even destroy the minority population. Hitler's Nazi movement in Germany in World War II and slavery in the United States are two of the more blatant examples of cultural destructiveness. In the United States, other recent examples of cultural destructiveness include boarding schools for Native Americans that purposely set out to eradicate the culture, purposefully denying people of color access to their natural helpers or healers, and removing children from their home on the basis of race. While it is rare for public officials to voice overt bigotry with respect to race, cultural destructiveness is evident in contemporary public discussions about gays and lesbians, for many people continue to publicly advocate the condemnation and eradication of that lifestyle.

Cultural Incapacity. In this next point on the continuum, organizations do not intentionally seek to be destructive, but neither do they exert any capacity to be helpful to minority groups. The system itself remains biased, but that bias is expressed in more subtle forms. People are ignorant or fearful of diverse groups and display a paternalistic posture toward them. Discrimination and segregation are common policies, and minority populations are given various messages that they are unwelcome.

Cultural Blindness. This point on the continuum is characterized by a well-intentioned desire to be unbiased. The expressed philosophy is that all people are the same and that color or culture should make no difference. But this attitude leads to ethnocentrism in the organization and delivery of helping services. Ethnocentric helping approaches and other dominant-culture attitudes and values are deemed universally applicable, with little regard for their relevancy to minority populations. Cultural blindness goes hand in hand with assimilation, which denigrates the unique strengths and capabilities of diverse groups and blames the victims for their problems. Examples of cultural blindness include foster care licensing standards that restrict licensure of extended family systems occupying one home, pretending not to notice the race or other diversity characteristic of a client, and exhibiting little motivation to learn more information about diverse groups.

Cultural Pre-competence. This point on the continuum is characterized by a sincere desire to improve services to minority populations. It is the beginning phase of movement toward genuine cultural competence, marked by efforts to recruit minority staff, train workers on cultural sensitivity, conduct needs assessments, and recruit representatives of the minority community to serve on committees and boards. This type of organization has begun the process toward cultural competence but lacks information and expertise on how to proceed. The danger here is that the organization will stop too soon and be satisfied with some level of "tokenism."

Cultural Competence. At this point of the continuum, organizations are proactive in their approach to diversity. They conduct continuous self-assessments, continuously expand their cultural knowledge and resources, and adapt service models to better meet the needs of minority populations. They view minority groups as distinctly different and each containing numerous subgroups. Representation of minority populations on staff and on policy boards goes beyond tokenism to significant and meaningful representation and influence.

Cultural Proficiency. Beyond the level of cultural competence, some organizations reach the level of cultural proficiency. At this level, cultural competence is totally ingrained within the operation of the organization. Diversity is not just respected, it is held in the highest esteem. Culturally proficient organizations advocate for cultural competence throughout the community, sponsor activities for improved relations among groups, and build the knowledge base for culturally competent practice by conducting research and sponsoring demonstration projects.

Cultural Mapping

The Culturagram

The culturagram is a practice tool that can help social workers understand and empower culturally diverse families (Congress, 1994). It has particular relevance for families of recent immigrants to the United States. The culturagram can help social workers individualize clients, thus avoiding generalizations stemming from general knowledge about a group. The culturagram provides a forum for the discussion of different aspects of the specific family, as depicted in the figure below:

FIGURE 7.1
Culturagram

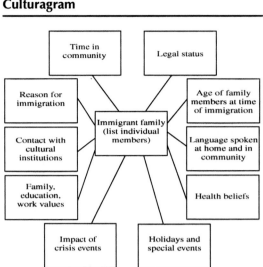

From E.P. Congress, "The use of culturagrams to assess and empower culturally diverse families." In Families in Society, *75, 531–539. Copyright © 1994 by Families International, Inc.*

The following aspects are included in the mapping process. Typically, information from all of these areas is not obtained in the first interview, when the social worker typically focuses on the first five areas.

Reasons for Immigration. Knowing the reasons for immigration helps the social worker understand the basic orientation and adjustment of the family to their current situation. Some immigrants are forced to leave their country, others leave to join relatives. Some come from urban areas, others from rural regions. Some want to return to their countries of origin, others view their status as permanent.

Length of Time in Community. Length of time in the community is associated with level of acculturation. The longer a family has been in the country, the more likely that members will have become accustomed to the laws, values, and lifestyles of the new community. Between generations, conflicts can arise between the "first generation"—those who immigrated to the country—and the "second generation"—those who were very young at the time of immigration or were born in the United States.

Legal or Undocumented Status. Most immigrants come to the country legally, including students who gain permission to come for a specific, temporary length of time. Social workers should tread lightly in this area, because some immigrants arrive illegally and are reluctant to discuss their situation for fear of deportation. Before exploring this area, social workers should have developed a trusting relationship in which the family feels reassured about confidentiality.

Age at Immigration. Young children tend to acculturate more quickly than parents. It is important to obtain this information for each family member, because often family members arrived in the country at different times. In this situation, the degree of acculturation may depend more on the length of time in the community, rather than age.

Spoken Language. The preferred language of a family member should be respected. Often, young children are bilingual and learn English sooner than parents. In some families, the native language is spoken at home, while English is spoken in public. The family's preferences in this area may necessitate translators or indicate the value of language courses.

Contact with Cultural Institutions. Contact with churches, ethnic schools, and social clubs is one way for families to maintain their cultural identity. Lack of contact with these institutions can lead to increased stress and maladaptive behavior if family members do not have sources for traditional supports.

Health Beliefs. The health beliefs of immigrants can be dramatically different from American customs and the American medical care system. Some cultures view health in very spiritualistic terms, while others minimize the psychological aspects of health and avoid mental health practitioners. Preventive medicine, including immunizations, may not be compatible with some cultures in which medical care is sought only when one is very ill.

Holidays and Special Events. Holidays are often celebrated according to religious beliefs and customs. Other special events, such as births, weddings, and funerals, may entail different emphasis and rituals than is common for the majority of

Americans. Such information should be included so that the practitioner is sensitive to and respectful of the unique ways that the immigrant family deals with these issues.

Crisis Events. Particular events or circumstances may be perceived as more stressful, and thus have more impact, within a certain culture. For example, the death of a grandparent would be more stressful in a family whose culture places high value on veneration of older family members. Sexual behavior among adolescent girls would be more stressful in a culture that places high value on female virginity before marriage.

Family, Education, and Work Values. Many traditional cultures place more emphasis on the needs of the collective (family) than on the needs of the individual. This cultural value can conflict with American society's staunch individualism and with the social work value of individual self-determination. Most immigrant families value education as a key to success, but this may conflict with the economic needs of the family and the necessity to work to assure short-term economic survival. Work can also be viewed as essential to self-esteem, so that unemployment can be degrading and humiliating. Sometimes traditional cultural norms dictate that the man is the primary breadwinner; in other cultures, all family members are expected to work.

Understanding Gay and Lesbian Adolescents

As mentioned in a previous section, the condemnation of gays and lesbians often is open, public, and religiously rationalized. To be openly gay or lesbian is to risk discrimination and prejudice. Many states have laws that define homosexual behavior as criminal. In this hostile context, it is increasingly important for social workers to be sensitive to the struggle of gay and lesbian teenagers to confront and accept their homosexuality.

Dempsey (1994) has offered an excellent overview of these issues with implications for social workers and health care providers. Identity development, the central developmental task of adolescence, can be even more traumatic for gay ado-

lescents because they perceive themselves as different, they lack positive role models, they lack peer support, and they are isolated from the mainstream. Because of the negative images of homosexuality and the lack of support, they often deny their own intuition about themselves and hide or suppress their sexual orientation. This denial of emotions can generalize to other feelings as well, so that homosexual adolescents can become cut off from their emotional selves.

According to Dempsey (who cites Troiden, 1988), there are four stages of identity development for homosexuals. The first stage, sensitization, begins before puberty. Here, the children realize that they are different from their same gender peers, but they rarely associate that difference with homosexuality. This association begins in the second stage, identity confusion. During adolescence, these young people begin to consider that their differentness might mean that they are gay, lesbian, or bisexual. Typically, youth deny these feelings and assume heterosexual roles. During the third stage, identity assumption, the young person begins to accept his or her homosexuality and share his or her identity with selected individuals. This third stage usually occurs in late adolescence or young adulthood, and is characterized by sexual experimentation and social contacts with other gays. The fourth and final stage is characterized by commitment to the homosexual identity. The individual becomes comfortable with the view of self as gay or lesbian, and finds it easier to live openly as such.

Most adolescents do not have the support or ability to sort out their identity confusion, so most homosexuals do not come out of the closet as teenagers. Because of the pressures, lack of support, and internal confusion, gay and lesbian youth are at increased risk for a wide range of problems including suicide, substance abuse, homelessness, dropping out of school, prostitution, and acquiring sexually transmitted diseases and AIDS. While not making assumptions about sexual orientation, practitioners need to view these factors as possible indicators of identity confusion spurred by a homosexual orientation. Gay adolescents need to hear that not all adults believe homosexuality is wrong. They need to link with support systems such as gay youth groups that can help overcome social isolation and provide positive role models. Sex education classes should address homosexuality in a nonjudgmental manner, so that teenagers struggling with homosexual identification can receive permission to consider their own identity in a nonjudgmental manner. Finally, teens may need help in how to approach their parents and friends regarding their sexual orientation and how to minimize their risk and exposure to homophobic violence and discrimination.

Gender Bias

In work with children, it is vitally important for social workers to combat the gender bias that girls in our society experience. Discrimination based on sex has a long history in this country, as numerous authors and feminists have documented. Of particular concern for the readers of this text is the decline in self-esteem among girls during the teenage years.

A study conducted by the American Association of University Women (AAUW) (1992) documented this decline in female self-esteem during adolescence, and laid much of the blame on school systems. Prior to adolescence, girls tend to outshine boys in many ways: they do better in school, have better social skills, and demonstrate a solid sense of self. During adolescence, many females suffer a significant decline in self-esteem that cannot be accounted for solely by the turmoil of adolescence itself. The increasingly sexist and violent messages that young women receive from the larger culture, particularly through the media, tend to undermine their self-esteem and confuse their sense of competence and identity (Pipher, 1994).

The way in which social stereotypes and pressures negatively impact the self-esteem of young female adolescents is dramatically depicted in the following essay.

The Age of Beauty

by Nancy Friday

The line between childhood and adolescence was marked by one horrible dress.

I had stood, all eagerness and impatience, while my sister's old evening dress was pinned on me before that fateful dance at the yacht club. I didn't even know enough to look critically at the mirror and see that the strapless gown didn't suit me, especially after the dark brown velvet straps had been added to keep the dress up on my flat chest. I placed no value on looks. Having not had this rite of passage explained to me, I hadn't a clue that beauty was the prerequisite to adolescent stardom. Certainly, this new longing for boys had made me awkward in their presence; but I had noticed that they were awkward, too. Accustomed to being chosen first for any team of girls, I didn't question success that night, couldn't remember failure, so carefully had I buried nursery angers under trophies of recent accomplishments. I'm sure I was prepared to solve any hesitancy the boys might have in approaching us girls by taking the initiative myself. Assuming responsibility was who I was. In recent years my life had been a great adventure, in which there had been no comparisons made to my mother and sister. In my mind, they were boring in their tedious arguing over my sister's looks and her evenings with boys.

That night at the yacht club marked the end of childhood, the finish of that adventure story with me as heroine. In one momentous night I took it all in and made my concession speech to myself. I watched my friends, whose leader I had been for years, watched them happy in the arms of desirable boys, and I recognized what they had that I lacked; saw it so clearly that I can recreate the film today, frame by frame: they had a look I lacked that went beyond beauty. It wasn't curls, breasts, prettiness, but a quality of acquiescence: the agreeable offer to be led instead of to lead. My own face was too eager, to open, too sure of itself. I needed a mask. I needed a new face that belied the intelligent leader inside and portrayed the little girl, no, the tiny, helpless baby who hadn't been held enough in the first years of life and had been waiting all these years for boys now to care for her.

I stood in my horrible dress, shoulder blades pressing into the wall, watching my dear friends dance by in the arms of handsome boys, with a frozen, ghastly smile on my face, denying I needed to be rescued. Why, even the girl who couldn't hit a ball danced by. Though they all whispered for me to hide in the ladies' room, I stood my ground.

Miserable as I was, I recognized the work ahead: the girl I had invented, so full of words waiting to be spoken and skills to be mastered, she had to be pushed down like an ugly jack-in-the-box. No boy was going to take a package like me.

A part of me was filled with rage at having to abandon what I thought to be a fine person. But I had no voice for rage. I belonged to a family of women who wept, and by not weeping I had made myself different from my mother and sister. But that night I became a woman; I wept and wept after someone's father drove me home while the rest of my group went off to a late party with boys. I showed my grief but not my rage. I did what most women still do: I swallowed anger, choked on it. I bowed my head, in part to be shorter, but also, like a cornered cow, to signal I had given up.

By morning I had buried and mourned my 11-year-old self, the leader, the actress, the tree climber, and had become an ardent beauty student. From now on I would ape my beautiful friends, smile the group smile, walk the group walk and, what with hanging my head and bending my knees, approximate as best I could the group look.

I have a photograph of myself taken in our yard on what looks like The First Day of Adolescence. I am sitting in a white wicker chair, hunched forward, staring at the ground, hands tightly clasped in my lap, swathed in the loser's agony of defeat. I remember the box camera aimed at me and that awful skirt and sweater, which had been my sister's—as had the awful dress at the yacht club, fine for a beauty but oh, so wrong for the tomboy I had been.

Twenty years later, I would go through the countless hours of physical therapy to realign my spine, which has never recovered from the bent-leg posture I mastered in learning the art of being less. Neither professional success, great friendships nor the love of men could recapture the self-confidence, the inner vision and yes, the kindness and generosity I owned before I lost myself in the external mirrors of adolescence.

It is probably true that adolescence itself is harder for girls than it is for boys (Eagle & Coleman, 1993). They begin to physically mature 2 years earlier than boys, causing self-consciousness, embarrassment, and isolation. The physical changes are themselves more dramatic than they are for boys. While boys' basic shape remains the same, girls' physical appearance changes markedly as breasts grow and hips en-large. And, of course, girls menstruate, and there is nothing in boys' experience that is comparable.

Yet much of the decline in self-esteem can be attributed to the ways in which society and its social institutions, especially school systems, treat females. According to the AAUW study, girls receive less attention from teachers than boys, girls are steered away from traditional male courses such as math and science, and books and curricula offer stereotypical images of women and ignore the contributions and experiences of females. Also, equal proportions of boys and girls have learning disabilities, yet boys are twice as likely to be identified as needing special help. Entry into adolescence corresponds with changes in the school environment (from elementary school to middle school and junior high) that do not match the needs of females. Girls tend to do better in collaborative situations rather than the competitive ones fostered in junior high and high schools. Girls prefer the smaller, more personal and intimate settings of elementary schools rather than the larger and more impersonal settings of the upper grades.

The loss in self-esteem during adolescence can trigger serious adjustment problems for females, including depression, eating disorders, dropping out of high school, and teenage pregnancy. During the teen years, male development is characterized by the need to separate and assert independence and autonomy, while female development depends more on attachment, relationships, connectedness to others (Gilligan, 1982). Social workers and other professionals need to tune in to the different ways in which females experience the world and encourage schools and social systems to do likewise, so that this decline in self-esteem is prevented or minimized.

Gender bias is not confined to females. Our society also has stereotypes of boys and male behavior that have led many experts to conclude that our culture is doing a poor job of raising boys. In a thorough examination of this problem, William Pollack (1998) concludes that there is widespread cultural confusion about how best to parent boys, and this confusion is transmitted to the boys themselves in the form of isolation and despair as boys try to adapt to outdated notions of masculinity. Boys are still taught to be tough, to hide their emotions, and to show no vulnerability. They are also expected to become independent and to separate from their mothers and families prematurely. Thus they are disconnected both from their own selves and from their families. Other commentators have focused on the impact of feminism on our ideas about masculinity; ideas are diametrically opposed to traditional models of masculinity. Thus, boys wonder whether they are supposed to be tough (traditional role) or sensitive (evolv-ing role). This struggle to respond to the feminist notions of appropriate gender roles has led to the formation of many male organizations and groups that seek to help men clarify what "real" masculinity is all about (Doyle, 1995). For Michael Gurian (1996), the key to raising successful, responsible, and sensitive men lies in recognizing that boys are biologically different than girls, and that we should encourage and positively channel, rather than stifle, boys' natural affinity for competition and aggression. If the essence of being male can be valued through positive role models, support for nuclear and extended families, community understanding and support, and activity-focused challenges that stimulate discussion of feelings, then the confusion about what it is to be male can be addressed.

The previous paragraph addresses the general socialization of boys into gender roles, a process that is itself confusing and potentially harmful. When one adds poverty, discrimination, poor schools, abuse, community violence, and drugs into the picture, the result is often angry young men who come to the attention of the juvenile justice system. Aaron Kipnis (1999) chronicles how our society is failing these young men and offers concrete suggestions for change, summarized below.

What Troubled Boys Need (adapted from Kipnis, 1999)

- Affordable education and literacy programs
- Job and skills training
- Association with "normal" people at work and school
- The attention of older men
- Spiritual experiences
- Psychological and substance abuse counseling
- The sealing of juvenile records
- Positive support and encouragement from family and community

Respect for Diversity and Difference in Child Welfare

Race and Child Welfare Services

In a comprehensive review of child welfare research that focused on the issue of race, the authors concluded that "families and children of color experience poorer outcomes and are provided with fewer services than Caucasian families and children" (Courtney, et al., 1996, p. 125). The differential treatment occurs across services, from family preservation to foster care to adoption. Family preservation models may not be suitable for or useful to families of color. In foster care, children of color receive fewer services, are likely to stay longer in care, and more likely to recidivate than are Caucasians. African American children are less likely to be adopted.

Underlying these issues is the problem of over-representation of minority races in the child welfare system. The number of children in foster care increased by 65% between 1984 and 1993 (Curtis, et al., 1995). The percentage of children of color in foster care has also steadily increased, and African American children are overrepresented in foster care (Scannapieco & Jackson, 1996). African American children were 15% of the total population of the 35 states surveyed in 1996, but totaled 48% of the children who entered out-of-home care, while the figures for Caucasians were 69% of the total population and 36% of the children in out-of-home placement (Petit, et al., 1999). Once in state care, minority-race children tend to stay longer: from 1988 to 1993, minority children in New York State stayed twice as long in care as whites, and in Illinois, African American children stayed almost five times as long as whites (Curtis, et al., 1995). Data from 18 states reporting indicated that African American and Native American children who left care in 1996 had been in care 22.5 months (median) compared to 18.6 months for Caucasians. For those still in care in 1996, African American children had spent a median 11.5 months in care, compared to 9.1 months for Caucasian children (Petit, et al., 1999).

How can this overrepresentation be explained? Is there more abuse and neglect among minorities, or do white professionals, in discriminatory fashion, single out minorities for attention? The latter explanation is the one that most minorities would advocate, and it is supported by national studies conducted by the U.S. Department of Health and Human Services. According to these studies of the incidence rates of child abuse and neglect, there are no significant race differences in the incidence of maltreatment or maltreatment-related injuries. Furthermore, according to the authors, these findings suggest that the differential representation of minorities in the child welfare population is likely due to differential treatment somewhere in the process (Sedlack & Broadhurst, 1996). In the case of Native Americans, Congress has acted to address these problems, as discussed in the following section.

The Indian Child Welfare Act of 1978, P.L. 95-608

Native Americans have historically experienced untoward levels of discrimination and disrespect in their dealings with the child welfare system (Matheson, 1996). Federal policy governing Indian affairs was characterized by forced acculturation, including forced religious conversions and forced placement of children in boarding schools and other institutions. The extent of the efforts at forced acculturation are shocking: between 1969 and 1974, at least 35% of Native American children were placed in foster homes and institutions (Matheson, 1996); in 1971 and 1972, more than 35,000 Native American children lived in institutions, most in boarding schools administered by the Bureau of Indian Affairs (Byler, 1977). To halt this cultural genocide, Indian leaders, after many years of struggle, were able to convince Congress to pass the Indian Child Welfare Act of 1978 (ICWA) (P.L. 95-608).

The ICWA creates procedural safeguards for the custody and placement of children. These procedural safeguards are summarized as follows:

Procedural Safeguards under the Indian Child Welfare Act of 1978 (adapted from Pecora, et al., 1992)

- Tribes are given exclusive jurisdiction over reservation Indian children.

(cont'd.)

- For non-reservation Indian children, state social workers must notify the parents and the tribe before taking custody, except in emergency situations.
- State jurisdiction over cases of non-reservation Indian children can be transferred to the tribal court at the request of the tribe or parent.
- If the tribe does not assume jurisdiction, the state social worker is required to give preference for placement first to the child's extended family, next to the tribe, then to other Indian families.
- Voluntary placements of Indian children for foster care or adoption must be well informed; consent must be in writing before a judge that certifies the consent was explained in a language that the parent understood.

Implementation of the ICWA has been fraught with inconsistencies and has achieved mixed results. Tribal and urban Indian agencies are responsible for administration, training, and monitoring of the ICWA, but political conflicts and power struggles among Indians themselves, coupled with inadequate funding to establish Indian child and family services, have impeded implementation (Matheson, 1996; Pecora, et al., 1992). A study of implementation in four states concluded that 53% of Native Americans under state jurisdiction were placed in non-Indian homes (Plantz, Hubbell, Barrett, & Dobrec, 1989). This statistic can be seen in a positive light as an improvement over past practices, or in a negative light as an unacceptable rate of crossracial placement. Implementation can be improved by increased funding for training and monitoring, agreements between states and tribes, and the employment and retention of Native American staff.

African American Kinship Care and Transracial Adoptions

The African American community has long been characterized by strong extended family bonds that have contributed to the resiliency of the community over time. In traditional African society, informal kinship bonds were a crucial aspect of the idea that the raising of children was a community responsibility. To cope with contemporary challenges of increased poverty, AIDS, reduction in formal service supports, and increased drug abuse, the traditional informal kinship care arrangements are being supplemented by more formal kinship care arrangements. Under formal kinship care, the state or county has official custody of the child, but a relative cares for the child. Social workers involved in these formal kinship care arrangements need to keep in mind that the relative caregiver does not view herself as a foster parent, but as a family member responding to the needs of the family. Permanency for the child can be ensured by working with the kinship triad of the child, the biological parents, and the caregiver relatives (Scannapieco & Jackson, 1996).

Issues of diversity and difference are at the heart of the controversy regarding crossracial (or transracial) adoptions, which most often involves placement of a minority-race or mixed-race child with a white adoptive couple (Cohen, 1992). Although current crossracial adoptions in the United States encompass adoption of Asian, Chinese, South American, and other foreign children by white Americans, the controversy over crossracial adoptions centers on the adoption of African American and Native Americans. With respect to the latter, the Indian Child Welfare Act of 1978 requires that preference be given first to the child's extended family, then to other members of the child's tribe, and then to other Native American families, before the child can be placed for adoption in a non-Indian home.

No comparable legislation exists on the adoption of African American children by white families. During the 1960s, adoption of black children by white families was seen as consistent with the civil rights movement and the spirit of racial integration (Shireman, 1994). The controversy over the practice exploded in the 1970s, when the National Association of Black Social Workers (NABSW), appalled that more than one-third of black children were adopted by white parents, officially condemned and opposed the practice (Cohen, 1992). Black professionals and the NABSW believed that black children in white homes would be deprived of the skills needed to function in black communities, would not learn how to cope in a racist society, and would fail to develop a positive identity (Jones & Else, 1979). Although subsequent research has appeared to indicate that black children raised in white homes do not suffer unduly from identity confusion, critics of the research maintain that the measures used to assess adjustment and identity development are inadequate (Shireman, 1994). Specifically, the measures assess general self-esteem and adjustment, rather than reference-group identity, which more accurately reflects the child's identification with the black culture. Hence, the apparent positive adjustment of these children could well be a form of denial of differences, which is an early stage of racial identity that can be destructive if not worked through. In any case, critics assert, the practice of systematically removing children from their culture amounts to cultural genocide.

Recent federal laws, the Multi-Ethnic Placement Act (MEPA) of 1994 and its follow-up Interethnic Adoption Provision Act (IAP) of 1996, now forbid agencies that receive federal funds from routinely making adoption decisions based on race (Pecora, et al., 2000). These laws were passed to address perceived discrimination in placement decisions in which interracial adoptions were discouraged or categorically denied. Now, child welfare workers cannot deny placement on the basis of race, but may consider race along with other factors in determining what is in the child's best interests.

Child-Rearing and Discipline Practices

Because some minority racial groups have higher rates of poverty, it is possible that the disproportionate representation of minority children in the child welfare system is due to the increased stress and other factors that accompany poverty. It is also possible that a predominantly white system discriminates against minorities through application of ethnocentric standards of child-rearing and discipline.

In order for social workers in child welfare to avoid judging a minority group by ethnocentric standards, it is important that they understand and appreciate the child-rearing and discipline practices of different cultures. Judgments about what is abuse and neglect must be based on the norms of a given culture, not on the ethnocentric application

of standards from the dominant culture to minority cultures. A brief review of some of these common child-rearing practices follows.

Readers are strongly cautioned not to use the information to stereotype: individual differences within cultures are varied. The following material may apply, in a general sense, to most of the members of the identified group, but the material that follows is based on summaries of the literature provided by Ho (1987).

African American. Child-rearing in the African American community is characterized by the importance of teaching young members how to be black in a white society. This responsibility is shared by the extended family and those with whom the family is close, including the religious community. Physical discipline is common in the African American community and is seen both as a means for the child to learn to be sensitive and as a means for teaching the child the importance of following the rules in the larger, white community to avoid confrontation with authorities (Willis, 1992).

Individualism is stressed, and there are few inhibitions on the expression of one's uniqueness. Both girls and boys are strongly encouraged to complete their education, and girls are taught to be self-sufficient and independent. Older siblings are expected to assume much of caretaking responsibilities for younger children, especially those over 3 years of age. This cultural norm may conflict with practices in the majority culture, so that social workers must guard against viewing this practice as an abrogation of parental responsibility or neglect of the younger or older sibling's needs.

Native American. In Native American cultures, the extended family and tribe play strong roles in the upbringing of children. Children are seen as individuals who are not entirely dependent on adults, who can make important decisions for themselves. Children are thought to learn best through observation and participation, not through direct instruction, commands, or physical punishment. Thus, it would be ethnocentric for social workers to expect directive, behavioral reinforcement approaches from biological parents. Native Americans tend to seek harmony with nature and other people, so that exerting control over anything or anybody is not valued. Also, it would be ethnocentric to view the common responsibility to raise children as being a sign of neglect on the part of the biological parents.

Hispanic American. The lines between parents and children tend to be clearly drawn in Hispanic families. The status of children is low compared to that of the parents, and children are expected to show respect to parents and other adults. Parenting roles also tend to be stratified, with the father's role being to discipline and control, and the mother's to nurture and support. Additionally, the father's role is to protect the mother and to insist that the children obey her.

The extended family is an important source of nurturance, guidance, and support in Hispanic families. Godparents selected at birth often play an important and active role, forming coparenting bonds with the child's parents. Godparents are also chosen at marriage, and may serve as mediators to the couple during troubled times. The relationship among cousins can be very much like a sibling relationship, and children are discouraged from forming close friends outside the extended family network. From an early age, siblings are assigned household chores and functions, with the oldest serving in supervisory capacities with authority over the younger siblings. During times of trouble, children can be transferred within the extended family to different nuclear families, a practice which should not be considered as abandonment or abrogation of parenting responsibility.

Asian American. Like the other groups discussed above, kinship ties are extremely important to Americans of Asian heritage. These ties take clear precedence over outside friendships and other social relationships. It is not unusual for several generations and extended kin to share a common domicile. Parent-child relationships are governed, in part, by concepts of obligation and shame. Family members are obligated to be kind, helpful, and compassionate to each other. Respect and obedience to elders is the child's greatest obligation. Asian families typically use shaming to reinforce these family obligations. Withdrawal of familial confidence and support can cause great anxiety to the individual in a culture in which family interdependence is so important.

Typically, the father is the primary disciplinarian and the mother is seen as more nurturing. After infancy, love and affection are not openly displayed, and children are taught to show no aggression under any circumstances. The eldest male child receives the most respect and is expected to be the most responsible. He is expected to be an active role model for the younger siblings, even into adulthood.

Parent Training Programs for Minorities. In recent years, several parent training programs have been developed for specific minority cultures (U.S. Department of Health and Human Services, 1991). The Effective Black Parenting Program was developed in the late 1970s by the Center for Improvement of Child Caring in Studio City, California. The cognitive-behavioral training program consists of 15 3-hour training sessions that focus on fostering effective communication, discipline, and health, as well as African American identity and self-esteem. The same center developed a similar program for Hispanic parents entitled Los Niños Bien Educados. A program for Native Americans, Positive Indian Parenting: Honoring Our Children by Honoring Our Traditions, was developed by the Northwest Indian Child Welfare Institute in Portland, Oregon. In eight sessions of 2–3 hours, participants are encouraged to explore and apply the values and attitudes of historic Indian child-rearing practices. The curriculum emphasizes oral tradition, story telling, the spiritual nature of child-rearing, and the role of the extended family.

Gay and Lesbian Youth in Foster Care

The situation for gay and lesbian youth in group homes can be quite traumatic (Wolfson, 1998). Many gay and lesbian youth report being verbally harassed and physically abused by other youth in these group homes. In response, they frequently run away from the group home, preferring the risks of homelessness and the streets to the continued harm of the group home. In addition, social workers and other staff members may not be trained on how to work with issues of sexuality when providing counseling and other services, or may themselves be biased.

In an attempt to protect these young people, and surround them with supportive staff, some cities have created group homes specifically for gay and lesbian youth. In Los Angeles, five such group homes serving 36 youth have been established by Gay and Lesbian Adolescent Social Services (GLASS). In these group homes, gay and lesbian youth find their sexuality validated, and they can be freed to work not only on issues surrounding their sexuality, but also other issues that may be present such as abuse, chemical dependency, and family issues.

While there are many positive aspects of this segregated living arrangement, there is also a potential downside, for some wonder whether being in an overly friendly environment is the best preparation for living in the "real world." Advocates respond that until these youth can be properly protected and supported in mainstream settings, they need the safety and comfort of the segregated group home to serve as a base from which to learn how to live in the more hostile, outside world (Wolfson, 1998).

Respect for Diversity and Difference in Children's Mental Health

Racial, Social Class, and Gender Bias in Assessments and Treatment

Studies on bias in the clinical judgment of mental health professionals have documented the existence of racial, social class, and gender bias in numerous diagnostic and treatment realms. In a thorough review of these studies, Garb (1997) summarizes the extent to which bias has been demonstrated in various empirical studies:

- African American and Hispanic people are more likely to be improperly diagnosed with schizophrenia than white clients.
- Mental health professionals who are not familiar with a client's culture are more likely to infer that psychopathology and maladaptive behaviors are present.
- The risk of violence tends to be overrated for African Americans and males and underrated for females.
- Middle-class individuals are more likely to be referred for psychotherapy than lower-class individuals.

- Females are more likely to be overdiagnosed with histrionic personality disorder and males with antisocial personality disorder.

The business of diagnosis and treatment of mental disorders in minority populations is fraught with controversy and complexity. Defining and measuring mental health and mental disorder is a challenging dilemma in any circumstance, as discussed in chapter 3. The mental health establishment has assumed that psychiatric symptoms are universally distributed and uniformly manifested, and this assumption has never been rigorously tested. Instruments used to measure mental health are seldom subjected to culturally grounded validity studies. Thus, the cross-cultural validity of many diagnostic categories is dubious at best. Studies of the prevalence rate of mental disorders among different races and cultures in the United States have yielded inconclusive results (Vega & Rumbaut, 1991). However, a recent review of the effects of race, ethnicity, and poverty on the mental health of children concluded that the prevalence of emotional disorders in African Americans, Native Americans, and Hispanics may well be less than the larger population, when poverty is controlled in the analysis (Samaan, 2000). That is, poverty is highly correlated with the prevalence of mental health disorders in children, but when poverty is controlled for as a factor, children from these minority groups have fewer mental health problems than whites. The authors attributed this situation to cultural factors such as social support, extended families, religious/spiritual factors, and maternal coping patterns that may serve to protect children from mental health problems.

Accurate assessment, including valid diagnosis, is essential to treatment planning, insurance reimbursement, and eventual alleviation of the problem. Overdiagnosis of minority populations can subject people to unwarranted interventions by the dominant culture, while underdiagnosis can prevent minorities from accessing the resources of the dominant culture. Misdiagnosis of minority populations can easily occur, due to cultural expression of symptomatology, unreliable research instruments and evaluation inventories, clinical bias and prejudice, and institutional racism. To ensure that misdiagnosis does not occur, mental health clinicians should familiarize themselves with the ways that mental health issues are expressed between and within different cultures. They should focus on the specific personal and cultural history of a client, including immigration status, level of cultural assimilation, religious beliefs, socioeconomic status, and experiences of racial oppression (Solomon, 1992).

Beyond diagnosis, there is concern that children and youth of color with the same or similar presenting problems receive different, more restrictive treatment than do their European American counterparts. A recent study of the utilization patterns of almost 3,000 youth with emotional and behavioral disorders served by the state mental health system in Virginia, revealed serious and troubling differences between African American and European Americans in the sample (Sheppard & Benjamin-Coleman, 2001). First of all, African Americans were overrepresented in the mental health system, with 41% of the sample compared to 23% of the overall state population. Second, analysis of records in the state's information management system revealed that more black (55%) than white youth (48%) received an out-of-home placement in the four-year study period. Third, despite little difference in presenting problems, blacks were three times as likely as whites to have placements in detention centers rather than hospitalizations. The need for cultural competence in the assessment and treatment of diverse populations is clear and compelling.

Cultural Competence in Mental Health

In mental health settings, culturally competent clinical practice includes viewing mental health issues from within the context of the cultural norms and experiences of the community. Ho (1987) has documented how traditional family therapy theories must be adapted to various cultures. For example, in Hispanic families, the father's typical role is to discipline, while the mother's is to nurture. This structure might readily be viewed by family systems therapists as overly rigid and the basis for an unhealthy alliance between mother and children that excludes the father. But in Hispanic families, it is the functional norm because the Hispanic wife's sense of family obligation and respect for hierarchy inhibit her from undermining the father or encouraging the children to disre-

spect him. In this situation, feminist therapists and those with egalitarian ideals for marriages must constantly confront their own biases to be effective. As long as the family members themselves are content with the situation and it works for them, the practitioner should refrain from imposing his or her own values.

Culturally competent mental health practice entails confrontation of ethnocentric bias in the predominant theories about the etiology and treatment of mental disorders. The Progressive Life Center in Washington, D.C., serving the African American community, has based its entire operation, including its theory of mental health interventions, on the foundation of African cultural values. Seven principles of healthy living, known as Nguzo Saba, provide the framework for assessment and treatment. These are unity, self-determination, collective work and responsibility, cooperative economics, purpose, creativity, and faith. Optimal mental health functioning is achieved in an environment characterized by harmony, interconnectedness, authenticity, and balance. Thus, compared to traditional mental health approaches, the approach at the Progressive Life Center is more action oriented, more visual, more spiritual, and more focused on interactions and relationships with the family and community (Benjamin & Isaacs-Shockley, 1996).

Culturally competent mental health clinicians must remain cognizant of the tension between mainstream mental health theories that emphasize adolescence as a time of individuation and the strong value of family loyalty that is prominent in many families of color. While the larger white culture stresses individualism, many minority cultures define members according to their roles and responsibilities in the family. Thus, family therapy, rather than individual therapy, would often be the preferred modality of treatment. Also, an adolescent's demand for greater freedom and individualization must not be perfunctorily labeled as "normal," but rather as an expression of a value that conflicts with the traditional values of the family and culture (Benjamin & Isaacs-Shockley, 1996).

Another tension between mainstream mental health professionals and some people of color is in the area of parental discipline practices. In a study of the views of the caretakers of 286 children with serious emotional disorders, Walker (2001) found that African American caregivers in the study voiced considerably more dissatisfaction than Caucasians with professional attitudes condemning the use of physical punishment. The author noted that it is the providers' attitudes that need to change in this area, because studies have shown that the use of physical discipline among African Americans does not seem to be associated with negative effects in children.

Cultural competence means giving careful consideration to the relationship between mental health conditions and the processes of acculturation and powerlessness. Acculturation makes many demands on the individual and can trigger heightened conflicts between the generations in a family. Cultural mapping (as presented in the culturagram above) can facilitate assessment of acculturation issues and allow for the reframing of many presenting problems. People of color who have experienced powerlessness can regain a sense of self-worth and mental well-being by learning how to assertively affect their environments.

Contrary to these recommendations, one empirical study found that most of its sampled professionals appeared to take a "color-blind" approach to therapy (Harper & Iwamsasa, 2000). The 155 participants in the survey all were cognitive-behavioral therapists who served adolescents; most (66.5%) were male, European American (92.9%), and held Ph.D. degrees (83.9%). When the presenting problem is not directly related to ethnicity, only one-fourth of the sample indicated that they would always or frequently discuss issues of ethnicity with their adolescent clients. When conducting therapy with an adolescent whose ethnic background was different than their own, only one-half reported that they would address this difference in therapy.

A final characteristic of culturally competent mental health practice is involvement in the larger community. At the Progressive Life Center in Washington, D.C., staff members are involved with churches, participate in radio and television talk shows, and function on community task forces. In addition, the agency invites the community to picnics, lectures, open houses, and rites of passage for youth. These rite-of-passage ceremonies are attended by community leaders and residents and signify that the youth has reached a level of maturity that warrants recognition and celebration (Benjamin & Isaacs-Shockley, 1996).

Although there is much said about the importance of involving minority families in organizations and systems change, there are few articles in the literature that detail examples of how this has been successfully accomplished in the real world. An outreach effort by the Federation of Families for Children's Mental Health has provided important lessons and guidelines for these efforts. As part of the Annie E. Casey Foundation's Urban Mental Health Initiative, the Federation of Families for Children's Mental Health (FFCMH) has successfully worked to engage and involve members of minority cultures in the activities of the FFCMH and in local systems of care (Huff & Telesford, 1994).

Like most parent advocacy organizations, the membership of the FFCMH was largely white and middle class until a Casey Foundation grant provided it with the impetus and resources to make a concerted effort to recruit and involve minority families. First, the federation organized focus groups in the targeted communities to hear directly from parents about their needs and experiences. Next, the federation identified local community leaders through churches, public housing councils, and Head Start programs, and listened to their ideas about how to outreach more parents. They held meetings within natural geographic boundaries of neighborhoods at times that were convenient to participants. They publicized meetings through flyers posted in Laundromats, churches, and other neighborhood centers of activity, through public service announcements on the radio, and through flyers sent home from school with children. Importantly, transportation was provided as needed, child care was available free of charge, and food was served at the meetings. For other organizations, it is vital to know that these intensive outreach efforts are necessary if real dialogue is to be established.

Identity Issues for Biracial Youth

Our tendency to categorize people according to their race obscures the fact that a large percentage of our population is biracial. Official census data and agency intake forms seldom offer the opportunity for people to identify themselves as biracial.

People of biracial heritage feel external pressure to label themselves as one category or another and internal pressure to resist this external pressure and somehow integrate their mixed heritage.

For children, the confusion and pressure can begin as early as the preschool years, when children become aware of racial differences, labels, and their own racial heritage. During adolescence, which is the prime time for identity development, biracial youth feel the tensions and confusions about racial identity most acutely. The development of a positive racial identity in children of black parents and white parents may be particularly complex because of the stark contrasts in the ways that each race has been valued by the larger society. Society has traditionally defined any person with any amount of black blood as a black person, but many parents and children resist this categorization. People of biracial heritage may never be fully accepted by either racial community, so it is imperative that they be given the tools and support to develop their own unique, integrated sense of self (McRoy & Freeman, 1986; Miller & Miller, 1990).

Social workers in mental health and school settings are well positioned to help adolescents directly and provide ideas and guidance to parents about how to help their child maintain a strong self-image. Anxieties about racial identity are seldom the presenting problem, but may well underlie other presenting problems such as poor academic achievement or aggressive behavior toward peers. In assessing any presenting problem involving a biracial child, the social worker needs to explore openly, with parents and child, the possibility the racial identity confusion may be contributing to the problem. Areas to be explored include the child, parents', and others' view of the child's racial identity; the child's level of expressed interest in learning more about his or her racial heritage, and the parents' response; role models for the child from each race; and social contacts with each race (McRoy & Freeman, 1986). For the parents of mixed-race children, the primary tasks are to counter societal messages which undermine self-esteem, validate uniqueness, and teach strategies for dealing with discrimination and racism (Miller & Miller, 1990).

CHAPTER 7 SUMMARY

This chapter on respect for diversity and difference highlighted the importance of culturally sensitive practice in this complex and increasingly diverse society. Prejudice and discrimination can appear in subtle forms that go beyond conscious, overt bias and bigotry. These forms include unknowingly applying different standards to different people, applying the same ethnocentric standard to all people, and minimizing the significance of an event or circumstance as seen through the eyes of the minority person. The chapter presented information on topics that can help the social work practitioner and administrator in their ongoing struggle to honor diversity and difference: the dynamics of powerlessness, the cultural competence continuum for organizations, the culturagram, issues for gay and lesbian adolescents, and gender bias.

The chapter concluded with an examination of how respect for diversity and difference applies in child welfare and children's mental health settings. In child welfare, topics included the overrepresentation of minority populations, the Indian Child Welfare Act of 1978, African American kinship care, transracial adoptions, child-raising practices, and gay and lesbian youth in foster care. Diversity issues targeted in children's mental health included bias in assessment and treatment, cultural competence, and identity issues for biracial youth.

CHAPTER 8

Pragmatic Perspective 5: Least Restrictive Alternative (LRA)

Overview

The least restrictive alternative (LRA) is both a philosophy and a legal principle. This chapter defines LRA and discusses its scope and relevance to social work in child and family settings. The concept of continuum of care is closely associated with LRA, and both concepts have been criticized from a variety of fronts. This section concludes with a discussion of how LRA can conflict with client choice, offering guidelines for resolving these situations. The chapter concludes with a discussion of the specific ways in which least restrictive alternative manifests itself in the child welfare and children's mental health service systems.

Least Restrictive Alternative: Definition, History, and Scope

The *least restrictive alternative* (LRA), in its broadest sense, is a principle which espouses that children and families who need services should receive those services in ways that are the least restrictive of their basic rights, particularly their right to personal liberty. In child welfare, the LRA principle is evident in family preservation programs that attempt to keep children out of the restrictive foster care system and within their families, where parents can exercise their parental rights. In mental health, LRA is evident in efforts to avoid hospitalization in favor of community-based services, and in legal safeguards against people being committed against their will. In education, LRA applies particularly in special education and the philosophy of "inclusion," which strives to serve children with special needs within their regular schools and classrooms whenever possible.

The least restrictive alternative is more than a general philosophy; it is a legal principle that has been a driving force for reform of the human services system for a number of years. Historically, service professionals have not enthusiastically embraced this principle. In fact, professionals have historically organized care in highly restrictive ways, in the belief that the high level of restrictiveness was in the client's best interest. In other words, professionals believed that the client's need for specialized, restrictive care outweighed the client's other needs and rights. Thus, in child welfare, abused and neglected children were judged to be best served outside their families by professional parents and social workers. In mental health, children with serious emotional and behavioral disorders were thought to be best served in hospitals and residential treatment centers where the professionals could control the environment and create a therapeutic milieu for change. In education, children with disabilities were thought by educational professionals to be best served in segregated classrooms and buildings, away from other children, where specially trained teachers could address their unique needs. Never mind that many children placed in foster care were abused and neglected, or lost all sense of permanence, while in foster care; never mind that children in hospitals lost vital connections with their families, peers, and communities, and were subjected to questionable treatment practices; never mind that children in segregated classrooms felt stigmatized and ostracized, and failed to learn. Professionals asserted, and some still assert, that these were the unfortunate, but necessary, prices to pay for the needed professional treatment.

The least restrictive alternative principle asserts that children and families can develop best when the professional treatment is offered in settings that are as normalized as possible. The LRA principle is associated with family preservation in child welfare, with deinstitutionalization in mental health, and with inclusion in special education. The LRA principle asserts that less restrictive environments are not only adequate to achievement of goals, they are superior. For example, in the mental health arena, a successful lawsuit in Massachusetts asserted that state hospital patients, if served in the community, would get better treatment because treatment components such as individualized programming, education, training, and experience in mundane tasks of everyday living were all likely to increase in community settings (Herr, Arons, & Wallace, 1983).

Despite years of legislation and court cases that have reaffirmed the importance of LRA, the principle remains controversial among some professionals, and among some parents as well. Even among those who grant that the old system was much too segregated and institutionally oriented, some express concern that strict adherence to LRA will swing the pendulum too far in the other direction. In child welfare, for example, these voices of caution agree that maybe too many children were unnecessarily placed in foster care in the past, but they worry that family preservation programs have blocked *necessary* placements so that children's safety in their own homes is compromised. In mental health, these people ask, aren't some kids' mental health problems so severe that long-term hospitalization or residential treatment is required? In education, will children with special needs receive the proper individual attention in regular classes, and won't some of them be so disruptive that they jeopardize the learning of the other students?

Because of these concerns, most officials believe that there will always be a place in the system for the more restrictive alternatives. Rather than LRA dictating care for all children and families, the more pragmatic principle will be "least restrictive alternative consistent with the child's needs" or "least restrictive alternative considering the best interests of the child." This terminology opens the door for consideration of higher levels of restrictiveness when it can be demonstrated that an individual child needs it in order to succeed.

Continuum of Care

At this juncture of the discussion of LRA, the term *continuum of care* is often invoked, referring to a system of care that provides various options for children and families at various levels of restrictiveness. Thus, in child welfare, the continuum of care regarding placement options would range from less to greater restrictiveness as follows: biological or adopted family, extended family (relatives), friends, foster family within the community, group home (including different levels of homes), locked facility. In mental health, the range of treatment would vary as follows: outpatient individual, group, and family; intensive day treatment (part of every day) or partial hospitalization (all day every day) in which child is in a treatment program during the day and is home at night; temporary hospitalization in community facility; long-term residential treatment. In special education, the continuum of care would be: full-time placement in regular classroom without attendant or teacher in classroom; full-time placement in regular classroom with support in the regular class provided by teacher or attendant; mostly regular classroom with some resource room or other specialized help outside of classroom; mostly special education classroom within regular school building; full-time special education classroom within regular school building; placement in special school within school district; placement outside of school district.

TABLE 8.1
Continuum of Care Across Three Major Settings

	Child Welfare Placement	Mental Health	Education
Least Restrictive	Biological or adopted family	Weekly outpatient	Regular classroom, full time
	Extended family (relatives)	Day treatment	Regular classroom, instructional support
	Friends	Partial hospital	Mostly regular classroom, part-time with outside resource room
	Foster family within the community	Short-term hospital in community	Mostly special education classroom in regular building
	Group home	Long-term residential treatment, outside community	Full-time special education classroom in regular building
Most Restrictive	Locked facility	State mental hospital	Special school within school district
			Placement outside school district

Critique of LRA and Continuum of Care Concepts

Although the related concepts of LRA and continuum of care are widely promulgated, some critics believe these concepts have serious flaws. Taylor (1987) identified several pitfalls that are important to consider. First, the concepts implicitly legitimize highly restrictive settings in various ways. Some advocates believe that state institutions and other highly restrictive environments should be abolished altogether because they are not appropriate for anybody, regardless of the severity of the disability. To these advocates, LRA and the continuum of care do not address the question of whether or not people *should be* restricted, but *to what extent.* Additionally, rather than focusing on the *least* restrictive setting, the continuum of care concept allows authorities to rationalize client movement from highly restrictive settings to *less* restrictive settings.

Second, the concepts equate level of segregation with intensity of services, because they assume that the most segregated, restrictive settings provide the highest intensity of services. But in fact, segregation and intensity of services are separate dimensions. Some highly segregated institutional settings provide very minimal service, whereas less restrictive community settings provide a wide array of support services. This issue is especially confusing to legislators, who want to believe that less restrictive settings can and should cost less money.

Third, the concepts suggest that people will be frequently uprooted as they move up or down the continuum ladder. This destroys any sense of permanence as relationships with family, friends, and peers are constantly disrupted. Additionally, children in more restrictive placements must demonstrate their "readiness" to move to a less restrictive level, even though most highly restrictive placements are not geared to prepare them for less restrictive levels, but, rather, to function within the more restrictive setting itself.

Connections/Relevance of LRA to Other Pragmatic Perspectives

The principle of LRA is particularly relevant with respect to pragmatic perspective 4, respect for diversity and difference. As discussed previously, there is strong statistical evidence that minority-race children are overrepresented in more restrictive environments (Scannapieco & Jackson, 1996; Harry, 1992).

Given this statistical evidence, one must ask whether minority-race children in fact need these higher levels of restrictiveness, or whether the system somehow discriminates against them. Regarding the former possibility, one would have to argue that there is something inherent about the children's race that necessitates higher levels of restrictiveness. For example, in explaining why a disproportionate number of African American children are in more restrictive levels in child welfare, one would have to argue that African American families, in general, abuse their children more often or more severely, are less responsive to treatment, have less supportive kinship networks, and/or care less about their children. It would be difficult and irresponsible to mount such arguments.

The alternative explanation about the disproportionate number of African American children in highly restrictive child welfare placements would focus on the different ways that African American families are treated by the child welfare system. Are African American children more likely to identified as abused and neglected because teachers, doctors, and others who report instances of abuse and neglect have a double standard for whites and blacks? Once identified, do social workers, judges, and others treat children and families differently based on race, whether consciously or unconsciously?

The relevance of LRA is not confined to diversity and difference. Because of the strong legal foundation for LRA, social workers can discover that this pragmatic perspective can dominate and override other pragmatic perspectives in the practical world of day-to-day decision making. The conflicts can be particularly dramatic with respect to pragmatic perspective 1, combating adult-centrism, and pragmatic perspective 2, family-centered practice. Both of these perspectives advocate for strong self-determination on the part of children and families. Experience suggests that most children and families' goals will be consistent with LRA. That is, most children and families want services that are community based and integrated with the mainstream as much as possible. Most children prefer to live with their families rather than in foster care; most children do not like hospitals; most children prefer to be in regular classrooms. Most parents prefer these alternatives also. In these situations, if there is a conflict, it is likely to be when the professionals recommend a higher level of restrictiveness. In this situation, the principles of LRA and family-centeredness should prevail over the professional recommendations.

Occasionally, however, a child and/or the child's parents may believe that it is in the best interest of the child to be in a restrictive placement, and the professionals disagree. The child and/or family may want foster care, hospitalization, or a full-time special education self-contained classroom, counter to the precepts of LRA and against the recommendations of the professionals involved. These conflicts between LRA and client self-determination are most challenging to the individual social worker and the system. There are limits to self-determination and family choice, and legal mandates are one of those limits.

Openly acknowledging the legal limits to self-determination is the key to maintaining a positive working relationship with the child and parents in these conflicted situations. The professionals can explain that all less restrictive alternatives must first be exhausted before the higher levels of restrictiveness can be considered. Concurrent with this discussion, the professional can ask the child or parent to be very specific about what problems or needs are to be satisfied by the higher level of restrictiveness. In child welfare and mental health, the parent will often reply that the child needs 24-hour supervision. The social worker's response is then to figure out a way for 24-hour supervision to occur without the higher placement. In special education, the parent might respond that the child will get more specialized, individual attention in a segregated classroom. The professional response could be to attempt to meet that need within the less restrictive framework, by assigning a teacher or aide to the child in the classroom or arranging for resource-room time. Thus, the need of the child and family is validated and attempts are made to address the need, but the attempts are different from (less restrictive than) what the child and family originally preferred.

The relevance of LRA can be seen with respect to pragmatic perspective 7, organization and financing, and pragmatic perspective 8, achieving outcomes, as will be discussed more fully in subsequent chapters. The principle of LRA is central to identifying and measuring outcomes in child welfare and mental health. When considering large groups of children in a community, success is often defined in terms of fewer children in foster care and hospitals. If LRA outcomes are to be achieved, then the service delivery system must be organized and financed so as to promote and encourage children living and learning in the most normal environments possible. As will be discussed in chapter 10, this will require dramatic changes in the traditional way of doing business.

Steps to Resolving Conflicts between LRA and Child/Parent Wishes

- **Step 1:** Acknowledge the disagreement between client preference and legal mandate. Inform and discuss the legal mandates of LRA as they apply to the current situation.
- **Step 2:** Inform and discuss that all less restrictive options must be attempted first.
- **Step 3:** Ask the clients to specify the need(s) that the more restrictive placement would address, in their mind.
- **Step 4:** Actively listen to client concerns and needs.
- **Step 5:** Develop an action plan to meet client needs in a less restrictive way.
- **Step 6:** Periodically review and update concerns/plan.
- **Step 7:** If child and/or family continue to decry progress, consider that their more restrictive plan may be the best, and move to implement it.

The relevance of LRA can be seen with respect to pragmatic perspective 7, organization and financing, and pragmatic perspective 8, achieving outcomes, as will be discussed more fully in subsequent chapters. The principle of LRA is central to identifying and measuring outcomes in child welfare and mental health. When considering large groups of children in a community, success is often defined in terms of fewer children in foster care and hospitals. If LRA outcomes are to be achieved, then the service delivery system must be organized and financed so as to promote and encourage children living and learning in the most normal environments possible. As will be discussed in chapter 10, this will require dramatic changes in the traditional way of doing business.

Least Restrictive Alternative in Child Welfare

The least restrictive alternative (LRA) is a powerful perspective in child welfare, guiding policy and practice in family preservation, reunification, foster care, group care, and adoptions. Maintaining children in their own homes is the preferred option identified in federal legislation (P.L. 96-272). If a child must be placed out-of-home in state custody, a continuum of care from least to most restrictive guides the placement decision. The language of the law specifically addresses the importance of the least restrictive alternative in provisions for case plans "designed to achieve placement in the least restrictive (most family like) setting available and in close proximity to the parents' home" (42 USC 675 [5] [a]). First, placement with relatives is considered, then family foster care, then lower-level to higher-level group homes that employ professional staff and houseparents, then placement in a locked and secure facility.

Child Safety and LRA

The trend toward family preservation and maintenance of children in their own homes has been met with some criticism by the press and some professionals who claim that the push to keep children in their families has jeopardized the safety of many children (Wald, 1988; Ingrassia & McCormick, 1994). Whereas the old system was weighted toward the highly restrictive end of the continuum of care, the current system, driven by LRA, may be weighted too heavily on the least restrictive end of the continuum, according to these critics. Family preservation, designed to prevent *unnecessary* placements, may in reality prevent many *necessary* placements.

The controversy about the impact of family preservation on the safety of children received national attention when Newsweek printed a feature article in April, 1994 (Ingrassia & McCormick, 1994). The article noted that 42% of the 1,300 kids who died as a result of abuse in 1993 had previously been reported to child protection services. Spotlighting specific cases of child deaths in Chicago, the article painted a bleak picture of the social welfare system, quoting several experts in the field of child welfare who believed that the emphasis on family preservation and reunification was compromising the safety of children. Some former advocates for family preservation have reversed their position. Patrick Murphy, a court-appointed guardian ad litem for abused and neglected children in Chicago, once exposed the injustice of the state seizing children from parents because of poverty alone. Now, he leads a crusade in Illinois to rein in family preservation and reunification programs that he believes unduly place children at risk.

Defenders of family preservation and LRA in child welfare counter that anecdotal evidence of the compromise of children's safety does not coincide with research documenting the overall safety and effectiveness of family preservation programs (Hartman, 1993). There is no guarantee that children will be safe in families, but neither is their safety assured in foster care, where as many as 30 children are abused out of every 1,000 in out-of-home care (Barthel, 1992). Family preservation programs vary widely in scope, intensity, and duration of service, and they were never intended to be a panacea for all of the ills of the child welfare system. If safety has been compromised, it is because family preservation is inadequately funded, and the economic, social, community, and health care resources to support troubled families are inadequate or unavailable.

Foster Care Placement and LRA

Most children enter foster placement because of state action to protect the children from abuse and neglect. Some children, especially teenagers, enter the foster care system through the voluntary requests of parents who feel they are not able to control or manage the behaviors of their acting-out teen. In these situations, the state may be forced to take custody because parents abdicate responsibility. The conflict between LRA and the family choice component of family-centeredness is evident: while the state would prefer that the child remain at home, the parents want the child out.

MacDonald (1992) has described a programmatic response for dealing with these situations. First, parents who request placement are offered counseling as an alternative. If they refuse, they are assigned a preplacement worker who meets with them for four sessions to facilitate the child's transition from home to foster care. In the first family session, the worker does not challenge the parent decision, but explains that the four sessions are part of the agency protocol for placing children, and planning for their futures. The second session focuses on the strengths of the child that will contribute to a successful placement. The third session deals with logistical problems such as visitation, parent-worker communication, and so forth. The fourth session is dedicated to tying up loose ends and dealing with the feelings of loss around the impending separation. The worker employs "future questioning" to help the family diffuse the intensity of the current situation and consider the consequences of their decision. For example, the worker might ask, "What are the qualities that the foster parents will most appreciate in your teen?" or "Who in the family will be the saddest when the child is placed in foster care?" By cooperating with the family, the worker at the same time indirectly introduces ideas that can create reconsideration of the decision and renewed motivation to work on the problems. In a pilot of this program, unnecessary placements were avoided in 12 of 17 families who participated.

Once a child is placed into foster care, for whatever reason, LRA espouses that the least restrictive placement be found, beginning with relative placement and family foster care. The New Zealand Family Group Conferences and the African American kinship placement programs, both described in previous chapters, are examples of efforts to keep children within kinship networks. Family foster care is undergoing change as well, as officials attempt to care for children in family foster homes rather than more restrictive group homes. But the number of foster parents is in decline, as was discussed in the previous chapter. The recruitment and retention of qualified foster parents is a major challenge to officials who want to operationalize LRA for children in state custody. Fewer foster parents are willing to take on the challenges of caring for the many difficult-to-care-for foster children such as children with HIV infection, crack-addicted and drug-exposed infants, and adolescents with drug involvement and/or behavioral and emotional problems. Foster parents work 24 hours a day for minimal financial compensation. More women, who have traditionally been the primary caregivers in foster care, now are employed outside the home.

To address these issues and enable difficult children to live in family settings, many in the field advocate for the professionalization of foster parenting (Pecora, et al., 1992). Professionalization would enhance the status and compensation for foster parents so that they would be viewed as essential members of the professional team. They would receive ongoing training and support, including respite care and quick access to social workers and other professional supports. Although some children would still need the structure and emotional distance provided by group homes and residential treatment, professional foster parents could become a point on the continuum of care between regular foster care and group home placement, thus serving many children who had previously been served in more restrictive placements. Widespread implementation of professional foster parenting has been impeded by lack of fiscal resources to pay for the added compensation, training, and support. But if resources are not allocated to enhance the attractiveness of foster parenting, then the availability of foster family homes can only be expected to decline. This decline would mean that increasingly higher numbers of foster children would live in group homes and institutions, undermining the principle of LRA.

Recent empirical research, summarized by Barfield and Petr (2002), has documented that LRA works in foster care: that is, family foster care has been shown to be more effective than group homes on a variety of outcome measures. Three articles in particular have strongly challenged the notion that group homes are better for any type of foster child. These three studies are summarized in the following research capsule. Together, they support the idea that group homes should only be used when foster homes are not available—if there were enough foster homes, there would be no advantage to placing children in group homes.

RESEARCH CAPSULE 1

Comparison of Family Foster Care with Group Homes

Study 1

Title Comparison of Two Community Alternatives to Incarceration for Chronic Juvenile Offenders

Authors Chamberlain, P. and Reid, J.

Publication *Consulting and Clinical Psychology,* 66, 4, 624–633, 1998.

Design and Sample Pre- and post-test comparison with random assignment of serious and chronic male juvenile offenders to one of two treatment groups: Group Care (GC) (n = 42); and Multidimensional Treatment Foster Care (MTFC) (n = 37). Sample averaged 76 days in detention during the year prior to the study, 13 previous arrests, and 4.6 felonies. Age of sample ranged from 12–17, with a mean of 14.9.

Interventions Group Care (GC) based on the Positive Peer Culture model that attempts to help youth develop pro-social skills by developing a peer culture in which peers help each other by giving positive feedback and confronting inappropriate behavior and thinking errors in daily group sessions that include problem solving. Multidimensional Treatment Foster Care (MTFC) was a comprehensive treatment model including recruitment, training, and support of foster parents, individual and family therapy, school consultation, and wraparound services during aftercare.

Results The foster care condition (MTFC) outperformed group home care on these outcome measures. All differences are statistically significant: fewer runaways (30.5% vs. 57.8%); percentage who completed program (73% vs. 36%); average days spent in lockup during year 1 of treatment (32 vs. 70—MTFC spent 60% fewer days total); mean number of criminal referrals at 1-year follow-up

(2.6 to 5.4); and time living with parents or relatives during first 12 months after enrollment (MTFC boys spent nearly twice as many days with living with family).

Study 2

Title Institutional Care: Risk from Family Background or Pattern of Rearing?
Authors Roy, P., Rutter, M., & Pickles, A.
Publication *Journal of Child Psychology and Psychiatry, 41*(2), 139–150.
Design and Sample Retrospective study of two matched groups who were placed out-of-home as infants (before age 12 months), and then received continuous care until age 6, in one of two placement settings: Group Care (GC) (n = 19) or Family Foster Care (FFC) (n = 19). The study sought to compare outcomes at age 6 for children with equivalent backgrounds who grew up in different placements. Groups were matched on various demographic characteristics, including level of psychopathology and social problems in the biological families. Data collection involved standardized instruments and involved teacher scores, classroom observations, caregiver ratings, and individual interviews of teachers and caregivers.
Interventions Family foster care was traditional family foster care provided by relatives or nonrelatives, with social service support. Group Care consisted of 24-hour group living with educational and therapeutic services provided by staff.
Results FFC children were significantly better on teacher ratings of disruptive behavior and hyperactivity; classroom behavioral observations were consistent with teacher ratings. Caregiver ratings revealed more emotional difficulties and unsociability in the GC children. Researchers concluded that GC predisposes young children to higher levels of problems, particularly hyperactivity and inattention.

Study 3

Title Satisfaction of Children in Out-of-Home Care
Authors Mech, E., Ludy-Dobson, C., & Huiseman, F. S.
Publication *Child Welfare, 78,* 53–69, 1999.
Design and Sample Random selection and stratified sampling of 1,100 Illinois children aged 5–18 in out-of-home placement in three settings: relative foster family, nonrelative foster family, and group care. Children were interviewed and instruments completed at 1-year intervals for 4 years. Satisfaction was assessed in areas of health, appearance, school, friends, fun activities, clothes, comfort, and food, place of residence, private space, sleep, family relationships, and happiness.
Interventions Details about the interventions in each setting were not given.
Results Few differences were found in the satisfaction of children in the two foster family situations. Large and significant differences were found between family foster care and group care. For example, children were asked if they felt loved and if they felt safe. Percentages that reported always feeling loved were 94% in kinship care, 82% in nonrelative foster care, and 46% in group care. Percentages reporting always feeling safe were 92% in both kinship and nonrelative foster care, and 64% in group care.

Permanency Planning and LRA

Another issue in child welfare is the potential for LRA and its implicit continuum of restrictiveness to conflict with the principles of permanency. If the goal of permanency planning is to create living situations that endure a lifetime, how does a continuum of care, with the image of children moving up and down the continuum, promote that goal? Once in foster care, children can move repeatedly, destroying any sense of permanence and continuity of relationships. Some of that movement is related to LRA, for as a child's behavior and needs change, so too does the level of placement. A child may begin in a foster family, then exhibit behavioral or emotional problems that trigger a different foster home placement, continue or escalate the behaviors, resulting in a group home or residential placement, then move back to yet a third foster family when the behavior and emotional stability improve. Meanwhile, prolonged efforts to reunite the child with the biological family may thwart efforts to place the child in a permanent adoptive home and confine the child to a long stay in foster care.

In order to minimize the conflicts between LRA and the principle of permanence, and thus reduce the length of stay in foster care, some state child welfare authorities have advocated aggressive and early resolution of the case plan in favor of reunification or adoption (Chestang & Heymann, 1973). Through what has come to be known as "dual case planning" or "concurrent planning," social workers simultaneously institute plans for reunification and adoption. While providing prompt, intense, and aggressive reunification services, the social workers and court establish clear criteria for reunification to be achieved within a set timeframe. If those reunification efforts do not succeed by the deadline, the child can be quickly adopted into a permanent home because planning for this event was done concurrent with the reunification efforts. As discussed in chapter 2, the Adoption and Safe Families Act of 1997 (ASFA) appears to have acted on these concerns by encouraging states to make speedier decisions about the permanency plan.

Least Restrictive Alternative in Children's Mental Health

Continuum of Care

The continuum of care for children in mental health settings ranges from long-term residential treatment to in-home family counseling and outpatient care. Between these two extremes are short-term hospitalization in the community and day treatment and partial hospitalization services. In the latter situation, the child participates in a structured treatment and education program during all or part of the day but lives at home. In special education, the continuum ranges from full-time placement in a special school to full-time placement in a regular classroom. Points along this continuum include full-time placement in a special education classroom in a regular school, and regular classroom placement with part-time instruction in an outside resource room. Since issues regarding the least restrictive alternative for children with emotional and behavioral problems in special education were discussed in the previous chapter, this section will focus on the continuum of care and least restrictive alternative in traditional mental health settings.

The tension between inpatient and outpatient care, or between institutional and community-based services, is longstanding (Petr & Spano, 1990). Despite federal and state initiatives to promote community-based care, institutional care continues to be overused, according to many experts. The community-based initiatives have succeeded in shifting the locus of institutional care from long-term public facilities (state hospitals) to short-term private hospitals. Professionals began to express concern for the dramatic rise in the rates of inpatient hospitalization rates in the late 1980s (Weithorn, 1988; Appelbaum, 1989; Eamon, 1994).

The closing of county and state mental hospitals was just one of the reasons behind the high hospitalization rates. These high rates of hospitalization have also been attributed to the lack of constitutional safeguards protecting children from unnecessary hospitalizations. In 1979, the U.S. Supreme Court, in *Parham v. J. R.,* ruled that the involuntary commitment of minors did not require the same due process safeguards afforded to adults (Weithorn, 1988). Parental discretion, in combination with the professional judgment of the admitting psychiatrist, was ruled sufficient. Even though some states have moved to pass legislation that makes commitment standards the same for children and adults (Appelbaum, 1989), the adultcentric ruling of the Supreme Court apparently was partly responsible for many unnecessary admissions of minors to psychiatric hospitals: perhaps as many as two-thirds of all psychiatric hospitalizations of youth are inappropriate (Weithorn, 1988). Another reason for high hospitalization rates has been the reluctance of insurance companies to pay for intensive outpatient care. Families felt forced to go the inpatient route because that is what their insurance would pay for. Private, for-profit hospitals, spurred by high reimbursement rates from insurance companies and lack of effective monitoring, have been accused of exploiting the troubles of middle-class families for monetary gain (Darnton, 1989).

If hospitalization of youth were an effective and cost-efficient strategy in achieving positive outcomes, these high rates might be justified. But little research on outcomes and effectiveness of hospitalization and residential treatment exists, and the cost of hospitalization and residential care ranges between $100 and $500 per day (Kutash & Rivera, 1996). Studies have consistently shown the superior cost-effectiveness of inten-

sive community-based programs of care (Eamon, 1994).

A recent, well-designed control group study demonstrated the effectiveness of Multisystemic Therapy (MST) compared to brief inpatient hospitalization. MST is a home-based family preservation model that was originally developed for serious and violent juvenile offenders (see chapter 3). A synopsis of this study is presented in the following research capsule.

RESEARCH CAPSULE 2

MST Can Prevent Hospitalization

Title Home-based Multisystemic Therapy as an Alternative to the Hospitalization of Youth in Psychiatric Crisis: Clinical Outcomes.

Authors Henngeler, S., Rowland, M., Randall, J., Ward, D. M., Pickral, S. G., Cunningham, P. B. Miller, S .L., Edwards, J., Zealberg, J., Hand, L. D., & Santos, A. B.

Publication *Journal of the American Academy of Child and Adolescent Psychiatry, 38*(11), 1331–1339, 1999.

Design and Sample One hundred and thirteen youth, aged 10–17, approved for emergency psychiatric hospitalization were randomly assigned to one of two treatment groups: MST (n = 57) or psychiatric inpatient treatment (n = 56). Clinical symptoms and consumer satisfaction were measured within 24 hours of recruitment, shortly after the hospitalized youth was released, and at the completion of MST services.

Interventions The MST program is based on nine core principles, discussed in chapter 3. The authors state that MST was modified for this population by increasing staff and frequency of supervision while decreasing caseloads from 5 to 3 to increase the intensity of treatment, focusing on family empowerment, strengths, and community resources. Families in the MST group were seen for an average of 123 days, for an average of 97 contact hours, and 44% were hospitalized at some point for an average of 3.8 days. The inpatient hospitalization program was behaviorally based milieu treatment with teams of providers including psychiatrists, a master's level social worker, a special education teacher, and the nursing staff. After the initial hospitalization, 20% were rehospitalized for an average of 15.6 days. Forty-two of the hospitalized group received some form of follow-up care in the community, averaging 8.5 hours.

Results Compared to the hospitalization group, the MST subjects experienced a 72% decrease in days hospitalized and a 59% decrease in days in other out-of-home placements. MST was more effective than emergency hospitalization at decreasing youth's externalizing symptoms, improving family functioning, and improving school attendance. Consumer satisfaction scores were higher for the MST group for both youth and caregivers. Hospitalization was more effective at improving self-esteem. The authors concluded that MST, combined with judicious access to placement, can be an effective alternative to emergency psychiatric hospitalization of children and adolescents.

By segregating children from their families, schools, and community, hospitalization makes it more difficult for the child to cope effectively within his or her natural environment. Hospitalization can foster dependency and loss of self-esteem for the stigmatized child. Children can be subjected to inappropriate restraint and seclusion (Darnton, 1989). Clearly, the decision to hospitalize is not an easy one, because the risks are high and the benefits uncertain.

Guidelines for Appropriate Hospitalization of Youth

Given the absence of empirical data to support hospitalization, and the negative outcomes that can result, what guidelines or criteria can the conscientious social worker use to determine when hospitalization is necessary and potentially productive? Answering this question requires consideration of the needs of the individual child and family at a particular time, and the ability of community resources to meet those needs. Just as with adults, the decision also depends on whether the admission is voluntary or involuntary. Many children's rights advocates would assert that the criteria for involuntary admission of children should be the same as that for adults: danger to self or others. If a child is suicidal or threatening others, the value of human life supersedes the child's right to treatment in a less restrictive environment.

But should there be no other involuntary commitments of children? And should some voluntary admissions be denied? What are legitimate reasons to hospitalize a child for emotional or behavioral disorders? Are there legitimate needs of the child and family that only a hospital environment can meet? For example, what about hospitalization for severe and acute change in child functioning? Are hospitals necessary, at times, to provide 24-hour supervision and structure? Are they useful for comprehensive (medical, neurological, psychological, social) evaluations and medication trials? Do they provide more intensive treatment? These are reasons for hospitalization that are often cited by frontline professionals: round-the-clock supervision and structure, capacity for comprehensive evaluations, monitoring of medication trials, and more intensive treatment.

Yet it must be asked whether or not these needs

could be met on an outpatient basis. Round-the-clock, 24-hour supervision and structure could potentially be provided in a child's home by hiring paraprofessional staff to be with the child at all times. There is no reason that comprehensive evaluations could not take place on an outpatient basis, if the agency and community were coordinated and organized to provide them, and they could be paid for. The organization and structure of hospitals, and the availability of the child, make comprehensive evaluations in hospitals appear efficient compared to the way most community outpatient services are organized, but this situation does not have to be perpetuated. The same holds for medication trials—in an ideal world, the monitoring of the effects of a medication could be accomplished on an outpatient basis. Intensive treatment in the form of daily therapy, structured activities, and milieu treatment can be provided in partial hospital and day treatment programs.

Thus, the need for hospitalization appears to be confined to the need for protection of self and others, if there is a community-based continuum of care that can provide intensive and comprehensive service. To avoid unnecessary hospitalization, this system of care must include capacity for 24-hour supervision, comprehensive interdisciplinary evaluations, close monitoring of medications, and day treatment or partial hospitalization services. If these are lacking in a community, families and social workers may be forced to use hospitals to meet the child and family needs.

In children's mental health, issues related to the principle of the least restrictive alternative confront the social worker on a weekly, if not daily, basis. Social workers in outpatient settings must often deal with questions and requests for hospitalization from family or other professionals. They may have to respond to marketing practices of private and for-profit hospitals. When intensive community-based services are not available, it may be hard to resist thinking that a short stay in a hospital would be a good thing. Social workers employed in these hospitals must guard against a conflict of interest when they are asked to engage in marketing practices. They can influence decisions about admissions, length of stay, and treatment philosophy so that hospitalization is reserved for the most severe problems when other approaches have failed, and the time spent in the hospital is viewed as an opportunity for children to improve transactions with their families, schools, and communities. At the policy level, social workers can work to ensure that comprehensive out-patient services are included in health insurance plans and that effective screening and utilization review procedures are in place to monitor admissions and length of stay.

CHAPTER 8 SUMMARY

The least restrictive alternative is both a practice philosophy and a legal principle. LRA asserts that services should be provided in a setting least restrictive of a person's personal liberties and rights. LRA has been a driving force in prevention of out-of-home placement efforts in child welfare, deinstitutionalization in mental health, and inclusion in special education.

Closely associated with LRA is the concept of continuum of care, which places services along of continuum of restrictiveness from high to low. Critics have found fault with both LRA and continuum of care, asserting that the concepts legitimize higher levels of restrictiveness, confuse level of restrictiveness and intensity of care, and thwart attainment of a sense of permanence.

The least restrictive alternative has not been universally endorsed by professionals, who have tended to promote higher levels of restrictiveness. Conflicts between parents and professionals will most likely revolve around parents and children wanting less restrictive alternatives than professionals. Occasionally, however, the situation is reversed, so that the parent and/or child believe that a higher level of restrictiveness is best, but are not afforded that choice. Because this situation involves a conflict between the pragmatic perspectives of family-centered practice and LRA, specific pragmatic suggestions for resolving the conflict were offered.

In the field of child welfare, LRA principles are highly relevant, from decisions about child safety to type of foster care placement, to decisions about permanency. In children's mental health, LRA is particularly applicable to the issue of appropriate hospitalization of youth.

CHAPTER 9

Pragmatic Perspective 6:
Ecological Perspective

Overview

The ecological perspective is firmly established as a hallmark of the social work profession. In this chapter, topics include the ecomap, case management, community involvement and ownership, and advocacy for systems change. Pragmatic implications focus on collaboration and teamwork and the danger of triangulation. The chapter concludes with applications of the ecological perspective to the child welfare and children's mental health systems of care.

Ecological Perspective: Introduction and Overview

The aspect of social work practice that most distinguishes it from other professions is the importance placed on the interactions between a client and the client's environment. For as long as social work has been a profession, its purview has been the interface between a client and his or her world. In recent years, this person-in-environment approach has been manifested in the ecological, or ecosystems, perspective (Germain, 1973; Germain & Gitterman, 1980; Meyer, 1983; Siporin, 1980). Borrowing from the science of ecology, the ecological perspective places individuals and their problems in their larger human and social contexts. Individuals are engaged in constant, reciprocal transactions with other human beings and other systems. In contrast to traditional psychological theory that conceptualizes individual problems as originating within the individual psyche, ecological theory looks to the interface of the person with the larger environment for the origin of individual problems and their solutions. Human behavior cannot be understood except in the context of the multiple connections and interactions that individuals have within their own human ecology.

It follows, then, that the environment must have adequate resources, including both formal services and informal supports, to assist families in meeting their needs. The environment must also encourage positive transactions between people and their environments if human needs are to be satisfied and difficulties overcome. These transactions between people and their environments involve how individuals interact with their family, friends, coworkers, and professional service providers. It also involves how well these external people and systems interact, communicate, and coordinate with each other. Fulfillment of human needs can be blocked by gaps in available resources, poor access to resources, inefficient coordination of resources, insufficient skills in the individuals who need and use resources, or unsuccessful transactions between individuals and their environmental systems.

Although the ecological perspective is perhaps best understood at the abstract and theoretical level, several specific techniques and activities are consistent with its emphasis on person-in-environment. These are examples of how social workers can implement the ecological perspective in their practice: using an ecomap, case management, community involvement and ownership, and advocacy for systems change.

Ecomaps

The scope of the ecological perspective is broad and complex, encompassing a holistic view of an individual within the larger sphere of family, friends, school, work, church, recreation, and social services. To assist the social worker in employing an ecological perspective with clients, Ann Hartman (1978) introduced the ecomap (figure 9.1). The ecomap is a paper-and pencil assessment and intervention tool that maps the relationships and interactions between a family and the major systems that are a part of the family's life. It captures in visual form the positive and negative connections between the family and the world. It demonstrates areas of strength as well as areas in which conflicts need resolution, bridges need to be built, or resources need to be accessed, developed, or mobilized. Environmental relationships typically assessed include friends, extended family, school, work, health care, social welfare, culture, religion, and recreation.

Because it is a tool that social work students are exposed to early in their education, a detailed discussion of the ecomap will not be presented here. It is important to emphasize, however, that the ecomap can be quite helpful in child and family settings to obtain a broad picture of the child's environment. The ecomap can be used to identify relationships and supports within the extended family. For the individual children themselves, the school is probably the most important social institution outside of the family. For that reason, special attention should be paid to the relationship of the child and family to the school when constructing a genogram. The ecomap can help the worker and family organize the relationship of the family to the school and other social institutions and service systems. Child welfare, mental health, juvenile justice, and health care are systems frequently involved in children's lives, especially those of children with multiple challenges. Also important

are the relationship of the parents to employment, income, housing, and transportation, all of which impact the stress level of the family and the child's overall well-being. The ecomap can also identify informal supports and activities, such as church, friendships, and recreation.

Case Management

Case management is a burgeoning intervention strategy consistent with the ecological perspective. Models of case management have been developed for a wide range of vulnerable populations. Unfortunately, case management has been poorly defined, and thus can mean something very different to different people. The literature contains varied conceptualizations or models of case management, adding to the confusion. Common to all models, however, is the function of linking clients with essential resources and empowering clients to function as independently as possible (Hepworth & Larsen, 1993). Case managers share the knowledge of community resources, skills in connecting clients with resources, and skills in following up to assure that services are delivered in a timely fashion.

Rothman (1991), recognizing that case management was used across many service systems but that "nobody quite knows what case management is," conducted a review of 132 articles and a survey of 48 case managers. In addition to the above roles, Rothman identified additional functions performed by some case managers depending on the situation and the setting. Interagency coordination enhances case management. The case manager arranges for policies and agreements, formal or informal, between agencies to help assure smooth referrals and follow-up. Many case managers also counsel clients with concrete information and practical advice about day-to-day issues of living such as housing, money management, and employment. In some mental health settings, psychotherapy is an additional function, as social workers may be both therapist and case manager for the same clients. Finally, case managers can engage in individual advocacy for a client, when services or resources are being withheld unfairly.

Recently, it has been noted that referring to clients as "cases" may be disrespectful and dehu-

FIGURE 9.1
Eco-Map

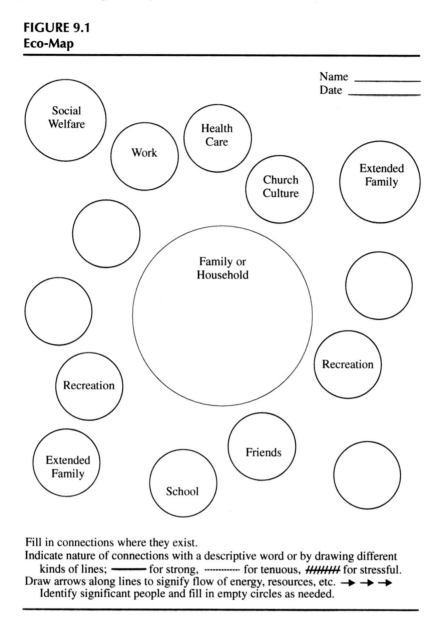

Name _____
Date _____

Fill in connections where they exist.
Indicate nature of connections with a descriptive word or by drawing different
kinds of lines; ——— for strong, ------------ for tenuous, ##### for stressful.
Draw arrows along lines to signify flow of energy, resources, etc. ➝ ➝ ➝
Identify significant people and fill in empty circles as needed.

A. Hartman, "Diagrammatic assessment of family relationships." In Social Casework, 59,
465–476. Copyright © 1978 by Families International, Inc.

manizing to the clients, and that "managing cases" may imply a level of professional control and paternalism inconsistent with the strengths perspective and with client empowerment. An alternative to the term *case management* is *integrated clinical care management* (ICCM) (Jackson, 1995). Although this latter term retains the idea of "management," it is clearer that it is the clinical care that is to be managed, not the person. Additionally, the goal of integration is specified in the title, thus clarifying to all the primary function of the position.

Community Involvement and Ownership

Senator and former First Lady Hillary Rodham Clinton (1996), among others, has quoted the African saying, "It takes a village to raise a child."

This phrase succinctly communicates the importance of the entire community in the successful rearing of children. Advocates of reform of the system of care for children and families have targeted the lack of citizen, neighborhood, and community commitment as a crucial variable that needs change. These efforts are true embodiments of the ecological perspective, because they target the larger environment, not individual clients, for change.

Many different strategies are being employed to achieve the goal of creating more healthy, nurturing, and supportive communities. At the client level, these include Big Brothers/Big Sisters for at-risk youth in the community, CASA and Citizen Review Boards in child welfare (Jennings, McDonald, & Henderson, 1996), community, full-service school programs in education (Dryfoos, 1994), and comprehensive planning efforts in

mental health (Jordan & Hernandez, 1990). The latter three initiatives will be discussed more fully later in this chapter; here, a brief introduction to each will suffice.

Big Brothers/Big Sisters is a community-based youth mentoring program that matches an adult with a boy or girl in hopes of forming a long-lasting, supportive relationship. It is an excellent example of community involvement of lay volunteers in the lives of at-risk children, primarily those from single-parent households. Professional staff members screen all applicants, arrange the matches, and provide training, orientation, and monitoring of the relationship over time. The matched pair will ideally spend 3–5 hours per week together over a year or longer. A recent, experimental design of the program demonstrated its effectiveness, as summarized in the research capsule below.

RESEARCH CAPSULE 3

Mentoring Works: Big Brothers/Big Sisters

Title Does Mentoring Work? An Impact Study of the Big Brothers Big Sisters Program.
Authors Grossman, J. B. and Tierney, J. P.
Publication *Evaluation Review, 22*(3), 403–426, 1998.
Design and Sample Experimental design with random selection and random assignment. Control group assigned to waiting list group for 18 months. Eight program sites nationwide; 10- to 16-year-olds from single-parent households, 487 in treatment group, 472 in control group; 43% lived in households receiving public assistance; 27% had experienced abuse; 62% male; 57% minority-race. Even though matches were not found for 22% of the treatment group, these unmatched children were not excluded in the data collection and analysis. Measurement instruments were self-assessment questionnaires.
Results Children in the treatment group had higher grades, attended school more often, reported better parental relationships and more parental trust, were less likely to initiate drug and alcohol use, and reported hitting others less often.

CASA programs and Citizen Review Boards (CRBs) are programs that attempt to get more citizen involvement and ownership in the lives and problems of children in child welfare. *CASA* stands for Court-appointed Special Advocate. Courts recruit and train regular citizens to follow and advocate for children who are placed in state cus-

tody. CASAs build a relationship with the child, the child's family and caregivers, and the professionals who work with the child, always urging the system to do its best for the child, and testifying in court if necessary. Citizen Review Boards consist of a panel of citizens, selected and trained by the courts, whose function is to provide a periodic, external review of the permanency status of children in state custody. Rather than formal court hearings, where rules and procedures can be intimidating to children and parents, CRBs meet informally with the child, parents, and professionals to ensure that case plans are being properly implemented. Neither CASAs nor CRBs have any independent legal authority—they can only make recommendations to judges and professionals.

Community-school programs seek to enlarge the mandate of public schools by transforming them into hubs of social service programs. Rather than their mission being to just educate children to the basic three *R*s of Reading, 'Riting, and 'Rithmetic, the community-school philosophy recognizes that children's learning is in large part dependent on their overall health and well being. Children learn better when they are not sick or hungry or subjected to violence at home. Thus, schools can best educate children by helping to meet the larger social needs that directly affect that learning. In one form or another, full-service schools become social agencies that attempt to address more then just the narrow educational needs of children.

In mental health, the concept of community has been incorporated in official policy and programming since the creation of community mental health centers through federal legislation in 1963 (Foley and Sharfstein, 1983). The creators of this legislation envisioned better mental health in local communities through the provision of quality, community-based treatment of problems that were identified and treated early, before they became debilitating. Recently, some communities, most notably Ventura County, California, have expanded further on the community concept by conducting thorough community-wide assessments of needs and goals (Jordan & Hernandez, 1990). Mental health centers formed formal interagency coalitions with other organizations in the community and offered services out in the community, rather than at the mental health offices.

Other community-building and community-wide ownership efforts include interagency coordinating councils, community planning councils, local governing authorities, and neighborhood revitalization programs. These efforts focus on collaboration and service integration, attempting to ensure that the community's system of care is coordinated and efficient. Only a brief description of each is presented here, as more extended discussion will be presented later in chapter 10 on pragmatic perspective 7, organization and financing, under the topic of service integration.

Interagency coordinating councils typically consist of professionals from various agencies who meet regularly to coordinate their efforts. These councils might produce written documents of interagency working agreements, referral procedures, or joint program planning. Community planning councils are similar in function to interagency coordinating councils, but they tend to be more broadly based in terms of their membership. Common citizens, business leaders, and consumers help plan for services in the community, so that the agency professionals do not operate in isolation. Local governing authorities, like community planning councils, are broad-based in their representation. Unlike interagency coordinating councils and community planning councils, local governing authorities have some responsibility and authority over financing, and they have sanctioning to hold social service agencies accountable for results. So, in addition to planning and coordinating services, local governing authorities can allocate funds and evaluate agency performance. Neighborhood revitalization efforts focus on improving the economic, social, health, and educational infrastructures of poor, blighted neighborhoods. They typically involve interagency coordination and service integration efforts, but also seek new sources of economic investment to revitalize a specific neighborhood.

Interagency Collaboration and Family-Centered Practice

Normally, interagency collaboration is characterized by a focus on professional coordination of services and programs, with little input from consumers. Walter and Petr (2000) have suggested that interagency collaboration is futile if it is not anchored in a shared value system that serves as the core unifying element of the efforts. They provide a vision and rationale for adopting family-centered values as this core, shared value base. If family-centered values were shared by all agencies, then their efforts would be consistent with the many

Indicators of Family-Centered Practice within Interagency Councils (adapted from Walter & Petr, 2000)

Mission Statement of Interagency Council

• All member organizations endorse family-centered principles
• Common community outcome objectives that support families

Membership of Interagency Council

• Includes families, youth, citizens, and frontline workers

Accountability to Family-Centered Outcomes

• Collection and use of aggregated data across agencies
• Case-level reviews to achieve outcomes
• Publicize success stories

Accountability to Family-Centered Values

• Regular checklist assessment ("accreditation") of agency practices
• Convene diverse focus groups

Maximize Family Decision making

• Grants to family organizations
• Formation of family-centered citizen case-review boards
• Promote family-centered values in the larger community
• Link and support informal support systems
• Recognize and honor exemplary businesses/agencies/individuals

Family-centered interagency collaboration would incorporate the family-centered principles discussed in chapter 5 into all aspects and levels of the interagency system. As the core, unifying values that all member agencies share, interagency councils would function to define and operationalize these values and hold member agencies accountable to them. Within organizations, the council would promote the guidelines for improving family-centeredness suggested in chapter 5. Between agencies, family-centered practices would include the following activities that would be overseen by the interagency council.

Advocacy for Systems Change

The direct provision of social work services to clients, including case management, can be criticized as being a conservative approach to human services that accepts the status quo in the system. Because case managers depend on friendly, cordial relationships with professionals in other settings, they may be reluctant to "rock the boat" by advocating strongly for their clients or for new services. Case management efforts often focus on linking clients to existing services rather than identifying and creating new services or different ways of doing business.

Advocacy is the process of working with and/or for clients to obtain services or resources, to modify policies and procedures that adversely affect clients, and to promote new legislation or policies that address and ameliorate adverse conditions (Hepworth & Larsen, 1993). Advocacy that focuses on the needs of an individual child or family is called *case advocacy*. When advocacy takes part on behalf of larger groups of people who are all adversely affected, it is often called *class advocacy*. Advocacy is often essential to improve social conditions and promote social justice. Advocacy is the appropriate response when clients are arbitrarily denied services or benefits to which they are entitled, when clients suffer discrimination, when gaps in services exist, and when organizational policies adversely affect the quality and quantity of services available.

In advocating for and with clients, social workers can employ numerous strategies and techniques. In case advocacy, they can present griev-

federal and state policies that emphasize the crucial role of the family. A family-centered value base would mitigate against the tendency of interagency coordinating councils to place their own networks at the center of their efforts, highlighting the interagency processes themselves rather than focusing on how those processes actually support families as consumers of services.

ances to organizational administrators, help clients appeal to review boards, and help clients access legal resources for the redress of grievances. Class advocacy activities include organizing client advocacy groups, developing petitions, conducting studies and surveys, educating the larger community, and providing expert testimony to policy-making bodies such as local and state governments. In perhaps its most radical form, class advocacy involves class action lawsuits filed on behalf of groups of aggrieved clients whose legal rights have been violated.

Pragmatic Implications: Collaboration and Teamwork

Social workers who operationalize the ecological perspective find that they are engaged with numerous other professionals both within and outside their own work setting. Thus, interprofessional collaboration and teamwork are essential components of successful practice.

Interprofessional collaboration and teamwork have several potential advantages. Because collaborative teams include a variety of professionals and paraprofessionals who can respond to different client needs, teams can be more holistic in approaching the needs of children and families. A more comprehensive program can be offered that meets more of the child and family's needs in a coordinated and integrated fashion. Staff members themselves can benefit from the process, as collaboration can be stimulating, reduce isolation, ease tensions and frustrations, and enhance feelings of value and professional worth (Toseland, Palmer-Ganeles, & Chapman, 1986).

Despite these potential advantages, interprofessional collaboration and teamwork should not be considered a panacea for solving client problems and meeting their needs. There is the danger of triangulation, as discussed in the next section below. To avoid triangulation and conflict, sanctions can be applied to pressure team members to conform to the majority view. Social workers can be pressured to present a united front to clients, even when the social worker disagrees with the team. In addition, teamwork and collaboration can be extremely time consuming, delaying the implementation of

services. If poor communication and conflict dominate the team, the quality of service to clients can suffer. Rather than a more comprehensive and holistic approach, the result of this poor teamwork can be increased fragmentation and discontinuity of service.

Skills Essential to Work Effectively in Collaborative Teams (adapted from Mailick & Ashley, 1981; Toseland, Palmer-Ganeles, & Chapman, 1986)

- Listen to and respect others' opinions
- Understand the implications of others' opinions
- Communicate directly and openly
- Recognize unique knowledge and expertise of others
- Defer to special knowledge when appropriate
- Develop maintain positive relationships with team members
- Be close enough to group to promote cooperation and mutual support, but maintain sufficient distance so that the group's norms will not be overwhelming.

Pragmatic Implications: The Danger of Triangulation

The ecological perspective may seem straightforward and simple to operationalize. In actuality, dealing with the many different people and organizations that comprise the human ecology of a family is quite complex and demanding. Implementing the ecological perspective involves collaboration and teamwork with a wide variety of organizations and professionals. In addition to surmounting the technical difficulties and demands of such seemingly simple and mundane tasks as getting people to attend a case conference, or even getting an agency representative to return a phone call, successful collaboration requires that practitioners be particularly attuned to the dangers of triangulation. Triangulation occurs when the worker inappropriately favors and "takes sides" with one of the multiple perspectives surrounding a child and family. The word *inappropriately* is key because it is sometimes appropriate, and in fact professionally responsible, to "take sides" when there is clear evidence of injustice, discrimination, or abuse, as discussed in the above advocacy section.

While strong and persistent advocacy may be required in the most egregious of situations, in most situations social workers are called upon to work collaboratively with a variety of professionals and family members, to be a member of a professional team that tries to reach consensus about the best course of action. As collaborator and team member, the social worker is sometimes called upon to be the mediator of conflict, a facilitator of improved communication and understanding. In these situations, it is not helpful to overly identify with one particular point of view. Improving the coordination of services and the interactions of individual clients with systems usually involves subtle diplomacy, tact, and the ability to accept, though not necessarily approve of, different points of view.

Consider, for example, the conflict that can arise in education settings between a teacher and a parent regarding what to do about a child's behavior at school and home. The teacher may feel that the parent is to blame for the child's behavior and be of the opinion that the focus of interventions should be targeted at the parent and the home environment. But the parent may feel that the teacher picks on her child and has unrealistically high expectations for children's behavior. For the school social worker in this situation, it would not be helpful to take one side over the other. The situation does not call for a "lawyer" approach in which the social worker works for one party, trying to convince the other of the correctness of his or her client's position. Neither should the social worker assume the "judge" role, in which he or she listens to both sides and then decides who is right. Both of these approaches would be examples of triangulation, in this situation.

The most productive approach, one that avoids triangulation, is to get the parties together, face to face, to iron out their disagreements. The social worker would help the parties see the other's point of view and find common ground, such as their common concern for the well-being of the child. Prior to the meeting, the social worker might coach the parent on how to assertively, but respectfully and tactfully, express her concerns; and the social worker might meet with the teacher to explain the social worker's role and the purpose of the meeting, so the teacher will not be expecting the social worker to be solely on the teacher's side.

This is, of course, easier said than done. There can be strong pressures on the social worker to take one side or the other. This can stem from pressure and confusion about who the client is, as was the case in conflicts between children, parents, and schools exemplified in the Randall Johnson case discussed in chapter 5. The reader will recall that this case example involved disagreements between the child, the teacher, and the parent. Told from the point of view of Jon, a social worker in the mental health center, it was recommended that Jon take a family-centered approach to the situation, to define the client as the family first. This did not mean that Jon should necessarily take a strong advocacy position for the parent against the school, but that the parent and family view should be validated in the sense that the family is seen as the primary client. The case was presented as an illustration of how a family-centered philosophy can help social workers focus on families as the unit of attention by defining the client as the family.

Now, consider the same situation from the point of view of Carmelita, the school social worker, rather than from the point of view of Jon at the mental health center. Suppose that the teacher has called Carmelita, the school social worker, for help. Being employed by the school district itself, Carmelita may feel pressure to work for the teacher as her primary client, and thus to take her side in the disagreement with the parent. Not only is the school paying Carmelita's salary, but there is in addition a culture within the organization (as in all organizations) to support and be loyal to one's colleagues. The teacher could understandably expect that Carmelita would agree with her plan for what should be done. On the other hand, Carmelita has been trained in her social work education program to think of children and families as her clients. She believes that social workers are employed by agencies, including schools, to help children and families by providing direct services and facilitating improvement in their interactions with their environment. She wants to combat adultcentrism and be family-centered, and she senses that taking the teacher's side would not be consistent with these goals.

The ecological approach, which focuses on improving the interactions between clients and their environments, would suggest that somehow Carmelita must work for the teacher, child, and parent *simultaneously* if she is to help the child do better in the school environment. Somehow, Carmelita must validate all points of view if she is to accomplish the goals of better communication and interaction between the parties. She does this by listening to, accepting, and understanding all positions, but agreeing with none.

Carmelita must accomplish all this while dealing with the additional pressure to be a messenger and go-between for the parties, a pressure that can lead to a different sort of triangulation. In this second form of triangulation, the worker does not actually take one side over another, but inappropriately carries messages back and forth between conflicting parties, allowing them to avoid direct contact and communication. Because face-to-face meetings can be hard to arrange in even nonconflictual situations because of work schedules and other commitments, it is tempting for the social worker to become a go-between. Although this strategy can be appropriate when the hostility between parties is extreme (the historical example of Henry Kissinger's shuttle diplomacy between Egypt and Israel comes to mind in this regard) or when schedules legitimately prevent a face-to-face meeting, the social worker's preferred strategy is to attempt to improve cooperation and coordination through direct communications.

Similar triangulation dangers exist in child welfare and mental health. Parallel situations exist in child welfare when the social worker is drawn into conflicts and disagreements that can arise between foster parents and biological parents, between court-appointed special advocates (CASAs) and lawyers representing the child, between group home parents and mental health professionals, or between any of the numerous players that are involved in a child and family's life. In mental health,

conflicts can arise between the psychiatrist and the parent regarding medications, between the group and individual therapist regarding the proper treatment plan, and between the parent and children regarding rules and consequences. At the community level, turf issues between agencies can result in competition and distrust rather than coordination.

Thus, the ecological perspective is a difficult and complex approach to operationalize because of the numerous potential conflicts and disagreements that can arise among the many players. It is therefore tempting for social workers to oversimplify their tasks by narrowly focusing their time and efforts on individual children, or on specific programs such as parent education, leaving the difficult, holistic, ecological efforts to someone else. But if social workers don't perform the ecological functions, who will? After all, the social workers may be the only professionals in the system with any training and expertise in this area.

Ecological Perspective in Child Welfare

The ecological perspective in child welfare recognizes that child abuse and neglect is highly correlated with environmental and system issues such as poverty, unemployment, and social isolation. Under stressful circumstances, it is easy to see how parents can easily displace their anger, frustration, and feelings of powerlessness onto their children. Thus it is appropriate for family preservation and other child welfare workers to utilize ecomaps, case management, community involvement, and case advocacy to ensure that the environmental impingements on children and families are reduced and their impact minimized.

Ecomaps and Case Management

Ecomaps are a useful tool to help children and families in the child welfare system identify the sources of environmental mismatch and stress. Using information from the ecomap, social workers can engage in case management activities to help families secure concrete resources, access needed services, and build informal support networks. Concrete resources include finances, shelter, and transportation. Services include day care, respite care, parent education, and individual or family counseling. Informal support networks include extended family, churches, and self-help support groups such as Parents Anonymous. Studies of effective family preservation programs have documented that this case management function is crucial to achieving successful client outcomes: "Short-term services can be effective when they include concrete services and the mobilization of community resources" (Berry, 1992, p. 321). These concrete services include teaching family care, supplemental parenting, medical care, help in securing food, and financial services. Not only is it important to create more nurturing and caring environments; clients must also learn the life skills necessary to more competently deal with the stresses and environmental challenges.

Community Involvement

In several areas of the country, child welfare officials are attempting to broaden the base of citizen involvement in the child welfare system through the formation of Citizen Review Boards (CRBs). As discussed in the previous chapter, the Adoption Assistance and Child Welfare Act of 1980 attempted to ensure permanency planning through systematic case planning and case review. These strategies are intended to result in better attention to the needs of the children in care, which in turn would lead to better foster care outcomes. Three types of case review exist to ensure adequate case planning for every child in foster care: judicial, administrative, and external citizen. CRBs involve community citizens in the external review process, and are typically used in combination with the other types of review.

A recent study documents the potential of CRBs (Jennings, et al., 1996). In this study, children were randomly assigned to CRB and control groups. The CRB comprised community citizens who received case information and conducted hearings to review and modify the case plan. CRB hearings were informal and were attended by all interested parties, including children, parents, other family members, substitute caregivers, mental health professionals, school personnel, guardians ad litem, and court-appointed special advocates. CRB hear-

ings were held at the time of initial referral by the judge, then at 3 months, 1 year, and 2 years.

Data were collected and analyzed for a total of 46 children in the review group and 39 in the control. Data regarding seven process variables and three outcome variables were collected. The seven process variables focused on extent of judicial determination of reasonable efforts, legal continuances, searches for relative placement options, the number of services planned and provided, and the time of the first and last permanency plans. The outcomes measured were the number of foster care placements experienced, the percentage of cases dismissed at each review, and the percentage of children in placements considered permanent.

Results indicated a consistent pattern favoring the CRB group, although differences did not reach statistical significance. Review cases were less likely than control cases to experience legal continuances, more services were planned and provided for children in the CRB group, permanency plans for children in the review group were more likely to contain specific goals, reunification with parents was the stated goal in a higher percentage of review cases, and a smaller percentage of children in the review group experienced multiple placements. Review cases averaged 64 fewer days under court jurisdiction than control cases. The authors concluded that external citizen review results in more specific and accurate case plans and better service provision and may allow children to achieve permanency more quickly.

To date, no study has measured other potential benefits of the CRB process. Regardless of the effect on outcomes such as those measured in the above study, CRBs may be worthwhile because they increase public involvement, understanding, and support for the child welfare system. Members of CRBs might become active in promoting legislative support to achieve lower worker caseloads and to initiate new programs. Parents and children may well feel less intimidated and experience a circle of community concern that lessens their sense of isolation and stigma. Foster care workers may appreciate the added manpower and creative problem solving that can be brought to the table on behalf of the children in their caseloads. As the field awaits more definitive studies of these and other more traditional variables, CRBs remain a promising type of case review whose potential has been documented.

Advocacy in Child Welfare

Case advocacy and class advocacy are both highly relevant to work with children and families in the child welfare system.

Case Advocacy. Children who have been abused and neglected are uniquely vulnerable because, unlike most other children, their parents are not usually their natural advocates. The need for case advocacy for individual children in the child welfare system was first recognized in law in the Child Abuse Prevention and Treatment Act of 1974 (P.L. 93-247) (Litzelfelner & Petr, 1997). The law required states to provide for the appointment of a guardian ad litem (GAL) in every judicial proceeding pertaining to alleged abuse and neglect of the child. The duties and qualifications of GALs were not specified in the legislation, but were left up to the states. GALs can be private attorneys, staff attorneys, or citizen volunteers, often called court-appointed special advocates (CASAs). GALs are expected to conduct an independent case evaluation and advocate for the interest of the child. Studies of the effectiveness of court-appointed attorneys serving as GALs have found that they typically had high caseloads and devoted very little time to individual cases (Condelli, 1988; Duquette & Ramsey, 1986).

The dissatisfaction with the effectiveness of court-appointed attorneys as GALs led to the establishment of CASA programs, which now number over 610 nationwide with more than 38,000 volunteers serving 129,000 children (National CASA Association, 1995). CASA programs enlist community volunteers to serve as GALs or as special, independent advocates. With only one case, or at most a very few, CASAs can provide the independent, thorough attention to the child's needs that the child deserves. CASAs have been shown to be an effective model of GAL in achieving positive outcomes for children. Children with CASA volunteers have been shown to be less likely to re-enter foster care (Abramson, 1991) more likely to be adopted (Abramson, 1991; Poertner & Press, 1990) and more likely to spend less time in out-of-home placement (Condelli, 1988) than children without CASAs. Despite their demonstrated effectiveness, only about 29% of the children involved in the child welfare system are represented by CASAs (National CASA Association, 1995).

Class Advocacy. Organizations such as the Child Welfare League of America and the Children's Defense Fund have long advocated for better laws and policies for abused children and their families. In addition to these efforts, class advocacy for children in the foster care system has recently proliferated through a number of lawsuits filed by legal right organizations such as the American Civil Liberties Union (ACLU) on behalf of the "class" of children in foster care. These suits are typically filed against state or local child welfare departments and assert that the department is violating the rights of foster children. These lawsuits have successfully challenged the adequacy and effectiveness of state child welfare systems nationwide. According to the New York Times (Pear, 1996), at least 21 states were operating all or part of their child welfare programs under court orders or consent decrees (agreements reached by the parties and approved by the court) in 1996. These 21 states were Alabama, Arkansas, California, Connecticut, Florida, Georgia, Illinois, Indiana, Kansas, Kentucky, Maryland, Massachusetts, Missouri, New Mexico, New York, Ohio, Pennsylvania, Rhode Island, Utah, Washington, and West Virginia, as well as the District of Columbia. The success of these lawsuits indicates widespread and serious problems for children and families who encounter the child welfare system.

In the District of Columbia, for example, at the end of a 3-week trial in 1991, the court declared the foster care system a "travesty" and ruled that the system violated the Constitution and many specific statutes (American Civil Liberties Union, 1993). Among other concerns, the Children's Rights Project of the ACLU charged that the district allowed reports of child abuse and neglect to go uninvestigated for weeks, removed children from homes without making reasonable efforts to keep the children in their families, maintained overcrowded foster homes, failed to monitor foster homes, maintained inadequate staffing with caseloads of over 100 children, allowed foster children to drift in foster care for an average of 5 years, and failed to apply for millions of dollars of federal aid to which its child welfare department was entitled.

In Connecticut, a suit by the Connecticut Civil Liberties Union resulted in a settlement and consent decree in 1991. In the consent decree, the state agreed to totally revamp its system. It hired 200 additional social workers and supervisors, established an academy to train them, offered parenting classes to all prospective foster and adoptive parents, increased the rates paid to foster parents, and infused the system with $5 million for new community services (American Civil Liberties Union, 1993). In Alabama, after a consent decree in 1992, the number of children in foster care has declined by 21%. In the Alabama counties that were first to carry out the decree, the average time spent in foster care declined from more than 300 days to 100 days (Pear, 1996).

While Connecticut and Alabama are cited as states in which lawsuits resulted in improved conditions for foster children, not all of the court orders and consent decrees have achieved the same degree of change. State responses to lawsuits and consent decrees vary widely. In Utah, a consent decree was reached 6 months after the lawsuit was filed by the National Center for Youth Law in 1994. But an independent review panel charged that the state was not fulfilling its responsibility in over half of the commitments it made in the consent decree. In Kansas City, Missouri, state compliance with the consent decree was so poor that a court cited the state for contempt and issued a new consent decree (Pear, 1996).

Because of the mixed results, the use of lawsuits to force compliance and improve the child welfare system is subject to debate and controversy. On the one hand, proponents of class action litigation point out that the children need protection of their rights and that states have failed to properly implement P.L. 96-272. They also argue that litigation can be used by state administrators to effectively leverage more dollars and resources for the child welfare system. On the other hand, lawsuits can trigger a defiant, defensive attitude that no court or compliance monitor can completely overcome. Fighting lawsuits and complying with consent decrees diverts valuable time, energy, and resources away from the direct provision of services to children and families in need. In Illinois,

the state reportedly paid almost $8 million to a private law firm to defend the state from lawsuits against its child welfare system (Pear, 1996). That $8 million conceivably could have been better spent directly on care of children. Recent court rulings have limited the scope of the legal foundation for such lawsuits, so that class advocacy in the future may, by necessity, involve advocacy to improve laws and their enforcement provisions at the federal and state levels, rather than lawsuits to force compliance to existing laws (Alexander & Alexander, 1995).

Ecological Perspective in Children's Mental Health

Interagency Collaboration and Service Integration

The needs of children with serious emotional and behavioral disorders and their families cross service systems, community agencies, and professional disciplines. With multiple problems and multiple needs, the importance of service integration at the client level through case management, and at systems level through interagency collaboration and planning, is paramount.

Wraparound. A promising intervention strategy that has been developed with children with serious emotional disorders and their families is the wraparound model (Burchard & Clarke, 1990; VanDenBerg, 1993). This model is attractive because it combines elements of case management, a strengths perspective, family-centeredness, and organization and funding of services into a coordinated and individualized circle of care for the child and family. Wraparound is targeted at those children who are involved with multiple systems of care, who are at risk for hospitalization or out-of-home placement, or who are returning from an institutional placement. The name *wraparound* stems from the objective of "wrapping around" an individualized array of supports and services that can meet the child and family's needs. An individual case manager or "resource coordinator" configures a wraparound team that consists of up to eight key people in the child and family's life, which may include extended family, clergy, and professionals from one or more agencies. At the center of this team are the child and family, whose needs and strengths in various life domains are identified by the team in a structured interview process. The team then identifies creative ways to meet those needs, which may or may not involve formal services.

A crucial component of the wraparound model, in its most developed form, is the second type of team that is involved: the community team. After the wraparound team has developed the wraparound plan, it is presented to the community team for funding. The community team consists of top officials from the major child-serving systems who have the authority to commit agency resources. This team is constituted to integrate funding streams for children's services, one child at a time, beginning with those who are at most risk for institutionalization and who require the most collaboration among service providers. Thus, unlike most case management models in which the case manager and client work in isolation, in the wraparound model the case manager and family have access to funding and support from the key actors at the family and the community levels. Rather than having to link and coordinate with separate resources and supports, one at a time, the group meetings at the family and community levels support communication and coordination between key actors and resources. The community team allows for flexible funding of both the traditional services that the family cannot afford and the new, unique, individualized services and supports unique to the child and family.

The wraparound process has been implemented in numerous sites nationwide. Although many benefits of the model have been reported, implementation has sometimes been problematic, as barriers to the implementation of the model and to achieving outcomes are sometimes formidable. Many of these barriers stem from the need for changes in attitudes, programming and funding. Some of the barriers that have been identified include family distrust of the system, fully implementing the strengths approach beyond identification and assessment, the amount of time required of team participants that leaves the coordinator burdened with many tasks, lack of support from coworkers, difficulty in funding individual plans, and overall lack of focus on assessing fidelity of

implementation on an ongoing basis (McGinty, McCammon, & Koeppen, 2001).

The empirical base for wraparound is not highly developed, but two studies with comparison groups have produced positive results. Evans, Armstrong, and Kuppinger (1998) reported on a small study that randomly assigned youth to treatment in a foster care condition (n=15) or to intensive case management that was consistent with a wraparound ideology (n=27). After one year, children in the case management group showed more improvement in behavior, mood, emotions, and role performance, but there was no difference between groups in family functioning. Clark and colleagues (1998) reported on a study that randomly assigned children placed in foster care to a program based on the wraparound ideology ($n = 54$) of a standard practices group ($n = 77$). The wraparound program increased permanent placements, decreased restrictiveness of living arrangement, and improved behavioral and school adjustment compared to the standard practices group. In both studies, fidelity of implementation was not assessed.

In order to address some of these implementation concerns and to better study the effectiveness of the wraparound model, its originators have developed a tool to measure the extent to which the model is actually implemented by its practitioners (Ermold, Bruns, Suter, Wimettee, & Burchard, 2000). The *Wraparound Fidelity Index* asks parents, youth, and facilitators to rate the degree to which the 11 components of the wraparound process are extent in their own situation. For example, to partially measure the implementation of the component of Parent Voice and Choice, parents are asked if they express opinions even if they are different from the rest of the team. To partially measure the implementation of the component Flexible Resources and Funding, parents and facilitators are asked if money is easily available to fund good new ideas for services and supports.

Interagency Collaboration and Planning. In a descriptive study of five highly regarded community initiatives to develop local systems of care, the authors concluded that a meaningful interagency structure was a vital key to success (Stroul, 1996). Interagency planning bodies in these communities went beyond the pro forma interagency groups that meet in many communities but accomplish little. In these successful communities, the interagency group made important decisions about community priorities, service development, financing, resource allocation, and information management.

Several factors seemed to distinguish these groups from similar groups in other communities that had little impact. First, the effective interagency task forces built on a long history of collaborative problem solving. Child-serving agencies shared the belief in collective ownership and shared responsibility for children with multiple needs. Second, the interagency task forces were made up of the top executives of each of the major child-serving agencies in the community. This level of participation underscores the commitment to collaboration and allows for the commitment of agency time and resources in a timely fashion. When top executive officers are allowed to send lower-level representatives, meetings are characterized by lots of talk and little action. Third, the successful interagency task forces retain an independent full- or part-time coordinator to organize and coordinate the work. Many other interagency task forces attempt to operate with staff employed by one of the participating agencies. This creates problems because these staff members have other full-time responsibilities and the work of the interagency group can be seen to be dominated by the agency employing the coordinator.

Even in these successful collaborations, coordination barriers remain. Usually, there exists ongoing tension between the goals of a system of care and goals of individual agencies. Collaboration can seem fragile because it too often depends highly on the leadership of a few key individuals. Different agencies may have different philosophies about the causes and effective treatments for children's problems. Also, despite general commitment to an interagency approach, if just a few key agencies—or even one—are less committed and uninvolved, progress can be slowed greatly.

Advocacy in Children's Mental Health

This section will highlight two of the major arenas for advocacy in the children's mental health system: family advocacy and child advocacy. Family advocacy efforts have evolved in the develop-

ment of voluntary state and national organizations, while child advocacy efforts have emanated from the federal government's program Protection and Advocacy for the Mentally Ill.

Family Advocacy. One of the consistent themes in CASSP and other systems-change efforts has been the importance of family involvement in the design, planning, and implementation of mental health services at both the client and systems levels. From the 1960s, parents of children with other disabilities, most notably mental retardation, have organized to influence their state systems of care. But the impetus for organizing a national parent advocacy organization for children with emotional and behavioral disorders did not begin until the mid-1980s, when two federal initiatives sparked momentum. First, CASSP required states to address the issue of family involvement. Second, the federal government funded the Research and Training Center on Family Support and Children's Mental Health at Portland State University, which in turn sponsored a series of regional conferences on parent-professional partnerships and family advocacy. In 1988, the center hosted a meeting to develop a 5-year plan for addressing key issues for families in the mental health system, and out of this meeting came a call for a national family advocacy organization. In 1989, the Federation of Families for Children's Mental Health was formed. The Federation has become a strong and effective voice at the national policy level, providing training and technical assistance to statewide family support networks in 28 states (Bryant-Comstock, Huff, & VanDenBerg, 1996).

Another national family advocacy organization is the National Alliance for the Mentally Ill Children and Adolescent Network (NAMI-CAN). The National Alliance for the Mentally Ill was formed in 1979 by parents of adults with serious, long-term mental illnesses. The organization became an effective advocate for change in the mental health system for adults. In 1988, NAMI-CAN was established to focus on the needs of members who had young children and adolescents with serious emotional and behavioral problems. NAMI-CAN focuses its efforts on children with neurobiological disorders and places emphasis on research to better understand the causes of these disorders (Bryant-Comstock, et al., 1996).

Protection and Advocacy Agencies. In 1975, Congress enacted legislation to create independent Protection and Advocacy agencies (P&As) in all U.S. states and territories to protect the human and civil rights of developmentally disabled people. In 1986, following hearings and investigations which substantiated abuse and neglect of mentally ill people in state psychiatric hospitals, Congress passed the Protection and Advocacy for Mentally Ill Individuals Act (P.L. 99-319), which extended similar protections to mentally ill individuals through the same P&A system. Under this legislation, P&As have the legal authority and public funding to protect and advocate for the rights of people with mental illness, including children (Petr & Poertner, 1989). The law gives P&As the authority to investigate reports of abuse and neglect in facilities that care for mentally ill people, including public and private hospitals, community facilities, and prisons. Abuse includes the usual acts of violence as well as the excessive use of force; neglect includes failure to carry out an appropriate individual treatment plan and discharge planning. Investigative authority extends to issues that arise during residency in, or 90 days after discharge from, such facilities. Staff members from P&As conduct both case advocacy and class advocacy to attempt to resolve complaints through counseling, negotiation, or litigation.

In FY 1994, the federal government allotted over $21 million for this program, and almost 19,000 individuals were served. Although 17% of these people were under age 20, states varied widely on the percentage of clients who were children. In 10 states, the percentage of clients under age 20 was less than 5%, while in 3 states (Kentucky, Maryland, and Pennsylvania) the percentage was 50% or more (Center for Mental Health Services, n.d.). The potential of the law to help children with emotional and behavioral disorders depends on the priorities set in each state.

The potential of this legislation in demonstrated in the recent activities of the P&A in New Mexico. The P&A agency filed a class action lawsuit on behalf of 1,000 children in state custody who were in need of mental health services but were not provided them. In addition, the P&A intervened to improve the situation for adolescents placed in seclusion in a locked cell located on an adult forensic unit, which housed adults facing criminal charges or committed by the state. While secluded in the cell that had only a concrete slab for a bed, the adolescents were exposed to adult patients' smearing of feces and prolonged screaming. As a result of negotiations with the facility, the hospital clinical director agreed that the seclusion cells should be used with neither adolescents nor adults (National Association of Protection and Advocacy Systems, 1995).

School-Linked Mental Health Services

Within school systems and communities, there is a growing movement to expand the purpose and scope of public schools by linking them more closely with other human services (Franklin & Streeter, 1995; Gardner, 1992). This linking is viewed as one way to address the need for service integration at the community level. Since schools are accessible and relatively stigma-free, proponents of school-linked services believe they are best situated to provide needed access to and coordination of services to children and families.

In many communities, one of the logical arenas for this linking to occur is between schools and mental health systems targeting children with serious emotional and behavioral disorders. Through joint funding and ownership, many mental health agencies and school districts have created day treatment programs combining therapeutic interventions with education to prevent the hospitalization and out-of-home placement of serious emotionally troubled children. Another, more recent type of collaborative effort is the use of school-based case managers and other types of interventions to develop individual service plans for children. One impetus for school involvement in these efforts has been the high cost paid by state and local education units to educate children in highly restrictive placements such as residential treatment centers. In Maryland, for example, the estimated cost for out-of-state care funded by education in FY 1992 was $30.7 million (Knitzer, 1996).

One of the foremost of these school-linked efforts in mental health is Project WRAP in

LaGrange, Illinois (Eber, 1993). In this project, the school system has taken the lead in developing an interagency community council whose purpose is to identify barriers to effective service delivery and redeploy resources. The philosophy strongly endorses the idea of inclusion for this population, and several programs have been developed to achieve this end. One is the Buddy Program, pairing children with emotional and behavioral disorders with a buddy from regular education to foster social interactions and better inclusion with regular students. Another is a Parent-to-Parent Support Program that provides mentors for parents whose children are experiencing difficulties. A third program within the overall structure of Project WRAP is the Wrap Around in School (WAIS) program that attempts to incorporate the wraparound model within the school. WAIS students have a family service manager, a team teacher, and in-school respite workers. Strong efforts are made to include WAIS students in regular in-school and after-school activities. This program model has expanded statewide in Illinois, and evaluations have shown positive results (Eber & Nelson, 1997). For children and families, benefits have included more successful transitions from residential settings to home, school, and community, prevention of out-of-home placements, and parent satisfaction with being included in decisions about services. System improvements have included additional family supports, systematic use of wraparound approaches, and placement of educators in leadership positions in local interagency networks.

CHAPTER 9 SUMMARY

The ecological perspective constitutes a broad view of human functioning that places importance on the reciprocal interactions between children, families, and their social environments. Social workers who use this perspective must strive to positively affect the responsiveness of the environment to the needs of children and families. Various techniques and strategies can be employed to help social workers and their clients understand the relevance of social systems for individual functioning and intervene to improve the relationship between individuals and the service system. These include ecomaps, case management, wraparound approaches, systems advocacy, interdisciplinary collaboration, and teamwork.

In taking an ecological perspective, the social worker is challenged to build consensus and cooperation among diverse and often competing perspectives. The danger of triangulation, or inappropriately taking sides in disagreements or conflicts, is a constant source of tension. At the same time, the pressure to reach consensus and validate all perspectives can be extremely time consuming and lead to compromise positions that do not adequately address client perspectives or adequately meet client needs. The emphasis that the ecological perspective places on cooperation, coordination, and consensus can conflict with combating adultcentrism, family-centered practice, the strengths perspective, and other pragmatic perspectives. Conflict can occur whenever other professionals do not act in accordance with these perspectives, and disagreement occurs about what is the best course of action. The social worker must continuously be aware of these potential conflicts and avoid seeing collaboration and consensus as an end in itself. Cooperation and collaboration are the means for achieving client outcomes and goals, not ends in themselves. Also under the umbrella of the ecological perspective are client advocacy and systems change, strategies social workers are obligated to employ when cooperative and collaborative approaches fail to achieve positive client outcomes.

The ecological perspective in child welfare was discussed in relation to ecomaps, case management, community involvement in the child welfare system via Citizen Review Boards, and advocacy at the case and class action levels. In children's mental health, discussion was focused on interagency collaboration, service integration, family advocacy, protection and advocacy agencies, and school-linked mental health services.

CHAPTER 10

Pragmatic Perspective 7: Organization and Financing

Overview

The organization and financing of services to children and families can appear to be chaotic and incomprehensible. The first sections of this chapter discuss current trends and reforms aimed at simplifying and streamlining service delivery. Topics include decentralization, block grants, privatization, managed care, and service integration. The final sections present ways in which organization and financing issues surface in child welfare and children's mental health.

Organization and Financing: Introduction and Overview

No social work student should embark into the world of social work in child and family settings without some knowledge of how the programs in these systems are organized and financed. If services are to meet individual and family needs and make any impact on the overall health and well-being of children and families, then they must be accessible, efficient, and affordable. A keen understanding of which services exist, how they can be accessed, and how they are paid for is crucial if social workers are to help clients negotiate the complex maze of the system. While child welfare, mental health, and education are organized to address specific categories of need, many children and their families cross over from system to system. Social workers in one system must have a general working knowledge of the other systems if they are to know how to help families access and utilize those other systems. From the client perspective, the system can appear to be a maze, because even though the needs of the families and children cross systems, those systems tend to be independent and uncoordinated.

Consider the situation of the Robinsons, a single-parent family that has multiple children with special needs.

CASE VIGNETTE: The Robinsons

Elizabeth Robinson works full-time at a local grocery store for a salary of $16,000 per year. Her medical insurance pays for medical care for her and her children, but not for mental health or dental care. Elizabeth has four children. Donna, 11, has difficulty in speech and hearing. She is in special education and receives individual speech therapy in the schools, but Elizabeth thinks Donna needs a thorough reevaluation from a private speech and hearing clinic, and perhaps additional speech and language therapy outside the school. Elroy, 8, has emotional and behavioral problems stemming from physical abuse he suffered at the hands of his father, who has since abandoned the family. Elroy receives special education services and has been recommended for individual and group therapy at the mental health center. Both Donna and Elroy need supervision after school until their mother returns from work. Tanya, 4, and Brian, 2, need full-day child care while their mother works. Both appear to be developmentally delayed and are in need of developmental evaluations. The family lives in a small, two-bedroom apartment, which Elizabeth feels is inadequate. She has applied for public housing subsidies to help her afford a bigger place. The family does not own a car, and the city they live in is of medium size with poor public transportation. School and mental health authorities would like Elizabeth to attend a parenting class to improve her communication and discipline with the children. Elizabeth is a recovering alcoholic who is expected to attend weekly alcohol therapy and weekly AA meetings.

The needs in this family are numerous, requiring a multitude of services, meetings, and appointments: special education, mental health, day care, after-school supervision, parenting education, alcohol counseling, transportation, developmental evaluations, and housing.

How are all those services to be paid for? How many different agencies and professionals will the children and family have to deal with? Will the children and family have to tell the same information about their history and situation to each and every one of the providers? Will any of the services be integrated or coordinated, or will the children and family feel that all the different professionals are working at cross-purposes or are duplicating services? Will professionals in the system view the family as "resistant," "dysfunctional," and "unmotivated" if they do not keep all the appointments or do not complete all of the "homework" the professionals assign? Will Elizabeth be reported for neglect if she does not do all that the professionals recommend? If Elizabeth sees the system itself as "dysfunctional," will she fight for better services or will she just exit the system by limiting or terminating the family's involvement?

If the organization and financing of services seems confusing from the family perspective, it may be no less chaotic from an organization administrator's perspective. In child welfare, public agencies are funded from a variety of federal, state, and local sources, depending on the program. Private child welfare agencies may receive federal, state, or local government grants, private funds from foundations, and fees for service paid by clients or insurance companies. Mental health agencies may receive funds from federal, state, and local tax dollars, private individuals paying fees for service, the local United Way organization, insurance companies, and foundations. School systems do not generally charge fees for service, and most of their funding is generated by local and state taxes, but they also receive federal funding for a variety of programs, notably special education.

Policy analysts have noted a strong relationship between the financing and organization of the social services system. The key operating principle is "What gets done is what gets paid for." For example, in child welfare, federal funds have long been available to help states pay for foster care, but until recently very little money was available for prevention of foster care placement, for reunification services, or for adoption. Hence, it was not surprising that some children were unnecessarily placed in foster care, and then spent a long time there once placed. Foster care is what was paid for; foster care is what was done.

In mental health, the financial system has been

based on the medical fee-for-service and insurance models. So it is not surprising that services are limited by how much the individual person or the person's insurance can pay. Jon, our mental health professional, may be of the professional opinion that Johnny, who is seriously troubled, needs 2 hours a week of individual therapy, 1 hour of group therapy, 1 hour per week of family therapy, and the mother 1 hour per week of individual therapy. This is not atypical for many situations, including sexual abuse. But if the family can afford only 1 hour per week, and they have limited insurance coverage, how many hours of therapy will be provided? Unless the agency has outside grant support, it will not be able to afford to provide more than what the mother and insurance can pay. This example depicts how professional practice is dramatically influenced by financial considerations. Where professional judgment and financial limits clash, the financial limits usually prevail.

There is universal agreement among policy analysts that the current organization and financing of children's services is in need of serious reform. It is fragmented, inflexible, uncoordinated, inefficient, wasteful, inaccessible, bureaucratic, noncomprehensive, and duplicative. The reasons for this disorganization are complex and not clearly understood. O'Looney (1993) believes that the disorganization stems from three characteristics of the system: it is predominantly public (governmental) as opposed to private; it is loosely, rather than tightly, organized; and it is largely noncompetitive. Services are organized by service and program categories, so that a family or child must meet eligibility standards to receive separately organized and funded services. The links between service programs and service systems are very loose and ill defined. A comprehensive, holistic approach is absent. Both agencies and clients waste time, because families have to deal with a number of different agencies to receive services, while agencies duplicate intake, service planning, evaluation, and even coordination services. The latter can occur when a family receives case management services from more than one agency, thus necessitating the coordination of the coordinators! Large public bureaucracies are said to stifle innovation and to promote incompetence through civil service regulations that have little relevance to performance.

A key operating principle in the reorganization

of the system is *decentralization.* Decentralization involves the diffusion of responsibility, planning, and implementation of services from the highest levels of an organization's structure toward those who are closer to the problems and issues (Barker, 1991). Decentralization can operate at all levels of a system: the federal government can defer to the states, the states to counties and cities, cities to neighborhoods. Within an agency, top-level administrators can delegate responsibility and authority down the hierarchy, so that direct-service professionals and clients have great flexibility and control in designing and implementing care plans.

One of the strategies for decentralization at the federal and state levels is the *block grant.* Block grants are a system of dispersing funds for health, education, or social welfare that permit recipient organizations to determine how best to distribute the money (Barker, 1991). The strategy is intended to consolidate and streamline the budget process, eliminating separate funding streams for individual and categorical programs. Block grants became very popular under the Reagan administration in the 1980s, particularly in the Omnibus Budget Reconciliation Act of 1981 (P.L. 97-35). Block grants are intended to increase flexibility, efficiency, and local control. Since block grants have also been associated with reductions in expenditures, critics assert that they are a covert way to cut funding. Critics also worry that too much local control can mean the diminution and erosion of standards and inappropriate targeting of funds.

Three other trends in the reorganization of services require more thorough discussion. The remainder of this chapter presents discussion of these three major, interrelated trends in the reform of the human services system: privatization, managed care, and service integration.

Privatization

The privatization of social services has been identified as 1 of the 10 new directions of change in society in the 1990s (Naisbitt & Aburdene, 1990). Although *privatization* is a broad term that can mean different things to different people, it generally refers to the increasing reliance on market forces, competition, and the private sector to provide services formerly provided by public or governmental agencies (Dorwat & Epstein, 1993).

Privatization is an outgrowth of popular political philosophies that hold that the private sector should be more dominant in all areas of the economy and human services, that the private sector can deliver goods and services more efficiently and effectively than the public sector.

A somewhat confusing privatization issue in the human services sector is that private agencies may be for-profit or not-for-profit. Not-for-profit private agencies have a long and valued history and tradition in social work and the human services. Charitable, religious organizations in child welfare and community mental health centers in mental health are examples of established not-for-profit organizations. For-profit agencies have only more recently come upon the human services scene, as exemplified in for-profit psychiatric hospitals that provide mental health care.

Because there have been few evaluations of the efficiency and effectiveness of privatization, both proponents and opponents argue its merits on rational and theoretical grounds (O'Looney, 1993). Proponents of privatization of human services argue that privatization will lead to more emphasis on performance and innovation with less emphasis on business as usual, more emphasis on rational decision making instead of political decision making, and more emphasis on accountability and consumer preference instead of the preferences of public administrators (Kettner & Martin, 1993). Proponents also claim that access to care and quality of care will be enhanced while costs are lowered (Dorwat & Epstein, 1993). These benefits would derive from the inherent differences between private and public organizations. Private sector employees can be held to higher standards than public civil service employees, and private sector employers have more latitude in rewarding good performance. Consumers have more choice in a private system, and thus more influence. Private agencies, due to competition, must change and adapt to survive. Public agencies have unnecessary administrative overhead and waste compared to leaner, streamlined private agencies.

Opponents of privatization argue that it will result in the opposite effects, especially in for-profit private agencies. Opponents claim that the profit motive will drive delivery of services, not quality of care. Access to services will be restricted and client choice will be minimized to cut costs and maximize profits. Because of competition between agencies, there may be few incentives for cooperation and service integration. In addition, some argue that the government has a poor track record in monitoring for theft and corruption in private contracts, and that private agencies pay workers less, provide fewer benefits, and offer less job security than do public agencies (Dorwat & Epstein, 1993). This latter objection strikes home with social workers who have made careers of public social service and have become accustomed to the job security, health benefits, and retirement programs that generally accompany employment in government.

Although thorough studies of the results of privatization are lacking, there is some research to indicate that consumers themselves prefer to receive services from private agencies. O'Looney (1993) reviewed these studies and concluded that consumers are generally more satisfied with private agencies, viewing them as more flexible, more responsive, and less stigmatizing. These results are associated with the higher status of private providers, the smaller size of private agencies, lower expectations of private providers by the consumers, a greater sense of confidentiality and safety, an enhanced feeling of choice about whether or not to use the services, and a greater sense of empowerment and influence. It is important to note that these consumer preferences do not necessarily reflect on the efficiency or effectiveness of the private agencies.

The arguments for and against privatization are summarized in the following box.

Arguments for and against Privatization of Public Services

For:

- More innovative
- More rational, less political decision making
- More emphasis on results and accountability
- Lowered costs
- Better quality care

(con't.)

- Better access to care
- More choice for consumers
- Higher satisfaction for consumers

Against:

- Decisions driven by costs and desire for profit
- Poorer quality care
- Poorer access to services
- Less choice for consumers
- Poorer pay and benefits to workers
- Less cooperation and service integration among providers

A principal means for privatization of human services is purchase-of-service contracting (POSC). Under POSC, public entities buy services for individual clients or for groups of clients from private providers, rather than providing the service and programming directly. Common examples of this include large cities contracting with a private company for sanitation services, or school districts contracting with private companies to provide bus transportation. In the child welfare arena, POSC can involve purchase of individual services, such as psychotherapy for a sexually abused child, or contracting of programs, such as the recruitment and training of foster parents.

The public purchase of private agency services blossomed in the 1970s and 1980s due to changes in the political climate, expansion of available federal funds for purchase of service, and the emphasis on quick start-up for programs. Public agencies reportedly favor POSC because it provides increased service flexibility, program innovation, and lower costs. Dangers of POSC include ambiguous lines of accountability, greater government influence in nonprofit agencies, and restriction of nonprofit agency discretion (Smith, 1989).

Although POSC has been a principal means to implement privatization, a study of 5 programs in 10 states (Kettner & Martin, 1993) concluded that the administrators of these programs have not necessarily viewed POSC as a way to enhance the goals of efficiency or effectiveness. In juxtaposition to advocates for privatization who cite efficiency and effectiveness as the prime advantages of privatization, administrators themselves have used POSC more to target specific needs, to build public-private partnerships by coordinating and maximizing public and private resources, to be responsive to political realities, and to maintain the business-as-usual stability of ongoing contracts that assure continuity of care. Efficiency and effectiveness were primary motivations only with programs such as employment training and specialized transportation, in which service volume and client outcomes were more easily quantifiable.

Another type of privatization, less frequently used, is vouchers. Vouchers have been advocated in the field of education, as a means to improve the quality of education and the responsiveness to consumers. Under voucher systems, public dollars, in the form of purchase-of-service vouchers, are provided directly to service recipients, rather than to organizations. The clients then use the voucher to purchase the designated service from the agency and provider of their choice. School vouchers, in which parents are given a set amount to purchase educational services, are a case in point. Voucher systems are viewed by many as a "purer" form of privatization because they more accurately apply the strengths of competition and choice characteristic of true market systems. However, voucher systems are criticized for paying little attention to standards and civil liberties. They also tend not to provide incentives for prevention activities or for focusing on results; instead, they tend to provide remedial services and to pay for the delivery of the service, not for results (O'Looney, 1993).

Privatization is a growing trend in child welfare, mental health, and education, although it takes a different form in each setting. In child welfare, privatization goes hand in hand with the trend toward downsizing in government. Some states are contracting entire statewide programs such as family preservation, adoption, and foster care to private contractors, thus reducing the number of government employees and the size of government. Under these POSCs, the role of the public social worker becomes one of referral of individual cases and monitoring of service contracts. In mental health, privatization has involved the dramatic increase in private provision of mental health care that was previously provided by public institutions. Responding to the demands created by deinstitutionalization and the growth of mental health riders in private insurance plans, the number of private, freestanding psychiatric hospitals tripled in the 1980s, and the number of psychiatric units in private community hospitals doubled (Dorwat & Epstein, 1993). In school systems, privatization can take the form of school vouchers, as previously mentioned, or it can take the form of purchase-of-service contracting. School districts can purchase specific services, such as transportation or special education services, or school districts can contract for the provision of the entire curriculum. Privatization can also be associated with managed care, as explained in the next section.

Managed Care

Managed care is a trend that originated in the health care system and has since begun to spread to other systems as well. Because many mental health settings operate as part of the larger health care system, managed care is especially relevant to that service system. Principles of managed care also apply to child welfare and to education settings, as will be discussed later in this section. First, the reader will become acquainted with an overview of managed care as it exists in the health care system.

What is managed care? In the health care field, managed care denotes a system of health care delivery that tries to exert control over and manage three aspects of care: cost, quality, and access (Kongstvedt, 1995). In the health care field, managed care has evolved because the traditional system of financing health care had driven up costs and overemphasized expensive treatments while eschewing more cost-effective prevention activities. The mechanism for financing health care in the traditional health care system was private insurance that paid for health care on a fee-for-service, as-needed basis. Under this system, the individual patient and physician determine what care is needed, and the fee for that care is billed to the patient's insurance company. The financial incentives for health care providers are to treat illnesses, not prevent them. Health care providers are paid when they perform treatments, so there

is an inherent financial incentive to be extremely thorough and cautious in treating illnesses, to order batteries of diagnostic tests and procedures, to hospitalize patients when their conditions even vaguely warrant it, and to keep patients in hospitals for long periods of time to ensure full and thorough recovery. This is not to say that physicians engaged in widespread fraud or malpractice. The financial system encouraged physicians to be thorough and cautious in their professional judgments and to err on the side of overtreatment, rather than undertreatment, in borderline cases. This system also had few financial disincentives for the patients themselves, because most of the cost of treatment was borne by insurance, and although insurance premiums would rise each year, much of that cost would be borne by employers. The issue of cost is seldom discussed between doctor and patient; if the patient has insurance, and the doctor recommends a treatment or procedure, then the patient complies. If the patient raises any question about cost, the question is likely to be not "What does that procedure cost?" but "Will that procedure be covered by my insurance?"

But while this traditional system promoted a high quality of treatment for those who are insured, it did so at a very high cost. It also did not promote prevention activities and it excluded from the system, or provided poorer quality of care to, those who did not have health insurance. Managed care is an attempt to control costs while providing an adequate level of health care to a larger segment of the population. In exerting controls, the choices of both patient and physician are restricted, as the organizational structure provides financial incentives for prevention and outpatient treatment. Basically, managed care allows for expensive outpatient treatments, hospitalization, and extended inpatient care only when they are documented to be absolutely necessary. Managed health care organizations are financially rewarded through cost savings when expensive care is avoided.

Managed care represents more than an evolution in health care. It represents a revolution, because the control of the payment and provision of services is wrested from the professional provider and placed with the managed care organization (MCO) itself (Giles, 1993). To reverse the focus from an inpatient, treatment orientation to an outpatient, prevention orientation, managed care systems typically use some form of capitation system to finance the care. *Capitation* is a form of compensation in which fixed dollar amounts are paid to providers for a population of people in advance of the delivery of services (Jackson, 1995). The prepaid amount must finance the provision of all contracted services. In effect, the health care insurance premiums of all patients are put into a central pool and used to pay for all of the inpatient and outpatient care needed by the patients enrolled. This pool of money must be *managed* so that it is not exhausted and depleted by expensive procedures. With only a set amount of dollars to work with, the financial incentive is to emphasize preventive care and early identification and treatment, not expensive diagnostic tests or inpatient care. The financial incentives in managed care are toward undertreatment, rather than overtreatment, as is the case in the traditional system.

In addition to these financial incentives, MCOs attempt to control costs yet ensure quality of care by establishing strict criteria for access to the system, especially for access to the expensive treatment options. Consumer choice is often restricted relative to choice of provider and access to specialists. Utilization-review procedures are instituted to evaluate the necessity, appropriateness, and efficiency in the use of medical services. Intensity and level of care is established by common protocols, not the individual judgment of professionals. Because of the increased focus on prevention and quality-review procedures, advocates of managed care claim that overall quality of care in man-

aged care systems is better than traditional fee-for-service systems. Additionally, they argue that the overall health of the population is improved because the lower costs allow more people to afford health insurance and thus to gain access to the health care system.

Managed care principles represent a new paradigm of service delivery affecting the provision of services beyond the health care system (Jackson, 1995). These principles apply particularly to mental health settings, because a large part of mental health services are organized and financed under the larger health care system. In the old paradigm, the provision of services is driven and controlled by professionals; in the new paradigm, provision is controlled by consumers and payers. In the old paradigm, the judgment of the experienced professional is sufficient to determine the level of care and intensity of treatment; in the new paradigm, level of care and intensity of services are guided by explicit criteria and clinical protocols accepted by industry professionals. In the old paradigm, longer treatment is deemed more effective than shorter treatment; in the new paradigm, time must be taken into consideration and minimized, placing greater trust in client's strengths and not fostering dependence. In the old paradigm, the focus is on the relationship with the client and other process issues; in the new paradigm, the focus is on accountability for results and measuring outcome. In the old paradigm, inpatient and outpatient treatments were separated and dichotomized; in the new paradigm, various options along a continuum of care, including prevention, are promoted.

Comparison of Service Paradigms (adapted from Jackson, 1995, p. 2.13)

Old Paradigm	*New Paradigm (Managed Care)*
Professional control of provision of services	Consumer and payer control
Professional judgment regarding level of care and intensity of services	Level of care and intensity guided by explicit criteria and clinical protocols
Longer treatment is better	Time-limited, strengths-oriented treatment is better
Focus on relationship and process	Focus on results and measuring outcome
Inpatient/outpatient treatment dichotomy	Continuum of care, including prevention

Because managed care restricts both consumer and professional choice, and because its incentives favor undertreatment rather than overtreatment, managed care is not wholly endorsed by either patients or health care providers. In the mental health arena, professionals have been particularly vocal in their opposition (Giles, 1993). The opposition centers on the belief that MCOs put dollars before patients, sacrifice the quality and quantity of inpatient care, and unduly restrict clinical judgment by substituting the opinions of outside utilization reviewers and generic clinical protocols driven by cost containment. Defenders of managed care counter that these objections are motivated by self-interest, that outpatient treatment for a variety of conditions has demonstrated as much or more success in achieving outcomes than inpatient treatment, that brief, goal-directed therapy has a higher level of scientific efficacy than long-term, insight-oriented treatments, and that protocols are necessary to ensure focused, efficient treatment that allows a greater quantity of clients to be served.

The trend toward managed care has important implications for social work practice. Managed care is a sterling example of how shifts in the organization and financing of services can cause drastic change at the direct practice level, as depicted in the above comparison of paradigms. Clearly, what gets done is what gets paid for. Still, social workers may find themselves well positioned in the managed care arena, because many of the skills and tasks required by managed care are grounded in traditional social work philosophy and techniques (Jackson, 1995). In addition to training in systems thinking, research, and goal-oriented problem solving, social workers are well prepared to assume the essential tasks of coordination and integration of services. Integrated clinical case managers (ICCMs) are needed in managed care systems to perform the core functions of linking clients to resources and coordinating care among various providers. There is some possibility, however, that the case manager role in MCOs could be restricted to administrative functions, to the exclusion of clinical, therapeutic services.

Social workers in managed mental health care systems may find themselves caught in real dilemmas involving split loyalties. Managed mental health care is consistent with some social work values and pragmatic perspectives, but it may conflict with others. For example, managed care restricts self-determination and choice by parents of children, and thus may not maximize the choice principle of family centeredness. On the other hand, managed care is compatible with the strengths principle of family centeredness, and managed care's continuum of care may actually result in more, albeit different, choices for families. In addition, managed care could make services available and affordable to more people, it promotes a strengths perspective, and it endorses care in the least restrictive environment.

In child welfare, managed care principles are beginning to appear in the way that certain child welfare services are organized and funded. Child welfare authorities are beginning to combine privatization with the capitation method of financing services. Here is an example of how it works. Using public dollars from various sources, suppose that a state child welfare governmental agency decides to institute purchase-of-service contracting (POSC) with private agencies for the administration of large programs, such as family preservation. *Family preservation* is the term used to describe intensive, home-based services provided to families who have children at risk for out-of-home placement and state custody. The goal of these programs is to ensure the safety and well-being of the children while maintaining them in their own family, thus preventing their placement into state custody. Suppose that family preservation services had previously been a public agency program; that is, public tax dollars hitherto had been used to pay for family preservation staff workers' salaries, benefits, office space and furniture, transportation, and other program expenses. In addition, the program has provided some "flexible funds" that could be spent for other goods and services, such as housing deposits, transportation, and individual psychotherapy, to help the children be safe in the home. In moving to a privatized, capitation system, the state child welfare agency computes what it has spent to provide service to an average client. It then contracts with a private agency to provide the same services for a capitated fee. Rather than reimburse the private agency for specific services provided, the state gives the private agency a set amount of dollars per family referred. The private agency will spend more on some families and less on others, but they must manage the dollars so that expensive services do not deplete the budget. The state specifies the continuum of services that are to be provided or available to clients, establishes the expected program outcomes, and monitors the performance of the contractor. The private agency has the flexibility to match client with need and to spend the dollars in the way that they think will be most efficient in achieving desired outcomes.

Service Integration

The term *service integration* refers to efforts to reduce the fragmentation of the service delivery system in order to improve efficiency and coordination. At the client level, service integration can be accomplished through use of case managers or integrated clinical care managers, as discussed in the above sections. At the systems level, service integration across service delivery systems can involve various initiatives, including interagency coordinating councils, community planning councils, local governing authorities, and neighborhood revitalization efforts. These types of efforts were briefly introduced in the previous chapter on the ecological perspective.

One vision of integrated, full-service networks takes the form of one-stop, multipurpose sites where families can come for an array of services to meet their needs (O'Looney, 1993). Similar to large discount department stores or mega-supermarkets, where a consumer can find groceries, banking outlets, dry cleaning, photo finishing, electronics and a variety of consumer goods, pharmacies, fast food, and other services, these one-stop family resource centers make it easier for children and families to access services such as mental health counseling, vocational training, child care, housing assistance, employment services, and parent education. The agencies that provide these services can more easily coordinate efforts, share information, and pool agency funds to meet needs. In addition, this type of service integration is potentially more efficient because professional and client time is better utilized. Duplication of professional tasks such as eligibility assessment, social history taking, and case management can be eliminated, thus saving agency resources and relieving the family of unnecessary

burden. Thus, service integration can be more effective in achieving positive outcomes because services are more accessible to clients, more comprehensive, more coordinated, and more efficient.

Service integration at the systems level has been spearheaded by private foundations; "in large measure, the pressure for reform and the emerging models for system improvement spring from the ambitious efforts of a few foundations that have themselves become more family-focused in defining their missions and interest areas" (Massinga & Cargal, 1991, p. 303). Notable among these foundations are the Annie E. Casey Foundation, the Ford Foundation, the W. K. Kellogg Foundation, the Edna McConnell Clark Foundation, and the Robert Wood Johnson Foundation.

As a case in point, the Annie E. Casey Foundation has focused its efforts at the state and local policy level, attempting to restructure and decategorize service systems so that they are better coordinated and less fragmented. In 1988, the foundation committed $20 million over 5 years to help Maryland, North Dakota, and Connecticut reform their child welfare systems. Another early foundation initiative was the New Futures program, which invested $50 million over a 5-year period to create school-based, integrated service systems to attack the problems of teen pregnancy and high dropout rates. In more recent years, the Casey Foundation's initiatives have broadened to encompass a wide range of family support and systems reform efforts. Because the Annie E. Casey Foundation is at the forefront of systems change, the foundation and its various programs will be highlighted to illustrate the broad range and types of systems reforms and service integration initiatives that have been undertaken in this country.

The Annie E. Casey Foundation was established in 1948 by Jim Casey, one of the founders of the United Parcel Service, and his siblings, who named the foundation after their mother. Because of his interest in foster care, much of the early work of the foundation centered on direct provision of long-term foster care and permanency planning through the Casey Family Services, a direct operating unit of the foundation. The goal of Casey Family Services is to create a model for the care of foster children that can be emulated by states and other private agencies. In the 1980s, the foundation expanded the scope of its operations to include the goal of improving the effectiveness of states and other major institutions serving disadvantaged children and their families. In 1994, the foundation approved over $60 million in grant awards, of which 19% was allocated to Casey Family Services. The remainder was targeted for systems reform in the areas of increasing awareness, strengthening management capacity, program demonstration and policy research, long-term comprehensive reform, and evaluation and dissemination (Annie E. Casey Foundation, 1994).

The largest share of the foundation's resources is expended in the area of long-term comprehensive reform of service delivery systems in a multitude of states and localities. Despite the diverse nature of the sites and programs, they are unified by common principles: "To develop effective services, we must first: decategorize funding and program boundaries; decentralize resource and policy decisions; develop collaborative governing bodies empowered to make decisions across youth-serving systems; enlarge the flexibility, discretion, and community rootedness of front-line decision making and practice; and be genuinely accountable for children and family outcomes" (p. 24).

Three of the foundation's recent long-term comprehensive reform initiatives have particular relevance for cross-system service integration. The foundation's Mental Health Initiative for Urban Children was launched in 1992 to help selected communities integrate mental health services into nonstigmatizing community settings such as churches, schools, and neighborhoods in a culturally competent manner. Neighborhoods in Miami, Boston, Houston, and Richmond were selected to participate in 1994. Activities at these sites focused on establishing local governing boards to manage resources, developing family advocacy and support groups, and piloting small service projects to test new service delivery models.

The foundation's Kentucky Education Reform initiative provides funding to help the state of Kentucky restructure its entire educational system. The restructuring includes decentralized school governance and performance-based rewards and sanctions for schools. A key component of that reform is the establishment of Family and Youth Resource Centers that integrate services by linking schools to other resources in the community. The

foundation is also providing support for increasing parental participation in the schools.

The foundation's Rebuilding Communities initiative was launched in 1993. This program is a 7-year, $15 million partnership with five community organizations to revitalize low-income neighborhoods. The initiative brings together residents, civic leaders, city government, religious institutions, businesses, and others to address issues. The Marshall Heights Community Development Organization in Washington, D.C., is one of the recipients of funds. This organization has a track record of providing "one-stop shopping" for community residents. From one organization, residents can obtain emergency food, temporary housing, homeownership assistance, employment referrals, and drug abuse prevention and treatment services. The support from the foundation will allow the organization to continue its approach and to expand its efforts to plan and manage the community's human services system from within.

In an ideal world, the citizens and professionals in a community would work together to establish clear agendas and goals for the children and families in their community. But no such structure currently exists in most communities. Who decides what is most important? Who holds agencies accountable for results? Who has the authority to allocate resources to address cross-system problems? Who mobilizes resources to address new problems? Who is responsible for the overall health and well-being of children and families in a community?

The most comprehensive and radical service integration initiatives involve restructuring of the governance, or authority, relationships between local, state, and federal levels, to focus more clearly on achieving specified goals and outcomes for children and families (Center for the Study of Social Policy, 1995; Melaville & Blank, 1993). The idea is to create a focal point for the reorganization and integration of the service system through local governing authorities that restructure the service system by improving the way that decisions are made and resources are deployed. These local governing authorities institute a decision-making process through which a local community takes responsibility for advancing broadly based strategies that achieve desired results for children and families.

States and communities that attempt this radical change must address five thorny implementation issues. First, the state must in some way sanction and authorize the new governance arrangements, so that the efforts are legitimized to the public and to the local service agencies. This mandate can come in the form of enabling legislation through the state legislature, or it can come directly from the executive branch via an executive order. Legislation has the advantage of indicating that the reform efforts are a broad-based public commitment, not a fad of current administrators. Second, states and local entities must define in some detail the shift in roles and responsibilities. Enabling legislation can outline these in only the broadest terms—details must be acceptable to all parties, and agreement can best be reached through a structured, interactive process. The long-term goal is to enable local communities to have the authority and responsibility for children's services, but this cannot be achieved overnight. The process begins with identifying specific results local governance bodies will pursue and establishing parameters for how they will pursue those desired results. Thus the third implementation issue is targeting a specific programmatic arena in which to begin to test out the new structures and relationships. In one state this might be family preservation in child welfare; in another it might be community schools. The danger is that these initiatives could be seen as just another program implemented within the given structure, rather than being seen as an example of how the new structures can work. Fourth, organizers need to be aware of the possible contradiction between local and state agendas. Communities tend to develop broad and more universal goals focused on health, safe neighborhoods, and thriving economies, while the state is more focused on achieving results for special needs populations, such as abused and neglected children. Finally, the new local structures must have the resources and capacities to carry out their new responsibilities. These include core staff to administer the local entity, ongoing training for staff, board members, and the general public, and data information systems that can provide up-to-date information about the health and welfare of the community. Funding of these capacities can be difficult to secure; state and local representatives must work together to obtain the needed supports and resources (Center for the Study of Social Policy, 1995).

Service Integration through Local Governance: Five Implementation Issues

1. State mandates for changing governance

2. Renegotiation of state and local responsibilities

3. The role of specific program strategies

4. Developing a community, not a state, agenda

5. Building local capacities to sustain the new governance structure

---

Organization and Financing in Child Welfare

Child welfare is primarily a state and local enterprise, involving the efforts of both public and private agencies (Costin, Bell, & Downs, 1991). Public agencies operate under the auspices of laws that define their responsibilities. Private agencies are of two types: not-for-profit, sometimes called voluntary child welfare agencies; and for-profit, sometimes called proprietary.

Federal, state, and local levels of government combine to provide public child welfare service. The federal government infuses the child welfare system with billions of dollars of support, and it requires that states meet certain conditions and standards to receive that support, but it does not organize or provide services directly. Administration of child welfare services rests with the states and their local subdivisions.

These respective roles have a long history, dating back at least to the passage of the Social Security Act of 1935. In this law, the federal government established the Aid to Dependent Children program, which provided grants to states to fund programs for the financial assistance of poor and dependent children, so that they could remain in their own homes rather than orphanages or almshouses. The law also contained provisions for states to receive federal grants for the provision of child welfare services for the protection and care of homeless, dependent, or neglected children and children at risk for delinquency. Federal funds generally pay a significant portion of the costs for child welfare programs, but not the full cost. States and localities must provide the difference through state and local tax funds (Costin, et al., 1991). Some state programs have traditionally operated with little or no federal funding. These include state orphanages, training schools, and other state institutions for the care of children which began to blossom in this country in the late 1800s as previously discussed in chapter 1.

As discussed in the previous chapter, the quality of public child welfare services has been questioned by numerous advocates and has been challenged in the courts through a number of lawsuits. In an effort to improve and ensure quality, several states have sought accreditation from the Council on Accreditation for Children and Family Services, based in New York. In 2000, 2 states, Oklahoma and Illinois, had achieved accreditation, 5 more states were in process, and 10 states were preparing to begin the process. Standards are set in areas such as staff training, intake procedures, caseloads, investigative procedures, foster home licensing, and recordkeeping. Although meeting these standards can cost the states more money, the results have been impressive in the areas of improved services to youth and boosting employee morale. For example, in Illinois, accreditation has been deemed a significant factor in achieving the following changes: the turnover rate was reduced from nearly 40% to 12%, the number of youth in custody dropped 25%, and caseloads have dropped to 18 per worker (Boyle, 2000).

Voluntary, not-for-profit agencies have a long history of providing care to needy children and families, predating the advent of public child welfare and continuing to expand even while public child welfare has grown. Not-for-profit child welfare agencies are generally formed and directed by a group of community citizens concerned about a specific problem or limited segment of the local child welfare system. Through a board of directors, the group assumes certain responsibilities with respect to policies and the supervision of professional staff. Funding for the agency may come from private donations, local fund-raising entities such as the United Way, or government contracts (POSCs). Many voluntary agencies are sponsored by sectarian organizations and may target children and families who belong to a certain religious group (Costin, et al., 1991).

Proprietary, for-profit child welfare agencies are not common in the provision of traditional child welfare services such as foster care or adoption. However, they are more common in related settings such as mental health, where for-profit psychiatric hospitals and psychotherapists in private practice serve many child welfare children and families. Also, recent privatization of traditional public agency responsibilities in foster care and adoption open the door to a greater role for proprietary agencies in the direct provision of child welfare services.

Federal funding for child welfare efforts comes in the form of an array of mostly categorical funding streams targeting specific programs and populations. Critics of this method of funding have charged that this financing mechanism favors out-of-home and residential care to the detriment of programs that encourage services in the least restrictive alternative. For example, in FY 1992, the funds appropriated specifically to support foster care were over $2 billion, while the appropriations for family reunification were only $50 million and for adoptions only slightly more than $200 million (Pecora, et al., 1992). Reform efforts have thus focused on changing the financing of programs so that funds can be used more creatively and flexibly to serve children and families more effectively in less restrictive environments. Block grants and managed care with privatization are two strategies that have been increasingly employed, as exemplified in the following discussions of decategorization in Iowa and privatization in Kansas.

Iowa Decategorization

In 1987, the Iowa legislature authorized demonstration projects to explore the effects of decategorization of child welfare services (Kimmich, 1995a). As Iowa was the first state in the country to attempt this way of reforming the child welfare system, much national attention in child welfare circles has been paid to its decategorization effort. The goal of this initiative, as outlined in state law, was to redirect funding toward more preventive, family-centered, and community-based services to reduce reliance on more restrictive, out-of-home and out-of-community services. To achieve this goal, the state changed the funding structure for child welfare services in the demonstration counties and required the counties to develop local, interagency planning bodies to collaborate on systems reform.

The changes in the funding structure were twofold. First, more than 30 categorical funding streams were combined into a single block grant to the counties, allowing them more flexibility to allocate resources for a full continuum of services. Second, the counties were allowed to keep and carry over any savings realized by serving families in these different, less restrictive ways. To accommodate these changes, each county formed an interagency structure of collaboration and a governing process for the decategorized child welfare fund. By 1995, one-third of Iowa's counties, accounting for two-thirds of Iowa's child population, were participating in the project.

An evaluation of the eight counties participating in the program at the end of 1992 was conducted by the Human Services Research Institute (Kimmich, 1995a; 1995b). Overall, the evaluation was favorable and the results are described as follows.

In sum, the evaluation concluded that "decategorization has made considerable change in the way human services agencies interact, in the array of services available, in the flexibility of funding, and in revitalizing families, front-line workers and service providers" (Kimmich, 1995a, p. vii).

Kansas Privatization Using Managed Care Principles

As previously discussed in this chapter, purchase-of-services contracting (POSC) has long been a common privatization feature of child welfare services. Public child welfare agencies contract with private providers for services such as family counseling, foster care, group home placement, and adoption, usually on an individual, case-by-case basis. Although this common practice has not been subjected to extensive evaluation, a recent study in Milwaukee, Wisconsin, has questioned the cost-effectiveness of private contracting for foster care services (Emspak, Zullo, & Rose, n.d.). This study concluded that the existing privatized foster care services in the county were more expensive and less effective in achieving permanency outcomes than were public foster care services provided directly by the county.

Selected Outcomes of Iowa Decategorization Program (adapted from Kimmich, 1995a and 1995b)

- Increased interagency collaboration occurred at both the family and systems levels.
- Families felt better served and workers felt more invested in the service system.
- Local contracting with provider agencies led to an increased array of preventive service options and gave providers flexibility in what services they provided, as well as where and when they provided services.
- More joint funding by multiple agencies occurred.
- Although families were not highly involved in overall service design and policy making, they experienced positive changes at the direct-service level. Families reported improvements in their relationship with workers, better knowledge of community resources, more extensive personal support networks, and greater involvement in community activities.
- Group care placements decreased, as did restrictiveness of placements, but these were not uniform across counties and it was not clear that the decreases could be attributed to the decategorization initiative.
- Decategorization, particularly the level of collaboration that must accompany it, demands a great deal of time and effort.

History and Background of Kansas Efforts.
Kansas is one of the first states to attempt to go beyond purchase-of-service contracting and to institute a privatized system utilizing principles of managed care to the organization and financing to its entire, statewide programs in family preservation, foster care, and adoption. Applying the capitation principle of managed care, in the form of case rates, to each of the three programs independently, the state has contracted with private service agencies to provide directly, or to subcontract for the provision of, a specified range of services to children and families for a specific period of time for a fixed amount of dollars per case. The private agency absorbs the costs exceeding the negotiated case rate and retains any unspent portions of the payments.

For family preservation, after a competitive bid process, contracts were awarded in 1996 in five regions of the state, with the case rate ranging from $3,274 to $3,750. Under the contract, the provider is paid one-third of the contracted, fixed amount upon referral. After 45 days of service, the provider is paid another one-third of the fixed amount. The final one-third is paid after 90 days of service. For that amount, the provider is expected to provide prevention of placement services and assume direct-service responsibility for a period of 12 months. In other words, the case must be kept eligible for services for 1 year: it can be closed, but it must be reopened with no additional payment if the family "reenters the system" within 1 year of referral. The range of services to be provided includes 24-hour initial response time and ongoing staff availability, formulation of a case plan within 10 days, 1-hour crisis response, in-home provision of services, and other concrete services and goods necessary to maintain the family. The contractor must collect data and report regularly on progress, so that the state can also monitor outcomes for children and families. The state intends to hold the contractor accountable for outcomes, such as "90% of families will not have confirmed abuse or neglect during program participation" and "80% of families will not have a child placed outside the home during program participation."

In the area of adoptions, the state awarded one statewide contract in 1996. The private agency is expected to serve about 900 children, at a case rate per child of $13,556. One-half of this amount is paid at referral, one-fourth when the child is placed with the adoptive family, and the final one-fourth when the adoption is legally finalized. The agency is expected to provide services to the family to maintain the placement for 18 months after finalization for no additional payment. The private agency is responsible to recruit, train, and support prospective adoptive families, as well as provide services to maintain the placement. Expected outcomes are clearly specified and include the following: "70% of children shall be placed with adoptive families within 180 days of receipt of the referral for adoption"; "90% of adoptive placements shall be finalized within 12 months of the placement date"; "90% of adoptive placements shall continue to be intact 18 months following finalization."

Implementation of this privatization initiative in the area of foster care is complex and challenging. The state of Kansas cares for more than 3,900 children in out-of-home placement to be covered under the contract, at a cost of approximately $56 million per year. Included in this amount are payments to foster/group care providers that cover food, shelter, school supplies, and child care for the foster parent working outside the home; foster parent recruitment and training; reintegration services; clothing allowances; nonmedical transportation; independent living services; and mental health treatment. The contractee is expected to provide all of these services for the fixed amount agreed upon per child. Juvenile offenders in out-of-home placement are not included, as the state is considering creating a new administrative structure to oversee their care and treatment.

In October 1996, Kansas awarded contracts to three private providers to cover the five regions of the state (two providers have contracted for two regions). The case rates range from $12,860 to $15,504. The payment system for the foster care contract is as follows: 25% of case rate paid at the time of referral; 25% after receipt of 60 day progress report or at case closure; 25% after receipt of 180-day case plan or at case closure; 25% when the child returns home or other permanency goal is achieved (living independently; referral to adoption contractor). For children reintegrated with their families, the contractor remains responsible for providing services for 12 months after the physical reintegration. If the child reenters foster care in that 12-month time period, the contractor is responsible for providing the out-of-home placement and services without additional funding. Children re-entering foster care after 12 months of reintegration are considered new referrals.

As with adoption and family preservation, the foster care contract includes monitoring of outcomes by the state. These include children being safe from maltreatment (95% of children in the care of the contractee will not experience abuse/neglect while in placement), children experiencing a minimal number of placements (90% of new referrals will have no more than three placement moves), children maintaining family, community, and cultural ties (70% of children will be placed within their boundaries of their geographic region), and children being reunified with their families (60% of children are returned to the family within 6 months; 90% do not re-enter state custody within 1 year).

In all of the contracts, the financial incentive for the private agency is to serve children for the least cost. This can be achieved by one or more of the following strategies: streamlining administration, keeping salaries and other costs low, serving children and families through less restrictive and less expensive alternatives, and preventing serious and costly problems from occurring. In foster care, the managed care approach clearly aligns fiscal incentives with the principle of the least restrictive alternative. If children can be reunified or cared for in relative homes and family foster care, then the contractee can minimize the costs and retain a greater share of the case rate. This reverses the former situation in which federal categorical payments provided fiscal incentives for long-term foster care. The requirement to serve the child for 12 months following reintegration prevents premature reintegration motivated solely by fiscal concerns.

Under the new system, the role of the public child welfare worker will be to investigate reports of abuse and neglect and serve as a single point of contact for the child and family. If the child is referred to family preservation, foster care, or adoption, the public child welfare professional continues to follow the case to provide continuity of care and to monitor progress.

Teresa Markowitz, MSW, Kansas Commissioner for Child and Family Services, is in charge of the design and implementation of the above initiatives. Rather than referring to these initiatives as "privatization" or "managed care," Ms. Markowitz prefers the term "managing outcomes" (Markowitz, personal communication, September 13, 1996). In emphasizing the outcome focus, Ms. Markowitz underlines the main goal of the initiatives: to achieve better outcomes for children and families. The reorganized system does emphasize a partnership with the private sector, and it does contain some principles of managed care. But the most important difference, in her opinion, is the focus on accountability for outcomes.

Consistent with this focus, state-level child welfare staff members are assigned to review and monitor the performance of the contracts. On-site teams review data and records and discuss areas of strength and needed improvement with the contracted provider. A contract for a thorough and ongoing external evaluation is under negotiation. This external review will provide data on a regular basis (monthly or quarterly) so that needed changes can be identified and instituted in a timely fashion.

Recent Developments and Changes in Kansas's Child Welfare System. Kansas's efforts to privatize child welfare services remain controversial. In operation since 1996, it offers the best current example of a competitive, privatized, managed care, outcome-focused approach to the delivery of child welfare services. State officials have acknowledged serious problems in initial implementation and have made many significant changes in the structure and financing of services, but they have not abandoned the effort. Implementation problems and key changes will be discussed in this section, and an overall assessment of the success or failure of the initiative will be presented in chapter 11.

Within the first weeks and months of privatization of foster care, many professionals and judges complained about serious implementation problems. A study of one county's experience (Petr & Johnson, 1999), initiated by Judge Jean Shepherd, compared children placed in the first 6 months of privatization (March—August 1997) with children who had been placed during the same 6-month period 1 year before privatization began (March—August 1996). Data for each group through September of the respective years were obtained from court files. Results consistently favored the 1996, pre-privatization group, which had significantly more time spent in first placement, fewer moves, and fewer runaway incidents in the time span reviewed. Kansas Action for Children, a statewide children's advocacy organization, issued a report in 1998 identifying many serious concerns, including poor planning, hurried implementation, lack of historical cost data to accurately develop case rates, confusion about public sector, private sector, and judicial roles, lack of a pool of experienced staff that could be hired on short notice by contractors, and flaws in the design of the managed care aspects of the system (Kansas Action for Children, 1998).

The case rate aspect for financing the new system was one of the most problematic features of the managed care design. In the initial first 4 years of privatization, the state found it necessary to provide an additional infusion of funds to the contractors, well above the contracted case rates. In foster care, contracted case rate payments totaled $178.7 million, but the state paid an additional $96.7 million in "risk-share" payments and $8.4 million outside the case rate (Kansas Action for Children, 2001). These additional funds were also provided to the adoption contractor in similar proportions, but that did not prevent the contractor from having such serious financial problems that they were forced to choose between paying subcontractors who provided daily care to children less than the contracted amount or declaring for bankruptcy (Kansas Action for Children, 2001).

The case rate method of financing was one of the aspects of the original design that was changed when the state reopened the bidding process for a new, 4-year contract period to begin in 2000. Instead of the case rate system described above, the new basis for payment is on a per-child, per-month basis. According to legislative testimony by a state official, "The financial review process created concerns regarding the viability of the case rate as the payment system for foster care. The primary concern was that the contractors did not have adequate control over when children returned home or moved to another permanency. . . . This left contractors in a situation where their financial risk could not be appropriately balanced with their case responsibility" (Kansas Action for Children, 2001). This change in financing alters the fiscal in-

centives inherent in the system. Under the original managed care system, despite its numerous problems, the case rate system did financially reward attainment of the permanency goals of reintegration and adoption. The infusion of cash over and beyond the case rate undermined this incentive, and the new financing system abandons this aspect of managed care altogether. Now, the fiscal incentive is for continued care in the system.

Another important change in the financing of this endeavor, related to the provision and financing of mental health services for children and youth in foster care, was made in September 2001 (Child Welfare and Mental Health Partnership Planning Process, 2001). From the beginning of Kansas's privatization efforts, the financing and provision of mental health services had been controversial. Traditionally, mental health services for foster children had been provided by community mental health centers (CMHCs) and other community mental health professionals, and financed on a fee-for-service basis through Medicaid. Under the first round of privatization, these Medicaid dollars were included in the contractor's case rates, and the contractor was expected to provide, or pay CMHCs and others to provide, all needed mental health services. Critics of this system alleged that contractors provided fewer services because of the fiscal incentives to do so. Contractors responded that they provided all necessary services, and that the case rate was not adequate to finance all of the services that were requested. After months of discussion, the state issued new guidelines for child welfare and mental health partnerships. These guidelines stipulated that the cost of mental health services for all children in the adoption contract and for the children in the foster care contract with the most severe mental health needs would no longer be included in the case rate. Thus, for these children, the private contractors no longer have the fiscal responsibility for payment of mental health services, and the CMHCs could again provide the services and bill Medicaid directly. For foster children, this new system is dependent upon a local, written partnership plan between the CMHC, local state child welfare office, and the private contractor.

The open bidding process, an inherent component of the competitive, privatized system, has itself been criticized. In 2000, the contracts for the delivery of the three services in the five regions of the state changed. In family preservation, three of the five contracts changed; in foster care, two of five changed; and in adoption, the one statewide contract changed hands (Kansas Action for Children, 2001). When a contract changes hands, there is a real potential for disruption in the continuity of service to children. For a contractor who loses a bid to renew services, the last 6 months means downsizing toward termination of services. Social workers look for new jobs, and foster parents wonder if they will be comfortable with the new contractor. For the new contractor, the first 6 months are devoted to hiring and training staff and setting up an infrastructure. What level of attention can be devoted to the children themselves during this year of transition?

Organization and Financing in Children's Mental Health

Nationwide System Reform

In recent years, something of a revolution has taken place in the organization and financing of children's mental health services. Much of the recent federal efforts in the children's mental health arena have been geared to developing a *system* of care for children and their families, to enhancing changes at the policy level that would have direct impact on the type and quality of care received by children and families. This was exemplified initially in the CASSP initiative in the mid-1980s, and most recently in 5-year grants to 22 sites to create community-based systems of care. The federal initiatives have sought to improve the access and availability of services, to develop leadership capacity and increased funding, to promote better coordination and collaboration among providers, to promote family participation in all aspects of service delivery, and to ensure cultural competency. The strategies the federal government has employed to achieve these goals include providing grants to states, communities, family organizations, and research centers; developing resource materials and technical assistance; disseminating information; requiring states to submit plans for a system of care to receive block grant funds; and collaborating with various state

and federal agencies and groups to enhance and promote changes (Lourie, Katz-Leavy, DeCarolis, & Quinlan, 1996).

In many states, these efforts have resulted in dramatic improvements. An evaluation of the first 10 states to receive CASSP funding concluded that they had made improvements in leadership capacity, local coordination of services, family participation, cultural responsiveness, and evaluation capacities (Schlenger, Etheridge, Hansen, Fairbank, & Onken, 1992). State departments of mental health have employed more staff members assigned to children's mental health, and the proportion of states with separate mental health budgets has risen from 18% in 1982 to 70% in 1993 (Davis, Yelton, Katz-Leavy, & Lourie, 1995).

These federal and state efforts have been joined by substantial investments from private foundations aimed at effecting change at the state and local levels. The Robert Wood Johnson Foundation's Mental Health Services Program for Youth (MHSPY) is a $20 million initiative focusing heavily on interagency collaboration, flexible and integrated financing, and shared governance. Currently, seven sites in seven different states are using 4-year implementation grants to restructure their children's mental health systems. Each site must designate a community authority and governance structure that integrates the efforts of all agencies serving children. Because MHSPY is a cross-system initiative, formal agreements between agencies attempt to decategorize service and funding so that the financing, policy, and service decisions will be flexibly made in response to the individual needs of the child and family (Cole, 1996).

The Annie E. Casey Foundation, spotlighted earlier in this text, awarded six planning grants in 1992 for its Mental Health Initiative for Urban Children. Sites in Florida, Massachusetts, Texas, and Virginia were awarded $3 million, 4-year implementation grants. The purpose of this initiative was to demonstrate the capacity to reform the system of services in poor, urban, minority communities. Each state targeted its efforts at the community level in high-poverty, inner-city neighborhoods: Miami's East Little Havana; Boston's Mission Hill, Highland Park, and Lower Roxbury; Houston's Third Ward; and Richmond's East End. Neighborhood-based control was critical to this initiative. State and local systems were to be restructured to be neighborhood based, with more local control over services. The initiative also promoted integration across multiple systems and targeting resources for prevention and early intervention. Mental health services were to be integrated into existing community settings in locations that are less stigmatizing, such as schools, churches, and recreation centers. A central component of the initiative was the involvement of families, as described in chapter 7 under pragmatic perspective 4, respect for diversity and difference. The foundation anticipated that these neighborhood programs could serve as models for other areas of the state and nation (King & Meyers, 1996).

Early experience with these projects has illuminated certain lessons. First, the project confirmed the stigma associated with "mental health," as both residents and officials avoided this phrase when referring to the project. Second, the neighborhoods and state authorities disagreed on how much of the financing and authority would be delegated to local neighborhood groups. Third, the project experienced more hurdles when more "naturally occurring" neighborhoods were merged for the purposes of the project. Conflicts between these neighborhoods exacerbated the conflicts between the state and the merged neighborhood. Fourth, the foundation staff members believed they underestimated the difficulty of achieving substantial system reform. The forces that create and maintain the existing systems are reluctant to change. Still, the staff believed that its own agenda was in basic harmony with state agendas for change, and that success could be achieved (King & Meyers, 1996).

The Ventura Planning Model

One of the most widely acclaimed and successful systems change efforts is that in Ventura County, California (Jordan & Hernandez, 1990; Hernandez & Goldman, 1996). This systems change effort began as a demonstration project authorized by state law in 1984. Concerned about the high costs of out-of-home and institutional placements, the California legislature enacted the law to create a comprehensive and coordinated system of mental health care for children that could be replicated in other counties in the state. Ventura County was chosen

as the demonstration site because of its comparatively strong record of collaboration among service agencies. The county had been able to reduce its average daily state hospital census from 14 to 3 by developing a community-based program that relied heavily on aggressive strengths-oriented and family-centered case management services to identify and create support services for the children and families.

The California legislation encouraged the community to build on its previous success through an interagency, strategic planning effort. This effort focused on five essential elements: (1) identifying target populations, (2) establishing measurable goals, (3) evaluation and continuous monitoring of client outcomes, (4) instituting an array of community-based services tailored to the needs of the targeted population, and (5) developing interagency partnerships.

Target Populations. The community was able to agree to target its efforts to those children and families with the greatest needs and challenges. Members of the target population have three common characteristics: (1) a diagnosable mental condition, (2) one or more functional impairments that place them at risk for out-of-home placement, and (3) serious behavioral symptoms such as psychosis, suicidal potential, or dangerousness to others. Of the county's 225,000 children and adolescents, the mental health system serves about 800 at any one time and 1,600 annually.

Measurable Goals and Evaluation of Client Outcomes. These characteristics distinguish Ventura County from many other interagency collaboration efforts and are described in the next chapter on pragmatic perspective 8, achieving outcomes.

An Array of Community-Based Services. In developing a full continuum of care, the community established standards to ensure quality of care, including cultural competency, family involvement, accessibility of services in natural settings such as schools and homes, and a strengths perspective. Services are organized into five subsystems, each of which has a Mental

Health Department supervisor. The Special Education/Mental Health Subsystem provides school-based day treatment, case management, respite care, emergency inpatient services, and intensive in-home services. Other systems of care are the Juvenile Justice/Mental Health Subsystem, the Child Welfare/Mental Health Subsystem, the Case Management Subsystem, and the Outpatient Services Subsystem.

Interagency Partnerships. The community understood that the target population crossed service systems and thus required a joint, coordinated effort. Written agreements between agencies form the basis for interagency communication and the integration of resources. The chief executive officers of the major child-serving organizations attend a monthly interagency meeting, and no substitutes can be sent in their stead. Other regular meetings are held at the midlevel and direct-service staff level to coordinate fiscal resources and discuss particularly difficult cases. The legally defined mechanism for beginning a multiagency planning process on behalf of a child is the development of an IEP for any child being considered for home teaching, day treatment, or out-of-home placement as a result of behavioral or emotional problems. Such children are assigned a case manager who becomes a part of the IEP team and initiates the interagency coordination.

Managed Care in Children's Mental Health

Because of their close affiliation with the health care system, children's mental health services are increasingly subject to the wave of managed care. Whether through private insurance obtained through place of employment or through the government Medicaid program, which is the nation's primary health insurance program for low-income people under age 65, the financing of mental health services is moving toward a managed care system. Many states have applied for, and been granted, "waivers" which allow them to implement comprehensive reforms in their Medicaid systems. These waivers allow states to change the list of covered services, change eligibility criteria, and mandate that Medicaid beneficiaries receive services through managed care plans. Fortunately,

these waivers are granted only on a temporary basis, subject to the state conducting an evaluation of the new system, including access to care and services utilization (Folcarelli, 1995).

To date, however, managed children's mental health care is largely untested, and the major question remains: Is managed care, in which cost control is a key organizing principle and indicator of success, compatible with the unique needs of children with mental disorders? A survey of three publicly administered managed care programs in three different states by Law (1995) revealed preliminary findings that appeared promising. North Carolina began a capitated managed care program in 10 areas in 1994, each of which had a single point of entry. Early results indicated a 39% reduction in inpatient days and increased utilization of alternatives to hospitalization. Data on client satisfaction, cost, inpatient length of stay, and provider participation were yet to be analyzed. In San Mateo County, California, an evaluation of a pilot managed care program for high-risk Medicaid recipients concluded that there were decreased costs per child, increased school attendance, and fewer out-of-home placements. In Washington State, a capitated system of managed care was recently implemented in four regions of the state. A preliminary evaluation of stakeholder perceptions conducted during the first year of implementation revealed that clients and families were generally positive about most aspects of the program, while providers were generally negative, feeling that the quality of care was compromised. Staff involved with implementation in these states reported that the thorniest issues in evaluating programs were the difficulty in defining and measuring appropriate outcomes, the need for multiple data sources, and the importance of an effective management information system.

The Health Care Reform Tracking Project (HCRTF) is a national study on managed mental health care for children with serious emotional and behavioral disorders enrolled in state Medicaid programs (Stroul, Pires, Armstrong, & Meyers, 1998). A survey of a range of key stakeholders in 10 states revealed mixed findings on the benefits and drawbacks of the managed care approach. In some states, the operation of the new system was hampered by too rapid implementation that did not include participation of families or mental health professionals in the planning and design, resulting in misinformation and unrealistic expectations. In 4 of the 10 states, respondents were concerned that lack of good historical data on utilization of services resulted in exceedingly low case rates, which in turn limited the services for enrollees. (This concern about the adequacy of case rates is echoed in the Kansas child welfare managed care initiative.) On the positive side, the survey revealed that the managed care reforms seemed to have resulted in greater access to mental health services, including an increase in the number of children receiving services and a reduction in waiting lists and other delays. In 7 states, managed care made it easier to obtain home- and community-based services, but in all 10 states it was more difficult to receive inpatient care. The trend in all 10 states was toward briefer, more problem-focused treatment approaches, which was welcomed by some but criticized by others. System-of-care principles such as a broad array of community services, family involvement, interagency coordination, and cultural competence were not likely to be implemented unless there was a strong mandate from the state that they be included as part of the managed care contract. Although greater accountability is listed as a potential benefit of managed care systems, this survey found that little was being done to track clinical outcomes (Stroul, et al., 1998).

In the private sector, an example of managed psychiatric care for adolescents is the Humana Michael Reese HMO (Barglow, Chandler, Molitor, & Offer, 1992). In this staff model HMO, subscribers are entitled to 30 days of inpatient psychiatric care per year, yet the average length of stay for adolescents in the acute care unit is 10 days. From the first day of admission, the purpose of the hospitalization is to prepare the adolescent and family for outpatient treatment. Most of the hospitalized adolescents enter the intensive outpatient treatment program, which also accepts referrals from the emergency room and outpatient clinic. This program offers 24 support services and a range of treatment modalities including day hospitalization, twice-weekly group therapy, parent education groups, and multifamily therapy. Financial incentives help steer the families to the outpatient program: 1 inpatient day is equivalent to 5 days in the intensive outpatient program. Upon completion of this short-term and intensive outpatient program, families are usually referred to long-term therapy in the community, which is not covered by the HMO. A phone survey evaluation of parents found that 71% of parents felt that the program had helped the family, 65% believed that the adolescent had improved significantly, and fewer than one-third of the adolescents were readmitted to the hospital. The hospital utilization rate was deemed "quite low"—5.94 adolescent hospital days per year for each 1,000 members.

CHAPTER 10 SUMMARY

The way services are organized and financed has a strong impact on both what social workers do and what children and families receive. The current service system for children is disorganized, fragmented, and costly. Sweeping reform of the service system is occurring on several fronts.

This chapter highlighted several recent and ongoing trends in the delivery of human services to children and families. The decentralization movement seeks to bring decision making and authority to lower and lower levels in the organizational hierarchy. Block grants attempt to streamline administration and improve flexibility by decategorizing program funding and decentralizing fiscal authority.

Three particular trends in the organization and financing of services are privatization, managed care, and service integration. Privatization involves a greater reliance on the private sector for the provision of services that traditionally have been delivered by public, governmental agencies. Purchase-of-service contracting (POSC) and vouchers are two mechanisms for privatization. Proponents assert that privatization is preferred by consumers, is more innovative, and costs less.

Managed care is a system of organizing and financing services that emerged in the health care field and has particular relevance to mental health settings. Under managed care, control is exerted over access to services and the level and intensity of care provided. Managed care is a radical change in that individual professional clinical judgment is replaced by standard protocols, and client access to expensive treatment options is restricted. Privatization and managed care are not inherently good or bad for clients; the crucial determining factor is implementation. Social workers should be vigilant in influencing the implementation of these initiatives so that clients' needs are the focus. Service integration strategies attempt to coordinate services and improve efficiency. Many different service integration strategies are being tested in various parts of the country, spearheaded by the efforts of various private foundations, notably the Annie E. Casey Foundation. After some years of experience, change efforts have proved more difficult, complex, and time consuming than first anticipated.

These concepts and issues were discussed primarily at the policy level, but all have direct implications for the practicing social worker at the direct-service level. The trend toward privatization means that jobs for social workers will increasingly occur in the private sector, where job security and fringe benefits may not be as strong as in the public sector. The trend toward managed care means that direct practice social workers will be asked to define client goals in specific, measurable terms and will be held more accountable for achieving those goals in the shortest amount of time possible. This will create tension for providers and clients, especially in the mental health arena, who have become accustomed to long-term and less goal-directed methods. The trend toward service integration will mean more social work jobs in the fields of clinical case management and administration of interagency councils, to reflect advances in integration at both the client and agency levels.

Organization and financing issues in child welfare were discussed in terms of history and traditional practices, as well as with respect to innovative reform efforts in Iowa and Kansas. In children's mental health, national reform efforts by foundations, the Ventura planning model, and managed care initiatives were highlighted.

CHAPTER 11

Pragmatic Perspective 8: Achieving Outcomes

Overview

A final trend in the delivery of services is focus on achieving outcomes. Measuring outcomes is important in holding programs accountable to their consumers and to the general public. While a laudable goal, the effort to establish and measure outcomes is fraught with controversy. This chapter discusses the obstacles to achieving an outcome focus, including resistance among providers, distinguishing process outcomes from final outcomes, potential conflict between individual and systems outcomes, deciding which outcomes are the most important to measure, difficulty and costs of measuring and interpreting outcomes, the relationship of funding to outcome, and prevention versus treatment. Despite these obstacles, both the child welfare system and the children's mental health systems have moved to an outcome focus, as discussed in the final sections of this chapter.

The Complex Process of Outcome Measurement

For years, critics of the system of care for children and families have decried the absence of an outcome focus. Outcomes are the measurable achievements, or end results, that services are designed to accomplish. In child welfare, programs could target outcomes such as reducing the incidence of child abuse and neglect, or raising the number of children safely served in their families instead of foster care. In mental health, programs could target outcomes such as reducing the number of disruptive behaviors of children with diagnosis of conduct disorder, or reducing the rate of attempted teenage suicide in a community. In education, programs could target outcomes such as improved reading comprehension, or lowering the high school dropout rate.

Only recently, through initiatives such as the Children's Defense Fund's *State of America's Children Yearbook* and the Annie E. Casey Foundation's Kid's Count Project, have accurate statistics about the health and well-being of children and families been well publicized. To people new to the social service and education systems, looking in from outside, it has been a shocking revelation that there is little or no accountability for results. Instead, services are funded from year to year with little or no information about how well those services are accomplishing their goals, about whether or not children and families are better off because of those services.

At first glance, focusing on outcomes seems to be simple, straightforward, and necessary. Systems that focus on outcomes, or results, should perform better and be more efficient. Without an outcome-based system, there has been no way to tell success from failure; no one knows which staff members, programs, or providers are effective; rewards are based on longevity, size of budget and staff, and avoidance of public crises; public support is difficult to mobilize, and collaboration is hindered because different professionals are working at cross-purposes (Rapp, Ruhlman, & Topp, 1994). But change to an outcome-based system also entails risk (Schorr, 1994). The public may underestimate how long it takes to achieve significant improvement in outcomes and become discouraged about the whole enterprise. To avoid this discouragement, funders and providers could confine their efforts to those clients and social problems that can show rapid and measurable results, to the exclusion of more serious problems and more needy clients. Some fear that outcome-based accountability could become a smokescreen behind which funding cutbacks will be made.

As more and more attention is paid to focusing on outcomes, it is becoming more and more clear that implementing this change is an extremely difficult and complex undertaking. Going beyond the rhetoric of outcomes means entering a world of pragmatic implementation replete with hurdles, barriers, and complications that are very difficult to overcome. Much of the rest of this section will consist of discussion and analysis of these implementation difficulties: (1) resistance among providers, (2) distinguishing process, or intermediate, outcomes from final outcomes, (3) potential conflicts between individual and system goals, (4) disagreement about which outcomes to track, (5) difficulty and cost in accurately measuring and interpreting outcomes, (6) relationship of funding to outcome, and (7) prevention versus treatment.

Resistance among Providers

Human service professionals tend to get very nervous when pressure is exerted on them to be more accountable for final results, especially when they have not been held accountable for results in the past. Change is threatening, especially change that can negatively affect one's livelihood. Traditionally, evaluation of human service professionals has often been perfunctory, brief, and episodic. If they are performed at all, evaluations have taken place once a year, rather than on an ongoing basis. Many professionals seem to have the attitude that their

---

Hopes and Fears of Results-Based Accountability (adapted from Schorr, 1994)

Hopes

- Communities will be more organized and intentional about how they support children and families.
- Public faith in public and private human services will be restored.
- Human service agencies will be freed from cumbersome rules that prevent them from operating flexibly to meet their clients' needs.

Fears

- Attempts to better the conditions of disadvantaged children and those with the most serious problems, whose progress is difficult to measure or takes a long time to occur, will be abandoned.
- Procedural protections and concerns for equity will be neglected.
- Professionals and agencies will be penalized for not achieving results, even though they try hard, are doing the best they can, and their work should not have been judged as directly effecting the measured outcome in the first place.

---

training has prepared them for their job and that elaborate evaluations are unnecessary, insulting, and intrusive. "I know what I'm doing, just leave me alone to do it" is a typical attitude. In addition to anxiety about change and accountability, professionals also raise many of the other issues discussed below, many of which are valid and legitimate concerns. Likewise, state bureaucrats and agency heads have been reluctant to collect and publicize data about their programs because they have believed it would only open them up for criticism. As long as they continue to get funding without having to be accountable for outcomes, what is the point in collecting information that may not look good and might draw negative attention to the agency and program?

The limited evaluations of professionals and programs that have occurred have tended to scrutinize the professional's own actions and behaviors, or the program's internal operations, not what clients have accomplished. Unlike salespeople and others in the business world who are evaluated on the basis of concrete results, such as number of sales closed, human service professionals are not used to such pressure to perform. Professionals and programs have looked at "inputs" and processes, not at final results. For example, teachers typically have been evaluated on how well prepared they are in their lesson plans, on their ability to control and discipline their students, on their dedication and willingness to work hard, on their ability to get along with other teachers and work cooperatively with parents. Mental health professionals are typically evaluated on their level of professional knowledge and interpersonal skill, on the number of clients they see in a week, on their ability to work with superiors and other professionals in a team approach, and on their willingness to take on difficult clients and other assignments. Child welfare agencies have typically reported on the number of services provided, the contact hours between workers and clients, and the size of worker caseloads.

Distinguishing Process Outcomes from Final Outcomes

Many of the above actions and attitudes could well have a direct positive effect on final outcome. For example, one could logically assert that discipline and control in a classroom are a necessary prerequisite for learning to occur. For a mental health professional to be effective, he or she must presumably have good interpersonal communication skills. Factors deemed necessary to achieve positive final outcomes are called by various names: process variables, intermediate outcomes, inputs, or means to the end. Evaluations of programs and professionals have traditionally focused on these process variables, partly because it is easier, more

convenient, and less costly to focus on them, partly because professionals themselves tend to focus on process rather than outcome in their helping efforts with clients, and partly in the belief that they do have a direct impact on outcome. Program evaluations, for example, have often focused on how the money was spent, the number of people that were served, the training that was provided to staff members, and the number of direct-service hours provided by the staff. In court orders to abusive parents, judges sometimes insist on and track attendance at parenting education classes or a minimum number of drug and alcohol counseling sessions, which are the means to achieving the end goals of changed parenting behavior. But hard data to back up the belief in the utility of these variables are often lacking. Certainly, attendance at parenting classes does not ensure change in abusive parenting behavior. Attendance at parenting classes may not even be a necessary, let alone sufficient, ingredient for change.

This confusion between process and outcome variables is one of the clear barriers to implementing an outcome-based based system. Even when this confusion is resolved and there is agreement to focus on results and final outcomes, it can be difficult to determine whether a given outcome is an intermediate outcome or a final result. Consider, for example, some of the indicators of health and well-being of children and families that are tracked by the Children's Defense Fund and by the Annie E. Casey Foundation's Kid's Count Project. Is not the rate of childhood immunizations a measure of process, not final outcome? Immunizations promote health and well-being, but they are not a measure of it. Is not the number of eligible children enrolled in Head Start programs a measure of process, not final outcome? Research has demonstrated that children who participate in Head Start learn more and better later in school; thus, the final outcome is amount learned, or the success achieved later in school, and participation in Head Start is documented as a means to achieve that end.

So, some measures of child and family well-being achieve the status of an outcome or final result, even though they are actually process variables, because the link is so strong between the measure and actual, final health and well-being of the population. Thus it would be a mistake to focus accountability efforts only on legitimate final results, because there are intermediate processes that have been shown to directly and dramatically affect those results. When this has been shown to be the case, it is perfectly acceptable, even desirable, to measure and track the process variable as a sort of "proxy" of the outcome variable.

There are other legitimate reasons to track process variables, even when they have no proven relationship to outcome. These center on ethical considerations that ensure that an attitude of "the ends justifies the means" does not permeate the field. One danger of a purely results-oriented system is that service providers could be encouraged to accomplish the ends by whatever means they chose, with no oversight about the ethics or morality of the means chosen. Just as it is not acceptable for a parent to achieve the result of improved child behavior through the means of severe daily beatings, neither is it acceptable for a professional or a program to achieve results through unacceptable means. It is thus important for evaluators to track some of the aforementioned variables, such as how the money was spent and how many direct-service hours were provided, not as indicators of success of the program but as a way to monitor that fraud or embezzlement did not occur in the handling of the money and that staff members did not sit around wasting their time. "Procedural protections will have to be maintained to protect against fraud, poor services, and inequities or discrimination based on race, gender, disability, or ethnic background" (Schorr, 1994, p. 7).

Finally, on the subject of process versus outcome variables, some variables are not easily classified as solely process or outcome, but are deemed important to measure regardless of their classification. For example, client satisfaction is sometimes viewed as an end in itself, but it can also be viewed as a means to achieve other ends. Although the statistical proof may be lacking, there is strong logic to the position that client satisfaction correlates strongly with achievement of goals. But even if there is no such correlation, client satisfaction is a goal that may be pursued in its own right. This is perfectly legitimate as long as there is no pretense that it is a measure of health and well-being. The same holds for other important aspects of service delivery such as family-centeredness and intera-

gency service coordination. There is a strong belief that family-centeredness and interagency service coordination are integral to achieving better outcomes, so they can be conceptualized as process variables. But some would assert that they are important in themselves, that they are ends to be achieved in and of themselves, even though they are not direct indicators of health and well-being.

Potential Conflict between Individual and Systems Goals

Resistance to accountability among professionals and confusion between process and outcome measures are only two of the barriers to an outcome-based approach. A third important issue concerns the potential for conflict between what is best for an individual child and family and what is best for the larger group or community. Individual goals are sometimes at odds with group goals. In our individualistic society, it is difficult for many to establish goals for a large group that may not fit for an individual family.

This issue has recently come to the fore in the child welfare field, in the area of family preservation. One of the expressed goals of family preservation initiatives is to keep as many children with their families, and out of foster care, as possible, by preventing unnecessary out-of-home placements. The outcome, or measure, that is then tracked statewide is the total number of children in state custody in foster care. At the program level, this same outcome drives the services provided. Prevention of placement becomes paramount, and families and workers feel they have failed if one or more of the children come into state custody. But for any individual family, out-of-home placement may be the necessary, best goal to achieve at a certain point in time. Rather than being viewed as a success, though, the statistics count this as a failure. A similar situation can exist in special education, where the system is being driven by the concepts of inclusion and least restrictive environment. Although programming for an individual child is still supposed to be based on individual need, it becomes more difficult to see the individual need for a restrictive placement in an atmosphere that advocates that most children need inclusion.

Deciding Which Outcomes Are Most Important to Track

A fourth implementation issue involves reaching agreement about which outcomes are the most important to track and measure. At every level, this involves disagreements among well-intentioned people who have different values and different priorities. When financial resources for tracking outcomes are limited (and resources for this are always limited if they exist at all), disagreements about where to prioritize are a given. Thus, one result of a movement toward outcome-based services will be a much more politicized environment in which various client and professional groups scramble to ensure that their own particular area of concern is not left out. Even within a single service sector, legitimate and valid conflicts arise. For example, in the health field, at the community level, is it more important to track and measure immunization rates, utilization of prenatal care, rates of teenage pregnancy, or level of poverty? All relate directly to health status. At the individual client level, which outcome is most important for an individual pregnant teenage woman and her family: immunization for her other young children, birth control to prevent future pregnancy, getting a job to reduce poverty, or some other goal, such as obtaining housing or stopping drug abuse, which are not even listed as the agency's program goals?

This issue is particularly relevant with respect to the inclusion of the disenfranchised in the priority setting process. Who, ultimately, decides which outcomes are most important? Professionals in direct-service positions? State and program administrators? Clients? Legislatures? Community planning councils? The outcome indicators important to the white, middle-class, adult, male, professional majority may not be those most relevant to the racial and ethnic minorities, to the poor, to children, to women, and to lay parents/consumers. For example, in the child welfare arena, legislators and policymakers may legitimately be interested in the number of children entering the foster care system each month, and how long children stay in foster care. They want to minimize this number to promote family stability and to save tax dollars. At the same time, members of the minority African American community believe that African American children are overrepresented in

the foster care system, and that they stay longer than white children. If the state officials fail to include African Americans in the planning and decide to set up a system to track the total numbers of children and the length of time they spend in care, but that information tracking system is not able to break out these statistics by race, then the agenda of the African American population will be neglected.

Difficulty and Costs of Measuring and Interpreting Outcomes

A fifth implementation issue involves the difficulty and cost involved in accurately measuring outcomes and then interpreting what the data mean. Even if professional resistance can be overcome, even if confusion about process and outcome variables can be sorted out, even if different levels of outcome are addressed, and even if disagreements about which outcomes are important can be resolved, there is no guarantee that the outcomes can be accurately measured for a reasonable cost, that the data collected will be valid or reliable, or that the results will be interpreted by all to have the same meaning. As social work students have learned in their research sequence, good evaluation research is costly and time consuming. Accurate and adequate sampling, data collection procedures, and reliability and validity of measurements are just a few of the issues affecting the validity of the results. And in the end, it is very difficult to establish a cause-and-effect relationship between interventions and outcomes. Whether it is the individual professional's interventions with a specific client or a program's interventions with a group of targeted clients, there are many other outside influences on clients that professionals and programs have no control over, influences which may be more powerful with respect to the measured outcome. Because the world of human services is so complex, it is extremely difficult and costly to isolate and control for all the variables. Thus, data about results are always subject to criticism. People who do not like the results can almost always find some flaw in the study that casts doubt on the accuracy of the data or can offer an alternative explanation for what the data mean.

Relationship of Funding to Outcome

Implementation of outcome-based approaches must consider the relationship of costs of the programs to outcome. Even if results have been achieved, were the results worth the cost? Could some other approach achieve the same result for less cost? Detailed cost-benefit analyses are almost always deemed too complex and too expensive, yet outcome-oriented funders and legislators will naturally perform their own informal, subjective, less rigorous cost-benefit analysis, answering for themselves the basic question "Do the results of these efforts justify their costs?" Because this question is so difficult to answer, and because of all the other complexities of outcomes approaches discussed above, there is a real danger that novice champions of an outcome-based approach can lose their enthusiasm and can quickly become cynical veterans who decide that putting the money directly into services, and forgetting about evaluation of results, is the most pragmatic and beneficial use of the limited amount of resources.

Prevention versus Treatment

Yet even these hardened souls have difficulty avoiding the final key issue that will be addressed in this section: should the limited resources be targeted for prevention of problems or for treatment? Prevention versus treatment is a critical issue that has received much attention. The systems of care for children and families in the United States have traditionally focused on treatment of problems after they occur. But prevention programs are deemed to have the most dramatic impact in the long term, while treatment is deemed necessary in the short term.

Discussion about prevention and treatment is sometimes inhibited because of lack of a clear distinction between the terms. Where does prevention end and treatment begin? For our discussion, *primary prevention* will refer to those programs and activities that aim to keep a problem from occurring in the first place. Immunizations against diseases are an excellent example of primary prevention efforts. The immunization is itself not treatment, because there is not disease to treat. *Secondary prevention* efforts seek early identification and treatment of a problem to prevent it

from becoming worse or more widespread. Regular mammogram screening to detect the early onset of breast cancer is an example of secondary prevention. If the cancer is identified early, treatment can prevent it from becoming more severe and life threatening. Secondary prevention acknowledges and supports treatment efforts, but views treatment as one legitimate tactic in the overall strategy of prevention. Like secondary prevention, *tertiary prevention* efforts also involve treatment, this time in a rehabilitative sense. In tertiary prevention, treatment is needed to prevent the long-range effects of the problem and to prevent its recurrence. Physical therapy procedures come to mind here. After a stroke, for example, physical therapy is instituted to minimize the effects of the stroke and to educate the person about how to prevent its recurrence. So primary prevention seeks to reduce the incidence of problems, secondary prevention seeks to reduce the duration and severity, and tertiary prevention seeks to reduce the level of impairment that may result from the problems (Caplan, 1964).

In the real world, distinctions between these types are often blurred, so that few programs can be assigned to just one category (Bloom, 1991). In child welfare, for example, family preservation programs can be viewed as primary prevention programs in the sense that they prevent the occurrence of out-of-home placement, as secondary prevention because they involve early identification and treatment of parenting problems and the effects of the child abuse, and as tertiary prevention in their efforts to minimize the impact of the abuse and rehabilitate the parents and children to prevent recurrence.

Many reports and experts have lamented the dearth of primary prevention programs in this country. Despite evidence that primary prevention can and does work (Roberts & Peterson, 1984), the system of care for children and families has continued to emphasize treatment over prevention. The reasons for this situation are complex. One issue is the tendency of social programs in the United States to be *residual* rather than *universal*. In the United States, with its traditional philosophy of rugged individualism, a person must be deemed worthy of assistance to get help from society. Hence, health and social programs require that people prove their eligibility for the service.

Eligibility usually involves proof of worthiness and inability to provide for oneself; in other words, they must have failed in their own attempts before asking for help. This *residual* philosophy contrasts with a *universal* philosophy that holds that all people have the same needs and that society should act to support them in meeting those needs. There are few universal programs in the United States other than public education and fire and police protection. The residual approach is treatment oriented, while the universal approach encourages primary prevention; hence the predominant residual philosophy results in a treatment-oriented system.

Furthermore, in our residual human services system, even prevention programs are highly influenced by the residual philosophy, so that prevention efforts tend to be of the secondary and tertiary varieties of prevention, in which treatment plays an active role. When primary prevention efforts are considered, they become diluted because of the complex nature of the identified problem and muddled by residual thinking, so that they lose their potential for universal impact. Consider, for example, the prevention of child abuse (Rodwell & Chambers, 1992). There are two ways to pursue the primary prevention of child abuse—that is, preventing the first occurrence of child abuse in families. One way is a universal approach, in which an entire population is exposed to a remedy for a factor that is believed to be causal. The United States has eschewed this approach because it requires long-term, massive commitments of resources targeted at causal factors such as poverty, the acceptability of violence in the culture, and the acceptance of corporal punishment of children. Instead, primary prevention of child abuse has focused on targeting particular individuals and families who are deemed at high risk for the first occurrence of child abuse. This second, residual way

to approach primary prevention, while less expensive, is fraught with difficulties. To begin with, it is very difficult to accurately identify the target population in advance of the occurrence of abuse. Some potential abusers are missed, while some of those who are not likely to abuse are falsely identified. In addition, the participants in these programs are stigmatized by their identification as potential abusers. Society cannot force those identified to participate, so how can such programs ensure they will serve all those identified? Even if the target population could be accurately identified, there is no reason to believe that all of those selected would agree to participate. Because neither approach to primary prevention of child abuse is feasible, secondary and tertiary prevention makes more sense.

A third issue is the difficulty the transition from a treatment-oriented system to a prevention-oriented one. Professionals have been trained and employed in a treatment-oriented educational and service system—how can they be retrained and re-employed? More importantly, if problems were actually prevented, what would the professionals do for work? Will there be enough jobs in a prevention system to support all of the displaced social workers? There is a vast industry for the treatment of health and social problems, an industry that has a vested interest in maintaining and perpetuating the jobs and incomes of those involved.

Prevention takes a long time to work. It is true that in the long run, in a primary prevention system, there will be many fewer people to treat, but what do we do in the meantime with all the people who need treatment now? Won't it be necessary to continue with treatment while we begin the prevention, and won't this then cost twice as much for a while? Changing professionals and finding the dollars are not easy tasks.

RESEARCH CAPSULE 4

Prevention Works

Study 1

Title Long Term Effects of an Early Childhood Intervention on Educational Achievement and Juvenile Arrest.
Authors Reynolds, A. J., Temple, J. A., Robertson, D. L., & Mann, E. A.

Publication *Journal of the American Medical Association, 285,* 2339–2346, 2001.

Design and Sample Fifteen-year follow-up study of 1,539 low-income, mostly African American children in Chicago born in 1980. Participants (n = 989) were compared to a matched-group cohort (n = 550).

Interventions Services were provided by the Chicago Child-Parent Center at 25 sites in the city. The program was administered by the public schools and consisted of comprehensive education, family and health services including half-day preschool for 3-and 4-year-olds, half- or full-day kindergarten, and school-age services for 6- to 9-year-olds. The children in the comparison group participated in less comprehensive early childhood programs.

Results Children who participated in the preschool treatment intervention for 1 or 2 years had significantly higher rates of high school completion, more years of completed education, lower rates of juvenile arrest, violent arrests, and school dropout. Children who participated from preschool through second or third grade experienced lower rates of grade retention and special education compared to those with less extensive participation.

Study 2

Title High/Scope Perry Preschool Program Effects at Age Twenty-Seven

Author Schweinhart, L. J. & Weikart, D. P.

Publication In *Social Programs That Work,* Jonathan Crane (Ed.), 1998, pp. 148–162, New York: Russell Sage.

Design and Sample Random assignment of 123 low-income preschoolers to treatment and no-treatment groups between 1962 and 1965. Treatment and control groups were quite similar at entry according to statistical analysis of demographic data. Treatment group (*n* = 58) attended High/Scope Perry Preschool Program; no-treatment group (*n* = 65) were not enrolled in a preschool program.

Interventions Treatment group participants were in classes of 20–25 3- and 4-year-olds attending preschool five mornings a week, for either 1 year (*n* = 13) or 2 years (*n* = 45). In addition to the classroom curriculum that emphasized daily routines, activity areas, and children's initiative, teachers made 90-minute weekly home visits to each child and mother, treating the parent as a full partner in the educational process.

Results Follow-up measures of outcome at regular intervals consistently favored the treatment group. At age 27, treatment group outcomes were dramatically better than the no-treatment group on these outcomes: number arrested five or more times (7% vs. 35%); number ever being on welfare (59% vs. 80%); number graduating from high school on time (66% vs. 45%); number earning more than $2,000 per month (29% vs. 7%); and number owning their own homes (36% vs. 13%). Furthermore, a cost-benefit analysis concluded that the program returned $7.16 for every dollar invested.

Study 3

Title Preventing Adolescent Drug Abuse through Life Skills Training: Theory, Methods, and Effectiveness

Author Botvin, G. J.

Publication In *Social Programs That Work,* Jonathan Crane (Ed.), 1998, pp. 225–257, New York: Russell Sage.

Design and Sample Review of numerous evaluations involving thousands of students. Evaluations used random assignment with schools, not individuals, as the unit of assignment.

Interventions Life Skills Training (LST) consists of 15 classes for 45 minutes each in the seventh grade, with booster sessions of 10 classes in the eighth grade and 5 classes in the ninth. There are three components to the curriculum: general self-management skills, general social skills, and information and skills specific to the problem of drug abuse. The booster sessions are designed to reinforce the core curriculum, focusing on the continued development of general life skills.

Results Follow-up measures conducted in the various studies consistently demonstrated large short-term reductions in self-reported use of cigarettes, alcohol, marijuana, and harder drugs. Some of the effects faded over time, but at the end of high school, the program has shown reduction of cigarette smoking by 20%, the incidence of drunkenness by 15%; and weekly marijuana use by 33%. Furthermore, the cost of the program is less than $75 per student.

Pragmatic Connections to Practice

This section has discussed and analyzed the trend toward outcome-based accountability in child and family services. For social work students, this is the arena in which previous coursework from the research sequence of the curriculum may attain newfound relevance. Barriers to implementing an outcome-based approach were identified, including resistance among providers, confusion between intermediate and final outcomes, conflicts between individual goals and program goals, difficulties in reaching agreement about which outcomes are most important, problems in the accurate measurement and interpretation of data, and deciding whether the outcomes are worth the cost required to achieve them. In addition to these barriers, policy makers and funding sources must grapple with the issue of determining whether to allocate limited resources to prevention or to treatment.

Whether the social work student plans to become a direct-service provider or an administrator, the pressure to document results will be increasing. At the direct-service level, this will mean establishing with clients clear goals and objectives that are periodically reviewed and regularly evaluating progress. In some settings, performance evaluations will be based on the success clients have in achieving these goals and objectives. This trend could result in both positive and negative consequences for the worker and client. On the positive side, this goal/outcome focus can assure that problems are identified and addressed in a timely, focused, and efficient fashion. Clients and workers will be less likely to waste time or be distracted from their work. On the other hand, there could be a tendency on the worker's part to avoid the more difficult, intractable client issues. Will the goals and objectives be the most serious and relevant, or will they be the ones that can be readily achieved? Another concern is that the program goal may conflict with and override the individual client goal, so that the services could become adultcentric, ethnocentric, and/or not client- and family-centered. If program and community outcomes are imposed from above and rigidly applied, will there be room for individualized case plans that address the unique needs of particular children and families?

At the administrative level, funding of programs will be more clearly tied to outcomes, so program administrators will need to be able to organize and implement data-based evaluations that provide funders with the necessary information on program performance. Administrators may implement more stringent evaluations of staff members, rewarding those who are most successful in helping clients achieve goals. If the old administrative slogan "what gets measured gets done" has any validity, then frontline workers will feel the pressure to align their own actions with the goals and outcomes to be measured.

At the community level, social workers may find that broad-based citizen groups target well-being goals for the community that they expect professionals to help achieve. Using the widely available *Kid's Count* data, citizen groups could track progress on one or more indicators from year to year, publicizing both the successes and failures.

This sort of community involvement and attention could make social services much more political, because those services that do not have direct bearing on the chosen indicators could become isolated, fighting for recognition and survival.

For the individual social worker in the system, the intertwinings between prevention and treatment can surface daily. A school social worker such as Carmelita, for example, evaluates children for special education who have emotional problems related to serious child abuse. Carmelita might become active in national and local efforts to prevent child abuse, having become convinced that fewer kids would need special education if child abuse could be prevented.

Jon, as a social worker in a mental health setting, might be frustrated with the lack of progress he sees in a 7-year-old girl. In supervision, the supervisor might point out that although things have not been progressing very far, neither have things gotten worse. The supervisor might then point out that Jon's efforts may well be holding the line and preventing the situation from becoming worse. Jon would thus come to see the value of his treatment efforts within the scope of prevention.

In child welfare, Susan might come to realize how the system is organized around treatment of child abuse and neglect, as evidenced by the amount of dollars expended to treat and deal with the problem after the fact compared to the amount of dollars and activities focused on primary prevention. Yet Susan sees daily the results of our failure to mount primary prevention programs. She knows that she cannot end poverty or change the attitudes and beliefs of society about violence, which would be primary prevention approaches to child abuse, but she can focus on secondary and tertiary prevention by working to identify child abuse early, minimize the negative impact on children, and prevent the recurrence of abuse and neglect in the families she serves. In doing so, she is working on another prevention goal as well, the prevention of out-of-home placement and state custody.

Achieving Outcomes in Child Welfare

The number of successful class action lawsuits filed against state child welfare systems nation-wide (discussed in chapter 9) is an indication of the failure, to date, of child welfare to achieve its stated objectives. In the child welfare arena, what are the indicators of client and system success? Are these indicators interrelated? Is there any potential contradiction between client indicators and system indicators?

Like any program or system of services, the child welfare system should be judged by how well it succeeds in attaining its goals and objectives. Goals must be measurable, and success must be defined as attainment of the goals. Put simply, the child welfare system has three principal goals: protection of children, preservation of families, and permanence for children. Although there may be debate about the best indicators for each of these goals, all of these goals are measurable to some degree, given adequate data collection and data analysis systems. For example, the protection of children can be measured, at both the individual and systems levels, by counting the number of confirmed instances of abuse and neglect. The preservation of families can be measured by counting the number of days that abused and neglected children live with their families, as compared to out-of-home placement. Permanency for children can be measured by counting the number of different placements that children experience over time.

But what are the norms for each of these measures? What is an acceptable rate of abuse and neglect in a population or in a family? How many children should be living with their families, and how many should be in out-of-home placement? What is an acceptable number of different placements for a population or for one child in a given time span? How, in other words, does one know when success has been achieved? In the Kansas example discussed above, goals have been stated in absolute terms: "90% of families will not have occurrence of abuse or neglect while participating in family preservation"; "80% of families will not have a child placed out of the home during participation in family preservation"; "70% of children placed in foster care will be reintegrated with their families in six months."

But these goals are somewhat arbitrary. They may sound reasonable, but do they in fact represent realistic and achievable norms or standards? An alternative way to measure success is in terms of improvement in the respective data, not the attainment of some absolute goal. Effectiveness and success are relative and depend on how success is defined. For example, a state or local child welfare system might well be judged successful in the area of child protection if there is a specified level of reduction in the number of confirmed instances of abuse or re-abuse, or a reduction in the number of children who are placed in foster care.

However, translating this same relative measure to specific families can be problematic. At the client level, the standard of success may be higher, because it is harder to tolerate any abuse that one experiences firsthand. Should a chronically abusive parent be reasonably expected to cease and desist all abuse immediately, or should child welfare officials be willing to accept a reduction in the frequency of abuse as a sign of success? To encourage optimism and success in families, it may be advisable to accept the latter reduction in frequency, and for a worker and family to define success so that they do, in fact, succeed. Yet, while it seems perfectly reasonable to hope for a 10–20% reduction in the number of confirmed cases of abuse and neglect in an entire state or metropolitan population, it doesn't seem quite right to settle for that level of improvement within an individual family. At the same time, a zero tolerance level may not be fair to the parents and to the spirit and goal of family preservation.

Thus, there are interactions and contradictions between the goals of child protection and family preservation. If the systemwide or client goal for child safety is set too high, then perhaps fewer families will be preserved. On the other hand, if the goals for family preservation are set too high, then children's safety will suffer. In other words, there may well be an inverse relationship between the goals of safety and family preservation, so that improvement in one will be offset by lack of progress in the other.

The goal of permanence also interacts with the other two goals. In many respects, for an individual child and family, the goal of permanence can be achieved only when the tensions between the other two goals have been resolved. One of the primary reasons for the impermanence of children in state custody is the inability of professionals in the system to agree on whether it is worth taking the safety risk associated with the child living at home in order to preserve the family. Thus, children go back and forth between foster care and home, as safety conditions get better or worse in the family. Although ASFA encourages states and judges to make a final decision regarding permanence within 12 months of placement, this is not always done. Some child welfare experts are recommending that a final decision about adoption or return home be made within 6 months, and that dual case planning be initiated for each possibility. But a "final" decision about return home is often far from definitive, and it may be neither final nor permanent. As stress, isolation, drug abuse, unemployment, and other factors mount in families, the risk of child abuse and neglect mounts. Adoption is not necessarily a permanent and final solution either, because many adoptive placements fail, or "disrupt." So, although the permanency goal of child welfare is often dependent on the resolution of the conflict between other two goals of safety and family preservation, resolution of that conflict is often temporary and does not guarantee permanence for the child.

Prevention versus Treatment

Another issue worthy of discussion is the potential for primary prevention to impact the rates of child abuse and neglect. Professionals who work with abused children yearn for the day when child abuse will be a thing of the past—a rare occurrence that affects very few children. The National Committee to Prevent Child Abuse (NCPCA), in 1992, launched a national initiative to prevent child abuse, called Healthy Families America (HFA) (Mitchel & Donnelly, 1993). HFA is a collaborative effort with the Ronald McDonald Children's Charities and the state of Hawaii, which was one of the first states to develop a statewide system for the prevention of child abuse through intensive home visitor services to parents of newborns. All 50 states are participating in the initiative, at varying degrees of involvement. The goal of the program is to provide all new parents, especially those at high risk for child maltreatment, with the education and support they need through a voluntary home visitor program. The program is based on the belief that if parents are educated and if they receive services and supports to relieve stress, then abuse and neglect are less likely to occur. The four components of the HFA effort are described below.

Healthy Families America: Critical Components (adapted from Mitchel & Donnelly, 1993)

Initiation of Services
- Services are delivered prenatally or at birth
- Universal intake targets all new parents in a given area
- Universal needs assessment identifies most at risk
- All services are voluntary
- Home visitation is the core service

Service Intensity and Duration
- Home visits are made at least once a week
- Services are available for the long term (3–5 years)

Content of Services
- Services are to be family-centered, addressing the needs of the child within the context of the family, and recognizing adults as primary decision makers
- Services are to be coordinated and emphasize linkages to health care and school readiness services
- Services are individualized and emphasize self-sufficiency and empowerment

Selection and Training of Service Providers
- Home visitors are selected on basis of personal qualities, not academic credentials or previous experience
- Workers receive ongoing training
- Workers receive 2 hours per week of supervision from professionals
- Worker caseloads are limited to 15

Attention to the potential of intense home visiting to prevent child abuse and neglect was stimulated by a study conducted by David Olds and associates, published in the prestigious journal *Pediatrics* in 1986 (Olds, Henderson, Chamberlin, & Tatelbaum, 1986). The study involved a randomized clinical trial in which high-risk, first-time mothers were assigned to one of four groups. The first group served as a control, and received no additional prenatal services from the research project, but did receive developmental screenings when children were aged 1 and 2. In addition to the screening services, the second group received free transportation to prenatal appointments and well-child care. The third group was provided with a nurse home-visitor during pregnancy, in addition to the screening and transportation services. Visits lasted a little over an hour, and occurred about once every two weeks. The fourth group received all of the services of group three, plus continued home visits until children were 2. Home visitors emphasized the strengths of the mothers and their families, educated the parents on fetal and infant development, involved family and friends in child care and support of the mother, and linked the family to other health and human services.

The program was able to document positive results for women deemed at highest risk, namely poor teenagers. Those in this category who were visited by a home visitor had fewer instances of verifiable child abuse and neglect in the first 2 years of the children's lives. Also, the parents were observed to restrict and punish their children less frequently, and their babies were seen less frequently in the emergency room in the first year of life. For all nurse-visited women, regardless of risk status, during the second year of the child's life, the babies of nurse-visited women were seen in the emergency room fewer times and were seen by physicians less frequently for accidents and poisonings.

One of the continuing barriers to effective implementation of child abuse prevention is lack of funding. Currently, the most widely available source of funding for child abuse prevention is children's trust funds (Daro, 1991). First conceived by Dr. Ray Helfer at Michigan State University in the 1970s, children's trust funds have been established in almost every state to provide a stable source of funding for child abuse prevention efforts. Generally, state law establishes the trust funds, and many receive additional money from private sources. States appropriate dollars to the funds through state income tax designations or portions of the fees charged for marriage licenses, birth certificates, or the like. Since 1984, the federal government has provided a 25% match to the dollars collected by the states.

Kansas Privatization Initiative

As discussed in chapter 10, the initiative in Kansas to privatize family preservation, foster care, and adoption services using a privatized, managed care approach has been controversial. In order to assess the first 4 years of the initiative and provide direction for action, an independent citizen organization, Kansas Action for Children (KAC), published a report in February, 2001, "The Kansas Child Welfare System: Where Are We, Where Should We Be Going?" (Kansas Action for Children, 2001). Unless otherwise noted, the information in the following section is derived from this report.

One of the hallmarks of the Kansas initiative was the emphasis on collection of outcome data, a feature that had not been a characteristic of the previous public system. As described above, performance standards were set in a variety of areas relative to the status of children in each of the three areas: family preservation, foster care, and adoption. According to available data, the KAC report concluded that standards related to safety had largely been met, while standards related to the permanence of children in care had largely not been met. For example, performance on the revised standard that 40% of children return home or achieve another permanent placement within 6 months of referral (the original standard had been 60%) was 27% in 1998 and 27% in 1999. This failure was deemed a significant weakness because lack of permanency had been a major fault of the old system.

The report criticized many other aspects of the initiative. Although family preservation programs generally met their performance goals of preventing placements for those families it served, other families most at risk for placement were often not referred for family preservation. In other words, many of the children coming into foster care did not have the benefit of family preservation services to attempt to avoid the need for placement. Coordination of services was problematic, due in part to the separate contracts for family preservation, foster care, and adoption. For example, these separate contracts for foster care and adoption made concurrent case planning very difficult, and thus

presented challenges for early adoption. The report noted the commendable attempt to track outcomes by establishing performance standards, but concluded that they were goals rather than standards, because it appeared they were not tied to accountability or consequences. Also, contractors had not obtained adequate response rates on required consumer satisfaction surveys, and there was no performance standard relative to children's overall well-being while in custody.

On a fiscal level, chapter 10 described how the case rate aspect of the managed care approach was severely tested and eventually was drastically changed (though not quite abandoned), so that part of the initiative can be deemed a failure. Early on, contractors succeeded in convincing the legislature to allocate millions of dollars to supplement the alleged inadequate case rates. Then in the second round of contracts, the case rate was changed to a monthly rate. With that change came a change in the fiscal incentive for contractors. In the original case rate system, the fiscal incentive was clearly toward family foster homes rather than group homes and institutions, and for timely achievement of reunification or adoption. Now that contractors are paid a monthly rate for each child, the fiscal incentive for foster care remains, but that for reunification and adoption no longer exists. The fiscal incentive now is for continued foster care, because contractors are paid only when the child continues in foster care. There are no savings for quick and timely reunification or adoption—when those outcomes occur, the foster care contractor loses the child and the income. Perhaps this fiscal incentive can be mitigated by an increased emphasis on achieving permanency outcomes, because the state still expects the contractor to work toward reunification and adoption, even though there is no fiscal incentive to do so.

In the midst of so much criticism, why is privatization in Kansas surviving? First, there may be strengths to the system in some regions that are hard to discern because of the lack of comparative data from the old, public system. For example, even though the contractors have never met the performance standard for permanent placement, they may be performing better in some areas of the state than the old, public system. Second, the political ideology that encourages privatization of government services remains strong. Third, and perhaps most important, there is now a political constituency that can and does advocate for services to the child welfare system. In the old, public system, the news media rarely took notice of the system, and the legislature rarely debated the needs of this population. Foster children, foster parents, and professionals had no strong organization to lobby on their behalf. When the executive and legislative branches built annual budgets, there was no effective voice to advocate on behalf of the child welfare system. Now, the delivery of child welfare services is a prominent issue in the news media and in the minds of legislatures. Outcomes and strategies for achieving them, including appropriate levels of funding, are now regularly discussed and debated. Private contractors, including powerful and influential people on their board of directors, advocate for better funding of services— that is, for better funding of the privatized system.

National Outcomes for Child Welfare System after ASFA

The federal government's General Accounting Office (GAO) (2002) issued a report on outcomes and other information in 2002, for fiscal years 1998 to 2000. Even though all states now report data to the federal government, it is difficult to establish the effects of ASFA because little reliable data are available from the pre-ASFA period. Also, changes from 1998 to 2000 may or may not be the result of the legislation itself. Still, the quality of current information is a vast improvement over the pre-ASFA period and will provide an excellent baseline for future years. Unless otherwise noted, data in the following sections are taken from the GAO report.

Foster Care Outcomes under ASFA. Reunification with families continues to be the most frequent permanency outcome for children in foster care. Most of those exiting were reunified with their families (55% in FY 2000), but 33% of those reunified in 1998 returned to foster care within 3 years. Of the 741,000 children who exited foster care in the fiscal years 1998–2000, the length of stay (LOS) averaged 1 year, with 31% in care from 1–11 months and 10% for 5 years or more. The median LOS varied dramatically from state to state, with Delaware's being five months and Illinois's being 4 years. Sixty-two percent of these children experienced only one or two placements

in care, while 10% had five or more placements while in care.

Adoption Outcomes under ASFA. According to the GAO report, the vast majority of those who were adopted between 1998 and 2000 were less than 12 years old (88%) and had one or more special needs (85%). In 1998, the LOS for adopted children averaged 43 months, and 41% had been in care more than 4 years. In 2000, the corresponding figures were 39 months and 34%, indicating some reduction in the time children await adoption. About 5% of adoptions were reported to have been disrupted prior to finalization.

As discussed in chapter 2, one of the major goals of the Adoption and Safe Families Act of 1997 was to promote adoption of children in foster care. Several key provisions of that legislation were designed to achieve that goal. These provisions included expedited timelines for earlier decisions regarding the termination of parental rights (the "fast track" and "15 of 22" provisions), the Adoption Incentive Program, which monetarily rewards states for increasing the number of adopted children above their baseline, requirements to conduct reasonable efforts toward adoption, permission to pursue the goal of adoption concurrent with reunification efforts, and efforts to reduce cross-state barriers to adoption.

The first two provisions listed were deemed especially crucial to achieving improved adoption outcomes. As Penelope Maza of the federal government's Children's Bureau stated, "The interaction between these two provisions is designed to have a significant impact on the number of children adopted from the public child welfare system and the length of time of the foster care experience until adoptions are finalized" (Maza, 2001, p. 1). The incentive payments have resulted in $42,510,000 being paid to 35 states during 1998, the first year that adoption incentive payments were made (Ledesma, 2000), and according to the GAO study, these dollars were used to recruit adoptive families, provide post adoption services, hire additional staff, and provide training, in that relative order.

Even before passage of this legislation, adoptions of children in the foster care system had been increasing, from about 15,000 in 1988 to 31,000 in 1997. This figure grew to 50,000 in 2000. Taking the previous rate of increase into account, it is estimated that there were an average of 11,000 extra children adopted per year in the 3 fiscal years following the passage of ASFA (Maza, 2001). This increase is substantial and has been attributed in large part to the provisions of ASFA.

However, the GAO study surveyed four states about their implementation of the "fast track" and "15 of 22" provisions and found fewer instances of their use than expected. This survey concluded that the "fast track" provision is rarely engaged. For example, in Maryland, of the 4,000 children who came into custody in FY 2000, only 36 were "fast-tracked." Also, in nine states that responded to the request for data on the "15 of 22" provision, most children who were reviewed at this point were not referred for filing of termination of parental rights (TPR). For example, in Oklahoma in 2000, filings were recommended on 1,027 children but not recommended for almost 3,000. Still, states reported that these figures seemed to be more than in the pre-ASFA period, and that the legislation had encouraged them to focus earlier on a permanency decision. States reported that barriers to speedier decisions included judges' reluctance to waive reasonable efforts, fears that waiving reasonable efforts would be counterproductive at the later TPR hearing, and various extenuating circumstances at the "15 of 22" hearing that made it not in the child's best interest to file a TPR petition.

The greatest challenge to maintaining these high rates of adoption may occur in the next few years, because termination of parental rights is increasing for older children, who, because of their age, are more difficult to adopt. It is likely that adoption workers will be searching for adoptive homes for increasingly older children for whom adoptive placements are not as readily accomplished (Maza, 2001).

Achieving Outcomes in Children's Mental Health

Goals of the Children's Mental Health System

Longitudinal studies of children with emotional and behavioral disorders reveal that these children fare quite poorly compared to youth in the general population, or youth with other types of disabilities (Wagner, 1995). High school students identified as Seriously Emotionally Disturbed (SED) miss more school, participate less in clubs and social groups, fail more courses, and drop out of high school in more numbers than other groups. As young adults, only 26% pursue postsecondary education compared to 68% of the general population. Fewer youth with SED are employed, married, and registered to vote. Three times as many SED youth are arrested within 1 year after high school.

These data from education, the trend toward managed care, the subsequent focus on evaluation of managed care systems, and the initiatives to reorganize systems of care have all brought increasing attention to the issue of outcomes. In children's mental health, what are the critical outcomes at the system and individual level, and what are some of the difficulties or barriers in defining, measuring, and achieving them?

As discussed in the previous section, there have been many recent initiatives to improve the system of care in children's mental health. Fortunately, most of these efforts have included an evaluation component, so there are considerable data about the goals, outcome indicators, and success of these system change efforts. Thirty of these systems-change efforts have been summarized by Stroul, McCormack & Zaro (1996).

The major goals, and common outcome indicators, of systems change in the children's mental health arena are the following.

Goals and Outcome Indicators of Children's Mental Health System
(adapted from Stroul, McCormack, & Zaro, 1996)

Goals:

- Develop and provide a full array of community-based services

- Reduce the reliance on restrictive treatment environments and out-of-home placements

- Increase interagency coordination and collaboration

- Provide flexible, individualized services tailored to the unique needs of each child and family

- Contain costs and demonstrate cost-effectiveness   *(cont'd.)*

Outcome Indicators:

* Type of residential living (placement)
* Utilization of inpatient and residential treatment as compared to less restrictive treatment
* Functioning of youth themselves
* Educational status of youth
* Law enforcement status of youth
* Level of family involvement and professional support
* Satisfaction with services
* Access to services
* Costs

The Ventura Planning Model's Approach to Outcomes

Promising results in some or all of the above outcome indicators were found in most of the 30 sites. However, not all of the sites have elaborate or extensive evaluation efforts. Probably the most advanced and comprehensive local system to track outcomes has been developed in Ventura County, California (Jordan & Hernandez, 1990; Hernandez & Goldman, 1996), whose system of care was described in chapter 10. The outcome focus of this interagency effort begins with a clear vision of the goals to be achieved, stated in measurable terms.

Measurable Goals of Ventura Planning Model (adapted from Hernandez & Goldman, 1996)

* Reduction in out-home placement
* Reduction in juvenile justice recidivism
* Reduction in psychiatric hospitalization
* Reduction in out-of-county non—public school placements
* Improved school performance and attendance

Ventura County was so successful at achieving its goals that the state of California adopted its model for statewide implementation. From 1985 to 1988, the county's state hospitalization rate dropped 68%, out-of-county non—public school placements declined 21%, and out-of-county court-ordered placements were reduced by 47%. Significant gains were documented in school attendance and academic performance for children in the project's day treatment program, and the number of juvenile incarcerations was down 22% (Jordan & Hernandez, 1990).

These goals were accomplished within the cost guidelines established by the state. In creating this program, the state developed an innovative way to examine the cost-benefits of the project. The state required that the project demonstrate either that 100% of the project's costs be offset by savings gained in reduced costs of institutional and out-of-home placements, or that 50% of the costs be offset with achievement of a set of client-oriented outcomes. This method demonstrated a commitment not just to saving money, but also to achieving positive outcomes for children, even if this meant spending more money. This way of defining success alleviated the pressure to achieve better outcomes at the same cost that many community-based programs experience. Cost avoidance was calculated at 66% of the program's $1.5 million budget, and all client-oriented measures exceeded expectations (Jordan & Hernandez, 1990).

The Fort Bragg Evaluation Project

Despite the generally favorable results reported above, the results of the large-scale Fort Bragg Evaluation Project, perhaps the most comprehensive and most thoroughly evaluated systems change effort, were mixed (Bickman, Summerfelt, & Foster, 1996). In this comparison study, a children's mental health system, providing a full continuum of care with few limits on service utilization was designed for 42,000 dependents of Fort Bragg military personnel in North Carolina, with funding from the Department of the Army. Two comparison sites that utilized the Army's traditional care system were included in the study. The demonstration site succeeded in achieving many of the desired outcomes, including implementing a full continuum of care for this large population. In comparison with the other sites, the demonstration site succeeded in increasing access to care and using less restrictive treatment options. Parents and adolescents in the demonstration expressed significantly greater satisfaction with services than those at the comparison sites.

However, in two important categories, the demonstration site did not outperform the comparison sites. First, regarding child and family outcomes, improvement was documented in both sites, but there was no superiority at the demonstration site. Second, the costs per child of the demonstration site were significantly higher than the comparison sites. This was due to longer duration of treatment, use of expensive intermediate-level services not available in the control sites, and lack of any effort to control costs through the limitation of services. Rather than limiting services, the demonstration site attempted to achieve lower costs through utilization of less restrictive and less costly types of care. Although these alternatives were much more heavily used, there was not a sufficiently significant corresponding drop in the use of traditional services to offset the cost.

Consumer Satisfaction

The Report on the Surgeon General's Conference on Children's Mental Health (Office of the Surgeon General) emphasized the need and value of getting parent and youth perspectives in the planning of mental health services. Most experts in the children's mental health field agree that consumer satisfaction is one of the important outcomes of service. That is, the more that parents, children, and youth are satisfied with services, the more likely that positive outcomes will be achieved. Although this notion has not been tested empirically, it stands to reason that dissatisfaction is a barrier to the therapeutic process and the helping relationship, and thus is an impediment to positive and focused goal achievement.

In Kansas, a statewide phone and mail survey has provided local community mental health centers (CMHCs), state mental health officials, and consumer groups with valuable information about parent and youth satisfaction. Parents of young children, and youth age 12 and above, are regularly surveyed on a variety of consumer satisfac-

tion items. Reports are generated for each of the 27 individual CMHCs, and these are also aggregated into a statewide report. State officials require that CMHCs engage in dialogue with consumers, staff, and other key stakeholders to study the strengths and weaknesses of their own reports, and to write a plan for how the center will target low areas of satisfaction for improvement.

Although results from Kansas may not be indicative of consumer satisfaction in other states, this study is the first large-scale study of consumer satisfaction and offers insights into areas that may be useful to other states as well. In the period from July, 2001, to February 2002, 1,091 parents and 361 youth completed surveys. Statewide, both parents and youth reported generally high levels of overall satisfaction with CMHC services, with some variance occurring with specific aspects of services. For example, parent satisfaction was greatest with the length of time between intake and services (93.7%) and much lower with the services they received in a crisis (74.6%). When asked to grade services, parents rated parent support worker and case management the highest (3.4 and 3.3 on 4-point scale), and respite care and independent living services lowest (2.8). Youth were most satisfied that workers did not blame them and were trustworthy (93% and 90.2%), and less satisfied with how the staff helped them plan for the future (78.9%). When analyzing the relationship of overall satisfaction to other variables, the statewide report found that overall satisfaction was correlated with satisfaction with specific aspects of service: time between intake and beginning services, worker turnover, crisis services, involvement in treatment planning, appointment times and location, and the level of family-centeredness of the mental health worker (Martin & Petr, 2002).

Current Challenges

The Fort Bragg Evaluation Project and the thrust toward managed care highlight the many challenges involved in attempting to measure and achieve outcomes in children's mental health. Challenges for achieving outcomes include individualizing outcomes in measurable terms, the complexity and scope of children's lives and the multiple influences on outcome, and the lack of empirical data about which interventions work best with which problems. Challenges for evaluating the effort to achieve outcome include accurate measurement of relevant outcome and cost on an individual basis, obtaining valid comparison groups, and overcoming logistical problems such as funding and information management.

These challenges are being addressed in the current evaluations of managed care systems, discussed above, and in a comprehensive federal study that is in process. Currently, the federal government is engaged in a large-scale evaluation of systems change that may shed light on the effectiveness of large-scale systems change efforts. As mentioned previously, in 1994, the Center for Mental Health Services funded 22 sites nationwide to create effective systems of care. This federal initiative includes a comprehensive 3-year evaluation that will study whether client-level and systems-level outcomes were achieved. Also, the evaluation will attempt to identify features of the system of care and communities that affected outcomes. The ongoing evaluation will collect descriptive data on clients, the type of services received, and their duration. At the client outcome level, data will be gathered relative to client behavioral and educational functioning, child and parent satisfaction, parent sense of empowerment, and the level of restrictiveness of placement and treatment. At the systems level, data will be obtained relative to interagency collaboration, availability and accessibility of services, family involvement, cultural competence, and costs (Stroul, McCormack & Zaro, 1996).

CHAPTER 11 SUMMARY

In contrast to the process orientation of traditional human services, the final pragmatic perspective emphasizes the importance of achieving outcomes. This perspective asserts that the effectiveness of services can be assured when professionals and organizations are held accountable for the health and well-being outcomes that services are designed to address. Implementation of an outcome focus is plagued by many technical and attitudinal barriers. These include resistance from professional providers and organizations, distinguishing process (intermediate) outcomes from final outcomes, potential conflicts between individual and systems goals, disagreements about which outcomes are the most important to track, the difficulty and cost of accurately measuring and interpreting outcomes, and prevention versus treatment.

At the direct-service level, social workers will experience added pressure to document that their efforts are achieving the goals set out by their clients and organizations. In both the child welfare and children's mental health systems, federal and state policymakers are insisting that outcomes be measured and accounted for, yet many of the early attempts to accomplish these goals have met with only limited success, due in part to the barriers and inherent complexities of the process that were outlined in the first section of the chapter.

Achieving outcomes in child welfare was discussed relative to prevention versus treatment issues, the outcomes of the Kansas privatization initiative, and current national outcome measures associated with ASFA. In children's mental health, the chapter reviewed outcomes of the Ventura planning model, the Fort Bragg evaluation project, and consumer satisfaction.

U N I T
II
Conclusion

Summary

This concludes unit II, which presented an overview of the eight pragmatic perspectives that dominate social work practice with children and families. Students should keep in mind that these eight perspectives sometimes overlap and sometimes contradict each other. For instance, combating adultcentrism (pragmatic perspective 1) overlaps with respect for diversity and difference (pragmatic perspective 4), as it speaks to the issues of differences between adults and children. the strengths perspective (pragmatic perspective 3) is an essential aspect of combating adultcentrism (pragmatic perspective 1), family-centered practice (pragmatic perspective 2), and respecting diversity and difference (pragmatic perspective 4). Combating adultcentrism (pragmatic perspective 1) may at times appear to be child-centered rather than family-centered (pragmatic perspective 2), and the practitioner will feel discomfort until the tension between the two perspectives is resolved. The organization and financing of certain services (pragmatic perspective 7) may encourage an individual rather than an ecological perspective (pragmatic perspective 6), and a deficiency rather than a strengths perspective (pragmatic perspective 3). An intense outcome focus at the program level (pragmatic perspective 8) may minimize the importance of individualizing outcomes relative to diverse populations (pragmatic perspective 4). The least restrictive alternative (pragmatic perspective 6) may be at odds with the informed-choice component of family-centered practice (pragmatic perspective 2).

At any one point in time, with any one particular client, in any one particular program and setting, the day-to-day work of the social worker may be guided more by one perspective than by another. Sometimes social workers must choose between competing perspectives. This is one reason why the real, hands-on social work with children and families is so difficult and complex: there is no one perspective, no single theory or approach that can guide practice in all situations. Competent, conscientious practitioners consider more than one perspective, sometimes even all eight, when they are trying to understand a situation and act responsibly. Detailed, in-depth case examples from child welfare and children's mental health are presented in chapters 12 and 13 to demonstrate how the pragmatic perspectives guide and influence case-level decisions.

If social work is a process of making purposeful use of oneself, then these perspectives can help the practitioner decide what is most purposeful in a given situation. However, there is no specific formula for their direct application. No single pragmatic perspective has the most dominance and relevance—no combination of perspectives take priority over others. This may frustrate students who, understandably, are seeking to simplify their work and interactions with clients. But the reality is that social work in child welfare and children's mental health is a complex undertaking, and simplistic formulas falsely lead the student to expect that the work is less difficult and frustrating than it really is. In the effort to simplify, the scope and focus of the work become so narrow that important issues and perspectives are ignored or neglected.

These eight pragmatic perspectives have pragmatic relevance at both the direct practice and the policy levels. The traditional system of care for children and families, including policies, programs, and professional attitudes, has not been organized or driven by these pragmatic perspectives. Instead, the system has been characterized by the opposite perspectives: it has been adultcentric, professional- and child-centered rather than family-centered, deficiency oriented rather than strengths focused, insensitive to diversity and culturally incompetent, dominated by restrictive environments instead of the least restrictive alternative, individually rather than ecologically focused, fragmented and inefficient, and focused on process rather than on achieving outcomes. Individual professionals, organizations, and policymakers are beginning to act in accordance with the eight perspectives presented here, but the magnitude and scope of the needed changes can be overwhelming to the beginning and seasoned social worker alike. On the surface, these eight perspectives may appear to be commonsense and simple to operationalize, but in the real world, where their opposites have dominated for so many years, they represent radical change. Thus, students may find that they must take considerable risk and encounter much resistance when they attempt to operationalize these perspectives in their agency settings.

The final unit of this book, comprising chapters 12 and 13, presents extensive, in-depth case examples of how the eight pragmatic perspectives apply, interrelate, and help determine best practices in the child welfare and children's mental health service systems.

Suggested Assignments and Learning Activities for Unit II

1. Conduct a 30-minute observation of children in a "natural" setting where they are interacting with each other, without adult interference. When in a natural setting such as a playground, what are children like? Did you discover anything about children, or about your own adultcentrism, in completing this activity?

2. Solicit children's opinions on some subject of interest to you or your agency.

3. Interview the staff of a family advocacy organization. What are their opinions about professionals and the current system of care? What do they see as barriers to achieving their goals?

4. Review the policies of your practicum agency with respect to family-centered principles. What are the areas of strength and weakness?

5. Conduct a self-assessment of your own unique strengths, especially as they pertain to work with children and families.

6. Identify the strengths in a new client.

7. Interview staff at your practicum agency about how LRA applies and tensions it is creating.

8. Read about and/or get firsthand experience of a culture different from your own.

9. Analyze the level of cultural competence in your practicum agency, using the guidelines presented in the text.

10. Find out what interagency coordinating councils exist in your community and visit one or more meetings. What is the focus of the group and are they succeeding?

11. Complete an ecomap with a client or on yourself.

12. Find out how your practicum agency is funded and analyze how that funding influences its operations, values, programs, etc.

13. Find out what data your agency keeps track of, why, and what the data is used for.

14. Find out what *Kid's Count* data say about your community, and whether/how the data are used by groups or agencies in your community.

15. Find out what your state law is concerning the reporting of abuse and neglect. Who are mandated reporters? What types of abuse are included, and how is each defined?

16. Write a position paper on whether or not white parents should be foster or adoptive parents for Native American, African American, or other children of color, and/or vice versa.

17. Complete an ecomap with a foster child's family.

18. Debate the following question: If quality foster family homes could be found for all foster children within their communities, would there be a need for group homes?

19. Find out what the state plan is in your state for the implementation of the Family Preservation and Family Support Program.

20. Find out if your state's child welfare system is operating under a court order or consent decree, and if it is, find out the terms and conditions of the order or decree. Is your state's child welfare system currently being sued?

21. Find out if Citizen Review Boards or CASA programs are operating in your community. Who administers the programs, how are they funded and staffed, how many children and volunteers are involved, etc.?

22. Find out how your state administers its children's trust fund for child abuse prevention. How much money is allocated and how is it spent?

23. For each of the case examples in chapters 12 and 13, construct an ecomap of the family's relationship with their environment, using the information given. What other information would you want/need to have to complete the ecomap?

24. In the field of child welfare, which single one of the eight pragmatic perspectives is most important, in your opinion? That is, which one, over all others, should the social worker try to operationalize if at all possible? Why?

25. Choose a case example or a program. Analyze the case or program from the point of view of the eight pragmatic perspectives. How is each perspective relevant to understanding and guiding policy and practice in the case or program? (Extended, in-depth case examples are presented in the two chapters that conclude this book.)

26. Investigate the licensure/certification laws in your state to find out the degree to which social work practice is regulated or limited in the mental health arena.

27. Read more about family genograms and construct one on your own family of origin or a client's. Be sure to incorporate strengths into your effort.

28. Interview children and staff in SED programs in your local schools. What do they like and dislike about their educational program for SED youth?

29. Find out if there is a Peer Mediation program in your local school district. Interview students and staff about their experiences and view of effectiveness.

30. Find out about the protection and advocacy agency in your state. Obtain a copy of its annual report and determine whether children with serious emotional disorders seem to be a priority. Interview the director or other staff about their services to this population.

31. Find out whether your state's Department of Mental Health has a separate budget and designated staff for children's mental health.

32. Help form a parent support group in a mental health agency or school special education program.

33. Visit an inpatient psychiatric treatment ward or residential treatment center in your area. Ask about the treatment program, including involvement of children and adolescents in decision making, cultural competence, level of family involvement, and use of seclusion and restraints.

34. Volunteer to be a Big Brother/Big Sister for a youth with emotional or behavioral problems.

35. Find out what outcome measures (if any) are routinely used at your local mental health agency.

36. Contact your city and county planning commissioners to find out whether the community has adopted any mental health goals for the children in the community.

37. Obtain your state plan for children's mental health; read and critique it. Submit your critique to the director of the state mental health department.

38. For each of the case examples presented in chapter 12, construct an ecomap of the family's relationship to the environment, using the information

provided. What additional information would you want/need to obtain to complete the ecomap?

39. If you have ever experienced working as a member of a professional team, write a short paper describing how you and your team dealt with disagreements. Was there pressure on you, like there was on Cynthia, to present a united front? Did team members accuse you of triangulation? How did you handle this pressure, and what was the eventual outcome in the case?

40. In the field of mental health, which of the eight pragmatic perspectives is the most important, in your opinion? Why? Rank the eight perspectives in terms of their importance and provide your rationale.

U N I T

III

Extensive Case Examples

This unit consists of in-depth analyses of two case examples from each of the two major service systems that are the focus of this book. Both chapters first present a narrative describing the child, the family, and the developments in the case over time. Next, the narrative is critiqued and analyzed utilizing the eight pragmatic perspectives as the analytic framework to conceptualize the practice and policy aspects of the progress of the case.

In chapter 12, two different types of case examples are discussed. The narrative for the first case example is a reprint from an issue of a popular professional journal, including two outside commentaries. Then, in contrast to the traditional professional views extent in that narrative, the text's analysis shows how adoption of the eight pragmatic perspectives would have led to different actions and decisions by the professionals involved. The second case example concerns reunification of a child in foster care with his biological mother, illustrating how complex and difficult the reunification process can be.

In chapter 13, two examples from the children's mental health system are analyzed. The first example, about Bill, depicts social work in a community mental health setting. The focus of this example is on "secondary prevention"—how services can be used to identify and work on problems before they become too severe. But the case demonstrates also that even "minor" problems can be complex and frustrating, as many different people must be involved and many different issues must be addressed. The second case example, that of Sharon, presents a more serious and chronic problem of adolescent depression. A suicide attempt and subsequent hospitalization are followed by intensive mental health and educational interventions that eventually prove to be successful.

As mentioned in the preface, all case examples developed by the author are entirely fictitious or are fictitious composites from the author's professional experience.

CHAPTER 12

Connections: Case Examples
from Child Welfare

Overview

This chapter presents in-depth analyses of two case examples of social work with children and families in the child welfare system. In both examples, a narrative describes the family and the developments in the case over time. Next, the narrative is critiqued and analyzed utilizing the eight pragmatic perspectives as the analytic framework used to conceptualize the practice and policy aspects of the case.

Case Example 1: The Sloan Family

The first case example was previously presented in the September/October 1990 issue of *Family Therapy Networker* (now called the *Psychotherapy Networker* and reprinted here with permission). This journal, which is highly readable and relevant to all social workers working with families, has an intriguing regular feature entitled the "Consultation Corner." In this section of the journal, family therapists present fairly detailed accounts of specific cases for commentary and reaction from experts in the field. This particular entry demonstrates the limitations of a purely clinical,

deficiency-oriented, family therapy approach to children and families with multiple, long-standing child welfare concerns. The reader is encouraged to read the narrative of the case and the two expert commentaries closely, noting any areas in which the reader agrees or disagrees with the comments of the two expert commentators. The reader is also encouraged to consider the ways in which the eight pragmatic perspectives presented in this text could guide and direct the workers in their approach to this challenging family. The author's own commentary, which could be viewed as an integrative child welfare approach, follows the reprint of the article.

Narrative

Consultation Corner

Edited by Charles H. Fishman

DRAWING THE LINE:

ARE SOME FAMILIES "UNTREATABLE"?

Overview

Family therapists are sometimes accused of having too much messianic fervor, a compulsion to help people who don't seem to be seeking help. But where does the therapist draw the line? Is it ever appropriate for a clinician to tell a family that he or she can't help them?

The major issue in the following case, submitted by an outpatient therapist at a large community mental health center, is one of treatability. The commentators tackle the question of what, if anything, can be done with a multiproblem family that has become the focus of a complex network of social and treatment services.

The Sloan family was referred to our community mental health center by a Head-start social worker. The mother, Amy Sloan, presented her 12-year-old son, Tom, as the one in need of help, although the family's history made it clear that the entire family had undergone serious traumas. Amy was concerned about Tom's acting out, not respecting curfews and staying out late, smoking marijuana, and doing poorly in school.

Amy, age 28 and Caucasian, is raising five of her seven children, of whom Tom is the oldest. Her husband, Neal, was shot and killed in a dispute over drugs 2 years ago on Tom's birthday; the family witnessed the shooting. Even before the shooting, the family had been seriously harassed by the small-town community because Neal, a drug user, had been infected with the AIDS virus. When the community learned that he had AIDS, they tried to set the family's house on fire, slashed the Sloans' car tires, and banned the children from school.

Amy took her children back to Chicago, her hometown, after Neal's death. Amy has tested HIV positive, and so has her 2-year-old daughter, who now lives with relatives in another state. Amy's 10-year-old son also lives apart from the family, with Amy's father.

Amy's boyfriend, Bob, who is her sister Jane's ex-husband, is the father of two of Jane's children, and possibly Amy's youngest. He takes an active role in disciplining all the children, although whether he has Amy or Jane's support in this is unclear. Stability, routines, and rules are lacking in the family. The oldest children go to school when they want, which is rarely, and stay out as late as they want. Mealtimes often consist of sandwiches, made by the children themselves, and bedtimes may be 8 p.m. or 2 a.m., depending on what is happening any given night. None of the adults in the family has held a job for more than a few weeks at a time.

Amy, her children, and Bob comprise one subsystem; her mother, Mae, Mae's invalid husband and two teenage sons represent a second subsystem; and Amy's sister Jane, her second husband and the three children represent a third. The subsystems exist in theory only. In reality, family relationships are so enmeshed, boundaries so unclear, and living arrangements so unstable that concepts such as "family," "mother," "father," and "home" have little meaning for the Sloans. All of these people have lived together at Mae's house at various times. Amy's children refer to both Mae and Amy as "mom" and Amy's 7- and 8-year-old daughters spend more time caring for Amy's 1-year-old than do any of the adults.

We made a home visit with the social worker for the intake. Amy greeted us at the door at noon, still in her nightgown. Tom was not present, although other children were in and out. Amy cried when she described Neal's death, and then changed the subject to her mother, Mae, who lived on the first floor of the building. She complained that Tom minded his grandmother but not her. She described her 7-year-old daughter's nightmares that Amy would leave, and said that when Amy couldn't sleep, this child would stay up all night with her. We talked about how difficult the last 2 years' events had been—Neal's death, moving back to Chicago, being a single mother, financial problems—and arranged to come back in two weeks.

As we were leaving with the social worker, two nurses from the Board of Health were coming in. We were struck by the thought of all the service providers working with this one family, and the family's apparent nonchalance about all these resources.

After visiting the Sloans, we talked about addressing issues of loss, and doing grief work with the mother and maybe some of the children. Since we saw so many issues and needs, we decided to assign two therapists to the case: one to ally with Tom, the identified patient, the other to support Amy, and both for family treatment. From the description of Tom's behavior and the daughter's nightmares, we felt that the children were all acting out their fear of losing Amy.

As it happened, we weren't able to focus on these core issues for any sustained period of time because we were always dealing with the crisis of the week. Many of these crises were brought about by the conflict between Amy and Mae. Their already volatile relationship was exacerbated when Amy was evicted from her apartment and the family moved in with Mae. After that, the conflicts regularly escalated until Amy could no longer tolerate the situation and moved out several times, suddenly and impulsively, sometimes taking the children and sometimes leaving them with Mae. Amy stayed in shelters, in Bob's van, or with friends, until she eventually would move back with Mae. We decided to include Mae in treatment.

The children are often used as pawns between Amy and Mae. Mae uses the children as a means of keeping Amy dependent on her and extracting money from Amy. Separation has been a difficult developmental task for several generations of this family. Amy and Jane remain psychologically and financially dependent on Mae, and Mae, age 54, reports that she only recently "cut the apron strings" with her own mother. Amy has only been able to separate when there has been another person—husband or boyfriend—available to bolster her fragile sense of self.

The flow of treatment was also interrupted by Amy's three arrests for alleged theft, drug dealing, and writing bad checks; by Tom's frequent run-ins with the police and school authorities; by violence in the home directed at Amy, Mae, or Jane by Amy's 18-year-old brother, Jim; by violence directed at Amy or Bob; and by a suicide attempt by Amy that resulted in a week of hospitalization.

Historically, Mae appears to have used the threat of psychiatric hospitalization as a source of power or control. Amy was hospitalized several times during her adolescence when Mae could not control her. Mae uses the same threat on Jim and Tom when they are out of control.

Violence is a means of communication and gives family members about their only feeling of being taken into account. Substance abuse is a long-standing problem; Amy's father was an alcoholic who abused Mae. The couple eventually separated, and Mae joined Al-Anon, while he joined Alcoholics Anonymous and stopped drinking. Amy has admitted that she abuses prescription drugs, particularly codeine.

Amy, like others in her family, exhibits characteristics of codependence, including a low sense of self, difficulty with impulse control, relationships with substance abusers, difficulty with trust, closeness and intimacy, need for control, and a willingness to rescue others from the consequences of their behavior.

To bolster their own self-esteem, the adults in the family attack or belittle one another. This dynamic holds true especially for Amy and Mae, who often function as competitive siblings. Because the adults are so preoccupied with defending themselves against each other, they neglect to nurture and promote the children's development. Whether dependent child or competitive sibling, Amy is not in charge of her children.

The lack of consistency and the instability of the children's physical and psychological environment has led to a confusion of roles and boundaries in the family.

How can we help this family separate and move on through the developmental stages?

How can Amy distance herself from her mother and focus on the children's needs as well as her own?

Amy has been unable to keep a job, unable to provide adequate physical and psychological stability for her children, and she has been arrested several times because she seems to be governed by her impulses and need for short-term gratification. How do we improve her ego functioning so that she considers the consequences of her behavior and can begin to do some long-range planning? Does involving Mae in treatment undermine our efforts to strengthen Amy's ego functioning?

Are we overextending ourselves as therapists? Our efforts with this family have done little to get them to focus on real problems, and we wonder if we are enabling the family to continue its feuding by helping them avoid some of the consequences of their irresponsibility. In spite of many efforts on our part to clarify our roles, both Amy and Mae continue to view therapists as "referees." Often they will call us, not with any service question, but simply to inform us what terrible thing the other has done. How can we assume a more therapeutic role with this family?

[By Charles H. Fishman, M.D.]

COMMENTARY NUMBER ONE: A SYSTEMIC APPROACH

[By Mara Selvini Palazzoli, Stefano Cirillo, Matteo Selvini, and Anna Maria Sorrentino]

Obviously, the Sloans are more challenging than the self-referred families usually seen in therapy, and therapists sometimes must do more to "take charge" of the clients' lives than their training prepares them to do. However, we still doubt that this particular family, as presented, can benefit much from family therapy just now. The therapists seem to be treating the Sloans as if they had voluntarily initiated therapy themselves, and as if the children were acting out fairly standard patterns of unresolved relational conflicts between the adults of two generations. But this family is hardly in a position to benefit from a traditional family therapy that stresses developmental tasks, boundaries, hierarchies, etc. Such concerns are clearly an unapproachable luxury for the Sloans at this point, who exhibit a multigenerational history of virtually nonexistent child care skills and no understanding at all of what children need from parents.

In this family, there are no parental role models, no reasonably defined schedules for meals and bedtime, no stable physical environment, no consistent, comprehensible rules, or dependable adult relationships. Amy is at present not capable of mothering; she can only grasp at fleeting relationships and alliances with people who temporarily seem to meet her enormous emotional needs and take her side in her interminable battles against her relatives. These conditions are incompatible with successful family therapy.

Nonetheless, there are ways of working with this family in which therapy might be a component. Given the chaotic state of the Sloan family, we would suggest, as a first step, that the children—including the ones not currently living with Amy— be placed in a residential care community, allowing Amy visiting and telephone privileges with them. Besides protecting the children, this step aims at rebuilding a sibling group in which each child no longer sees him or herself as a pathological case (Tom, a juvenile delinquent; Sue, a girl suffering from nightmares; Patricia, a baby infected with AIDS), but just one of seven siblings neglected by an inadequate parent.

If, after careful evaluation, Amy looks as if she could benefit from therapy, the children could go from the residential community to a foster family until their mother seems competent to care for them. The children's father, or fathers, if they can be found and prove reliable, should be treated as well.

If Amy does not appear treatable, then the children should be put up for adoption. The very threat of permanently losing her children might spur Amy into a more adult attitude about both therapy and her responsibilities as a mother. In effect, acting to protect the children first, before beginning therapy, sets up a contractual premise with Amy, that if she wants her children back, she must prove that she can become a better mother. If forced to look at the consequences of her neglect and irresponsibility, she may begin to perceive her children as individuals with their own needs, rather than pawns in the chronic warfare with her mother, father and sister. (We would also like more information about the father and sister, and their relationship to Amy.) Only at this point could Amy realistically benefit from therapy (alone and in sessions with the other adults in her life) and become aware of her own needs and frustrations. Any new insights about herself and any maturity Amy gains during therapy will be revealed in her interaction with her children.

Even if Amy's therapy fails, the children will at least get the message that the family problems are not their fault. This awareness will help them overcome their almost inevitable guilt about not being "good" children. On the other hand, the knowledge that their mother was herself incapacitated will enable them to give up any vengeful, self-destroying grudge against her.

On the whole, this case seems emblematic of a certain "psychotherapism" that inclines therapists to ignore contextual realities in the belief that all problems are amenable to clinical intervention. But engaging in therapy without some sort of responsible commitment or contract almost guarantees failure, particularly with a family that is predisposed by their long-term situation to look upon the therapists as just two more in an endless stream of official functionaries running through their lives.

Such therapeutic dead-ends reinforce the public tendency to scapegoat mental health professionals for the deficiencies of the welfare system, and give the impression that the therapists are somehow responsible for the never-ending cycles of neglect, abuse, and poverty characteristic of such families. On the other hand, the implied belief of the therapists that therapy solves every problem kills any impulse for public authorities to develop more innovative plans and find new resources for child protection.

COMMENTARY NUMBER TWO: AN INTERGENERATIONAL APPROACH

[By James L. Framo]

The poet Dorothy Parker once wrote, "When I was young and bold and strong, oh right was right and wrong was wrong. With plume on high and flag unfurled I rode away to right the world. But now I'm old and good and bad are woven in a crazy plaid. I sit and say the world is so and he is wise who lets it go."

There was a time when I would have zealously taken on the challenge of treating the Sloans—a family in which drugs and violence are a way of life; in which boundaries are diffuse and fluid and family roles are interchangeable; in which the kids are parentified, out of control, and do not know whom to respond to as parents; in which the reality issues (money and medical problems) are overwhelming; in which mother and grandmother alternate between hostility and mutual dependency; and in which men are either dead, disabled, or irrelevant. But when you are young, optimistic, full of energy, confident of your theoretical grasp of problems and equipped with a grab bag of techniques, you believe you can help everybody. Maybe this is why schizophrenics respond so well to the enthusiasm of new psychiatric residents, and psychology and social work students.

All kinds of ideas about treating the Sloans would have occurred to me in those early days, like finding a female cotherapist to work with me and getting all the family members I could find to come in—mother, her mother, her father, her mother's mother, her sister, her brothers, her children. I certainly would have made an extra effort to see the fathers of the young children as well as the mother's father, and grandfather, even if I had to contact them myself or make a home visit.

I would have also decided which "family" or subsystem would make the most promising therapeutic target. I might have chosen to get to the struggle between the mother and grandmother by conducting a family-of-origin session with the mother and all the members of her original family, even though an intergenerational approach is usually less effective with crisis-focused families.

I might also have elected to do what the therapists did in this case—work with the mother and children, isolating this sub-unit, validating mother as a person, and strengthening her role as a parent. I might have chosen to do family therapy with the whole melange, and explicitly taken charge, given directives, or even taken the hard line myself with these children and tried to bring order out of chaos.

Years ago I might have put the family in a multiple-family group, a useful modality in which tumultuous families learn to help each other. Or I might have called in a consultant to conduct some social network sessions. I might also have brought together the various professional helpers who were involved with the family in order to coordinate their efforts and to deal with practical matters. This is the kind of work Dick Auerswald used to do. A host of community resources could be called upon: referrals to drug treatment programs and centers for the treatment of AIDS, mother could be enrolled in parenting skills classes or in a Tough Love group; various family members could be involved in psychoeducational programs. I might even have considered placing the children elsewhere—although this is a step I never undertake without evidence of severe child abuse.

While I might have tried all these different approaches 30 years ago, my experience since then has taught me that it is unlikely that any would have brought about any meaningful change in this case. What middle-class therapists refer to as "disorganized, chaotic, multi-problem families" are in fact highly organized, patterned, and ordered. These families fall roughly into three categories:

1. Families who do not seek help manage to muddle through on their own, and extricate themselves from spiraling cycles of hopelessness. When in crisis, some of these families make use of a network of informal helpers.

2. Families who, despite massive problems, will profit from professional help. They will respond positively to skillful interventions offered by trustworthy and caring professionals who understand the everyday reality issues these families face.

3. Families who will sabotage and frustrate every attempt to help them.

Families in this last category seem to exist in greater numbers than their actual incidence because they are involved with multiple agencies, many of which are working at cross-purposes. Their voluminous records, sometimes extending back for generations, fill up agency file cabinets. These families, in a sense, make parents out of society as they overutilize police services, social agencies, and other institutions. They have a strong sense of entitlement, feeling that the world owes them what they have been deprived of. They may project their helplessness and despair onto professional helpers who, after a while, reflect the families' inner state by themselves feeling helpless and impotent. Since they have no control over their own lives, they may attempt to control or even punish the therapist. Eventually the helpers become frustrated and, if they are not masochistic, they act out against, or get rid of, the family.

One way that the therapist can recognize this type of family is his or her sense of relief when they cancel appointments. As a matter of fact, such families don't make appointments that fit clinic hours; they show up or call when they need help. Helpers who do therapy with these families sometimes discover that, unbeknownst to the therapists, some family members are engaging in behaviors (e.g., drug dealing) outside the sessions and laughing up their sleeves about how they have duped their shrinks. When they find this out, the therapists feel betrayed and ask themselves, "Is the effort worth it when there are so many workable situations I can put my energy into?"

Years of practice with families of every income level have done much to dispel my old omnipotent fantasies about being able to help all the families I see. I don't know whether or not the Sloans are untreatable, I do know that I would not treat them. My decision has nothing to do with their socioeconomic level. I have seen families that I concluded were untreatable (by me) in all populations and class levels. The fact is that my own intergenerational approach, where adults meet with parents and siblings to deal with the hard issues between them, requires a minimal amount of motivation, honesty, and cooperation. The description in this case suggests none of these characteristics are present in the Sloans.

At the present time, I supervise and teach students who are on the front lines, seeing difficult families like the Sloans. I try to help these students develop a treatment philosophy that can guide them in this challenging work. I emphasize the difference between the therapist's view of what is therapeutic and the family's perspective. I encourage them to understand the family's world and its values. I press them to look for the strengths and resources in the family. I always ask, "Where is the father?" and try to counteract the tendency of many young therapists to exclude fathers from treatment.

But in addition to helping students find more effective ways to treat difficult cases, I also try to help them decide when it is advisable to let a case go. I sometimes quote an old family-therapist friend, Oscar Weiner, who used to say, "You can't want more for people than they want for themselves." For myself, I try not to remember another old saying: "Those who can, do. Those who can't, teach."

Commentary and Analysis: The Eight Pragmatic Perspectives

The Sloan family clearly presents daunting challenges to the child welfare, mental health, and education systems. In contrast to the two commentaries presented in the journal, the following commentary views the family situation from a broad child welfare perspective, using the eight pragmatic perspectives to clarify and focus the work with the family.

Pragmatic Perspective 1: Combating Adultcentrism. Both the therapists and the commentators displayed high levels of adultcentrism with respect to this family. There is no indication that any of the children were interviewed individually to obtain their input and perspectives on the problems. The conclusion that the children "were all acting out their fear of losing Amy" is an interpretation that appears to be based on the therapists' orientation and predisposition rather than on clinical interviews with the children. Neither of the commentaries addressed the importance of understanding the children's perspectives. Commentary 1 paid some attention to the experience of the children in suggesting that it was important for them to get the message that the family problems were not their fault. But the suggestion that the children would receive this message if they were removed from the home is based on an entirely adultcentric assumption about how children feel. Some children may experience removal as an indication of their parents' culpability, but many others may see it as confirmation that they themselves were responsible for the breakup of the family. Tom, whose behavior has gotten him in trouble with school and law enforcement authorities, in not likely to view his removal as reflecting on his mother's parenting, and, in any case, probably should not be encouraged to excuse his behavior in such a fashion. Young children are especially inclined to idealize their parents and disinclined to blame their parents for anything, so the assumption that they would view their removal as evidence of parent incapacity is highly questionable.

The way to combat adultcentrism with the Sloans would be to encourage maximum participation and involvement of the children in the pro-

cess. This would include individual attention and interviews for each of the children in the household. For Tom, a focus on loss and grief issues might be appropriate, but so might a focus on negotiation, communication, and assuming responsibility in the household. Interventions should be based, in part, on the perspective, temperament, and point of view of the individual child, and not solely on the parent or therapist's preconceived notions about why children behave the way they do. In addition, combating adultcentrism would involve focusing on the children's strengths and capabilities, none of which were mentioned by the therapists or the commentators. More on how the therapists could have operationalized the strengths perspective with these children is offered below under pragmatic perspective 3.

Pragmatic Perspective 2: Family-Centered Practice. The reader will recall that family-centered practice involves three central elements: the family as the unit of attention, maximizing family choice, and a strengths perspective.

Clearly, the therapists and the commentators viewed the family as the unit of attention. The children's issues and needs were viewed in the context of their family, not in isolation. Yet, initially, the boundaries of the family were somewhat narrowly defined as the traditional nuclear family. Despite early indications that extended family, especially Mae, the grandmother, were highly involved with the children and mother, the therapists did not expand the boundaries of the unit of attention until later in the process, after several incidents in which Mae was directly involved. Even then, there is little indication that extended-family members other than Mae were brought into the process. Also, as Framo astutely asked in commentary 2, "Where is the father?" A boyfriend and father figure, Bob, is mentioned at the beginning of the case, but his role in the therapy process is never clearly identified. Also, the fathers of the younger children are not mentioned, and Amy's father is not involved in the process. It appears that the therapists unduly limited the unit of attention to the exclusion of some very important potential resources.

Regarding the element of maximizing family choice, the therapists had many opportunities to attend to this element, but largely ignored those opportunities. In the beginning, they could have asked Amy, Bob, and the children to identify the significant players in the extended family constellation who should be involved in the process. In effect, the family could have been given the opportunity to define its own boundaries and voice opinions about who should be involved. Instead, the therapists showed a clear bias in favor of a nuclear family structure and unduly criticized the negative aspects of extended family involvement without considering the potential positive aspects. Family members also could have been asked to identify their needs and goals for the therapy. Instead, the therapists appeared to define the "core issues" with little indication as to whether or not the family agreed with the assessment. The narrative does indicate that Amy was primarily concerned about Tom's behavior, but what were the views of other family members on the presenting problem, and did the family agree that the "real" issues were loss and grief related? Framo, in commentary 2, acknowledges some of these same concerns in calling for those who work with these types of families to understand the family's world and its values, and to be aware that there is a difference between the therapist's view of what is therapeutic and the family's perspective.

Finally, neither the therapists nor the commentators considered the potential strengths in this family. Like many professionals in the field, they were deficiency oriented and failed even to attempt to identify or utilize strengths in the family. For example, the therapists appeared to view the extended family's involvement in the nuclear family as having only pathological consequences for the family due to the "enmeshment" and lack of appropriate boundaries, without consideration of possible positive effects that could accrue from the closeness, support, and potential resources that could be tapped and developed.

Pragmatic Perspective 3: Strengths Perspective. As mentioned above, a lack of a strengths perspective was apparent in the discussion of this case, at both the child and family levels. The case narrative and commentaries are excellent educational tools to demonstrate how thoroughly the pathological deficiency model permeates the thinking of many professionals.

At the child level, the adultcentric tendency to view children as inadequate or incompetent, and thus primarily in need of socialization and social control, was evident in the narrative. Granted, Tom had serious behavioral problems that demanded attention and remediation, but is Tom to be defined solely and purely as an acting-out child? What are his interests, strengths, aspirations, and competencies? Does he have friends? What does he have going for him? Is he good at art, sports, computers, or music? What does he hope to be when he grows up, and how does he plan to get there?

Most important, a solutions-focused perspective would focus on the times when Tom has *not* been in trouble, the times when he has been relatively successful, and attempt to find solutions in these exceptions to the problem. The same applies to all of the other children—what strengths and resources have they used to cope with the situation, when have they been successful, and what was different about those times?

At the family level, therapists missed several opportunities to explore strengths and build on exceptions to problems. Even in this limited, deficiency-oriented narrative, one can find at least four instances of clues to strengths and exceptions that could be more actively explored. For example, it is important to note that this is a *voluntary* client system, referred by a Head Start social worker. The mother, Amy, is concerned about her son's behavior and has asked for help. Compared to other situations with *involuntary* clients, there is a level of motivation here that should be noted, acknowledged, and nurtured. Second, the therapists note that Mae, the grandmother, has "only recently" been able to "cut the apron strings" with her own mother. In the reported context of enmeshment and poor boundaries, isn't this a positive sign and a significant change? Instead of denigrating the accomplishment by referring to as occurring "only recently," could not this be viewed as an incredible achievement, as a strength which Mae could build on in her relationships with her own children? If enmeshment is a problem, and Mae has some experience with *solving* the problem, could that experience not be shared as a model for the rest of the family? Third, the therapists note that Amy reports that Tom minds his grandmother, Mae, but not Amy. The therapists appear to view this as a deficiency. Could it not be viewed as a strength and as an exception? Isn't this information about Tom's capability, as well as about strength in the family system? Tom *can* behave in some situations, and someone within the family system knows how to help him do that. Fourth, the therapists note, almost parenthetically, that Mae and Amy's father have successfully dealt with previous alcoholism—Mae by joining Al-Anon and the father by joining AA and stopping drinking. But rather than viewing these events as strengths and successes, the therapists somehow manage to frame them as deficits by noting, "substance abuse is a long-standing problem." Perhaps it is more accurate, and productive, to say that "substance abuse is a long-standing problem that some members of the family have been able to successfully conquer."

Pragmatic Perspective 4: Respect for Diversity and Difference. This is a Caucasian family, so issues regarding respect and diversity for minority cultures do not apply in this case. However, pretend that the family was reported to be African American, Native American, Hispanic, or Asian American. With this change in the description of the family, would anything change in the approach to the family, in the way that the problems were understood, or the interventions? What should the therapists do to respect diversity and difference if this were a minority-race family? For example, would it be advisable to have a therapist of the same race as the family? Would issues of power and disenfranchisement, as discussed by Pinderhughes and summarized in chapter 4, be an appropriate focus of the work? If this were a minority-race family, would (should) the role of the extended family be viewed more positively—would (should) the so-called enmeshment and lack of boundaries be viewed differently?

Pragmatic Perspective 5: Least Restrictive Alternative. This perspective is highly relevant to the analysis of this case, because this is the type of family that is seen in many intensive family preservation services (IFPS) programs. The recommendation for out-of-home placement, made by the authors of commentary 1, reflects the thinking of many professionals and the general public when confronted with families such as the Sloans.

In graduate courses that this author has taught, and in which this case example was used, fully half of the students in some classes have supported placement of the children. Commentary 1 reflects the values and hopes of many professionals regarding the value of foster care and residential treatment—that removal of the children will spur the parents to change, and that the placement will be therapeutic for the children.

But, ignoring for the moment that there is no reported physical abuse or sexual abuse of the children, that the specific nature and severity of neglect has not been established, that the removal of the children guarantees neither parental change nor better conditions for the children, and that the children would most likely be split up to different foster and group homes, the important question, under the Adoption Assistance and Child Welfare Act of 1980 (P.L. 96-272), is "Were reasonable efforts made to maintain these children in their own family?" Consideration of placement and foster care should not be made until reasonable efforts to prevent placement have been made.

So, knowing only what has been presented in the narrative about the case, what would constitute reasonable efforts for the Sloans, and were they being made? To answer this question, one must first determine what the problem is that is placing the children at risk for out-of-home placement. As Framo states in commentary 2, "I might even have considered placing the children elsewhere—although this is a step I never undertake without evidence of severe child abuse." Since there is no indication of physical abuse or sexual abuse, a case for removal would have to be made on the basis of emotional abuse or neglect. The narrative reports a high level of violence in the home, and although none of the violence is reported to be directed at the children, a case could be made that exposure of the children to that violence constitutes emotional or psychological abuse. As far as neglect is concerned, a case could be made that the children, especially Tom, lack adequate parental supervision, but there is not enough information to judge about medical, educational, or physical neglect. Clearly, Tom needs more structure, discipline, and parental supervision to get his behavior under control. So a case can be made for the children being at risk for out-of-home placement due to the emotional abuse accompanying the violence in the home, and due to the neglect inherent in the lack of adequate parental supervision.

Given this information, the reasonable efforts to prevent placement should then focus on reducing or eliminating violence in the family and on developing adequate supervision of the children, especially Tom. In this light, it is interesting to note that the focus of the therapists on grief and loss issues as the "core issues" would be appropriate only if grief and loss directly related to the violence or the lack of parental supervision. A case could certainly be made that there is a direct relationship. But other explanations and interventions could also be appropriate, including some of those suggested by Framo, such as coordination of the efforts of all the service professionals, referrals to drug treatment programs, and parenting skills classes. In addition, anger management therapy or training, respite care, attendant care for Tom, and IFPS services could be components of a reasonable efforts case plan. As a final resort, voluntary placement of the children with other relatives could be attempted to avoid state custody. Unless more of these services had been attempted than was indicated, and unless the extent of abuse and neglect was more severe than reported, it would be appropriate to institute more thorough reasonable efforts before removing the children.

Pragmatic Perspective 6: Ecological Perspective. The narrative is not specific about the number and types of services the Sloans were receiving from various agencies in the community, but it is implied that they did participate in a substantial number. Construction of an ecomap with the family could help the worker and families organize these many contacts and relationships into some more ordered picture that could help reduce the sense of chaos in the family's relationships with outsiders.

In addition, the ecomap might reveal successful informal supports that could be built upon, and identify relationships with significant others that needed particular focus and attention. After mapping out the existing and needed informal supports and formal services, a case manager could be employed to help the family negotiate all of the systems involved and coordinate the efforts of all of the service providers, in a fashion similar to the "social network sessions" Framo mentions. Part of this case management activity could involve systems advocacy for the family or individuals within the family. For instance, Tom and Amy might need help in obtaining special educational services for Tom, who might qualify for these services but might not have received them to date.

These case management activities would be included in the reasonable efforts plan, particularly as they applied directly to the two major problems identified in the previous section that were placing the children at risk for out-of-home placement: violence in the home and supervision of the children. Attendant care, a service which matches a child in need of supervision with an adult paraprofessional for certain times of the day and week, is one possible service a case manager could arrange to help keep Tom out of trouble at those times in which he is most vulnerable. Another service that might be needed is inpatient drug and alcohol treatment for mother Amy, because her drug use may be interfering with her ability to parent Tom and the other children. Ideally, in a family-centered approach, Amy and the younger children would be admitted together to the treatment facility, so that the relationships can be strengthened rather than weakened during the period of treatment.

Pragmatic Perspective 7: Organization and Financing. Extensive information about the level and extent of community services is not provided in the narrative, but it is implied that the family benefits from various categorical services delivered by different agencies and professionals, in an uncoordinated fashion. The payment source for the mental health therapists themselves is not provided either, but because this is a poor family, we can assume that they are not paying out of pocket, that there is grant support from some source for the therapists' time.

For our purposes, let's suppose that the Sloan family has come to the attention of the child welfare authorities, and that a case plan has been written to deliver an array of services in the spirit of reasonable efforts to prevent removal of the five children. These services would focus on two related goals: (1) reducing violence in the home through intensive, in-home family preservation services and anger management training, and (2) securing adequate supervision of the children,

especially Tom, through IFPS parental skills training, attendant care, and drug treatment for the
mother (either outpatient or inpatient, depending on results of drug/alcohol evaluation). (With
more information about the family gained from
the ecomap, many more services might well be included, but for the sake of simplicity, we'll proceed
with those mentioned.) The reasonable efforts case
plan, in abbreviated fashion, might look something
like the following.

Reasonable Efforts Case Plan for the Sloan Family (abbreviated)

I. Problems/issues related to abuse and/or neglect that place the children at risk for
placement:

Problem 1: Extensive violence in the family, though not directed at the children.

Problem 2: Lack of adequate parental supervision of children, especially Tom, related
in part to drug abuse by the mother.

II. Services planned to address the problems:

Problem 1: (a) IFPS to provide family therapy to identify roots of violence and develop
alternative coping behaviors; (b) anger management training for several
family members through group classes provided at mental health center.

Problem 2: (a) IFPS to provide parenting skills training for parents to learn effective
ways to structure and supervise children's activities. IFPS and parents
will observe and talk with Mae to discover how she gets Tom to behave;
(b) attendant care to provide supervision to Tom at his most vulnerable
times; (c) drug/alcohol evaluation for Amy, with follow-up outpatient
or inpatient treatment, as recommended. Parents of Amy will offer
suggestions based on how they have successfully overcome and coped
with alcoholism; (d) IFPS and family will identify natural resources within
extended family and community to model parenting skills and to provide
supervision for kids.

III. Strengths to build on:

1. Clients, including mother Amy, have voluntarily sought help.
2. Tom behaves when Mae is watching him.
3. Some members of the family have been able to overcome alcoholism.
4. Mae has improved her relationship with her own mother, which may help her in
her relationship with her daughter.

As previously mentioned, the actual case plan
might well involve many more services and supports than those listed above. But even considering the basic list above, who will provide those
services and how will they be paid for? Will the
services be organized under one roof, for easy access by the family? Will they be coordinated so
that the family experiences the total impact of the
whole range of services rather than each separate
service in relatively impotent isolation? The family, being at or near the poverty level, cannot be
expected to pay for all of the services, so how are
they to be financed?

If the state has flexibility in the use of its foster
care dollars, some or all of these services can be
paid for through reallocation of foster care dollars.
Rather than use the foster care allocation to support
the five Sloan children in out-of-home placement,
this money can be used instead to pay for the services that support them safely in their own home.
These flexible dollars could be expended in one of
three ways: direct provision of the services by the
state, purchase-of-service contracting (POSC) on
an individual service basis, or POSC on a capitated
basis.

Under the first option, the state itself would

provide the services and employ the staff necessary to deliver the services. The state would have "in-house" IFPS, anger management training groups, attendant care, and drug and alcohol services. Because the services would be provided by the state, they would be considered public social services. The second two options would be considered forms of privatization. Under the first privatization option, the state social worker would refer the Sloan family to individual and separate private agencies that provide IFPS, anger management, attendant care, and drug/alcohol services. Each of the services would be paid for separately, on a fee-for-service basis, under billing procedures established by the state. Under the second privatization option, the state would contract with one private agency to provide whatever services referred families needed and reimburse the agency a set fee per family for a given period of time. Under this capitation option, the private agency would have an array of services and providers available and would pay for them from the pooled, capitated amount they received from the state for each and all of the families referred. Some families would need more services and some less, but, unlike a fee-for-service POSC, the private agency would have to manage the pooled, capitated amount so that all families received what they needed under the POSC contract. The three ways to organize and finance these services are depicted in figure 12.1.

Pragmatic Perspective 8: Achieving Outcomes. With the Sloan family, as with all other clients, success should be measured by whether or not the desired outcomes were achieved. In this case, then, it follows that the plan outlined above would be judged successful if (1) the children remained at home and (2) the children were no longer neglected in terms of violence in the home and lack of supervision.

The first goal appears to be a simple one to measure: either the children stay with their family or they are removed to state custody. But the situation is really not quite so dichotomous. What if the children go to live with extended family, but do not come into custody? What if Tom enters inpatient psychiatric treatment for several days? In some states, a child can come into state custody but not be removed from the home—the custody allows for greater levels of supervision and

agency involvement. Each of these three options lies somewhere between the overly simplified dichotomous options, and researchers and clinicians must consider them in any accounting of success.

Regarding the second goal, the tendency toward dichotomous thinking can complicate matters here as well. Most likely, the end result of the helping efforts will be not the absence of violence, nor perfect parenting. Somehow, a standard of "good enough" parenting must be established, not a standard of perfect or ideal parenting. Is it realistic for the measurable objective in the case plan to be no violence of any kind, ever? No, a realistic goal would be for some significant reduction in the level of violence. Or is it realistic to think that Tom will never get into any trouble at school or with the law, that he will be supervised at all times, and that Amy will learn how to effectively parent him at all times? No, again, a more realistic goal is for some level of improvement in these areas.

Looking at success as a continuum, rather than as a dichotomy, allows for realistic goals to be established and for people thus to experience success. But even when the standard is realistic, it may still be difficult to measure progress. Will the level of violence in the home be measured from self-report of the family, by the observation of professionals, or by the number of police calls to the home? Will the level of supervision and parental competence be measured by self-report, direct observation by professionals, or the number of reports to child welfare for lack of supervision?

Because these final outcomes are so difficult to measure validly, it is tempting for the professionals to look to the process (intermediate) variables for indications of success, rather than at the final outcomes. The process variables for the violence in the family might be the motivation and cooperation of the parents—did they attend anger management classes and did they work with IFPS on the problems? Likewise for the parental supervision issues. In the original narrative, grief and loss issues were hypothesized to be the "core issues." If the family were to deal directly with these, then that would be another indication of achieving success with an intermediate outcome, and the professionals might have more faith that the violence and lack of supervision would subside. If drug use was believed to be a direct impediment to adequate parenting, then completion of drug treatment might be

FIGURE 12.1
Organization and Financing of Sloan Family Reasonable Efforts Case Plan.

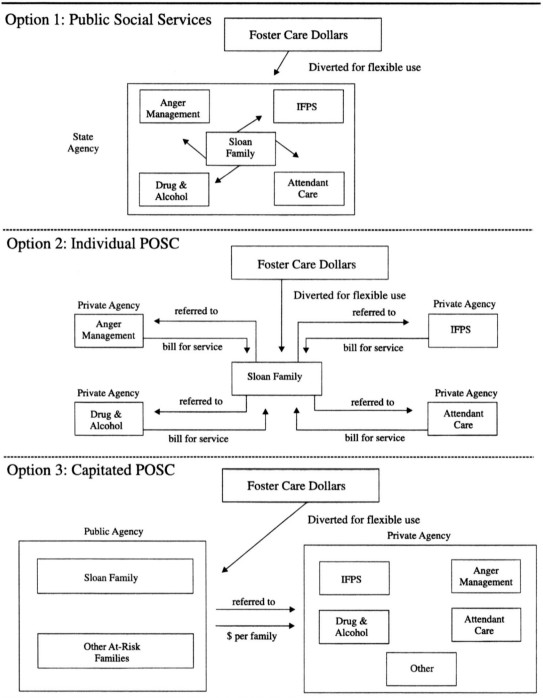

viewed as the end result, rather than as a means to accomplish the goal.

In the real, pragmatic world, then, success in the case plan will be judged in a relative sense. Did the family try hard and did they make some progress? Are the children at less risk of neglect than when the services started? Is there substantially less violence in the home? But there may be no clear-cut answers to these questions, because different professionals and family members may disagree about how hard somebody tried, how much progress was made, or whether a certain level of reduction in violence was "substantial." This ambiguity and difference of opinion are two of the factors that make child welfare work so challenging.

It is interesting to speculate about whether or not the Sloan family might have benefited from a primary prevention program, before the problems became so complex and difficult to treat. What if, at the time Tom was born, Amy had received home visits from a program designed to prevent the occurrence of child abuse and neglect, like those described in the preceding chapter. If Amy had received early help in parenting, been educated about community resources, and been offered early help with drug and alcohol, could the problems described in the narrative have been averted?

Case Example 2: Victor

This case example centers on issues related to reunification of children in state custody. As the case demonstrates, successful reunification can be a complex, time-consuming process with many complex decision points. The case illustrates how the pragmatic perspectives can help the worker make purposeful decisions and how they can provide an overall structure and organization that adds clarity and direction to those decisions.

Narrative

Overview. Victor was an 11-year-old African American male placed in state custody because of a combination of physical abuse on the part of his mother, Anita, and her inability to control and supervise Victor. Victor displayed many defiant behaviors, including refusing to do chores or look after his two younger siblings, smoking cigarettes, being out late at night without parent permission, and disobeying school rules, which resulted in several in-school suspensions and detentions. (Victor and his family also have numerous strengths, which will be discussed in later paragraphs.) According to Anita, she used physical punishment (hitting with a belt) only as a last resort after all else had failed, including a brief hospitalization in the psychiatric ward of the local hospital. On three occasions, school personnel reported bruises to child welfare authorities, who confirmed abuse on all three occasions. After the first report, intensive in-home family preservation services were initiated to prevent placement, but after the second and third incidents, when Victor displayed extreme anger at Anita and Anita did not think she herself could control her own anger, it was decided Victor's safety could not be assured in the home. Temporary state custody was obtained in court and the state instituted aggressive reintegration efforts through its specialized, in-house reunification program. The case was assigned to Brenda, herself an African American with several years experience in child welfare and reunification.

Background. Brenda learned that Victor was the oldest of Anita's four children, each of whom had different fathers. The other children were Amanda, 8, Rasheed, 6, and Cynthia, 3. Victor's own father's whereabouts were unknown, and the fathers of each of his younger siblings had lived with the family several months or years after the birth of each of the siblings. Victor had gotten along fairly well with the last one, Michael, who still lived in the community but had limited contact with Victor and the other children. Michael and Anita had split up a year ago, and Anita was currently involved with a man named Jerome, whom Victor had met only a few times.

Brenda also learned that Victor was extremely intelligent, having tested in the gifted range at school. He also had demonstrated musical talent and loved rap music. Anita had a strong employment history, having worked as an LPN at a local hospital for the last 5 years. She aspired to return to school to become an RN. Jerome was a mechanic who attended church regularly, and he had convinced Anita to join the church as well. Amanda and Rasheed did well at school and had no special education needs, but did get into trouble occasionally. Cynthia was home or at the sitter's during the day, and had chronic health problems that necessitated regular visits to health care professionals.

Support from Anita's extended family was limited. Her only brother lived in a different state, and she and her parents, who lived in a neighboring town, were in constant conflict. Anita's parents were very religious and criticized Anita for her instability with men and her use of alcohol. Despite the constant conflict, Anita believed in the importance of her children knowing their grandparents, and she and her family visited the grandparents regularly.

Case Plan. Victor had been placed temporarily in an emergency shelter and was waiting for a placement in a foster home or group home when Brenda began work on the case. Brenda took control of this placement process, deciding that Victor would be best served in a group home within the community, based on several complicating factors. There was an African American foster family willing to take Victor in another region of the state, about 150 miles away. The group home had white houseparents and mostly white staff and white children, so the decision was a difficult one for Brenda. The mother, Anita, had preferred the group home, while Victor himself had requested an African American foster family, and preferred that option even though it would mean that he would see his mother and siblings less often. Another complicating factor was that Victor stated that his first choice was to live with his grandparents. While Victor was still in the emergency shelter, Brenda had explored this option but found that the grandparents were reluctant to take on this responsibility due to their age and poor health. Also, Anita was vehemently opposed to this option because she felt her parents would turn Victor against her. Brenda ultimately opted for the group home because its close proximity allowed for frequent visits between Anita and Victor, and because Victor would not have to change schools.

Brenda's first step was to write a case plan establishing goals and objectives that all of the parties could agree to. The state's goal was reintegration, which Anita wanted as well, but Victor was so angry with his mother for the abuse and the hospitalization that he stated he never wanted to live with her again. He also reported that she drank all the time and he was tired of having to deal with so many different men intruding into the family. The grandparents were ambivalent: they wanted Victor to live with his mother, but only if she changed. They hinted that if reintegration failed, they would take Victor, but they were not direct or clear on this point.

Given this situation, Brenda decided that reintegration was the appropriate immediate goal, and that living with the grandparents would be the second choice if reintegration failed. Knowing that reunification involved more than physical reintegration, Brenda made plans with the group home for frequent visits between Victor and his family, and between Victor and his grandparents, to maintain emotional connections. To achieve the goal of reintegration with Anita, the following objectives and methods for achieving the objectives were agreed to in the case plan:

Victor's Case Plan

1. Anita will learn to parent without violence. This objective will be accomplished through attending Effective Black Parenting classes and working with Brenda in the home. Success in achieving this objective will be demonstrated in Anita's parenting of the younger children, during home visits and during a trial reintegration period.

2. Since Anita's parenting ability is adversely affected by her alcohol abuse, Anita will cease all drinking. This objective will be accomplished through outpatient drug counseling and attendance at weekly AA meetings. Success will be demonstrated by Anita's sobriety as attested to by family, friends, employer, and others.

3. Victor will work on his anger at his mother. This will be accomplished through individual work with Brenda and joint meetings with Brenda and his mother. Success will be demonstrated when he is able to make a commitment to trying to live with her again.

4. Victor will maintain emotional connections to his mother, siblings, and grandparents through regular visits, arranged by the group home at times that do not conflict with group home structure and activities.

5. Victor will improve his behavior with respect to obeying adults, including his mother and school authorities. This objective will be accomplished through a point and level system at the group home, special education intervention at the school, and in the parenting work that Anita undertakes with Effective Black Parenting classes and her work with Brenda. Success will be documented by attaining the highest level at the group home, having no suspensions or detentions at school, and obeying Anita's rules to her satisfaction during visits home.

6. All of the professionals will acknowledge and build on strengths within the family. These strengths include their ability to participate in decision making, Victor's intelligence and musical talents, Anita's employment history, and the level of motivation of all concerned.

The target date for reintegration was set at 6 months from the time of removal from the home. Reintegration was eventually achieved, but not until a full year had elapsed. Progress in the case was compromised by many different factors, as is discussed in the following paragraphs.

Case Progress: First 3 Months. In the first 3 months, progress was substantial, to the point that Anita felt ready to take Victor back and Brenda seriously considered recommending that Victor return to his mother's care. Regarding the first two goals, Anita did quite well, but it seemed that nobody except Brenda believed the change was for real or would last. Anita completed the Effective Black Parenting classes with distinction, as the instructors made special note of her participation, motivation, and investment. Brenda had observed much improvement in Anita's parenting of the younger children, although Anita acknowledged that it was much harder to control her anger when Brenda was not present. Anita also attended outpatient alcohol counseling and AA meetings, with no reports of drunkenness.

Victor also made early progress, but it was not enough for the professionals involved to recommend that he go home. In relation to the anger at his mother, after several weeks of refusing to meet with Anita, he had begun to work directly on his anger with Brenda in individual and family sessions. He talked about the physical punishment and how humiliated and powerless he had felt. He also talked about his anger at the brief hospitalization, which he felt he had been tricked into and during which he felt like an imprisoned criminal. He had been forced to take medication and had been placed in restraints and seclusion for brief periods during his 2-week stay.

To his credit, Victor had been able to express this directly to his mother in joint sessions, and she had responded quite appropriately, acknowledging that the abuse was wrong and that she understood his feelings about the hospitalization. Victor talked also about his anger at her choice of men and her alcoholism, articulating his concerns in a way that demonstrated his intellectual intelligence and psychological insight. Brenda complimented Victor on his ability to communicate clearly and also praised Anita for having taught him how to express himself so well. While hearing Victor out and validating his feelings, Anita at the same time made it clear that she was trying hard to change and that she would still expect that Victor follow the rules. She also let Victor know that she was continuing her relationship with Jerome, and that he and Victor would have to learn to get along. Although the anger was subsiding and Victor was allowing discussion of his return home, he continued to adamantly oppose reintegration.

Victor's behavior at the group home and school had only recently begun to improve. He initially rebelled against the point and level system, accusing the group home staff of being prejudiced against him. When Brenda looked into the accusation, the group home vehemently denied any prejudicial treatment. However, Brenda helped them see that the root of Victor's complaints lay in his feelings of disconnectedness to the African American community, so the group home agreed to allow Victor to participate in a weekend group for young African American males, and they connected him with an African American Big Brother through the local Big Brother/Big Sister organization. These compromises helped take the edge off Victor's defiant attitude, and he began to earn more points in the level system.

At school, the special education staff was slow to evaluate Victor for BD (behavior disordered) services. He had previously been tested as gifted, but had not been evaluated for BD services. At the end of three months, the evaluation had been completed and an Individual Education Plan (IEP) had been set in place that combined gifted and behavioral disordered services. In the meantime, however, Victor had continued to act up and had received four detentions and two in-school suspensions.

The visitations for Victor with his mother and grandparents did not go according to schedule. The group home insisted that home visits were an earned privilege, and Victor seldom had earned the points necessary. Instead of home visits, the group home allowed relatives to visit at the home, but these were generally brief and irregular, due to difficulties in coordinating everybody's schedules and transportation.

First CRB Hearing. In that community, the juvenile court judge had begun an "early review" of children placed into state custody through citizen review boards (CRBs). The CRB would review progress and make recommendations for changes

in the case plan at 3 months and 6-month intervals thereafter. So, at the end of 3 months, Brenda reviewed the progress in the case and struggled with what to recommend at the CRB hearing. On the one hand, Anita had made tremendous progress, and Brenda believed that she was serious about changing. Her relationship with Jerome was much more solid than previous relationships, she was parenting the children better, she was maintaining sobriety, and she was interacting with appropriate empathy and boundaries with Victor. On the other hand, there had been few home visits to test the situation, Anita's progress might prove to be short-lived, Victor was still refusing to go home, and Victor's behavior had only recently begun to improve.

At the CRB hearing, all of the people involved in the case gave their opinions about progress toward reunification. Anita documented her own progress and requested that Victor return home immediately. She felt that he would be safe and that she could deal with his anger and misbehavior with the help of Jerome and Brenda. Victor spoke loudly of his anger at his mother and said he refused to go home. The grandparents said they thought Victor was a "good boy" and that Anita had not really changed. They complained that they did not get to see Victor very often, and that it was difficult for them to travel to the group home at their age. The group home staff recommended at least 6 more months of care, stating that Victor needed time to successfully complete their program. The volunteer Court Appointed Special Advocate (CASA) recommended continued placement because she wanted Anita to demonstrate change over a longer period of time. The school personnel reported on Victor's behavior and the results of their evaluation, but had no opinion about whether or not he should return home.

Brenda decided to recommend increased home visits and continuation of the reintegration plan, with an eye to physical reintegration within 3 to 6 months. Her main rationale for delay was not that she distrusted that Anita had really changed, nor that she was concerned about Victor's continued behavior problems, but most of all because Victor was still so angry at his mother. Brenda feared that if the system forced Victor to return home, he would run away and/or rebel so defiantly that he would have to return to foster care. Brenda wanted to give things just a little more time to come together so the family could experience success with the reintegration.

The CRB recommended, and the judge later concurred, that Victor remain in foster care, with the goal of physical reintegration by the next CRB hearing in 6 months. They noted the progress that Anita had made and encouraged her to continue it. They recommended more frequent and intensive family counseling, and more frequent visits home. They admonished Victor for remaining so defiant, and urged him to "get with the program."

Case Progress: Months 4 to 9. During the 6 months between CRB hearings, progress was mixed. Both Anita and Victor experienced ups and downs that necessitated changes in the case plan.

Initially, Anita was quite disappointed with the CRB's recommendation and judge's decision, to the extent that she returned to some of her previous behaviors. She canceled several appointments with Brenda, she missed AA meetings and alcohol counseling sessions, and she reverted to use of physical punishment with the younger children. During this time, child welfare's protective services received two reports that Anita was neglecting the health needs of Cynthia, the 3-year-old. After several weeks of this behavior, Brenda was able to have a long talk with Anita, during which Anita tearfully expressed her anger, disappointment, and feelings of powerlessness after the CRB hearing. Brenda validated those feelings and talked with her about how she could regain some feelings of control and influence. Anita wanted increased visits with Victor, more family sessions to include Jerome (whom she was planning to marry), more support from her parents, who she felt had influence over Victor and could help him be less angry at her, and more involvement with the school in developing an educational plan for Victor.

Anita also felt that she and Victor were receiving too many conflicting messages from all the service providers regarding how to deal with Victor's behavior. The group home and school targeted different behaviors and used different consequences, while the CASA and school staff were telling Anita that she should never spank her children or use any form of physical discipline. Brenda supported these concerns and suggested that Anita

could, with Brenda's help, arrange and chair a conference in which she discussed these issues with Brenda, Victor, the CASA, Victor's grandparents, group home staff, and school staff. Anita was uncomfortable with such a large meeting, but she did meet separately with her parents, group home staff, and school staff to discuss her wishes and concerns. Brenda attended all of these meetings and arranged child care for the other children so that Anita could attend. She assisted Anita in saying what she wanted to say, but she made it clear to Brenda and the other staff members that Anita had called the meeting and was in charge.

Even though Anita did not get all of the changes she wanted, the process empowered her and she soon regained all of the lost ground in parenting and alcohol counseling. Brenda agreed to increased family sessions that focused on (1) Victor communicating in words when he is upset rather than being sullen or acting out his anger, (2) Victor developing a relationship with Jerome, in which Jerome's role was not to be the disciplinarian, and (3) Victor spending adequate time with Anita to rebuild the relationship on a more positive foundation. The meeting with the group home achieved only partial results, because the group home refused to allow home visits regardless of Victor's behavior. However, they did allow more visits at the residence and they supported more frequent family sessions.

The meeting between Anita and Victor's grandparents also had mixed results. The grandparents were only able to criticize Anita in her presence, but individually with Brenda, they were able to hear and trust the progress that Brenda reported, and they understood the need for them to actively encourage Victor to work toward going home. With this support from the grandparents, and with continued direct communication between Victor and Anita and Anita's appropriate responses, Victor's anger subsided and he signed on to the reintegration goal about 2 months after the CRB hearing.

The meeting with the school staff achieved creative and positive results. Anita reviewed the IEP, questioning the rigid behavior modification program that had been developed. While Anita understood the need for this type of programming to some extent, she did not feel that Victor was responding to this approach very well at the group home. She asked that the school re-evaluate Victor, spending more time observing his behavior and attempting to discover what he responded to. In the course of doing this, the school discovered that Victor was much less of a behavior problem when he was intellectually challenged and engaged, and that he never was a behavior problem was he was involved in music activities. As a result of this discovery, the school personnel were able to devise an educational program that integrated music and intellectual challenges more fully into his instruction, and this decreased the number of behavioral incidents.

Second CRB Hearing. By the second CRB hearing, several weekend home visits had gone successfully and Brenda was more confident that reintegration would succeed. Anita had maintained her sobriety, she had continued to demonstrate adequate parenting skills (although she still spanked the children with an open hand occasionally), and she and Jerome had gotten married. Although there were still issues to be worked out in the family, Brenda felt that it was safe for Victor to return. Some recent new developments increased the risk and stress in the family: Anita was due to have a baby in 2 months, both Anita and Jerome had lost their jobs, and their car was broken down. Also, while Victor had done well at school, he had never reached the highest level at the group home, because his behavior there was still problematic. Despite these less than ideal circumstances, Brenda strongly recommended immediate return home.

Concurring with this recommendation were the grandparents and Victor himself. However, the CASA and the group home staff strongly recommended that there needed to be a longer transition time. They wanted weekend visits to be continued and extended to allow for adjustment to the new baby, for at least one of the parents to regain employment, for the car to get fixed, and for Victor to reach the highest level at the group home. The CASA also felt that Anita should not have custody until she had stopped the use of physical punishment altogether. Although Brenda argued that the current situation (unemployment, pregnancy, use of physical punishment, and level of Victor's misbehavior) would not be cause for removal from the home, and thus should delay reintegration, the CRB agreed with the CASA and group home parents (except on the physical punishment issue),

stating that a cautious approach was in order. In that state, a child could not be returned home without court approval, so Brenda and the family had no choice but to delay reintegration.

Despite their disappointment and anger, Brenda and the family were able to continue the progress; Jerome got a job, the car was fixed, and the baby was born healthy. Victor never did reach the highest level at the group home, but the judge approved Victor's going home 3 months after the second CRB hearing, which was 1 year after placement. This created some hard feelings between Brenda and the group home staff, who let Brenda know that she should no longer consider the group home a placement resource for her foster children. Overall, Brenda was relieved that the family was able to maintain progress and overcome their disappointment, because she had known of families who had pretty much given up when they felt that the system had overoptimistic expectations.

Commentary and Analysis: The Eight Pragmatic Perspectives

Hopefully, in reading the narrative of this case, the reader was able to identify pragmatic ways in which some of the pragmatic perspectives applied. This commentary discusses how the eight pragmatic perspectives guided or affected the decisions and progress in the case.

Pragmatic Perspective 1: Combating Adultcentrism. Several examples of adultcentrism, and efforts to combat adultcentrism, are evident in this case narrative.

Adultcentric attitudes were most displayed by the group home staff and school personnel, whose strict behavior modification approach emphasized social control and minimized Victor's strengths and abilities. Clearly, some degree of socialization was called for to address Victor's behaviors, but a balance between socialization and self-determination was absent. Brenda and Anita were able to get the school to modify its IEP, but the group home's program was so institutionalized and applicable to all of the residents that they were unable to individualize the program for Victor. This hard-line approach served only to intensify Victor's opposition, as he felt he could not back down or save face.

The reader may have mistakenly identified Brenda's decision to place Victor in a group home, rather than with the grandparents or the foster home, which were Victor's preferences, as an example of adultcentrism. There are limits on self-determination, and combating adultcentrism does not mean doing whatever the child wants in all cases. What it does mean is seeking out the perspective of the child, seriously considering it, and explaining the ultimate decision. This is what Brenda did, so she was not acting in adultcentric fashion when she placed him in the group home.

An outstanding illustration of combating adultcentrism was evident in the way that Brenda patiently dealt with Victor's anger about the abuse/hospitalization and his initial refusal to go home. Essentially, she used active listening techniques to validate his feelings without approving of his ultimate decision. Her approach exemplified the idea that the helper accepts, but does not necessarily approve. While patiently listening to Victor's anger, Brenda remained completely neutral on the issue of whether or not he should or would return home. Rather than saying, "I understand that you are angry, but you just have to go home, and that's final," Brenda, through her words and actions, said, "I understand that you are angry and that you do not want to go home. I can see how you would feel that way." If Victor asked specifically about whether or not he had to go home, Brenda would reply, "I know you really don't want to. I also know that your mother really wants you to try. It's hard for me to know what's best." She also afforded Victor some choice about meeting with his mother to discuss the issue. If Victor had refused over a long period of time to meet with his mother, Brenda might have needed to be more insistent that he give it a try, but her initial approach of maximizing Victor's self determination worked for him, so that more heavy-handed approaches were not necessary.

Of course, it is impossible to predict whether a more forceful, adultcentric approach would have achieved reintegration faster or not. At the 3-month CRB hearing, Brenda's judgment was that forcing Victor would be too risky—this might achieve earlier reintegration, but one that was tenuous and fragile and that could lead to a longer stay in foster care in the long run. It is also possible, as Anita had asserted, that Victor would

have adjusted well despite being forced to return home.

Pragmatic Perspective 2: Family-Centered Practice. For the most part, Brenda was strongly family-centered in her approach. Her strong support for reunification—including physical reintegration with the mother, community placement near the mother, and frequent visits to promote emotional connectedness—was the foundation for her active family-centered approach.

Brenda listened to Anita when she indicated that her own parents and her fiancé, Jerome, needed to be involved and included in the unit of attention. An even more complete and thorough family-centered approach would have been to ask Anita and Victor whether either of them wanted for the biological father or Michael, the most recent stepfather, or any significant others such as clergy or neighbors, to be involved.

The element of maximizing family choice was also evident in Brenda's approach, although, as with combating adultcentrism, there were limits to the extent of self-determination. Brenda sought Anita's involvement and opinions about a wide range of subjects and decisions, but Anita did not always get what she wanted. The most dramatic example of this was when Brenda and the CRB decided that Victor would not return home after the first 3 months, despite Anita's strong desire that he do so. The safety of the child was Brenda's primary concern, and this concern took precedence over the principle of maximizing family choice. Also, since Victor must be considered a member of the family, there was no consensus among all family members about which choice was best.

Pragmatic Perspective 3: Strengths Perspective. With both Victor and Anita, a strengths perspective was critical to successful resolution of the case.

With Victor, Brenda operationalized a strengths perspective in her validation of his perspective, in her belief that he was a competent and capable person who could form valid opinions about his situation. She communicated a belief in his ability to improve his behavior and recognized his expressed need to visit frequently with his grandparents. She pointed out his strengths and helped the school make use of those strengths in his educational plan. Also, as will be discussed more in the next subsection, Brenda listened to Victor's complaints about discrimination by the group home parents and helped him rectify the situation. Other workers might have dismissed his concerns as the whining of a child who wasn't getting something he wanted.

With Anita, Brenda supported her early changes in sobriety and parenting, and, unlike Anita's parents and others, expressed confidence that she could maintain the changes. Most importantly, Brenda helped Anita believe in herself and take control of the situation by encouraging her to assert her concerns about the case plan and progress to all of those involved, and to be in charge of the meetings with professionals. The reader should be cautioned that not all parents would be ready to assume this level of assertiveness and responsibility, and some might experience a worker's encouragement as quite *dis*empowering. It is a misapplication of the strengths perspective to insist that a client exploit a strength or ability that they truly do not have. But in this case, Anita had the motivation and the capacity, with Brenda's support, to take charge of an area of her life in which she had felt quite powerless.

Pragmatic Perspective 4: Respect for Diversity and Difference. Respect for diversity and difference guided practice in the matching of worker and client, the handling of the accusations of discrimination at the group home, the approach to physical discipline and referral to Effective Black Parenting, and the way in which Anita was encouraged to reverse long-standing feelings of victimization.

At the beginning of the reunification effort, trust and rapport between the worker and client were more readily established because both the mother, Anita, and the worker, Brenda, were African American females. This is not to say that such a match guaranteed trust and rapport, or that a white male could not have established trust and rapport. But in most cases, it is easier for clients to develop trust and rapport with people who have had similar experiences. It is not *necessary* to have been an alcoholic to work with alcoholics, or to have been a parent to work with parents, or to be Native American to work with Native Americans, but it is often preferred. Ideally, Anita would have been given some choice about this in the beginning, but

staffing realities often narrow choice in matching clients with workers.

When Victor complained that the group home staff was treating him differently than the other children because of his race, Brenda took those complaints seriously and discussed them with the staff. Brenda was not able to confirm the accusations, but she was able to use the occasion as an opportunity to address Victor's identity development as it related to his racial heritage. The weekend group and Big Brother were intended to help Victor solidify a positive identification as an African American male.

Physical discipline had been a long-standing practice in Anita's family, as it is in many African American families. Brenda respected this cultural practice not by insisting that all physical discipline cease, but by helping Anita learn new skills that could supplement the physical discipline and assign it to be used as a last resort. The Effective Black Parenting curriculum also reinforced this approach. (See chapter 7 for a description of Effective Black Parenting.)

When Anita expressed her feelings of disappointment and powerlessness in the face of the CRB decision for Victor to remain in custody, Brenda and Anita discovered that the roots of these feelings lay in the racism and sexism that Anita had experienced as an African American female. By helping Anita assert herself and her needs with respect to Victor and his care, Brenda helped Anita to influence more than just the immediate situation. Brenda hoped that his experience would generalize to other situations as well, so that Anita would be able to exert influence and control in other areas of her life.

Pragmatic Perspective 5: Least Restrictive Alternative. As was discussed in previous chapters, the least restrictive alternative principle is a driving force in federal legislation that sets child welfare policy, and in child welfare practice. Initiation of placement prevention services for Victor and his family, reunification services, and consideration of the least restrictive living situation are consistent with this principle.

A group home placement for Victor was not, strictly speaking, the least restrictive alternative. Placement with relatives or in a foster family are less restrictive options than a group home, and both of these options were available to Brenda. However, as explained above, placement with the grandparents of foster family would have necessitated placement outside the community and a change in schools for Victor. Placement with the grandparents also would have been in direct contradiction of the mother's wishes. This case illustrates the complexity of placement decisions and is a testimony against the blind and inflexible application of any one principle to child welfare decisions. In this case, in Brenda's professional judgment, Victor's needs related to stability (school and community) and frequent contact with his mother outweighed his needs for placement with relatives or a family of the same race. If the grandparents had lived in the community and gotten along well with the mother, or if a same-race foster family could have been found in the community, Brenda's decision may have been different.

Given the same situation, another worker might have opted for placement with the grandparents or the foster family. There is no one right decision in situations like this, for each has a positive and a negative side. Certainly there was a downside to the decision that Brenda made. The group home was indeed a more restrictive setting because of its rules and its level system. Victor did not adapt particularly well to this setting, and visits between Victor and his family were less frequent than hoped for. The racial mismatch also created tension, and Brenda had to intervene regarding Victor's claims of discrimination. But there also would have been a downside to placement with the grandparents or the African American foster family. This case illustrates how no one practice principle can take absolute precedence in decision making. Ideally, one would like to secure placement in the least restrictive alternative, placement in the community, placement with relatives, and placement in the same race and culture, but in the real world, it is not always possible to accomplish all of these with one placement.

Pragmatic Perspective 6: Ecological Perspective. The initial reunification case plan reflected the importance of the environment in lives of Victor and his family. Brenda assumed some case management functions in referring Victor to the group home, arranging for visits, connecting Anita with Effective Black Parenting and alcohol

counseling, and facilitating communication between Brenda and the service providers. She also attempted to see that the services were coordinated; for example, she made sure that the behavioral programs for Victor initiated by the group home, school, and mother were similar and not operating in contradiction to each other. Brenda engaged in systems advocacy when she encouraged Anita to meet with various providers and assert her need for changes in how the system was treating her and Victor. The larger environment was also represented in community participation in the CRB and CASA activities.

Because there were so many services and extended family members involved, the situation was ripe for triangulation. Brenda had to make sure that communication channels were open, else one or another of the providers could have worked at counter-purposes or undermined the efforts of the other. For example, when Anita expressed dissatisfaction with the different approaches to dealing with Victor's behaviors, the group home could have discredited the school program and undermined their efforts, or vice versa. Instead, a joint meeting resulted in clearer identification of target behaviors and similar consequences. With respect to the issue of Anita using physical punishment, the CASA and school staff could have continued to criticize Anita, which would have undermined her authority and credibility with Victor. Instead, they listened to Anita, Brenda, and the Effective Black Parenting teacher and did not triangulate with Victor against his mother.

In all of these collaborative efforts, the most tension for Brenda, and the most difficult situation to avoid triangulation, was in the relationships among herself, Victor, and the group home staff. Brenda found that she disagreed with the group home on several issues, but she did not want to criticize the group home parents in front of Victor for fear of undermining their authority with him. When Victor accused the group home of discrimination, she tended to agree with Victor, but she did not want to alienate the houseparents by publicly stating this. In this instance she was able to focus on a common, related issue of Victor's identity development, which defused the situation and helped the parties work toward a mutual goal. Regarding visitation, Brenda knew that the houseparents would not budge on the issue of home visits being contingent on Victor's behavior, and that she, Victor, and Anita would have to live with it. The only alternative was to place Victor elsewhere, and even if there had been viable alternatives, the move would have disrupted Victor's fragile sense of stability. Rather than bemoan the group home's policy to Anita and Victor, Brenda quietly accepted it (without openly approving of it) and encouraged the family to do likewise.

With respect to the issue of Victor returning home, Brenda had to publicly disagree with the houseparents, who then claimed that her lack of support was causing conflict between them and Victor: "How can we now expect him to behave and progress in the level system, when he says he'll be going home anyway, so why bother!" Brenda had previously met with the houseparents privately, trying to reach a compromise about the expectations and timetable for return home, but had not succeeded. Brenda realized that this was one of the "turf" battles between group homes and state child welfare officials that hopefully would be resolved at a higher policy level. The "turf" issue boiled down to the question of who was in control, reflecting a fundamental difference between the child-centered philosophy of the private, nonprofit group homes and the family-centered philosophy and reunification agenda of the state child welfare agency. Resolution of the conflict could depend on reform in the organization and financing of group home services, as described in the next subsection.

Pragmatic Perspective 7: Organization and Financing. The different services provided in this case were provided by different agencies in different locations by different staff members. One of the reasons Brenda did not recommend and arrange for even more services was that this would have involved more to coordinate and more opinions to deal with, as well as more appointments for the family to keep. Because Brenda herself was able to provide family and individual counseling, these services did not have to be arranged separately. All of the services were paid through various means and resources. The Effective Black Parenting classes were supported by a foundation grant, so Anita had only to pay a small registration fee. Anita's alcohol counseling was paid for, in part, by her insurance through work, and in part by Anita herself by way of a sliding-fee scale.

Brenda's own services were supported by a federal/state grant. The services at the school were provided at no cost to the family through special education funding. The group home was paid on a per-diem basis by the state under a long-standing POSC arrangement.

Change in the organization and financing of group home placements is one way to resolve the conflict between group homes and child welfare discussed in the previous subsection. In this conflict, the state's emphasis on family reintegration runs counter to the group homes' emphasis on child treatment and rehabilitation. The key to resolving this conflict would be to structure the financing of services so that the state's goals and the means of financing services are consistent and compatible, not contradictory. In the above situation, in which group homes are paid a per-diem rate for the care of the children, the financial incentive is for long-term treatment. Financially speaking, the discharge of a child from a group home threatens the group home's very survival, because it does not get paid for empty beds. Thus, the child-focused, child-treatment philosophy is reinforced by the financing mechanism. To change the group home philosophy toward its own family-centered, reunification philosophy, the state may need to change the way it finances group care, so that the financial incentives are more in line with the philosophy.

Several options are open to the state in this regard. First, it could retain the POSC on an individual-child basis, but guarantee the group home a certain number of days of care, or a certain total amount of financial support, so that the group home would not lose money if beds were not full. Rather than reimburse per child per day, the group home might be awarded a block amount under a standing contract to serve a set number of children. Another option would be for the state to operate its own group homes with state employees. The group home would operate under a budget, no immediate penalty would result if beds were not always full, workers would be trained in family-centered practice and reunification, and in this manner the state could bring the organization and financing in line with the philosophy.

A third, more radical approach to resolving the conflict would be a privatized, managed care approach to foster care. This way of reorganizing and refinancing the foster care system is currently being pioneered in the state of Kansas. Under the privatized, managed care approach, foster care services, including residential group home care, are contracted to a single private agency. The state pays the contractee a certain amount of dollars per child for the care of that child, whether that child stays in care for 1 day or 5 years. Thus, similar to managed care, reimbursement is capitated and the contractee must provide the full range of services, including residential group care and reunification services, for all referred children for the capitated amount. The budget for the private agency is thus determined by the pooled dollars from each child in care. The financial incentives in this type of reorganization are similar to those for managed health care. The incentive for the agency is to provide care in the least restrictive (also the least expensive) alternative: in foster family homes and in the child's family of origin. Such an emphasis could harbinger a resurgence of foster parenting, in that the private agency might pay more to foster parents because it would still cost less than group homes. Since care in group homes and residential treatment facilities is so expensive and thus such a drain on the pooled budget, it does not behoove the organization to keep children for long periods of time in expensive placements. Reunification, foster family homes, and adoptions are the most cost-effective ways to use the pooled dollars. However, the dangers and disadvantages of approach are similar to managed care in health and mental health. With so much emphasis on less expensive care, will children who need more expensive care actually receive it? Will children be returned too fast to unsafe family situations? Will cost-cutting measures of the agency reduce the level of quality of the care provided in the more expensive options?

Pragmatic Perspective 8: Achieving Outcomes. The desired outcomes in this case were specified in the reunification plan, as listed above in the narrative. The overall goal of physical reintegration

stemmed directly from the mandates of P.L. 96-272. This goal was achieved in 1 year, which was twice as long as originally planned.

To achieve the overall goal, most of the five original objectives were met. The mother, Anita, demonstrated the ability to learn new parenting skills and to apply them to her other children as well as to Victor. She also was able to maintain sobriety, which was on the case plan because it directly related to her parenting ability. If Anita had been able to drink without it contributing to her abusive behavior, then it would have been inappropriate for this objective to have been on the reintegration plan. The objective of frequent visits to assure emotional connections to mother and grandparents was only partially met, as these were more infrequent than planned. For his part, Victor was able to overcome his anger at his mother and to improve his behavior to some extent.

A strength of this case was the way in which Brenda was able to focus everyone on the goal of reintegration and on ameliorating the conditions and factors that led to removal. She did not allow extraneous or unrelated issues to dominate, despite the perspectives of the CASA, group home staff, and some members of the CRB. A minor weakness in the case plan was the linking of Victor's behavior at school to reintegration. Victor was not, and probably never would have been, removed from home because of his behavior at school. Although Victor's general behavior stemmed in part from lack of adequate supervision and structure from his mother, Anita, it is questionable whether Anita should be held accountable for his behavior at school, where she is not directly involved in his supervision. This situation reflects the tendency for professionals to add standards and increase expectations once a child is removed. Sure, we want abused kids to do their homework and behave at school, but should that be a condition for their going back home? Or might such a condition foster the child's sense that there is something wrong with him or her, that he or she was to blame for the breakup of the family?

CHAPTER 13

Connections: Case Examples from Children's Mental Health

Overview

This chapter presents in-depth analyses of two case examples of social work with children and families in mental health settings. As in chapter 12, a narrative describes the child, family, and developments in the case over time. Then the narrative is critiqued and analyzed, using the eight pragmatic perspectives to conceptualize the practice and policy aspects of the case. The reader is reminded that these extended case examples are intended to reflect the real world of social work. Thus, mistakes are made, conflicts arise and are not completely resolved, and not all goals are fully achieved.

The two case examples differ in the seriousness of the presenting problem and the level and intensity of services. The first case example about Bill illustrates the early identification and treatment function of outpatient mental health services. Problems with a young child are identified and ameliorated so that more serious problems are hopefully prevented from occurring at a later time. In the second case example regarding Sharon, a seriously depressed, suicidal teenager and her family receive a variety of services and supports over several months to improve and maintain her functioning.

Case Example 1: Bill

This case example concerns the mental health of a 5-year-old boy having behavioral problems at home and at school. The setting is the children's division of the outpatient department of a local mental health center. A key to successful intervention is the way in which the therapist frames and conceptualizes the issues and then involves the significant adults in modifying the child's environment so that his needs are better met.

Overview and Narrative

Presenting Problems and Identifying Information. Bill is a 5-year-old biracial child who was brought by his mother and stepfather to see Jon at the mental health center because of increasing aggressiveness at school and home. Bill attends a day care center in the mornings (the same one he has attended since age 3), and a public school kindergarten in the afternoons. For the last several weeks, according to the parents, Bill has been getting in serious physical fights with two other children at the day care center and three other children at public school kindergarten in the afternoons. At home, Bill has begun to talk back to and argue with his stepfather, Joe, attempting to bite and kick him on two occasions.

Bill's mother, Francine, who is white, and father, Don, who is African American, were divorced when Bill was a little over 1 year old. Frances married Joe, her second husband, who is white, 2 years ago. Don was remarried to Coreen, who is African American, 3 years ago, and they have a 1-year-old girl, Samantha. Bill has no other siblings.

Assessment Phase. Francine phoned for the initial "intake" appointment at the mental health center and gave the above information over the phone. Jon began the assessment process by interviewing the family (Bill, Francine, and Joe) altogether for about 30 minutes, then interviewing Bill individually for almost an hour. In the family interview, Jon asked each person about his or her perspectives and concerns. Francine began by reiterating the above concerns about Bill's behavior. Joe con-

curred and added that he and Bill had not gotten along particularly well ever since he married Francine. Bill was fairly quiet in the family interview but did acknowledge that he was getting in trouble at school a lot lately and that he didn't like it when he got so mad. Both Francine and Joe were able to list strengths and positive qualities they saw in Bill—he is imaginative, smart, and funny. The family meeting ended with a mutually agreed upon plan for the assessment and information-gathering phase: Jon would meet alone with Bill that day, then with Francine and Joe alone the following week to get more information. In the meantime, Jon asked and obtained permission to contact both the day care center and the kindergarten teacher to obtain their perspectives. Jon also asked if it would be helpful and advisable for him to talk with Don and Corona, but Francine preferred to wait on this.

In the individual interview with Bill, Jon asked open-ended questions to elicit responses that helped Jon form hypotheses for understanding Bill and the roots of Bill's behavior. A partial transcript of the interview follows.

JON: I want to play sort of a game with you, where I ask you some questions about all sorts of stuff and you just answer whatever you want. It's not a test; there aren't any right or wrong answers. It goes like this: If you had three wishes, and all three wishes could come true, what would you wish for?

BILL: (Takes his time, thinks for a while, glancing at Joe several times) That my birthday was every day.

JON: OK. I'm going to write these down so I don't forget them. What would be your second wish?

BILL: That I wouldn't have to go to school every day.

JON: OK. And the third wish?

BILL: (Pauses, then brightens, smiles, and talks faster) To have a real baby alligator and he'd never grow up to be a big one.

JON: OK. Now, here's a new one. If you had a million dollars, and you could do with it whatever you wanted, what would you do with it?

BILL: Ummmm . . . Spend it so I could rent a movie and I'd be in the movie.

JOE: Tell me again? I'm not sure I got that.

BILL: Well, you know, like you rent movies and give them to a friend and I'd be in the movie.

JOE: OK, I got it. Now, if you could be anything you wanted to be when you grow up, what would you be?

BILL: (Quickly) A doctor. I always wanted to be a doctor.

JON: OK. How come?

BILL: Because it's good health to be a doctor.

JON: I see. Doctors are pretty healthy people?

BILL: Yes!

JON: OK. Now here's a different question. What is the best thing that ever happened to you in your whole life?

BILL: (Pause, looking thoughtful) You mean the neatest thing?

JON: Yeah, the best, neatest thing that ever happened.

BILL: (Pause, looking up to Jon) When somebody else's house caught on fire and I could go watch it on fire.

JON: Ummmm. Can you tell me more about that?

BILL: (Nods, but diverts eyes and attention to a toy.)

JON: Like, did this happen in your neighborhood?

BILL: (Shrugs, continues to play with toy, doesn't answer.)

JON: OK. Well, so what is the worst thing that ever happened to you, the very baddest and awfulest thing?

BILL: (Somewhat slowly and tentatively) When I spilled milk and it stuck to my shoes and my Mom didn't like it.

JON: Oh, I see. What happened next?

BILL: (Quiet voice, smiling, almost a question) She spanked me.

JON: She spanked you. I noticed that you're almost laughing when you say that.

BILL: (Deep breath and grinning) Yeah, that's kind of a joke. I made that up. Are you going to tell my parents what I say?

JON: (Surprised and caught off guard) Well, usually I tell them what we talk about, because they are your parents and all. Do you want me to tell them everything?

BILL: (Shrugs, looks away, begins to play with a stuffed rabbit.)

JON: OK. Well, let's see here if there's more questions I want to ask. Sometimes, when I ask kids what's the worst thing that ever happened to them, you know what they say? If their parents have gotten a divorce? Some of the kids say that the divorce was the worst thing that happened.

BILL: (Stops playing with the rabbit, looks thoughtful.)

JON: Of course, other kids say it was the best thing because their parents were always fighting and stuff.

BILL: (Quiet) Ummm. Fighting a lot. (Begins to play with the stuffed rabbit.) This rabbit needs its diaper changed—it peed all over itself!

JON: (Redirecting) What do you think about your parents getting a divorce?

BILL: (Settles down, pause) Kind of sad.

JON: Yeah. Lots of kids feel that way. Lots of them feel mad and other things too.

BILL: (Pause) You want to hear something horrible?

JON: You want to tell me something horrible?

BILL: (Nodding.) I hate Joe. (Nervous laugh and smiling.)

JON: (Slowly) You say you hate Joe. And you are smiling and kind of laughing. I'm mixed up. I don't understand.

BILL: No, I do hate Joe. It's true.

JON: I see. How come?

BILL: Because he's fat and has a beard and I don't like that.

JON: OK. So do you want to tell me more?

BILL: Well, it's a secret. I only told you.

JON: Uh huh. And do you want me to keep the secret?

BILL: I thought you said you had to tell my parents what we talk about.

JON: Well, sometimes I do and sometimes I don't. I'm not sure whether you do or don't want me to tell them about this.

BILL: (Nods and then begins playing with puppets and stuffed animals, who are fighting and needing changes in their diapers.)

JON: So did you decide about whether you want me to tell your parents?

BILL: (Ignores question and continues to play.)

JON: I see that you are wanting to play some more but our time is almost up. I need to talk a few minutes with your parents before you all go. How about if I tell them that you and I talked and one of the things we talked about was all the changes from the divorce and how you are having a hard time adjusting to all the new people and everything?

BILL: OK. And I wish I didn't have to go back and forth between my mom and dad's houses so much.

JON: OK. Do you want to stay here while I talk to your parents or should I talk with them alone?

BILL: Stay here.

Jon had another appointment waiting so was able to meet with the family for only about 5 minutes. He told Francine and Joe that he would talk with them more about their perspective and about what he and Bill had discussed when they came back for the next appointment.

That night, Jon received a phone call from Joe stating that he and Francine needed a crisis appointment the next day. On the way home in the car, Bill had suddenly announced that he hated Joe and that he didn't want to stay at his Mom's house. This led to a heated discussion between Joe and Francine about their divergent parenting styles and the conflicts they have about disciplining and parenting Bill. Jon talked with Joe briefly on the phone, asked that he and Francine not talk any further that night so that they could cool off, and scheduled an appointment for early the next day.

Before this appointment, Jon considered what he had learned from Bill and this incident that might help him understand the presenting problem. From the interview with Bill, there were indications that Bill was struggling with developmental issues involved with new transitions and expectations that accompany entering public school. Specifically, Bill stated that one of his wishes was to not have to go to school. Also, he wished for a baby alligator that would never grow up, a possible reflection of his view of himself. There were also indications that Bill felt stressed by the visitation schedule and that he experienced his relationship with Joe as conflict-filled and problematic. Apparently, Bill had, with considerable ambivalence, hoped that Jon would somehow let Francine and Joe know his feelings and communicate his concerns. Jon felt he had made a mistake in not being more tuned in to this issue and wished he had had more time with Bill to have figured out a better response. When Jon did not do what Bill had apparently hoped, Bill decided to "let the cat out of the bag" himself on the car ride home. Jon was not sure how to understand some of Bill's other responses, especially his comments about watching the house on fire as the best (neatest) thing that had ever happened to him, and the retracted comment about his mother spanking him over spilled milk. Finally, Jon noted that many of Bill's responses indicated an age-appropriate egocentrism—wanting to have a birthday everyday and wanting to be an actor or central character in a movie.

In the meeting with Francine and Joe, Jon hoped to understand their parenting conflicts better, especially any link there might be to the presenting problem behavior. He also planned to share his impressions of Bill, share his uncertainty about the meaning and context of the fire and spanking comments, and obtain more information about the divorce and the current custody/visitation arrangements. He hoped that Francine and Joe could provide insights and clarification about how best to understand Bill's behavior and how best to proceed.

During the meeting with Francine and Joe, they began by sharing the history and nature of their parenting relationship. Francine felt that her own style was strong on nurturance and fostering of creativity, and that she had perhaps been too permissive with Bill during the time between the divorce and the marriage to Joe. She tended to view Joe as adding needed limits and discipline to Bill's life, but she felt he was sometimes too strict and controlling. Joe agreed that he felt in the disciplinary role and that Bill needed to grow up and quit acting like such a baby. Apparently, the night before, Francine had threatened divorce if Joe did not modify his stance with Bill, and Joe felt anxious about this threat. Getting these issues out on the table seemed to relieve the tension somewhat, and both parents agreed that they wanted to work out their parenting differences and stay married.

Jon also learned that relations were strained between Francine and Don and their spouses. The divorce agreement was for joint custody, with Bill staying about half the time at each household. Each week and weekends were split, so that Bill went back and forth between households every week, and had been doing this for 3 years. Francine and Don also were in conflict over how Bill was to be raised regarding racial identity: Don wanted Bill to be raised with a strong African American cultural and racial identity, while Francine hoped Bill could develop a biracial identity that integrated both white and African American values and culture.

Jon shared data and impressions from his interview with Bill, asking Francine and Joe for help in understanding Bill's comments about the house on fire and the spanking. They reported that, to their knowledge, Bill had never witnessed a house burning, nor had he seen a movie with that content recently. They noted that Bill had an intense level of imagination, and that he often played by himself for hours, inventing imaginary games and stories that he sometimes became so involved in that he seemed to have trouble reorienting to the world. Perhaps the story of the house on fire reflected

of his intense imagination. Francine denied ever having spanked Bill for spilling his milk or for anything else. Joe acknowledged having spanked Bill with his open hand on a few occasions, but never over spilled milk. Perhaps Bill's comment reflected his concern over the potential consequences of his recent misbehavior.

At this point, Jon and the family agreed to the following plan. Jon would finish the assessment phase of the work by talking with school personnel at both the day care center and the regular school, by meeting again with Bill individually, and by meeting with Don and Corona. In the meantime, because of the acute conflict between Joe and Francine regarding parenting, Jon scheduled two appointments within the next week to address their conflicts in parenting.

Jon learned the following information from the school personnel. The day care center teacher confirmed that Bill had been coming to the center for several years, and that his behavior had become a problem only in the last few weeks. She described Bill as a quiet child who usually preferred to play by himself, creating imaginary games and stories. In the last few weeks, conflicts with other kids broke out during group activity times, when the staff organized games and activities focused on the children's social development. At the public school, the kindergarten teacher described Bill as one of the most immature of her students. He had a hard time sitting still in class, listening to and carrying out directions, and playing with other kids. He tended to be singled out and teased by other kids during recess, and he sometimes responded with anger and aggression when they didn't leave him alone. Bill also had been hostile to the teacher, sometimes ignoring her, other times talking back and loudly refusing to do what he was asked. Both teachers were able to list Bill's strengths of intelligence and creativity, although the kindergarten teacher did so only after some hesitation.

From Bill's father, Don, and stepmother, Corona, Jon learned that Don was quite dissatisfied with the custody arrangement. He wanted full residential custody, as he believed that Bill needed a stronger sense of permanence and his own home was more stable and predictable than Francine's. Don said that Bill did not display any angry or aggressive behaviors when at Don's house. He believed that the aggression at home and school was not as bad as reported, and that a firm and consistent response was all that was needed to correct it. Don confirmed that he wanted Bill to be raised in an environment that more fully honored and celebrated his African American heritage, but voiced doubt that Jon, being white, would understand or appreciate that concern.

The second interview with Bill was dominated by themes similar to the first interview. During the free-play time, Bill initiated play with the stuffed animals, who consistently got into trouble, were punished, and then became babies who needed their diapers changed. During talk time, Bill reiterated his negative feelings about Joe, but said he did not want to live all the time at Don's because he would miss his mother.

In the two crisis meetings with Francine and Joe, Jon was able to help them move toward resolution of their parenting conflicts. The strategy involved each moving toward the other in parenting style and working harder to present a united front. Francine resolved to be more active in disciplining Bill, and Joe agreed to take a back seat in this regard, taking the role of Francine's behind-the-scenes "coach" regarding discipline. When Bill acted up, they agreed to jointly decide what the consequence should be, and have Francine implement and enforce the consequences. Joe would let Bill know that he agreed with Francine, and that she was in charge. Meanwhile, Joe would work on developing a more positive relationship with Bill, finding ways and times to play and interact with Bill in fun ways rather than interacting only around discipline. In this endeavor, Francine would act as Joe's coach, as she was deemed the expert on how to nurture, stimulate, and have fun with kids. Jon was thus able to turn negatives into positives: Joe was viewed not as a harsh, rigid disciplinarian but as the authority on discipline who could share and teach his knowledge to Francine; Francine was viewed not as a permissive, indulgent parent but as the authority on how to develop positive relationships with kids. Each could help the other move toward a more well-rounded parenting approach. This general strategy was suggested by Jon, and after asking questions and modifying several details, the parents agreed.

Intervention Plan. With the above information in hand, Jon used the assessment guidelines for avoiding blame (presented in chapter 6) with Francine and Joe to arrive at a mutual understanding of the presenting problem (Bill's aggression) and a plan for addressing the problem. The assessment phase of the process is intended to answer the question "Why at this particular time is this particular child engaging in this behavior?" The intervention plan is then based on this understanding.

The first level of understanding on the assessment guide is consideration of the presenting problem as a behavior within the normal range of functioning for children of that age and culture. Jon, Francine, and Joe all agreed that Bill's behavior was more aggressive than the norm—the teachers both had noted the "abnormal" nature of the behavior. Jon noted that Don and Corona differed on this point, but he agreed that Bill's aggression was serious enough to attend to.

The second question to consider is whether Bill was "born that way"—whether temperament and constitutional makeup play a part in the behavior. This level of understanding was also ruled out, as Bill seemed normally to be a quiet and introspective child, not physically active or aggressive.

The third level of understanding is consideration of Bill's behavior as a learned behavior. Has the behavior been modeled or reinforced in any way? There was no indication of a pattern of aggression or violence in either Francine or Don's household, nor at the school settings, and both sets of parents restricted Bill's exposure to violence on TV and movies, so the modeling hypothesis did not seem relevant. As regards reinforcement, Bill was receiving added attention (albeit negative attention) as a result of the behaviors, and the consequences for the misbehavior were different at home, school, and the day care center. But Bill, as an only child, received lots of positive attention regardless of his behavior, so it was difficult to view attention as the "reward" for the misbehavior. Improvements in the consistency and immediacy of consequences in the various settings were needed, although these were not seen as the primary focus of intervention.

The fourth level of understanding, viewing the behavior as reflective of an adjustment issue, had considerable merit. Developmentally, Bill was at a stage in which he was asked to be more grown-up, while he himself seemed to prefer to remain a younger child, who, like the alligator, never grew up. He was inclined toward solitary play and imaginary games, while most children his age were more interested in playing with other kids and being physically active. Situationally, Bill was continuing to cope with a divorce situation that was becoming more difficult to adjust to in positive ways. His frequent changes in residence between his mother's and father's were not helping him establish a sense of permanence and consistency, and conflicts with Joe had been increasing. It seemed reasonable to Jon and the parents that Bill's aggressive behavior could reflect his increasing frustration at dealing with these adjustment issues.

The fifth level of understanding did not seem to apply in Bill's case. There was no history of severe trauma that could account for the increased aggressive behavior at this time. Although the separation and divorce could have been experienced as a traumatic event, Bill now seemed more focused on the current adjustment issues relative to the divorce, rather than the original event.

Thus, Jon and the family were able to frame the presenting problem in a context that helped them understand the behavior and led them to strategies for resolving the behavior. In order not to excuse the behavior, part of the intervention plan focused on the behavior itself and on consistent consequences for the misbehavior. But the primary interventions focused on the developmental and divorce adjustment issues that were seen to be driving the behavior. The plan, then, consisted of the following.

Intervention Plan for Bill's Aggressive Behavior

Goal: Reduce or eliminate Bill's inappropriate aggression at home and school

Objectives to Achieve Goal:

1. Address developmental adjustment issues. Bill needed to be gently but consistently encouraged to leave childhood behind and experience the positives of "growing up." Perhaps adults had not appreciated how hard this would be for Bill, so a more concerted and gentle approach was called for. Using Bill's creativity and smarts, adults could help him make connections with other children with similar strengths and interests. Parents could make a more concerted effort to have Bill invite other kids over to play. Bill could be assigned household chores and responsibilities commensurate with his age, receiving an allowance in return.

2. Address divorce adjustment issues. Francine and Don agreed to meet with Jon to attempt to work out a new custody/visitation arrangement that afforded Bill a greater sense of stability and permanence. Francine and Joe agreed to continue to address their parenting conflicts, so that Bill experienced less conflict and a more unified approach to his behavior. Finally, individual play therapy for Bill was recommended to help him express and integrate his feelings about both the developmental and divorce adjustment issues.

3. Address specific behavior. As part of their work with Jon, Joe and Francine would work to establish clear limits and consequences for Bill's misbehavior, and rewards for desired behavior. Jon would also coordinate with the day care center, the public school teacher, and the school social worker so that Bill experienced similar consequences in different settings.

This plan viewed Bill's behavior as a complex and multifaceted problem that required interventions on several fronts: individual work with Bill, parenting work with Francine and Joe, divorce work with Francine and Don, and case coordination with the two different schools.

Progress and Outcome. Sufficient progress was made on all the objectives so that within 6 months, and a total of 20 face-to-face sessions, complaints about Bill's aggression had ceased and mental health counseling was terminated.

On the developmental front, Bill responded well to the initiation of allowance for chores. At both Francine and Don's households, Bill was put in charge of picking up his room, taking out small sacks of trash and garbage, and helping to dry the dishes on occasion. For these chores, he received $2 a week. The parents and schoolteacher were able to find a computer class for children his age where he met two new friends. In addition, the parents enrolled Bill in a karate class, which served both to channel his aggression into an appropriate form and structure as well as to provide opportunities for social interaction. Bill was shy and reluctant to participate at first, so Joe agreed to enroll with Bill in a parent-child class, and this activity became a primary source of fun for the two.

On the parenting front, Francine and Joe were able to continue their progress in parenting. It was difficult for each to change parenting styles, and Jon had to help them understand the difference between coaching and preaching, but both were satisfied with the improvements. Meetings between Francine and Don were tense, as Don initially insisted on full custody. When Francine remained firm and Don's lawyer advised him that he did not have strong grounds for full custody, they were able to work out a new arrangement for joint custody. Under this new arrangement, Bill stayed for nine weeks at one residence, with visits to the other family every other weekend. The summer was split into six-week intervals. Bill himself did not fully comprehend the time frames involved, but was delighted that he would not have to go back and forth so often. Francine also agreed to do more to expose Bill to African American culture, including allowing Don to take Bill to his church every Sunday.

Regarding the specific aggressive behavior, Francine and Joe were able to agree on consequences that Francine then implemented. The consequences involved losing TV time and access to favorite toys. The parents were careful not to implement consequences that contradicted other objectives: they did not restrict Bill from computer or karate class or from time with Joe; they did not restrict him to his room, where he would be reinforced for solitary, fantasy play; and they did not assign him extra chores, which would have muddled the positive thrust and intent of the chores. If Bill was aggressive at school, the school initiated time out, informed the parents, and the parents initiated a consequence at home as well. Although Francine was agreeable to initiate a reward system for not being aggressive at school, Joe and the teachers objected that this seemed too much like a bribe, and that rewards should be reserved for behavior that is exceptional, not that minimally conforms to acceptable standards. In the end, they decided to delay a reward system until the effect of the consequences for misbehavior could be assessed. Although the teachers were too busy to complete detailed behavioral scales on Bill, they reported reduced problems, especially after the first 6 weeks of work with the families. Since Don and Corona said they did not experience behavior problems with Bill, they were not pressured to coordinate consequences with Francine or the school.

Although individual therapy had been recommended, the family and Jon were not able to implement this recommendation due to the financial cost and the priority placed on the other interventions. For several weeks, Jon met weekly with Francine and Joe as well as with Francine and Don, so that there seemed to be little time or money for individual therapy. Jon did "check in" with Bill on an individual basis on four occasions during the 6 months, so Jon was able to monitor how Bill was experiencing the interventions.

At school, a new development that occurred after about 3 months required considerable energy and cooperation among the parents, Jon, and school personnel. The kindergarten teacher recommended that the parents enroll Bill in a transition first grade classroom, called T-1. In that school district, children who seemed not quite ready for first grade due to delayed social, emotional, or intellectual development could enroll in the T-1 classroom without being officially classified as special education students. In smaller classes with individualized attention, the idea was that these children could receive the help they needed to succeed in the first grade. Bill was recommended because of his social and emotional, not intellectual, development. Francine and Don had several meetings with the school and with each other to weigh the pros and cons of the recommendation. At first they rejected the idea because of the potential stigma and because Bill was intellectually capable. But after visiting the T-1 classroom and visiting more with the teachers, they opted to enroll Bill in T-1 for the next academic year. Bill himself expressed a preference for regular class, but the parents explained their reasoning and their belief that a child at his age should not have the ultimate say in such a decision.

Commentary and Analysis: Eight Pragmatic Perspectives

Pragmatic Perspective 1: Combating Adultcentrism. Adultcentrism was manifested in this case in several ways. First and foremost, the entry of the child into the public school system signaled a new and intense focus on socialization and mild forms of social control. Bill was expected to sit in his chair, follow rules and schedules, and behave in a more adult manner than he had been expected to at home or at preschool. Little allowance had been made for his unique, individual situation and level of development: all the children in kindergarten were expected to conform to the adult rules and standards, demonstrating that a principal purpose of kindergarten was socialization.

Additionally, little attempt had been made to understand Bill's perspective on the problem, to seek his input into understanding the problem and finding solutions. At home, the mother and stepfather were polarized at two ends of the adultcentrism continuum. The mother's nurturing, nondemanding stance, at one end of the continuum, didn't allow Bill's strengths and capabilities to shine through because little was expected of him. At the other end of the continuum, his stepfather's demanding socialization stance didn't allow for Bill's uniqueness and individual needs.

To combat adultcentrism, the social worker interviewed Bill separately, using age-appropriate interviewing techniques, to gain a better understanding about how Bill viewed the situation and what was important to him. The worker honored and respected that input and helped communicate that perspective to the adults, who in turn were able to validate and act appropriately on the information. The mother and stepfather tried to move more toward each other to present a unified parenting approach that was more realistic in its expectations of Bill and his behavior, combining sensitivity to his needs with confidence in his abilities to grow. The biological mother and father changed their custody arrangement to more accurately reflect Bill's needs and preferences rather than their own. At school, the teacher continued to expect that Bill follow the rules, but was more patient and understanding when he struggled, viewing his behavior as reflective of a developmental struggle rather than willful opposition to her authority. Additionally, the school personnel worked to improve his peer social skills and assessed his appropriateness for the individualized T-1 classroom.

Behavior modification principles, whose adultcentric propensities have been previously noted, were employed with Bill through the use of time out and consequences at home. These principles were employed to achieve necessary and positive socialized behavior, and caution was maintained so that undue social control did not result. This caution manifested in several ways. First, only aggressive behaviors that were clearly outside the norm were targeted. Second, consequences were age appropriate and limited in duration. Third, Bill had some choice in the consequences that were employed—about which TV programs and toys to give up. Fourth, Bill was not forbidden to be himself. Bill enjoyed fantasy, solitary time, and imaginary games. These behaviors were not directly targeted for behavioral intervention, and he was allowed to continue to enjoy this kind of time and activity while being encouraged to pursue new activities as well.

Pragmatic Perspective 2: Family-Centered Practice. Family-centered practice involves three key components. The first, focusing on the family as the unit of attention, guided the social work efforts because Bill's family was seen as his most important resource and strength. The family was defined as Bill and the parents defined it, to include both households. The worker helped Bill by helping his family help him. A child-centered intervention would likely have targeted Bill himself for intervention, helping him to adjust and change through individual play therapy or behavior modification.

The second component of family-centeredness is informed choice. Rather than tell the parents how they should understand the problem and advise them on how they should solve it, the worker provided them with information and options. Specifically, the worker informed them about Bill's point of view and asked them how this information fit with their perspective. He shared the assessment guideline and worked with them to arrive at a mutual understanding of the problem. He offered choices for intervention from individual therapy to school coordination to parent meetings to divorce custody sessions, discussing the pros, cons, and costs of each, and allowing them to prioritize. When in crisis, choices for meeting times were available. Throughout, Jon offered professional opinion and information when asked for it, but emphasized that he was working for the family, and that their own decisions would guide the process.

The third component of family-centered practice is the strengths perspective. The help offered allowed the family to grow and problem solve, without placing them in family therapy. The latter would have been more of a deficit-oriented intervention in which the cause of Bill's problem was seen as originating within pathological family dynamics. A professional-centered role would have been to diagnose the family pathology and treat it, leaving the parents feeling at fault and blamed for the circumstances. For example, the professional-centered practitioner might have told the mother and stepfather that their parenting disagreements reflected marital discord that was being deflected to the child and acted out by him. Or the professional might have searched for multigenerational patterns that would provide insight on why family anxiety was being expressed by the child in this particular way. Instead, the social worker defined the problem not in terms of pathology and deficit, but in terms of how the family could help Bill conquer his developmental hurdle and adjust better to the divorce.

Pragmatic Perspective 3: Strengths Perspective. The social worker communicated a strengths perspective by respectfully communicating the belief that all of the parties (child, parents, school personnel) were able to make competent decisions and choices, by pointing out strengths and positives in the behaviors and attitudes of all parties, by focusing on solutions rather than past mistakes, by choosing to frame ambiguous or challenging behaviors and attitudes positively rather than negatively, and by framing an understanding of the problem in the least pathological, least blaming terms.

The worker communicated his belief in the competence of all parties to make competent decisions in several ways. With Bill himself, the worker offered choices in the interviews (e.g., play or talk time), encouraged the parents to offer him some choice in the consequences for his misbehavior, and sought Bill's opinion about the changes in time spent at each household and the issue of T-1. With Francine and Joe, Jon encouraged dialogue and direct communication regarding decisions about discipline, rather than telling them what the best decision was. Jon accepted their view and definition of the problem and their needs, rather than impose his own. With Francine and Don, Jon again facilitated communication and kept the discussion focused on the issues at hand, but did not decide for them which arrangement was best. With school personnel, Jon resisted giving recommendations about how they should handle Bill's behavior, deferring to their own judgment, experience, and expertise. Jon did suggest that it might be helpful to have someone observe Bill's behavior on the playground in detail, to discover exceptions to the times of Bill's misbehavior, but the school staff members were unable to find anyone with the time to devote to this task, and Jon's time to do this could not be paid for.

Throughout the process, Jon pointed out and drew upon the strengths and positives of Bill and the family. Bill's intelligence, creativity, and sense of humor were validated and incorporated into the intervention plans. The worker noted the strengths in the parents and family such as their concern for him, their ability to talk and communicate, their involvement in his school and other activities, their seeking help, and their willingness to allow the worker to try to better understand and communicate Bill's point of view.

Jon did not dwell on the past or encourage the parents to feel guilty or to blame for Bill's troubles. Francine was inclined toward blaming herself, stating that she was too permissive with Bill in the first months and years after the divorce. She also worried that the joint custody arrangement had contributed to Bill's insecurity and consequent aggressiveness. While Jon listened to these concerns, he did not dwell on them, and he expressed confidence that then, as now, Francine did the best she could and made decisions that she thought were in Bill's best interests. In meetings between Francine and Don, Jon deflected the tendency of each to blame the other for the past, and encouraged them to focus on present common concerns and solutions.

Jon was able to frame several "negative" attitudes and behaviors in a positive light. Bill's aggressiveness with other children, while unacceptable in its extreme form, was an attempt at standing up for himself and not allowing others to berate him, which was a positive sign in a quiet and potentially nonassertive child. Francine and Joe's respective parenting styles, while problematic in the extreme, represented expertise that could be taught and shared with the other. When Francine, Joe, and the school balked at instituting rewards for Bill's positive behaviors, this was not viewed as resistance or rigidity on their part. Instead, Jon respected their position and viewed it as a strength that they could assert their own perspective and views.

Finally, Jon operationalized a strengths perspective by eschewing an exclusive pathological, deficiency orientation in the assessment and understanding of the problem, normalizing it without minimizing it. Bill's problems were framed as understandable, almost normal reactions to the stresses associated with his age, school situation, and divorce; yet they were serious enough to warrant attention. Rather than labeling Bill's behavior as "conduct disorder" or "depression" or "oppositional-defiant disorder," Jon and the family viewed the behavior as an issue of adjustment. This framed the issue in a nonblaming way that

identified both Bill and the larger environment for change.

Pragmatic Perspective 4: Respect for Diversity and Difference. Jon's respect for diversity and difference were crucial in his interactions with Don regarding sensitivity to the racial issues involved in Bill's biracial heritage. When Don challenged Jon's sensitivity to racial issues, rather than viewing this as hostile and resistant behavior, Jon complimented Don on his openness and courage in bringing up a delicate subject. Jon acknowledged that he had limited experience in the area and expressed hope that Don would educate him further. Jon offered to include an African American staff person in the meetings with Don and Francine, but Don declined, stating that Jon clearly had an interest in being fair and that he would reserve the right to do this later, if the need arose. Jon validated Don's concerns in the discussions with Francine and supported their plan to have Francine focus more on this potentially problematic area of Bill's development.

Additionally, Don expressed some concern that Bill was being singled out by the school for T-1 placement due to his race. He asked Jon whether a white child who exhibited the same behaviors would be singled out. When Francine and Don met directly with the school staff, these concerns were largely alleviated, though Don never fully embraced the decision for T-1 placement.

Pragmatic Perspective 5: Least Restrictive Alternative. The issue of least restrictive alternative arose both in relation to the level of services offered in the mental health system and in the schools. Through the mental health center, services were provided on an outpatient, not an inpatient basis. Although extended inpatient care is unusual for a child so young, an inpatient evaluation might have been recommended by other professionals less oriented toward providing care in the least restrictive alternative. The least restrictive environment was also evident in the initiation of computer and karate classes, which were normal, informal services, not formal therapy groups.

The recommendation by the schools for T-1 placement clearly triggered concerns about the least restrictive alternative. While T-1 was deemed the most appropriate placement, it was also more restrictive in that it segregated and thus stigmatized Bill to some extent. Although this stigma was mitigated somewhat by the absence of a special education label, the principle of inclusion was violated by the segregation into a "special" class. As with more traditional special education placements, the parents struggled with whether the benefits derived from attention to Bill's individual needs outweighed the negatives of the segregation and stigma. These decisions are never easy, and Jon took the appropriate course of pointing out the pros and cons to the parents, but not letting his own biases interfere with their deliberations.

Pragmatic Perspective 6: Ecological Perspective. The ecological perspective was manifested in Jon's attention to the crucial role of Bill's immediate environment in the assessment and intervention stages. Clearly, the interactions and fit between Bill and his environment needed improvement. Due to the crisis nature of the early contacts with the parents, Jon never completed a formal ecomap with the family, which might have revealed additional areas of concern and focus. Although case management services were not needed to access essential concrete services such as housing, employment, and transportation, changes in Bill's immediate environment and coordination among the various parents and school personnel were vital to the successful outcome. Environmental changes included changes in the custody arrangement, changes in Francine and Joe's parenting approach, T-1 placement, initiation of more exposure to African American culture, and use of informal and natural community supports such as computer and karate classes.

Accessing the latter informal resources is a good example of the use of the ecological concept in a way that social workers sometimes neglect. Often, social workers are so knowledgeable about and attuned to the formal resources in a community that they overlook the power and impact of the informal support networks in a community. To guard against this tendency, when social workers identify a need in a child or family, it is important to first determine whether that need can be met through existing, informal, natural helping networks. Bill had the needs to develop a sense of competence, improve his social skills and interactions, and channel his aggression. While these needs could have been met through individual or group therapy, they also could have been, and were, met through engaging in normal activities provided to all children in a community.

Pragmatic Perspective 7: Organization and Financing. In this example, the financing mechanisms for service had a definite effect on the nature and types of services provided. This example demonstrates that "what gets done is what gets paid for." Francine and Joe's health insurance, through Francine's employer, included a mental health rider of the managed care, health maintenance organization type. This policy allowed for limited reimbursement of outpatient and inpatient mental health treatment. Jon's mental health center was a contracted provider of these mental health services. Before making the initial appointment, Francine had to call the insurance company for preauthorization for the initial assessment; the company would pay for up to 2 1/2 hours. In Bill's case, this amounted to the first intake session (1 1/2 hours) plus the one crisis session (1 hour).

After that, Jon had to receive authorization for continued services. Since his diagnosis was adjustment reaction rather than a more serious mental illness, the managed care company's protocols authorized only four outpatient visits. This was quickly consumed in parent conferences with Francine and Joe, and one meeting with Don and Corona. After those four sessions, the managed care company initially refused to authorize more sessions, but Francine and Joe came anyway, because they did not feel they could stop the process. The mental health center established a sliding-scale fee, based on ability to pay, while the parents appealed the insurance company's decision. Meanwhile, individual therapy was not implemented because of the cost to the parents, and Jon's time spent on the phone with school personnel was not reimbursed. Eventually, the company paid for four additional visits, after Jon and the parents had communicated several times by phone and in writing to the company, but this still left numerous sessions unreimbursed.

The meetings involving Francine and Don were not covered by either of their insurance policies, so they agreed to split the cost, again on a sliding-scale fee. This was a cumbersome arrangement for the mental health center's financial office, and both

Francine and Don spent many hours getting their bills corrected and straightened out with the financial office. Jon also had to spend considerable time with the financial office clarifying information and verifying information given by the clients.

This method of payment constrained service delivery in several ways. First, Jon felt pressure to assign a more serious diagnosis that would warrant more sessions. Even Francine and Joe asked if this were not possible, so that their insurance would cover more fully. Second, the full intervention plan could not be implemented: the recommended individual therapy sessions were curtailed, meetings and phone conversations with school personnel were kept to an absolute minimum, and there was no funding to pay for Jon to observe Bill at school and on the playground, nor to consult actively with the teachers. Third, much time and energy was deflected from finding solutions to Bill's problems to finding ways to pay for the services.

Pragmatic Perspective 8: Achieving Outcomes. At the individual case level, success was achieved regarding the initial goal, as reported by the parents and teachers. No objective behavioral scales or measurements were used to document this success, however, and it would have been an improvement had the parents and teachers been willing to do this. Jon found that many clients and professionals resisted objective measures of progress, viewing them as a time and energy drain that, in any case, only confirmed and underlined what they already knew. Nevertheless, Jon himself continuously asked "How is the progress?" and "Are we almost there yet?" to keep the key actors focused on the goal. Jon did have to complete his own assessment of progress for the insurance company.

This case demonstrates how complicated even relatively "simple" cases can be, and the importance of working on several environmental fronts at the same time to achieve success, even with a so-called minor problem of adjustment reaction. Jon was asked by his supervisor: "Could success have been achieved in shorter than 6 months and fewer than 20 sessions, as the insurance company protocols indicated?" Jon replied, "That depends on how you define success. Yes, Bill's behavior improved considerably after 6 weeks, but I felt that this progress was fragile and would be short-

lived unless Joe and Francine continued their parenting work and Francine and Don resolved the custody and T-1 issue. Yes, we could have applied a Band-Aid, but it would have soon come off, and the child and family would have returned, perhaps with more serious problems."

Jon's comments reinforce the prevention aspects of this case. Jon saw this as a clear opportunity for early intervention and the prevention of more serious problems. Because of the commitment and resources of this family, a thorough and relatively comprehensive approach was possible. In many other families, this level of service simply would not have been possible. Perhaps Bill will not now need special education services. Perhaps Francine and Joe's marriage was saved. Perhaps Bill's racial identity and self-esteem will be stronger, so that he does not become depressed as a teenager. It is difficult, if not impossible, to document that Jon's work prevented negative outcomes. Even if all of those outcomes come to pass, who is to say that involvement with Jon was responsible? If Bill doesn't eventually need special education, who is to say that he would have needed it anyway? Maybe the marriage would not have failed in any case, or maybe it survived because of other factors. While it is possible to study effects of prevention efforts on large groups of people over time, for practitioners like Jon who work with individual clients, belief in the prevention impact of their work is largely a matter of faith.

Case Example 2: Sharon

This example describes a much more serious and chronic situation than Bill's case. The subject, Sharon, was seriously depressed to the point of attempting suicide. Her case example is described from the point of view of the case manager, Cynthia. Over the course of several months, Sharon received numerous mental health and other services. The mental health services included inpatient psychiatric services at a local psychiatric hospital, outpatient individual therapy utilizing a cognitive-behavioral approach, day hospital treatment, family therapy, medication therapy, attendant care, and case management from Cynthia. Cynthia succeeded in coordinating all of these mental health services as well as special education, respite care, employment, and transportation. Cynthia also assisted the family by helping Sharon's mother find child care for the younger siblings and complete renovations on their house that afforded Sharon more privacy.

Overview and Narrative

Presenting Problems and Identifying Information. Sharon is a 15-year-old white female who was admitted to County Psychiatric Center after being seen in the emergency room for an overdose of sleeping pills. Her best friend, Donna, just happened to stop by to visit, discovered her unconscious on the floor, and called for an ambulance. For several days prior to this incident, Sharon had been withdrawing from people, sleeping 15 hours per day, missing school, and complaining to her mother that nobody liked her. Her mother at first attributed her behavior to teenage moodiness, but later urged her to get psychiatric help, which Sharon refused to do.

Sharon lives with her divorced mother, Joan, and four younger siblings (Paul, 12, Eric, 7, Louise, 4, and Kathy, 2) in a small, three-bedroom home on the outskirts of town. Her father, who is also the father of Paul and Eric, has not been heard from since he left the family 6 years ago. Louise and Kathy were born out of wedlock and their fathers are not present. Joan has a history of severe depression, has herself attempted suicide twice, and takes part in group therapy and a medication clinic at the local mental health center. Joan is not employed and supports the family with welfare payments (AFDC), food stamps, and disability payments for her depression. Joan's parents live in the community and sometimes have offered to help Joan with finances and child care, but Joan usually has refused their offers because she does not want to be dependent on them.

Assessment Phase. Cynthia, who is African American, was assigned to be Sharon's case manager, responsible for arranging discharge and coordinating aftercare. This was a new position funded by a case management grant obtained by the local mental health center. She met with Sharon after she had been on the psychiatric unit for 3 days. The initial interview focused on Cynthia explaining her role to Sharon and learning Sharon's problems,

interests, and aspirations. During this interview, Sharon complained about the treatment she was receiving from the hospital staff. Sharon felt that the group therapy was too structured, too much like a classroom at school: "They just lecture to us about stuff we already know." She felt that the antidepressant medication was helping and didn't understand why she couldn't be discharged back home so she could go back to school. She did not want to talk about her suicide attempt, and denied that she was thinking any more about harming herself. Cynthia informed her that her exact discharge date was up to her doctor, but that it seemed encouraging that Sharon was so eager to return to her home and community, and it was Cynthia's job to help plan for the discharge so that everything would run smoothly.

Cynthia invited Sharon to talk more about her and the things that Sharon felt needed to be different to avoid her being hospitalized again. Slowly, Sharon told Cynthia about herself and her family, mostly focusing on negatives so that Cynthia had to reach for positives and strengths. Sharon said she hated living in the small house, where she had to share a small room with her two younger sisters. Her mother expected her to baby-sit the younger kids "all the time," but Sharon wanted to get a job as soon as she turned 16 next month, and this was a source of conflict with her mother. She also disliked school, and was thinking about dropping out after she turned 16. Sharon didn't care what kind of job she got, and didn't feel she had any particular talents or abilities that she could use in a job. Sharon said that Donna was her best, and almost only friend. She didn't have a boyfriend and seldom dated boys. She thought that boys didn't like her because she was fat (Sharon was 30 pounds overweight). Before the conversation ended, Sharon complained again about the group therapy and asked if she had to participate. She also wanted to know when she could visit her mother and siblings.

Next, Cynthia talked with the hospital staff. Most of them were negative and pessimistic about Sharon and her lack of progress. The admitting psychiatrist, Dr. Thomas, said that Sharon's desire to return home was premature considering the seriousness of the suicide attempt, the long history of depression, and previous suicide attempts at ages 13 and 14. The psychiatrist felt that Sharon was minimizing the risk so that she could be discharged and perhaps attempt suicide again. He wanted her to remain on the unit for at least 6 weeks to be sure that she was properly supervised, her medication was properly monitored, and she regularly attended individual, group, and family therapy. He wanted to see Sharon progress to the point that the risk of suicide was strongly diminished on discharge. He also thought it would take at least 6 weeks for Cynthia to arrange for the needed supports in the community.

The nurses and attending staff noted that Sharon still wanted to sleep most of the day and they had to almost push her out of bed to attend group therapy and other activities. They said that Sharon was withdrawn, hostile, and uncooperative. They dismissed her complaints about group therapy as "resistance to treatment." Regarding visits with the family, the staff reported that Sharon was "not ready" for these, but if she and the family insisted, they could visit briefly in the evenings as long as staff members were present to help make the visit therapeutic. A family therapist from the mental health center staff would soon be assigned to begin family therapy. After allowing staff members to air their negative feelings about Sharon, Cynthia asked if they had noted any positive behaviors or attitudes. Initially, the staff was silent, but then workers were able to acknowledge that Sharon had not expressed any suicidal thoughts or made any suicidal gestures, and took her medication without complaint. One staff member had observed some signs of energy and life when Sharon had interacted with two of the younger children on the unit. Sharon had played a game with one of the children and had been seen laughing and joking with him.

For the next step in the assessment process, Cynthia went to Sharon's home to visit with Sharon's mother, Joan. Joan was pleased to see Cynthia and her first question was about when she could visit Sharon at the hospital. Joan asked how Sharon was progressing, but expressed worry and fear when Cynthia said that Sharon wanted to come home as soon as possible. When Cynthia told Joan about the psychiatrist's recommendation for a minimum 6-week stay, Joan seemed relieved and stated that she could be sure that Sharon was safe at the hospital. Joan apologized for the small and cramped quarters, offering that she knew Sharon needed more privacy but asserting that she could

not afford a bigger place. She questioned why Sharon would attempt suicide again, and blamed herself for not dragging Sharon to a psychiatrist before the suicide attempt. Cynthia explained that her own role would be to help plan for discharge and aftercare, and asked what Joan felt was needed for Sharon to live successfully at home. Joan stated that Sharon needed to take her medication regularly, stay around people, go to individual therapy, and do her schoolwork. Joan also felt that a larger residence would reduce the stresses enormously, as would getting a dependable family car for transportation.

Cynthia proceeded to construct an ecomap with Joan. This process revealed important aspects of the family's ecology and pinpointed areas for Cynthia's intervention. The relationship with the extended family was depicted as somewhat tense and filled with conflict. Joan's parents lived nearby and often offered help, but Joan viewed them as critical rather than supportive. The whereabouts of Sharon's father were unknown, and neither Joan nor Sharon wanted to find him. Joan's relationship with social service agencies was generally supportive, especially with the mental health center. She needed better housing and transportation, and this was identified as an area for Cynthia's intervention. Sharon's relationship with school was mixed—she was pretty smart and got better-than-average grades, but she didn't like school and wanted to graduate as soon as possible. She was not particularly close to any of her teachers and she did not participate in sports or other activities. Donna was depicted as a source of support, but other friends were lacking, so that Sharon's support system was confined to her nuclear family and Donna. Neither Sharon nor the family participated in church or religious activities.

As the interview with Joan progressed, Sharon's siblings began to come home from school, and they all were eager to hear about their older sister. Cynthia learned that Paul and Eric were both good at sports but struggled with academics. Eric had been identified as learning disabled and received help in a resource room an hour each day. Louise and Kathy stayed home with their mother all day. Both seemed healthy and well cared for. There was some concern about Louise's speech development, and she was scheduled for an evaluation with the school district's preschool special education team. Cynthia asked about meeting with Joan's parents, but Joan said they would refuse to meet with Cynthia "because you're black—they are real prejudiced." When all the family was present, it was hard to get a word in edgewise, as the children were very active and talkative. Joan, in contrast, was quiet and lower in energy, which may have been a reflection of her disability. As Cynthia was leaving, Sharon's friend Donna arrived to visit the family and questioned Cynthia about Sharon's status. Donna claimed that she was mystified about what triggered Sharon's suicide attempt, and wanted to visit her as soon as possible.

As a final step in the assessment process, Cynthia visited the high school Sharon attended to visit with the special education staff there. Cynthia learned that Sharon had been in special education as a child with serious emotional and behavioral disorders since she was 12. Her current IEP called for inclusion in regular classrooms with one class period a day in the special education resource room for extra help and counseling. Staff members were reluctant to have Sharon return to regular school. They thought that given the seriousness and long history of depression, long-term residential treatment (up to 6 months) with discharge to a day hospital was the best course of action.

Case Plan. After Sharon had been in the hospital for 1 week, the hospital staff met with Cynthia, the special education staff, and the mental health therapists to develop a plan of treatment, discharge, and aftercare. Individual and family therapy had begun with Jon, the outpatient mental health therapist who would be continuing after hospitalization. In addition, Cynthia had been able to arrange for visits between Sharon, her mother, her siblings, and her friend Donna. Group therapy at the hospital was conducted by a psychiatric nurse and social

work student. As admitting physician, the psychiatrist chaired the staff meeting and first directed discussion to understanding the contributing factors to Sharon's depression and suicide attempt.

Regarding the question "Why at this particular time is this particular child engaging in this particular behavior?" staff members agreed that Sharon's suicide attempt and depression could not be considered within a "normal" range for her age. They concluded that several factors likely contributed to the depression. First, Sharon's constitutional makeup and innate temperament indicated that there were biological/genetic contributions to the depression. Her mother, Joan, and Joan's mother both had struggled with serious and chronic depression. Second, Sharon was struggling to adjust to the struggles of adolescent identity formation, her cramped living situation, her dissatisfaction with school and social life, and her role in the family as child care provider to her siblings. Third, some of Sharon's depression may have been learned or conditioned from observing her mother and from her own cognitive processes that reinforced a negative self-concept. The role of trauma in the depression was not known to be a major contributing factor, as both Sharon and Joan had consistently denied any major traumatic events. As far as the trigger for the suicide attempt, the staff had learned little about what had led up to Sharon taking the pills. Sharon had refused to discuss details and no one in the family knew much about the precipitating events.

The team agreed that the case plan for Sharon should be multidimensional, to address all of the potential contributing factors to her depression and to minimize the risk for another suicide attempt. The initial plan was designed to address goals for Sharon's hospital stay, discharge, and aftercare, as follows.

Sharon's Initial Case Plan

1. Hospital Stay
   • *Goal of hospitalization:* Sharon's depression will become stabilized and under control so that the risk of suicide is minimized.
   • *Means to achieve the goal:* Medication, individual, group, and family therapy will be utilized to achieve the goal. Individual and group therapy will be primarily cognitive-behavioral, to help Sharon reverse the negative thinking and destructive

(cont'd.)

thought patterns that are self-defeating, while building a more positive self-image through accomplishing self-identified goals and tasks. Family therapy will focus on the relationship between Sharon and her mother, focusing on negotiation of issues such as Sharon's responsibility for care of the younger children, privacy, and the limits on Sharon's freedom. In all of the modalities, therapists will encourage Sharon to discuss more fully the events that precipitated the suicide attempt, so that further interventions can be based on ameliorating the precipitating factors. Also, the possibility of past trauma as a contributing factor will be more fully explored to either confirm or rule out this possibility.

2. Discharge Planning and Aftercare

A tentative discharge date is set for 6 weeks from the date of admission. The exact discharge date will depend on (a) progress made by Sharon and (b) successful arrangement of services to be in place on discharge. Indicators of Sharon's progress and readiness for discharge will be: (1) taking medication without fail; (2) discussing precipitants of suicide attempt; (3) developing realistic plan to address precipitants (4) accomplishing three self-identified goals, or making good progress toward their accomplishment; (5) identifying a plan of support and action for dealing with depressive episodes. Arrangement and coordination of aftercare is Cynthia's responsibility. Issues and needs to be addressed are coordination of mental health services, medication compliance, special education programming (including consideration of day hospital treatment and placement), responsibilities in the home, adequate supervision, social supports, adequacy of living space, transportation, and possible employment.

The above plan represented a compromise among team members. Special education staff, and some members of the hospital staff, believed that Sharon needed long-term inpatient care, and that discharge home in 6 weeks, even if it was to day treatment, was premature and risky. Cynthia, on the other hand, had argued for earlier discharge, asserting that it was possible to meet all the purposes of inpatient treatment on an outpatient and day treatment basis.

Progress in Hospital. Sharon was disappointed to learn that the team did not recommend her immediate discharge home. She protested to Cynthia that the team was only seeing her weaknesses and did not show enough faith in her strengths and abilities. Joan, however, liked the plan and encouraged Sharon to work hard in her therapy so she could be discharged as soon as possible.

Progress began to be made in *individual therapy,* where Sharon began to focus on her self-defeating thought processes and how her depressed feelings were in part the result of these

cognitive patterns. Bob, the therapist, used several cognitive-behavioral techniques, including cognitive restructuring, to help her with this (Stark, Raffaelle, & Reysa, 1994). First, he encouraged Sharon to self-monitor her feelings in a daily log. In the log, Sharon identified times when she experienced strong feelings, either negative or positive, and rated the strength of these using a self-anchored scale from 1 to 10. Next, she wrote what was happening in the situation, what she was doing, and what she was thinking at the time. She began to link positive feelings with positive thoughts about herself and the situation. She discovered that her thought processes associated with depressed and negative feelings invariably involved blaming and criticizing herself for being lazy, stupid, ugly, etc. Later, for the negative feelings, Sharon answered the question "What is the evidence for and against the thoughts?" The next step was to list alternative, more positive ways to think about the situation and what would happen if those ways of thinking were true. This process encouraged

Sharon to recognize when depressed feelings were beginning to occur and to activate her thinking self to combat them by evaluating whether or not she was irrationally distorting the situation.

In addition, Bob helped Sharon evaluate areas in which her negative self-evaluations were accurate—areas for self-improvement. Sharon set and met three goals in the first 3 weeks of therapy. First, she succeeded in initiating three separate conversations with other adolescents on the unit, to combat her tendency to be withdrawn. Second, she identified an area of talent and interest on which she could build: caring for younger children. Third, she met a goal of setting her own alarm clock and getting herself up for 5 days in a row.

Finally, Bob was able to help Sharon talk about the events precipitating the suicide attempt. He learned that, in addition to all of the stresses mentioned above, Sharon had experienced a falling out with her friend Donna. The tension in the relationship had been building as both friends felt closer to each other and had begun to express their affection physically. Sharon had decided that she herself most probably was lesbian, but Donna had been repulsed by the thought of herself as lesbian, and had sought to distance herself from Sharon. Feeling rejected, Sharon had become despondent and attempted to harm herself. This information led Bob to focus some of the individual sessions on Sharon's self-identification as a lesbian and on her relationship with Donna, who was invited to sessions to discuss the relationship. Donna and Sharon decided to remain "just friends," and Sharon accepted this limit to the relationship. Using cognitive techniques, Bob helped Sharon analyze situations in which she felt rejected and make plans at those times for talking to others and getting support rather than attempting to hurt herself.

In *family therapy,* this issue was a sensitive and potentially volatile one, because Sharon was not sure how her mother would respond to her sexual orientation. Bob helped her plan how to approach her mother and helped them discuss it openly. Eventually, a few weeks after discharge from the hospital, Joan was able to accept Sharon's sexuality and this source of support and validation did much to help Sharon's self-esteem. Both Bob and Joan helped Sharon think about how and when to "come out" with other relatives and friends.

Meanwhile, Sharon and Joan began to negotiate Sharon's responsibilities with the younger siblings. This included help from Cynthia in arranging for respite and other child care, as described below. Discussion of the conflict-ridden issue of Sharon working or finishing school was postponed until after discharge.

The *group therapy* in the hospital was not successful. Sharon continued to resent the structured format of the group and the leaders refused to change the way the group was conducted. This led to increased tension between Sharon and the hospital staff members, who continued to refer to her as "uncooperative" and "resistive."

The *discharge planning* and *case management* activities focused on having adequate supervision and services in place on discharge. Sharon did not want to return to the high school, but neither did she want to enter the day treatment program on discharge. Sharon insisted that she wanted to get a job, live at home for a couple of years, and take the GED. Cynthia arranged for a meeting of the day treatment staff, special education personnel, Sharon, and her mother to discuss these goals. Although it was a somewhat unusual, the day treatment center eventually agreed to consider these goals after she began the program on discharge. Although this consideration did not at first translate into active support, their eventual decision to actively support her plans was influenced by Joan's and Cynthia's advocacy for the plan (described below) and by the Transition to Adulthood initiative within special education.

In addition to planning for the day treatment program, Cynthia worked to address the areas of child care responsibilities, supervision, social supports, and adequate living space at home. Joan's need for a break from the kids was met through respite care services provided 10 hours per week and additional child care provided by Joan's parents. Even though Joan hated to rely on her parents, Cynthia helped her see that this was better than relying too much on Sharon. Sharon's role in child care for her siblings would be reduced by half on discharge. Supervision of Sharon in the evening hours, to guard against suicide, was addressed on an as-needed basis. Sharon contracted to let her mother, her therapist Jon, or Cynthia know when she was feeling down so that attendant care could be arranged. Sharon had made sufficient progress in the hospital for the adults to accept this plan. Regarding social supports, Sharon agreed to try to expand her circle of support beyond family, Donna, and the mental health professionals. Accomplishing this would be a goal of the day treatment program.

Securing the concrete needs of the family in terms of adequate living space and transportation consumed much of Cynthia's time. By getting donations of material from a variety of sources and obtaining volunteer labor, Cynthia was able to arrange for a room addition to be built on the family's home. Although this room was not completed at discharge, the team agreed that this alone was not reason to keep Sharon in the hospital.

Repairing the car to ensure adequate transportation proved to be problematic. Although the grant under which Cynthia was hired included flexible funds for such purposes, professionals and administrators balked at using the funds in this way. The cost of repairs, estimated at $750, was not the central barrier. Objections centered more on the dependency that this might encourage, and the number of monetary requests from Joan and others that might ensue. The flexible funds were limited, and the needs of clients were great. The grant committee postponed decision on Cynthia's request, pending development of clear policy guidelines for use of those dollars.

With progress demonstrated and most essential services in place, Sharon was discharged to home and the day treatment program 26 days after admission. A "care team" was established to coordinate care and services for Sharon. This team consisted of Sharon, Joan, Cynthia, Bob, Dr. Thomas, and Michelle, who was a special education teacher at the day treatment program.

Progress in Aftercare. The day treatment program consisted of both educational and a therapeutic components. Students from grades 8–12 attended, with older students grouped separately from younger ones for classes and group therapy. Although the staff members had assured Sharon that they would consider her plan for working and getting a GED, Sharon found herself in classrooms with a traditional focus, and she was told "we'll discuss that next week" whenever she requested a change. Both the mother, Joan, and the adult staff at the day treatment believed that it was best for

Sharon to return to the high school and graduate with her class. They saw her wish to do otherwise as an attempt to run away from her problems, rather than face them.

Sharon persisted in bringing up the issue in family therapy, telling her mother that she could not accept or tolerate the current situation. Joan did not know whether to be firm or to give in to Sharon's demands. Bob encouraged her to seek some sort of compromise, if possible, as did most of the parents in a parent support group that Cynthia had referred Joan to.

The situation became more complex and volatile when additional pressures and setbacks occurred. About 1 month after discharge, Sharon began to "forget" to take her medication, and did not follow thorough on her cognitive-behavioral program in individual therapy. In group therapy at the day treatment program, she was quiet and refused to participate. Many days she refused even to get out of bed. In addition to the stresses at home and school, and her strong disappointment about what she saw as adults thwarting her plans and goals, Sharon suffered some interpersonal setbacks with peers. Feeling the burden of shouldering her "secret" about being a lesbian, she suddenly decided to come out to several peers. Unfortunately, some of her peers reacted with shock and criticism, then participated in taunting and teasing her. Despite the support of her mother and Bob, who both admired her strength and courage in revealing her sexual orientation, Sharon began to sleep more and make negative remarks about herself.

Sharon's increasing symptoms of depression prompted Cynthia, Bob, and Michelle to initiate attendant care for supervision in the evenings and to and from the day treatment program. When Joan refused to let Sharon go out on a date with a new female friend, Sharon left the house, angry and defiant. No one, including the police, was able to find her for 2 days. Then, one of Sharon's schoolmates told Michelle that Sharon was camping with a friend at a local lake campground. Joan called an emergency meeting of the care team to discuss what to do. Joan brought two parents from the parent support group with her, one of whom, named Barbara, was a staff person for a local parent advocacy organization associated with the Federation of Families for Children's Mental Health.

The psychiatrist, Dr. Thomas, called the meeting to order and offered the strong opinion that the police should be sent to the lake campground to pick Sharon up and take her to be hospitalized. He said that her behavior was putting her at risk and that the adults should be firm in setting limits and protecting her from herself. Michelle agreed, expressing concern for Sharon's safety and the inability of the staff to ensure 24-hour supervision. Cynthia was not sure that this was best and wondered if some middle ground could be reached. Bob agreed that Sharon was slipping badly, but wondered if a heavy-handed response would only increase her hostility and defiance.

At this point, Barbara asked why all the professionals were acting like it was their decision to make, not Joan's. Sherrie said that Joan should be the one in charge of the meeting and that they all should be listening to Joan and helping Joan think through what to do. She then asked Joan to share what she had been thinking and state what sort of help she wanted from the group. Joan said she was torn between taking a firm, tough stance or talking with Sharon and offering some sort of compromises on the job and girlfriend situation. Joan felt that perhaps the adults had not put enough faith in Sharon, and noted that Sharon did well in the hospital when she could see clearly that she could influence the date of discharge, and she was allowed to set her own goals. Joan wondered if the team was making a mistake in not supporting Sharon's goals of employment and a GED, which seemed to be very important to Sharon. Michelle and Dr. Thomas said that any compromise would be giving in, that Sharon needed to see that she could not manipulate the situation. Cynthia and Bob, on the other hand, reflected on how hard this decision must be for Joan, and asked how they could help. Joan asked that either Bob or Cynthia accompany her to the campground to talk with Sharon. As Bob had appointments scheduled all day and was reluctant to cancel them, Cynthia agreed to go with Joan. Dr. Thomas and Michelle protested, stating that they would clearly document in the records that Joan was acting against their advice.

On the way to the lake, Cynthia and Joan discussed how to approach Sharon. Joan wanted to take along some fast-food hamburgers and fries as a sort of peace offering that would also communicate how much she cared about Sharon's welfare.

Cynthia agreed that was a great idea. If Sharon was hostile, threatened suicide, and/or refused to discuss and compromise, then Joan would call the police and have her hospitalized. If Sharon was willing to discuss the situation and reach some sort of compromise, then Sharon could come back home.

When they arrived, Sharon seemed taken aback and disarmed by Joan's peace offering. She, Cynthia, and Joan were able to talk at length about recent events and Joan shared how difficult it was to decide what was best to do. After much discussion, Joan agreed to support Sharon's goals of seeking employment and obtaining a GED. She also agreed to meet Sharon's new female friend and negotiate times and circumstances under which they could see each other. In return, Sharon compromised by agreeing to stay in the day treatment program and use her time there to study for the GED. Sharon also agreed to resume taking her medication regularly, actively participate in individual therapy, and allow attendant care supervision in the evenings for the next 2 weeks.

The next day, Sharon, Cynthia, and Joan met with Michelle and the day treatment staff to advocate for a change in the educational program. With reluctance, the staff agreed to develop an individual educational program (IEP) that would prepare Cynthia for the GED, and to drop the plan for her to return to the regular high school. They also agreed to help her find employment, or job training. As it worked out, Cynthia and school staff were able to get Sharon placed on an apprenticeship basis at a local child care center. In addition to the GED, Sharon began to take courses to certify her as a preschool teacher's aide.

At home, Sharon continued to occasionally care for her siblings, but on a less frequent basis, as respite care and grandparents filled in at other times. Sharon enjoyed the privacy afforded by her new bedroom addition, and this extra space helped reduce stress in the household. The family continued to struggle to obtain reliable transportation, as the grant committee established a policy that flexible funds could be used only to a maximum of $400.00, and not at all for car repairs. Sharon was allowed increasing freedom to see her new friend contingent on her improved cooperation with school and therapy, and her willingness to discuss the ups and downs of the relationship with

Joan and her therapist. In individual and group therapy, Sharon came to accept her depression as a disability that she would have to cope with for the rest of her life, rather than as something that could be cured. Although there were many minor setbacks in the next few months, and services continued for a year, Sharon was able to complete her GED at age 17, become certified as a preschool teacher's aide, and move out on her own shortly after her 18th birthday. No more suicide attempts or hospitalizations occurred in this time frame. Cynthia continued to provide support and case management throughout. Sometimes this involvement centered on obtaining a new resource, sometimes it centered on providing help and support during crisis in the evenings or on weekends, sometimes it involved listening to Sharon and her mother, or helping them negotiate an issue when Jon was not available.

Commentary and Analysis: The Eight Pragmatic Perspectives

Pragmatic Perspective 1: Combating Adultcentrism. Adultcentric bias was manifested early in the process by the parent, Joan, and the professionals. In the hospital, no one, except perhaps Cynthia, listened to Sharon's thoughts and ideas about the group therapy and early discharge. There may well have been good reason not to do all of what Sharon wanted, but there was no good reason not to listen to her point of view. The dialogue might have produced some sort of compromise, rather than a unilateral decision. Even if no compromise resulted, at least the adults would have communicated respect by listening to Sharon's ideas. The group leaders refused to listen to Sharon's feedback or change the format of the group, and Sharon continued to refuse to actively participate. What effect on participation and motivation of group members would have resulted if the group therapists had allowed the group members to establish the agenda and goals for the group? Fortunately, the discharge plan was constructed such that Sharon had an opportunity to reduce her time in the hospital, and thus have some power in the situation.

Later, Joan and the professional staff continued to demonstrate adultcentrism when they did not seriously discuss Sharon's educational and vocational goals. Sharon was implicitly viewed as incompetent, and the adults communicated, "We know what is best." Again, there was little room for compromise and Sharon felt powerless and childlike. Rather than respond to Sharon's wishes with a considered and respectful "Maybe," the adults bluntly said "No." The exasperation Sharon felt contributed to her lack of motivation and poor progress. Joan and some of the staff members were determined not to be "manipulated," and viewed compromise as "giving in." But Cynthia and Bob validated how difficult the decision must be for Joan and assisted her in reaching a compromise that she felt good about.

This was a turning point in the progress in the case. Adultcentrism did not cause the depression, but it blocked progress. As a soon-to-be adult, Sharon needed the adults to recognize her developmental needs for self-determination and negotiation; instead, she was treated as a young, incompetent child. Cynthia's efforts to combat her own adultcentrism influenced how she worked with both Sharon and Joan, and ultimately helped change the course of Sharon's life.

Pragmatic Perspective 2: Family-Centered Practice. Some aspects of care for Sharon were not family-centered. On admission, the hospital staff seemed to view Sharon herself as the unit of attention, rather than her family. This was exemplified in the failure to set up family visits and family counseling in a timely fashion. When the professionals met after 1 week to establish a case plan, no one thought about inviting Sharon or her mother to the meeting. This professional-centered and child-focused approach implicitly undermined the role of the family and denigrated the competence of both Sharon and Joan. These types of staff-only meetings are common in mental health settings and are rarely questioned. But they signify professional arrogance and elitism by excluding the child and parent from the decision making and presuming that the professionals play the most important role in the life of the child.

Later, due to the assertive efforts of Barbara, the family advocate, and support from Cynthia and Bob, a much more family-centered approach developed. When Joan called the emergency meeting of the care team, she was at first ignored by the professionals. When Barbara confronted the group about its usurping Joan's parental role and responsibility, a major shift occurred. With Joan clearly in charge of the meeting and responsible for the ultimate decision, the professional role shifted to working *for* Joan, not just *with* her. The professionals might still offer opinions and advice, but Joan was free to accept or reject these. Fortunately, Cynthia and Bob were willing to help Joan implement the plan that she thought was best.

It is interesting to speculate about what might have happened had Cynthia and Bob not been so supportive. With all of the professionals aligned against her, would Joan have followed the professional advice to send the police to pick up Sharon, or with Barbara's help, would she have tried to do what she thought was best? In an ideal world, Joan would have been afforded choice about the mental health staff she worked with, and could have "fired" the professionals that were not working well with her. In reality, this choice is very limited, due to limited staff and the administrative complexities of affording consumers such choices. Joan may have been able to change case manager or therapist, but often there is only one psychiatrist to choose from.

Close readers and critics of the family-centered philosophy might point out that this discussion appears to represent a "parent-centered" rather than a family-centered approach. Clearly, as the head of the household, Joan deserves respect and acknowledgment of her primary decision-making role. In this sense, family-centered practice does have a flavor of parent-centeredness about it. But what makes this example *family*-centered is the way in which Sharon and her siblings and extended family were included in the process. This was in contrast to a child-centered approach, which would have excluded or marginalized the family, or a parent-centered approach, which would have minimized the role of Sharon. In fact, Sharon's ideas and opinions were honored and respected, and the role of the professionals was to help the parent and child negotiate a compromise. The fact that this negotiation was not between two equals (for children and parents are not equals in most families) does not mean that the approach should be labeled parent-centered.

Pragmatic Perspective 3: Strengths Perspective. A strengths perspective is essential to combating

adultcentrism and to family-centered practice, and thus was evident in work with both Sharon and the family. A strengths perspective was crucial in helping Sharon combat her low self-esteem, in helping her achieve her goal of employment, in helping her feel comfortable with her sexual orientation, and in reinforcing her confidence in her own ability to make decisions.

In helping build her self-esteem, the individual therapy did not focus only on those times in which she felt depressed. In a fashion akin to solutions-focused therapy, Sharon was asked to identify and analyze the times she did not feel depressed, when she in fact felt elated or confident or contented. Both Bob and Sharon asked her to list her strengths and to direct her attention toward them. One result of this was the identification of potential employment as a child care provider. Sharon liked young children, had experience caring for them, and was good at it. With regards to the sensitive issue of sexual orientation, Cynthia and Bob validated her sexuality rather than criticizing or admonishing her. They did not view homosexuality as deviant, and thus did not try to change her or talk her out of being lesbian. Joan's eventual support and validation were powerful self-concept builders. When Sharon was taunted and ostracized by some of her schoolmates for being gay, the professionals did not question or criticize her decision to come out; instead, they communicated respect for her courage and conviction.

A strengths perspective was demonstrated toward the family by not blaming Joan for Sharon's difficulties, by respecting Joan's role and responsibilities as a parent, and by emphasizing what family members did well as individuals and as a group. Some family therapists would have looked for the source of Sharon's depression in the family dynamics—the interpersonal relationships among family members, particularly between Joan and Sharon. Instead, Bob focused on the complex etiology of the depression, including its biological components. This use of a disability model of depression helped Sharon and the family focus on coping with the condition, not finding a cause and curing it.

Focus on family dynamics was restricted to present, not past, issues that related to Sharon's developmental needs, including the need for negotiation and compromise. This focus normalized or "depathologized" the issues and thus lowered the family's defensiveness. By communicating respect for Joan's parenting role, the staff reinforced Joan's sense of competence and capability. "If they think I should be the one to make decisions, they must think I'm a pretty strong and capable person!" thought Joan. Of course Barbara, the family advocate, was the most active and strongest supporter of Joan in this regard. Whenever she met with the family, Cynthia opened and closed each meeting with a brief acknowledgment of recent positives in the family's life. Cynthia noted how energetic and verbal the siblings were, helped Joan see how well family members communicated with and cared about each other, and noted how few arguments there were despite the stresses of cramped living quarters, Joan's and Sharon's depression, and the noise of the young children. They connected these positive family attributes to Joan's good parenting.

The overall effect of these individual instances of the strengths perspective was a working context that communicated a sense of positive expectations and confidence. This was not a Pollyanna approach in which problems were ignored and minimized. Instead, professionals communicated the belief that the problems did not mean that the family members were crazy or deviant, but that they were struggling and they had the capability of making things better for themselves. This working context enabled the family to believe more strongly in themselves and to develop a sense of confidence in their abilities.

Pragmatic Perspective 4: Respect for Diversity and Difference. There were two major issues in which respect for diversity and difference were crucial to a successful outcome: Sharon's sexual orientation and the conflict between Cynthia and Sharon's grandparents regarding Cynthia's race.

The way in which staff and Joan responded to Sharon's sexual orientation was crucial to her self-esteem, as discussed above. In addition, Sharon's negative experiences with her peers after coming out spurred school staff to initiate two important programs. First, they formed a diversity committee, made up of staff and students, whose goal was to combat prejudice within the school. This committee sponsored forums, provided teachers with educational materials, and drew posters with pictures and slogans that honored diversity. Second,

they worked with the mental health center to form a confidential support group for gay and lesbian teenagers. In the group, members offered support and validation to each other, so that their sense of isolation was reduced. They discussed forming an open group or "club" at the high school, but decided that such a group would only open them to taunting and criticism from other students, and they were not ready to take on those battles.

The second issue is one in which many social workers of color find themselves, but which is not addressed in many educational programs. The focus of educational material on diversity is frequently on the situation of white worker and minority-race client, rather than minority-race worker and white client. But Cynthia found herself in the latter situation in which racism on the part of her client's grandparents was threatening to impede her effectiveness. The grandparents' support was needed, specifically for child care of Sharon's younger siblings, and generally to support their daughter Joan in her parenting role. Cynthia did not want to alienate the grandparents or do anything that would undermine that support. So although she was angry with them, she did not want to act on that anger by excluding them from the process.

But neither did she want to silently accept racist treatment. If she did not meet them face-to-face, wouldn't that be acquiescence to prejudice? But if she did meet face-to-face, the grandparents might refuse to work with her, which would thwart the prospects of a reconciliation between Joan and her parents. With the help of her supervisor, Joan decided to contact the grandparents by letter and phone to explain her role with Sharon and to offer the grandparents the choice of working with herself or with Bob on the identified issues. Her supervisor helped her see that this was an approach that she might have taken with the grandparents even if she hadn't been informed of their prejudice. This way of contacting the grandparents communicated that Cynthia was a reality in Sharon's life, that that she was not going to go away, and that she was a competent professional with a job to do. It also afforded them an opportunity to work on the issues, albeit with someone else. But Cynthia decided that her professional responsibility was to see that the grandparents worked with *someone*, because this was in Sharon's best interests.

To confront the grandparents about their racism would have been acting on Cynthia's issues and needs, not Sharon's or Joan's, and thus would not have been directly related to her professional function.

Pragmatic Perspective 5: Least Restrictive Alternative. The issue of least restrictive alternative, and its companion concept of continuum of care, both played prominent roles in the decisions, directions, and disagreements that occurred in this case. From the initial hospitalization, the focus of staff, parent, and child decision making was focused on what supports and restrictions were necessary for Sharon's treatment.

Initially, Sharon wanted the least restrictive choice of immediate return to her home with little supervision. The psychiatrist and hospital staff insisted on a longer stay, and Cynthia argues for early release with many supports and adequate supervision in place. According to the guidelines on hospitalization discussed under this same heading in chapter 8, hospitalization was a cautious, yet reasonable decision considering the safety issue and risk. Staff members also would have been justified in releasing Sharon earlier if adequate, 24-hour supervision could be assured, and if intensive treatment, comparable to that received in the hospital, could be initiated. In other words, if the purposes or functions of the hospitalization—supervision of safety and intensive treatment—could have been assured on an outpatient basis, then hospitalization would not have been necessary.

The continuum of care was exemplified in the day treatment program. Imagine the dilemma if this stage in the continuum of care had not been available, and the choice was between the two polar extremes along the continuum: inpatient care and weekly outpatient therapy. Not only did the day treatment program provide intense therapy, supervision, and education, it also included services such as attendant care and in-home family therapy. It is easy to see how children with serious mental health difficulties used to spend long periods of time in the hospital. If the only choices are outpatient therapy without attendant care and other supports, or inpatient treatment, then youth like Sharon would have had to spend long periods in the hospital to ensure adequate supervision and intensive treatment.

Disagreements about the least restrictive alternative were again the focal point of the case when Sharon ran away to the campground. Here, the hospitalization option was being advocated because of Sharon's history of suicidal behavior and her recent setbacks. But in this case, following the same guidelines of the previous chapter, hospitalization would not have been justified unless there was a clear indication of danger to self or others. Previous history does not necessarily predict current behavior. There was no indication that Sharon was in fact suicidal at this point. She had not attempted to hurt herself, and she had not even threatened to hurt herself. Therefore, the mother's response was the appropriate one. Although she did not state her intentions in these same words, what she wanted to do was to "assess the situation." She wanted to meet with Sharon to see if she would be cooperative or if she was in danger of hurting herself. Dr. Thomas and Michelle's recommendation for hospitalization was premature because it was not based on a current and accurate assessment of Sharon's status.

The application of the principle of least restrictive environment to the educational system was not so cut and dried. The special education program at the day treatment program was segregated outside of the mainstream, yet Sharon did not want to return to the regular classes at the regular high school. Her own wishes were less in sync with LRA than those of the adults in the situation. Thus, there was some tension between combating adult-centrism and least restrictive environment, and in the end, the principles of least restrictive environment were judged less important than affording Sharon a sense of power and control over her own life.

Pragmatic Perspective 6: Ecological Perspective. The use of the ecomap and the case management tasks of Cynthia's work were two aspects of the ecological perspective that were illustrated by this case. The ecomap helped the family get a feel for how they fit with their environment, identifying several areas for Cynthia's intervention. The case management activities illustrated how effective case management focuses on obtaining and strengthening both formal service, such as family therapy and special education, and informal supports, such as volunteer labor for the room addition and grandparent provision of child care. Cynthia's case management functions were not restricted to resource acquisition and coordination, however. She also was available to the family for crisis intervention and emotional support. Early in her case management career, Cynthia and others had attempted to define her role more narrowly, restricting her activities to resource acquisition and coordination. But as this case example illustrates, case managers are often the ones who spend the most time with families, know them the best, and have the most flexible schedules. So when crises like Sharon's running away occur, case managers are often the ones most trusted and most available to respond.

This case also illustrated the difficulties of working in a collaborative, team context when disagreements arise between the professionals. During the runaway crisis, Cynthia and Bob disagreed strongly with Dr. Thomas and Michelle over the need for hospitalization. Taking a more family-centered and less adultcentric approach, Cynthia and Bob wanted to allow Joan and Sharon an opportunity to solve their issues without resorting to such drastic, and highly restrictive, means.

The experienced reader might recognize their actions as quite courageous and even highly unusual. In professional mental health circles, it is often rare to find open disagreement among staff. Disagreement, if voiced, is to occur behind the scenes, out of earshot of the family. In dealings with the family, the staff is expected to present a "united front." So, in many situations, there would have been extreme pressure on Cynthia and Bob to quietly carry out the opinion or decision of the higher-ranking members or the majority on the team.

Practicing social work in a manner consistent with the eight pragmatic perspectives presented in this book does often require courage, assertiveness, and a pioneer, trailblazing spirit. This willingness to disagree and take risks can open one to scorn and criticism from other professionals. This professional derision can involve accusations of triangulation (siding with the client against the professionals) and/or undermining professional collaboration.

But neither of these criticisms is justified. Social workers' first ethical and legal obligation is to their clients, not to other professionals. In this case example, to accuse Cynthia of triangulation in "siding" with Joan is to display both a double standard and a misuse of the term *triangulation*. What the professionals really wanted was for Cynthia to side with them against Joan. Somehow, this is not seen as a form of triangulation! Why the double standard? Triangulation is a phenomenon that was originally applied to family systems, to describe inappropriate, emotionally reactive, and long-standing patterns of behavior that caused problems in a family (Nichols & Schwartz, 1995). In Cynthia's case, the so-called triangulation is neither inappropriate, emotionally reactive, nor long-standing. Her behavior may cause a temporary problem and conflict in the functioning of the team, but this conflict is caused by legitimate professional disagreement based on rational, not emotional, considerations. If Cynthia displayed a long-standing pattern of disagreement associated with her own emotional needs and anxieties around conflict, then the issue of triangulation might be considered.

But can professionals disagree and still collaborate? If collaboration must entail consensus or unanimity, then the answer is no. In this way of thinking, all open professional disagreement is inappropriate. But in dealing with the complex and uncertain world of children and families, there will be, and in fact must be, disagreement. The definition and operationalization of collaboration must have room for disagreement among professionals. It may be helpful to think of case-level professional collaboration as occurring with the child and the family, not in isolation. Thus, the purpose of professional collaboration and teamwork is not to make decisions about the child and family, but to present the child and family with the best information and professional opinion available. Consistent with the tenets of family-centered practice, the role of the professional is to work for the family. Families have the capacity to receive and process disagreement, just as they have the capacity to weigh the pros and cons of various courses of action.

So Cynthia was not guilty of triangulation or of undermining collaboration. Dr. Thomas and Michelle were the ones who, in fact, were triangulating and undermining collaboration. If they had offered their opinions and recommendations to Joan in the spirit of helping her think through her options, with respect for her role as the decision-maker, then there would have been no issue about others on the team offering differing opinions. Disagreement among professionals is only a problem when the professionals on the team adhere to a professional culture in which the professionals presume to know best. In the attempt to appropriate the decision making from the family, the professionals want clients to think that they all think the same way so that their power is increased: "If we disagree, then, God forbid, the family will make its own decision!"

Pragmatic Perspective 7: Organization and Financing. In this case example, funding for the various services and supports came from many different sources. Medicaid, the federal health insurance program for poor and disabled, paid for most of the mental health services, including attendant care and respite care. When Cynthia's case management activities exceeded the Medicaid limit, the case management grant from the state paid for her time. Education costs were paid by the school district. The house was renovated by private donations of material and labor.

Because the day treatment program was a collaborative effort of the child welfare, mental health, and education agencies, a breakdown of its organization and financing will be detailed here. (Facts and figures in this discussion are based on the actual operation of the Westside Alternative School in Hays, Kansas.)

The purpose of the day treatment program is to prevent the unnecessary out-of-home placement of youth having serious emotional or behavioral problems. The program enrolls between 27 and 33 children at any one time. The program employs 11 staff members: 2 teachers, 1 teacher paraprofessional, 5 case managers, 1 therapist, 1 principal and program manager, and 1 secretary. Nine essential services were provided by the day treatment program: individualized education, partial hospital, daily group counseling, daily home contact, weekly family night, weekly in-home family counseling, 24-hour in-home crisis assistance, attendant care, and case management.

The daily schedule is as follows.

8:15–9:00	Group therapy
9:00–11:30	Academics
11:30–11:55	Lunch
11:55–12:20	Independent living skills
12:20–1:00	Academics
1:00–1:40	Group therapy
1:40–2:40	Physical education
2:40–3:15	"Store," graph daily progress, relax

For students who stay until 5:00 p.m.:

2:45–3:15	Stress management
3:15–4:30	Recreation, homework, arts/crafts, or positive practice activities
4:30–5:00	"Store," graph daily progress, relax

Students earn points in six areas of student performance, and the grade for a class is calculated by the total number of points earned in all six areas: attendance, social behavior, assignment completion and accuracy, applying classroom learning, group work, motivation, and cooperation. A 12-step level system is used to track student performance on academics and behavior. This level system is used to determine when a student is ready to be placed full- or part-time in a regular school.

The day treatment program's annual cost is approximately $11,200 per child: $8,700 for mental health services and $2,700 for education services. Medicaid is the primary funding source for mental health services. For children who do not have Medicaid, funds are made available by the school district and the local public child welfare department. The educational costs are funded primarily by the local budget and special education funds. The costs and funding for the day treatment program are described in the following charts.

Costs for Westside Alternative School, Hays, KS

Education Costs, 1994–1995

Staff (3): $74,505
Building Lease: $23,095
Transportation: $10,500
Building Maintenance: $5,000
Copying: $4,500
Computer: $2,000
Inservice/Supplemental: $2,000
Total: $121,600
Annual education costs per child: $2,700

> *Mental Health Costs, 1994*
>
> Staff (8): $227,953
> Indirect: $120,698
> Building Lease: $27,510
> Travel & Child Incentives: $12,978
> Total: $389,139
> Annual mental health costs per child:
>   approximately $8,500

Pragmatic Perspective 8: Achieving Outcomes.
While in the hospital, the objectives that needed to be accomplished for Sharon to be discharged were stated in specific terms (see above narrative), and she was able to achieve most of them. After discharge, her progress declined for a period of time until the situation came to a critical juncture, and then after the meeting at the campground with her mother and Cynthia, progress again was attained. Disagreement between Sharon and the adults about the educational and vocational goals highly affected the progress on the mental health goals. Thus, the case illustrates how goals and progress in various areas are intertwined. It also illustrates the importance of client-directed goals, and how adultcentrism can negatively affect goal attainment.

Sharon's case also illustrates the relationship between individual and systems goals. In Sharon's case, her decline in progress would not have been noted on typical systems-level measurements of outcome. That is, she was not rehospitalized, placed out of the home, or treated for another sui-

cide attempt. Her lack of progress was noted only at the individual level in her refusing to attend or participate in the day treatment program and individual therapy, sleeping more, and making more self-deprecating remarks. These could have led to events that would have been noted in systems-level statistics, but these were prevented by changing the case plan. The level of individual depression cannot be measured at the community level, but the level of individual depression is linked to hospitalization rates and number of suicide attempts, which can be.

Although Sharon's individual mental health goals were "in sync" with the systems goals, her educational goals were not. In Sharon's community, one systems-level indicator of child well-being was "school performance and attendance in regular classrooms." These goals were also what the adults wanted for Sharon at her individual level. When Sharon convinced the adults that she did not want or need to attend regular school or take regular classes, her individual goals and needs were somewhat in conflict with the community goals and needs. She continued to attend the day treatment program, not the regular school. Due to her individualized learning based on passing the GED, she was not enrolled in any regular classes. Some adults continued to disagree with her own goals and plans and saw the eventual outcome as a failure, not a success, because she quit school to go to work. These adults had strong beliefs and values with respect to the importance of traditional high school education. Others believed that the outcomes for Sharon were a success at the individual level, but not at the systems level.

REFERENCES

Abramson, S. (1991). Use of court-appointed advocates to assist permanency planning for minority children. *Child Welfare, 70,* 477–487.

Alderette, P., & deGraffenreid, D. F. (1986). Nonorganic failure-to-thrive syndrome and the family system. *Social Work, 31,* 207–211.

Alexander, R., Jr., & Alexander, C. L. (1995). The impact of Suter v. Artist M. on foster care policy. *Social Work, 40,* 543–548.

Allan, G. (1991). Family group conferences: A lawyer's perspective. In R. Wilcox, D. Smith, J. Moore, A. Hewitt, G. Allan, H. Walker, M. Ropata, L. Monu, & T. Featherstone, *Family decisionmaking/family group conferences: Practitioner's views* (section 6, pp. 1–7). Lower Hutt, New Zealand: Practitioner's Publishing.

Allen, M. (1992, Fall). Redefining family reunification. *The Prevention Report,* 5–7.

Allen, M., Kakavas, A., & Zalenski, J. (1994, Spring). Family preservation and support services: Omnibus reconciliation act of 1993. *The Prevention Report,* 1–5.

Allen, R. I., & Petr, C. G. (1996). Towards developing standards and measurements for family-centered practice in family support programs. In G. Singer, L. Powers, & A. Olson (Eds.), *Redefining family support: Innovations in public-private partnerships* (pp. 57–88). Baltimore: Paul H. Brookes.

Allen, R. I., Petr, C. G., & Brown, B. F. C. (1995). *Family-centered behavior scale and user's manual.* Lawrence, KS: University of Kansas Beach Center on Families and Disability.

Allen-Meares, P. (1995). *Social work with children and adolescents.* White Plains, NY: Longman.

Allen-Meares, P., Washington, R. O., & Welsh, B. L. (Eds.). (1996). *Social work services in schools* (2nd ed.). Boston: Allyn and Bacon.

American Association of University Women. (1992). *How schools shortchange girls: A study of major findings on girls and education.* Washington, DC: American Association of University Women Educational Foundation.

American Civil Liberties Union. (1993). *A force for change: Children's rights project.* New York: American Civil Liberties Union.

American Psychiatric Association. (1987). *Diagnostic and statistical manual of mental disorders* (3rd rev. ed.). Washington, DC: Author.

American Psychiatric Association. (1994). *Diagnostic and statistical manual of mental disorders: DSM IV.* (4th ed.). Washington, DC: Author.

Ames, L. B., Metraux, R., & Walker, R. (1995). *Adolescent Rorschach responses: Developmental trends from 10 to 16 years.* Northvale, NJ: Jason Aronson.

Annie E. Casey Foundation. (1994). *The Annie E. Casey Foundation 1994 Annual Report.* Baltimore: Annie E. Casey Foundation.

Annie E. Casey Foundation. (2000). *Kid's count data book.* Baltimore: Annie E. Casey Foundation.

Appelbaum, P. S. (1989). Admitting children to psychiatric hospitals: A controversy revived. *Hospital and Community Psychiatry, 40,* 334–335.

Aries, P. (1962). *Centuries of childhood.* London: Jonathan Cape.

Artiles, A. J., & Trent, S. C. (1994). Overrepresentation of minority students in special education: A continuing debate. *The Journal of Special Education, 27,* 410–437.

Association for the Advancement of Behavior Therapy. (1981). *Graduate study in behavior therapy: Social work departments.* New York: Author.

Aust, P. H. (1981). Using the Life Story Book in treatment of children in placement. *Child Welfare, 60,* 535–536, 553–560.

Barfield, S. K., and Petr, C. G. (2002). *Group care for children and adolescents.* Lawrence, KS: University of Kansas School of Social Welfare.

Barglow, P., Chandler, S., Molitor, N., & Offer, D. (1992). Managed psychiatric care for adolescents: Problems and possibilities. In J. L. Feldman and R. J. Fitzpatrick (Eds.), *Managed mental health care: Administrative and clinical issues* (pp. 261–272). Washington, DC: American Psychiatric Press.

Barker, R. L. (1991). *The social work dictionary.* (2nd ed.). Silver Spring, MD: National Association of Social Workers.

Barkley, R. A. (1995). *Taking charge of ADHD: The complete, authoritative guide for parents.* New York: Guilford Press.

Barkley, R. A., Conners, C. K., Barclay, A., Gadow, K. Gittleman, R. Sprague, R., & Swanson, J. (1991). *Task force report: The appropriate role of clinical child psychologists in the prescribing of psychoactive medication for children.* Washington, DC: American Psychological Association.

Barth, R. P. (1988). Disruption in older child adoptions. *Public Welfare, 46,* 23–29.

Barth, R. P. (1990). Theories guiding home-based intensive family preservation services. In J. K. Whittaker, J. Kinney, E. M. Tracy, & C. Booth (Eds.), *Reaching high-risk families: Intensive family preservation in human services* (pp. 89–112). New York: Aldine de Gruyter.

Barth, R. P. (1992). Adoption. In P. J. Pecora, J. K. Whittaker, & A. N. Maluccio (Eds.), *The child welfare challenge: Policy, practice, and research* (pp. 361–398). New York: Aldine de Gruyter.

Barth, R. P. (1994). Shared family care: Child protection and family preservation. *Social Work, 39,* 515–524.

Barth, R. P., & Berry, M. B. (1987, March). Outcomes of child welfare services under permanency planning. *Social Service Review,* 71–90.

Barth, R. P., Berry, M., Yoshikami, R., Goodfield, R. K., & Carson, M. L. (1988). Predicting adoption disruption. *Social Work, 33,* 227–233.

Barthel, J. (1992). *For children's sake: The promise of family preservation.* New York: Winchell.

Benedict, R. (1934). *Patterns of culture.* Boston: Houghton Mifflin.

Benjamin, M. P., & Isaacs-Shockley, M. (1996). Culturally competent service approaches. In B. A. Stroul (Ed.), *Children's mental health: Creating systems of care in a changing society* (pp. 475–491). Baltimore: Paul H. Brookes.

Bergman, A. I., & Singer, G. H. S. (1996). The thinking behind new public policy. In G. Singer, L. Powers, & A. Olson (Eds.), *Redefining family support:*

Innovations in public-private partnerships (pp. 435–463). Baltimore: Paul H. Brookes.

Berman, A. L., & Jobes, D. (1991). *Adolescent suicide: Assessment and intervention.* Washington, DC: American Psychological Association.

Berry, M. (1992). An evaluation of family preservation services: Fitting agency services to family needs. *Social Work, 37,* 314–321.

Bickman, L., Summerfelt, W. T., & Foster, M. (1996). Research on systems of care: Implications of the Fort Bragg evaluation. In B. A. Stroul (Ed.), *Children's mental health: Creating systems of care in a changing society* (pp. 337–355). Baltimore: Paul H. Brookes.

Birt, C. J. (1956). Family-centered project of St. Paul. *Social Work, 1,* 41–47.

Bloom, M. (1991). Primary prevention: Theory, issues, methods, and programs. In A. R. Roberts (Ed), *Contemporary perspectives on crisis intervention and prevention.* Englewood Cliffs, NJ: Prentice Hall.

Boat, B. W., & Everson, M. D. (1988). The anatomical doll project: An overview. Unpublished manuscript, Department of Psychiatry, University of North Carolina, Chapel Hill.

Botvin, G. J. (1998) Preventing adolescent drug abuse through life skills training: Theory, methods, and effectiveness. In J. Crane (Ed.), *Social programs that work* (pp. 225–257). New York: Russell Sage.

Boyle, P. (2000). Accreditation boosts child welfare in Illinois. *Youth Today, 9*(8), 5–6.

Bremner, R. H. (Ed.). (1971). *Children and youth in America* (Vol. 2). Cambridge: Harvard University Press.

Brodzinsky, D. M. (1993). Long-term outcomes in adoption. *The Future of Children, 3*(1), 152–166.

Bryant-Comstock, S, Huff, B., & VanDenBerg, J. (1996). The evolution of the family advocacy movement. In B. A. Stroul (Ed.), *Children's mental health: Creating systems of care in a changing society* (pp. 359–374). Baltimore: Paul H. Brookes.

Burchard, J. D., & Clarke, R. T. (1990). The role of individualized care in a service delivery system for children and adolescents with severely maladjusted behavior. *The Journal of Mental Health Administration, 17*(1), 48–60.

Bureau of the Census. (1927). *Children under institutional care, 1923.* Washington, DC: U.S. Government Printing Office.

Burns, R. C. (1982). *Self-growth in families: Kinetic family drawings research and application.* New York: Brunner/Mazel.

Bush, M. (1980). Institutions for dependent and

neglected children: A therapeutic option of choice or a last resort? *American Journal of Orthopsychiatry, 50,* 239–255.

Bush, M., & Gordon, A. C. (1982, July). The case for involving children in child welfare decisions. *Social Work,* 309–314.

Butterfield, W. H., & Cobb, N. H. (1994). Cognitive-behavioral treatment of children and adolescents. In D. K. Granvold (Ed.), *Cognitive and behavioral treatment: Methods and applications* (pp. 65–89). Pacific Grove, CA: Brooks/Cole.

Byler, W. (1977). *The destruction of American Indian families.* New York: Association on American Indian Affairs.

Caplan, G. (1964). *Principles of preventive psychiatry.* New York: Basic Books.

Center for Mental Health Services. (n.d.) *Fiscal year 1994 report on activities under Public Law 99-319.* Washington, DC: Author.

Center for the Study of Social Policy. (1995). *Changing governance to achieve better results for children and families: A working paper.* Washington, DC: Center for the Study of Social Policy.

Chamberlin, R. W. (1996). Primary prevention and the family resource movement. In G. Singer, L. Powers, & A. Olson (Eds.), *Redefining family support: Innovations in public-private partnerships* (pp. 115–133). Baltimore: Paul H. Brookes.

Chan, S. (1990). Early intervention with culturally diverse families of infants and toddlers with disabilities. *Infants and Young Children, 3*(2), 78–87.

Chapin, R. K. (1995). Social policy development: The strengths perspective. *Social Work, 40,* 506–514.

Chestang, L. W., & Heymann, I. (1973). Reducing length of foster care. *Social Work, 18,* 88–92.

Child rights become law. (1990). *Action for Children, 5*(2), 1, 4.

Child Welfare and Mental Health Partnership Planning Process. (2001, September). Memorandum from Joyce Allegrucci and Laura Howard. Topeka, KS: Kansas Department of Social and Rehabilitation Services.

Child Welfare and Mental Health Partnership Planning Process. (2001, September). Topeka, KS: Kansas Department of Social and Rehabilitation Services.

Children's Defense Fund. (1995). *The state of America's children yearbook: 1995.* Washington, DC: Author.

Children's Defense Fund. (2001). *The state of America's children yearbook: 2001.* Washington, DC: Author.

Children's Defense Fund. (1990). *Children 1990: A report card, briefing book, and action primer.* Washington DC: Author.

Choi, J. K. (2000). Valuing the voice of our young people. *Focal Point, 14*(2), 9, 10.

Clapp, G. (1988). *Child study research: Current perspectives and applications.* Lexington, MA: D. C. Heath & Co.

Clark, H., Prange, M., Lee, B., Stewart, E., McDonald, B., & Boyd, L. (1998). An individualized wraparound process for children in foster care with emotional/behavioral disturbances: Follow-up findings and implications from a controlled study. In M. E. Epstein, K. Kutash, & A. Duchnowski (Eds.), *Outcomes for children and youth with behavioral and emotional disorders and their families: Programs and evaluation best practices* (pp. 513–542). Austin, TX: Pro-Ed Publishing.

Clark, H. B., Deschenes, N., & Jones, J. (2000). A framework for the development and operation of a transition system. In H. B. Clark & M. Davis (Eds.) *Transition to adulthood: A resource for assisting young people with emotional or behavioral difficulties* (pp. 29–54). Baltimore: Paul H. Brookes.

Clinton, H. R. (1996). *It takes a village, and other lessons children teach us.* New York: Simon & Schuster.

Coady, N. (1993). The worker-client relationship revisited. *Families in Society, 75,* 291–300.

Cohen, N. A. (1992). The continuum of child welfare services. In N. A. Cohen (Ed.), *Child welfare: A multicultural focus* (pp. 39–83). Boston: Allyn and Bacon.

Cole, R. F. (1996). The Robert Wood Johnson Foundation's mental health services program for youth. In B. A. Stroul (Ed.), *Children's mental health: Creating systems of care in a changing society* (pp. 235–248). Baltimore: Paul H. Brookes.

Collins, B., & Collins, T. (1990). Parent-professional relationships in the treatment of seriously emotionally disturbed children and adolescents. *Social Work, 35,* 522–527.

Compton, B. R., & Galaway, B. (1989). *Social work processes* (4th ed.). Belmont, CA: Wadsworth.

Condelli, L. (1988). *National evaluation of the impact of guardian ad litem in child abuse and neglect judicial proceedings.* Washington, DC: CSR, Inc.

Congress, E. P. (1994). The use of culturagrams to assess and empower culturally diverse families. *Families in Society, 75,* 531–539.

Connolly, M., & McKenzie, M. (1997). *Effective*

participatory practice: Family group conferencing in child protection. New York: Aldine de Gruyter.

Conte, J. R. (1986). *A look at child sexual abuse.* Chicago: National Committee for the Prevention of Child Abuse.

Cook, T. D., & Reichardt, C. S. (Eds.). (1979). *Qualitative and quantitative methods in evaluation research.* Beverly Hills, CA: Sage.

Costin, L. B., Bell, C. J., & Downs, S. W. (1991). *Child welfare: Policies and practice* (4th edition). New York: Longman.

Courtney, M. E., Barth, R. P., Berrick, J. D., Brooks, D., Needell, B., & Park, L. (1996). Race and child welfare services: Past research and future directions. *Child Welfare, 75*(2), 99–137.

Cowger, C. (1994). Assessing client strengths: Clinical assessment for empowerment. *Social Work, 39*(3), 262–268.

Coyle, J. T. (2000). Psychotropic drug use in very young children. *Journal of the American Medical Association, 283*(8), 1059–1060.

Crissey, M. S. (1992). Some research revisited. In M. Kessler, S. E. Goldston, & J. M. Joffe (Eds.), *The present and future of prevention* (pp. 41–54). Newbury Park, CA: Sage.

Cross, T. L. (1988). Services to minority populations: Cultural competence continuum. *Focal Point, 3*(1), 1–4.

Crouch, J. L. (1994). Does abuse as a child result in irreparable harm in adulthood? Yes. In E. Gambrill & T. J. Stein (Eds.), *Controversial issues in child welfare* (pp. 29–33). Boston: Allyn and Bacon.

Curtis, P. A., Boyd, J. D., Liepold, M., & Petit, M. (1995). *Child abuse and neglect: A look at the states. The CWLA stat book.* Washington, DC: Child Welfare League of America.

Darnton, N. (1989, July 31). Committed youth. *Newsweek,* 66–69.

Daro, D. (1991). Strategies and models in child abuse prevention. In A. R. Roberts (Ed.), *Contemporary perspectives on crisis intervention and prevention* (pp. 161–184). Englewood Cliffs, NJ: Prentice Hall.

Davis, M., Yelton, S. Katz-Leavy, J., & Lourie, I. (1995). Unclaimed children revisited: The status of state children's mental health service systems. *Journal of Mental Health Administration, 22*(2), 142–166.

De Jong, P., & Miller, S. D. (1995). How to interview for client strengths. *Social Work, 40,* 729–736.

de Shazer, S. (1985). *Keys to solution in brief therapy.* New York: Norton.

Dempsey, C. L. (1994). Health and social issues of

gay, lesbian, and bisexual adolescents. *Families in Society, 75,* 160–167.

Denzin, N. K. (1977). *Childhood socialization.* San Francisco: Jossey-Bass.

Deschenes, N., & Clark, H. B. (2001). Best practices in transition programs for youth with emotional and behavioral difficulties. *Focal Point, 15* (1), 14–17.

DiLeo, J. H. (1983). *Interpreting children's drawings.* New York: Brunner/Mazel.

Diorio, W. D. (1992). Parental perceptions of the authority of public child welfare caseworkers. *Families in Society, 73,* 222–235.

Dorwat, R. A., & Epstein, S. S. (1993). *Privatization and mental health care: A fragile balance.* Westport, CN: Auburn House.

Dougherty, D. (1988). Children's mental health problems and services: Current federal efforts and policy considerations. *American Psychologist, 43,* 808–812.

Downs S. A., Costin L. B., & McFadden, E. J. (1996). *Child welfare and family services: Policies and practice.* White Plains, NY: Longman.

Doyle, J. A. (1995). *The male experience* (3rd ed.). Madison, WI: Brown & Benchmark Publishers.

Dryfoos, J. G. (1994). *Full-service schools: A revolution in health and social services for children, youth, and families.* San Francisco: Jossey-Bass Publishers.

Dunst, C. J. (1991). Implementation of the individualized family service plan. In M. J. McGonigel, R. K. Kaufmann, and B. H. Johnson (Eds.), *Guidelines and recommended practices for the individualized family service plan* (2nd ed., pp. 67–78). Bethesda, MD: Association for the Care of Children's Health.

Dunst, C. J., Trivette, C. M., Davis, M., and Cornwell, J. (1988). Enabling and empowering families of children with health impairments. *Children's Health Care, 17*(2), 71–81.

Dunst, C. J., Johanson, C. Trivette, C. M., Hamby, D. (1991). Family-oriented early intervention policies and practices: Family-centered or not? *Exceptional Children, 58,* 115–126.

Dunst, C. J., Trivette, C. M., Starnes, A. L., Hamby, D. W., & Gordon, N. J. (1993). *Building and evaluating family support initiatives.* Baltimore: Paul H. Brookes.

Duquette, D. N., & Ramsey, S. H. (1987). Representation of children in child abuse and neglect cases: An empirical look at what constitutes effective representation. *Journal of Law Review, 20,* 341–408.

Eagle, C. J., & Coleman, C. (1993). *All that she can be: Helping your daughter achieve her full potential and maintain her self-esteem during the critical years of adolescence.* New York: Simon and Schuster.

Eamon, M. K. Institutionalizing children and adolescents in private psychiatric hospitals. *Social Work, 39,* 588–594.

Early, T., & Poertner, J. (1993). Case management for families and children. *Focal Point, 7*(1), 1–4.

Early, T. (2001). Measures for practice with families from a strengths perspective. *Families in Society, 82*(3), 225–232.

Eber, L., & Nelson, M. (1997). School-based wraparound planning: Integrating services for students with emotional and behavioral needs. *American Journal of Orthopsychiatry, 67*(3), 385–395.

Eber, L. (1993). *Project WRAP: Interagency systems change through a school-based model.* LaGrange, IL: LaGrange Area Department of Special Education.

Emery, R. E. (1988). *Marriage, divorce, and children's adjustment.* Newbury Park, CA: Sage.

Emspak, F., Zullo, R., & Rose, S. J. (n.d.). *Privatizing child protective services in Milwaukee County: An analysis and comparison of public and private systems.* Milwaukee, WI: The Institute for Wisconsin's Future.

Epstein, M. (1999). The development and validation of a scale to assess the emotional and behavioral strengths of children and adolescents. *Remedial and Special Education, 20*(5), 258–262.

Ermold, J. M., Bruns, E. J., Suter, J. C., Wimette, J., & Burchard, J. D. (2000). *A user's manual to the Wraparound Fidelity Index: Version 2.0* Burlington, VT: University of Vermont Department of Psychology.

Evans, G. (1993). *Foster care facts and figures.* Houston: National Foster Parent Association.

Evans, M. E., Armstrong, M. I., & Kuppinger, a. d. (1998). Family-centered intensive case management: A step toward understanding individualized care. *Journal of Child and Family Studies, 5*(1), 55–65.

Fahlberg, V. I. (1991). Preparing older children for adoption. In E. D. Hibbs (Ed.), *Adoption: International perspectives* (pp. 103–113). Madison, CT: International Universities Press.

Fein, E., & Staff, I. (1993). Last best change: Findings from a reunification services program. *Child Welfare, 72,* 25–40.

Fenton, J., Batavia, A., & Roody, D. S. (1993). *Proposed policy statement for NIDRR on constituency-oriented research and dissemination (CORD).* Washington, DC: National Institute on Disability and Rehabilitation Research.

Fine, G., & Bordon, J. R. (1989). Parents Involved Network Project: Support and advocacy training for parents. In R. M. Friedman, A. J. Duchnowski, & E. L. Henderson (Eds.). *Advocacy on behalf of children with serious emotional problems* (pp. 68–78). Springfield, IL: Charles C. Thomas.

Fine, G. A., & Sandstrom, K. L. (1988). *Knowing children: Participant observation with minors.* Newbury Park, CA: Sage.

Finkelhor, D., & Browne, A. (1986). Initial and long term effects: A conceptual framework. In D. Finkelhor (Ed.), *A sourcebook on child sexual abuse* (pp. 180–198). Beverly Hills, CA: Sage.

Finkelhor, D. (1979). *Sexually victimized children.* New York: Free Press.

Finkelstein, N. E. (1980). Family-centered group care. *Child Welfare, 59,* 33–41.

Firman, C. (1993). On families, foster care, and the prawning industry. *Family Resource Coalition Report, 1*(2), 9–11.

Folcarelli, C. (1995). Federal assessments of state health care reform: Medicaid section 1115 waiver evaluations. *TABrief, 1*(2), 4–5.

Foley, H. A., & Sharfstein, S. S. (1983). *Madness and government: Who cares for the mentally ill?* Washington, DC: American Psychiatric Press.

Franklin, C., & Streeter, C. L. (1995). School reform: Linking public schools with human services. *Social Work, 40,* 773–782.

Freeman, E. M. (1995). School social work overview. In *Encyclopedia of Social Work* (19th ed., pp. 2087–2089). Washington, DC: National Association of Social Workers.

Friedman, R. M., Kutash, K., & Duchnowski, A. J. (1996). The population of concern: Defining the issues. In B. A. Stroul (Ed.), *Children's mental health: Creating systems of care in a changing society* (pp. 69–96). Baltimore: Paul H. Brookes.

Friesen, B. J., & Koroloff, N. M. (1990). Family-centered services: Implications for mental health administration and research. *Journal of Mental Health Administration, 17*(1), 13–25.

Gallup, (1988). A study of the parental experience of American parents. Chicago, IL: Family Resource Coalition.

Garb, H. N. (1997). Race bias, social class bias, and gender bias in clinical judgment. *Clinical Psychology: Science and Practice, 4*(2), 99–119.

Garbarino, J., Stott, F. M., & Faculty of the Erickson Institute. (1989). *What children can tell us: Eliciting, interpreting, and evaluating information from children.* San Francisco: Jossey-Bass.

Gardner, S. L., (1992). Key issues in developing school-linked, integrated services. *The Future of Children, 2*(1), 85–94.

General Accounting Office. (2002). Foster care: Recent legislation helps states focus on finding permanent homes for children, but long-standing barriers remain (GAO-02–585). Washington DC: U.S. Government Printing Office.

George, R. M. (1990). The reunification process in substitute care. *Social Service Review, 64,* 422–457.

Gergan, K. J. (1983). *Toward transformation in social knowledge.* New York: Springer-Verlag.

Germain, C. (1973). An ecological perspective in casework practice. *Social Casework, 54,* 323–330.

Germain, C., and Gitterman, A. (1980). *The life model of social work practice.* New York: Columbia University Press.

Giaretto, H. A. (1981). A comprehensive child sexual abuse treatment program. In P. B. Mrazek & C. H. Kempe (Eds.), *Sexually abused children and their families* (pp. 179–198). Elmsford, NY: Pergamon Press.

Gil, E. (1991). *The healing power of play: Working with abused children.* New York: Guilford Press.

Giles, T. R. (1993). *Managed mental health care: A guide for practitioners, employers, and hospital administrators.* Boston: Allyn and Bacon.

Gilligan, C. (1982). *In a different voice: Psychological theory and women's development.* Cambridge, MA: Harvard University Press.

Glassner, B. (1976). Kid society. *Urban Education, 11*(1), 5–21.

Goldenberg, I., & Goldenberg, H. (1991). *Family therapy: An overview.* (3rd ed.). Pacific Grove, CA: Brooks/Cole.

Goldstein, H. (1990). Strength or pathology: Ethical and rhetorical contrasts in approaches to practice. *Families in Society, 71*(5), 267–276.

Goode, D. (1986). Kids, cultures, and innocents. *Human Studies, 9,* 85–106.

Goodman, G., & Aman, C. (1987, April). Children's use of anatomically correct dolls to report an event. Paper presented at the biennial meeting of the Society for Research in Child Development, Baltimore, MD.

Graziano, A. M., & Bythell, D. L. (1983). Failures in child behavior therapy. In E. B. Foa and P. Emmelkamp (Eds.), *Failures in behavior therapy* (pp. 406–424). New York: John Wiley and Sons.

Grossman, J. B., & Tierney, J. P. (1998). Does mentoring work? An impact study of the Big Brothers/Big Sisters program. *Evaluation Review, 22*(3), 403–426.

Grotberg, E. H. (1976). Child development. In E. H. Grotberg (Ed.), *Two hundred years of children* (pp. 391–420). Washington, DC: U.S. Department of Health, Education, and Welfare, Office of Child Development.

Gurian, M. (1996). *The wonder of boys.* New York: Penguin Putnam.

Gustavsson, N. (1995). Emotional problems of children and adolescents. In P. Allen-Meares, *Social work with children and adolescents* (pp. 97–116). White Plains, NY: Longman.

Halleck, S. L. (1963). The impact of professional dishonesty on behavior of disturbed adolescents. *Social Work, 8,* 48–56.

Hanson, J. (1987). *The legacy of child saving revisited: Toward a new model of practice.* Unpublished manuscript, University of Kansas.

Hanson, R. F., & Spratt, E. G. (2000). Reactive attachment disorder: What we know about the disorder and implications for treatment. *Child Maltreatment, 5*(2), 137–145.

Harper, G. W., & Iwamasa, G. Y. (2000). Cognitive-behavioral therapy with minority adolescents: Therapist perspectives. *Cognitive and Behavioral Practice, 7,* 37–53.

Harry, B. (1992). *Cultural diversity, families, and the special education system: Communication and empowerment.* New York: Teachers College Press.

Hartman, A. (1978). Diagrammatic assessment of family relationships. *Social Casework, 59,* 465–476.

Hartman, A. (1990). Children in a careless society. *Social Work, 35,* 483–484.

Hartman, A. (1993). Family preservation under attack. *Social Work, 38,* 509–512.

Henggeler, S. W., Schoenwald, S. K. Borduin, C. M., Rowland, M. D., & Cunningham, P. B. (1998). *Multisystemic treatment of antisocial behavior in children and adolescents.* New York: Guilford Press.

Henggeler, S., Rowland, M., Randall, J., Ward, D. M., Pickral, S. G., Cunningham, P. B., Miller, S. L., Edwards, J., Zealberg, J., Hand, L. D., & Santos, A. B. (1999). Home-based multisystemic therapy as an alternative to the hospitalization of youth in psychiatric crisis: Clinical outcomes. *Journal of the American Academy of Child and Adolescent Psychiatry, 38*(11), 1331–1341.

Hepworth, D. H., & Larsen, J. (1993). *Direct social work practice: Theory and skills* (4th ed.). Belmont, CA: Brooks/Cole.

Herbert, M. (1989). *Working with children and their families.* Chicago: Lyceum Books.

Hernandez, M., & Goldman, S. K. (1996). A local

approach to system development: Ventura County, California. In B. A. Stroul (Ed.), *Children's mental health: Creating systems of care in a changing society* (pp. 177–196). Baltimore: Paul H. Brookes.

Herr, S. S., Arons, S., & Wallace, R. E. (1983). *Legal Rights and Mental Health Care.* Lexington, MA: Lexington Books.

Hess, p. m., & Folaron, G. (1991). Ambivalences: A challenge to permanency for children. *Child Welfare, 70,* 403–424.

Hicks, B. B. (1990). *Youth suicide: A comprehensive manual for prevention and intervention.* Bloomington, IN: National Education Service.

Ho, M. K. (1987). *Family therapy with ethnic minorities.* Newbury Park, CA: Sage.

Hodges, K., Wong, M. M., & Latessa, M. (1998). Use of the child and adolescent functional assessment scale as an outcome measure in clinical settings. *The Journal of Behavioral and Health Services Research, 25*(3), 325–336.

Hoffman, L. (1981). *Foundations of family therapy.* New York: Basic Books.

Huff, B., & Telesford, M. C. (1994). Outreach efforts to involve families of color in the Federation of Families for Children's Mental Health. *Focal Point, 8*(2), 10–12.

Ingrassia, M., & McCormick, J. (1994, April 25). Why leave children with bad parents? *Newsweek,* 52–56, 58.

Jackson, V. H. (Ed.) (1995). *Managed care resource guide for social workers in agency settings.* Washington, DC: National Association of Social Workers Press.

James Bell Associates. (1996). Final report on analysis of 1995 five-year state plans: Family preservation and family support services implementation study. Arlington, VA: Author.

James, B. (1994). *Handbook for treatment of attachment-trauma problems in children.* New York: Free Press.

Jennings, M. A., McDonald, T., & Henderson, R. A. (1996). Early citizen review: Does it make a difference? *Social Work, 41,* 224–231.

Jensen, P. S., Bhatara, V. S., Vitiello, B., Hoagwood K., Feil, M., & Burke, L. B. (1999). Psychoactive medication prescribing practices for U.S. children: Gaps between research and clinical practice. *Journal of the American Academy of Child and Adolescent Psychiatry, 38,* 557–565.

Jensen, P. S., Vitiello, B., Leonard, H., & Laughren, T. P. (1994). Design and methodology issues for clinical treatment trials in children and adolescents. *Psychopharmacology Bulletin, 30*(1), 3–8.

Jerrell, J. M., & Larsen, J. K. (1986). Community mental health services in transition: Who is benefiting? *American Journal of Orthopsychiatry, 56*(1), 78–88.

Johnson, H. (1986). Emerging concerns in family therapy. *Social Work, 31*(4), 299–305.

Johnson, H. C. (1989). The disruptive child: Problems of definition. *Social Casework, 70,* 469–478.

Johnson, L. C. (1989). *Social work practice: A generalist approach* (3rd ed.). Boston: Allyn and Bacon.

Johnston, J. R. (1994). High-conflict divorce. *The Future of Children, 4*(1), 165–182.

Jones, c. e., & Else, J. F. (1979). Racial and cultural issues in adoption. *Child Welfare, 58,* 373–382.

Jones, T. M., Garlow, J. A., Turnbull, H. R., & Barber, P. A. (1996). Family empowerment in a family support program. In G. Singer, L. Powers, & A. Olson (Eds.), *Redefining family support: Innovations in public-private partnerships* (pp. 87–112). Baltimore: Paul H. Brookes.

Jordan, A., & Rodway, M. R. (1984). Correlates of effective foster parenting. *Social Work Research and Abstracts, 20,* 27–31.

Jordan, D. D., & Hernandez, M. (1990). The Ventura planning model: A proposal for mental health reform. *The Journal of Mental Health Administration, 17*(1), 26–60.

Kadushin, A. (1980). *Child welfare services* (3rd ed.). New York: Macmillan.

Kaduson, G. K., & Schaefor, c. e. (Eds.). (2000). *Short-term play therapy for children.* New York: Guilford Press.

Kagan, J. (1984). Continuity and change in the opening years of life. In R. N. Emde & R. J. Harmon (Eds.), *Continuities and discontinuities in development* (pp. 15–44). New York: Plenum Press.

Kagan, R., & Schlosberg, S. (1989). *Families in perpetual crisis.* New York: W. W. Norton and Company.

Kagan, R. M., & Reid, W. J. (1986). Critical factors in the adoption of emotionally disturbed youths. *Child Welfare, 65*(1), 63–73.

Kalter, N., & Schreier, S. (1994). Developmental facilitation groups for children of divorce: The elementary school model. In C. W. LeCroy (Ed.), *Handbook of child and adolescent treatment manuals* (pp. 307–342). New York: Lexington Books.

Kansas Action for Children. (1998). *Privatization of child welfare services in Kansas: A child advocacy perspective.* Topeka, KS: Author.

Kansas Action for Children. (2001). *The Kansas child welfare system: Where are we? Where are we going?* Topeka, KS: Author.

Kempe, C. H., Silverman, F., Steele, B., Droegmueller, W., & Silver, H. (1962). The battered child syndrome. *Journal of the American Medical Association, 181,* 17–24.

Kettner, p. m., & Martin, L. L. (1993). Purchase of service contracting in the 1990s: Have expectations been met? *Journal of Sociology and Social Welfare, 20*(2), 89–102.

Kimmich, M. (1995a). *Iowa decategorization as a strategy for comprehensive community-based planning: Lessons learned from implementation.* Salem, OR: Human Services Research Institute.

Kimmich, M. (1995b). *Iowa decategorization and statewide child welfare reform: An outcome evaluation.* Salem, OR: Human Services Research Institute.

King, B., & Meyers, J. (1996). The Annie E. Casey Foundation's mental health initiative for urban children. In B. A. Stroul (Ed.), *Children's mental health: Creating systems of care in a changing society* (pp. 249–261). Baltimore: Paul H. Brookes.

Kinney, J. Haapala, D. Booth, C., & Leavit, S. (1990). The homebuilders model. In J. K. Whittaker, J. Kinney, E. M. Tracy, & C. Booth (Eds.), *Reaching high-risk families: Intensive family preservation in human services* (pp. 31–64). New York: Aldine de Gruyter.

Kipnis, A. (1999). *Angry young men.* San Francisco: Jossey-Bass.

Kirby, L. D., & Fraser, M. W. (1997). Risk and resilience in childhood. In M. W. Fraser (Ed.), *Risk and resilience in childhood: An ecological perspective* (pp. 10–33). Washington, DC: NASW Press.

Kirk, W. G. (1993). *Adolescent suicide: A school-based approach to assessment and intervention.* Champaign, IL: Research Press.

Klepsch, M., & Logie, L. (1982). *Children draw and tell. An introduction to the uses of children's human figure drawings.* New York: Brunner/Mazel.

Knitzer, J. (1982). *Unclaimed children.* Washington, DC: Children's Defense Fund.

Knitzer, J. (1996). The role of education in systems of care. In B. A. Stroul (Ed.), *Children's mental health: Creating systems of care in a changing society* (pp. 197–213). Baltimore: Paul H. Brookes.

Knitzer, J., Steinberg, Z., & Fleisch, B. (1990). *At the schoolhouse door: An examination of programs and policies for children with behavioral and emotional problems.* New York: Bank Street College of Education.

Kongstvedt, P. R. (1995). *Essentials of managed health care.* Gaithersburg, MD: Aspen Publishers.

Kreiger, R., Maluccio, A., & Pine, B. (1991). *Teaching family reunification: A sourcebook.* West Hartford, CT: Center for the Study of Child Welfare, University of Connecticut School of Social Work.

Krener, P. K., & Mancina, R. A. (1994). Informed consent of informed coercion? Decision-making in pediatric psychopharmacology. *Journal of Child and Adolescent Psychopharmacology, 4*(3), 183–200.

Kresnak, J. (2001). Police take custody of abuse probes. *Youth Today, 10*(4), 1, 42–44.

Kutash, K., & Rivera, V. R. (1996). *What works in children's mental health services? Uncovering answers to critical questions.* Baltimore: Paul H. Brookes.

Lahti, J. (1982). A follow-up study of foster children in permanent placements. *Social Service Review, 56,* 556–571.

Langley, P. A. (1991). The coming of age of family policy. *Families in Society, 72,* 116–120.

Law, c. e. (1995). Evaluating children's managed mental health care. *TA Brief, 1*(2), 2–4.

LeCroy, C. W. (1994). Social skills training. In C. W. LeCroy (Ed.), *Handbook of child and adolescent treatment manuals* (pp. 126–169). New York: Lexington Books.

Ledesma, K. (2000). Incentive payments reinvested in program improvement. *The Roundtable, 14*(1), 1–2.

Leviton, A., Mueller, M., & Kauffman, C. (1992). The family-centered consultation model: Practical applications for professionals. *Infants and Young Children, 4*(3), 1–8.

Lindsey, D. (1994). *The welfare of children.* New York: Oxford University Press.

Litzelfelner, P., & Petr, C. (1997). Case advocacy in child welfare. *Social Work, 42,* 392–402.

Lourie, I. S., Katz-Leavy, J., DeCarolis, G., & Quinlan, W. A. (1996). The role of the federal government. In B. A. Stroul (Ed.), *Children's mental health: Creating systems of care in a changing society* (pp. 99–114). Baltimore: Paul H. Brookes.

Lucco, A. A. (1991). Assessment of the school-age child. *Families in Society, 72,* 394–408.

Lyons, J. S., Baerger, D. R., Quigley, P., Erlich, J., & Griffin, E. (2001). Mental health service needs of juvenile offenders: A comparison of detention, incarceration, and treatment settings. *Children's Services: Social Policy, Research, and Practice, 4*(2), 69–85.

MacDonald, G. D. (1992). Accepting parental responsibility: "Future questioning" as a means to avoid foster home placement of children. *Child Welfare, 71,* 3–17.

Mack, D. (1997). *The assault on parenthood: How our culture undermines the family.* New York: Simon and Schuster.

Mackay, R. W. (1973). Conceptions of children and models of socialization. In R. Turner (Ed.), *Ethnomethodology* (pp. 180–195). Baltimore: Penguin.

Mahler, M., Pine, F., & Bergman, A. (1975). *The psychological birth of the human infant: Symbiosis and individuation.* New York: Basic Books.

Mailick, M. D., & Ashley, A. A. (1981). Politics of interprofessional collaboration: Challenge to advocacy. *Social Casework, 62,* 131–137.

Making reasonable efforts: Steps for keeping families together. (n.d.). National Council of Juvenile and Family Court Judges, Child Welfare League of America, Youth Law Center, National Center for Youth Law.

Malekoff, A. (2001). The power of group work with kids: A practitioner's reflection on strengths-based practice. *Families in Society, 82,* 243–248.

Maluccio, A. N., Fein, E., & Olmstead, K. A. (1986). *Permanency planning for children: concepts and methods.* New York: Tavistock.

Maluccio, A. N., Krieger, R., & Pine, B. A. (Eds.) (1990). *Preparing adolescents for life after foster care: The central role of foster parents.* Washington, DC: Child Welfare League of America.

Marston, D., & Heistad, D. (1994). Assessing collaborative inclusion as an effective model for the delivery of special education services. *Diagnostique: Professional Bulletin of the Council for Educational Diagnostic Services, 19*(4), 51–67.

Martin, J. S., & Petr, C. G. (2002). *Kansas consumer satisfaction survey, children's mental health: Statewide summary Round 4.* Lawrence, KS: University of Kansas School of Social Welfare.

Massinga, R. W., & Cargal, J. (1991). Foundations and family-based services: support, innovation, and leadership. *Families in Society, 72,* 301–309.

Matheson, L. (1996). The politics of the Indian child welfare act. *Social Work, 41,* 232–235.

Maza, P. L. (2001). The age factor in adoptions. *The Roundtable: Journal of the National Resource Center for Special Needs Adoption, 16*(1), 1,3.

McCurdy, M. A., & Daro, D. (1993). *Current trends in child abuse reporting and fatalities: The results of the 1992 annual fifty-state survey.* Chicago:

National Committee for the Prevention of Child Abuse.

McDermott, M. T. (1993). Agency versus independent adoption: The case for independent adoption. *The Future of Children, 3*(1), 146–152.

McDonald, T., & Marks, J. (1991). A review of risk factors assessed in child protective services. *Social Service Review, 65*(1), 112–132.

McGinty, K., McCammon, S. L., & Koeppen, V. P. (2001). The complexities of implementing a wraparound approach to service provision: A view from the field. *Journal of Family Social Work, 5*(3) 95–109.

McGoldrick, M., & Gerson, R. (1985). *Genograms in family assessment.* New York: W. W. Norton and Co.

McKenzie, J. K. (1993). Adoption of children with special needs. *The Future of Children, 3*(1), 62–76.

McMahon, M. O. (1996). *The general method of social work practice: A generalist perspective.* (3rd ed.). Boston: Allyn and Bacon.

McRoy, R. G., & Freeman, E. (1986). Racial-identity issues among mixed race children. *Social Work in Education, 8*(3), 164–174.

Meckel, R. (1985). Protecting the innocents: Age segregation and the early child welfare movement. *Social Service Review, 59,* 455–475.

Melaville, A. I., & Blank, M. J. (1993). *Together we can: A guide for crafting a profamily system in education and human services.* Washington, DC: U.S. Government Printing Office.

Mellor, D., & Storer, S. (1995). Support groups for children in alternate care: A largely untapped therapeutic resource. *Child Welfare, 74,* 905–918.

Melton, G. (1982). Children's rights: Where are the children? *American Journal of Orthopsychiatry, 52*(3), 530–538.

Merriam-Webster's collegiate dictionary (10th ed.). (1993). Springfield, MA: Merriam-Webster.

Meyer, C. (Ed.). (1983). *Clinical social work in the ecosystems perspective.* New York: Columbia University Press.

Miller, J. (1993). *Seattle's family support centers at one year.* Seattle, WA: Department of Housing and Human Services.

Miller, R. L., & Miller, B. (1990). Mothering the biracial child: Bridging the gaps between African-American and White parenting styles. *Women and Therapy, 10,* 169–179.

Mitchel, L., & Donnelly, A. C. (1993). Health families America: Building a national system. *The APSAC Advisor, 6*(4), 9, 10, 27.

Monteleone, J. A., Glaze, S., & Bly, K. M. (1994).

Sexual abuse: An overview. In J. A. Monteleone & A. E. Brodeur (Eds.), *Child maltreatment: A clinical guide and reference* (pp. 113–131). St. Louis, MO: G. W. Medical Publishing.

Munkel, W. I. (1994). Neglect and abandonment. In J. A. Monteleone & A. E. Brodeur (Eds.), *Child maltreatment: A clinical guide and reference* (pp. 241–257). St. Louis, MO: G. W. Medical Publishing.

Murphy, D. L., & Lee, I. M. (1991). *Family-centered program rating scale: User's manual.* Lawrence, KS: University of Kansas Beach Center on Families and Disability.

Naisbitt, J., & Aburdene, P. (1990). *Megatrends 2000: New directions for the 1990s.* New York: William Morrow and Co.

National Association of Protection and Advocacy Systems. (1995). *NAPAS Annual Report, 1994–1995.* Washington, DC: Author.

National CASA Association. (1995). *Report of the 1995 program survey.* Seattle, WA: National CASA Association.

National Commission on Children. (1991). *Beyond rhetoric: A new agenda for children and families: Final report of the national commission on children.* Washington, DC: U.S. Government Printing Office.

National Institute of Mental Health. (1991). *Treatment of children with mental disorders.* Washington, DC: U.S. Government Printing Office.

National Institute of Mental Health. (2001). *Treatment of children with mental disorders.* Retrieved December 18, 2002, from www.nimh.nih.gov/publicat/childqa.cfm.

Nelson, K., Saunders, E., & Landsman, M. J. (1990). *Chronic neglect in perspective: A study of chronically neglecting families in a large metropolitan county: final report.* Oakdale: National Resource Center of Family Based Services, University of Iowa.

Nichols, M. P., & Schwartz, R. C. (1995). *Family therapy: concepts and methods.* (3rd ed.). Boston: Allyn and Bacon.

O'Looney, J. (1993, December). Beyond privatization and service integration: Organizational models for service delivery. *Social Service Review, 501–534.*

Olds, D. L., Henderson, C. R., Jr., Chamberlin, R., & Tatelbaum, R. (1986). Preventing child abuse and neglect: A randomized trial of nurse home visitation. *Pediatrics, 78*(1), 65–78.

Orten, J. D., & Rich, L. L. (1988). A model for the assessment of incestuous families. *Social Casework, 69,* 611–619.

Pardeck, J. T., & Pardeck, J. A. (1987). Bibliothrapy

for children in foster care and adoption. *Child Welfare, 66,* 269–278.

Pear, R. (1996, March 17). Many states fail to meet mandates on child welfare. *New York Times,* pp. A1, A14.

Pearl, P. S. (1994). Emotional abuse. In J. A. Monteleone & A. E. Brodeur (Eds.), *Child maltreatment: A clinical guide and reference* (pp. 259–283). St. Louis, MO: G. W. Medical Publishing.

Pecora, P. J., Whittaker, J. K., & Maluccio, A. N. (1992). *The child welfare challenge: Policy, practice, and research.* New York: Aldine de Gruyter.

Pecora, P. J., Whittaker, J. K., Maluccio, A. N., & Barth, R. P. (2000). *The child welfare challenge* (2nd ed.). New York: Aldine de Gruyter.

Pelton, L. H. (1998). Commentary: How we can better protect children from abuse and neglect. *The Future of Children, 8*(1), 126–129.

Petit, M. R., Curtis, P. A., Woodruff, K., Arnold, L., Feagans, L., & Ang, J. (1999). *Child abuse and neglect: A look at the states. The CWLA stat book.* Washington, DC: Child Welfare League of America Press.

Petr, C. G. (1988). The worker-client relationship: A general systems perspective. *Social Casework, 69*(10), 620–626.

Petr, C. G. (1992). Adultcentrism in practice with children.

Petr, C. G., & Allen, R. I. (1999). Family-centered professional behavior: Frequency and importance to parents. *Journal of Emotional and Behavioral Disorders, 5*(4), 196–204.

Petr, C. G., & Barney, D. D. (1993). Reasonable efforts for children with disabilities: The parents' perspective. *Social Work, 38,* 247–255.

Petr, C. G., & Entriken, C. (1995). Service system barriers to reunification. *Families in Society, 76,* 523–532.

Petr, C. G., & Johnson, I. (1999). Privatization of foster care in Kansas: A cautionary tale. *Social Work, 44*(3), 263–267.

Petr, C. G., Holtquist, S., & Martin, J. S. (2000). Consumer-run organizations for youth. *Psychiatric Rehabilitation Journal, 24*(2), 142–148.

Petr, C. G., & Poertner, J. (1989). Protection and advocacy for the mentally ill: New hope for emotionally disturbed children? *Community Mental Health Journal, 25*(2), 156–163.

Petr, C. G., & Spano, R. N., (1990). Evolution of social services for children with emotional disorders. *Social Work, 35*(3), 228–234.

Phillips, K. (1990). *The politics of rich and poor:*

Wealth and the American electorate in the Reagan aftermath. New York: Random House.

Pincus, A., & Minahan, A. (1973). *Social work practice: Model and method.* Itasca, IL: F. E. Peacock.

Pinderhughes, E. (1995). Empowering diverse populations: Family practice in the 21st century. *Families in Society, 76,* 131–140.

Pipher, M. (1994). *Reviving Ophelia: Saving the selves of adolescent girls.* New York: Ballantine Books.

Plantz, M. C., Hubbell, R., Barrett, B. J., & Dobrec, A. (1989). Indian Child Welfare Act: A status report. *Children Today, 18,* 24–29.

Poertner, J., & Press, A. (1990). Who best represents the interests of the child in court? *Child Welfare, 69,* 537–549.

Poertner, J., & Ronnau, J. (1992). A strengths approach to children with emotional disabilities. In D. Saleebey (Ed.), *The strengths perspective in social work practice* (pp. 111–121). New York: Longman.

Polansky, N. A., Chalmers, M. A., Buttenweiser, E., & Williams, D. P. (1981). *Damaged parents: An anatomy of child neglect.* Chicago: University of Chicago Press.

Pollack, W. (1998). *Real boys: Rescuing our sons from the myths of boyhood.* New York: Henry Holt and Company.

Radin, N. (1989). School social work practice: Past, present, and future trends. *Social work in Education, 11,* 213–225.

Rapp, C. A., & Poertner, J. (1992). *Social administration: A client-centered approach.* New York: Longman.

Rapp, C. A., Ruhlman, L., & Topp, D. (1994). *Creating a results based system for kansas child welfare.* Lawrence, KS: University of Kansas School of Social Welfare.

Reid, W. J., Kagan, R. M., Kaminsky, A., & Helmer, K. (1987). Adoptions of older institutionalized youth. *Social Casework, 68*(3), 140–149.

Reynolds, A. J., Temple, J. A., Robertson, D. L., & Mann, E. A. (2001). Long-term effects of an early childhood intervention on educational achievement and juvenile arrest. *Journal of the American Medical Association, 285,* 2339–2346.

Rindeleisch, N., & Rabb, J. (1984). How much of a problem is residential mistreatment in child welfare institutions? *Child Abuse and Neglect, 8*(1), 33–40.

Roan, S. (2000, April 3). Teens: They're often the patients the health-care system forgot. *Los Angeles Times,* A15.

Roberts, M. C., & Peterson, L. (Eds.) (1984). *Prevention of problems in childhood: Psychological research and applications.* New York: John Wiley & Sons.

Rodwell, M. K., and Chambers, D. E. (1992). Primary prevention of child abuse: Is it really possible? *Journal of Sociology and Social Welfare, 19,* 159–175.

Rosenthal, J. A. (1993). Outcomes of adoption of children with special needs. *The Future of Children, 3*(1), 77–88.

Rothman, J. (1991). A model of case management: Toward empirically based practice. *Social Work, 36,* 521–528.

Rounds, K. A., Weil, M., & Bishop, K. K. (1994). Practice with culturally diverse families of young children with disabilities. *Families in Society, 75*(1), 3–14.

Russell, D. E. (1983). The incidence and prevalence of intrafamilial and extrafamilial sexual abuse of female children. *Child Abuse and Neglect, 7,* 133–146.

Saleebey, D. (1996). The strengths perspective in social work practice: Extensions and cautions. *Social Work, 41,* 296–305.

Saleebey, D. (Ed.). (1992). *The strengths perspective in social work practice.* New York: Longman.

Samaan, R. A. (2000). The influences of race, ethnicity, and poverty on the mental health of children. *Journal of Health Care for the Poor and Underserved, 11*(1), 100–110.

Sanchirico, A., & Jablonka, K. (2000). Keeping foster children connected to their biological parents: The impact of foster parent training and support. *Child and Adolescent Social Work Journal, 17*(3), 185–203.

Sands, R. G. (1991). *Clinical social work practice in community mental health.* New York: Macmillan.

Scannapieco, M., & Jackson, S. (1996). Kinship care: The African American response to family preservation. *Social Work, 41,* 190–196.

Schlenger, W. E., Etheridge, R. M., Hansen, D. J., Fairbank, D. W., & Onken, J. (1992). Evaluation of state efforts to improve systems of care for children and adolescents with severe emotional disturbances: The CASSP initial cohort study. *The Journal of Mental Health Adminisration, 19,* 131–142.

Schorr, L. B. (1994). *The case for shifting to results-based accountability.* Washington, D: Center for the Study of Social Policy.

Schrag, P. (1978). *Mind control.* New York: Pantheon Books.

Schweinhart, L. J., & Weikart, D. P. (1998). High/Scope Perry preschool program effects at age twenty-seven. In J. Crane (Ed.), *Social Programs That Work* (pp. 148–162). New York: Russell Sage.

Sedlack, A. J., & Broadhurst, D. D. (1996). *Third national incidence study of child abuse and neglect.* [Final Report.] Washington, DC: U.S. Department of Health and Human Services.

Sgroi, S. M. (1982). *Handbook of clinical intervention in child sexual abuse.* Lexington, MA: Lexington Books.

Sheppard, V. B., & Benjamin-Coleman, R. (2001). Determinants of service placement patterns for youth with serious emotional and behavioral disturbances. *Community Mental Health Journal, 37*(1), 53–65.

Sherman, A. (1994). *Wasting America's future: The Children's Defense Fund report on the costs of child poverty.* Children's Defense Fund. Boston: Beacon Press.

Shireman, J. (1994). Should transracial adoptions be permitted? In E. Gambrill & T. J. Stein (Eds.), *Controversial issues in child welfare* (pp. 246–260). Boston: Allyn and Bacon.

Siegel, M. G. (1987). *Psychological testing from early childhood through adolescence—A developmental and psychodynamic approach.* Madison, CT: International University Press.

Singer, G. H. S., Powers, L. E., & Olson, A. L. (1996). *Redefining family support: Innovations in public-private partnerships.* Baltimore: Paul H. Brookes.

Siporin, M. (1980). Ecological systems theory in social work. *Journal of Sociology and Social Welfare, 7,* 507–532.

Sivan, A. B., Schor, D. P., Koeppl, G. K., & Noble, L. D. (1988). Interaction of normal children with anatomical dolls. *Child Abuse and Neglect, 12,* 295–304.

Smith, S. (1996). Georgia family organization plays key role in delivery of children's mental health services. *Focal Point, 10*(2), 11–13.

Smith, S. R. (1989). The changing politics of child welfare services: New roles for the government and the nonprofit sectors. *Child Welfare, 68,* 289–299.

Smoller, J. W. (1986). The etiology and treatment of childhood. In G. C. Ellenbogen (Ed.), *Oral sadism and the vegetarian personality* (pp. 3–14). New York: Ballentine Books.

Snow, C. W. (1989). *Infant development.* Englewood Cliffs, NJ: Prentice Hall.

Solomon, A. (1992). Clinical diagnosis among diverse populations: A multicultural perspective. *Families in Society, 73,* 371–377.

Sorenson, G. (1995, June). *Discipline of students with*

disabilities: An update. A Legal Memorandum. Reston, VA: National Association of Secondary School Principals.

Specht, H. (1988). *New directions for social work practice.* Englewood Cliffs, NJ: Prentice Hall.

Staff. (1923). *Child Welfare League of America Bulletin, 2*(7).

Staff. (1928). *Child Welfare League of America Bulletin, 7*(1).

Staff. (1994). Major increase in support for children's mental health. *Update: Research and Training Center for Children's Mental Health, 8*(1), 1, 4.

Stark, K. D., Raffaelle, L., & Reysa, A. (1994). The treatment of depressed children: A skills training approach to working with children and families. In C. W. LeCroy (Ed.), *Handbook of child and adolescent treatment manuals* (pp. 343–397). New York: Lexington Books.

Stempler, B. L., & Glass, M. S. (Eds.) (1996). *Social group work today and tomorrow: Moving from theory to advanced training and practice.* New York: Haworth Press.

Stern, D. (1985). *The interpersonal world of the infant.* New York: Basic Books.

Stevenson, L. (2000). Bringing youth to the table in systems of care. *Focal Point, 14*(2), 16–18.

Stolz, S. B. (1978). *Ethical issues in behavior modification.* San Francisco: Jossey-Bass.

Stone, L. J., Smith, H. T., & Murphy, L. B. (Eds.). (1973). *The competent infant.* New York: Basic Books.

Stroul, B. A. (1996). Profiles of local systems of care. In B. A. Stroul (Ed.), *Children's mental health: Creating systems of care in a changing society* (pp. 149–176). Baltimore: Paul H. Brookes.

Stroul, B. A., McCormack, M., & Zaro, S. M. (1996). Measuring outcomes in systems of care. In B. A. Stroul (Ed.), *Children's mental health: Creating systems of care in a changing society* (pp. 313–355). Baltimore: Paul H. Brookes.

Stroul, B. A., Pires, S. A., Armstrong, M. L., & Meyers, J. C. (1998). The impact of managed care on mental health services for children and their families. *The Future of Children, 8*(2), 119–133.

Summers, J. A., Behr, S. K., & Turnbull, A. P. (1988). Positive adaptation and coping strengths of families who have children with disabilities. In G. Singer & L. Irvin (Eds.), *Support for caregiving families: Enabling positive adaptation to disability* (pp. 27–40). Baltimore: Paul H. Brookes Publishing.

Summers, J. A., Turnbull, A. P., Campbell, M., Benson, H., Siegel-Causey, E., & Dell'Oliver, C. (1989). *A family-friendly IFSP process: Model outline.*

Lawrence, KS: Beach Center on Families and Disability, University of Kansas.

Sumner, W. G. (1906). *Folkways.* New York: Ginn.

Tannen, N. (1996). A family-designed system of care: Families first in Essex County, New York. In B. A. Stroul (Ed.), *Children's mental health: Creating systems of care in a changing society* (pp. 375–388). Baltimore: Paul H. Brookes.

Taylor, S. J. (1987). Continuum traps. In S. J. Taylor, D. Biklen, & J. Knoll (Eds.), *Community integration for people with severe disabilities* (pp. 25–35). New York: Teacher's College Press.

Thyer, B. (Ed.). (1989). *Behavioral family therapy.* Springfield, IL: Thomas.

Toseland, R. W., Palmer-Ganeles, J., & Chapman, D. (1986). Teamwork in psychiatric settings. *Social Work, 31,* 46–52.

Tower, K. D. (1994). Consumer-centered social work practice: Restoring client self-determination. *Social Work, 39,* 191–196.

Trattner, W. I. (1974). *From poor law to welfare state.* New York: Free Press.

Troiden, R. R. (1988). Homosexual identity development. *Journal of Adolescent Health Care, 9,* 105–113.

Turnbull, A. P., & Summers, J. A. (1987). From parent involvement to family support: Evolution to revolution. In S. M. Pueschel, C. Tingey, J. E. Rynders, A. C. Crocker, & D. M. Crutcher (Eds.), *New perspectives on Down Syndrome: Proceedings of the state-of-the-art conference* (pp. 289–306). Baltimore: Paul H. Brookes Publishing.

Turnbull, A. P., Turnbull, H. R., Shank, M., & Leal, D. (1995). *Exceptional lives: Special education in today's schools.* Englewood Cliffs, NJ: Merrill, Prentice Hall.

Turnbull, H. R., III & Turnbull, A. P. (1990). *Families, professionals, and exceptionality: A special partnership* (2nd ed.). Columbus, OH: Merrill.

Turnbull, H. R., & Turnbull, A. P. (2000). *Free appropriate public education: The law and children with disabilities* (6th ed.). Denver, CO: Love Publishing.

U.S. Bureau of the Census. (1991). *Statistical abstract of the United States.* Washington, DC: U.S. Government Printing Office.

U.S. Department of Health and Human Services. (1988). *Study findings, study of national incidence of child abuse and neglect.* Washington, DC: U.S. Government Printing Office.

U.S. Department of Health and Human Services. (1991). *Parent training is prevention: Preventing alcohol and other drug problems among youth in the family.* Rockville, MD: Office for Substance Abuse Prevention.

U.S. Department of Health and Human Services. (1996). *National incidence study of child abuse and neglect.* Washington, DC: U.S. Government Printing Office.

U.S. Department of Health and Human Services. (1999). *Mental Health: A Report of the Surgeon General.* Rockville, MD: U.S. Department of Health and Human Services, Substance Abuse and Mental Health Services Administration, Center for Mental Health Services, National Institutes of Health, National Institute of Mental Health. Retrieved January 8, 2003, from www.surgeongeneral.gov/library/mentalhealth/home.html.

U.S. Department of Health and Human Services. (2000). *Report of the Surgeon General's conference on children's mental health: A national action agenda.* Rockville, MD: U.S. Department of Health and Human Services, Substance Abuse and Mental Health Services Administration, Center for Mental Health Services, National Institutes of Health, National Institute of Mental Health. Retrieved January 8, 2003, from www.surgeongeneral.gov/topics/cmh/childreport.htm.

Umbreit, M. S. (1991). Mediation of youth conflict: A multi-system perspective. *Child and Adolescent Social Work, 8,* 141–153.

Vaillant, G. E. (1984). The disadvantages of DSM-III outweigh its advantages. *American Journal of Psychiatry, 141,* 542–545.

VanDenBerg, J. (1993). Integration of individualized services into the system of care for children and adolescents with emotional disabilities. *Administration and Policy in Mental Health, 20*(4), 247–258.

Vaughn, S., & Schumm, J. S. (1995). Responsible inclusion for students with learning disabilities. *Journal of Learning Disabilities, 28,* 264–270.

Vega, W. A., & Rumbaut, R. G. (1991). Ethnic minorities and mental health. *Annual Review of Sociology, 17,* 351–383.

Verry, E. (1939). Problems facing children who have had a relatively long period of institutional care. *Child Welfare League of America Bulletin, 18*(2), 2–4.

Wachtel, E. F. (1994). *Treating troubled children and their families.* New York: Guilford Press.

Wagner, M. M. (1995). Outcomes for youths with serious emotional disturbance in secondary school and early adulthood. *The Future of Children, 5*(2), 90–112.

Wakefield, J. C. (1992a). The concept of mental

disorder: On the boundary between biological fact and social values. *American Psychologist, 47,* 373–388.

Wakefield, J. C. (1992b). Disorder as harmful dysfunction: A conceptual critique of DSM-III-R's definition of mental disorder. *Psychological Review, 99,* 232–247.

Waksler, F. (1986). Studying children: Phenomenological insights. *Human Studies, 9,* 71–82.

Wald, M. S. (1988). Family preservation services: Are we moving too fast? *Public Welfare, 46*(3), 33–38, 46.

Waldman, I. D., Lilienfeld, S. O., & Lahey, B. B. (1995). Toward construct validity in the childhood disruptive behavior disorders: Classification and diagnosis in *DSM-IV* and beyond. In T. H. Ollendick & R. J. Prinz (Eds.), *Advances in clinical child psychology* (Vol. 17, pp. 323–363). New York: Plenum Press.

Walker, J. S. (2001). Caregivers' views on the cultural appropriateness of services for children with emotional or behavioral disorders. *Journal of Child and Family Studies, 10,* 315–331.

Walter, J. L., & Peller, J. E. (1992). *Becoming solutions-focused in brief therapy.* New York: Brunner/Mazel.

Walter, U. M., & Petr, C. G. (2000). A template for family-centered interagency collaboration. *Families in Society, 81*(5), 494–503.

Walton, E., Fraser, M. W., Lewis, R. E., Pecora, P. J., Walton, W. K. (1993). In-home family-focused reunification: An experimental study. *Child Welfare, 72,* 473–487.

Warner, A. G. (1922). *American charities* (3rd ed.). New York: Crowell.

Webb, N. B. (1996). *Social work practice with children.* New York: Guilford.

Webb, N. B. (Ed.). (1991). Play therapy with children in crisis: A casebook for practitioners. New York: Guilford Press.

Weick, A., & Saleebey, D. (1995). Supporting family strengths: orienting policy and practice toward the 21st century. *Families in Society, 76*(3), 141–149.

Weick, A., Rapp, C., Sullivan, W. P., & Kisthardt, W. (1989). A strengths perspective for social work practice. *Social Work, 34,* 350–354.

Weisman, M. (1994). When parents are not in the best interests of the child. *Atlantic Monthly, 274*(1), 43–63.

Weissbourd, B. (1987). A brief history of family support programs. In S. Kagan, D. Powell,

B. Weissbourd, & E. Zigler (Eds.), *America's family support programs* (pp. 38–56). New Haven, CT: Yale University Press.

Weithorn, L. A. (1989). Mental hospitalization of troubled youth: an analysis of skyrocketing admission rates. *Stanford Law Review, 40,* 773–838.

White, S., Strom, G., & Santilli, G. (1986). A clinical protocol for interviewing young children with the sexually anatomically correct dolls. Unpublished manuscript, Case Western Reserve School of Medicine, Cleveland, OH.

Whitman, A. (1939). The contribution of child caring agencies in solving problems of mental disorder. *Child Welfare League of America Bulletin, 18*(3), 1–2, 8.

Whittaker, J. K., & Tracy, E. M. (1990). Family preservation services and education for social work practice: Stimulus and response. In J. K. Whittaker, J. Kinney, E. M. Tracy, & C. Booth (Eds.), *Reaching high-risk families: Intensive family preservation in human services* (pp. 1–11). New York: Aldine de Gruyter.

Wilensky, H. L., & Lebeaux, C. N. (1958). *Industrial Society and Social Welfare.* New York: Russell Sage Foundation.

Willis, W. (1992). Families with African American roots. In E. W. Lynch and M. J. Hanson (Eds.), *Developing cross-cultural competence: A guide for working with young children and their families* (pp. 121–150). Baltimore: Paul H. Brookes.

Wodrich, D. L. (1994). *Attention deficit hyperactivity disorder: What every parent wants to know.* Baltimore: Paul H. Brookes.

Wodrich, D. L. (1997). *Children's psychological testing: A guide for nonpsychologists* (3rd ed.). Baltimore: Paul H. Brookes.

Wohl, A., & Kaufman, B. (1985). *Silent screams and hidden cries.* New York: Brunner/Mazel.

Wolfson, J. (1998). Gay youth find safe haven in GLASS houses. *Youth Today, 7*(7), 1, 34–36.

Yanok, J., & Derubertis, D. (1989). Comparative study of parental participation in regular and special education programs. *Exceptional Children, 56*(3), 195–199.

Zastrow, C. (1993). *Social work with groups* (3rd ed.). Chicago: Nelson-Hall.

Zito, J. M., Safer, D. J., dosReis, S., Gardner, J. F., Boles, M., & Lynch, F. (2000). Trends in prescribing of psychotropic medications to preschoolers. *Journal of the American Medical Association, 283*(8), 1025–1030.

INDEX

CPSIA information can be obtained at www.ICGtesting.com
Printed in the USA
LVOW11*0822010813

345690LV00002B/2/P